Major Problems in
American Business History

MAJOR PROBLEMS IN AMERICAN HISTORY SERIES

GENERAL EDITOR
THOMAS G. PATERSON

Major Problems in American Business History

DOCUMENTS AND ESSAYS

EDITED BY

REGINA LEE BLASZCZYK

UNIVERSITY OF PENNSYLVANIA

PHILIP B. SCRANTON

RUTGERS UNIVERSITY

HOUGHTON MIFFLIN COMPANY
Boston   New York

To our colleagues in the
Business History Conference.

Publisher: Charles Hartford
Senior Consulting Editor: Jean L. Woy
Senior Development Editor: Julie Swasey
Associate Project Editor: Teresa Huang
Editorial Assistant: Katherine Leahey
Senior Art and Design Coordinator: Jill Haber
Senior Photo Editor: Jennifer Meyer Dare
Composition Buyer: Chuck Dutton
Senior Manufacturing Coordinator: Renée Ostrowski
Senior Marketing Manager: Sandra McGuire
Marketing Assistant: Molly Parke

Cover image: Mural, painted by John McCoy II for E. I. du Pont de Nemours & Company's exhibit at the New York World's Fair, 1939. Hagley Museum and Library, Wilmington, Del. (see Chapter 11, p. 336).

Printed in the U.S.A.

Library of Congress Control Number: 2001133228

ISBN: 0-618-04426-4

23456789-MP-09 08 07 06

Contents

CHAPTER 3
Merchants and Commercial Networks in the Atlantic World, 1680–1790
Page 68

CHAPTER 4
Public and Private Interests in the Transition to Industrialization, 1790–1860
Page 107

CHAPTER 5
Doing Business in the Slave South, 1800–1860
Page 137

CHAPTER 6
Inventing American Industry, 1810–1890
Page 172

C H A P T E R   7
Technology in the Age of Big Business, 1870–1920
Page 208

C H A P T E R   8
The Age of the Octopus: Business and the Reform Impulse, 1876–1920
Page 240

C H A P T E R   9
The Many Faces of Entrepreneurship, 1840–1930
Page 272

C H A P T E R   1 0
Satisfaction Guaranteed? American Business and the Rise of Consumer Society, 1900–1940
Page 296

CHAPTER 11
*Times of Crisis: From the Stock Market Crash
Through World War II, 1929–1945*
Page 334

CHAPTER 12
Postwar Challenges and Opportunities:
The Culture of Affluence and the Cold War, 1945–1980
Page 372

CHAPTER 13
Business and the Public Interest: Corporate Responsibility
for Environment, Health, and Safety, 1945–2005
Page 408

Preface

Wal-Mart is the most respected name in American business—and one of the most vilified. Founded in 1962, this Arkansas-based global retailer, which operates more than 5,000 stores on four continents, has grown phenomenally over the past four decades by emphasizing "Every Day Low Prices." No other company in the world sells more bicycles, books, CDs, dog food, toothpaste, DVDs, magazines, and toys. *Fortune*, America's leading business magazine, has included Wal-Mart among the "100 Best Companies to Work For" and named it the "Most Admired Company in America." On the other hand, Wal-Mart's success and size have made it a global symbol of business power, drawing the wrath of outspoken critics. This megalith, which controls 42 percent of the world's general merchandise market and whose 2005 sales topped $285 billion, has come to symbolize the destruction of American downtowns, overseas sweatshop manufacturing, exploitive labor practices, censorship of merchandise, and environmental blight. Wal-Mart's dark underbelly contrasts sharply with the wholesome, small town, all-American image it promotes in TV commercials and advertising circulars.

What should concerned citizens think about the Janus face of Wal-Mart? How can we fairly evaluate Wal-Mart's contributions to society and the critiques against it? American business history—the study of how American enterprise developed, operated, and evolved in the past, interacting with individuals, institutions, and governments—can help us make sense of Wal-Mart. Business history cannot forecast economic trends or predict corporate successes and failures, but it can inform our understanding of business's proper role in the economy and society. The past shows us, for example, that several themes in the Wal-Mart story have deep historical roots. A faith in the pursuit of happiness through free enterprise, international trade, family values, suburban living, and mass consumption has long undergirded the American way, as explored to varying degrees in Chapters 2, 3, 4, 9, 12, and 15 of this book. Just as important, history reveals that some Americans have always been skeptical of business behemoths, believing "The Corporation" antithetical to individual freedom, community values, and the earth's ecology. Antifederalists and Jacksonian Democrats crusaded against banks in the 1780s and 1830s; progressive lawyer Louis Brandeis battled "The Octopus" of big business in the 1910s; and insurance company physicians lashed out against "Big Tobacco" during the 1980s. Each warned Americans about the dangers of unbridled corporate power, subjects treated in Chapters 3, 4, 8, and 13. These historical examples put the Wal-Mart debate in context, showing how questions about abundance, giantism, and private interests have preoccupied Americans since the foundations of the republic. Chapters 14 and 15, moreover, consider Wal-Mart's place in the service sector and the role of American multinationals in the global economy.

As the story of Wal-Mart demonstrates, there are many compelling reasons to study the history of American business. First, people who run their own companies can learn a good deal from it. History shows that small and midsized businesses, including "mom and pop" enterprises, have always been vital to the U.S. economy, much as they are today. At the start of the twenty-first century, there were 4.5 million corporations, 16.4 million non-farm proprietorships, and 1.6 million partnerships in the United States. Many of these 22.5 million enterprises were small companies, including newsstands, coffee shops, local plumbers, real-estate brokerages, general contractors, and the franchises of national chains. These firms added value to American life, providing consumers with food, goods, and services not within the scope of large corporations, while functioning as vehicles of upward mobility for minorities and immigrants. Their predecessors were the dockside storekeepers, tavern proprietors, itinerant peddlers, neighborhood drug stores, home economists, corner grocers, local restaurants, and agricultural growers considered in Chapters 3, 5, 9, 10, 11, and 13.

Second, history can help to explain the complex relationship—sometimes feisty, sometimes cozy, and never dull—among business, government, and politics. Today's lawmakers spend their days grappling with distended federal agencies, budget deficits, and trade imbalances, while firms navigate the complicated regulatory framework and dangerously litigious environment. Frustration runs high over rules and regulations, probes and investigations, and interminable lawsuits and opaque judicial decisions. It is easy to lose sight of the reasons for this apparatus. Studying the past reveals the problems, issues, and obstacles that gave birth to government intervention, instilling an appreciation of the necessity for labor unions, antitrust legislation, minimum wage laws, and ecological protections—subjects considered in Chapters 6, 7, 8, 11, and 13.

Finally, business history illuminates the ways in which the drive for greater human dignity, liberty, and civil rights has been at the core of the American experience over four centuries. Managers at the Hudson's Bay Company who traded with North American Indians (Chapter 3); U.S. senators who debated slavery's extension into Kansas (Chapter 5); and General Motors labor economists who negotiated with auto workers during New Deal (Chapter 11) tried to balance economic imperatives, cultural differences, and social pressures. The profit motive exerted powerful sway, but factors such as race, gender, ethnicity, social class, and consumer choice acted as countervailing forces that influenced decision makers in telephony, pharmaceuticals, department stores, airlines, advertising, and baseball.

Major Problems in American Business History considers how American enterprise evolved over the past four hundred years, tracing the nation's shift from an agricultural to a service economy. It focuses on the lives of people doing business— on their hopes, dreams, decisions, and struggles. It assumes that a variety of experience is valuable, and that we can learn something from shopkeepers, plantation owners, factory managers, and big business executives. Instructors who emphasize traditional topics, such as institution building, business–government relations, political economy, and multinationals, will find important coverage in this volume. Professors curious about the gender, class, racial, ethnic, and cultural dimensions of American enterprise will find much, too. Attention to business and culture is rapidly reshaping the discipline, particularly among members of the Business History

Conference (BHC), the major international organization in business history. This volume seeks to capture some of that variety and excitement.

This book showcases research by multiple generations of business historians, featuring classic writings and recent scholarship. The mix of documents and essays shows students that there is no "one best way" to study business history. There are as many approaches as there are questions, issues, and scholars. We hope, moreover, to demonstrate that American enterprise has a rich, invigorating past. Economic concerns have always motivated Americans, making business a historical topic equal in significance to politics, religion, reform, labor, gender, immigration, social thought, and race. Through the lens of business history, we can better comprehend important current issues and events.

This book is part of a textbook series, Major Problems in American History, designed for upper-division college courses. Volumes in the Major Problems series present documents and essays that focus on a particular period or a specialized topic in U.S. history. This volume is intended to serve as the primary or secondary text in lecture courses and seminars on American business history. It might also be used as a supplementary text in classes on the history of technology, economic history, American civilization, American studies, or general U.S. history.

Business historians relish case studies, sometimes organizing their books around a series of them to explore larger questions. This volume follows that pattern. Each chapter has an introduction, primary sources, essays, and a bibliography. Each chapter's introduction puts it in historical context, discussing a period, topic, or theme and suggesting ways to think about a problem or set of problems that historians consider important. Each introduction identifies the topics under analysis, reviews the major interpretations, discusses seminal approaches, and poses important questions. The documents in each chapter provide the voices of men and women engaged in some aspect of business enterprise. The essays in each chapter show how scholars approach similar topics from different viewpoints. The head notes labeled "Documents" and "Essays" explain how the primary and secondary sources relate to the chapter's overarching themes. These notes are designed to help students make connections. Finally, the short bibliographies, "Further Reading," list major works that students can explore for book reviews or in-depth study and research.

The chapters in *Major Problems in American Business History* are arranged thematically and chronologically, allowing instructors to emphasize topics or periods in their courses. Every chapter is organized around a set of issues specific to a period, linking business and economic history to one or more major themes in American history. Chapters 2 and 3, for example, consider debates about capitalism in early America, trade networks in the Atlantic world, and the impact of merchants on the political economy. Chapters 8 and 11 situate transformations in American business and technology within major reform movements, namely, the Progressive Era and New Deal. Other themes central to American history, such as slavery, technology, consumerism, the military-industrial-academic complex, and environmentalism, provide the organizational motifs for Chapters 5, 7, 10, 12, and 13. Aspects of the international economy and globalization are considered in Chapters 2, 3, 6, 10, 12, 14, and 15.

In New England and the Delaware Valley, several institutions enabled us to complete *Major Problems in American Business History*. At Boston University,

Bruce J. Schulman supported this project during his tenure as director of the American and New England Studies Program by funding Regina Lee Blaszczyk's research assistant. In this capacity, American studies Ph.D. student Paul "V." Schmitz diligently retrieved countless articles from the business press on subjects from Hollywood to hotels. At the University of Pennsylvania, Ruth Schwartz Cowan has graciously hosted Reggie's appointment as a visiting scholar in the Department of the History and Sociology of Science, providing access to the fabulous resources at Van Pelt and Lippincott Libraries and to a community of scholars genuinely interested in how business, technology, science, and culture intersect. Elsewhere in Philadelphia, the Chemical Heritage Foundation advanced this project in various ways, courtesy of Arnold Thackray, Ron Reynolds, Miriam Schaefer, and John Van Ness. At Rutgers University, Dean Margaret Marsh and history department chair Andrew Lees have long supported Philip B. Scranton's research in business and technological history. Moreover, discussions with colleagues Paul Israel, Susan Schrepfer, Howard Gillette, and Mike Geselowitz have been immensely valuable to Phil, as has been his two years chairing the Rutgers Center for Historical Analysis project, Industrial Environments.

In nearby Wilmington, Delaware, the Hagley Museum and Library holds unparalleled collections in the history of American enterprise. The most senior scholar in American business history, Alfred D. Chandler, Jr., once described Hagley as the nation's foremost library in American business and economic history. He was right. Created to preserve du Pont family and Du Pont Company materials, Hagley over the past few decades has expanded its collections to include manuscripts, photographs, and imprints that document the full scope of American enterprise. Two former managers, director Glenn Porter and archivist Michael Nash, launched this collecting initiative, which is being continued by George Vogt, Terry Snyder, and Lynn Catanese. Through the Hagley Center for the Study of Business, Technology, and Society, we enjoyed unfettered access to these collections, aided by resourceful librarians and archivists. In the Hagley Center, seminars and conferences always get the intellectual juices flowing, thanks to Roger Horowitz's imaginative programming.

From the inception, Houghton Mifflin's Senior Consulting Editor Jean L. Woy shared her expansive ideas for the project and helped to determine its fundamental outline. Along with series editor Thomas G. Paterson, Jean envisioned a highly accessible reader with chapters that linked developments in business and the economy to mainstream topics in American history. These editorial concerns dovetailed nicely with new work in business history that was making those connections. The synergy shaped this reader into a book that exposes students to historical interactions among business enterprise, economic development, and political, social, and cultural trends.

At the editorial and production stages, several Houghton Mifflin staff played key roles. We'd especially like to thank Senior Development Editors Fran Gay and Julie Swasey for helping to guide the writing and revision process and Associate Project Editor Teresa Huang for shepherding the project from manuscript to bound book.

Over the project's duration, countless colleagues put in their welcomed two cents, much to the book's benefit. The reviewers who commented on the annotated table of contents deserve special thanks: Jonathan J. Bean, Southern Illinois University at Carbondale; Colleen A. Dunlavy, University of Wisconsin–Madison; Pamela Walker

Laird, University of Colorado–Denver; Mark H. Rose, Florida Atlantic University; and Steven W. Usselman, Georgia Institute of Technology. These scholars will see their influence in this volume, which is much better due to their feedback.

During the volume's gestation, numerous archivists, historians, and librarians shared ideas, manuscripts, and other sources. Unfortunately, we were unable to include all of the stimulating material provided by these generous colleagues. We are grateful to Janet Abbate, Glen Asner, Chris Baer, William H. Becker, Sven Beckert, Mansel G. Blackford, David Brock, Ann M. Carlos, W. Bernard Carlson, Joe Conley, Tracey Deutsch, Nathan L. Ensmenger, Louis Ferleger, John Fleckner, Patrick Fridenson, Walter A. Friedman, Tiffany M. Gill, Hugh S. Gorman, Linda Gross, David Hancock, Howell John Harris, Ellen Hartigan-O'Connor, Susan Hengel, Sheldon Hochheiser, Roger Horowitz, David A. Hounshell, Richard R. John, Peter Kolchin, Gary Kulik, Stuart W. Leslie, Laura Linard, Kenneth J. Lipartito, Christopher McKenna, Marge McNinch, Mary O'Sullivan, Edwin J. Perkins, Shari Ratchet, Rosalind Remer, Donna Rilling, Christine Meisner Rosen, Fath Davis Ruffins, David B. Sicilia, Kathryn Steen, Marc J. Stern, Rohit Daniel Wadhwani, Marsha Warrick, and Jon Williams. We extend special thanks to Bruce J. Schulman and Geoffrey Jones, who read the narratives for Chapters 12–14 and Chapter 15, respectively, with critical eyes.

Friends and family have especially provided encouragement and support. Phil, as always over the last two decades, is deeply grateful for Virginia McIntosh's love and realism, and to his late mother, Della Scranton, for passing down the joy of learning. As ever, Nina and Bill Walls watched from the sidelines, quietly supportive and eager to see Reggie's next project in print. Most important, Reggie thanks Lee O'Neill, who provided the love, inspiration, and managerial insight that brought this project to completion.

R. L. B.
P. B. S.

Major Problems in
American Business History

CHAPTER
1

Business and Us

In 1925, Republican President Calvin Coolidge addressed the American Society of
Newspaper Editors and coined a phrase that became a mainstay of American
culture: "The chief business of the American people is business." Coolidge's catchy
comment is often quoted by historians describing the procorporate policies of the
Republican administrations in the 1920s. But his remarks are relevant in a broader
way. They capture something so deep-rooted that it is often overlooked by those
who study the many facets of American history, from society and culture to gender
and race relations.

In the mid-1920s—as now and before—business was the driving force in
American life, the raison d'être for millions of Americans striving to find a place
in the social order, a glimpse at the good life, and a piece of the action. To be sure,
other things mattered more to many Americans. Some took greater inspiration
from God, or more comfort from friends and family. Others valued solidarity with
their union brethren, racial groups, and ethnic communities. Still others revered
higher pursuits, bowing to the demands of literature, art, and science. Whether
they acknowledged it or not, these people shared a common thread. One way or
another, everyone earned a livelihood—through manual labor, white-collar
work, or a wisely invested trust fund. Business enterprise was the mechanism that
generated jobs, profits, dividends, and prosperity. Capitalism linked evangelical
preachers, mom-and-pop storekeepers, corporate executives, and ladies and gentlemen of leisure in a uniquely American economic culture.

Historians who study American enterprise know these fundamental facts.
Digging beneath the surface, these scholars seek to understand how the many
varieties of business, from peddlers' push carts to multinational corporations, made
the economy work. They try to learn how the people who ran businesses made decisions that affected the market basket of products, determined the wages and work-
days of millions of people, and shaped entire industries, geographic regions, and
economic sectors.

Business historians know that entrepreneurs, like other historical actors, were
influenced by their backgrounds, experiences, and prejudices. They suffered from
the same weaknesses that plagued the rest of humanity. Business historians look
beyond such stereotypes as "robber barons" and "global capitalism" to shine a light
on the commercial foundations of the American experience.

E S S A Y S

In the first essay, Philip B. Scranton, coeditor of this volume, explains why business history is a valuable area of study for college students. He surveys everyday experiences with reference to their economic significance, underlining the premise that business lies at the heart of American culture. What are the Classic Choices, Strategy Angles, and Big Ideas? How can they help us understand the history of business?

Next, Alfred D. Chandler, Jr., the Straus Professor of Business Administration Emeritus at the Harvard Business School and author of the Pulitzer Prize–winning book, *The Visible Hand: The Managerial Revolution in American Business* (1977), looks at a key economic development that preoccupied business historians who came of age between the 1940s and the 1960s. As part of this generation, Chandler sought to understand the ascent of U.S. business to global leadership in the postwar era. He found the roots of that growth in the period from 1860 to 1930, when big business came to dominate some American industries. In the second essay, Chandler outlines his seminal theory about the rise of big business. What factors contributed to this development? What roles did markets, technology, and managers play? How were cultural issues involved?

In the third essay, Mary A. Yeager, associate professor of history at the University of California–Los Angeles and editor of *Women in Business* (1999), breaks away from Chandler's approach and offers an alternative vision for business history. Yeager argues that the economic world should be viewed from the bottom up, that is, from the perspective of women in business. She values the experiences of farm women, shopkeepers, midwives, nurses, servants, and office workers who sustained the capitalist system from its inception. How might Yeager's perspective allow for an interpretation of business that is sensitive to culture, politics, and law?

In the fourth essay, David Vogel, the Soloman Lee Distinguished Professor of Business Ethics at the Haas School of Business at the University of California, Berkeley, examines the relationship between business, government, and politics in the United States, with reference to other capitalist economies. Writing in the 1980s, Vogel was influenced by Washington debate over whether a national industrial policy would help business cope with a flagging economy. In this context, he argues against the widespread perception of business and government as adversaries. Taking a historical perspective, Vogel sees the federal government and American enterprise entwined in a beneficial symbiosis that dates back to the early nineteenth century. How does Vogel's analysis help explain business-government relations in our own time? How does this symbiosis explain American economic culture?

The final essay is jointly authored by Christine Meisner Rosen, associate professor of business and public policy at the Haas School of Business at the University of California, Berkeley, and Christopher C. Sellers, associate professor of history at the State University of New York, Stony Brook. Rosen and Sellers propose a new focus for business history, stressing the interface of enterprise and the environment. They draw on theoretical models developed by industrial ecologists to outline a research agenda that would allow for a fuller understanding of business's relationship to the natural world. Because this approach is so new, you won't find many examples of "ecocultural" business history in this volume. The research has yet to be done! How do culture and nature intersect with business in this research agenda?

Why Study Business History?

PHILIP B. SCRANTON

If you've gotten this far, holding this book in your hands, perhaps paging through it, you have already made (or are considering making) a *business decision:* investing your time and money (or someone else's money) in a term's worth of American business history. You have considered alternative uses for that time and money, at least within the curriculum's rules and your major's options. You're assessing what benefits you might gain from incurring these costs in cash and in effort. All these are business judgments, not just because they relate to money, but because they involve investing, uncertainty, commitments, institutions, and, given class size limits, a version of marketplace supply and demand. This is much more complex than buying a cup of yogurt.

The judgments you're making also have a *history*—a history of decisions about your academic investments that trails behind you as you move through college years. Some were brilliant choices and yielded terrific returns; some not so great. Some you had to make because courses were required; some you chose because of pressure from family ("Get a job!") or friends. Yet for others you had as wide a field for selection as your schedule and interests allowed. Your transcript (the accounting) represents your history of decisions and efforts, but like all accounts it delivers only a few basic bits of information. Your memories, your notes, your books, papers, and exams, your files of e-mails are all sources richer than the transcript; its only virtue is being a compact summary.

The history of your academic investments also has a *context,* both a series of settings and a trail intersecting a broader history. Searching "context" in your memory's Google™, you'll find a variety of conversations and debates about selecting this college and that major or career track. You'll find your personal and family history of investments in schooling before undergraduate years, and, as well, the values, beliefs, and expectations that underlay both earlier and current efforts. Without breaking a sweat, you'll locate a cluster of key institutions forming a background to your choices (family and school, of course, but also churches, teams, workplaces, and so on). And you'll realize that the government of the country you grew up in (and the one you live in now, if that's different) was making choices and making history all the while—that its institutions, laws, conflicts, and economy have influenced in a very deep way your options for investing. Over the decades, governments have supported most elementary and secondary schooling and have provided the roads you now drive, loans for college expenses, and funds for your university's buildings and for research. Thus many of your choices up to this moment have been deeply informed by history, by institutions, and by business as well.

Overall, history and context provide foundations for and meaning to choices, in business, and otherwise. In the United States, the decisions and efforts of businessfolks over the last three centuries have fundamentally shaped and reacted to this

---

Written for this volume by Philip B. Scranton.

nation's dilemmas, crises, and challenges (from replacing the slave economy to manufacturing weapons in wartime to battling global competitors). Now, if you're still with me, I'd like to try and sketch out the benefits you can reap from expanding your knowledge of business and history—the assets you'll take away from investing a term's work. My suggestion is that there are three clusters of these take-aways. I'll call them Classic Choices, Strategy Angles, and Big Ideas.

Classic Choices

Enterprises and the people who own or manage them have to make a series of fundamental choices about what they do and how they're going to do it. Perhaps the most basic is deciding whether they will be involved more in production of goods and services or more in the exchange side of the market economy. The kind of business you have and how it fits into our economic and social context is deeply affected by whether you're making something or making it possible to exchange something someone else has made. Early in American history, most everyone was a producer—farming, fishing, hunting and trapping animals for food and fur, crafting furniture and necessaries. Still there were quite a few businesses buying these products and trading them—haulers and boatmen moving tobacco or grain, dockworkers and warehouse folks moving and storing imports and exports, merchants cutting deals, retailers in cities like Boston or New Orleans, all working on the exchange side. Over the centuries, the proportions changed in three ways:

1. More producers offered services (though many manufactured goods) and fewer were committed to agriculture and extraction of resources from land and water.
2. The business of exchange swelled to massive proportions (railroads, highway, sea and air shipments, advertising, shopping malls, online buying/selling, and global trading).
3. A sizable share of American work became centered not on business but in government, the military, education, and nonprofits, though all were deeply connected to money, technology, and the economy.

Why did these changes come to pass? Good question; seek answers ahead.

Business people have to choose as well between entrepreneurship and management and, in either case, decide how to proceed. It's been often said that, even in these days of gigantic corporations, Americans seek to run their own businesses almost as much as they did a hundred years ago or more. Yet being an entrepreneur can be a lonely and risky job; hence so often small start-ups are family based and family run, which generates advantages and dilemmas (Such as? What might they be?). Being a nonfamily clerk or manager in a family business has long been a dead-end job, unless a strategic marriage into the family could be arranged. In a corporation, though, with its bureaucracy and many subdivided responsibilities, there could be room to rise on the basis of talent and accomplishment (until recently, chiefly for white males), rather than because of bloodlines or weddings. Of course, you'd never own the place, and chances were that you'd never become a CEO, running a whole firm, but the tradeoffs for investing your time and energy usually looked positive. After all, it would take some really arrogant or clumsy fools to ruin a great enterprise, or some ugly turn of history, or some unexpected shift in the business context. Yet beyond the Rockefellers, Carnegies, Morgans, and Gateses—icons of American business success—there was no shortage of great fools, producing shocking bankruptcies (Enron, perhaps?) or slow, agonizing declines. Risk lay all round those making business and career decisions, and risk changed over time. How and why? This you'll see in the documents, stories, and commentaries ahead.

The last classic business choice is between conflict and collaboration, inside and outside the firm. If you're in an entrepreneurial production business (making furniture, say), as soon as your sales grow so that you can't do everything yourself and you have to start hiring workers, the choice is there. Do you command these folks like a military officer or do you treat them like partners, like collaborators in making things? Better, when do you command and when do you collaborate, and why in each case? In a managerial organization, the same issues arise. Most have a chart of responsibilities and supervision, a formal division of labor; but how do you actually do the work? As a team member (when the team leader gets all the credit)? As a hard-driving striver (whom everyone else despises)? As sometimes one and sometimes the other (you opportunist!)? As so often with history, in some times and places, one choice works brilliantly, and in others, the same choice can bring disaster. For example, in the 1920s Henry Ford ran his classic Model T automobile plant in a top-down, driving fashion, paying good wages in a harsh, my-way-or-the-highway regime. Yet during the Great Depression, workers eventually rebelled, violence exploded during a series of company attacks on union campaigners, and Ford lost market momentum, falling behind General Motors in market share.

Meanwhile, companies building the machinery for auto manufacturing realized that their skilled metalworkers were their biggest assets, so even in the depression managers strove to avoid layoffs and sustain the cooperation between shop and office that had long been central to innovation.

Outside the firm, in the wider world and its markets, choosing between conflict and collaboration is a major challenge. We're used to thinking about competition as a naturally good thing, but we infrequently ask "Good for whom?" Theorists tell us competition benefits consumers through lower prices and benefits the whole economy, in a Darwinian way, by killing off weak enterprises and pushing the fitter ones to innovate in technology, marketing, service, and so forth. Of course, the theorists aren't speaking from the position of actual businessfolk looking out for the future. Having run a business for almost fifteen years (a bookstore), I can tell you that competition is nasty stuff; it threatens your profits, prosperity, even your survival as an enterprise. So as the eighteenth-century Scottish economist Adam Smith observed, it's entirely natural for business owners and managers to "conspire against the public interest," meaning to try and find some way to get out of each other's way and make a living by minimizing competition. At times, big corporations have similar interests, acting in a "corespective" fashion, so as to divide even global markets among a small group of companies. This is what the great electrical corporations did in the late nineteenth century, as Westinghouse and General Electric in the United States split the world market for power systems with Germany's Siemens and AEG. Of course, such collaboration, whether territorial market-sharing, agreements on pricing or the movements of prices, rejecting disruptive innovations or sharing in inventing them, is always vulnerable to shifts in technical or consumption trends or in the political and economic context. New competitors start business and old agreements falter, markets shrink in a depression that creates mad price-cutting so as to hold clients, or governments make such agreements illegal. Yet the incentive to collaborate and avoid competition and survive rivals the incentive to compete in order to grab more of the market and earn big money. Like the others, this classic choice is with us still and gets made over and again, even within one enterprise.

Strategy Angles

Given the classic choices they cannot avoid making (and revising), business owners and managers have to come up with strategies that will guide them in achieving their goals (such as increasing profitability, expanding market share, fostering innovation, or selling the company and taking an early retirement). There may be others, but the four angles that I consider important historically are organizational, problem-solving, persuasion, and ethical strategies. They're intertwined with the choices and the contexts but are pretty basic, and their characteristics change over time.

If you operate a managerial, exchange-oriented, competitive firm (say brokering travel services to business), do you want to have the same organizational structure as an entrepreneurial, product-oriented, collaborative firm (say a maker of military weapons components)? Doubtful. In the twenty-first century, your travel-service brokerage needs to be agile, to have rapid abilities to add and drop staff, who need to be talented in communications (personal and networked), a wholly different set of challenges and resources than a business travel agency confronted in 1950, when your principal tool was a long-distance telephone connection. Similarly, a half-century ago, a company would expect to make weapons parts based on detailed specifications military agencies provided; nowadays your weapons components builder needs a research and development (R&D) unit; long-term knowledge of engineering, materials, and testing; durable links with subcontractors and armed forces' purchasers; and a mass of high-tech machinery (along with the skilled workers to run it with precision). One situation today demands a flat, flexible organization, the other an elaborate hierarchy or network accumulating and retaining specialized competencies, and both were different a half-century ago. Overall, organization and operation are mutually reinforcing, and a mismatch between the two can spell disaster. Historically, this often has come when an enterprise designed for one purpose tried to add or shift to something different without realizing that its current organization had to be redesigned as well, as you may see. For example, the DuPont corporation's early success was based on making a few varieties of gunpowder and explosives. When, after 1910, the enterprise entered the business of making synthetic dyes for fabrics and paints, its management, accounting, and inventory systems were not set up to deal with thousands of varieties of products. DuPont lost money hand over fist until reorganizations addressed this mismatch.

Problem-solving strategies are critical to all organizations (and individuals too), but organizations (and individuals) certainly face dramatically different sets of problems across time and space. Historically, the key was being creative about proposing solutions. An urban factory owner just after the Civil War would worry almost as much about fires as about products and markets, but insurance companies either refused to write policies for manufacturers or charged huge premiums. What to do? One strategy was to collaborate and create manufacturers' own insurance companies. A second was to contract with a broker to secure many small insurance policies, each from a different carrier. Alternatively, factory owners could recondition their buildings to limit the rate fires could advance, in time adding sprinklers or powerful fire hoses on each floor. They could also sell off their current plants and build new ones with all the latest fire-retardant and fire-protection features. One problem, yet at least four solutions—and that's crucial. Here's why.

Managers focused on efficiency often believe there's only one best way to solve a problem, but they're imagining that all the possible solutions are comparable along some basic criterion (cost, usually). The solutions offered earlier, though, weren't primarily about cost; they were about strategy options—create a new institution, use a middleman to negotiate, remodel your building, or start fresh. In real businesses, historical or current-day, figuring out what the problem is, then crafting a variety of strategic solutions, can create a pathway out of the swamp. One-dimensional thinking can lead you straight to the crocodiles.

Strategies for persuasion include marketing and advertising, of course, but you've probably heard enough about that just by living in our ad-saturated society. Marketing is about persuading people to spend, but businesses have (and always have had) a great deal more strategic persuading to do. How do you persuade the bank to extend your loan six months? How do you persuade your clients in St. Louis to pay their overdue bills so you can rid yourself of that bank loan? How to persuade your staff to work harder in the rush season when they fear they'll be laid off once demand slackens? In reading business letters (or nowadays, e-mails), poring over policy petitions, or exploring bankruptcy court depositions, business historians learn what arguments entrepreneurs and managers thought were convincing in the past (or in bankruptcies, what arguments failed). Many of the same issues San Francisco merchants and Chicago meatpackers faced in 1900 remain with us, just styled in different ways on different scales. Their strategies for persuasion can teach us still.

Last, businessfolk have to define ethical strategies in order to act in a world where both competition and collaboration may break the law and assault moral and religious values. You can try to ruin a competitor's advantage by widely circulating rumors that his products cause cancer, but you could get sued for slander and shunned by your congregation for shameless lying. You could agree with other banks and big retailers to hike credit card interest rates all at once together, but might face antitrust prosecution for conspiracy and collusion. At what point does aggressive behavior by owners or managers to gain an advantage in the marketplace turn into evil action? What would you *not* do to make money? Why do others do these things?

Think about slave trading, the use of others' slaves in business or agriculture, being a merchant trading in the products of slave labor, being a consumer smoking slave-cured tobacco or wearing slave-harvested cotton made into a shirt or skirt. All these things once were surely legal, but where would *you* have drawn the line? Why would others draw it somewhere else? Is business immoral at its foundations, or are there just bad apples threatening to spoil the barrel? Two sorts of historical context matter very much here—a business person's individual history and values and the larger environment of culture and society in which that person lives. In the crisis of World War II, the United States decreed nationwide rationing of key commodities—gasoline, tires, meat, butter, and so forth. Just as during Prohibition, some Americans made serious money by evading the regulations and the law. How would you compare the two contexts, the 1920s and the 1940s? How would you assess such businesses' actions, ethically and morally?

Many business decisions involve ethical strategies and moral commitments. Recognize that this can involve suspending moral standards in one part of an individual's life (the business part) and sustaining such standards in another part (being a good parent, giving to church and charity). Or the reverse, being fair, precise, and honest in business and a cruel parent—humans are strange that way. In the chapters that follow, you might look for the ethical dilemmas facing individuals and institutions, think about alternatives to the choices people made, and consider what decisions you would have made were you transplanted into their times and circumstances. When you stretch yourself back into time like that, history can genuinely "come alive."

Big Ideas

If studying three hundred years of American business history is not to seem like a forced march across rocky ground, we'll need some big ideas to lift us up so we can see big sections of the landscape we're trying to understand (and see it change). Big ideas will allow us to develop perspectives on the history unfolding below us. They will aid us in organizing ways of thinking about it analytically and critically. After all, the point is not just to encounter the past, but to understand it and make judgments about what is usable today in that mass of tangled experience. Big ideas help us untangle threads of information and weave them into stories, explanations, arguments, and criticisms. They help, but we have to do the work. I'll offer here four concepts, some familiar, others perhaps new to you. There are many more, of course; these are just my favorite four: (1) complexity, (2) capitalism, (3) business, state, and society, and (4) unintended consequences and unacknowledged assumptions.

Complexity is controversial, as we're often told to "Keep It Simple, Stupid." Complexity is about complications, about situations that aren't what they seem on the surface, about causes that have multiple effects or an effect that arises from multiple causes. Complexity is a challenge in that we ache for simplicity, all the while knowing that our lives aren't simple, our politics and culture aren't simple, and history, for certain, wasn't simple. Business history encourages us to embrace complexity rather than wishing or washing it away. Consider an eighteenth-century transoceanic trading "adventure." So many things had to break right for it to be successful: decent weather, an absence of pirates, no plague among the crew, an honest captain, a sturdy vessel, accurate navigation (or pretty near so), demand for the outbound cargo at the ports visited, a supply there of goods in exchange that had high value back home, no sudden outbreaks of war. So why was the voyage successful? All of the above. Why did it fail? One or two things went wrong. This opens a nice point—failure often seems much easier to explain than success, but be careful: there are complex failures just as there are, sometimes, simple successes.

Capitalism is another controversial big idea—not just because there was a twentieth-century contest between capitalist and socialist/communist systems, traces of which remain with us. The term "capitalism" has generated a great deal of fuss first, because it has enormous moral and practical weight, assessed differently by different observers and actors, and second, because it has a hotly contested history.

Here we need to distinguish between "business," the making and trading of things and services, which has been going on for millennia, and "capitalism," which is a particular way of doing business invented, depending on your point of view, some- where between 1500 and 1750, somewhere in Europe, and exported from there. From where I sit, what is distinctive about capitalism is not profit seeking, or private property, or money exchanges, or credit, or corruption, but a *relentless drive for improvement, expansion, and control, defined and channeled through economic in- stitutions (usually firms) and their interactions, and involving technological change.* It's not universal, even now, and in America, it spread irregularly across the land- scape through the eighteenth and nineteenth centuries—how, when, and where (and under what definition of capitalism) are questions historians continue to debate. After all, in the 1700s and 1800s, some family farms strove for simple self-sufficiency and, like the Amish still, disdained most new technologies and avoided expansion. They were involved in markets to a degree, but they weren't capitalists, in my view. My definition is hardly the only one, so as you work, you might test to see where it fits and where it fails.

Because we built and inhabit a capitalist economy, the relations between busi- ness, the state, and our society are an important focus, the third big idea. The state (governments at all levels) has long been crucial here, for its leaders and employees actively construct the environment in which enterprise can (or cannot) function. States create the rules of the market game and enforce them, well or badly. States build the society's defenses and promote creation of transport and information infrastructures. By ignoring some things, states allow their unregulated develop- ment (e.g., religious congregations, community associations, chat rooms). By being active, states define what fairness means, what money we shall use, what consti- tutes proper or antisocial behavior, what boundaries we may establish or cross without interference.

For their part, businesses can be both social and antisocial, and much of this has to do with boundaries. Inside a business there's a minisociety—a network of social relations, routines and rules, an environment with conflicts, divisions of labor, alliances, exchanges, sometimes special languages. To operate and endure, that minisociety cannot be dysfunctional, even though many nasty things may happen. It cannot block achieving its goals, descend into civil war, or be looted by one or another party. Outside, our business must create social, as well as economic, rela- tions with other businesses and institutions, *for whose fate we're not responsible.* That's the boundary point. Nor are the others responsible for our survival, and no business or collection of businesses is responsible for the general welfare of society. At this juncture, the great divide begins. Is the general welfare of society sustained simply by permitting businesses, individually and collectively, to operate with a minimum of interference from the state, as Adam Smith and his descendants assert? By contrast, is the general welfare of society threatened by the anarchy of business competition and by collaborations that "conspire against the public interest," as Adam Smith also observed and as regulators argue?

Perhaps business and the state are locked in a perpetual tug of war over power and authority in society, over the shifting boundaries between the economic and the political. One has laws, courts, and armies; the other has stacks of money and the keys to innovation. In American business history, we can see that push-pull contest and will also notice that the government is ever-present in business decisions and institutions. It defends the nation in which business happens, prints the currencies for settling accounts, sets the rules for contracts, and funds the courts we need for handling disputes. Rather like business, the state refers to a collection of interlinked institutions that develop interests, advance them, and get into battles with one another at times. Keep an eye out for these institutions and watch as their interests shift with the tides of politics.

Last, here's a big idea you've probably heard of and its partner, less familiar. Unintended consequences are a product of human purposes put into action. We try to do something and, whether or not we succeed, often something else also happens, maybe many things we had not planned on. In finishing a business project, you stay up late, pound the Internet, and generate a smashing presentation to clients, which, as you intended, impresses your boss and marks you as a rising star. Oops, your colleagues in the office start stealing your lunch and doing ugly things to your computer. Worse, the also-impressed clients offer you a job at their headquarters, a thousand miles away. Now what?

The argument for unintended consequences operates in business history as well. Railroads after 1850 often competed by cutting rates to secure market share, but when one line's reductions triggered a flood of other lines' equal or greater cuts, a "rate war" broke out and none of them could make a profit. One observer even argued that the logic of railway competition was "bankruptcy for all." No one intended that outcome, and it took financier J. P. Morgan to sort things out. Although many appreciated Morgan's efforts, others condemned his "Money Trust," as you'll see.

Unacknowledged assumptions are the unstated premises we hold in the back of our minds as we undertake actions. In that sense, they're prior conditions for action, whereas unintended consequences arrive in its aftermath. Let's say you're an investor during the wave of mergers that started in the late 1890s (generating U.S. Steel, among other giant firms). One of your friends is promoting a merger of wagon- and carriage-building companies and shows you the prospectus—rising population so an expanding market, a current business depression making prices low for buying companies, and so forth. You buy $50,000 worth of the stock, and in a decade you've lost every penny. What were your unacknowledged assumptions? At least that horse-drawn vehicles were here to stay, and perhaps also that a big carriage and wagon corporation would be more efficient and more profitable than scattered small and midsized companies. However, the automobile arrives and carriage markets contract sharply. Moreover, carriage buyers want so many different models that big companies can't make them any cheaper than smaller competitors. Wrong on both, you lose!

Unacknowledged assumptions may run the other way, of course. You may presume that change is always happening, and, being an optimist, look for investments at the cutting edges of technology or trade. You might get rich in software or go broke in the dot-com smash, or both. The meaning here: beneath our rational calculations, in this case about investing, our fundamental dispositions and assumptions also figure into our decisions. As you analyze business history, perhaps you can identify assumptions that lie behind others' decisions in other times.

Well, I started all this with your decision to pick up this book and fan through the pages, perhaps to invest in a term of American business history. Chances are, if you've read to the end of this section, you've made that investment and are looking forward to returns on it. As I've suggested here, learning about business history reaches far beyond the immediate subject matter to involve you in debates about decision making, persuasion, institutions, complexity, strategy, capitalism, ethics, the proper role of business and the state, and much more. Thus you can expect that the returns on your time and effort will be positive, perhaps substantial, in the weeks ahead. With any luck, all the unintended consequences will be on the plus side as well. Enjoy!

What Is a Firm?

ALFRED D. CHANDLER, JR.

1. Introduction

"What is a firm?" the title to this session asks. The answer seems to be easy. A firm is a legal entity—one that signs contracts with its suppliers, distributors, employees and often customers. It is also an administrative entity, for if there is a division of labor within the firm, or it carries out more than a single activity, a team of managers is needed to coordinate and monitor these different activities. Once established, a firm becomes a pool of learned skills, physical facilities and liquid capital. Finally, "for profit" firms have been and still are the instruments in capitalist economies for the production and distribution of current goods and services and for the planning and allocation for future production and distribution.

I think most economists would agree on these four attributes of the firm. I, as a historian who has spent a career in examining the operations and practices of business firms, have had little trouble in locating information on literally hundreds of individual enterprises, each of which played a part in the creation and development of modern industries and modern economies. Nor do individuals have difficulty in defining the firms in which they work or the securities of those in which they invest.

If the firm is so easy to identify, why then do we have a session on "What is a firm?" It is one that concerns economists more than economic historians, for it is less a question of economic practice than economic theory. Ronald Coase first raised the question years ago when he asked: If accepted theory assumes that the coordination of the flow of goods and services is done through the price mechanisms, "why is such an organization necessary?" Therefore, he continued, "our task is to discover why a firm emerges at all in a specialized exchange economy."

As an economic historian I've concentrated on practice rather than theory. In *The Visible Hand* I investigated the beginnings and subsequent development of what I term the modern multi-unit enterprise (a firm consisting of more than a single plant, shop, or office) in American transportation, communication, production and distribution. In *Scale and Scope*, published in 1990, I focused on the history of the modern industrial firm—the most complex and the most transforming of modern business enterprises—from the 1880s, when such firms first appeared, through World War II. I did so by comparing the fortunes of more than 200 of the largest firms in the three

Alfred D. Chandler, Jr., "What Is a Firm?" *European Economic Review* 36 (1992): 483–492.

major industrial economies—those of the United States, Britain and Germany—which until the Great Depression produced two-thirds of the world's output of industrial goods.

What I plan to do in this paper is: first to describe the similarities in the historical beginnings and continuing evolution of these enterprises, and then outline my explanation for these similarities. Finally, I relate my explanation of these "empirical regularities" to four economic theories of the firm—the neoclassical, the principal-agent, the transaction cost, and the evolutionary. That is, I attempt to indicate the value of these theories for explaining the beginnings and growth of modern industrial enterprises.

2. Regularities Described

The basic similarities in the collective history of the approximately 800 industrial firms were that a new type of enterprise appeared suddenly in the last two decades of the 19th century, that such firms continued to cluster in industries with the same characteristics throughout the 20th century, and that they were created and continued to grow in much the same manner. There industrial firms first appeared as modern transportation and communication networks were completed—networks that themselves were built, operated, enlarged and coordinated by large hierarchical firms. By the 1880s the new railroad, telegraph, steamship and cable systems made possible a totally unprecedented high volume, steady and regularly scheduled flow of goods and information through national and the international economies. Never before could manufacturers order large amounts of supplies and expect their delivery within, say, a week; or could they promise their customers comparable large-scale deliveries on some specific date. The new potential for greatly increased speed and volume of production of goods generated a wave of technological innovations that swept through Western Europe and the United States during the last decades of the 19th century creating what historians have properly termed the Second Industrial Revolution.

New industries appeared. Old ones were transformed. The making of steel, copper and aluminum; the refining of oil and sugar; the processing of grain and other agricultural products; and the canning and bottling of the products thus processed were all transformed. In chemicals new processes produced man-made dyes, medicines, fibers and fertilizers. New mass produced office, agricultural and sewing machines quickly came on the market as did heavy machinery for a wide variety of industrial uses. The most revolutionary of the new technologies were those that generated and transmitted electricity for lighting, urban traction and industrial power. These new industries drove economic growth and played a critical role in the rapid reshaping of commercial, agrarian, and rural economies into modern, urban industrial ones. The newly formed enterprises that created and expanded these industries almost immediately began to compete in international markets.

Firms in these industries differed from older ones such as textiles, apparel, furniture, lumber, leather, publishing and printing, ship building and mining. They were far more capital-intensive, that is the ratio of capital to labor per unit of output was much greater. And they were able to exploit far more effectively the economies of scale and scope. In the new capital-intensive industries large plants had significant cost advantage over smaller ones. Up to a minimum efficient scale (determined by the nature of the technology and the size of the market) long-run cost per unit of output dropped much more quickly as the volume of output increased than was the case in the older labor-intensive industries. Many too benefited from the economies of scope—that is, those economies resulting from making a number of different products in a single factory or works using much the same raw and semi-finished materials and much the same intermediary processes of production.

Nevertheless, as I wrote in *Scale and Scope:*

> These potential cost advantages could not be fully realized unless a constant flow of materials through the plant or factory was maintained to assure effective capacity utilization. If the realized volume of flow fell below capacity, the actual costs per unit rose rapidly. They did so because fixed costs remained much higher and "sunk costs" (the original capital investment) were also much higher than in the more labor-intensive industries. Thus, the two decisive figures in determining costs and profits were (and still are) rated capacity and throughput, or the amount actually processed within a specified time period. . . . In the capital-intensive industries the throughout needed to maintain minimum efficient scale required careful coordination not only of the flow through the processes of production but also the flow of inputs from suppliers and the flow of outputs through intermediaries to final users.
>
> Such coordination did not, indeed could not, happen automatically. It demanded the constant attention of a managerial team or hierarchy. The potential economies of scale and scope, as measured by rated capacity, are the physical characteristics of the production facilities. The actual economies of scale and scope, as measured by throughput, are organizational. Such economies depend on knowledge, skill, experience, and teamwork—on the organized human capabilities essential to exploit the potential of technological processes.

These enterprises in the new capital-intensive industries began and continued to grow in similar ways. All exploited the cost advantage of scale and scope. Nevertheless, investment in production facilities large enough to exploit these advantages were in themselves not enough. Two other sets of investments had to be made. The entrepreneurs organizing these enterprises had to create a national and then international marketing and distributing organization. They also had to recruit teams of lower and middle managers to coordinate the flow of products through the processes of production and distribution and teams of top managers to monitor current operations and to plan and allocate resources for future ones. The first firms to make the three-pronged set of investments in manufacturing, marketing, and management essential to exploit fully the economies of scale and scope quickly dominated their industries. Most continued to do so for decades.

The tripartite investment gave the first to make it—that is, the first movers—powerful advantages. To benefit from comparable costs, challengers had to construct plants of comparable size and do so after the first movers had already begun to work out the "bugs" in the new production processes. The challengers had to create distribution and selling organizations to capture markets where first movers were already established. They had to recruit management teams to compete with those already well down the learning curve in their specialized activities of production, distribution, and (in technologically advanced industries) research and development. Challengers did appear, but only a few.

The three-pronged investment led to the creation of the modern multi-unit industrial enterprise in those industries where the cost advantages of the economies of scale and scope were the greatest. So from their beginnings in the 1880s they concentrated in the capital-intensive industries. The structure of these industries became, after a short shakedown period, and remained oligopolistic.

In the new or transformed capital-intensive, oligopolistic industries price remained a significant competitive weapon. But these firms competed even more forcefully through functional and strategic efficiency; that is, by carrying out more capably processes of production and distribution, by improving both product and process through systematic research and development, by locating more suitable sources of supply, by providing more effective marketing services, by product differentiation (in branded packaged products primarily through advertising), and finally by moving more quickly into expanding markets and out of declining ones. The test of such competition was changing market share and in the new oligopolistic industries market share and profits changed constantly.

Such oligopolistic competition in these capital-intensive industries sharpened the product-specific capabilities of workers and managers. These capabilities plus retained earnings from profits of the new technologies became the basis for the continuing growth of these managerial enterprises. Firms did grow by combining with competitors (horizontal combination) or by moving backward to control materials and forward to control outlets (vertical integration); but they took these routes usually in response to specific historical situations.

For most, the long-term continuing strategy of growth was expansion into new markets—either into new geographical or product markets. The move into geographically distant areas was normally based on the competitive advantage of organizational capabilities developed from exploiting economies of scale. Moves into related product markets rested more on capabilities developed from the exploitation of the economies of scope. Such organizational capabilities honed by oligopolistic competition provided the dynamic for the continuing growth of such firms, of the industries which they dominated, and of the national economies in which they operated.

3. Explaining the Regularities

Thus the key concept I use to explain the similarities in the beginnings and growth of modern industrial enterprises is that of organizational capabilities. These capabilities were created during the learning process involved in bringing a new or greatly improved technology on stream, in coming to know the requirements of markets for new or improved products, the availability and reliability of suppliers, the intricacies of recruiting and training managers and workers. These capabilities were the collective physical facilities and human skills as they were organized within the enterprise. They included the physical assets of each of the many operating units—the factories, the selling and other offices, and the research laboratories—and of more importance the functional and administrative skills of the employees in such units. But only if these skills were carefully coordinated and integrated could an enterprise achieve the economies of scale and scope that were needed to compete and to continue to grow.

Such managerial skills were based on learning carried on within the different levels of the hierarchy—the operating units, the functional departments, and, as the firm grew, the product and geographical divisions and, of course, the corporate offices. Such learning was a process of trial and error, feedback and evaluation. It is more organizational than individual. Even the skills of individuals depended on the organizational setting in which they were developed and used. If these company-specific and industry-specific capabilities continued to be enhanced by constant learning about products, processes, customers, suppliers and other workers and managers within the firm, the enterprise was usually able to remain competitive and profitable. If not, its market position deteriorated.

The creation, maintenance and expansion of such capabilities permitted American and German firms in the two decades before World War I to drive quickly British firms out of international markets and even Britain's own domestic one in most of the capital-intensive industries of the Second Industrial Revolution. They made it possible for German enterprises to regain swiftly their position in world markets after a decade of war, defeat and inflation between 1914 and 1924, and to come back again in the 1950s after a far more devastating war.

So too organizational learning permitted Japanese firms, first to carry out a massive transfer of technology from the west to Japan. Then once their domestic market became large enough to permit the building of enterprises large enough to exploit fully the economies of scale and scope, they developed organizational capabilities necessary to provide competitive advantage in international markets. Finally the economies that followed the Soviet model by relying on central planning agencies—Gossnap and Gosplan in Soviet Russia—to coordinate current flows of goods through the processes of production and distribution and to allocate resources for future production and distribution prevented managers in units of production and distribution from learning how to coordinate effectively flows of goods from suppliers and to markets based on information and knowledge about current facilities, available supplies and market demand. The failure to develop such capabilities has been central to the disintegration of these centrally planned economies.

4. Organizational Capabilities and the Theory of the Firm

How then do established theories of the firm—neoclassical, principal-agent, transaction cost and evolutionary theories—relate to this historical description of and explanation for the development of the modern industrial firm that has transformed industries and economies in the past century and a half? How do these theories contribute to an explanation of economic growth and transformation?

The first two—the neoclassical and principal-agent theory—contribute little in their present abstract formulations. The neoclassical theory views the firm as a legal entity with a production set (a set of feasible production plans) from which a manager, acting rationally with full information, chooses the set most likely to maximize profits or present value of the firm. Principal-agent theory accepts the neoclassical firm as a production set but gives it a managerial hierarchy. The advocates of this theory concentrate on the abilities of the "owners" to discipline the managers with whom they have contracted to choose and implement the production plans, but who may manage the firm in their own interest rather than for that of the owners. The proponents of agency theory concern themselves with the owners' problems of coping with asymmetric information, measurement of performance, and incentives. Both theories see the firm as a legal entity that contracts with outsiders—suppliers, dealers, financial institutions and the like—and insiders—workers and managers. But neither deals with the firm's physical facilities, and human skills and the resulting revenues on which the current profitability and future health of the enterprise depend.

Transaction cost theory has more relevance to the historical story and the explanatory concept of organizational capabilities precisely because it does incorporate investment in facilities and skills. Because it does, I have learned much from its practitioners, particularly Oliver Williamson. The theory focuses on transactions. As Williamson emphasizes, micro-economic activity is organized to economize on costs of production *and* transactions. At issue is whether the costs of transactions carried out by the enterprise are lower by relying on the market (where they are defined through contractual agreements) or by internalizing them within the firm. Such costs are reduced through internalization when firms make investments in highly specialized physical facilities and in human skills based on specialized learning. That is, these specialized assets can only be used for the production and distribution of specific products or services. So they lose value if deployed to other activities. This is particularly the case when a contractual arrangement involves many continuing transactions.

The reason is, Williamson argues, that long-term contracts are difficult to define, because the contracting parties cannot obtain all the necessary information. They act rationally, but this rationality is bounded. Moreover, the different parties involved, acting for their own self-interest, may suppress information, that is, they may act opportunistically often with guile. In Williamson's words: "Any attempt to deal seriously with the study of economic organization must come to terms with the combined ramifications of bounded rationality and opportunism in conjunction with asset-specificity."

The basic difference between myself and Williamson is that for Williamson: "The transaction is the basic unit of analysis." For me it is the firm and its physical and human assets. If the firm is the unit of analysis, instead of the transaction, asset specificity still remains significant; but the specific nature of the facilities and skills are more significant than bounded rationality and opportunism to the shaping of decisions as to internalizing transactions and, therefore, in determining the boundaries between firm and market. For example, in the new capital-intensive industries the need for the firm to monitor high level throughput was much greater than in the older labor-intensive ones. Therefore, whereas firms in the capital-intensive industries internalized distribution, those in the labor-intensive ones continued to rely on independent distributors. Moreover, in capital-intensive industries the pressure to internalize varied with the source of supplies, nature of technology of production, and the size and requirements of markets. So too the pressure for backward integration varied as an industry grew and its leaders expanded into more distant markets.

An understanding of the specific characteristics of a firm's assets, particularly its learned organizational skills, is even more useful than an understanding of the impact of bounded rationality and opportunism on transactions involving those assets in explaining the continued growth of firms into new foreign and related product markets. Knowledge gained in creating a wholesaling organization led to the building of a comparable one in a foreign market. When such markets grew to a size that permitted the establishment of plants of minimum efficient scale, firms used their learned skills to build the new facilities. The number and location of the plants built abroad reflected the minimum efficient scale (mes) of the technology of production and the size of the markets. Thus steel, copper and aluminum plants where mes was very high were rarely built abroad; but in food and machinery many processing or assembling plants were built or acquired in foreign lands.

So too the organizational skills developed in one function often gave the firm a competitive advantage in a related product market. The move into new markets based on competitive advantage in one function required the building of complementary facilities and skills, and, in turn, trained managers in the ways of seeking out and capturing market opportunities. For example, in the years since World War II such organizational skills permitted business machine companies to become first-movers in mainframe computers, over-the-counter drug companies to become first-movers in the new antibiotic prescription drugs, chemical companies to move out of commodities into specialty chemicals and oil companies to replace chemical firms in the production of petrochemicals. Thus in analyzing the continued development of existing industries and the building of new ones, the firm would seem to be a more promising unit of analysis than the transaction, and the concept of the organizational capabilities that permit it to remain competitive, and therefore profitable, in national and international markets more pertinent than those of bounded rationality and opportunism.

This is why I'm sympathetic to the recently articulated evolutionary theory of the firm, first made explicit by Richard Nelson and Sidney Winter in their *An Evolutionary Theory of Economic Change* published in 1982. As Winter notes, their emphasis is placed on production rather than exchange. On the other hand, he continues, "[neoclassical] orthodoxy and transactions costs economics, place deal-structuring at center stage, and cast the economics of production and cost in a supporting role."

The central concept of Nelson and Winter is that of routines. "In evolutionary economics, the specifics of the ways firms relate to owners, customers, and input suppliers are subsumed under the heading of organizational routines." They define "'routine' in a highly flexible way, much as 'program' (or, indeed, 'routine') is used in computer programming." For them "routines are the skills of the organization" that in turn become its "genes."

In a recent, still to be published, paper Nelson, building on his and Winter's past work and the more recent writings of David Teece, Giovanni Dosi, William Lazonick and myself, presents "An Emerging Theory of Dynamic Firm Capabilities." Here he focuses on "three different, if strongly related features of a firm that must be recognized if one is to describe it adequately: its strategy, its structure, and its core capabilities." For Nelson the strategy and structure of firms, not the transactions in which they are involved, shape its capabilities. For him strategy is "what scholars of management mean, as contrasted with game theorists. I mean a set of broad commitments made by a firm that define and rationalize its objectives and how it intends to pursue them." "My concept of structure," he continues, "also is orthodox, as is my belief that strategy tends to define a desired firm structured in a general way, but not the details. Structure involves how a firm is organized and governed, how decisions are actually made and carried out, and thus largely determines what it actually does, given the broad strategy." Finally, "[s]trategy and structure call forth and mold organizational capabilities, but what an organization can do well has something of a life of its own."

5. Towards a Dynamic Theory of the Firm

The emerging theory of dynamic firm capabilities is of great value to the economic historian, for it recognizes the centrality of the processes of production and distribution and of organizational learning in the creation, development and transformation of those processes. It also emphasizes differences in production and distribution technologies and activities of different industries and different sectors. For me personally this emerging theory will be of particular value in further historical analyses. By focusing more sharply on organizational learning, I should be able to say more about why functional and strategic competition in modern capitalistic economies play a larger role in changing market share and profit than does price, to explain more carefully the success and failure of enterprises to grow by moving into new regional or related product markets, and to analyze more precisely the competitive success or failure of national industries and even national economies in which these firms operate.

Like the builders of the evolutionary theory of the firm, I see agency and transaction cost theory of value to the economic historian but within the framework of evolutionary theory. Like them, I am convinced that the unit of analysis in developing a relevant theory of the firm must be the firm, not the contractual arrangements or transactions that it carries out. Only by focusing on the firm can micro-economic theory explain why this legal, contracting, transacting entity has been in the past the instrument in capitalist economies for carrying out the processes of production and distribution, of increasing (or hampering) productivity, economic growth and transformation. Only by focusing on the firm can theory predict the firm's continuing role as an instrument of economic growth and transformation, and be of value for developing policies and procedures for maintaining industrial productivity and competitiveness in an increasingly global economy.

Considering Businesswomen

MARY A. YEAGER

A focus on women opens the way for a more culturally-centered and politically-aware business history, one that is likely to alter the way we have looked at business people, business institutions, and their relationship to society as a whole, for better or worse. Some societies have been more business-oriented than others, generating an expanding and vibrant middle class to cement the link between production and consumption. They have harnessed the energies of business people and institutions in a way that has more often expanded than constricted the opportunities and economic and political rights of others. No society has produced a business system as open to women as to men, where women have outnumbered men as owners, managers or workers.

From the vantage point of women, "business" and business activities acquire new meaning and significance. Business emerges as a rather humdrum practical affair,

Mary A. Yeager, ed., *Women in Business,* vol. I (Cheltenham, UK; Northampton, Mass.: Edward Elgar, 1999), pp. xvi–xxi.

where money is made rather than accumulated, where growth and expansion is the exception rather than the rule, where management is more a high-wire balancing act between home and work than learned skill. For most of the women considered, here and one suspects, for most businessmen as well, business was more often than not, simply "work"—a way to make a living and survive. In fact, business was often such an integral part of women's lives that some steadfastly refused to distinguish business from life. Business was, after all, little more than another transition stage in their own lives. "You . . . can never think of me as a business woman," [Zora Putnam] Wilkins cautioned her daughter in 1910. "That is because I make a business of life and living my business." "Business is just life," American real estate entrepreneur Edith Mae Cummings wrote in 1929, "and we had life before we had business."

In portraying women in business and the business activities of women, [we can] . . . recognize that women, as individuals and as groups, never fully coincide with specifically defined roles or activities. Women, like men, engage in multifaceted roles with connections and discontinuities spread unevenly over their lifetimes. Their roles as business people are but a slice of their lives at any one point in time. The various dimensions of their lives influence how they perceive their opportunities and how they manage and organize their lives inside and outside of business.

Yet focus on business requires that it be differentiated from other activities, relations and patterns of actions and outcomes if we are to understand women's lives and experiences as a whole and the role that business has played in shaping their thoughts and actions. So vague was the original meaning and use of the term when it first appeared in English sometime in the 15th century, that most scholars have ignored its etymology. "Business" meant "busy-ness," or continual action, the doing of some activity, with no particular identity attached. Unmoored from its historical context, the word has been used and interpreted in a variety of ways. "Business" has been used as a noun, to indicate any profit or money-making activity; as an adjective to describe men and women, as in "businesswoman or businessman"; and as an adverb to denote how something is done, as in a "business-like" manner. It has been used to denote innovative and entrepreneurial as well as routine behaviour. It has referred to decisions for organizing the production and distribution of goods and services for profit. It has even served as a euphemism for sexual intercourse.

The only constancy in the meaning and usage of the term "business" has been an unexamined and unexplained gender bias that has more often than not masqueraded as gender neutrality. Despite the fact that men have long controlled, dominated and defined the business world, the history of business has been written as if sex and gender have not mattered, at least not in ways that have significantly affected the conduct, structure and performance of business institutions. Business may describe a particular kind of activity or decision-making capability. It may describe what a man or woman does. It may even impart an "identity" to a man or woman. But what business does or does not do; what business is or is not, has little to do with the sexual or gendered identities of people engaged in business.

A re-examination of the etymology of the term reveals that "business" may well be one of the more stubbornly gendered words and activities of our time. The meanings and usages of the word evolved from a long, drawn-out gendering process by which the business activities which were most talked about, analysed and valued came to be associated more intimately with men than with women; more often with production than with distribution and consumption; more with decision-making and leadership than with mere participation in exchange; more with profit than income maintenance or sustenance; more with firms than with families; more with formal, for-profit exchange in private markets than with informal, barter or non-pecuniary transactions; and, finally, more with goods than with services.

A journey through history reminds us that gendering processes evolved differently over the centuries and came to be interpreted in a variety of ways by different societies over time. It underscores business' humble origins in the everyday world of commerce and exchange. In its earliest formulations, "busy-ness" aptly described the continual interaction of a variety of producers, traders and consumers, in constant motion between home and village or town, exchanging goods and services, transacting deals, making and broadening markets from one location to another "dickering"; negotiating, over matters of money and meaning, over costs, prices and values. The "clamor of the marketplace, as [the French social historian] Fernand Braudel so colourfully describes, was easy to hear and fascinating to watch. So audible and magical was the spontaneity of exchange in the marketplace, so socially intertwined with daily living was market exchange, that the individual identities of people participating in the market were unremarkable. In the beginning there were simply markets made by women and men participating in the business of exchange.

Market exchange was not a business conducted by equals, however. Nor did it lead to equitable results. By the 16th century, the term "business" had come to describe a person's official or professional duties as a whole, a stated occupation or trade. It was also more consistently and systematically associated with men than with women, and with long distance more often than local trade. These changes in the use and meaning of the term foreshadowed the 17th-century appearance of a "man-of-business" who devoted less time and energy to public affairs of state and more time to private money-making activities in unregulated markets. Although it can be argued that "Man" carried universal connotations, historians generally, and business historians in particular, following a record left primarily by men in business, have interpreted "Man" as male. Already by the 17th or early 18th centuries, business had become an affair defined largely by certain groups of men in business and one considered by most societies to be conducted primarily by men in business.

Neither Braudel nor business historians seem to have noticed that the women who had helped to churn "the wheels of commerce" had mysteriously disappeared into a "varied and active [market] proletariat," while a handful of elite merchants and their families built social hierarchies over women's heads. Sometime between the period that Braudel colourfully calls the birth of the "ordinary" market economy in the 15th century and "the capitalism of the real businessmen" in the 16th to 17th centuries, women dropped out of sight, or at least out of the sight of historians and of men in business. The "clamour" of ordinary markets was reduced to an inaudible hum. Scholarly ears picked up only the controlled melodies of the more visible and "powerful merchants" who constructed business "firms" out of the kin and family networks that pushed them out into the world and up the social ladders that stretched between family, economy and state. With the instruments of exchange in hand and the "power apparatus" engaged, men were described as pushing capitalism into and out of one sector after another, spilling its costs and benefits unequally, beyond national borders into the world economy.

Had Braudel and other historians looked more carefully and probed more deeply the gendered origins and evolution of business, they might well have seen that not all women everywhere went quietly into the night when men pushed themselves onto centre stage. Although the recorded history of business suggests a predominantly masculine-oriented set of images, there were also important moments strewn across the history of capitalism where women challenged cultural traditions and imparted their own set of meanings and significance to the term "business." One such "moment" occurred in ante-bellum America, when the word "business" had come to mark distinctly new "masculine" and "feminine" identities. The double-billed appearance of the words "businessman" and "businesswoman" signalled a new and disturbing development in the business world. The expansion of markets, fuelled in part by an energetic, growth-oriented government and the spread of transportation improvements, had widened opportunities for everyone, including women. Those few women who dared to compete with men in business threatened a virtual war between the sexes.

The *Southern Literary Messenger* recorded the trials and tribulations of one "universally recognized businesswoman," Mrs Jemima Jowers Leathers. When Jemima refused to take orders from her businessman husband, either at home or in her own business, her husband, Jeptha exploded: "I'll have my way or die!" To which Jemima was reported to have said: "You may have your way and die, too, for what I care, but I'll show you that I'll do as I please with my own business!" What began as a domestic dispute triggered by Jemima's success in business, ended when the Legislature acted "to divorce Jemima Leathers from her husband, Jeptha Leathers, and to confer upon the said Jemima the powers and privileges of a Fem. sole."

This example, one of many scattered across the business landscape, underscores the significance of investigating those unusual moments of everyday economic life that swirl beneath the broader contours of capitalism. Instead of Braudel's grand vision of capitalism, the history of women in business suggests a complex gendering process underway in the family and home, in the market and state. It was as much a political as an economic process, making some people leaders and others followers. Knowing more about why this process evolved when and in the way it did to produce different outcomes for men and for women is the important challenge for scholars of women in business. Etymology may not reveal the contested interpretations and negotiations, or the power struggles involved in the fight for meaning and significance. But if considered alongside the record of economic change more generally, it yields some important clues.

The delineation of distinct spheres of activity to differentiate those associated with family, economy and state marked the continuation of a process of change that enabled those men who commanded more resources and more power (often by drawing on resources of family or clan) to achieve monopoly control of violence, which in turn laid the basis for the state's comparative advantage in supplying protection and business' advantage in production, trade and exchange. These respective advantages were neither equally matched nor distributed evenly across societies over time. However, privileged access to society's resources, and the ability to organize and mobilize those resources to protect and provision society, created social hierarchies that divided communities into small groups of elites at the top and a mass of commoners at the bottom.

The "man of business" grew up with both the state and the market from a pivotal and strategic position in the family. Upon decisions about who and what to protect, and what and when to produce and exchange, hinged the fates of state-makers, market-builders, families and clans. Forced to grow up together, states, markets and families became social laboratories for organizational learning, laboratories whose entrants were sexually and socially gendered, and whose capabilities for organization expanded or receded as they confronted and overcame the differential constraints and opportunities that enveloped their lives. Both in governing and in provisioning, families and clans, however defined or constituted, came to play a vital role as key social units and collectivities that made the decisions that defined the range and limits of economic activity. Decisions about production and reproduction, often in unconscious rhythms with the ups and downs of economic life, and in constant struggle and negotiation with the state or alternative governing forms, manifested biological and cultural differences between men and women.

A complex series of interrelated decisions underlay the contested construction of a series of boundaries and spheres that distinguished the private and public roles of men and women and the functions and obligations of private and public institutions. The answers to questions concerning who was excluded from which activities, when and for what reason, reflected not only the distribution of power and resources, but also the sources of societal imagination and inertia. Most importantly, perhaps, the process of boundary construction created mutual links of dependency between three different and asymmetrical systems of social organization that conditioned the lives and perceptions of people who criss-crossed the boundaries of families and firms, the market and the state. Just as people engaged in transacting business in the market began to develop their own mechanisms and methods of production, reproduction and control in relation to their families and kin and particular life circumstances, so too did people involved in building and running the state develop the machinery to govern, sometimes in cooperation with, sometimes in opposition against, various merchant and business groups. The systems were not always compatible nor even complementary. Sometimes they clashed, causing social upheaval and re-organization; always they continued to change as people interacted with each other and with the earth's resources. Whatever the case, activities within, between, and across the intersecting spheres shaped the histories of the people in business and the business systems that evolved.

When [Wilkins] and Cummings spoke of business as just another aspect of life, they did not single out their families, firms, the market or the state. For them, business involved negotiating boundaries across and around these institutions. For these two American women in the 1920s, business appeared to present far more opportunities than constraints. For other women in different societies, or even for other American women and men, business was just as likely to be an additional load rather than a lodestar. It depended on context, culture and circumstances.

To probe the changing meaning and usages of the word "business," then, it is important to piece together from the raw materials of evolving civilizations around the globe the activities and functions, the values and attitudes, the symbols and rituals, that have merged to produce the changing realities and images of business and of the people who engage in business activities. The term "business" did not acquire singular meaning overnight in a particular region at a particular point in time. Business accumulated different meanings over time as different individuals and groups engaged in commerce and exchange with other individuals and groups. Business was both cause and consequence of changing civilizations.

To define "business" from the standpoint of women, we need to situate business very broadly in four interrelated and interactive systems of organization: the family, the firm, the market and the state. If participation in decisions involving the production, distribution and sale of goods and services for a profit is considered an irrevocable characteristic of business, distinguishing it from all other institutions and activities, then we need to consider women as decision-makers first and foremost and to include decisions about reproduction and marriage with those of money-making and production for profit. By broadening our conceptualization of decisions and decision-making to incorporate joint decision-making strategies in the family, we are better positioned to determine to what extent these areas of decision-making influence the attitudes, behaviour and performance of men and women in business. We need to think more about how women's decisions regarding marriage and families facilitated or obstructed their business careers and/or those of their partners and husbands. Decisions about whether to marry and have children, decisions about housework and job work, are all decisions which influence women's and men's attitudes and behaviour with regard to business and society's attitudes to business people. If the term "businessman" is used to designate "anyone who participates in decisions for organizing the production and distribution of goods and services for profit," we nevertheless need a culturally and socially conditioned view of economic activity that incorporates the gendered identities of business people as they move in and out of families, firms, markets and states.

Do Business and Government Get Along?

DAVID VOGEL

The relationship between the American government and American business—particularly big business—has been generally regarded as an adversarial one, in sharp contrast to the more co-operative relationships that appear to be more common in other capitalist societies. Yet it is by no means clear that the relationship between business and government in the United States is as distinctive as most scholars have assumed. Certainly popular antagonisms toward large firms is not a uniquely American phenomenon; it has also characterized domestic politics in other capitalist societies, including Germany, France, and Britain. Compared with other capitalist nations, the relationship between workers, farmers, and small businessmen, on the one hand, and big business, on the other, have not been noticeably conflictual in the United States. American unions have been relatively weak and moderate, American farmers have accommodated themselves to the imperatives of large-scale industrial development since the 1920s, and, except in a limited number of policy areas,

David Vogel, "Government-Industry Relations in the United States: An Overview," in *Comparative Government-Industry Relations: Western Europe, the United States, and Japan,* ed. Stephen Wilks and Maurice Wright (Oxford: Clarendon Press, 1987), pp. 106–113.

American small businessmen have not been an important factor in American politics for nearly a century. Only middle-class reform groups have been more influential in America than in other capitalist nations. On balance, it would be hard to make a case that large firms in America enjoy less political influence *vis-à-vis* other sectors of the economy than their counterparts in other capitalist polities.

What, then, is distinctive about business–government relations in the United States? America does remain unique in the scope and complexity of its laws and regulations that restrict management prerogatives in a wide variety of areas. The most obvious example is anti-trust policy: no other capitalist nation has sought to establish such a wide variety of legal controls over the terms of competition. As a former chairman of the board of Du Pont put it, "Why is it that my American colleagues and I are being constantly taken to court—made to stand trial—for activities that our counterparts in Britain and other parts of Europe are knighted or given peerages and comparable honors for?" Likewise, no other capitalist nation has established so many rules that restrict exports of goods and services. These range from the Foreign Corrupt Practices Act to a variety of trade embargoes and restrictions on the sale of particular products to specific countries.

Yet, while these restrictions may be annoying to particular firms, their aggregate impact on the competitive position of American industry is rather modest. The enforcement of America's anti-trust laws has been highly selective and has not resulted in levels of market concentration significantly different from those of other capitalist nations. In recent years, the American government has not hesitated to encourage mergers on the part of marginal firms or permit co-operation among firms in the more dynamic sectors of the economy. And while some rules and regulations have certainly restricted exports, on balance, American foreign policy over the last half-century has been highly supportive of American foreign trade and investment.

It is true that over the last two decades, the level of conflict between government officials and corporate managers over the making and implementation of policy in areas such as occupational health and safety, environmental and consumer protection, and equal employment has been substantially greater in the United States than in any other capitalist nation. No other capitalist nation has provided middle-class reform groups with such extensive opportunities to participate in the policy process nor erected so many legal and procedural obstacles to prevent business–government co-operation in the making and enforcement of regulatory policies. As a result, the politics of government regulation of corporate social conduct in the United States have been relatively adversarial.

Yet, at the same time, if one compares the actual implementation of regulatory policy in the United States with that of other capitalist nations, it does not appear that, in the final analysis, American officials have been any less sensitive to the costs of compliance than their counterparts in other capitalist nations. As in the case of anti-trust policy, American controls over corporate social conduct may be far stricter than in other capitalist polities, but their enforcement has been highly selective. For all the numerous, and well-documented, "horror stories" about the effects of particular regulatory policies on various firms and industries, the burden they have placed on the American economy does not appear to differ significantly from those imposed on firms in other capitalist nations; indeed the United States spends a smaller proportion of its GNP on pollution control than does Japan. It is the way

American regulatory policies are made, not the costs of complying with them, that distinguishes government regulation in America from other capitalist nations.

Moreover, it is important to keep the nature of conflict between business and government in America in perspective. Government regulation represents one of the relatively few areas in which there has been considerable antagonism between business and government in the United States. But, even in this policy area, conflict has been the exception, not the rule. Most importantly, economic regulation in the United States has only rarely challenged management prerogatives; in most cases the initiative for regulation came from the regulated industries themselves. America's current efforts at economic deregulation primarily involve conflicts *among* particular firms and industries, not *between* business and government. Prior to the mid-1960s, the regulation of corporate social conduct was handled primarily at the state level and for the most part it was relatively co-operative. It only became relatively adversarial in the mid-1960s, and the level of conflict has diminished considerably since the late 1970s. The close quasi-corporatist ties between defense contractors and the Department of Defense, farmers and the Department of Agriculture, real estate developers and builders and the Department of Housing, and bio-enginering firms and NIH are the norm, not the exception, of business–government relations in the United States.

Moreover, business–government relations in America have always been relatively co-operative at the state level. During the first half of the nineteenth century, state and local governments played a critical role in promoting the expansion of American agriculture, primarily through financing and organizing the development of the nation's infrastructure: more than two-thirds of the 4,000 miles of canals constructed in the United States prior to the Civil War were financed by state governments. From the outset of the industrial revolution, states competed actively with each other in seeking to attract new investments, while, over the last century, creating a good "business climate" has been a majority priority of most state governments. Although a few states did pursue anti-growth policies during the 1970s, more recently virtually all state governments have become much more active in seeking to improve the performance of their economies. The emergence of Silicon Valley in northern California has created a model of government–business–university co-operation which other states are now trying to duplicate. Every state now has some form of an economic development agency; in thirty of the fifty states, this agency has cabinet-level status and in several states its budget exceeds $100 million. Such agencies typically employ a variety of means of attracting investment, including direct financial assistance, tax incentives, training assistance, and special programmes, such as the establishment of low-cost industrial sites.

Corporate Political Participation

What also makes the pattern of business–government relations in the United States distinctive is the nature of corporate political participation. Unlike in other capitalist nations, where there exist a wide array of official and quasi-official channels through which business can regularly communicate its views to public officials, in America corporate political participation tends to be much more *ad hoc* in nature. While in other capitalist nations the consultation of industry by government is assumed, in America it must constantly be asserted; business enjoys few privileges not enjoyed by other interest groups. Business may be no less influential in the United States than in other capitalist nations, but in America its influence comes at a price: companies must invest substantial resources if they are to affect public sector decisions.

For example, if a company or trade association wants to affect a government regulatory policy, it must prepare expert testimony for both congressional committee hearings and agency rule-making proceedings, hire lawyers who can then take an appeal against an agency decision to the federal courts, and then, if necessary, entrust its lobbyists to seek to have the regulatory statute amended in the legislature. The later strategy may require the company to enter into alliances with other interest groups, mobilize its shareholders and employees to write to or visit their representatives in Washington, and mount a nation-wide public relations campaign designed to influence press coverage of the issue. Each of these efforts involves a considerable expenditure of corporate resources.

By any index, the scope of government intervention in the economy has increased enormously over the last two decades. The American government has become more active in both regulating and promoting business than at any time in its history. As a function of the deregulation of banking and telecommunications, the increase in government spending as a proportion of GNP since 1965, the expansion of social regulation, the growing internationalization of the American economy, and the significant expansion of the Defense budge, the corporate strategy of American firms has become increasingly dependent on government decisions. From this perspective, Reagan has not so much reversed the direction of the New Deal as accelerated it.

The result has been an unprecedented expansion in the amount of resources business firms devote to the political process. For example, in 1961 only 130 firms were represented by registered lobbyists in Washington, DC, and of these only 50 had their own Washington staffs. By 1979, 650 firms had their own registered lobbyists and 247 had full-time employees in the nation's capital. While only a small minority of *Fortune* 500 companies had public affairs offices in 1970, a decade later more than 80 per cent had established such units. In 1974 there were 89 corporate political action committees; by 1982 there were 1,555. Corporate public relations programmes and efforts to build "grass roots" support among employees, stockholders, and community groups were relatively rare prior to 1970; they have now become an important component of virtually every effort on the part of the business community to influence public policy. In addition, the American business community has devoted enormous resources toward influencing the climate of intellectual opinion, through its sponsorship of conferences, publications, and academic research. These efforts have, on balance, proved extremely effective. The relative degree of political power exercised by business at both the federal and state levels increased significantly between 1977 and 1985. Business became much more successful both at shaping the political agenda and in influencing the outcomes of a variety of particular public policies, particularly in the areas of tax policy and government regulation.

America continues to differ from other capitalist nations, not only in the resources companies devote to affecting public policy, but also in the decentralized nature of that participation. In spite of its heightened politicization, the American business community, like all other interest groups in American society, remains politically fragmented: there is no peak organization capable of representing the views and interests of American business as a whole.

Over the last century, a number of organizations, including the Chamber of Commerce during the Progressive Era, the National Association of Manufacturers during the 1930s, the Committee for Economic Development during the 1960s and the Business Roundtable during the 1970s, have sought to play such a role. But their efforts have invariably floundered. Even trade associations in America have been far less important than in Europe or Japan; their role atrophied still further during the 1970s as companies became more diversified. In fact, over the last fifteen years, the nature of corporate political participation has become even more fragmented, with individual firms themselves becoming the most important political units. [D. B.] Yoffie and [J. L.] Badaracco write:

> A company with a politically active senior executive, a corporate public affairs staff, a PAC, its own media identity, a Washington law firm, and a Washington office or lobbyist has an independent apparatus for political action. It has its own information, contacts, and bargaining chips. It can lobby in Congress, negotiate with executive agencies, and take court action. Such a company can still work, in the traditional ways, through its industry association or through umbrella groups like the Chamber of Commerce. But it can also act on its own.

Finally, compared to other capitalist nations, business–government relations in America have also been less stable. Over the last century the United States has experienced three major changes in the role of government in the economy. The first, associated with the Progressive Era, occurred between the turn of the century and the First World War. The second was the New Deal, which dominated American politics during the 1930s. The third, which still lacks a convenient label, took place between the middle of the 1960s and the middle of the 1970s; it was associated with a major increase in the scope of federal controls over corporate decisions in the areas of personnel policy, environmental and consumer protection, and occupational health and safety. The political turbulence associated with the reforms instituted during each period served to reinforce the long-standing belief of American corporate executives that the American political process is both unpredictable and potentially threatening to their prerogatives. As one executive put it at a business meeting in 1975, at the height of the most recent reform period, "My industry is regulated up to its neck. You are regulated up to your knees. And the tide is coming in." Since then, of course, the influence of business over public policy has significantly increased, yet the perception of vulnerability expressed in this quotation remains a permanent feature of American business culture.

Conclusion

This paper has argued that business–government relations in America have been less distinctive than has been commonly assumed. It has primarily focused on the area of industrial policy, since students of business–government relations have frequently argued that it is precisely the inability of America to develop a coherent set of sectoral policies that reveals the distinctiveness of the American political system. We have suggested that America does have a highly developed set of industrial policies, which, on balance, appear to be no more or less coherent, consistent, or successful than those of its major industrial competitors. It now appears that the period of *laissez-faire* capitalism, far from establishing the future course of business–government relations in America, may instead come to be seen as a historical anomaly. In many respects we have come full circle: American business–government relations over the last half-century increasingly resemble the pattern of "state mercantilism" of the first half of the nineteenth century. The only difference is that the former period of co-operation took place primarily at the state level, while, in recent years, the federal role has become much more important. Yet, in a sense, the fundamental dynamics are similar: just as the states financed the construction of canals and roadways in order to enable their citizens to compete more effectively with those of other states, so can many of the recent promotional policies of NASA and the Department of Defense be viewed as an effort to enable American industry to become more internationally competitive.

What does continue to make America distinctive is not so much the effect of its public policies on business as the way in which they are made. Precisely because American politics are highly pluralist and fragmented, companies have been forced to devote substantially greater resources to public affairs than in other capitalist nations. While some firms have cut back on their political activity since Reagan's election, the overall level of political involvement of American business remains extremely high by historical standards. And it is likely to remain so in the foreseeable future—particularly as issues surrounding the international competitiveness of American industry continue to occupy a prominent place on the nation's political agenda. The increased politicization of business represents one of the most significant changes in business–government relations in America over the last two decades.

Business and the Environment

CHRISTINE MEISNER ROSEN and CHRISTOPHER C. SELLERS

Business history has never paid much attention to the environment. Brushing aside the firm's reliance and impact on the natural world, early business historians zeroed in on the role of the entrepreneur in big business's rise. They found it easy to truncate, marginalize or altogether ignore the physical processes by which the stuff of nature—"raw" materials—was carved or coaxed out of mountains, forests, and deserts, channeled into factories and squeezed and cajoled into commodities. They scarcely considered the ever-changing varieties of "waste" generated by businesses and customers, which so often infiltrated, polluted, and otherwise altered the world beyond factory and office. They devoted equally little attention to the effects of resource extraction and use on plants, animals, land, air, or water, much less entire ecosystems and climate.

The emergence of Chandlerian institutional history perpetuated this neglect. The organizational approach encouraged business historians to focus on the dynamics of corporate management and the internal evolution of the firm. Its adherents impressed upon their colleagues the value of analyzing how corporate managers responded to market conditions beyond the firm's walls, through strategies and organizational

Christine Meisner Rosen and Christopher C. Sellers, "The Nature of the Firm: Towards an Ecocultural History of Business," *Business History Review* 73 (Winter 1999): 577–579, 584, 587–596. Reprinted by permission of the *Business History Review*. Copyright © 1999 by the President and Fellows of Harvard College; all rights reserved.

structures. Although there was nothing in this approach that would have prevented them from examining how firms organized themselves to manage natural resource utilization, pollution control, or any other aspect of the interface between the corporation and the environment, Chandler and his followers chose to concentrate on matters relating to vertical integration and the evolution of the large, diversified, multi-divisional industrial corporation. In the process of investigating these admittedly important aspects of the rise of big business, they continued to ignore the subject of big business's dependence and impact on the natural world. Their inattention persisted despite the fact that they wrote at a time of mounting public outcry over industrial pollution and increasing conflict between business and an ascendant environmental movement.

We hope . . . [to] impress upon business historians the richness, relevance, and importance of questions about business's interface with the natural environment. An environmentally-minded business history will, we contend, restore crucial materialist dimensions to the field: not just the concreteness of money and markets, but of fire, rock, dust and smoke. We also believe there are few more promising avenues for integrating business history into larger historic panoramas or for ushering the field through a cultural turn. . . .

A first step in opening the borderlands between environmental and business history is to acknowledge that we have, as a discipline, tended to treat industrial impacts like pollution as well as most other environmental dimensions of business activity as if they were what economists call "externalities." Externalities are "social costs" or "spill-over effects" of economic activity, which may impact buyers and sellers as well as bystanders in a given economic transaction, but are not priced into the transaction itself. As such, they are distinct from the conventional economic costs internalized by the price mechanism of the market system in which business managers operate. And as such, they have long been widely accepted as naturally outside or beyond the scope of the businessman's economic calculations, unless artificially internalized into the market by regulation. . . .

In contrast, what we have discovered in our own historical research . . . is that when environmental impacts like pollution do come to be perceived as "problems," they do not stay "external" to economic actors for long. Instead they stir increasing deliberations and engagements among those concerned, including business managers. The environment is thereby brought within the cultural sphere of those who manage business organizations. It influences their thoughts and actions, whether as managerial decision-makers within the firm or as civic actors beyond it.

Like other members of society, business managers do not line up in a monolithic fashion in opposition to pollution control and other forms of environmental protection. As one of us, Christine Meisner Rosen, showed in an article, . . . a group of Chicago businessmen near the turn of the century became involved in anti-smoke campaigns. They took it upon themselves to clean up their own as well as their fellow business owners' smoke stacks, some of whom strongly opposed their efforts. However "social" or "external" the cost of smoke pollution may have been in theory, many business people saw their own advocacy of smoke reform as pivotal to maintaining their reputation both among their fellows and among actual or potential customers in Chicago and elsewhere. Theirs was an "altruism" with a steady eye to the bottom line.

Moreover, once we move to consider the entire range of business dealings with material[s] throughput and its impacts, it becomes clear that what can seem "external" to business calculations in one era can become a carefully figured entry on corporate balance sheets in another. In his book, *Hazards of the Job,* Christopher Sellers showed how industrial diseases arising among workers in lead factories and mines remained largely external to the economic calculations as well as the awareness of American owners and managers in the late nineteenth century. Once a hue and cry were raised within and without the factory, however, and especially once an industrial hygiene expertise and a workers' compensation system began to hold firms accountable for some of these costs, companies started to pay experts to assess and remedy these "problems."

In sum, rather than writing off business' environmental relations as "externalities," we propose that business historians treat the environmental dependencies and impacts of business just as they have treated market conditions and labor relations. We urge our colleagues in business and environmental history alike to investigate the ways in which people in industry have viewed, used, and otherwise managed natural resources and allowed, palliated, or ignored the environmental consequences. Take a look at how managers have responded to the existing possibilities and constraints of the physical world, as well as those posed by markets, economics, technologies, social and governmental demands. Test the hypothesis that managers in specific industries knowingly managed their firms' environmental impacts in ways that harmed or benefited natural ecosystems or human health. Consider whether firms reduced pollution and mitigated other environmental problems, not only in reaction to court decisions and regulation, but also in order to maximize profits or to enhance the personal goals of individual managers.

For a starting point, we take our cue from the integrative vision of the young Karl Marx: ". . . the celebrated 'unity of man with nature' has always existed in industry, just like the 'struggle' of man with nature." . . . All business activities involve the direct or indirect manipulation of materials and energy derived from the natural world. This involvement can be as glaringly obvious as the clear-cutting of a forest, or as subtle and covert as the nearly invisible electronic sinews grounding global hedge funds and the vast and growing commerce of the Internet. Whatever the level of visibility, an environmental history of business must keep an eye on the "natural" origins of the physical stuff used in economic production. It must trace the environmental metamorphoses and impacts that result, as well as the operative notions of "nature" and the "natural" that guide and constrain such transformations. Seen in this light, questions about the environment are not peripheral but central to business history. They are a basic dimension of what business is about.

Industrial ecologists have laid out a useful framework for conceptualizing this unity between business and nature. They have developed a theoretical model of an "industrial ecosystem" that describes the flows of material and energy that connect business with the natural world. Materials and energy flow from the natural world into the industrial system and back out again in a continuous and never ending feedback loop. Stages in these currents divide roughly into three: one, the transformations by which natural resources are extracted from the earth and converted into raw materials and mechanical energy; two, the manufacturing operations by which these material and energy flows are worked and reworked into useable or saleable products; and three, those processes and practices by which manufactured products come to be distributed to and used and disposed by consumers.

All three of these stages in the flow of materials and energy between business and the natural world generate "wastes" that can become "pollution." Though the content and definition of these terms may vary drastically across time and place, . . . resource extraction, manufacture, and consumption all eventually give rise to excess or residual materials, from the brine of oil wells and the smoke of industrial boilers to peeling house paint. Treated or untreated, these inevitable discards return directly to the natural world, where they eventually decay or degrade over time—unless managers or consumers shunt them back into the production and consumption loop by reprocessing and reusing them. . . . [T]hese wastes could have powerful consequences that managers could not ignore.

Business managers and institutions play an active role in directing the flow of energy, materials, and wastes, through all the stages of production and consumption in the earth's industrial ecosystem. In so doing, they deeply influence how the rest of society emits waste and interacts with and impacts on the natural world. Most business historians are quite familiar with the effects that mines and factories have had on the air people breathe, the water they drink, and the physical landscape in which they live, work, raise families, and engage in recreational activities, even if these subjects are not often addressed in their historical work. What is important about the industrial ecology concept is that it directs attention to how flows of energy, material, and waste within industry affect the world beyond the factory and office when they move into the realm of the society that consumes the fruits of industrial production. . . . [T]his outflow could bring toxic chemicals directly into the homes and schools of ordinary Americans. It has also led to animal and plant extinctions and other less drastic forms of natural eco-system change and may be causing global climate change. Industrial ecology points toward management's role in fostering the consumption that drives such broad environmental change, as an important facet of the historical relationship between business and the environment.

At the same time, we also need to recognize where, for our purposes, the analytical model distilled by industrial ecologists falls short. A theory developed by engineers, industrial ecology focuses heavily on quantitatively analyzing material and energy flows as they move through industrial ecosystems. It also devotes a great deal of attention to the development of more environmentally benign product designs and manufacturing systems and the creation of waste exchanges and other engineering systems, in an effort to close material and energy flows to bring them more in line with the closed loop flows characteristic of natural biological ecosystems. As yet, however, it offers only the crudest of tools for grappling with the symbolic or strategic dimensions of managerial decisions, especially those dealing with marketing, advertising, public relations, and even philanthropy, which may sustain or alter the flow of commodities past the factory or office door. Nor does it adequately contend with how changing understandings and values may alter decisions about the streaming of energy or material within the workplace as well as without. Not least of its limitations, it gives minimal attention to how market factors shape the managerial thoughts and actions that direct the flow of energy and materials through industrial ecosystems. In contrast, we've seen fit to craft an approach to business history that is at once *eco*logical and *eco*nomic and *cultural.*

No matter what aspect of business's co-evolution with the natural world a business historian may choose to tackle, he or she will confront a wide array of questions and challenges. . . . [W]e have settled upon several themes and guidelines that we feel are critical to an *ecocultural* approach to business history.

One of the most important themes is technology. From flaked rocks and other simple hand tools, to water, steam, and electric powered machinery and the modern computer, technology has shaped economic production in a myriad of ways since ancient times. Many of the most important stories waiting to be told in the ecocultural history of business pivot around some technological change, whether in energy sources, shop floor processes, or extractive machinery. . . . [T]echnology has served as an instrument both by which business managers exploited and/or degraded the environment and as a tool by which they sought to rectify the damage. We must address both sides of this historical potential.

A second theme is the role of the market, a topic as central to an ecocultural business history as it is to the other more conventional aspects of our discipline. The market has shaped business's interactions with the natural environment in truly powerful ways. It is, as we all know, the primary engine of business's development and so a major determinant of business's impact on water, air, land, climate, and biological ecosystems. With all its imperfections (including environmental externalities), it set the prices that determined when and where managers chose to invest in the technologies that allowed them to extract raw materials from the earth and process them into manufactured goods. It was the mechanism through which consumers discovered the prices of those goods and purchased them. It provided the signals that enabled managers to decide whether it made economic sense to invest in technologies to abate pollution and other environmental harms.

The market did not operate in a vacuum, however. A third theme with which ecocultural business historians must grapple is the role of the government in shaping the interactions between business and the natural world. We cannot address the role that the marketplace played as a driver, mediator and shaper of the material flows of materials through the industrial ecosystem without studying the role of the state. Through its allocation of property rights, its adjudication of court cases, its regulation of economic activity, its ownership of natural resources, its decisions to go to war, and other activities, government has played a crucial role in structuring the institutions that define the market signals to which business managers responded. It has also imposed rules and requirements on business that sometimes forced managers to take actions that conflicted with or changed those signals. Government figures prominently . . . , not just as an actual or potential environmental regulator, but as an advisor to industry, the creator of demand for manufactured goods, and a shaper of values and attitudes.

While the ecocultural history of business shares these three themes with other approaches, its distinctiveness resides in the guidelines by which it addresses them. First, the ecocultural perspective in business history consistently focuses on the cultural shaping of the interface between business and the environment. "Culture" here includes the ideas, values, and assumptions of business managers regarding what is good, bad, technically and economically feasible with regard to environmental issues—as well as those of environmentalists, government regulators, judges, scientists and the public as a whole. For instance, to understand the impact of either markets or the state in the history of environmental management, it is necessary that we examine the critical role that managerial (and non-managerial) *perceptions* of cost and "interest" played in the economics and politics of pollution control. We must not assume that these ideas are necessarily objective measures of reality. Our historical actors may have believed that their ideas accurately reflected economic, political, technological, or ecological reality, but notions about economic and political self-interest have proven at least as mutable as ideas about the workings of nature. . . .

As business historians, it is important that we examine the environmental impacts of culture at the level of the individual firm or industry, at least to the extent the primary sources permit this. We must be sensitive to the fact that individual managers at different companies typically exhibited a range of attitudes toward environmental issues. Management attitudes and practices also varied across different industries. We need to try to understand the reasons for these differences as well as analyze their consequences—for the development of business, as well as the evolution of the natural world.

We must also explore the values and experiences of ordinary factory workers. Direct contact with the raw materials and machinery of production often made workers the first witnesses to the environmental consequences of managerial decisions. From their ranks came the earliest victims of industrial materials later decried as environmental toxins, like lead paint and pesticides. Communities of working families have historically borne witness to their suffering as well as to the worst environmental disasters wrought by corporations, from Donora to Love Canal to Bhopal. Depending on era and topic, the ecocultural historian of business may find workers' experiences as revealing and important as those of the managers who direct their labor, a valuable counterpoint from which to evaluate the significance of the attitudes and values expressed by high ranking executives and other business managers and professionals.

In addition to these micro-level aspects of business culture, however, we must address more macro cultural dimensions of the business-environment interface. Broader societal and national cultural contexts shaped the values and attitudes that managers and workers and others brought to the subject of business's use and abuse of the natural world. One of the most surprising discoveries . . . is the powerful role that national cultures played in how business people and government regulators made sense of and dealt with pollution and other environmental problems. Further grappling with this dynamic requires that American business historians pay more attention to work being done by business historians in Europe, Asia, and elsewhere. While one of the most exciting contributions of the Chandlerian business historians has been the world-wide similarities they have documented in the evolution of corporate organization, the ecocultural perspective may better enable us to understand how, over time, differences in national cultures led to different managerial experiences even in similarly organized firms.

Throughout, another fundamental guideline for ecocultural inquiries into business history must be to maintain a steady attentiveness to the physical world with which business people and their enterprises interact. One of our most important tasks is to incorporate analysis of the material world into our study of the evolution of the firm. We need to explore how business managers responded to the opportunities as well as the constraints offered up by their material surroundings. Environmental history has deep roots in historical approaches that attribute agency to influences and forces beyond the social or cultural activities of humanity—to climate, geography, pests, disease vectors and the like. Business historians can profit by following suit. We need to recognize the agency of the physical world, even as we attend to the agency of business. This is to say that we need to address both the matter of how business has been shaped by the physical world and the matter of how managers have in their turn managed that interaction. From the vantagepoint of this dual focus, business historians can provide a unique perspective on one of environmental history's chief concerns: the dialectical, interactive dance between human and non-human agency in history.

. . . [C]ulling and interpreting the evidence to write nature into business history poses a variety of methodological difficulties. Society, culture, even markets arise out of the fabric of human talk, evidence of which we can often obtain through documentary records. Alas, however, many of the natural world's physical actors and influences, from smoke or lead dust to perturbations of climate, register fitfully in the documentary leavings on which historians must rely.

Today's scientific accounts of environmental agents and dynamics can help us overcome this hurdle, aiding our understanding of the environmental conditions to which past business managers (and government regulators, and ordinary citizens) responded. We can make use of contemporary research bearing upon those aspects of nature about which we plan to write, whether in biology, chemistry, physics, or other natural sciences. Applying modern science to the past presents further dilemmas, however, since the knowledge and awareness in other times and places often proves so different from today's claims. Fortunately, those more Western and industrialized societies which environmental historians of business will likely study offer at least some precursor body of written knowledge on most environmental dynamics and effects we will choose to investigate. Often it has been compiled by some earlier group of scientific professionals.

We nonetheless think it necessary for ecocultural historians of business to contend with the culturally rooted dimensions of knowledge, rather than relying entirely upon the "truth" of modern science to explain everything. We also need to make sense of the often dramatic differences between past and present claims about the physical world, rather than simply dismissing the old assumptions and understandings as incorrect. Economists' notions of "information" and "uncertainty," while they provide some tools for dealing with such questions, can only go so far. Taking our cue from the work of anthropologists and cultural studies of science, we urge business historians to piece together how nature and its operations looked to past business people and their experts. However mistaken today's science may initially make business people in other times and places appear, ecocultural historians may find that the past natural knowledge or expertise on which their business subjects relied had its own internal sense and coherence. Understanding how different groups socially and culturally constructed nature in the past—what they believed certain rocks were and could become, what harms they thought a metal to cause—will strengthen our explanations of past business behavior. For while business decisions had objective impacts on the physical world that today's science may better comprehend, managers often made those decisions quite rationally in the context of their convictions about that world. We need to take seriously both past and present knowledge about nature in order more fully to fathom the history of the business/environment interface.

This brief list of desiderata for an ecocultural approach to business history is far from exhaustive. It should nevertheless be enough to give our readers a sense of where we'd like to see the field go, and how to get there. Of course, the greatest challenges come as we pursue more than just a couple of these themes and guidelines and seek to weave them together into coherent and illuminating narratives.

 F U R T H E R   R E A D I N G

Atack, Jeremy, and Peter Passell. *A New Economic View of American History: From Colonial Times to 1940*, 2d ed. (1994).

Blackford, Mansel G. *The Rise of Modern Business in Great Britain, the United States, and Japan*, 2d ed. (1998).

———, and K. Austin Kerr. *Business Enterprise in American History*, 3d ed. (1994).

Bruchey, Stuart. *Enterprise: The Dynamic Economy of a Free People* (1990).

———. *The Wealth of the Nation: An Economic History of the United States* (1988).

Chandler, Alfred D., Jr. *Scale and Scope: The Dynamics of Industrial Capitalism* (1990).

———. *Strategy and Structure: Chapters in the History of the Industrial Enterprise* (1962).

———, and Richard S. Tedlow. *The Coming of Managerial Capitalism: A Casebook on the History of American Economic Institutions* (1985).

Childs, William R., et al., eds. *Business and Industry* (2003).

Cochran, Thomas C. *Business in American Life: A History* (1972).

Engerman, Stanley L., and Robert E. Gallman. *The Cambridge Economic History of the United States*, 3 vols. (1996–2000).

Galambos, Louis, and Joseph Pratt. *The Rise of the Corporate Commonwealth: United States Business and Public Policy in the Twentieth Century* (1988).

Laird, Pamela Walker. *Pull: Networking and Success Since Benjamin Franklin* (2006).

Lipartito, Kenneth J., and David B. Sicilia, eds. *Constructing Corporate America: History, Politics, Culture* (2004).

McCraw, Thomas K. *American Business, 1920–2000: How It Worked* (2000).

———, ed. *Creating Modern Capitalism: How Entrepreneurs, Companies, and Countries Triumphed in Three Industrial Revolutions* (1997).

Miller, William, ed. *Men in Business: Essays on the Historical Role of the Entrepreneur* (1979).

North, Douglass C. *The Economic Growth of the United States, 1790–1860* (1961).

Tedlow, Richard S. *Giants of Enterprise: Seven Business Innovators and the Empires They Built* (2001).

Schweikart, Larry. *The Entrepreneurial Adventure: A History of Business in the United States* (2000).

Whaples, Robert, and Dianne C. Betts, eds. *Historical Perspectives on the American Economy: Selected Readings* (1995).

CHAPTER
2

Capitalism in

Early America

Writing in 1959, the historian Carl N. Degler, in Out of Our Past: The Forces
That Shaped Modern America, *examined British America from the vantage
point of the people who freely emigrated there. Degler believed that, as an extension
of the world's most developed Protestant nation, these colonies attracted people who
valued individual achievement and material gain. In his view, British emigrants
saw business as a way of life. People with modest ambitions hoped to prosper by
running farms, stores, and workshops. Those with grander ideas obtained private
charters from provincial legislatures to finance and manage new towns, while
some, like William Penn, secured proprietary land grants from the crown and
became the nation's first large real-estate developers. Degler was not the first
historian to argue that capitalist practices and Protestant ideals shaped British
America. Since the late 1800s, progressive historians had embraced this point
of view. In the 1960s, Degler's snappy phrase—"capitalism came in the first
ships"—captivated a generation of scholars anxious to understand the roots of
America's rise to global economic supremacy.*

*Today, some business historians follow in Degler's footsteps, equating early
American capitalism with old-fashioned hard work and the determination to
succeed. Other scholars, influenced by developments in social history, see things
differently. Some challenge this emphasis on the domination of business values
and capitalist institutions, arguing that many colonists were foremost motivated
by religious beliefs, political ideals, or highly localized traditional cultures. Others
remind us that official British America did not acknowledge large segments of the
population. Slaves, servants, Indians, and most women could not own property
or engage in contractual relations. No amount of ambition would enable their
advancement. Others have focused on everyday operations to illustrate how
even the best-intended colonial businesses were sometimes stifled by the lack of
markets and infrastructure.*

*These documents and essays provide the opportunity to think further
about the meaning of capitalism and business introduced by Philip B. Scranton
and Mary A. Yeager in Chapter 1. What is capitalism, and how does it relate to*

business? How did religion, community, and kinship networks support or contra-dict capitalist institutions and business values? What role did geography play in economic development?

D O C U M E N T S

Documents 1 and 2 show that artisans and tradesmen who ran small colonial busi-nesses could have disparate experiences, influenced by temperament, circumstances, and culture. As one of British America's most illustrious self-made men, Benjamin Franklin—who wore the hats of a printer, publisher, and inventor—rose from obscurity to prominence, personifying what the eminent German sociologist Max Weber later called "the spirit of capitalism." A prolific writer, Franklin sought to inspire others by publishing upbeat recipes for success in his famous quarterly, *Poor Richard's Almanac* (1733–1758), and in pamphlets such as *Advice to a Young Tradesman* (Document 1). In Franklin's eyes, the pursuit of commerce went hand-in-hand with the fundamental tenets of Protestantism, which in part held that dili-gence and hard work in this world would be rewarded in the afterlife. In contrast, other businessmen questioned the compatibility of commerce and Christian values. In Document 2, the devout Philadelphia Quaker John Woolman, a shopkeeper and tailor, explains his growing disgust with the retail trade. As a storekeeper, he came to see credit, liquor, and fashion as sources of moral corruption. Impelled by his Christian conscience, Woolman eventually left retailing to focus on tailoring and orchard tending.

Generally, the British government prohibited the colonies from establishing certain types of manufacturing facilities to protect its ready market for goods made in English factories. The British Board of Trade encouraged the colonies to produce the raw materials needed by these industries: raw wool, cotton, flax, lumber, whale oil, and bar iron. When mills, furnaces, and other capitalist ventures for producing these exports appeared on the countryside, some colonists resented the encroachment. Sometimes, conflict erupted over the use of natural resources. Documents 3 and 4 are petitions to Rhode Island authorities regarding the dis-position of the colony's rivers, which farmers claimed as their fishing preserve, iron masters saw as an energy source, and commercial fishermen used to earn their livelihoods.

Documents 5 and 6 present two views on commercial development in Florida once the area came under British domain after the Seven Years' War, or the French and Indian War (1756–1763). In Document 5, promoter Alexander Clúny compares the advantages of Florida's coasts, with the aim of attracting British settlers. Although he favors West Florida, Clúny describes East Florida as an asset to the British empire. He sees it as a potential source of agricultural exports such as rice, indigo, silk, wine, and cochineal (an ingredient in red textile dye), and as a strategic trading post with access to the Spanish colonies. In Document 6, Henry Laurens (1724–1792), a promi-nent planter and merchant from South Carolina, strongly advises his business associate, the London merchant Richard Oswald, against establishing a 20,000-acre plantation at Mosquito's Bite in East Florida. He cites the "want of Neighbours, Navigation, & Markets" and the difficulty of managing a slave workforce in this isolated environment as reasons to reconsider the investment.

1. Benjamin Franklin Coaches an Ambitious Tradesman, 1748

TO MY FRIEND, A. B.:

As you have desired it of me, I write the following hints, which have been of service to me, and may, if observed, be so to you.

Remember, that *time* is money. He that can earn ten shillings a day by his labour, and goes abroad, or sits idle, one half of that day, though he spends but sixpence during his diversion or idleness, ought not to reckon *that* the only expense; he has really spent, or rather thrown away, five shillings besides.

Remember, that *credit* is money. If a man lets his money lie in my hands after it is due, he gives me the interest, or so much as I can make of it during that time. This amounts to a considerable sum where a man has good and large credit, and makes good use of it.

Remember, that money is of the prolific, generating nature. Money can beget money, and its offspring can beget more, and so on. Five shillings turned is six, turned again it is seven and three-pence, and so on till it becomes an hundred pounds. The more there is of it, the more it produces every turning, so that the profits rise quicker and quicker. He that kills a breeding sow, destroys all her offspring to the thousandth generation. He that murders a crown, destroys all that it might have produced, even scores of pounds.

Remember, that six pounds a year is but a groat a day. For this little sum (which may be daily wasted either in time or expense unperceived) a man of credit may, on his own security, have the constant possession and use of an hundred pounds. So much in stock, briskly turned by an industrious man, produces great advantage.

Remember this saying, *The good paymaster is lord of another man's purse.* He that is known to pay punctually and exactly to the time he promises, may at any time, and on any occasion, raise all the money his friends can spare. This is sometimes of great use. After industry and frugality, nothing contributes more to the raising of a young man in the world than punctuality and justice in all his dealings; therefore never keep borrowed money an hour beyond the time you promised, lest a disappointment shut up your friend's purse for ever.

The most trifling actions that affect a man's credit are to be regarded. The sound of your hammer at five in the morning, or nine at night, heard by a creditor, makes him easy six months longer; but, if he sees you at a billiard-table, or hears your voice at a tavern, when you should be at work, he sends for his money the next day; demands it, before he can receive it, in a lump.

It shows, besides, that you are mindful of what you owe; it makes you appear a careful as well as an honest man, and that still increases your credit.

Beware of thinking all your own that you possess, and of living accordingly. It is a mistake that many people who have credit fall into. To prevent this, keep an exact account for some time, both of your expenses and your income. If you take the pains

Benjamin Franklin, "Advice to a Young Tradesman," in Albert H. Smyth, ed., *The Writings of Benjamin Franklin,* vol. 2 (New York: Macmillan, 1905), pp. 370–372. This document can also be found in Stuart Bruchey, ed., *The Colonial Merchant: Sources and Readings* (New York: Harcourt, Brace & World, 1966), pp. 113–114.

at first to mention particulars, it will have this good effect: you will discover how wonderfully small, trifling expenses mount up to large sums, and will discern what might have been, and may for the future be saved, without occasioning any great inconvenience.

In short, the way to wealth, if you desire it, is as plain as the way to market. It depends chiefly on two words, *industry* and *frugality;* that is, waste neither *time* nor *money,* but make the best use of both. Without industry and frugality nothing will do, and with them every thing. He that gets all he can honestly, and saves all he gets (necessary expenses excepted), will certainly become *rich,* if that Being who governs the world, to whom all should look for a blessing on their honest endeavours, doth not, in his wise providence, otherwise determine.

AN OLD TRADESMAN.

2. John Woolman's Christian Conscience Impels Him to Leave Retailing, 1756

Until this year, 1756, I continued to retail goods, besides following my trade as a tailor; about which time I grew uneasy on account of my business growing too cumbersome. I had begun with selling trimmings for garments, and from thence proceeded to sell cloths and linens; and at length, having got a considerable shop of goods, my trade increased every year, and the way to large business appeared open, but I felt a stop in my mind.

Through the mercies of the Almighty, I had, in a good degree, learned to be content with a plain way of living. I had but a small family; and, on serious consideration, believed truth did not require me to engage much in cumbering affairs. It had been my general practice to buy and sell things really useful. Things that served chiefly to please the vain mind in people, I was not easy to trade in; seldom did it; and whenever I did I found it weaken me as a Christian.

The increase of business became my burden; for though my natural inclination was toward merchandise, yet I believed truth required me to live more free from outward cumbers; and there was now a strife in my mind between the two. In this exercise my prayers were put up to the Lord, who graciously heard me, and gave me a heart resigned to his holy will. Then I lessened my outward business, and, as I had opportunity, told my customers of my intentions, that they might consider what shop to turn to; and in a while I wholly laid down merchandise, and followed my trade as a tailor by myself, having no apprentice. I also had a nursery of apple-trees, in which I employed some of my time in hoeing, grafting, trimming, and inoculating. In merchandise it is the custom where I lived to sell chiefly on credit, and poor people often get in debt; when payment is expected, not having wherewith to pay, their creditors often sue for it at law. Having frequently observed occurrences of this kind, I found it good for me to advise poor people to take such goods as were most useful, and not costly.

In the time of trading I had an opportunity of seeing that the too liberal use of spirituous liquors and the custom of wearing too costly apparel led some people into great inconveniences; and that these two things appear to be often connected

The Journal of John Woolman (Boston: James R. Osgood and Co., 1871), pp. 90–94.

with each other. By not attending to that use of things which is consistent with universal righteousness, there is an increase of labor which extends beyond what our Heavenly Father intends for us. And by great labor, and often by much sweating, there is even among such as are not drunkards a craving of liquors to revive the spirits; that partly by the luxurious drinking of some, and partly by the drinking of others (led to it through immoderate labor), very great quantities of rum are every year expended in our colonies; the greater part of which we should have no need of, did we steadily attend to pure wisdom.

When men take pleasure in feeling their minds elevated with strong drink, and so indulge their appetite as to disorder their understandings, neglect their duty as members of a family or civil society, and cast off all regard to religion, their case is much to be pitied. And where those whose lives are for the most part regular, and whose examples have a strong influence on the minds of others, adhere to some customs which powerfully draw to the use of more strong liquor than pure wisdom allows, it hinders the spreading of the spirit of meekness, and strengthens the hands of the more excessive drinkers. This is a case to be lamented.

Every degree of luxury hath some connection with evil; and if those who profess to be disciples of Christ, and are looked upon as leaders of the people, have that mind in them which was also in Christ, and so stand separate from every wrong way, it is a means of help to the weaker. As I have sometimes been much spent in the heat and have taken spirits to revive me, I have found by experience, that in such circumstances the mind is not so calm, nor so fitly disposed for Divine meditation, as when all such extremes are avoided. I have felt an increasing care to attend to that Holy Spirit which sets right bounds to our desires, and leads those who faithfully follow it to apply all the gifts of Divine Providence to the purposes for which they were intended. Did those who have the care of great estates attend with singleness of heart to this heavenly Instructor, which so opens and enlarges the mind as to cause men to love their neighbors as themselves, they would have wisdom given them to manage their concerns, without employing some people in providing the luxuries of life, or others in laboring too hard; but for want of steadily regarding this principle of Divine love, a selfish spirit takes place in the minds of people, which is attended with darkness and manifold confusions in the world.

Though trading in things useful is an honest employ, yet through the great number of superfluities which are bought and sold, and through the corruption of the times, they who apply to merchandise for a living have great need to be well experienced in that precept which the Prophet Jeremiah laid down for his scribe: "Seekest thou great things for thyself? seek them not."

3. Farmers Ask the Rhode Island Assembly to Regulate Commercial Fishing, 1766

To the Honorable General Assembly of the Colony of Rhode Island . . . at South Kingstown in Kings County on the last Monday of February 1766

We the subscribers, your humble petitioners, the inhabitants of the County of Kings County Most Humbly shew—

Rhode Island Petitions, vol. 13, part 2, p. 10, Rhode Island State Archives, Providence, R.I.

That Although there hath been many wise and good acts made and passed by the Honorable Assembly of the Colony, from time to time, in order that the Alewives and other fish may not be obstructed in their proper course up Pawcatuck River, Which the acts have all as yet proved Ineffectual, and the course of the fish up the River being so obstructed by Ways, Dams, Seines, and Snaring and Threshing the River with Boats, Canoes, and Poles both night and Day, that Skim off all the fish and stopped their course up the River, and Many Poor people, who were greatly relieved by catching the Alewives for the support of their families are now denied that privilege that Divine providence had bestowed upon them. For all them that hath Dams and Ways built on the river near the Mouth of the same, stop the fish and engross all the fishing to themselves, and then sell the fish to Back Inhabitants on the River at an Extravagant price, which so obstructing and hindering the fish from their proper course upon the River, Hath almost already entirely ruined the course of the fish, Which if not remanded will not only stop the course of Alewives and small fish, but obstruct and hinder the course of Bass and other fish that frequent the river and its Bay adjoining; which is an unspeakable advantage to the poor inhabitants of the County; & also to many of the inhabitants of New London County (who join on the river are now enforcing a petition at their Assembly of this Kind).

Therefore, we Humbly pray that your Honors would be pleased to take the same into your wise consideration, and in your wisdom, order . . . that hence forth and for the future, that no Seine shall be drawn in the River, from Pawcatuck Rock up stream nor in any of the Branches of the River, from the Rock up stream, from the first day of March to the first day of June following, Annually. And that no wares shall be erected on the River, or any of the branches up stream from the Rock, during the term from the first day of March, to the first day of June, as afore, Annually. And all Dams shall be clearly opened twenty foot wide on the River in good Water, as Low as the Natural Bottom of the River; and shall be opened by the first day of March and continue opened until the first of June, Annually. And that no person or persons shall drive the River or Branches with Boats, Canoes, Poles, or Stones, in order to obstruct the course of the fish during the Term Annually. And that there shall be annually chosen two . . . men in Each Town adjoining the River in the Kings County, who shall inspect into the fishing in the River and whoever doth not open his or their Dam agreeable to the Act at their Direction shall be fined fifty pounds lawful money to be received before any two or more Justices of the Peace in the Kings County, from which there shall be no appeal, and Execution be awarded Immediately, and any proper writ shall bring the offender to trial and the oath or oaths of the Inspectors shall convict any person and their said Dam or Dams shall be opened by the Inspectors at their Direction at the Cost of the Owner. And any person or persons being found by the Inspectors or any lawful Witness to have a Ware on the River, or Draw a Seine in, or Drive the fish in the River during the Term, or any of the Branches of the River, up stream from the Rock shall render a fine of fifty pounds, and any two Lawful . . . [?] shall convict them as afore. And that no person shall fish in the River or any of the Branches up stream from the Rock, with any net. . . .

And if Complaint be Exhibited under Oath by the Inspector, Inspectors, or by Two Lawful Witnesses against any person or persons for any of the offences within five Days after it is Committed, before any Justice of the Peace in Kings County, Complaint shall stand good against offender three years, tho he be absent of Government.

And If any of the Inspectors neglect or refuse to do their duty (after being properly Engaged) to open a proper fish course, shall suffer the same like penalty . . . every week during their . . . Neglect, to be remanded in Manner and form as afore.

4. Iron Masters Petition Rhode Island Lawmakers for Water Rights, 1769

To the Honorable General Assembly now held at Providence the last Monday in February 1769.

The Petition of Stephen Hopkins, Nicholas Brown, Joseph Brown, John Brown, Moses Brown, Jabez Bowen Jun., and Rufus Hopkins, all of said Providence herewith.

That they have, at a vast expense purchased a Bank of Ore, and erected a very large Furnace for making Pig-Metal, upon a branch of Patuscet [Pawtuxet] River in Scituate, and have moreover for the accommodating their works purchased divers great Tracks of Wood land, about said Furnace, made ready and been at great Charge otherwise for carrying on this Business—That the Pigs made there have succeeded so well that they propose to keep the Furnace blowing as steadily as may be, but find they are like to be obstructed therein from the twenty first day of April to the first of June annually by the Operation of an Act of this Colony, made in the Year 1735, to prevent the Fish from being hindered in their Courses up the Fresh Rivers. The Nature of their Works, and the Process of their Business is such, that while the Furnace is in Blast, it will not be possible for them to leave and keep open such a Way through the Dam for the Fish to pass, as the Law requires.

Under this Difficulty they make their application to the Honorable Assembly for Relief; and make no Doubt, but if it should appear to your Honours, that an inconsiderable Fishery above the Furnace, at a Season when the Labour of the People is most needful, will not in any Measure equal the advantages which might be derived to the Community by the carrying on of a large and useful manufacture.

That this is the Case will appear when the Assembly are truly informed of the Quality of Pigs that may be made in a week, under suitable management and the number of Hands, who must be consequentially employed.—The extending of Manufactures, especially of such as are necessary hath been the Policy of all wise States: and at this Time of Difficulty the extension of the Iron Business, which is the most useful in Nature, we hope will meet with all due Countenance from the Assembly of this Colony.

Things being under this Situation, they humbly pray that notwithstanding said Law, or any Plank [?] thereof they may be permitted to keep their Furnace a going at any Season without being obliged to leave or keep open any Way for the Fish to pass through the Dam—begging leave to observe that however holsome a Law may be in general, yet in many Instances a universal Observation of it may be detrimental to the Community. And in the present case, if they be held to said Law it will be

Rhode Island Petitions, vol. 13, p. 77, Rhode Island State Archives, Providence, R.I.

the utmost Detriment to them, as the Spring Season is the best to begin a Blast, and will prevent carrying it into the Winter.

Step. Hopkins
Nich. Brown
Joseph Brown
John Brown
Moses Brown
Jabez Bowen, Jr.
Rufus Hopkins

5. Promoter Alexander Clúny Extols Florida's Virtues, 1770

We are at length arrived at *Florida,* the Boundary of the *British* Empire, and consequently the End of our Travels on the Continent of *America.* A new Acquisition of Territory is always the Subject of much Speculation and Controversy. This of *Florida* has been so much and so contrarily described, since it came into our Possession, that a Word on either Side of the Question is sure of meeting Contradiction. In such Cases, the middle Way is generally held to be the safest; in this it is certainly the right; the Advantages and Disadvantages, the Praise and Dispraise of this Country being equally exaggerated in every Particular, and that from the same Motive of Self-Interest. This will appear when it is considered who the Persons are, who have given such Descriptions.

The People, who have obtained Grants of Lands in *Florida,* and want to settle or sell them, represent the whole Country as a *Canaan,* "flowing with Milk and Honey," in order to tempt Purchasers, or allure Adventurers to go thither with them. The Army, who have been sent there to take and keep the Possession, exclaim against it as an *Aceldama,* "a Field of Blood," designed to be the Burying Place of all Strangers, who are so unhappy as to go there.

Contradictory as these Representations are, it is not so difficult, as it may appear, to reconcile them. The Sea-Coasts, where the Fortresses, judged necessary for protecting the Navigation and maintaining the Possession, have been erected, are barren and unhealthy in an extream Degree. The inland Country, from the Commencement of the Hills, is healthful, and not only fertile in all it's aboriginal Productions; but also fit to produce many exotick to it, in the highest Perfection. All necessary therefore to decide between the different Characters, drawn with equal Warmth and Confidence of Assertion, of *Florida,* is to distinguish between those two Parts of it, and give to each it's own. The Consequence in respect to the former is obvious. Of the latter, it is not mine to judge. All that comes within my Province, being to point out the Advantages, in a commercial View, which this Country is capable of producing to *Great Britain.*

Alexander Clúny, *The American Traveller; Containing Observations on the Present State, Culture and Commerce of the Colonies in America, and the Further Improvements of Which They Are Capable* ([Philadelphia?]: 1770), pp. 77–79.

Florida is divided, like *Carolina,* into two Provinces of the same Name, and distinguished only by their Situation on the *Eastern* or *Western* Sides of the Country.

Most of the Disadvantages, indiscriminately imputed to the whole Country, should be confined to *East Florida,* which is for the greater Part a flat, sandy, and almost barren Desert. The most considerable Fortress and Port for Trade in this Province is *St. Augustine.*

It is not to be expected, that a Settlement so new, and under such Circumstances, can have yet made any very considerable Advances in Trade. Our Exports to *St. Augustine* consist of the same Commodities, as those to the neighbouring Provinces of *Georgia* and *Carolina,* and amount to about £ 7,000 annually. Imports from thence, we have yet received none worth bringing to Account.

It must not be concluded from hence though, that the Country is incapable of producing any Commodities proper for Exportation, or that it may not be brought to rake off much greater Quantities of ours, than it does at present. The Contrary is the Fact, in both Instances. With proper Cultivation it will produce Rice, Indigo, Silk, Wines and Cochineal [a vivid red dye], so as to be brought into Commerce on advantageous Terms. The Importance of these Articles requires no Proof. The last in particular will be one of the most advantageous Additions that can be made to our commercial Stock, as it enters deeply into the Manufacturing of some of our most valuable Commodities, for which Purpose we are now obliged to purchase it from others, at what Price they please to impose; whereas, if we produce it ourselves, we shall not only save the greater Part of that Price, and thereby be enabled to carry those Manufactures to Market on cheaper Terms, than we can at present; but also to turn the Scales, and set our own Price upon it to other Countries.

The Importance of this Colony though arises not from the immediate Produce of this or any other Article, however important in itself; but from the Advantage of it's Situation, indeed of the whole Country of *Florida,* for carrying on a Trade with the *Spanish* Colonies; it being certain, that a regular Intercourse might be established with them, which would open a Vent for the Commodities of *Great Britain,* and yield Returns for them in Gold and Silver, the most profitable of all Kinds of Commerce, to an Amount superior to any Trade we have.

6. Merchant-Planter Henry Laurens Reflects on Florida's Challenges, 1766

It is almost unnecessary for me to enter upon the affair of your once intended connexion with Governor Grant in a Tract of Twenty Thousand Acres Land in East Florida since he has wrote you his own sentiments & determination on that Subject; it will be enough to remark that upon His Excellency's appeal to me whether he was bound to continue or rather renew his Partnership? I replied in general terms that he was not, taking for my Warrant, your Letter to him & particularly your words to me in the 24th February, "if he chuses to *resume the original Plan*

Henry Laurens to Richard Oswald, August 12, 1766, extract enclosed in Henry Laurens to James Grant, September 18, 1766, in George C. Rogers et al., eds., *The Papers of Henry Laurens,* vol. 5: *Sept. 1, 1765–July 31, 1768* (Columbia: University of South Carolina Press, 1976), pp. 155–158.

you were ready to go on with him." So far as to an obligation. But at the same time I said it seem'd to me to be rather a point of delicacy between you two & rather too delicate for my judgement in the absence of one Party & having a high an equal regard for both. But, Sir, upon the whole it must be to either of you or to you alone a bagatelle business whether you are connected or not since if you disapprove or are not so very fond of the scheme as you were at first you may so easily & without loss withdraw from it. Your Negroes, Governor Grant assures me are increased in number & worth more than they cost. The Land & implements cannot have cost much. I had a very great desire to see & traverse the spot intended for you but there is no practicable Road yet & the only conveyance by Water was in a small Pilot Boat crouded with your Negroes & that within three days of my first arrival at St. Augustine. Mr. Moncrief an ingenious diligent Young Man who went down upon that occasion & return'd thro many perils on the Sea beach reported to me that the Major part of it was exceeding good, capable of producing Indigo & Sugar in abundance, & that the fresh Marshes (part of your Tract) will make as fine Rice fields as any in America. How good a judge he is of the qualities of Land I know not, but admitting all that he says to be very true yet I fear you will never make any great progress there for want of Neighbours, Navigation, & Markets convenient either for disposing or Shipping off your produce as well as the distance from the eye & attention of a faithful friend on which Account your Negroes will be exposed to many extraordinary dangers & expences. Allowing your whole 20,000 Acres to be good which I am sure they are not, partly from my own observation of the Country as you shall hear presently but more from the information of other People who have traveled over & explored all that part of the Coast; yet the adjacent Lands on all hands are mean, consequently you will have no Neighbours or none but such as will be a pest to your settlements. The Navigation into the Musquito River is at all times bad & sometimes scarcely any Bar at all, within it is very shoal indeed, & you will have none better than that of Musquitoes neigher to you than St. Mary's, to which Ships may not resort in any Numbers these Twenty Years, so that in fact you will have no Port that you can depend upon nearer than Savanna & may be when you get there you may be obliged to come away to this place.

If you have no Neighbours or no good ones your Negroes will be exposed to the arbitrary power of an Overseer & perhaps sometimes tempted to knock him in the head & file off in a Body. The Man that I have engaged for you brought me exceeding good credentials of his ability & integrity from under the hands of two or three Gentlemen of undoubted worth, yet in this short space he has had many quarrels with your Negroes & the Governor does not speak so well of him. I went three several times in different directions to the River St. John's by which means I saw the Mid-Land Country & both Shores of that vast River from the great Lake to the Ocean a distance of One Hundred & thirty computed Miles. That River runs nearly paralel with the Sea therefore I must have been at one time or other within Ten Miles of Musquito & not more than Fifteen or twenty from your Estate, all that Midland between St. John's & Augustine is base indeed its produce chiefly Pine Trees of an inferior growth & some Swamps of Bay & Cypress of a Sandy foundation, hence in my opinion its inhabitants will never be numerous & I have been well assured that the Soil Southward of Musquito as far as the Cape & beyond it is of the same & a worse stamp. This consideration led me to say you would you must be under disadvantages for want of Neighbours. Governor Grant I am certain of it will take all possible care to restrain an Overseer & to keep your Plantation in general in good order, but he cannot mend the other evils if they are evils. I should have been wanting in my duty to so good a friend as Mr. Oswald especially when he seems to rely upon me if I had not said so much of my apprehensions where his Interest is concern'd & it will give me a vast deal of pleasure to find after a Year or two's experience that I have been quite mistaken, & while I say this from a pure motive of service to one friend I am sure of differing in opinion with & incuring a very hearty scold from another as soon as he is apprized of the contents of this Letter which he shall not be these two Years from me but any body else may send him a true Copy of it. I know when his first heat is over he will commend my honesty & lament my ignorance. I dont say that no Man can make Money at Musquitoes, yes probably twenty or thirty industrious families with frugal living at one quarter the expence of your Overseer, & an hundred times the labour that any Mere Overseer will be at, might get Bread & even in a course of Years earn some Negroes. But I do sincerely believe that Mr. Oswald will never make a penny there unless it shall be hereafter by the Sale of his Land to some such People.

Upon the River St. John's there are some Tracts of Sandy high Land abounding with Live Oak of immense dimensions, several large Islands in the River full of Trees of good sorts & a Swamp on the West (upper) side of it cover'd with fine Cypress, Tupelo, Ash, & Maple which I believe will produce Rice in abundance & after three or four Years it may be greatly improved in Indigo perhaps Sugar, &Ca., if the Winters will allow the growth but the Navigation of that River too is very bad. No Vessel that draws above Nine feet Water ought to attempt it. They tell you there is sometimes 15 feet on the Bar, it may be so, but I believe it very seldom happens & within the Mouth & all above it is full of large & troublesome Shoals. Some People have lately return'd to Augustine who had been round the Cape to make a survey of the Lands of Bay-Tempo as they pretended but probably on a scheme of Trade; be that as it may, I am told they report nothing favourable of the Soil. So that upon the whole I do not think *East Florida* will ever be valuable to Britain as a *Plantation*. But this is my own private opinion founded upon no great experience & therefore I mean to confine it if you please between our selves.

 E S S A Y S

First, Edwin J. Perkins, professor emeritus at the University of Southern California and a specialist in early American economic and financial history, argues that business values have been part of American culture since the first British settlements. Examining eight major groups—merchants, artisans, farmers, indentured servants, slaves, laborers, sailors, and women—Perkins shows that much of the free population of British America pursued upward mobility and created a culture that valued savings, a strong market orientation, and positive attitudes toward wealth. In Perkins's view, colonists were stalwart go-getters, whose unbridled entrepreneurial spirit fueled institutional change and business growth after the American Revolution. An entrepreneur is an innovator who welcomes economic risk. As you read, keep in mind that Perkins's essay is a synthesis that draws on the published work of other scholars (secondary sources) rather than original documents from the period (primary sources). What are the pros and cons of writing economic history using secondary sources?

In the second essay, Gary Kulik, adjunct professor in the Winterthur Program in Early American Culture at the University of Delaware, examines the legal battles over water rights between back country farmers and some of the first industrial capitalists in Rhode Island. In Kulik's account, Rhode Island farmers possessed a world view that revered rural life, and their "country" perspective was at odds with the emerging international economy. These farmers used the courts to challenge commercial interests for control of the colony's rivers. They did not entirely oppose the introduction of blast furnaces or cotton mills. Instead, they insisted that others simply respect their right to fish. Consider how Kulik's argument, based on the persistence of the farmers' rural values, stands in relation to Perkins's thesis.

Finally, Professor David Hancock, a historian of early America and the Atlantic world at The University of Michigan–Ann Arbor, examines Mosquito's Bite plantation, a short-lived Florida venture by the London merchant Richard Oswald, to explain the difficulties facing businesspeople who had transatlantic investments in the American colonies. Oswald belonged to a network of London-based merchant capitalists who accumulated vast fortunes as shippers, traders, government contractors, and slavers in the British Atlantic world. When the Treaty of Paris (1763) ended the Seven Years' War and expanded the British territories, these merchants established American plantations to grow sugar, rice, and indigo for European markets. Some investments by these absentee owners succeeded, whereas others—including Oswald's Florida plantation—failed. Hancock shows how the harsh material realities on the imperial periphery—such as soil and climate, the lack of an infrastructure, and managerial incompetence—could thwart the efforts of even the most experienced entrepreneurs. How does Hancock's analysis, based on the extensive use of merchant letters, reorient Perkins's discussion of the entrepreneurial spirit?

The Entrepreneurial Spirit in Colonial America

EDWIN J. PERKINS

Entrepreneurial attitudes and strategies for upward economic mobility pervaded the free population of the British North American colonies throughout the first two centuries of European settlement. These attributes were shared by the vast majority of colonial households: not only by merchants, but by artisans, most farmers (including many tenants), indentured servants, unmarried and still youthful day laborers, and even a few exceptional slaves operating in the urban self-hire market. In retrospect, the business and social historian Thomas Cochran was on the mark when he first stressed the revolutionary character of the American economic system and the depth of business values within the society.

In the larger perspective of U.S. history, historians should henceforth stress that the majority of the free population from colonial times forward were active participants in an economic, social, and political system heavily imbued with entrepreneurial values—a system characterized by high savings rates, a market orientation, and positive attitudes toward the accumulation of wealth. How wide a swath did the business sector cut in the U.S. colonial past? It encompassed most occupational

Edwin J. Perkins, "The Entrepreneurial Spirit in Colonial America: The Foundation of Modern Business History," *Business History Review* 63 (Spring 1989): 169–186. Reprinted by permission of the *Business History Review.* Copyright © 1989 by the President and Fellows of Harvard College; all rights reserved.

groups even in that earlier preindustrial era. This theme remains one vital part of an abiding continuity in American history from 1607 to the present. . . .

Components of the "Entrepreneurial" Group

. . . Members of the mercantile community were among the most active full-fledged entrepreneurs in colonial society. Merchants accounted for 2 to 5 percent of aggregate employment, with greater concentrations in port cities and towns. In addition to facilitating the exchange of goods in internal and foreign markets, they were the conduits for the extension of credit from areas with surplus working capital down through the chain of mercantile firms to the final consumers. The source for much of the credit that supported the carrying of inventories and the sale of imported goods in the colonial market can be traced to British traders and manufacturers. . . . [V]irtually all historians have agreed that these wholesalers ranked high among the legitimate precursors of nineteenth-century entrepreneurs.

Not every merchant conformed to the bold entrepreneurial model, however. Like some farmers and artisans, a few shopkeepers were content merely to reach a comfortable living standard, with no aspirations for acquiring greater wealth. These merchants were content to operate small- to medium-scale businesses, avoiding the risks of an expanded inventory. Meanwhile, at the top of the mercantile pyramid, some merchants who had accumulated great wealth through their involvement in risky ventures subsequently became exceedingly conservative and focused their energies mainly on preserving existing capital. Thomas Doerflinger has explained how many formerly successful merchant households in Philadelphia withdrew from trading activities and invested their funds in urban rental properties. Thus, though the mercantile sector included a higher percentage of active entrepreneurs within its ranks than other occupational groups, some merchants were not consistently bold risk-takers, and some tried to protect previously accumulated assets from the threat of possible losses.

In addition to merchants, many, if not most, artisans deserve inclusion in any discussion of the preindustrial roots of American entrepreneurship. . . . These workers can be viewed as laborers, since they produced various goods using hand tools; at the same time, master artisans may be classified with equal validity as the owners and managers of small business firms. Most operated proprietorships, or occasionally worked in partnerships with one or two other men. Youthful apprentices and journeymen were subordinate employees, but usually their dependent status was merely a temporary stage along the route to independence. By their early thirties, most craft workers were married and self-employed, although exceptions to this generalization might be found in a large urban area such as Philadelphia, where a substantial number of craft workers remained journeymen employees throughout their working lives.

Master artisans owned their own tools, maintained inventories of raw materials and goods-in-process, accepted orders from customers, managed their daily schedules, handled their own monies and accounts, and generally performed all the functions typically associated with the operation of small business enterprises, past and present. Of course, some artisans had no grander ambition than to remain independent, small-scale producers—that is, "maintainers"—but most artisans were prevented from expanding their scale of operations, irrespective of their attitude about possible opportunities beyond the local market, by limited access to distant markets resulting from inadequate transportation services.

Mounting evidence from analyses of estates suggests that moderately successful artisans frequently owned a few acres near their homes suitable for limited cultivation, and that an even larger number maintained a sufficient number of livestock—cows, cattle, hogs, and chickens—to provide a steady source of meat, milk, and eggs for their households. In Philadelphia, the largest port city over the last quarter-century of the colonial era, master artisans frequently occupied homes whose values, or rents, were comparable to the residences of the small and medium-sized merchants who composed the majority of the mercantile community. We also know that many of the new manufacturing establishments created after independence to serve wider markets were organized and managed by persons who had initially operated small artisan shops and later made the transition to employer status. Thus the entrepreneurial tradition that emerged on a grander scale in the nineteenth century can be traced as validly to the activities of colonial artisans as to any other occupational category.

A substantial share of farm households also legitimately belongs in the entrepreneurial camp. Farm workers made up from 60 to 85 percent of the free colonial work force—with the exact percentage depending on geographical location and how we categorize persons also engaged on a part-time basis in related pursuits, such as crafts and occasional day labor. The criterion for the assignment of farm households to the business and entrepreneurial sector hinges on whether they aimed at the steady accumulation of property—in land, livestock, bonded labor, fences, barns, or other productive assets. The distinction lies between farmers seeking further capital formation and farmers content to maintain existing levels of productivity. . . .

. . . [C]onsidering the thirteen colonies as a whole, the vast majority of farm households in the middle and southern colonies, plus a fair share of those in New England, were seeking the means to further material advancement for themselves and their children. . . .

Entrepreneurially oriented farm households had several important characteristics in common. First, they tended to defer immediate consumption and to save a healthy share of their annual income; those savings were invested in making capital improvements to their properties. This investment behavior was exhibited mainly through non-pecuniary activities such as clearing forests, constructing barns, building fences, and otherwise augmenting the productive capacity of their farms. These farmers tried to expand the total agricultural output of their lands by hiring extra labor to plant and harvest more cropland than was required for a comfortable subsistence. Households then faced several options in the disposition of surpluses. On the one hand, they could sell excess output in the marketplace and use the sale proceeds to purchase other goods or services designed to satisfy their desires for immediate consumption, or, alternatively, they could follow investment strategies leading to the improvement of their productive capacity.

Among the prime vehicles for agricultural investment were livestock herds. Two strategies, pursued either separately or in combination, led to capital accumulation. Surplus foodstuffs could be withheld from sale in the marketplace and fed to livestock—mainly cattle and hogs—thus increasing meat and dairy supplies available to members of the household in later periods. Another investment strategy, and one that the first and second generations of landowners often chose, was to concentrate on building livestock herds by deferring the slaughter of females and adding more animals to breeding stock; by postponing immediate gratification from a tastier and more varied diet, the household could enjoy enhanced income in subsequent years either from increased meat consumption or from the sale of surplus livestock in the marketplace.

These strategies of saving and investment were employed not only by independent yeomen who held title to their own farms, but also by numerous colonial tenant households as well. . . .

For younger households, headed by single or married males under the age of thirty-five, tenancy was often strictly a voluntary, temporary career stage that aided in the accumulation of wealth and subsequently led to land ownership and independence. Even some persons with sufficient financial resources to purchase unimproved land close to the frontier opted instead for tenancy status on improved farms that already possessed the potential for higher yields and better access to waiting markets. Rental terms were frequently attractive to potential tenants for several reasons. . . . In short, the supply of rental properties was large relative to the supply of potential tenants, which translated into a reasonable level of rents, whether paid in cash or in kind.

Colonial tenants with an entrepreneurial orientation frequently used their initial capital stock plus the sums saved from yearly profits to invest in a series of productive assets. In the southern and middle colonies, many tenants decided to invest surplus funds in human capital—servants or slaves—before moving on to acquire their own cropland. Some devoted their surpluses to building livestock herds. Others used their own labor and surplus funds to make leasehold improvements on rented properties. When their leases expired, some tenants, notably in Maryland, were allowed to remove the easily portable assets. . . .

In villages and towns, artisans frequently leased small farms, a few fields, or even more commonly pasturage for their livestock. Most craft workers maintained at least one cow for dairy products, plus several cattle, sheep, or hogs. The income generated from collateral agricultural activities, in the form of either food consumption in the home or sale in the marketplace, supplemented the earnings from regular craft work. In addition to helping to care for the livestock, the wives and children of male artisans were often engaged part-time in agricultural pursuits and thus made substantial contributions to household income.

Although some Marxist historians may vehemently disagree, I believe southern planters and other farmers with investments in indentured servants or slaves qualify for inclusion in the entrepreneurially oriented classification because they sent bonded workers out into the fields with the aim of producing surpluses for sale in the marketplace. The prime markets for many of these products—especially tobacco, rice, and indigo—were located overseas. Farmers with investments in other human beings normally sought to expand the scope of future operations; the profits expropriated from their bonded workers were frequently reinvested in additional land and labor. In the South, moderately successful planters tried to emulate their more prosperous neighbors, hoping one day that they or one of their progeny might eventually reach the elevated status of "great planter." Large planters hired overseers for their huge work forces. This practice of employing full-time supervisors who did not hold an ownership stake in the business enterprise was a forerunner of developments relating to the emergence of an independent managerial class in manufacturing firms and railroads in the nineteenth century. . . .

Another group that, on balance, deserves inclusion in the ranks of the entre-preneurially oriented are indentured servants. . . . Most existing accounts of inden-tured servants not only place them exclusively within the working-class sector, but also depict them as persons grossly exploited by their owners, in a manner similar to slaves. But the similarities between servitude and slavery have been overemphasized to the neglect of the vast differences in their origins and outcomes. Except for that 10 percent or so of the total who were transported to North America from England's crowded jails in the eighteenth century, most servants voluntarily agreed to busi-ness contracts covering a period ranging from four to seven years. Slaves, in con-trast, were involuntary captives, and the term of their service was indefinite—usually not only for their own lifetimes, but also for the lifetimes of all future generations unless manumitted.

Servants are best viewed as ambitious persons who elected to make an invest-ment in their personal welfare based on an exchange of labor services over a fixed term of years for the benefit of regaining complete freedom in a new society where opportunities were vastly greater than in Europe. They risked an uncertain fate in a distant land because of a desire to increase appreciably the chance of eventually acquiring ownership of their own farm or artisan shop. . . .

In all, over a quarter-million Europeans chose to trade a temporary claim on their future economic output for the immediate financing required to transport them to a new environment where land was inexpensive and thus accessible to persons with limited assets. The vast majority traveled to the Chesapeake region or to the middle colonies, with few arriving in New England or the Lower South. Servants swapped one service for another: their own future labor units were traded for long-distance transportation, plus regular meals and some clothing. Prospective migrants negotiated the terms of their individual indenture contracts before their departure from European ports. A few people were kidnapped and shipped overseas involun-tarily, but most transactions took place in generally competitive markets involving numerous merchant contractors.

Prospective migrants bargained over the final geographical destination, length of contract, and the size of freedom dues at the expiration of their term. The inclu-sion of freedom dues was crucial, because these sums provided the financial resources to start a new life on a higher economic plane; in many cases the money was a good start toward making the down payment on a small farm, the purchase of a few head of livestock, or the acquisition of the tools required to stock an artisan's shop. Persons with craft skills or the ability to read and write were usually in a position to bargain for the most favorable contractual terms. Females, who generally entered domestic service, were in significantly shorter supply than males, and they generally obtained more favorable contracts requiring fewer months of labor. . . .

. . . Males normally labored in the fields or in the shop, often performing the same tasks as their employers; females were usually engaged in domestic service—cooking, washing, child care, feeding livestock, and other related house-hold duties. The status of servants was clearly subordinate, and they were routinely called on to perform the least desirable work assignments. Once freed, however, their previous condition of servitude was no handicap on the road to upward social and economic mobility.

In sum, markets in servant contracts functioned fairly efficiently from an economic standpoint, since all parties involved in these transactions, including those persons agreeing to the indentures, usually received the services agreed on in advance. If English merchants or colonial owners failed to live up to the terms of the written agreement, servants had the legal right to take the offending parties to court for breach of contract—although it should be noted that the court system was controlled by local property holders, who were rarely sympathetic to the complaints of bonded workers. An owner judged to be acting in violation of a servant's contract could be penalized, however, through a reduction in the term of required service or, in extreme cases, the granting of immediate freedom. The most frequent offense was the failure to pay freedom dues on the expiration of a contract, and suits alleging nonpayment were common in local courts. . . .

In addition to most indentured servants, a majority of those persons performing what was usually termed "common" or "day" labor also had a budding entrepreneurial orientation. In discussions of the colonial economy, historians have invariably assigned participants in these markets to the lower classes, since analyses of estates reveal that such workers tended to have few material possessions. Such persons also accounted for a large share of the population, comprising one-third or more of all adults in most regions. How, then, can one argue for the inclusion of so many visibly poor individuals within the entrepreneurial classification? The answer is revealed by an examination of the age distribution of common laborers. . . .

Prior to marriage in their early to mid-twenties, male youths routinely worked in the fields of nearby farms, and occasionally in an artisan shop, and young females assisted older women in neighboring households with domestic chores. These activities brought in a modest income and, perhaps equally important, the exposure to other family economic units served as a learning experience, since it acquainted these young people with the traditional roles of husbands and wives within an independent household. . . .

Youths of both sexes usually saved a substantial share of their modest earnings and used those sums, along with inheritances, to assist in financing the formation of their own new households. Despite the relatively high percentage of workers performing common labor for low wages, this generally youthful group did not form the core of a permanently deprived class of workers. Most youths engaged in common labor in the colonial period anticipated marriage and immediate promotion to landowner sometime before age thirty. The fundamental position of this stratum of society can be assessed, therefore, not by observing how its members fared economically as youths, but rather by considering the general level of wealth they had achieved on reaching middle age. By that criterion, most colonial youths clearly belong within the mainstream of an economic system imbued with enterprising attitudes.

The Excluded Groups

Enslaved blacks constitute the largest group of workers excluded from the entrepreneurial ranks. By the 1770s they made up just over 20 percent of the total population of the thirteen colonies. Unlike indentured servants, most slaves had no hope for a more prosperous future—either for themselves or for their children. This hopeless-ness was especially prevalent in rural areas, where the overwhelming number of slaves resided.

In a few towns and cities, however, some urban slaves were granted permis-sion to hire out their labor to third parties, sharing their earnings with owners on the basis of some prearranged formula. The system of self-hire was most common in Charleston, where blacks were a majority, and many slaves in that South Carolina port were engaged full-time in a variety of artisan activities. These slave artisans frequently maintained their own shops, and some were able to accumulate suffi-cient earnings to purchase freedom from accommodating owners. In his recent study of black employment patterns in Charleston, Philip Morgan has labeled some of these workers slave entrepreneurs. His categorization appears justified, because these bonded workers had the means of steadily accumulating property, with the goal of enhancing permanently their general welfare. Enterprising slaves nevertheless con-stituted only a minuscule fraction of the total slave population in the colonies.

The vast majority of sailors employed on vessels in ports all along the coast-line constitute another small but recognizable occupational group that should be excluded from any entrepreneurial classification. Colonial ships carried a substantial share of British and American cargoes in the North Atlantic trade, and they com-pletely dominated the coastal trade, a rapidly growing market in the last quarter of the colonial era. These vessels provided employment in jobs requiring little advance training for thousands of sailors at relatively low wages and, more important, in positions with few opportunities for advancement. Even in this instance, however, a few enterprising sailors who managed to survive the hazards of multiple voyages did move up to higher paying positions—first as mariners and perhaps later even to ship captain, a responsible job generating a fairly steady income.

In rural areas there existed a very small category of adult workers, over the age of thirty and usually never married, who continued to seek employment as day laborers throughout their working lives. Probably no more than 2 or 3 percent of the entire free rural population fit within this lowly occupational group. In urban areas, which accounted for a mere 7 percent of colonial population in 1775, the number of poor day laborers was probably relatively greater—perhaps as high as 10 percent of the overall work force.

What about women? Did they possess an entrepreneurial orientation? This question is difficult to answer satisfactorily because we need to distinguish, first, be-tween married women and widows and, second, between women as individuals and as members of household units. Since by law and custom, males—mostly fathers or husbands (but sometimes brothers or other close relatives)—usually exerted control over the property of daughters and wives, the vast majority of women, when consid-ered as individuals, cannot have functioned as entrepreneurs. For example, a married woman could not sign a legal contract without the permission of her husband.

If, however, we view colonial society from the perspective of the household unit, then the issue becomes clouded. Most wives identified with the acquisitive traits of their spouses and contributed through their labor activities to the shared goal of accumulating property and enhancing economic opportunities for the benefit of their immediate families and the later welfare of their children. Seen in this light, wives may be considered as full participants in households with an entrepreneurial outlook. They contributed by providing essential domestic services and by working in the fields at critical periods such as the annual harvest; in addition, the output from supplementary housewifery activities, such as churning butter and spinning thread, generated extra income for consumption or investment in productive assets.

Widows were more diverse in wealth and income, and that diversity is revealed in this group's linkage to the entrepreneurial spirit. Most widows were far removed from that concept, especially women beyond their prime childbearing years, roughly age forty. Under English law, widows normally received a dower—a one-third lifetime interest in the property of their deceased spouses. Although settlement terms differed depending on the number, age, and sex of surviving children and grandchildren, most widows aimed at conserving their remaining assets and eking out a modest living. Younger widows with several children, older widows without male teenagers still residing at home, and the few single women who had never married together constituted a group that consistently ranked among the households with the lowest incomes and wealth.

On the other hand, a small minority of widows and unmarried daughters who gained control over substantial property through inheritance were able to exercise a quasi-entrepreneurial role in society. These propertied women had free rein to manage their enterprises, including the hiring and firing of employees and the legal right to negotiate contracts of all varieties. They could sue and be sued. Moreover, women who had inherited ownership of farms, artisan shops, or mercantile firms were generally accepted by the commercial community and encouraged to behave in a businesslike manner. Law and custom were generally conducive to the accumulation of further wealth, although some colonies had restrictions on the ability of women to purchase additional land. Of course a woman owner could not exercise complete discretion in decision making, since, like her male counterparts, she was limited by custom to hiring only males as assistants for any position with supervisory authority and responsibility. Males as a gender group possessed the opportunity to start their work careers in entry-level positions (overseers, supercargoes, clerks) and to accumulate sufficient experience and savings to move gradually toward independent status. Women, in contrast, either began their business careers as full-fledged owner-managers, or they did not participate in the business world at all.

If women owners exercised all the power and authority of males in identical positions, then why use the prefix "quasi" to describe their seemingly entrepreneurial activities? The explanation relates not to their daily activities, but rather to their motivation and goals. Women were not expected to oversee the operations of farms and commercial enterprises because of a personal desire to succeed in the business world; in addition, they were generally not allowed to pass on the bulk of accumulated wealth to daughters or to other female relatives. Rather, they were viewed as persons who had assumed power in the marketplace on a strictly temporary basis as a result of extraordinary circumstances, conserving and expanding assets for male progeny or male relatives until some future date. So long as it was clearly understood that ownership and control were eventually destined for transfer to a male somewhere within the family structure, it was perfectly acceptable for a woman to assume the burden of business responsibilities following the death of a husband or father.

Therefore, such women are best viewed as persons functioning primarily as trustees for future generations of males. The situation is reasonably analogous to the powers occasionally assumed by a queen mother in Europe when acting as regent for an underage son who was heir to the throne. Because of limitations imposed by custom and law on their right to dispose of their property and the business enterprises periodically coming under their managerial control, colonial women even in the most favorable circumstances remained strictly on the periphery of the entrepreneurial class.

Farmers and the Anticommercial Impulse in New England

GARY KULIK

Conflict between farmers and mill owners in the early eighteenth century was rare for several reasons. Mill owners were not a separate "industrial" interest, for much of what constituted industrial production in the eighteenth century—the grinding of grain, the sawing of wood, the fulling of woolen cloth—was closely tied to agriculture. Farmers and mill owners were thus integral parts of a single and largely undifferentiated economy, and most mill owners did at least some farming. Moreover, the work of mill owners was either seasonal or episodic. For grain millers who worked largely in the fall, or for the proprietors of small sawmills who worked only when work was available, it was no particular hardship to construct a fishway or to open a portion of their dam during the annual fish runs. They might resent having to do so, but it did not threaten their livelihood.

The farmers, grain millers, and sawyers of the Rhode Island interior sought their livelihoods in an economy only tenuously tied to market production. Unlike the fertile coastal lands of southern Rhode Island, home of the pastoral economy of the Narragansett planters, the colony's northern and western lands were poor and unproductive. Backcountry farmers tended small herds of livestock and cultivated few market crops. Most of what they grew they consumed themselves. A few northern Rhode Island farmers raised small amounts of tobacco and flaxseed oil for international markets, yet the area produced so few provisions for the European or West Indian trade that Providence merchants had to send their agents into central Massachusetts to fill their ships. Local markets were also thin. Providence, the only city of northern Rhode Island, had no market house until 1774; like Boston, it was a net importer of food. In such an economy, the availability of free fish in the countryside was important. And river fish were generally consumed by those who caught them. Such fish were rarely marketed, for backcountry farmers could not compete, even if they wished, with the ocean fisheries of the Atlantic coast. The relative absence of a market economy muted tensions over water rights. As long as the economic stakes were low, conflict could be accommodated. But the stakes would not remain low.

Conflict over water rights increased in Rhode Island with the introduction of blast furnaces at mid-century. Unlike gristmills and sawmills, furnaces depended on wage labor, were fully committed to market production, and required continuous amounts

Gary Kulik, "Dams, Fish, and Farmers: Defense of Public Rights in Eighteenth-Century Rhode Island," in Steven Hahn and Jonathan Prude, eds., *The Countryside in the Age of Capitalist Transformation* (Chapel Hill: University of North Carolina Press, 1985), pp. 33–40, 45–46. Copyright © 1985 by University of North Carolina Press. Used by permission of the publisher.

of waterpower. No other enterprises placed comparable demands on the colony's rivers and streams, because furnaces operated around the clock, for months at a time. No other users of waterpower were as concerned with both technical efficiency and profit.

The Furnace Unity provoked the colony's first serious conflict. Owned by two Boston merchants and located on the Blackstone River about 9 miles above Paw-tucket Falls, the Unity cast hollowware for both local and regional markets as well as cannon and shot used in King George's War. On 27 April 1748 upstream residents claimed before the local justice of the peace that the furnace's dam hindered the passage of fish. The judge agreed, and ordered that "the said Dam should be broken and a way made through the same," by April of the following year. The two owners, referring to the plaintiffs as "certain malicious persons," petitioned the General Assembly in October 1748 to void the court's directive. The owners claimed that salt-water fish were not hindered, that breaking the dam would not promote the passage of fish, and moreover, would spoil a "useful grist mill now standing in such dam." The owners, however, made no claim for the local utility of the furnace. Their petition was signed by thirty-seven freemen. Even if some of them were furnace workers, it is apparent that local opinion was divided. The General Assembly agreed with the furnace owners and their supporters, its reasoning unknown, and preserved the dam.

Any other solution might have threatened the very existence of the furnace. Not only did blast furnaces have to be run continuously, they were customarily put in blast in the spring, in the midst of the annual fish runs. New England winters were too severe for prolonged outdoor work, and winter frosts adversely affected furnace operation. In the fall, water was likely to be scarce. And the summer, in the words of one ironmaster, was "too hot for the constitution of the workmen to endure it." Only the spring offered ideal weather and plentiful water. Knowing this, the owners of Furnace Unity had taken no chances. They drafted a carefully worded petition, and cogently argued their case before the Assembly. The stakes were high. Though local opinion was divided, the decision of the local justice of the peace had given notice of a culture that placed a higher value on public and customary rights than on economic development in the hands of absentee ironmasters. Moreover, such values had been legitimated by local authority. The furnace owners had prevailed only by appealing over the heads of that authority, to colonywide interests apparently more amenable to their influence. Ironmasters would not always be so successful.

Public conflict over fish intensified sharply in the years after 1765, as iron-masters sought exemption from the colony's Fish Acts. Farmers, in response, came to defend their rights with a new sense of urgency—an urgency shaped by the Revolutionary crisis. The rising conflict over fish was clearly the product of that extraordinary convergence of economic and ideological change which marked the years from 1765 to 1776.

By the 1760s, population growth was pressing against the limits of available economic resources. In the settled portions of New England, land had grown scarce, and so apparently had the numbers of river fish. The Swedish naturalist Peter Kalm, in his travels through New England, reported the claims of Boston-area farmers that fish were in short supply and that mill dams were the cause. Some ironmasters thus appeared to be profiting from their control of an increasingly scarce public resource.

The objections of farmers, which at some other time might simply have festered beneath the surface of public life, achieved both voice and legitimacy in the context of the American Revolution.

The growth of a contentious and popularly based politics in the years after 1765 encouraged backcountry farmers to seek redress for their grievances, and their grievances struck a louder and more responsive chord than they had a decade earlier. The issues they raised about dams, fish, and water rights had no direct connection to the momentous issues of the Revolution, but they drew upon a common sensibility—distrust of corrupt and arbitrary power. Farmers saw their rights to fish threatened by powerful ironmasters closely tied to the colony's political leadership and intent, so they believed, on turning manifestly public resources to private advantage. In responding to these threats, farmers sought to defend both their specific economic interests and their sense of public virtue, for the public good, as they understood it, demanded that individual economic rights be subordinated to the general will.

Concerns such as these derived their resonance from Anglo-American "Country thought," a cluster of ideas about power and liberty, virtue and corruption, private interests and public good, associated with the English Commonwealthmen and widely accessible to colonists during the final third of the eighteenth century. Country thought provided the language of patriot resistance at its most articulate levels. It was a language of moral regeneration, inspired by classical antiquity, implicitly anticapitalist, suspicious of wealth, power, and the influence of commerce. Historians are divided about the extent to which the Commonwealth tradition impelled the less articulate farmers, mechanics, and laborers of the colonial seaboard. The evidence from Rhode Island is sketchy but suggestive. The petitions of the colony's backcountry farmers were the product of their immediate experience, not an explicit expression of the Commonwealth tradition. But Country sensibilities lent shape to that experience, structured its meaning, and legitimated its expression. It was no accident that conflict over fish and conflict over empire overlapped in time and elicited similar fears—the fear of arbitrary power and corrupting influence, and the fear that rapacious private interests might overwhelm a fragile, and traditionally defined, public good.

Consider the pattern of conflict. In August 1765, Stephan Hopkins, Israel Wilkinson, and Nicholas Brown and his partners petitioned the Rhode Island General Assembly for an exemption to the Fish Act of 1735. They sought to build an iron furnace on the north branch of the Pawtuxet River. This was the Hope Furnace, the colony's largest and best known. Its supporters were men of prominence. Stephan Hopkins would later serve as colonial governor. Nicholas Brown's partners were his brothers John, Joseph, and Moses—the "Browns of Providence Plantations"—one of the colony's wealthiest families. In addition, Moses Brown, who would later play a critical role in the beginnings of the American textile industry, was a member of the Assembly's lower house. That body quickly granted the company's petition. The upper house, however, initially sought to defer the issue until meetings of local residents could be held. No record of such meetings survives, and the upper house eventually concurred. But it did so only after stipulating that the furnace owners construct a fishway whose effectiveness would be judged by three knowledgeable freemen. If these freemen decided that the fishway was unsuccessful, then the Act of 1735 would apply. Despite the furnace owners' formidable influence, they had not been wholly successful. The full efficiency of the Hope Furnace had been sacrificed to preserve a customary entitlement to fish. A century later, the first historian of Providence County claimed that this decision, along with other similar water-rights decisions, "tended greatly to retard the progress of manufacture." In this case, however, the retardation was only temporary. Four years later, the owners submitted another petition requesting full exemption from the Act of 1735. This time, with Stephan Hopkins himself in the governor's chair, it was granted.

The colony's major furnace owners had succeeded, though not easily and not without opposition. Smaller mill owners were not as fortunate. Farmers were becoming increasingly prickly about their rights to fish, and suspicious, not only of ironmasters, but of all mill owners. In May 1766, sixty upcountry farmers in the Pawtuxet Valley presented a petition to the Assembly opposing the effort of Samuel Greene to build a corn mill near Gorton's Pond. The farmers claimed that Greene's proposed mill would block the passage of fish, and, in addition, was unnecessary to the local economy. Their community already had a corn mill. In June, Greene formally applied for an exemption to the colony's Fish Act. The Assembly deferred its decision while demanding that Greene, in the interim, comply with the law. It never again acted on the question, effectively denying Greene his exemption. Samuel Greene had less influence than the colony's ironmasters, and popular pressure was mounting.

During the same year, three other petitions arrived in the Assembly raising new issues and introducing new protagonists. Mill owners and ironmasters were not the only ones to threaten the rights of farmers; so too did commercial fishermen. In February 1766, thirty-three farmers living near the Pawcatuck River asked the Assembly to regulate the use of fishing nets. Some farmers used small nets during the spring runs to catch as many fish as they could, curing them to eat throughout the year. But it was commercial fishermen, whose presence first became an issue in this period, who made extensive use of large nets and whose actions fundamentally threatened supplies of fish. Deploying their nets directly downstream of mill dams, they used the dams as barriers to trap migratory fish. Carefully maneuvering their boats, they drove the great spring schools toward their nets. The petitioners, invoking a "moral economy" of a kind revealed in E. P. Thompson's studies of eighteenth-century England, claimed that these commercial fishermen then charged an "extravagant price," depriving poor families of fish "that Divine Providence had bestowed upon them." They requested that the Assembly outlaw the use of nets annually from 1 March to 1 June, and that it impose a fine of 50 pounds on those who failed to open their dams during the spring runs. In May, over seventy residents of Cranston forwarded a petition to the legislature protesting the "great neglect of timely opening of mill dams," and demanding stiff penalties for those using nets at Pawtuxet Falls. And in August, residents of Westerly and Hopkinton submitted a third petition asserting that the current laws protecting fish were ineffective and had thus done "great damage [to] the poor." They too wanted stiffer laws mandating the opening of dams and restricting the use of nets. The General Assembly listened, and in February 1767 passed an act prohibiting the use of nets, or seines, from 25 March to 1 June on the entire Pawcatuck River and on a specified area below Pawtuxet Falls.

The popular pressure of these years was also evident at Pawtucket Falls on the Blackstone River. By the 1760s, the Jenckes family had dammed Sargeant's Trench and built two anchor shops upon it, converting what had originally been a fishway into a power canal. The rise of shipbuilding in Providence provided the incentive. Upcountry farmers did not immediately protest this abridgment of their rights, but in October 1761, John Dexter of Cumberland, along with seventeen others, requested that the General Assembly authorize a lottery to pay for improvements at the falls. Dexter and his fellow petitioners claimed that a great many fish of "several sorts" entered the river below the falls, but could not pass easily upstream. For 1,000 pounds, Dexter argued, a new fish passage could be constructed to allow fish "that choose fresh water to pass with ease." The Assembly granted the request.

Dexter's petition was signed by all of the mill owners then working at Pawtucket Falls—David and Hugh Kennedy, James and Nehemiah Bucklin, and seven members of the Jenckes family. They no doubt believed that supporting a new fishway was far preferable to giving up their rights in Sargeant's Trench, on which upcountry farmers might well have insisted. Farmers and mill owners at Pawtucket Falls were not yet in conflict, though their interests were clearly beginning to diverge. The new fishway worked, at least for a time. The General Assembly later claimed that the lottery had demonstrated its "public utility," benefiting farmers above the falls—"especially the poorer Sort of People."

By 1773, however, backcountry farmers had come to believe that the fishway was ineffective; now they convinced the Assembly to push the issue one critical step further. In August of that year the Assembly passed legislation with the ominous title, "An act making it lawful to break down and blow up Rocks at Pawtucket Falls to let fish pass up." The traditional common-law remedy for river obstructions had been affirmed by statute. It was now legal "for any person or persons whatsoever, at their own proper expense, to blow up or break down any rock or rocks in the falls . . . that obstruct the passage of fish up the said river, the said river being hereby declared a public river." The act was a major victory for northern Rhode Island farmers, clearly and unambiguously affirming the importance attached both to fish and to public rights.

The act was also more than the mill owners at the falls were willing to tolerate. The Jenckeses, the Bucklins, and one Richard Fenner, a miller on the west bank, responded to the Assembly at its next session. Asserting that they had been "peaceably and quietly possessed" of their mill privileges for decades, and that they had gone to great expense to maintain watermills frequently subject to floods, they did not now want to face the hazards of new law which would empower anyone "to judge of the propriety of destroying the dams at the Falls." Any person, they claimed, able to "procure a pound of gunpowder, actuated by the worst motives, may at any time in the space of a few hours, blow our interest to the amount of several thousands of dollars to irretrievable destruction." They requested that the law be repealed, and ninety-three freemen who signed their petition agreed with them—their numbers testimony to a growing divisiveness based on diverging economic interests.

Although it did not repeal the law, the Assembly in June 1774 claimed that it had been "misunderstood," and that "many Disadvantages have happened." The "Disadvantages" were not specified, but the Assembly formed a committee consisting of Stephan Hopkins, Darius Sessions, and Moses Brown—two of whom, as owners of the Hope Furnace, had a direct stake in amending the Fish Acts—to see that the new act was "truely executed." No rocks could be removed unless under their direction.

Yet removal proceeded. Moses Brown later testified that "he directed the blowers where not to blow," as fishways were created on both sides of the falls. These fishways, once again, seemed to work. A later petition asserted that "country" interests had been secured and that fishing continued to prove valuable, "particularly to the poorer inhabitants." The same petition also claimed that the mill privileges had not been damaged, although on this there is contrary evidence. Testifying in a later unrelated case, one Israel Arnold asserted that the mills lay idle, and the dam unrepaired, for three to four years after the blastings at Pawtucket Falls.

This victory for the farmers of northern Rhode Island came at the expense not of the colony's ironmasters—whose efforts to exempt themselves from the Fish Acts had initially provoked conflict—but at the expense of a less powerful group of grain millers, blacksmiths, and fullers. This was the first time in Rhode Island's history that farmers and the owners of small mills had seriously contested each other. In doing so, they revealed the distance that had come to separate their interests.

Now firmly tied to a market economy based upon shipbuilding and commerce, the mill owners of Pawtucket Falls were far less willing to accommodate the needs of farmers than their ancestors had been fifty years earlier. The rise of Providence port had made the difference. What had once been a fishway, mutually constructed by farmers and mill owners, was now a power canal. The colony's waterpower increasingly served the needs of an international economy. The economic stakes were higher and some men had come to believe that the public good now required that customary rights to fish be subordinated to the needs of commerce and manufacturing.

The farmers of the northern Rhode Island backcountry disagreed. Unlike some of their mill-owning neighbors, they had not grown more closely tied to a market economy. And they remained intent on protecting their rights to fish, even if that meant discouraging the full commercial use of the colony's rivers. The ferment of the Revolutionary years had given them the voice and the opportunity to reclaim rights once unambiguously theirs. They would continue their efforts to uphold those rights into the nineteenth century. But their power to do so would diminish. . . .

Conflict over dams and fishing rights in eighteenth-century Rhode Island was, at heart, a conflict over the coming of industrial capitalism. The annual spring migration of salmon, shad, and alewives furnished the noncommercial farmers of the Rhode Island backcountry with an important source of food. Their rights to fish were protected by both law and custom. Sawyers, grain millers, and other owners of small rural mills closely linked to local farm economies, easily accommodated those rights. The owners of blast furnaces, the first capitalists in the countryside, could not. Their technology and their capital investment required the intensive use of waterpower. As they sought to alter older patterns of river use, they also tried to alter the laws that protected the fishing rights of farmers. The conflict that furnace owners provoked paralleled the years of crisis leading to the American Revolution.

Farmers defended not just their economy, but their sense of public right and public virtue. They feared, not only the loss of fish, but the unrestrained pursuit of private advantage by mill owners. They were disturbed by the power of mill owners to impress their will on courts and legislatures. And as events would demonstrate, they had reason. Their apprehension had no direct connection to the issues of the Revolution, but drew upon a common sensibility—a sensibility expressed in Anglo-American Country thought. Country sensibilities lent shape to the experience of farmers and legitimated their concerns. Rhode Island farmers defended their fishing rights most effectively during the years from 1765 to 1772. After the Revolution, they continued to defend those rights, upholding an ideal of public virtue anticapitalist in its implications. Then their power declined. The growing commercial uses of waterpower, in particular the rise of cotton mills, fundamentally eroded the fishing rights of farmers. The pattern of conflict over dams and fish in eighteenth-century Rhode Island reveals the complex and contested nature of the American transition to industrial capitalism.

Planting East Florida: The Harsh Reality of Mosquito's Bite Plantation

DAVID HANCOCK

Florida captured Oswald's imagination. . . . Idealizing metaphors tumbled forth from his pen whenever he sat down to write about the possibilities for Florida planting. It was a "Paradise," a "New Canaan," a "desert in bloom" in the New World. How and why Oswald was first drawn to planting a country that was "by no means known" is not exactly clear. . . . But the "good reports" he heard about this territory in early 1764 meshed with his planting aspirations: he believed he could make money by establishing a plantation and reselling it in five or seven years; and it gave him an opportunity to conduct experiments and promote improvements that would satisfy his love of new techniques.

Oswald had to move quickly, for the settlement of Florida proceeded at a brisk pace. George III opened up the land to settlers on October 7, 1763, and appointed Colonel James Grant its Governor the following day. Public advertisements requesting private applications to the Board of Trade soon appeared in metropolitan, regional, and colonial newspapers and magazines. Eventually, the settlement of Florida came to dwarf all other contemporaneous plantation schemes in the number of acres granted. In addition to establishing his own plantations, Oswald was the single most important force in putting and keeping together a Florida planter group. He "plumped" for the colony by getting friends and acquaintances to become grantees, by supplying them with material assistance, and by providing them with moral support once they were bitten by the Florida bug.

As an impresario, Oswald made his greatest contribution in attracting planters. Of the 286 Privy Council orders authorizing survey of plantation lands, 62 (22%) went to men whom Oswald had known before 1763 in his capacity as commission merchant, army contractor, or Scots expatriate. To friends and strangers alike, he boasted that "no people in the world" live "more comfortably than the people in America." Oswald described the country in compelling terms to all who would listen. With a pitch combining uncharacteristic hyperbole with commonsense argument, he gathered together a group of grantees remarkable for its "note and ability." Military and contracting contacts formed the core. Such men, he believed, were well equipped to cope with the social dislocation of new communities; they were used to dealing

David Hancock, *Citizens of the World: London Merchants and the Integration of the British Atlantic Community, 1735–1785* (New York: Cambridge University Press, 1995), pp. 154–157, 159–160, 162–170. Reprinted by permission of Cambridge University Press.

with unknown peoples and regions; and their skills could be put to good use in taming a wilderness. With military men among the planters, there "would be still a greater degree of Security in a New Settlement." Merchants, too, shared many of the same qualities, and Oswald called on others like himself, especially those who possessed an army experience and an international clientele, to settle estates in Florida's hinterland.

Oswald also used his position as a commission merchant to assist operations in the new colony. To other planters, he recommended surveyors, overseers, and skilled laborers. Because he was in the business of supplying American planters with provisions, Oswald was able to send what the Florida estates needed, often before the planters knew that they needed it. Their greatest need was manpower, especially slaves, and among the grantees Oswald was the only slave trader. By 1770, he had sent three ships laden with slave cargo from his slave factory in Sierra Leone to East Florida. In the metropolis, he received planters' crops, chiefly indigo, and handled their sale.

Oswald also provided moral support to the planters. Known as "the Oracle" of "the East Florida Society," an informal drinking, discussion, and information group of Florida investors who met at the Shakespeare's Head in the West End of the City to discuss mutual planting concerns, Oswald gave freely to its members, in order to keep them "in good humour" and "to inspire better hopes." In an informal setting, whether coffeehouse, counting-house, or townhouse, Oswald did what he could "to spirit on those who had taken up the Idea" of planting, encouraging the disheartened and reviving flagging energies with practical observations about the possibilities for agricultural improvement.

As a grantee, Oswald wasted no time in pursuing his own project. In early May 1764, he devised an extensive plan of settlement, proposing a joint plantation venture with Governor Grant and outlining the expected stages of development in a lengthy memorandum; several months later, in early July, he was the third to file a request for land with the Privy Council; and, within ten days, he received an authorization to proceed with a survey of 20,000 acres. The Governor arrived in the colony in late August 1764 and, after two unsuccessful attempts, succeeded in fixing the boundaries of his and Oswald's settlement.

The 20,000 acres were located in the wedge formed by the confluence of the Halifax River and the Timoka Creek, approximately forty-five miles south of St. Augustine, a land generally referred to as "the Mosquitoes" after the nearby Mosquito Inlet (now, the Ponce de Leon Inlet) which opened onto the Atlantic. Oswald divided the grant into five settlements and focused his attention on the Mount Oswald Settlement, at the northernmost tip of the grant. His slaves cleared 400 acres, a quarter of which were river swamp dammed "with large and sufficient banks, drains, floodgates, &c.," and then readied them for indigo. Above the marsh, they raised a superintendent's dwelling house ($40' \times 20'$) that was "framed, & weatherboarded, shingled & glazed," an overseer's house ($20' \times 16'$), a kitchen, a large barn ($60' \times 30'$), a corn warehouse, a stable, and other outbuildings. Toward the end of the decade, they built a string of lesser settlements. . . . But it was on the fifth settlement, ominously called "Swamp," that Oswald expended his greatest energies, for it was at Swamp that he processed sugar. Here, in 1770, he erected a single-story overseer's house "built of very good materials and good workmanship," grain and sugar warehouses, a distillery, and a mill; he cleared 300 acres on the high, relatively dry ground between the Halifax and the Timoka; and he planted them with cane.

Despite the excitement, the Florida planting experiment failed. Oswald's grant was a bog, useless for anything but "indifferent" indigo or rice; and East Florida was, for Oswald and most planters, a swamp of an investment. By the time of the peace negotiations of 1782, . . . Oswald's characteristic understatement took on a tone of bitterness: East Florida was "a more tempting Country than it really is." Oswald and others witnessed (indeed, tolerated) one loss after another. Only 6 percent of the original Privy Council orders authorizing survey were processed and planted, comprising 1 percent of Florida territory. Apart from Governor Grant and perhaps one or two other planters, no large-scale grantee made a profit. Until 1770, the colony sent next to nothing to market. . . . During the American Revolution, the grantees' properties fell to enemy hands, employees deserted, and slaves rebelled. Independence and the return of Florida to Spain settled the matter. . . .

. . . Like nearly all the Florida planters, Oswald could not decide what to plant, nor would he stick with a crop long enough to make it pay. Under his original joint venture scheme, he vehemently rejected Laurens's idea of planting rice, thinking it was the wrong crop for a virtuous farmer to cultivate and preferring cotton and sugar, before acquiescing in Governor Grant's desire to cultivate indigo. After his partnership with Grant was dissolved, . . . he shifted his attentions among grapes, figs, cotton, and sugar. No one crop ever gave structure to Oswald's operations in Florida.

When he returned to his original idea of growing sugar, the merchant took sides in a rivalry that was dividing the absentee planters in London—a contest between . . . the indigo producers and . . . the sugar producers. . . . Oswald resolved "to go vigorously" into sugar so as to one day "vye with the West Indies in that Article." . . . From Jamaica, he brought an expert in sugar cultivation to supervise the planting. In 1775, he adopted a new French method for cutting sugar that had been successfully tried in New Orleans, and he erected a grinding mill according to the latest design.

The mill was as much a miscalculation as the sugar it ground, since it produced only a small amount of sugar each day and, when used, broke the slaves' legs. Both mistakes are revealing of the error underlying the entire plantation scheme: improvement programs devised and approved in Britain were not a sure guide to success in plantation America. The Swamp Settlement, it turned out, was "too far to the Northward for a Sugar Plantation." . . .

Oswald's planting schemes were also frustrated by a lack of infrastructure, both informational and material, and he worked to eradicate the problem. With respect to news about his plantation, this merchant who feasted on facts received a meager, unsatisfactory diet. Early reports on Florida planting by Adam Gordon, William Stork, Andrew Turnbull, and writers for the *Gentleman's Magazine* were positive, but vague. Subsequent overseers' accounts were no better. As late as May 1769, Oswald was still "pretty much in the dark"; suspense vexed him and, he believed, killed the interest of others. The planters, he explained to Governor Grant, were "fond of the notion of their foreign possessions"; they liked to talk about them and, "sometimes like us Farmers, to illustrate [them] to the utmost." Yet the planters never received accurate, detailed accounts of the lands they had been granted: reports were never sent, and remittances were "in suspense."

Oswald's grant had been surveyed in late 1764, and a patent issued on the strength of the survey, yet Oswald never received a copy of either the survey or a map of the plantation. In mid-1766, Henry Laurens traveled to St. Augustine to resurvey the land, but he was unable to make it to the Mosquitoes, since the only conveyance was a small pilot boat packed with Oswald's slaves and overseer. A Scots engineer named James Moncrieff did manage to squeeze into the boat, visit the plantation, and make a favorable report, yet even this account did not contain the level of specificity desired by Oswald or Laurens. Oswald continually pleaded with his overseers to send frequent and full reports of every aspect of plantation life. In response to one overseer's account, which he found "very general or rather imperfect," he outlined the contents of a model report:

> Where there's a surface of 30 sqr miles, I should think a good many particulars might be furnished that would be entertaining to a party concerned, such as—the Trees & Vegetables—in the different soils, the sort of soils—proportion of each—their fitness for differt products—pasture—levels—game—fish & ca.—Oeconomie & expence of Slaves—Regulations on the managing & working them & ca.

So it was that he grilled his employees with plantation questions and plagued them with requests for botanical specimens. It was Oswald's firm belief that his overseers should spend several hours each week writing him memoranda on the state of the estate. By autumn 1769, one overseer had had enough, and went so far as to beg the Governor to "stop his [Oswald's] mouth," but Grant knew it was useless. The only things that would satisfy the omnivore would be "twelve sheets of answers," plus vials of soil.

A lack of reliable information about his plantations went hand-in-hand with a lack of material infrastructure. Oswald reveled in the chance "of making some new Experiments Sutable to the nature of the Climate & Soil" which the "generality of New Settlers could not venture to attempt," for he believed that the experiments would not only build a richer, more workable soil and vegetation base but also, with the additional people involved in the administration of the experiments, facilitate the flow of information. When he introduced sugar, he brought in Jamaica experts who had mastered the art of cultivating cane; when he planted corn, he sought advice from Bengal. To his Florida plantations, he brought not only new machines like a contraption for pounding rice and new animals bred for strength in swamp cultivation and resistant to swamp disease, but also experts from other colonies and countries whom he could trust to report back to him. Yet, at the same time, he knew that the soil and mechanical experiments conducted by these experts would come to nought if no attention was paid to "other Circumstances of the Country," even if he was fully apprised of the outcome. Since improved plantations were useless if isolated, Oswald, as well as Mill, Herries, and Grant, backed numerous public works projects in Florida: lighthouses, harbors, canals, bridges, and roads. Their most successful project—a 150-mile carriage road from Fort Barrington to St. Augustine that was funded primarily by private subscription—strove to create "an universal Communication easy in time" where before had stood only a trail that was easily flooded and completely lacking in bridges or ferries.

In addition to the difficulty of isolating appropriate crops, and wanting usable infrastructure, finding reliable managers also bedeviled Oswald's planting in Florida.

... [I]n Oswald's case the problem of finding honest, competent managers ruined him. ... Trustworthy supervisors were difficult to find, yet the success of the operation depended on them. Oswald had hoped to rely on direct acquaintance, as usual. Contacts he made in Germany were an important source. He invited a Mr. Gessner who had worked for him for four years in Germany and now wanted a job in America. Gessner was "clever enough, active, & faithful," he spoke and wrote German, French, and English well and, best, as a European, he could be used to attract Germans "from the Northwd & back Settlements." When Gessner declined the invitation, Oswald turned to his men already in America. He delegated the responsibility for making an application of survey to his friend and correspondent John Graham of Savannah. Soon after a patent was granted, he named Governor Grant to manage lower-level appointments and on-site operations, and he asked Henry Laurens to supply provisions and laborers.

At this point, Oswald's planning broke down, and he ceased to rely on known men for his planting. A string of inept overseers, whose appointments he had allowed others to make and whose backgrounds he knew but sketchily, obstructed progress. A chronology of Oswald's mishaps is instructive. His first overseer—Samuel Huey— was found by Laurens, and accompanied the Charlestonian to Florida in May 1766. But Huey was "a drunken, good for nothing fellow," unfit "for the sole management of a Plantation." The Deputy Clerk of the Florida Council visited the estate several times that fall and "put Hewie upon his guard," but all for nought. The overseer was idle and negligent, incurred extraordinary expenses, and embezzled the plantation of its provisions. While fishing one day late in the year, he drowned while plantation slaves looked on. His death was barely lamented; the loss of the two slaves who went down in the same boat was greater.

Oswald hoped that Huey's successor, an American Indian named Johnson whom Laurens also hired, would "behave above the rank of common Carolinian Fugitives, to save his Scalp a whole Year." It was believed that he "must be discreet & carry a steady command," if he was to avoid a similar fate, since the blacks, who had allowed Huey to drown, "love those of their own colour least." (The Europeans believed that black slaves considered the Indians as blacks.) The Governor directed Johnson to raise provisions and plant indigo. At the same time, he placed him under the surveillance of two of Oswald's friends who had moved to Florida to supervise their own plantations. Johnson executed his job well for the first year and became "a favorite" of the neighbors. Finding "everything neglected & in confusion," he raised enough provisions to supply the slaves already in place and feed the thirty who were sent there during the course of the year. But Johnson had "a wandering disposition," and the Governor could not prevail upon him to stay at his post. One day in 1767 he walked off into the swamp and was not heard from again.

Oswald generally experienced problems with his white managers. He was unable to procure and keep seasoned, reliable overseers; those he employed provided him with useless information, if that. For most of the time, he was "pretty much in the dark as to data." So, in the early 1770s, he returned to the pool of army and commercial talent with which he was personally acquainted. When one of his mariners talked of retiring after fourteen years of service in the shipping lanes, and when another of his captains was to be deprived of his livelihood by the sale of a ship, Oswald moved them to "the Mosquitoes" where they served as overseers. Only in the years just preceding the outbreak of the Revolution did Oswald begin to send overseers who possessed some commitment to service, and some experience growing plantation crops and living in the American hinterland. But by then it was too late.

Despite his hopes, Oswald's superintendents and overseers were "unseasoned" men unused to the climate and uneducated in the ways of plantation cultivation. As Sir Alexander pointed out, "estates never thrive under new [or young] Overseers." By the time the overseers gained experience, they figured out that they could make more money managing their own estates elsewhere, and fled. The economic incentives to break one's contract and leave before the indenture had expired were great. And even when an overseer stayed long enough to write an account of his activities, it was difficult to obtain information from a man coping with a wilderness. The situation faced by a Florida planter vis-à-vis a Florida overseer was dramatically different from that faced by a Grenada planter vis-à-vis his employee. A Caribbean planter had other ways to learn about the state of affairs of his island and the operation on his plantation; a Florida landowner did not. Thus, only three years into his planting, Oswald realized that the grant was a morass into which sank all employees with whom he had no "personal knowledge." These Florida investments never saw a return, in large measure because on-site supervision by reliable relatives or friends was not sustained, as it was on the associates' more successful Caribbean estates to the south. Business success in East Florida, Oswald came to realize, was prevented by "taking up wrong notions." These he likened to an arch: "if one brick fails, the whole fabrick falls." In his own estimation, "wrong notions" were the work of unreliable managers whose imprecise, vague reporting and lack of commitment had led him astray.

In addition to these three reasons for the failure of the Florida project—difficulties in isolating crops, obtaining information and infrastructure, and finding reliable managers—Oswald's own plantations suffered from the additional handicap of an ambivalence about his goals. To Oswald, America represented not only a business venture but also an unlimited opportunity to conduct experiments and promote "improvements." As Jack Greene reminds us, "The people who created and perpetuated the new societies of colonial British America sought not merely wealth and personal independence as individuals and the welfare of their families, but also the social goal of improved societies that would guarantee the independence they hoped to achieve and enable them to enjoy its fruits." This was true for both settlers and planters. But the combination of motivations could have dire consequences. Florida was a business venture that Oswald kept treating as an experiment, with neither a clear model to copy nor a clear road to follow. Oswald's uncertainty about crops never allowed any one crop to reach wide-scale cultivation, and his penchant for throwing good money after bad severely retarded his plantations. Experiment marked the entire Florida scheme to an extent not known in Oswald's other commercial ventures.

The associate's Florida planting had an eleemosynary, sometimes utopian aspect to it. "The desire of promoting an enterprize productive of both national advantage and private interest" propelled him to lay down "the strictest conditions of Improvement," not only for his investments but also for new settlers he had never met and with whom he had little in common. So Oswald strove to relieve the destitute but deserving poor of Britain by providing them a home in Florida, in much the same way that Grant worked to establish "a good retreat" for penitent prostitutes of London there, and for "indigent familys who struggle under many difficulties in a less favourable soil & climate." Although this strain of philanthropy, expressing little concern for profit, was entirely foreign to the associates' more purely commercial undertakings, it surfaced late in life in their American planting. In planting America, Oswald thought of himself as a virtuous leader in a community where agriculture and commerce were linked.

 F U R T H E R   R E A D I N G

Bailyn, Bernard. *Voyagers to the West: A Passage in the Peopling of America on the Eve of the Revolution* (1986).
Galenson, David W. "The Rise and Fall of Indentured Servitude in the Americas: An Economic Analysis." *Journal of Economic History* 44 (March 1984): 1–26.
————. *White Servitude in Colonial America: An Economic Analysis* (1981).
Green, Jack P., and J. R. Pole, eds. *Colonial British America: Essays in the New History of the Early Modern Era* (1984).
Grubb, Farley. "The Statutory Regulation of Colonial Servitude." *Explorations in Economic History* 37 (January 2000): 42–75.
Henretta, James A. *The Origins of American Capitalism: Collected Essays* (1991).
Heyrman, Christine. *Commerce and Culture: The Maritime Communities of Colonial Massachusetts, 1690–1750* (1984).
Matson, Cathy, ed. *The Economy of Early America: Historical Perspectives and New Directions* (2005).
McCusker, John J., and Russell R. Menard. *The Economy of British America, 1607–1789* (1985).
Perkins, Edwin J. *The Economy of Colonial America*, 2d ed. (1988).
Rothenberg, Winifred Barr. *From Market-Places to a Market Economy: The Transformation of Rural Massachusetts, 1750–1850* (1992).
Schweitzer, Mary M. *Custom and Contract: Household, Government, and the Economy in Colonial Pennsylvania* (1987).
Ulrich, Laurel Thatcher. *Good Wives: Image and Reality in the Lives of Women in Northern New England, 1650–1750* (1980).
Walton, Gary M., and James F. Shephard. *The Economic Rise of Early America* (1979).
Wood, Gordon S. "Was America Born Capitalist?" *Wilson Quarterly* 23 (Spring 1999): 36–46.

Merchants and Commercial Networks in the Atlantic World, 1680–1790

Today, "network" and "networking" are terms describing the interconnectedness of business in our high-technology global environment. Computer, telecommunications, broadcasting, and electrical "networks" and professional "networking" are so integral to contemporary business that it is hard to imagine a world without these technologies and cultural practices.

Three centuries ago, networks also figured into business practice, providing the glue that held together the business realm. Although there were no electronic devices, there was a web of human relations. From Europe, a system of personal contacts and related institutional arrangements cast an invisible net across the Atlantic Ocean to Africa and the Americas to form a large international trading sphere that historians call "the Atlantic world." In this space, interlocking networks—built on communication and trust between acquaintances—linked businesses, institutions, and countries.

The people who mastered networking to create this commercial web were the merchants. In the mid-eighteenth century, the term "merchant" most often referred to a wholesale trader involved in international commerce. In the colonies, it sometimes described retail shopkeepers, planters who imported and exported, and the resident representatives of large trading companies. North American prosperity depended on the British demand for staples, such as wheat, tobacco, indigo, lumber, pig iron, and whale oil. These exports provided colonists with the cash or credit required to purchase imported European and Asian goods, both luxuries and necessities. Whether in London or Jamaica, New York or Charleston, merchants tied into commercial networks oversaw the procurement, shipment, and sale of these goods and managed the complex financial arrangements that under-pinned those transactions.

Why did networks exist, and what functions did they serve? The business realm of the British Atlantic world was highly fragmented. As we saw in Chapter 2, it consisted of thousands of small businesses run by sole proprietors or partners.

Exceptions included a few large trading companies, such as the Royal Africa Company, the British East India Company, and the Hudson's Bay Company, which operated under charters of incorporation granted by the British government. In this atomized world, somebody or something had to coordinate the flow of goods, services, and information. In the eighteenth century, the famous Scottish political economist Adam Smith claimed that "the invisible hand" of the market took charge. Today, historians recognize the importance of human agency and business institutions to economic activity. They also argue that merchants worked alongside market mechanisms to orchestrate business.

In Chapter 2, we read about Richard Oswald, a London merchant who unsuccessfully tried his hand at running a Florida plantation. Oswald's broader story provides a good segue into this chapter on commercial networks. As David Hancock has shown in Citizens of the World: London Merchants and the Integration of the British Atlantic Community, 1735–1785 *(1995), Oswald belonged to a circle of upstart London-based merchants, who invested in global trade. As trust developed within the clique, members shared resources and confidential news about markets, competition, and investment decisions. Each merchant contributed information from his wider experience. Thus by networking, the group reduced both the costs and the risks of doing business in an international market that had relatively poor communications across distances.*

D O C U M E N T S

Historians learn about commercial networks from several types of primary sources: government reports, customs books, account books, bills of exchange, securities ledgers, travelogs, advertisements, artifacts, and letters. We know that merchants forged networks in face-to-face interactions at counting houses, docks, taverns, churches, and exchanges. We also know that they sustained those networks across long distances through confidential letters entrusted to ship captains.

Documents 1 to 3 contain letters illustrating some of the opportunities and challenges faced by colonial businessmen involved in transatlantic trade. In 1686, William Fitzhugh (1651–1701) was a prosperous thirty-five-year-old Chesapeake Bay planter, who had lived in the new land for fifteen years. He belonged to a coterie of Virginian planters whose commercial activities also included trading, storekeeping, and flour milling. These men typically bought tobacco from smaller planters and shipped it to market along with their own. In turn, they imported English merchandise and retailed it to their neighbors. After more than a dozen years, Fitzhugh tired of this routine and tried to sell out. Written as a sales pitch, Fitzhugh's letter to Ralph Smith of Bristol, England, is the best surviving portrait of a seventeenth-century Chesapeake plantation (Document 1). While Fitzhugh vividly describes his well-tended farm, he does not mention the seven indentured servants, including a carpenter, glazier, and bookkeeper, who worked for him.

Some merchants took advantage of the ongoing wars between the European colonial powers to develop lucrative smuggling businesses. Bostonian Thomas Hancock established a legitimate trade between his hometown, Newfoundland, and London, selling oil and other whale products harvested from the north Atlantic. During the War of Jenkins' Ear and King George's War (1739–1748), Hancock expanded into the profitable—and illicit—trade between Boston, Holland, and the Caribbean. Hancock's vessels sailed to forbidden French and Dutch colonies in the West Indies where they traded salted fish for tropical luxuries such as molasses, indigo, and lignum vitae (the source of a valuable drug). They proceeded to Amsterdam to exchange the tropical goods for European wares before returning to Cape Cod where they smuggled in the continental contraband. Hancock's 1742 letter to his Scottish agents in Amsterdam describes part of one such covert voyage (Document 2).

In Document 3, a letter written by New York merchant Gerard G. Beekman (1719–1797) sheds light on another important aspect of transatlantic trade. Throughout his career, Beekman vigorously pursued the flaxseed business, shipping seeds grown in the northern colonies to Ireland for the linen industry. Eventually, he got involved in slaving. In 1749, Beekman discusses insurance on slave shipments and strategies for managing the human cargo.

Visual and material culture constitute another source of information about eighteenth-century commercial activities. In Document 4, a frontier agent of the Hudson's Bay Company writes to the London office for manufactured goods to refresh his inventory. His letter suggests that Indians were discerning consumers, who demanded quality merchandise. What does it tell us about material life and transatlantic networks? In Document 5, a billhead for shopkeeper Lewis Deblois illustrates the facade of his Boston store and lists the English imports that he carried. What types of products does Deblois describe, and why does he focus on those goods? What can we learn about colonial retailing and shopping from the images?

Documents 6 to 9 explore the activities of Philadelphia's Federalist merchants during the revolutionary era. Initially connected by a trade network, these merchants bonded around Federalist politics, lobbying for political reform to safeguard the interests of finance, trade, and foreign affairs. Combined with the third essay by Thomas Doerflinger, these Philadelphia sources show how businessmen and their networks helped to shape American politics, government, and law from the earliest years of the republic.

As inflation escalated during the American Revolution (1774–1783), Pennsylvania's farmers and artisans blamed big-city merchants. In Document 6, eighty merchants respond to this critique in a letter published in 1779 by the newspaper *Pennsylvania Packet*. Putting their financial knowledge to good use, the merchants propose a commercial policy that would ensure the continuation of unregulated trade while curtailing inflation. Their scheme was not adopted, and the conflict persisted. In Document 7, frustrated trader Tench Coxe draws up plans for a business association or chamber of commerce. Although Coxe's vision never materialized, his 1784 proposal aimed to unite Philadelphia merchants, guard commercial interests against the country, and generally promote trade, industry, and economic growth. How do these sources reveal the links between commercial networks and institution-building?

The dissonance between Pennsylvania's merchants and farmers, urban elites and country people, reflected the larger national political crisis rooted in the deficiencies of the Articles of Confederation. By 1786, Philadelphia merchants perceived the need for a stronger national government, and many rallied behind the Federalist effort to create a new Constitution. Antifederalists resisted this effort. In Document 8, the famous Antifederalist pamphleteer, George Bryan, attacks the Federalist merchants. In an essay published under the pseudonym "Centinel," Bryan claims that greed and ambition motivated their political activism. The Antifederalist suspicion of wealth and power cast a long shadow, feeding antibusiness sentiment for decades.

Document 9 shows one Philadelphia merchant's enthusiasm for the nation's economic future. Buoyed by the prospect of the Constitution's ratification, Levi Hollingsworth in 1788 urges one of his London contacts to follow in his footsteps and invest in western lands. The new federal government, he writes, will be most conducive to commerce, and westward expansion will prove profitable.

1. Virginia Merchant-Planter William Fitzhugh Describes His Tobacco Plantation, 1686

Doctr. Ralph Smith   April 22nd. 1686

In order to the Exchange you promised to make for me, & I desired you to proceed therein, to say to Exchange an Estate of Inheritance in land there of two or three hundred pound a year, or in houses in any Town of three or four hundred pound a year, I shall be something particular in the relation of my concerns here, that is to go in return thereof. As first the Plantation where I now live contains a thousand Acres, at least 700 Acres of it being rich thicket, the remainder good hearty plantable land, without any waste either by Marshes or great Swamps the Commodiousness, conveniency, & pleasantness your self well knows, upon it there is three Quarters well furnished, with all necessary houses, ground & fencing, together with a choice crew of Negroes at each plantation, most of them this Country born, the remainder as likely as most in Virginia, there being twenty nine in all, with Stocks of cattle & hogs at each Quarter, upon the same land is my own Dwelling house, furnished with all accomodations for a comfortable & gentile living, as a very good dwelling house, with 13 Rooms in it, four of the best of them hung, nine of them plentifully furnished with all things necessary & convenient, & all houses for use well furnished with brick Chimneys, four good Cellars, a Dairy, Dovecoat, Stable, Barn, Hen house Kitchen & all other conveniencys, & all in a manner new, a large Orchard of about 2500 Apple trees most grafted, well fenced with a Locust fence, which is as durable as most brick walls, a Garden a hundred foot square, well pailed in, a Yeard wherein is most of the foresaid necessary houses, pallizado'd in with locust Punchens, which is as good as if it were walled in, & more lasting than any of our bricks, together with a good Stock of Cattle hogs horses, Mares, sheep &c, & necessary servants belonging to it, for the supply and support thereof. About a mile & half distance a good water Grist miln, whose tole I find sufficient to find my own family with wheat & Indian corn for our necessitys & occasions Up the River in this Country three tracts of land more, one of them contains 21996 Acres another 500 acres, & one other 1000 Acres, all good convenient & commodious Seats, & wch. in a few years will yield a considerable annual Income. A Stock of Tobo. with the Crops & good debts lying out of about 250000lb. besides sufficient of almost all sorts of goods, to supply the familys & the Quarter's occasions for two if not three years. Thus I have given you some particulars, which I thus deduce, the yearly Crops of corn & Tobo. together with the surplusage of meat more than will serve the family's use, will amount annually to 60000lb. Tobo. wch. at 10 shillings ℔ Ct. is 300£ annum, & the Negroes increase being all young, & a considerable parcel of breeders, will keep that Stock good for ever. The stock of Tobo. managed with an inland trade, will yearly yield 60000lb. Tobo. without hazard or risque, which will be both clear without charge of housekeeping, or Disbursements for Servants cloathing. The Orchard in a very few years will yield a large supply to plentifull house keeping, or if better

Colonel William Fitzhugh to Dr. Ralph Smith, April 22, 1686, in Richard Beale Davis, *William Fitzhugh and His Chesapeake World, 1676–1701: The Fitzhugh Letters and Other Documents* (Chapel Hill: University of North Carolina Press and the Virginia Historical Society, 1963), pp. 175–176.

husbanded, yield at least 15000lb. Tobo. annual Income. What I have not particularly mentioned, your own knowledge in my affairs is able to supply, if any are so desirous to deal for the Estate without the stock of Tobo. I shall be ready & willing, but I will make no fractions of that, either all or none at all shall go. I have so fully discoursd you in the affair, that I shall add no farther instructions, but leave it to your prudent & carefull management, & would advise that if any Overtures of such a nature should happen, immediately give an account thereof to Mr. Nicholas Hayward Notary publick near the Exchange London, both of the person treating, & the place Scituation, Quantity & quality of the Estate, who will take speedy & effectual care, to give me a full & ready account thereof, which I hope you will ꝑ all opportunitys do to

To Doctr. Ralph Smith in Bristol   Sir Your   W. ff.

2. Boston Merchant Thomas Hancock Launches a Covert Voyage to Amsterdam, 1742

Messrs. Tho. & Adrian Hopes.   Boston. N. Eng^d. April 12th, 1742.

Gentlemen,

This covers you[r] Bill of Lading for 168 Tons of Chipt. N. River Chipt Logwood Twelve baggs of Cotton and Eight hundred Horns Shipt unboard the Brigantine Charming Lydia Simon Gross master Consigned yourselves, which I wish safe to your Hands and to a Good Markett, you will find it a Cargo of Choise Good New River Chipt wood & I Expect will yeald me a Better price than Commonly wood is sold at, when please God the Vessell arrives, I doubt not of your Disposeing of the Cargo to my best advantage, and the neet proceeds thereof Invest in the things mentioned in the Inclosed Invoice, which Ship to me per the above mentioned Brigantine Charming Lydia, & I earnestly Intreat the favour of you Gentlemen to Procure the Goods for me at the very Cheepest prizes, & Good Goods, & let them be packt up in the Safest Cheepest & best manner, my Request is Likewise that you give Capt. Gross the Quickest Dispatch, having a Cargo Ready for her Return, I hope She may not Stay with you above Ten or Twelve Days, and if War Continues please to Insure for me one half my Interest of Vessell & Cargo, Valueing the Vessell in this case at but £500 Sterling, and Should there be war with France & Spain two, then Insure my whol Interests, but if Peace with above powers Insure nothing. I have no Goods shipt but my own and no Letters sent to any body here but that Comes under Cover to me. Should Capt. Gross & Capt. Frost be both in Holland [at] the Same Time, I Desire you if you can to Sell the Charming Lydia if She will fetch 4500 Gilders or upwards, but not [less]. . . . She is a Good Vessell & Carrys well, and in this case send my [Effects] home in Capt. Frost, & my People, if you cant make [arrangements for them?] to be Discharged there—but in Case Capt. Gross's Vessell Dont Sell, & you have Opportunity to Sell Capt. Frost's Brigantine the Three Friends for the prices we fixt her at to the master, we Desire you to Do it

Thomas Hancock, Boston, to Thomas & Adrian Hopes, Amsterdam, April 12, 1742, in W. T. Baxter, *The House of Hancock: Business in Boston, 1724–1775* (Cambridge, Mass.: Harvard University Press, 1945), pp. 90–91.

& Send the Effects of Vessell & Cargo & men home in Capt. Gross, I rely much upon your honour Gentlemen that you Serve my Interests to the utmost of your power in Every Particular as to Sales & Returns, and Doubt not of your Doing me Strict Justice in Both. I have been advised by a good friend to consign this Cargo to a Certain house in Amsterdam, but my Principel is not to Exchange houses while I have Justice & good Treatment, which I Depend upon from you. The Cotton I have sent for a Tryal the contents of which is Inclosed as I Received it from Statia, make the best of it, its Good I had it from St. Eustatia & it Cost me Dear, dont let me be a Looser by it.—if it answers I Shall Ship you a Greater Quantity which I have now by me.—the Letters Capt. Gross Delivers you for London pray Send per very first post, pray write me by way of London & by any other opportunity that may offer if you can buy me a Sett of Riging for a Brigantine or Snow of 120 or 130 ton Little worse for ware at the price a Little higher than kings Junk [= secondhand naval ropes?] I'd have you do it & send with my other Goods, or Should Capt. Gross meet with what he thinks will do, please to pay for it. The Letters you send me by way of London Inclose to Francis Wilks Esq. & Co. who will always forward them the first opportunity.—pray Let me know what Sorts of flowered Silks & Damasks may be had with you & Send me the Pattens of Some of them, with the Prizes—Capt. Gross has Two Tons of wood which please Deliver him freight free & allow him Portledge of 2 p.c. upon the wood & Expense 2/6 per Day. Let my paper be packt in Bales of a middle Sizes. Note the things [to] be sent if a French war & if no French War Don't Send them, be [certain] to write me if Whale oyle or bone or any Particular [articles?] which may be mett with here will answer with you. . . .

3. New York Merchant Gerard G. Beekman Insures Slave Cargo from Africa, 1749

To Robert Shaw and William Snell, London, Jan. 20, 1749

By Antilope Captain Emory.

My Last to you was the 1 November with Coppy of what wrote You Via Derrey to Which I refer You have Also Coppey of what I wrote you by Bryant hereinclosed, which I hope is Come Safe to hand. Inclosed You have Two first Bills of Exchange one of 20 and the other of Thirty pounds Sterling Drawn on Captain Thomas Levitt in warwick Street near Golden Square London. When in Cash for the Same please to Credit my account for the Same. if Said Bills Should be protested pray advance so much for me as to Git the following Insurances made for my account. I am Concerned in a fine Brigantine aprim[e] Sailors Saild 2 Days ago for the Coast of Africa with a fair wind the Captain Extreamly well acquainted have bin several Voiages there. hes a Sober honist and Industerous man the vessell mounts 6 Carrage guns 4 pounder 8 Swivell and Small etc. In proportion Suitable She is also now New Sheaded has 4 anchors and all her Cables new, so that on the Whole she is well found

Gerard G. Beekman, New York, to Robert Shaw and William Snell, London, January 20, 1749, Gerard G. Beekman letters, Beekman Family Papers, New-York Historical Society, New York, N.Y. This document can also be found in Philip L. White, ed., *The Beekman Mercantile Papers, 1746–1799,* vol. 1 (New York: New-York Historical Society, 1956), pp. 73–74.

is to bring back if they Can 60 80 or 100 Small Slaves and not to go up the bites a slaveing to risque the Sailors health. is first to touch at Gambia or Surloon and so to touch all the Coast a long down as far to Leward as annamaboe his orders is to returne from the Coast so as to make [sure] that he gits hear before Cold wether Setts in next fall. The Reason of my being so particular is to Prevent Any Disputes arrising In case of Loss Misfortune and at the Same time am in hopes of the Vessell is so good and well found etc. that it may Save me one or two per Cent on the Premium. Now the Insurance I request youl make for my account. I hope youl git done at the Cheapest rate and Lett the underwritters be good viz One [on] the Brigantine Revenge Hur Tackles and Apparel James Holmes Master at and from New York to and at Gambia on the Coast of Africa with the liberty to Touch all the Coast along down to annimabo and at and from the Coast of Africa back again to New York the Sum of one hundred and fifty Pounds Sterling and that on my account. The above have done in as Cheap a manner as You Can But as to Insurance on the Cargo Chuse to Limmit if you Can have it Done at or under Twelve per Cent then git it Done out and home in the Same Manner as above. Do Have it done if not to be done at 12 or under then have it done as Chease [cheap] as you Can only out on the Cargo till it is safe arrived at Annamabo. The sum I would have inSured on the Cargo is One hundred and fifty Pounds Sterling and that on all risques, mortality of the negroes Only Excepted. I think I have bin as particular as possible. I don't know but Two Much to make it Troublesom to your I Shall write you by next ship and order some Insured one [on] a Large Snow and Sloop I am Concerned in bound to Ireland and the Other to Medaria [Madeira]. Your Complyance with advice by first Vessell will very much Oblige him who you may Very freely Command.

4. A Hudson's Bay Factor Orders Merchandise for His Indian Customers, 1739

Right Honourable Sirs, With submission, this we humbly beg leave to observe to your honours, according to your honours' orders, 1738 (paragraph the 7th) the Indians dislike of particular goods, their refusal and the reason for the same, to the best of our knowledge; with a true and exact account of goods not holding the number, measure and weight as per invoice, likewise the badness of provisions, etc.

1. Beads large pearl, the Indians dislikes for the colour, both large and heavy, the shape not being for the use they put them to, which is to hang at their nose, ears, and to make belts etc., so being few or none traded and lying useless in the factory, according to your honours' desire I send them home, as your honours will find the same mentioned as per invoice; as likewise all such as is sent home.

2. Kettles they complain of, for their being small for the weight, of a very bad shape, the handles hanging over the side too far, the ears too weak. The kettles they like is of a round high shape, light, strong ears, and the handles to lap just upon the side of the kettle.

James Isham, Fort York, to Hudson's Bay Company, London, July 20, 1739, in K. G. Davies, ed., *Letters from Hudson Bay, 1703–40* (London: Hudson's Bay Record Society, 1965), pp. 278–280, 282.

3. Their refusal of kettles is kettles of twelve quarts, they being large and heavy, not but some would trade them if they could, but the reason is, there is not one Indian in thirty that is able to purchase one, so lying useless in the factory, I send them home as aforementioned.

4. Powder they complain is of an ashy colour, very weak and foul, and of too large a grain; they finding when they put a little in their hand, it rubs to dust very soon, which is all the reason of dislike I can give for it.

5. Blankets, is only their complaint of being too short by six or nine inches, they answering very well in shape, make and colour.

6. Cloth is their general complaint, of its being too narrow, weak and thin, and of little service. It's their fashion if it's an end of cloth, to wear it at bottom, if not to wear the list at the side.

7. Buttons is very weak shanked and quickly breaks; though size, shape and make, answers extraordinary well.

8. Combs also answers for shape and make, there being no complaint, only very weak.

9. Fire steels is very faulty, gives but little first, and full large.

10. Gunworms is very unhandy, being short and too wide for a ramrod, they being obliged to put a piece of paper round the ramrod before the worm will be fast, by which reason they lose many a deer etc. before they have time to draw the small shot to put a ball in.

11. Flints French, is noways pleasing to Indians, they being for the most part very unshapeable for a gun.

12. Gloves yarn, are noways pleasing nor serviceable to Indians and none taken up by our men, so lying useless in the factory, I have sent them home as aforementioned.

13. Hatchets answers extraordinary well lately, only the small hatchets are full large.

14. Knives are noways pleasing to the natives, they being very bad blades and worse handles, especially jack knives.

15. Tobacco tongs lies useless in the factory, and few or none traded, for which reason I have sent them home, according to your honours' desire. The only reason I can give for the Indians dislike is they are of no service to them, but to take a piece of fire up with to light their pipe; but they take their knives to be more handy, not only so but for the most part they strike light to a piece of wood called (posoging) and so light their pipe with a piece, which is all the reason I can give for the dislike of the same.

16. Twine is their complaint of being very weak and uneven, being as thick as pack-thread in some places and as thin as thread in other places, and of a small size.

17. Powder horns they dislike for being so crooked for the most part, and very weak and thin in some places; they like for the most part straight horns.

18. Rings is too wide, the generality of the female sex having small fingers.

19. Those are the only things of dislike of trading goods to the best of my knowledge, and according to your honours' desire, have sent home samples of most part which is pleasing to Indians, and most conducive to your honours' interest. . . .

31. Pipes, we do assure your honours is so much broke when we receive them that we are in great want of the same, for in eighteen gross received from England, we shall not have much above twelve gross, the rest being so short that they are of no service. With submission to your honours, if they was put in cask or larger

boxes with more straw between each lay, it would preserve them very much from being broke.

32. Pipes is great encouragement to Indians especially leading Indians, for when they come with a gang of Indians, we give them a pipe and pipe of tobacco, which they are extremely thankful for; but when they are broke so that we have not way withal to supply them, they make a great many words and say if they went to another place they would be better received (meaning your grand enemy the French), when at the same time it's not in my power to help them, only promising with good words they shall have them for the future, when at the same time it's precarious whether I can make my words good or not, they being broke so as aforementioned. This I do assure your honours is not the first time of being so, they being the same for some time, which I find is a disencouragement to Indians.

5. Boston Shopkeeper Lewis Deblois Advertises the Latest London Goods, 1757

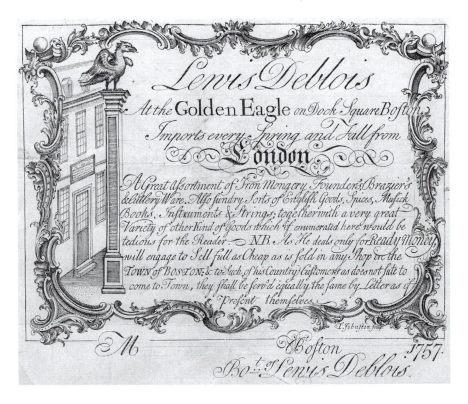

Billhead, Lewis Deblois, Boston, Mass., 1757, in Joseph Downs Collection of Manuscripts and Printed Ephemera, Winterthur Museum & Library, Winterthur, Del. Courtesy The Winterthur Library: Joseph Downs Collection of Manuscripts and Printed Ephemera, # 66×152.

6. Revolutionary Era Merchants Explain the Causes of Inflation, 1779

We are to observe to you, that if you wish to remove an effect you must begin by removing the causes, and not hope to wither the causes by lopping off their consequences. You think of limiting the prices of imported articles, but these prices depend upon various incidents. First, upon the price of our own productions, they upon the price of the labour to produce them, that upon the price of the necessaries of life to sustain it, those again in a great degree upon the quantity of our money; and all upon the winds, the seasons, the ravages of war, the calls for militia, for carters, for batteau men, horses, and a thousand other contingencies, which it is not in human prudence to foresee, to obviate, to regulate, or to provide for. Secondly, upon the prices of vessels and their outfits, which rest on the same fluctuation of uncertainties with the former. And, thirdly, upon the premium of insurance founded on the risk of a voyage, which is to be estimated by the events of the moment. If then you would limit the prices of foreign articles you must enable a merchant to get his goods freighted upon moderate terms, fix the prices of goods he is to expect and open an insurance for a low premium. But until these things be accomplished, you may indeed by an act of power force away the property of men at such rates as you may think proper to allow but like him who owned the goose which had laid golden eggs, you will cut off the source of all further supplies, and like him too, when you do repent, you will repent in vain. . . .

Perhaps we may be asked our opinion as to the measures which we conceive necessary for the purposes we have in view with our fellow citizens, and which it is so much our particular interests to prosecute. We do not hesitate to give this question an immediate answer. The first thing necessary is to take off the embargo, and every other regulation and limitation of commerce, and to prevent the unnecessary purchase of wheat, flour and other necessaries at remote places by commissaries and quartermasters. Secondly, to fix the value of the money borrowed by the continent, and in so doing to give a sufficient advantage as an inducement to the lenders that sums may be by that means obtained for the public exigencies without farther emissions. Thirdly, to enable merchants to make remittances abroad at a low rate in the way of exchange. And fourthly, to levy taxes on one, two or three pence in the pound monthly upon the actual value of estates estimated according to the prices of such articles, native and foreign, as may be taken for a standard. . . . Measures like these, we will venture to say, would immediately arrest the depreciation in its present state, and daily restore our money by just degrees to its pristine value, without distressing the people, and render it the immediate, as it certainly is, the remote interest of every man to begin the lowering of prices with his own commodities, without setting arbitrary rules for his neighbours, and to induce them to lower theirs simply by restraining from the purchase of those things which are too dear. If after all, regulations should be necessary, they ought to be laid on the necessaries and not on the luxuries of life. Nor can it at any time be justifiable to oblige one man to part with his

---

Pennsylvania Packet, or The General Advertiser Extraordinary, September 10, 1779.

property merely to gratify the palate of another. Still less can any reason be conceived for laying a ruinous tax on the industrious merchant, that drunkenness of the most dangerous and pernicious kind may be rendered cheap, yet such is the effect of a limitation on the price of rum.

7. Tench Coxe Proposes a Chamber of Commerce, 1784

The purpose for which should be initiated—

To unite the mercantile Body.

To form a city interest, that may create some small counterbalance for the too great weight of the Country interest in the state.

To regulate the commissions of sales, purchases, agencies, and negotiations which are extremely uncertain and various.

To restore the ancient intercourse that subsisted between the different parts in the city, and by a mutual exchange of private kindness and public services to restore our old good humor, and promote the trade and interests of the state.

To promote the perfection of such manufactures as are adapted to our situation, and particularly of our principal raw staples, as wheat, Indian corn, hemp, iron, lumber, etc., all of which are carried on to a very beneficial degree and are exported to our great advantage. In executing this the saving of the dear articles of labor, provisions, & rents may be effected in great measure by the use of water works. This country, the middle states especially, abound with mill seats, and [it] appears to me that it would be very useful to have a return made of all these mill seats *near* this city, upon navigable water & within 50 miles of it. . . .

To increase the facility of bringing our produce to market by the improvement of our two fresh waters the Delaware & Schuylkill, as well as our other rivers and our roads, also by building Canals.

To form something which perhaps might be properly enough called the Merchants Court to adjust disputes arising among mercantile men. This is an important object and point of convenience. This duty falls heavy now upon a few, who [?] through a good deal of it. It might be well to arrange this matter so that the parties might pay something to these referees or to the public or both. In London, [where a similar set up exists, it is said that] for each referee this must be a capital business, much larger than the sums to which transactions usually run here. It might also form a source from whence an annual income might be drawn to defray the continuous great expenses of the Chamber.

The fisheries of this country require our particular attention, and I think would pay us well for it. If the French and English can make that trade do so far from home as Newfoundland, . . . the New England states, and Cape Horn, I cannot see an impediment in our way.

To ascertain the line that should be drawn between our own states and those of foreigners, and lay the same before the assembly of these states. This cannot be so well done as by the merchants & a few cannot do it so well as them collectively.

Tench Coxe, "Plan of a Chamber of Commerce and a List of the Merchants of Philadelphia," October 21, 1784, pp. 9–12, Tench Coxe Papers, Correspondence and General Papers, microfilm reel 46, Historical Society of Pennsylvania, Philadelphia, Pa.

Besides, as long as it continues only generally interesting to all individuals alike, no one will take the lead. This would not be the case if it fell to . . . 28 or 30 to exert themselves in compliance with this engagement.

A consistent correspondence between the mercantile bodies of this and other of our cities upon new discoveries in trade or the arts must be very useful. Every new regulation, measure, or scheme adopted in any place should be handed in its digested form from one to another. It would therefore be very useful to have such a chamber in New York, Boston, Baltimore, Charleston, etc.

Attention should be paid to making useful some business property belonging to the merchants—for the purpose of building coffee houses, exchanges, etc., which serves as the [. . . ?] till they are collected into a body. . . .

The Chamber of Commerce might in my opinion institute a very useful Mercantile School in which should be taught the modes of calculating the exchanges, weights, and measures of foreign countries, tonnages of ships and the quantity of the various kinds of goods they would carry, the different kinds of manufactures or rather modes of manufacture by samples.

8. Antifederalist George Bryan Attacks the Merchant Junto, 1788

The merchant, immersed in schemes of wealth, seldom extends his views beyond the immediate object of gain; he blindly pursues his seeming interest, and sees not the latent mischief; therefore it is, that he is the last to take the alarm when public liberty is threatened. This may account for the infatuation of some of our merchants, who, elated with the imaginary prospect of an improved commerce under the new government, overlook all danger: they do not consider that commerce is the handmaid of liberty, a plant of free growth that withers under the hand of despotism, that every concern of individuals will be sacrificed to the gratification of the men in power, who will institute injurious monopolies and shackle commerce with every device of avarice; and that property of every species will be held at the will and pleasure of rulers.

If the nature of the case did not give birth to these well founded apprehensions, the principles and characters of the authors and advocates of the measure ought. View the monopolizing spirit of the principal of them. See him converting a bank, instituted for common benefit, to his own and creatures' emoluments, and by the aid thereof, controlling the credit of the state, and dictating the measures of government. View the vassalage of our merchants, the thraldom of the city of Philadelphia, and the extinction of that spirit of independency in most of its citizens so essential to freedom. View this Collosus attempting to grasp the commerce of America and meeting with a sudden repulse—in the midst of his immense career, receiving a shock that threatens his very existence. View the desperate fortunes of

[George Bryan], Centinel, No. VIII, *The Independent Gazetteer; or, The Chronicle of Freedom,* January 2, 1788. This document can also be found in John Bach McMaster and Frederick D. Stone, *Pennsylvania and the Federal Constitution, 1787–1788* (Philadelphia: Historical Society of Pennsylvania, 1888), pp. 625–626.

many of his coadjutors and dependants, particularly the bankrupt situation of the principal instrument under the *great man* in promoting the new government, whose superlative arrogance, ambition and rapacity, would need the spoils of thousands to gratify; view his towering aspect—he would have no bowels of compassion for the oppressed, he would *overlook* all their sufferings. Recollect the strenuous and unremitted exertions of these men, for years past, to destroy our admirable Constitution, whose object is to secure equal liberty and advantages to all, and the great obstacle in the way of their ambitious schemes, and then answer whether these apprehensions are chimerical, whether such characters will be less ambitious, less avaricious, more moderate, when the privileges, property, and every concern of the people of the United States shall lie at their mercy, when they shall be in possession of absolute sway?

9. A Merchant-Speculator Encourages Europeans to Invest in Western Land, 1788

Mr. Mark Pragers   Good Sir/ I anxiously expected Letters from you by every Ship from London. Capt. Sutton hath arrived at the Port. Capt Willet yet at Sea I trust by him I shall be informed of your receiving the Patents and Map of the Lands with other Papers—recommended by me to your Care from my Friend Mr. Enoch Story of London on this business. I beg to suggest to you the satisfaction that would probably arrise to any Gentleman or Company that may incline to purchase a Landed Estate on the Continent by sending an agent over to view the Lands, their [Situation] Soil Climate and other local advantages and as Mr. Wynkoop and myself have two resident Agents in the Kentucky Country viz Mr. Parker & Mr. Mindinghall late one of the Clerks at the Bank whom I presume you will remember—we can with great Conveniency direct such agent to them—This plan will obviate every doubt in the minds of European Purchasers as to the reality of the Purchase or the perfect Security of the Title & Possession and the certainty as to the Quality and almost incredible Fertility of the Lands as well as the Laws Manners Produce & flattering Prospects of the Western Country—& the many advantages that will result from such a Negotiation and in Truth I know of no Speculation in America equal to that now committed to your Patronage & Care—The quantity of Lands we possess in that Country are 300,000 acres in Tracts from 50 to 100,000 acres in a body: great part of which is of a prime Quality fit for Cotton Hemp Flax Tobacco Corn Wheat Rye & Grapes— Some Slips of the Burgundy Vine were sent to Lexington, the Capital of the Country last Spring & thrive amazingly. The Settlements are increasing very fast & the migration from the interior parts of America to Kentucke the last Fall is computed to 20,000 People. The Indians are not troublesome in that Quarter which will soon be rendered perfectly safe by the Settlements now forming on the Muskingham & other parts of the foederal Lands. Those on the back of the State of Georgia it is otherwise

Levi Hollingsworth to Mark Pragers, April 21, 1788, Levi Hollingsworth Letterbook, vol. 2 (1786–1791), pp. 228–230, Hollingsworth Papers, Historical Society of Pennsylvania, Philadelphia, Pa.

with but the Distance from Georgia to Kentucke is at least 50 miles. I have the pleasure to inform you that the new Constitution hath been adopted by every state that have convened for the Discussion of the Question. Maryland met yesterday at Anapolis five sixths of the members returned are Foederal & I am certain will ratify the Government. The Commerce of this City seems to revive a little this Spring. Great Quantities of wheat are shiping off for Portugal & flour for Spain & I flatter myself that on the foederal Government taking place a new Spring will be given to trade and agriculture throughout the States. I cannot help mentioning to you the Loss of my dear Daughter Lydia. You know how dear she was to me & her disconsolate mother. God Bless and preserve you. His ways are unsearchable & his Providence indisputable.   Yours LH

 # E S S A Y S

These essays consider different aspects of the merchant experience in the networked transatlantic economy. The first essay is by Kenneth Morgan, a professor of history in the School of International Studies at Brunel University in West London, who has published extensively on Anglo-American commerce. Morgan provides a sweeping overview of the transatlantic trade, with special reference to slavery. He shows how British mercantilism, embodied in the Navigation Acts, fostered a protected market throughout Britain's Atlantic empire. Official intervention by the British government created institutions that facilitated the development of trade networks for buying and selling human beings.

Whereas Morgan's essay casts a wide net, the next two essays focus more tightly on particular moments, places, and people. Ann M. Carlos, professor of economics at the University of Colorado in Boulder, and Frank D. Lewis, professor of economics at Queen's University in Kingston, Ontario, Canada, examine the fur-trade operations of the Hudson's Bay Company. From the late 1600s to the early 1900s, this chartered London company dominated the North American fur trade. The firm depended on Indians to hunt beaver and deliver pelts to its wilderness posts, providing European goods as payment. Drawing on letter books and ledgers, Carlos and Lewis examine exchanges among the Indians, frontier agents, and the London office. How is this case study connected to the broader story about commercial networks?

Finally, Thomas Doerflinger, a securities analyst and author of the Bancroft Prize–winning book, *The Vigorous Spirit of Enterprise: Merchants and Economic Development in Revolutionary Philadelphia* (1986), reinterprets Philadelphia's merchant community in the newly formed United States. Before the American Revolution, Philadelphia was British America's largest port, and Quaker wholesalers dominated the city. The revolution (1774–1783) burst this powerhouse asunder. A new merchant coalition seized power and began reshaping the political economy. Led by financier Robert Morris (1734–1806), these self-described Republicans helped Congress to create national institutions for advancing commerce and industry. The Bank of North America (1781), for example, embodied their convictions that a strong central bank would stabilize the economy. In 1787–1788, this newly powerful merchant group supported the Federalist Party, played a seminal role in forming the fiscal and economic policies of the federal government, and shaped the sections of the U.S. Constitution dealing with economic matters.

British Merchants, the Slave Trade, and the Transatlantic Economy

KENNETH MORGAN

Slave plantations began to flourish in the British Empire in the mid-seventeenth century. During the ensuing century they grew considerably in size, number and significance. By 1750 the black population of the British Empire totalled around 555,000, with some 295,000 living in the Caribbean and 247,000 in North America. In mainland North America, slaves worked principally on tobacco plantations in Virginia and Maryland (the Chesapeake region) and on rice and indigo plantations in South Carolina and Georgia (the Lower South). They were also found in smaller numbers, not always on plantations, in North Carolina, East Florida, the Mississippi Valley, the middle colonies of Pennsylvania, New Jersey and New York, and New England (notably in Rhode Island). Slaves dominated the labour force of sugar, coffee and cocoa plantations throughout the West Indies, both in the largest British island, Jamaica, and in a series of British possessions in the Windward and Leeward Islands of the eastern Caribbean.

Slave estates needed plenty of land and capital for planting staple crops, and for various buildings, including cooling and drying houses, water mills, distilleries, refineries and slave quarters. Plantations could contain between 50 and 350 slaves, with sugar estates requiring a larger labour force than those catering for other staple crops. The system of chattel slavery, based on racial discrimination and severe legal codes, meant that the offspring of slaves were themselves born into slavery. Because of a high death rate on many plantations, through a combination of hard work, disease and poor diet, the supply of slaves, especially to the West Indies, needed regular replenishment. The eighteenth century was the period when British slave trading was at its peak; some 3 million slaves were carried in British vessels to the Americas during that century, more than by any other European power. . . .

The Transatlantic Economy

The plantations and other British possessions in the New World were supplied by ships, goods and people that formed part of an ever-expanding, integrated transatlantic economy. Geographically, this trading complex embraced 2,000 miles of the west African coast, a free trading zone open to all the European powers; the Atlantic wine islands (Madeira, the Azores, the Canaries); ports in continental Europe such as Lisbon, Malaga, Amsterdam and Hamburg; the thirteen mainland North American colonies that became the United States plus Florida; the Canadian maritime provinces; the Caribbean islands, the Bay of Honduras and the Mosquito Shore in central America; and ports in Britain and Ireland. Vessels criss-crossed the ocean from London, Bristol, Liverpool and Glasgow to Boston, New York, Philadelphia,

Kenneth Morgan, *Slavery, Atlantic Trade and the British Economy, 1660–1800* (Cambridge: Cambridge University Press, 2000), pp. 9–10, 12–18, 21–24. Reprinted by permission of Cambridge University Press.

Charleston and Kingston, to name only the most prominent ports, and slaving vessels ranged down the west African coast from Senegambia to Angola.

Some trades operated on a bilateral basis, with vessels shuttling to and fro between ports; but since much British overseas trade in the age of sail was dominated either by full export cargoes or substantial import cargoes but rarely by both, a number of important multilateral trades grew up. Because of this imbalance in commodity flows, merchants based in New England or Pennsylvania and New York paid for the goods they received from Britain by shipping, freight and commodity earnings in the provision trades to southern Europe and the West Indies. By this means, they compensated for the lack of a staple commodity to provide regular direct returns and made up much of their trade deficit with Britain. In 1768–72, for which fairly full data are available, the North American colonists incurred a current account deficit of about £40,000 per annum, compensating for their deficit in commodity trade with Great Britain and Ireland by earning significant credits in the sale of ships to the mother country plus commissions, insurance, freighting goods and shipment of specie. . . .

Overseas trade operated under the framework of five Navigation Acts, passed between 1651 and 1696. These provided a large protected market for British manufactures within the empire by confining oceanic trade with the mother country mainly to British-owned and British-manned vessels and by prohibiting the manufacture of various products in the colonies. All colonial and European commodities were to be shipped to Britain or a British colony. An exception was made for certain enumerated commodities, including rice, tobacco, sugar, indigo and naval stores, which could be exported outside the British Empire after first being landed at a British port. . . . The Navigation Laws encouraged Britain to become an entrepôt for importing colonial staples and thus stimulated various re-export trades. They were intended to boost British shipping activity and the number of seamen to give strength to the navy in wartime. This system of protectionism involved placing tariffs on foreign-produced wares and elaborate customs procedures. The Staple Act of 1663, in addition, stipulated that, with a few exceptions, European goods destined for the English Atlantic colonies should be placed aboard ship at an English or Welsh port for shipment across the ocean.

The Navigation Acts lay at the heart of an "old colonial system" based on mercantilism in which the wealth and sea power of Britain were intended to grow by confining the benefits of empire to the state and its own subjects. They were viewed as a buttress against the economic rivalry of the continental European trading powers. Though subject to various revisions, the Navigation Laws lasted until 1849. They allowed much more flexible patterns of commerce, notably multilateral trade, than the strict controls imposed by Spain on its American dominions, whereby Atlantic shipping was mainly undertaken in bilateral fleets between one Spanish port and a few entrepôts in the Caribbean and South America. Nevertheless, by the late eighteenth century some leading economic commentators, notably Adam Smith and Josiah Tucker, considered that the Navigation Acts proved a burden to Britain's economic development and that they should be overturned in favour of free trade. But the protectionist system served Hanoverian Britain well, and free trade, despite the advocacy of some high-profile commentators, flourished only some time after Queen Victoria came to the throne. From time to time some historians have argued that enumerated commodities imposed economic costs on the colonies, but the current consensus is that the burdens of the Navigation Acts for the North American colonies was small.

Merchants established important commercial connections throughout Britain's Atlantic empire. They travelled between ports or sent captains, agents or supercargoes overseas to conduct business. West India merchants frequently served apprenticeships in the Caribbean, and some were involved in partnerships with personnel based in both Britain and the Caribbean. Scottish factors opened stores in the Chesapeake, especially in piedmont areas, where they sold an array of imported goods and dealt with tobacco customers. Some London firms had social and mercantile connections throughout the Atlantic trading world. Overseas ports had contingents of British merchants. For instance, Lisbon had a community of English merchants and Philadelphia attracted English and Irish businessmen who were socially mobile and searching for economic opportunity. Hanoverian London was home to an international community of merchants and became the leading world centre of finance and trade, a position wrested from Amsterdam in the early eighteenth century. Some London merchants with origins in Scotland, Ireland and the English provinces flourished in Atlantic trade in the mid-eighteenth century, building up interlocking business activities in government funds, military contracting, the slave trade, shipping and landownership in North America, the Caribbean and Britain.

These and other merchant groups established intricate business relations with colonial counterparts, basing their connections on reputation, honour, creditworthiness and sometimes kinship ties. Risk and uncertainty were central parts of economic enterprise throughout the early modern trading world. Small wonder, then, that personal attributes of probity and trust were essential for consolidating business links in a commercial world in which factors in transatlantic areas were often better placed to make entrepreneurial decisions than their principals. In all these commercial and shipping connections, slavery and the slave trade were central to transatlantic enterprise and to making the British a greater oceanic trading nation than its principal maritime rivals, the French and the Dutch. In *The African Trade, the Great Pillar and Support of the British Plantation Trade* (1745), the mercantilist writer Malachy Postlethwayt summed up this situation by referring to the British Empire as "a magnificent superstructure of American commerce and naval power on an African foundation."

As this quotation implies, the great circle of commercial exchange was supported with protection on the high seas afforded by the Royal Navy and privateering vessels in the many war years between 1660 and 1800. Britain was at war for 55 of 140 years in that period. These wars had a significant colonial component. Moreover, Britain achieved naval hegemony over the French, its chief colonial rival, over this period. The War of the League of Augsburg (1689–97) and the War of the Spanish Succession (1702–13) both partially involved conflict between the French and the English in the Atlantic. The War of Jenkins' Ear (1739–42) was rooted in rivalries with Spain in the Caribbean. The War of the Austrian Succession (1742–48) partly involved a power struggle with the French in the same theatre of conflict. The Seven Years' War (1756–63) witnessed the triumph of British hegemony over France in North America. The first British Empire began to crumble, however, with the loss of the American colonies in the War of Independence (1776–83), a conflict that also witnessed struggles between European maritime rivals in the West Indies. The first years of the wars against revolutionary France (1793–1801) saw renewed Anglo-French conflict in that theatre, exacerbated by the huge slave rebellion in Saint-Domingue.

Thus Britain's consolidation of a marine empire overseas involved considerable struggle and international rivalry. Trade was often interrupted; freight and insurance rates increased; and convoy protection was needed for commerce with the Caribbean. British privateers based in London, Liverpool, Bristol and the Channel Islands helped to stem the tide of depredations by foreign shipping. More important, the navy overcame most of the challenges it faced from war on the high seas. Britain maintained a wartime fleet of between 185 and 350 vessels in the first half of the eighteenth century, partly augmented by a construction programme and partly by capturing good-quality enemy shipping. By this means, it could establish supremacy over the combined fleets of France and Spain. Thus in the wars between 1739 and 1763 the British, despite danger and alarms, preserved their sugar colonies from invasion and economic catastrophe; the French suffered far more in these wars than the British. The navy enforced the Navigation Acts and gradually secured command of the English Channel against French and Spanish rivalry; by consolidating British security vis-à-vis their main European maritime rivals, command of the world was feasible.

In addition, the taxes collected by the British fiscal-military state to back military power were substantial; without them the economic benefits accruing to Britain from the colonies would have been seriously impaired. Taxes collected rose by a multiplier of 14.4 in the period 1688–1815 and successive governments borrowed extensively to fund the national debt. In wartime British governments could borrow large sums of money at several percentage points lower than those the king of France could achieve. . . . [T]hese monies served to bolster naval and military forces. They enabled the state to support overseas trading activity on a substantial scale. By these means, the eighteenth-century British people became second only to the Dutch as the most heavily taxed subjects in Europe. The bureaucracy of the British state grew and became more efficient with the development of government offices such as the Admiralty, Customs, Excise, the Board of Trade, the Treasury Board, the Victualling Board and the Colonial Office. British sinews of power in the eighteenth century were thus heavily centred on naval, financial and bureaucratic resources. . . .

The Growth of Overseas Trade

. . . English retained imports grew from £5.8 million to £23.9 million between the same two sets of years [1700–01 and 1797–98]. This growth was accompanied by a market shift in the pattern of trade: the transatlantic sector expanded while trade with Europe experienced relative decline. In 1700–01, the colonies in the New World accounted for 11 per cent of the value of English exports and for 20 per cent of imports. In other words, Europe still dominated British overseas trade at the start of the eighteenth century. This pattern changed, however, over subsequent decades. By 1772–73, North America and the West Indies took 38 per cent of exports and provided 39 per cent of imports. By 1797–98, North America and the West Indies received 57 per cent of British exports and supplied 32 per cent of imports.

Re-exports grew fivefold from £2,136,000 in 1700–01 to £11,802,000 in 1797–98. They were mainly supplied to European ports and included many colonial commodities such as tobacco, sugar, rice and coffee. . . . As Jacob M. Price has noted, re-exports "helped pay for the imports of all those useful raw materials from northern Europe—especially iron, flax, hemp, masts, deals, pitch, and tar—that kept thousands of sailors and tens of thousands of workers busy in Britain."

British exports sent across the Atlantic were mainly finished manufactured wares such as textiles, hardware, metalware and glassware. Imports from the Americas were dominated by sugar, tobacco, rice, coffee, raw cotton, wheat, naval stores, dyestuffs and other products increasingly in demand with British and European consumers. The most lucrative of these products were staple commodities grown in the tropical or semi-tropical colonies rather than in temperate zones, exotic fruits that gradually but inexorably became important components of the British diet. During the eighteenth century, British foreign trade changed from being largely an exchange of woollens for raw materials to being based on a wider range of manufactured exports exchanged for foodstuffs. Refined sugar became a significant part of the British diet in the eighteenth century; per capita consumption increased from 1 lb to 25 lb between 1670 and 1770, with many ordinary folk, as well as wealthier consumers, acquiring a sweet tooth. Tobacco in the form of snuff or cut or roll tobacco, smoked in clay pipes, reached a domestic market in which demand was limited and inelastic; but tobacco was an important re-exported commodity to France, the Netherlands and Germany. Rice was another significant re-exported staple that usually had a small market in Britain, because home-grown foodstuffs plus high import duties on rice deterred its mass consumption.

Invisible aspects of trade unrepresented in the customs figures expanded the scope of British overseas trading activity; they augmented the revenues from the export of British commodities overseas and covered up some of the deficits on the balance of commodity trade. In 1740 Robert Dinwiddie estimated that the amount of cash, dyes, drugs, cocoa and other commodities imported to the British plantations through trade with the Spanish and French possessions in the Americas amounted to £425,000 annually. Prize goods, mainly from the Caribbean, had an annual average value of £438,794 in the Seven Years War. In 1691 Jamaica's bullion exports were worth £100,000. Some £2,368,484 worth of bullion alone was sent to England from the West Indies in the period 1748–65. The increasingly interdependent nature of seaborne commerce meant that large imports of hemp, flax, timber and naval stores from the Baltic region were partly fuelled by the growth of demand for shipbuilding materials for vessels plying Atlantic shipping routes. . . .

The sheer scope of the changes in British foreign trade in the century after 1660 was striking when compared with what came before. Whereas overseas commerce had been concentrated for centuries on shipping with European ports and with a limited range and value of exports and imports, oceanic trade in the century after the restoration of the Stuart monarchy extended its geographical scope across the globe and augmented the types of goods found in ships' cargoes as well as their value. Important trades that were to some extent invisible in customs records, notably the Atlantic slave trade, became prominent in connection with British overseas territories in this period. The increasing sophistication and interdependence of the eighteenth-century Atlantic economy led to greater levels of capitalisation in foreign trade and more specialised commercial processes, such as the extension of credit ties, the evolution of complex mercantile practices and the growth in the size and market power of merchant firms.

Fur Trading on the Frontier: The Hudson's Bay Company and Indian Consumers

ANN M. CARLOS and FRANK D. LEWIS

The Hudson's Bay Company exchanged European trade goods for furs with Native Americans over a period that extends from the late seventeenth through the twentieth century. That experience provides an ideal case study of how a firm with little initial knowledge of its consumers developed a successful and enduring relationship with them. The Hudson's Bay Company received its charter in 1670, allowing it to trade for furs in the hinterland of Hudson Bay. Although the French had been trading through Quebec City and Montreal since the early 1600s, the English company was a new venture operating in a new area. At first, conflict between Britain and France prevented the Hudson's Bay Company from gaining secure control of its posts, but with the signing of the Treaty of Utrecht in 1713 the hinterland of Hudson Bay was defined as British, and the Company began to trade actively.

During the eighteenth century, the expanding fur trade reflected the growth of the European hatting and felting industries, which were primarily based on beaver pelts. Although beaver could be found in many parts of North America, the highest quality pelts came from the drainage basin of Hudson Bay, where only Native Americans hunted and trapped beaver; Indians thus were the primary agents in a market bartering furs for European commodities. Through this process Indians gained access to goods—both producer and consumer—previously unknown. We focus on the marketing of goods by the Hudson's Bay Company and the role played by Native traders in determining the quality and selection of goods made available for purchase.

The extensive data set preserved in the Hudson's Bay Company's archives provides a detailed view of the interaction between those who were supplying European goods and those who were supplying the furs. The trade accounts, letters, and other correspondence between the trading posts and the head office suggest that the Hudson's Bay Company was committed to learning about its consumers and to offering goods that were most in demand. They began by providing goods similar to those in the more easterly trade, but they also experimented with goods that Indians had not yet seen. The records reveal that the Native Americans in the region were demanding consumers, concerned not only with the quantity of the goods they received but also with their quality and variety. In a world where neither side was in a position to coerce the other, Natives' preferences played a major role in the conduct of the trade. . . .

From the start, the Hudson's Bay Company was aware that it was working in an unknown cultural environment, and one of its goals was to learn about the reactions of Native traders to price and other dimensions of the trade. In essence, this is

Ann M. Carlos and Frank D. Lewis, "Marketing in the Land of Hudson Bay: Indian Consumers and the Hudson's Bay Company, 1670–1770," *Enterprise and Society* 3 (June 2002): 286–290, 292–293, 297–298, 300, 302–310, 312–315. Copyright © 2002. Reprinted by permission of Oxford University Press.

the problem facing any multinational; success depends on the ability to breach the cultural divide. . . . We believe that the Hudson's Bay Company traversed the cultural divide successfully because it was willing both to incorporate Native trading traditions and to listen to its consumers.

The Trade at York Factory: A Brief History

Soon after receiving its charter, the Hudson's Bay Company established several trading posts: Rupert's House on the eastern side of James Bay in 1671, followed in quick succession by Fort Albany on the Albany River, and Moose Factory on the Moose and Abitibi Rivers. The French, operating along the St. Lawrence from Montreal, quite naturally saw the Company as a potential threat, and their reaction in 1686 was to capture Fort Albany and Rupert's House, although both posts were returned in 1693. Despite the conflict and uncertainty, the Hudson's Bay Company maintained its foothold in the region and gradually expanded its trading area. In 1684 the Company established Port Nelson, later renamed York Factory, and five years later built Fort Churchill. Even these more remote trading posts were not physically secure from French incursion. It was only after the Treaty of Utrecht was signed in 1713 and the drainage basin of Hudson Bay was declared English that the immediate risk of military conquest ended. The economic rivalry with the French continued, however, until their rule in Canada ended in 1763. English and Scottish merchants operating from Montreal also offered competition until the Hudson's Bay Company and Northwest Company merged in 1821. Our analysis here focuses on the trade through York Factory to 1770. . . .

York Factory, located on Hudson Bay at the mouth of the Nelson River, was by far the largest of the Hudson's Bay Company's trading posts. From 1713 to 1738 it faced little competition, but in the mid-1730s French traders began to move into the hinterland of York Factory, establishing their own trading posts and intercepting Indian groups en route to the Bay. . . .

During the eighteenth century, York Factory served a hinterland of nearly one million square kilometers. In 1720 the western territories of the Hudson's Bay Company, from James Bay to the headwaters of the Churchill River, were controlled by Algonquian-speaking Cree bands, while in the lands along the southwestern boundaries two Cree allies held sway: the Siouan-speaking Assiniboine and the Algonquian-speaking Ojibwa. Native populations in the region can only be estimated, of course, but available figures for the three main groups that occupied the York Factory trading hinterland suggest that Western Cree numbered 4,500; Northern Ojibwa, 1,400; and Plains Assiniboine, 2,700. . . . The size of the trading groups coming down to the Bay ranged from small bands to large groups, and decisions concerning who would come down to trade were made at the household or community level. The Company was able to exert pressure only through moral suasion and the goods they offered once Native traders had come down to the post. . . .

The European Goods Received by Native Traders, 1716–1770

. . . Indian traders purchased a wide variety of goods, which we have grouped into a few broad categories: producer goods, household goods, alcohol and tobacco, and other luxuries. Some of these commodities, among them kettles, guns, and blankets, came in different sizes and weights, and the jewelry items came in a wide range of types. Even ignoring the variations within commodity definition, Indian traders in a typical year could select among sixty to seventy different goods.

We have defined producer goods as those used mainly for hunting game. Guns and related supplies dominated the producer goods category, accounting for 70 to 80 percent of goods in this group in terms of value. Before 1720 Natives spent more than 60 percent of their income from the fur trade on producer goods. During the 1720s and through the 1730s, however, the share fell to between 40 and 50 percent; and starting in the early 1740s and continuing to 1770, the producer goods share declined to about 30 percent of expenditures. Guns came to play a less important role in demand. This change in consumption over the period does not reflect the gun merely as a durable item that did not need frequent replacement, because the quantity of powder and shot also declined. In fact, in the harsh local climate, guns were not that durable.

The household goods category contains those commodities used most directly in food preparation and for warmth. Kettles and blankets predominated, with awls and fire steels being minor items. Over the same period, the household goods share in expenditure also declined, from about 10 percent to just over 5 percent. The decline in the producer and household goods shares of Native expenditure was off-set by an increase in the share of expenditure on what we term luxury items. To refine further the nature of expenditures on these goods, we have broken them into three broad categories: tobacco and related items, alcohol and related items, and other luxury goods, including beads, cloth, jewelry, and vermillion among a long list of goods.

For much of the period, the most important luxury good purchased by Indians was tobacco. There were a few large year-to-year fluctuations, but for the most part, tobacco consumption as a share of total expenditure remained in the 15–20 percent range. Over the same period, the share of expenditure on alcohol increased steadily, albeit from an extremely low level. Indeed, in the early period, no alcohol was received in trade (though it was consumed during the ritual portion of trading), and until 1730 it remained a relatively minor item, with a share of about 5 percent. With the rise in fur prices after 1738, however, the share of expenditures on alcohol increased markedly, equaling or surpassing that for tobacco from 1750 to the end of the period. . . .

Among the wide variety of luxury goods that also gained in expenditure share, the most important by far was cloth. Purchases of cloth, in fact, exceeded those of alcohol through much of the period. Overall, the share of expenditure on "other luxuries" increased from about 15 percent in the early years to almost 30 percent by the end of the period. The luxury goods category contains many of the commodities that we find in the probate inventories in Europe and colonial America during the same period: beads, buttons, handkerchiefs, hats, lace, mirrors, rings, trunks, earrings, and medals.

The breakdown of purchases . . . documents a remarkable transformation in the consumption basket of the Native Americans trading at York Factory. As Kathryn Braund has noted in the context of a more southerly trade, "The improved tools meant that traditional tasks were completed faster and better" as "metal replaced stone, bone and shell." Interestingly, the superiority of this European iron technology to its stone, bone, or shell counterpart has generally been taken as a given.

Yet the changes in consumption patterns evident in the York Factory data force questions about the nature of the goods presented for purchase. While the trade data describe the quantitative changes that were occurring, the correspondence between the head office and managers at the posts illustrates the thinking of the Company with regard to marketing strategy and, relating to that, the role played by Native traders in the choices that were being made about the quality and types of goods being sent to the Bay.

Marketing to Native Americans: Language

A feature of the long-distance trades that has received very little comment is the frequency with which buyers and sellers spoke different languages. In some cases a barter trade can take place by relying on gestures or a basic pidgin; but the range of goods sold by the Hudson's Bay Company, and the elaborate trading processes and accompanying rituals, speak of a complex market relationship that evolved over many years. Hudson's Bay Company managers would have spoken early modern English, while Native Americans coming to York Factory spoke Algonquian Cree. As languages go, English morphology is relatively simple, especially in comparison to Native American languages, which are very complex. In the repeated transactions that were to occur, the way in which the Company approached communication with the Native Americans reflects the Company's view of the Indians as consumers.

The Hudson's Bay Company entered the fur trade with the intention of being a repeat actor. Despite the early wars with France, it built posts around the coastline of Hudson Bay—Fort Albany, Eastmain, York Factory, and Fort Churchill. The Company hired salaried managers to act on its behalf, and . . . through the use of positive incentives such as efficiency wages and gratuities, and through the close monitoring of accounts, the Company was effective in reducing the level of its managers' opportunism. Indeed, the Company sought to create a social system that made managers and workers feel part of a family. To this end, the London directors indentured boys from Christ's Hospital London who were educated in writing and arithmetic to be apprentice managers. In the general letter of 1689, the committee laid out its views of these apprentices: "[T]hey all write faire hands and Cast accompts, and being young will easily attaine the Lingua and bee trained up in our service and if you think such Ladds may be useful in a few years to send up with the Indians wee have thoughts yearely or every other year to take the like or a greater number from the said Hospital." By the end of the eighteenth century, many of the Company's major post factors and managers came from this group.

This letter, written during a time of instability around Hudson Bay, indicates that Company directors in London clearly recognized a need to have managers who could communicate with the customers. They were sending to Hudson Bay 14-year-old boys who would learn not only the trade but also the language. The Company saw the responsibility for facilitating communication as its own, rather than that of the Native Americans coming down to trade. If we think of the trade as a repeated game with the same post managers but often different Native traders coming down to the Bay, it becomes apparent why the Company had a greater incentive to invest in these communication skills than the Indians. . . .

Marketing to Native Americans: The Quality Dimension

The Hudson's Bay Company account books document the changing structure of the trade as consumption shifted from producer and household goods into luxury goods. The trade did more than just present Native Americans with an Iron Age technology; it also meant access to textiles, blankets, lace, thimbles, mirrors, alcohol, and tobacco. One of the most striking features of the letters exchanged between the post factors and the head office in London, as well as the letters from the directors of the Company to their factors, is the evidence they contain of the vital role played by Native traders in determining both the types and the quality of the commodities provided. Even though they might have journeyed several hundred miles to engage in trade, Indian traders were not willing to accept just any commodity that the Company chose to send over to its posts. . . .

Thus, very early on, the head office was aware that the Company's trade goods had to meet the standards of the Indians, and the interactions between post managers and Native traders quickly became the mechanism used to ensure that the commodities sent were satisfactory. . . .

Metal goods—guns, hatchets, knives, ice chisels, scrapers—were an important component of the trade, especially in the first half of our period, and the quality of these goods was, as noted, a major trading issue. . . . [T]here was, in fact, a serious underlying problem that did take many years to understand. The properties of metal in temperate climates and in extreme conditions are not the same. Metal products are prone to severe structural weaknesses during extreme winter conditions. In addition, water that gets into cracks can cause frost wedging. So guns could burst when fired and hatchets break.

The Indians quickly realized that flaws of any sort led to problems and were very choosy about the metal products they purchased. Indeed, although the head office often asked about the type of handles and the color of the wood, . . . post factor James Knight wrote back, "I have never knowd the Indians stand much upon the handles so the blades were but good." And in the same letter he continued: "I very seldom see that there is any manner of notice taken as ye colour of ye stocks so the lock and barrell is good and well stocked, and [the] sett of some for light colourd others for Dark is as their fancy deads." . . .

The directors had pursued a number of different strategies to deal with the metal failures, including, as noted, purchasing more expensive guns. Of course, the directors had to make the vendors understand what happened to their products in northern climates, a process that took many years. In addition, given that the problem seemed to lie in Hudson Bay, the Company sent out an armorer to each post, one of whose jobs it was to examine all guns on arrival at the factory to ensure that they met the required specifications and to repair guns when possible, whether new or used. The Company also had some metal products made at the Bay posts. That tactic produced its own difficulties, however: in 1728 Macklish had to ask the Company to send out better bar iron so that the smith could make ice chisels and scrapers without cracks and flaws. By 1742 the York Factory daily post journal notes that one of the major activities of the smith during the winter was to make scrapers and bayonets for the trade. . . .

The body of correspondence between the Hudson's Bay Company posts and the head office in London documents both Indian reluctance to purchase commodities that they considered inferior and the Company's continuous efforts to provide trade items with the correct attributes. In trying to decide on the correct attributes, the head office continuously required the post factors to send samples and explicit descriptions of the goods most desired. The problem facing the Company on the quality dimension was compounded when French traders moved into the York Factory hinterland. As Arthur Ray has noted, Native traders were quick to take advantage of the new situation. As early as 1728, even before the French had penetrated the area, the factor at York Factory wrote, "Never was any man so upbraided with our Powder, Kettles and Hatchets, than we have been this summer by all the Natives, Especially by those that border near the French." By the end of the 1730s, French traders had begun to set up posts within the drainage basin of York Factory. Quality issues now became confounded by issues of competition. . . .

Marketing to Native Americans: New Commodities

In creating a trade in furs with Native Americans, the Hudson's Bay Company had to provide goods with the proper specifications. As a result, Indian traders were able to buy guns, hatchets, cloth, kettles, knives, and twine better suited to their environment and needs. At the same time, the head office was always in search of new goods that would entice more Indians or more furs or specific furs in for trade at the posts. Throughout the period discussed here, the London directors sent out samples of goods that they hoped would find a market and, to the extent that there was a demand, instructions about specific items for which the "new goods" might be traded. Thus, these new commodities had the dual purpose of attracting more trade and, when possible, of generating trade in particular pelts, such as parchment beaver or martins, that were in high demand on the London market. . . .

In 1712 the directors sent out some brass "handcuffs" (bracelets) that would trade only for martins and at a price of four martins per pair. The handcuffs never sold—not because the Indians did not use them, but rather because they manufactured their own. When requested by the London committee to buy back old kettles, the chief factor at York Factory answered that he could not do so because the Indians "always converted them into fine handcuffs and pouches which is of greater value with them then twice the price of the kettles." Despite these failures, the Company continued its strategy of testing new commodities. The letter of 1732 notes, "[Y]ou will find by the Invoice a dozen silk handkerchiefs and one doz of trunks which we send you by way of trial *to see how Indians like them* and would have you rate them . . . the handkerchiefs at one and a half beaver each and the trunks at two beaver each." . . . [T]here was a demand for both of these items, especially for trunks.

With the movement of French traders into the region, the directors tried to use such new goods as a way to gain market share. . . . Unfortunately, unlike the trunks, brass collars did not sell and, two years later, the factories were told that "since the brass collars are not esteemed by the Indians according to their value we desire you would dispose of them in the best manner you can." In 1743 the Company sent out earrings that also did not sell. But nearly all of the new varieties of beads . . . were very successful.

Despite the occasional failures described here, a whole range of luxury items did sell and in fact grew as a share of Indian expenditure: beads, combs, magnifying glasses, looking glasses or mirrors, sashes, scissors, thimbles, and shoes. Although these commodities mirror the inventories of European and colonial households alike, no argument is being made here that Native Americans used these commodities in the same ways. Indeed, the Company's failure to sell brass collars, earrings, and sheepskins speaks directly to the independence of Native consumers.

Conclusions

The Hudson's Bay Company was a trading company. Its very existence depended on its ability to supply those commodities that would entice Native traders to its posts. Indeed, during the period examined here, Indian traders were not only freely coming down to York Factory, but most were journeying long distances to engage in trade. Despite the long journeys, the traders would not buy goods that failed to meet their specifications or interests.

The directors in London used the trade indents or accounts and the reports of the salaried managers to determine which commodities sold. Company managers learned Cree to help with their marketing and, from the correspondence, it is apparent that treating the Indians with respect was viewed as of paramount importance. Not only did the directors try to provide commodities that met the required specifications through use of samples and descriptions provided by the post factors, but the Company continually sent out new goods to "see if the Indians liked them." The rejection of some of these goods speaks only to the independence of Native consumers—it was their preferences that were paramount in determining which goods the Hudson's Bay Company shipped to Bayside posts. The evidence confirms that Indians were not only participating in the consumer revolution through the quantity of goods they were buying; they were also including variety and quality in their calculations as key dimensions of their consumption decisions, and the Hudson's Bay Company responded to these dimensions.

Philadelphia Merchants and the Rise of Federalist Power in the New Nation

THOMAS M. DOERFLINGER

By rupturing the economic and governmental framework of colonial Pennsylvania, the Revolution transformed the political apathy of the merchant community, turning it for the first time into an articulate interest group. Only a handful of merchants became active politicians, but these leaders pursued goals supported by the trading body as a whole. At the state level, they battled the radical Presbyterian faction that had seized power in 1776, and in national affairs they attempted to expand the power of the central government, particularly its power to tax. Toughened and tutored by a decade of bitter controversy and strategically situated in the capital of the nation, the merchants were well positioned to spearhead the drive for a Federal Constitution.

Thomas M. Doerflinger, *A Vigorous Spirit of Enterprise: Merchants and Economic Development in Revolutionary Philadelphia* (Chapel Hill: University of North Carolina Press, 1986), pp. 251–261, 266–280.

Indeed, it is doubtful whether any other local occupational group in the nation did more to advance the Federalist cause.

This activism was a dramatic departure from the pre-Revolutionary political behavior of the merchants. During the colonial period, . . . Philadelphia traders tended to leave politics to wealthy gentlemen and professionals who had higher social status, better education, and more free time to devote to public life. Moreover, in the period 1750–1770 the merchant group was divided almost evenly between Anglican supporters of the proprietor and Quaker adherents to the assembly faction. Lacking unity or effective leadership, the merchants were unable to control the flow of events between 1764 and 1776, and they were, in any case, ambivalent about the Revolutionary movement. The merchants' opposition to British encroachments on American liberties, though sincere enough, was tempered by compelling counter-vailing considerations, including their transatlantic connections and attachment to the empire, their deep suspicion of Presbyterian influence on the Revolutionary movement, and the benefits they were deriving from the general economic prosperity of the prewar period. For all these reasons, the merchants had ultimately been more obstructionist than supportive of the Revolution; they were too pragmatic, material-istic, and elitist to lead the drive toward Independence. But these very qualities made them particularly well suited to shape events after 1776. Once Independence was an established fact, Americans were suddenly confronted with the problem of how to transform the nation from a Revolutionary idea into a functioning state. There was much work to be done. The practical shortcomings of the Confederation rapidly became clear, and merchants, as energetic managers well versed in commerce and finance, took the lead in building a more efficient governmental framework.

This process went forward in two distinct stages. Between 1781 and 1784 a small but powerful band of Nationalists in Congress and the army, led by [the Philadelphia merchant] Robert Morris, tried to centralize fiscal and administrative activities. De-spite some success, the rationale for their unpopular initiatives was undercut by the return of peace. But as the nation drifted and floundered in the 1780s, a far wider segment of the Philadelphia commercial community became mobilized behind the cause of constitutional reform. Stung by commercial depression and alarmed by the attack on the Bank of North America and the return of paper money, the merchants were disgusted by the inability of Congress to regulate commerce, pay its foreign debts, and maintain order. No doubt they exaggerated the objective severity of these problems. But after their harrowing wartime experience of monetary collapse and popular tyranny, Philadelphia traders were not inclined to take chances.

The Pennsylvania Revolution

Paradoxically enough, the very moderation of Pennsylvania, so evident in the decade before 1776, gave rise to an extremely radical state government once the separation from England was finally effected. Stubbornly refusing to declare Independence in June 1776, the colony's assembly became politically irrelevant and was superseded by the network of Revolutionary committees that had emerged in Philadelphia to coordinate the war effort and to discipline tories. The leaders of this shadow govern-ment were primarily artisans, shopkeepers, tradesmen, and middle-class professionals who wished to eradicate the aristocratic character of the provincial government by drafting a truly democratic constitution for the new state. Pennsylvania's constitution of 1776 permitted all taxpayers to vote, and legislative authority was concentrated in a unicameral legislature that was elected annually. The executive function was lodged in the Supreme Executive Council, composed of one popularly elected representative from each county. Together with the assembly, this council elected a president, who was largely a figurehead. Appointed by the council for only a seven-year term, and dependent on the assembly for its salary, the Supreme Court was no more capable of independent action than the executive, particularly since judicial salaries were set by the assembly. And lest the assembly itself somehow manage to thwart the will of the people, the constitution ingeniously provided for the election, every seven years, of a Council of Censors to review recent legislation and to ensure that it was consistent with the spirit of the constitution.

Although largely the work of coffeehouse radicals from Philadelphia, the Pennsylvania constitution was nurtured and protected primarily by Scotch-Irish Presbyterians from the western counties, who formed the core of the Constitutionalist party. Westerners had been excluded from politics in provincial days, when the frontier counties were underrepresented in the assembly, but after 1776 they gained political leverage for two reasons. The new state constitution, by allotting an equal number of seats to each county until 1779, gave the sparsely settled western counties disproportionate power in the assembly. Second, even in the eastern counties the Constitutionalists wielded great strength as a result of the test acts they introduced requiring all citizens to swear their allegiance to the independent state of Pennsylvania before they could vote. Until its repeal in 1787, this requirement effectively disenfranchised Quakers, German Pietists, and many other loyalists, who constituted a large bloc of the electorate that strongly disapproved of the Constitutionalists' regime. . . .

Initially the Constitutionalists faced little organized opposition. . . . However, in March 1779 eighty-two people met in Philadelphia to form the Republican Society, whose stated purpose was to secure repeal of the new constitution, on the grounds that its "general tendency and operation will be to join the qualities of the different extremes of bad government. It will produce general weakness, inactivity and confusion; intermixed with sudden and violent fits of despotism, injustice and cruelty." Although it claimed to represent no particular interest or faction, the Republican Society was dominated by conservative Anglican whigs from the eastern counties. More important for our purposes, at least ten of the eighty-two were staff officers, and thirty-five were merchants [including a new group of Anglican merchants]. . . .

Thanks to the careful analysis of Philadelphia's social elite by Stephen Brobeck, we can trace precisely the ascent of the Anglican merchants to the pinnacle of political and social life. Brobeck has found that of the forty-six people who composed the pre-Revolutionary Anglican elite in Philadelphia, eleven formed a particularly prominent and cohesive core group, which was dominated by the Penn family and the family of Chief Justice William Allen. Nine of the eleven elite leaders in this prewar period were officeholders or professionals, and only two were active merchants. Holding positions in the provincial Council, the Philadelphia City Corporation, and the proprietary government, these were the well-connected gentlemen who had traditionally dominated political affairs in the colony. The Revolution did not treat such men kindly. The Penns and Allens, along with such allied families as the Chews, Hamiltons, and Shippens, generally were loyalist. Some family members were attainted for treason, others had property confiscated or lost lucrative proprietary offices, and still others fled Philadelphia to live in Europe or in other parts of America.

Coinciding with the voluntary withdrawal of Quaker grandees from politics, the destruction of the proprietary leadership created a power vacuum in Pennsylvania's upper class at precisely the time when agrarian radicalism was on the rise. Into this vacuum stepped wealthy Philadelphia businessmen who had been relatively inferior members of the Anglican elite on the eve of the Revolution: Robert Morris, Thomas Willing, Thomas Fitzsimons, J. M. Nesbitt, John Nixon, George Clymer, Samuel Meredith, Henry Hill, and the brilliant lawyer James Wilson, who was a newcomer to the Anglican elite. Wilson was a reckless land speculator who eventually went to debtors' prison, and his eight colleagues were active merchants who were still building their fortune. These people were the workhorses of the Republican faction. They wrote pamphlets, ran for office, addressed caucuses, circulated petitions, and plotted strategy. In addition to membership in the Republican Society, nearly all of them were leaders of the Bank of North America founded in 1781, and four of them were delegates to the Constitutional Convention in 1787. . . .

Because the majority of Philadelphia's merchants were conservative Anglicans and whigs, they naturally supported the Republican faction in its endless fight with the political heirs of Oliver Cromwell. But there was another issue that bound traders together even more strongly, because it struck at the heart of their livelihood: the problem of inflation and price controls. As prices rose from month to month during the war, social antagonism increased proportionally. By 1779, when prices were rising at a compound rate of 17 percent a month, the issue had spilled out of the statehouse and into the streets. Perplexed by the paradox of unaffordable provisions in a region of agricultural abundance, the little people of Pennsylvania, some of whom were mobilized in well-organized militia units, blamed inflation on wealthy tories who were allegedly manipulating commodity markets and refusing to accept Continental money. . . .

. . . As we have seen, the merchants were tormented by inflation throughout the war. They lost thousands of pounds in book debts that were paid off in depreciated currency, and their commercial operations were deranged by violent fluctuations in the price level. Yet, ironically, the merchants themselves were blamed for the currency collapse; and in addition to all of the inevitable military barriers to wartime trade, they had to grapple with mobs, regulations, committees, investigations, and price-fixing. In a memorandum to the Philadelphia Price Committee, eighty leading merchants defended the free market with reckless candor, even going so far as to liken engrossers (who purchased commodities in expectation of a price rise) to a wise and provident ship captain who puts his crew on short rations before provisions become truly scarce. As for the solution to inflation, the merchants insisted that it could not be ended simply by making it illegal. "If you wish to remove an effect you must begin by removing the causes, and not hope to wither the causes by lopping off the[ir] consequences." The cause of inflation, the merchants insisted, was not the perfidy of engrossers and monopolizers, but the "quantity of [our] money[;] . . . the winds, the seasons, the ravages of war, the calls for militia, for carters, for batteau men, horses and a thousand other contingencies," as well as the high prices of vessels and of maritime insurance. Here was an issue that nearly every merchant—Quaker or

Anglican, rich or middling, tory or whig—could understand, and it was an issue that continued to unite the trading body until 1788. Currency, the merchants knew, was the "grand instrument of commerce"; without it, trade itself could not go on. The monetary chaos of the war years and the searing experience with mob rule in 1779 taught them to take nothing for granted in protecting the integrity of the currency.

The Counterrevolution in Congress

The disorders that rocked Philadelphia in 1779 were part of a larger national crisis that nearly paralyzed the Revolutionary effort. Although Congress stopped issuing paper money in the fall of 1779, it was too late to stave off the total collapse of the Continental dollar, which in turn destroyed the system of staff departments managed by Jeremiah Wadsworth and Nathanael Greene. Henceforth, the army would have to live off clumsy and uncertain requisitions from the states or simply take what it needed from local farmers. The final collapse of the logistical system coincided with the most severe winter on record. Washington's troops were pushed toward starvation and mutiny as they huddled in the deep snow near Morristown, New Jersey. The spring of 1780 brought fresh disasters. After capturing Charleston in May, the British army sliced northward into North Carolina and, before the American victory at Kings Mountain in October, seemed to be gaining firm control of the entire lower South. The treason of Benedict Arnold in 1780 and the mutiny of the Pennsylvania line in 1781 further battered American morale.

This confluence of crises discredited the makeshift attempt by Congress to wage war with a profusion of paper money and the committee system. Fresh methods and new leadership were needed, and both were supplied by businessmen from the middle states, including several members of Pennsylvania's Republican faction. In the spring of 1780 Philadelphia's merchants lent assistance to the Continental army by forming the Bank of Pennsylvania, which was not a bank at all, but, rather, a collective loan by private citizens to a nearly bankrupt nation. The bank's managers scoured Pennsylvania for flour and made some timely deliveries to the destitute army. In the spring of 1781 the involvement of Philadelphia's traders in the rescue of the Independence movement proceeded a step further as Robert Morris was appointed superintendent of finance and vested with broad powers to reform the nation's fiscal and administrative affairs. Efficient and elitist, Morris gathered around himself a group of like-minded supporters who intended to curb democratic localism by strengthening the hand of Congress. Such men as Jeremiah Wadsworth, Timothy Pickering, Silas Deane, and Morris himself discovered the need for centralization while serving as suppliers to the army; others—James Madison, Gouverneur Morris, James Wilson, Alexander Hamilton, and George Washington among them—had done so while serving in Congress or the army. These Nationalists, as they are called by historians, were supported by many congressmen from the South, where Independence hung by a thread, but the core of the faction's support came from the middle states. Although some of them were men of distinguished social background, these Nationalists tended to be a materialistic, hard-driving, upwardly mobile lot, not averse to fusing public and private affairs in order to enhance their estates. The spirit of 1776 was not what drove them. Centralized power disturbed them far less than the licentiousness of the people and the shortsighted localism of state legislatures.

These acquisitive men of affairs hoped that a vigorous government and an enterprising citizenry would turn the United States into a state of "power, consequence, and grandeur."

It was no coincidence that the Nationalists drew their primary support from the middle states—precisely the area that had approached Independence with the greatest caution. Both phenomena—fear of the break with England and support for a stronger Revolutionary government—were inspired by the intrinsic conservatism of the region's leaders. Anglican businessmen and gentlemen from Pennsylvania and New York were far less suspicious of the centralized power and unbridled materialism embodied in the Nationalist program than were most Virginia planters and New England congregationalists. Indeed, many whigs viewed with alarm the spreading power of the Colossus from Philadelphia, the Great Man who embodied at once the most dangerous qualities of a prime minister, a financial manipulator, and a merchant prince. . . .

. . . Using Great Britain as a model, Morris attempted to strengthen the Federal government by restoring its credit and uniting its interests with those of the propertied classes. He shored up the public credit with his private wealth and created the Bank of North America, which, though controlled by private investors, provided financial assistance to the government. Morris also attempted to consolidate and enlarge the federal debt and consistently opposed the efforts of certain state legislatures—including Pennsylvania's—to assume responsibility for portions of the nation's financial obligations. So long as the central government had debts, it had a reason to tax, and the centerpiece of Morris's program was a 5 percent customs duty on imports, which he hoped would be only the first plank in a solid fiscal foundation for the government. In the future he intended to add taxes on polls, property, and commodities. By paying the interest on the Federal debt, these revenues would not only secure the loyalty of bondholders to the national government but would also transfer capital to moneyed men who would use it to build up the economy. In the realm of administrative reform Morris achieved major economies by abolishing many superfluous departments and employing private contractors to supply the army.

In the three years that he was in office, Morris achieved extraordinary success in rationalizing the operations of the Revolutionary government. Indeed, he was too successful: after the reduction of the British threat in the Battle of Yorktown, the impulse to strengthen the central government subsided. Morris did his best to keep the pressure on Congress by pursuing fiscal policies that made both the Federal bondholders and the Continental soldiers dependent on Federal revenues. But the basis of the Nationalists' support was too narrow, both geographically and ideologically, for them to prevail in peacetime. Even the impost, which had wide backing in Congress, was never adopted by all thirteen states. By January 1784 an opponent of the Nationalists could gloat, "Their schemes are now entirely defeated; their web is broken, which they have with so much art and industry been for several years spinning."

The Commercial Context of Constitutional Reform

. . . By 1787 the merchant community was broadly mobilized in favor of the Federal Constitution and was able to make a major contribution toward ratification.

The political outlook of merchants was shaped by business conditions during the 1780s. . . .

In essence, the depression of the 1780s resembled that of the 1760s: merchants imported too many dry goods on credit, many of them went broke, and a widespread contraction of economic activity followed. But the depression of the eighties was considerably more distressing for several reasons. Whereas the collapse of the dry goods trade in 1760 had been cushioned by continued prosperity in the provision trade between 1760 and 1763, in the mid-eighties both the dry goods and shipping trades were depressed. Moreover, the contraction of the sixties followed years of great prosperity during the Seven Years' War, whereas merchants had to endure the downturn of 1784–1788 after living through eight years of economic chaos during the Revolution. By 1788, commercial stagnation seemed to have replaced the commercial expansion of colonial days. The value of Philadelphia exports in 1787 was only 20 percent higher than in 1773, while the merchant community had grown by about 50 percent and Pennsylvania's population had risen by about 40 percent. A merchant in 1787 could look back on only one or two good years in the preceding decade, as against six or seven years of economic confusion. The basis of the economy had no less promise in 1787 than it had in 1760 or 1775: Pennsylvania was needed as a primary source of food for the slaves, peasants, and workers of the Atlantic world. But for over a decade the shock of war and the contingencies of the business cycle had curtailed the merchants' ability to serve these markets. Only when famine stalked Europe in 1789 did foodstuff exports finally explode, but it must be emphasized that there was no gradual and steady growth in the economy from 1783 to 1789. . . . [O]ne reason for the boom of the 1790s, widely recognized at the time, was that the adoption of the Constitution and the introduction of Hamilton's financial program markedly increased the confidence of businessmen—both foreign and domestic—in the American economy.

The Shaping of a Federalist Consensus

Thus there can be little doubt that the merchants approached the political issues of the 1780s from a position of extreme financial weakness. Their economic difficulties were not directly caused by the debility of national government under the Articles of Confederation, but the merchants had logical reasons for fearing that government policies or government weakness would seriously *compound* their financial problems instead of alleviating them. The chief danger was inflation. Like most market operators, the merchants had short memories; they tended to overlook the success of paper money during the colonial period and to focus instead on the horrors of inflation during the Revolution. And the merchants knew that inflation would be particularly devastating at this stage in the business cycle because they were owed large sums by shopkeepers and artisans, to whom they had sold dry goods on credit in 1783 and 1784. If Pennsylvania issued large amounts of paper money, these debts would be paid off just as they had been during the Revolution—with depreciated paper dollars. In sum, the business cycle, the memory of economic problems during the Revolution, and the leading policy issues of the day meshed precisely in the 1780s to politicize the merchants. Far more than in the 1760s or 1770s, political issues over which the merchants had some control struck at the heart of their business activities.

The paper money issue in Pennsylvania was inextricably bound up with the Bank of North America. . . . Although founded to strengthen the national government, the bank was owned by private shareholders and made short-term commercial loans to merchants and other businessmen. Apart from deposits, its liabilities consisted of notes that could be redeemed at the bank for gold, and these notes circulated in the economy as a form of private currency. The bank was a remarkably successful institution that earned large profits by providing a financial service that was much in demand.

Originally identified with Robert Morris and other Republicans, the bank widened its support in 1784 by shrewdly absorbing an opposing group of merchants who wished to establish a bank of their own. . . . Thereafter the bank's shareholders included merchants of every political stripe, a fact of great importance in ensuring the political unity of the merchant community.

The bank and most traders feared paper money during the 1780s, but cheap money had two influential constituencies. A small but powerful group of securities speculators, led by merchants Charles Pettit and Blair McClenachan, backed it as a way for Pennsylvania to assume its share of the Federal debt and to pay the interest and principle thereon. . . . A second and far more broadly based source of support for paper money was Pennsylvania's agrarian interest. Before the war, the provincial government issued paper money in the form of loans to farmers secured by the farmers' own lands. This land bank, as it were, had worked well, because it simultaneously performed three functions: Pennsylvania's economy received a circulating medium, the provincial government earned interest on the loans, and the farmers received loans with which to finance property improvements. During the 1780s farmers were understandably eager to revive this successful institution, and paper money would be particularly welcome in the midst of a depression, when hard money was so difficult to obtain. . . .

Despite the success of paper money in colonial times and the responsible nature of the current issue, the merchants categorically rejected the legislature's scheme. The memory of the Revolution was too recent and their financial condition too precarious for them to do otherwise. In a mass meeting the merchants approved, almost unanimously, a resolution stating: "Money being the grand instrument of commerce, and the measure of value, it is an indispensable condition of it that its own value be determined and known. . . . Gold and Silver alone possess this property, and no substitute for them can safely be relied on as a medium of commerce, which has an intrinsic principle of fluctuation. . . . It plainly appears, from the many abortive and ruinous attempts made since the revolution, that Government has it not always in its power to give to paper money this indispensible property of gold and silver." . . .

Once it became entangled in the paper money issue, the bank became the target of Presbyterian politicians in the assembly, who repealed its charter in September 1785. Hatred of the bank existed on three related levels. In the technical realm of economic policy, the bank was blamed for the economy's current ills. It allegedly encouraged overtrading and mercantile bankruptcies by enticing traders to borrow too much from the bank. It was accused of reducing the supply of hard money by allowing depositors to withdraw specie and ship it to Europe and by paying specie dividends to foreign shareholders. . . .

Following directly from this economic indictment was the more general social criticism of the bank that it favored the state's commercial interest—considered an unscrupulous band of ambitious aristocrats—at the expense of farmers and tradesmen. "The commercial interest is already too powerful, and an overbalance to the landed interest," it was said. "They have no need of so energetic an institution to give springs to their action, which is already too great." Impelled by "an amazing desire to accumulate wealth," the merchants would form a dangerous aristocracy that would threaten the liberties of their social inferiors. Just as the great banker Lorenzo de Medici had seized control of Renaissance Florence, so would Pennsylvania become the fiefdom of Robert Morris and his Republican junto. . . .

The attack on the bank and passage of the paper money bill underscored the economic weakness and political isolation of the merchant community. By importing excessive amounts of dry goods and selling them on credit, Philadelphia's wholesalers had already put a gun to their heads. Now the radicals in the assembly proposed to pull the trigger by flooding the state with paper money. In addition, the government of New Jersey threatened to compound the problem by issuing a currency of its own. Rural shopkeepers and mechanics would pay their debts, all right— with depreciated paper. Already racked by a decade of financial chaos, the merchants would have to endure another round of expropriation through inflation. Meanwhile, the merchants' own solution to the monetary problems of the war years, the Bank of North America, had been nearly destroyed.

In their private correspondence the merchants described how the assembly's actions had undermined confidence in the economy. "Our Assembly at their last Setting publish'd a Bill for consideration, to take away the Bank Charter & destroy it," wrote Benjamin Fuller. "You cannot conceive the effect it has had on Trade in general, little or no Money sturring for any Article, and produce falling hourly— this with the horrors of an Approaching paper Currency has thrown all kind of business into confusion & each man is fearfull of his Neighbour—All at present is Gloom." Stephen Collins, in the winter of 1785, wrote: "I think I shall not import more than half so many Good in the fall as I have wrote for in the spring, my courage more & more fails me and much more from the appearances of Publick afairs then from Trade being overdon, that will work its own cure. N Jersey are now pushing for a large Sum of Paper mony to be a Tender in Discharge of any Debts within the state. What but the Devel could Induce such a measure." . . .

The prospect of further financial disarray was only the worst problem facing the merchants in the mid-eighties; they were also concerned about the failure of Congress to protect American commerce. In 1783 Great Britain issued an order banning American ships in the British West Indies, and the merchants formed a committee to encourage an effective response to this commercial discrimination. Yet it was doubted whether a league of separate states could successfully spar with European nations. John Chaloner wrote in 1784: "Our Merchants Grumble much at the Regulations of trade in Europe. I doubt much Congress being furnished with sufficient powers from the several states to Counteract the policy of Great Britain & France. No Individual state will adopt particular measures because it will throw the trade from her to her Neighbour—So I fear we must grin & bear it." This pessimistic assessment was not unjustified. Delaware's refusal to pass a duty comparable to Pennsylvania's encouraged smuggling into the latter state, and New Jersey and Connecticut feuded with New York for placing tonnage duties on small coastal vessels. And this conflict in interstate trade was mirrored by civil disorder within the nation—an issue about which the merchants had become particularly sensitive after the unrest of 1778 and 1779. Glumly reviewing the various theaters of conflict in 1784—land wars arising from confused titles in Pennsylvania's Wyoming Valley, border clashes between New Yorkers and Vermonters, a border dispute between New York and Massachusetts—John Chaloner concluded, "All this must bring about a dissolution of the present Confederation or else increase its powers & authorities sufficient to protest all the Subjects of America—at present it is but a Shadow."

If it was to gain substance, instead of remaining a shadow, the Continental Congress needed two things above all else: money and talented leadership. In the mid-1780s it had neither. After six years of begging state legislatures for an impost, Congress was rebuffed by New York in 1786, and the issue seemed settled finally. Lacking an independent source of funds, Congress had to parcel out the public debt to the state governments and finance operations with requisitions from the states, which often had better things to do with the money. The resulting poverty made Congress nearly incapable of energetic administration; it even defaulted on its debt to France. So desperate were its finances that Rufus King confided to Elbridge Gerry, "You may depend on it, that the Treasury now is literally without a penny." Weak and demoralized, Congress attracted second-rate politicians. Remarked one observer of the body, "Had you been present you would have trembled for your country, to have *seen,* and *heard,* and *observed* the men who composed its rulers." And leadership seemed no better in the state governments, which were controlled by men of narrow vision and limited ability who had never traveled widely or considered the problems of the nation as a whole. Inevitably, the manifold deficiencies of the Confederation reduced the standing of the United States. . . .

Merchants and the Federalist Coup

Though no single problem was fatal in itself, the deficiencies of the Confederation were numerous and alarming. A severe if temporary commercial depression had been exacerbated by the threat of paper money, the attack on the bank, and a weak commercial policy, while civil disorder and political disarray called into question the very future of the country. These problems were not likely to be solved—indeed, had in part been created—by an impotent Congress and erratic state legislatures. With uncharacteristic unanimity and fervor the merchants forecast the calamitous fate awaiting the country. "The Affairs of this Country is going fast into Convulsions and I am Opinion Blood will be the Consequence before many Years pass or a great Change of some kind must take Place," wrote Benjamin Fuller. "You ask my political oppinion as to the new Constitution," wrote Levi Hollingsworth in 1788. "I answer that I am for the Unconditional adoption of it—nothing else can save America from general Ruin, in my judgement." . . .

The bleak prospects of the nation were all the more distressing because a simple change of government offered the prospect of prosperity and greatness for the United States. As William Bingham wrote in the spring of 1787: "[America] wants nothing now but a strong efficient Government, which will command Respect & Confidence abroad, & act with Vigour & Energy at home. . . . I am convinced that all our political Misfortunes flow from the Weakness of our federal Government." Another trader remarked, "I flatter myself that on the foederal Government taking place a new Spring will be given to Trade and agriculture throughout the States." . . .

Thus the merchants believed that the nation was at a crossroads. One avenue led to weakness, chaos, and poverty; the other, to order and abundance.

By 1787 the merchant community was in a position to translate this dichotomous assessment of the nation's future into a concrete political program. For it was no longer the apolitical, religiously divided occupational group of 1765 or the war-torn body of 1779. The trials of war and the disappointments of peace had united and mobilized the merchants, preparing them for effective political action in 1787. This process began with the emergence in 1779 of the Republican faction, and the proliferation of economic problems mobilized the merchants still further, forcing them to convene to formulate common political positions on price controls, commercial policy, paper money, and other matters. The Bank of North America also became a major bulwark of mercantile unity, as we have noted. Though controlled by the Morris clique, the bank served hundreds of merchant depositors and borrowers, and the second stock issue of 1784 attracted the funds of dozens of merchants, including Quakers and Anglican tories, who normally distrusted Morris. The emergence of the traders as an interest group was reflected in the effort of Tench Coxe, albeit unsuccessful, to form a chamber of commerce whose express purpose was to "unite the mercantile Body" and to "form a city interest that may create some small counterbalance for the too great weight of the Country interest in this state."

The political mobilization of the merchant community exemplified a general reorientation in America's political structure during the Revolution. Political life in the colonial period reflected the paradigm of mixed government, in which there was a correspondence between political institutions (governor, council, legislature) and social strata (royalty, aristocracy, and commoners). Following this model, merchants had left politics to their social superiors, the independent gentlemen. The destruction of traditional political elites, the upsurge in popular political participation, and the emergence of divisive economic issues during the war had eroded the values of mixed government and converted occupational groups into organized, articulate political factions. In Philadelphia it was the artisans who united first. Originally organized to prolong the profitable commercial boycott of 1769–1770, mechanics used diverse methods to shoulder their way into the city's political structure. They held a number of mass meetings before the war, formed the Patriotic Society in 1772, and played a major role in the Committee of Observation and Inspection that controlled the city between 1775 and 1777. By 1781 the state's western farmers had seized control of a still stronger level of power, the Pennsylvania Assembly, whose leaders self-consciously defended the state's agricultural interests.

Partly in reaction to the mobilization of artisans and farmers, merchants also combined to defend their particular interests. Because traders were deeply divided by the Revolution, this process was not complete until 1786. The recasting of political participation along occupational lines was remarked upon by contemporaries and seemed to be a fundamental trait of modern republics. As James Madison observed in Federalist 10: "The most common and durable source of factions has been the various and unequal distribution of property. . . . A landed interest, a manufacturing interest, a mercantile interest, a moneyed interest, with many lesser interests, grow up of necessity in civilized nations, and divide them into different classes, actuated by different sentiments and views." Such an analysis would have been irrelevant to colonial Pennsylvania, whose political life consisted of "jousting at the top" by well-born gentlemen. But political deference had fallen prey to the popular mobilization and economic fragmentation of the Revolutionary era.

The merchants used their newfound unity with telling effect in the Federalist revolution of 1787–1788. One Antifederalist pamphleteer remarked at "the infatuation of some of our merchants, who, elated with the imaginary prospect of an improved commerce under the new government, overlook all danger." Pennsylvania's lone delegate to the Annapolis convention was a merchant, Tench Coxe, as were four of the state's eight representatives to the Constitutional Convention: Robert Morris, Thomas Fitzsimons, Thomas Mifflin, and George Clymer. A fifth delegate, James Wilson, was a close associate of Robert Morris, and a sixth, Gouverneur Morris, was also a staunch Nationalist and an occasional business associate of Morris. And traders played a prominent role in the virtual coup d'etat that constituted the state's ratification procedure. Eager to get the tortuous series of state ratifying conventions off to an auspicious start, Federalist merchants in the Pennsylvania Assembly pressured the House in December 1787 into calling a state convention at once—before western opponents of the Constitution could rally their forces. Outnumbered but not outwitted, resourceful Antifederalists paralyzed the House by refusing to enter the chamber, thus depriving it of a quorum. But the Federalists matched cunning with force by allowing a mob to drag two recalcitrant absentees into the statehouse to watch the process of ratification begin.

Such Philadelphia traders as Tench Coxe, Pelatiah Webster, and Timothy Pickering also fought aggressively in the propaganda war of 1788, filling the public prints and their private correspondence with tedious defenses of the new government. Coxe credited himself with nearly thirty separate publications, and he eagerly traced the course of ratification in state after state by soliciting friends on the spot for the latest news. The important position of merchants in the Federalist revolution was revealed no less clearly by the Antifederalist critique of the movement. In the proposed new institutions of a senate and a presidency, writer after writer detected the plot of an opulent aristocracy to trample the liberties of the people. In Pennsylvania this "conspiracy of the well-born" was identified by the influential pamphleteer Centinel (George Bryan) with the Republican clique headed by Robert Morris and James Wilson. These men were portrayed as a band of ambitious plutocrats whose appetite for power and wealth knew no bounds:

> View the monopolizing spirit of the principal of them. See him converting a bank, instituted for common benefit, to his own and creatures' emoluments, and by the aid thereof, controlling the credit of the state, and dictating the measures of government. . . . Recollect the strenuous and unremitted exertions of these men, for years past, to destroy our admirable Constitution. . . . [A]nd then answer whether these apprehensions are chimerical, whether such characters will be less ambitious, less avaricious, more moderate, when the privileges, property, and every concern of the people of the United States shall lie at their mercy, when they shall be in possession of absolute sway?

Bryan's indictment of Pennsylvania's Republicans, who were now leading national Federalists, contained more than a kernel of truth. The Revolution had indeed given rise to a group of fortune builders in Philadelphia, far richer and more powerful than most pre-Revolutionary merchants. . . . [T]hey moved aggressively into many new fields in the two decades after 1775, and Robert Morris was involved in almost all of them. In the year that Bryan penned his indictment of the Federalists, Robert Morris monopolized the tobacco trade with France, headed a mercantile firm that handled 4 percent of Philadelphia's imports, controlled the port's only bank, dealt largely in public securities, and was about to sell multimillion-acre tracts in western New York to some of the richest men in Europe. A large proportion of the arriviste merchants of Philadelphia were associates of this Colossus, and Alexander Hamilton's generous financial plan would soon make some of them richer still. By the mid-nineties these merchants would lay claim to millions of unsettled acres in states from Maine to Georgia, acreage they intended to sell in lucrative little pieces to individual pioneers. So Bryan's analysis was exaggerated but not totally implausible. He correctly perceived the swollen, multifaceted ambitions—political, social, and financial—of the Federalist leaders in Pennsylvania. This is not to suggest that the merchants were motivated purely by the prospect of private gain. On the contrary, they were farsighted patriots possessed of a fresh, compelling vision of national greatness, and they made great sacrifices to turn this vision into reality. But they were disposed where possible to make the most of these sacrifices, and in 1787 and 1788 public and private interest meshed with uncommon nicety.

It may be said, then, that the Constitution did have economic origins. . . . [M]any important Federalists pursued constitutional reform in order to solve tangible political and economic problems that not only endangered the future of the nation but also injured their own businesses. The origins of the Constitution are distorted if these economic problems are minimized and the Federalist movement is interpreted simply as an exercise in constitutional reform driven by the ideals of republicanism. Even James Madison, a far more disinterested Federalist than the typical merchant, knew that "most of our political evils may be traced up to our commercial ones." The relevance of Madison's remark to the actual work of the convention is demonstrated by the many clauses of the document that addressed specific "commercial evils" prevalent in the 1780s. It was no accident that the Constitution gave the federal government the power to tax, to regulate commerce, to pay the national debt, to coin money, to issue patents for inventories, to grant letters of marque and reprisal, and to suppress insurrections. Federalist merchants, quite simply, had gotten what they wanted: a stable constitutional framework within which they could prosper. This is exactly what they would proceed to accomplish in the heady years of economic expansion between 1789 and 1792.

 # FURTHER READING

Bailyn, Bernard. *New England Merchants in the Seventeenth Century* (1955).
Beard, Charles A. *An Economic Interpretation of the Constitution of the United States* (1913).
Breen, T. H. *The Marketplace of Revolution: How Consumer Politics Shaped American Independence* (2004).
Casson, Mark, and Mary B. Rose. "Institutions and the Evolution of Modern Business: Introduction." *Business History* 39 (1997): 1–8.
Cooke, Jacob E. *Tench Coxe and the Early Republic* (1978).
Devine, T. M. *The Tobacco Lords: A Study of the Tobacco Merchants of Glasgow and Their Trading Activities, c. 1740–1790* (1975).

Dunn, Richard S. *Sugar and Slaves: The Rise of the Planter Class in the English West Indies, 1624–1713* (2000).

Engel, Marc, and Joseph A. Ernst. "An Economic Interpretation of the American Revolution." *William and Mary Quarterly,* 3d ser., 29 (January 1972): 3–32.

Hancock, David. *Citizens of the World: London Merchants and the Integration of the British Atlantic Community, 1735–1785* (1995).

Hoffman, Ronald, et al., eds. *The Economy of Early America: The Revolutionary Period, 1763–1790* (1988).

Matson, Cathy. *Merchants and Empire: Trading in Colonial New York* (1998).

McCusker, John J. *Essays in the Economic History of the Atlantic World* (1997).

———, and Kenneth Morgan, eds. *The Early Modern Atlantic Economy* (2000).

Morgan, Kenneth. *Bristol and the Atlantic Trade in the Eighteenth Century* (1993).

———. *Slavery and Servitude in Colonial North America: A Short History* (2001).

Pearson, Robin, and David Richardson. "Business Networking in the Industrial Revolution." *Economic History Review* 54, no. 4 (2001): 657–679.

Price, Jacob M. *Overseas Trade and Traders: Essays on Some Commercial, Financial, and Political Challenges Facing British Atlantic Merchants, 1600–1775* (1996).

———. *Tobacco in Atlantic Trade: The Chesapeake, London, and Glasgow, 1675–1775* (1995).

White, Philip L. *The Beekmans of New York in Politics and Commerce, 1647–1877* (1956).

CHAPTER
4

Public and Private Interests
in the Transition to
Industrialization, 1790–1860

In the early years of the republic, Americans faced the daunting task of establishing a new economy. Their colonial British heritage provided some economic lessons. Accustomed to mercantilism, Americans admitted that there were advantages to government rules and regulations that protected business while encouraging agriculture and commerce. But their revolutionary heritage yielded contradictory political lessons. Influenced by the ideas of John Locke, some Americans began to think that government power should be constrained and that business should be given a loose rein. In the end, Americans differed in the degree to which they favored "more" or "less" government, "more" or "less" unfettered business enterprise. In politics, this debate initially materialized in the struggle between Federalists and Antifederalists glimpsed in the last chapter. Ultimately, it evolved into the struggle between Alexander Hamilton and Thomas Jefferson, who in the public eye came to symbolize "government for business" and "government for the people," respectively.

In reality, the situation was not so black and white. As Larry Schweikart noted in The Entrepreneurial Adventure *(2000), Hamilton and Jefferson both embraced mercantilist doctrine on some occasions and a market orientation on others. They shared a vision of economic expansion, although they disagreed on the scope and the means. Hamilton did more than anyone in the early republic to shape the institutional structure of American business. He envisioned a strong federal government directing aspects of the economy, but he was suspicious of elites and pessimistic about the common people. Hamilton's legacy—a strong federal government charged with planning and orchestrating national economic growth—reflected his desire to protect the public interest against private greed and to foster a national market rather than a lot of local ones. In contrast, Jefferson contributed to the nation's business climate through land and trade policies that encouraged westward expansion and a boom in international commerce. While Jefferson envisioned an agrarian America, he also imagined a nation of small-scale entrepreneurial farmers.*

The struggle between these world views did not end with Hamilton's death in an 1804 duel. These conflicting and complementary ideas about the relationship between business and government materialized in politics and the courts into the nineteenth century. The years between 1790 and 1860 were a transitional moment for American business. As we shall see in Chapters 5 and 6, private enterprise of all types and sizes flourished, whether in Southern plantations, markets, and forges or in Northern textile mills, ports, and workshops. The rapid expansion of key business institutions—turnpikes, canals, ports, banks, stock markets, and corporations—and other salient features of industrial capitalism—a stable currency, a sympathetic legal system, dramatic technical innovations like the steamboat, the railroads, and the telegraph, giant factories, and consumer markets—frightened some Americans. Charges of "monopoly" and "privilege" culminated in a cry for reform that would ensure the rights of the people, leading to the Jacksonian political revolution of the 1830s. The transition to industrial capitalism was not clear and easy.

 D O C U M E N T S

By the early 1800s, some men of capital began to see the corporation as an institution promising substantial benefits, such as limited liability, existence in perpetuity, and openness to small investors. With the growing interest, questions arose about the corporation's legal rights, ultimately forcing the courts to resolve the issues.

Documents 1 through 4 contain materials related to important U.S. Supreme Court decisions defining the legal concept of the corporation. The first two documents are drawn from opinions by John Marshall, who served as chief justice from 1801 to 1835. A staunch Federalist, Marshall believed that the economy needed a solid legal foundation, and he sought to create this bedrock by safeguarding property rights and the sanctity of contracts. His court took the first steps toward putting the corporation on the same footing as a person and treating it as a protected property owner with legal rights. The Marshall Court was fundamentally conservative, and its decisions met the approval of businessmen searching for secure investment vehicles.

The Marshall Court ruled on several important cases about corporations. In 1809, it decided *Bank of the United States v. Deveaux*, which explored the right of the corporation to sue in federal court. Document 1 is Marshall's opinion, stating that the corporation is an "artificial being" and "not a citizen." He goes to on to say that "real persons" can sue "under their corporate name." This meant that shareholders, acting as individual citizens, can sue and be sued on behalf of their corporation.

Document 2 is Marshall's opinion in *Dartmouth College v. Woodward* (1819), a case that focused on contract and the corporation. In a reform effort, the New Hampshire legislature had amended Dartmouth's 1769 royal charter, so as to oust entrenched Federalist trustees in favor of political appointees. The trustees questioned the action's constitutionality. When the case reached the high court, the college's attorneys contended that New Hampshire lawmakers, by altering the colonial charter of incorporation, had violated the right of contract. The U.S. Supreme Court concurred, as shown in Document 2. By interpreting the Constitution's contract clause as a means of protecting corporate charters from state intervention, the Marshall Court set limits on the state's power to regulate them.

Documents 3 and 4 draw from the writings of Associate Justice Joseph Story, who served on the U.S. Supreme Court under Marshall, and his successor Roger B. Taney, a dedicated Democrat who believed in free competition. Early in the Taney Court (1836–1864), Story upheld Marshall's view of the corporation, dissenting on cases such as *Charles River Bridge v. Warren Bridge* (1837) on the issue of special privilege. Eventually he started to think more progressively. In Document 3, Story ponders the relationship between the corporation and bankruptcy law in an 1840 letter to attorney Daniel Webster. In Document 4, he writes to jurist James Kent in 1844 shortly after the Taney Court had overturned *Bank of the United States v. Deveaux.* Then, in *Louisville Railroad Co. v. Leston,* the court ruled that a corporation is a citizen of the state that granted its charter, having the right to sue and be sued in multiple jurisdictions. Story reflects on the *Deveaux* decision, admitting that the Marshall Court may have been shortsighted.

In the 1820s and 1830s, few topics stirred more political and economic debate than banking and its relationship to wealth and power. In national politics, major controversies over the Second Bank of the United States and the protective tariff pitted the Jacksonian Democrats, who feared the concentration of economic power, against the National Democrats and later the Whigs, who sought to expand industry, trade, and finance. The renewal of the Second Bank's charter was a key issue in the 1832 presidential campaign. After his election, President Andrew Jackson declined to recharter the bank, so the nation's largest business institution shriveled to death by 1841. Troubles multiplied when unrestrained state banks started freely issuing paper money, a British recession dampened the market for cotton exports, and Jackson tinkered with the federal surplus earned from the sale of western lands. As Cathy Matson's essay in this chapter shows, the Panic of 1837 gripped the economy, affecting the flow of cash, the availability of credit, and the stability of state and local banks. At the heart of these economic upheavals lay disagreements, dating from the revolutionary era.

The next two documents present opposing views on banks. In Document 5, Boston businessman Nathan Appleton evaluates the need for more banks. Appleton had a fortune made in manufacturing and commerce, which he reinvested in many New England textile mills, banks, and insurance companies. With his financial success and secure position atop the social order, this Boston Brahmin embodied the "special privilege" that Jacksonian Democrats loathed. Originally published in 1831, Appleton's essay counts banks among the institutions that benefit society, providing that these corporations are free from excess government regulation, such as taxes.

In Document 6, William M. Gouge, a financial journalist and clerk of the U.S. Treasury under Jackson, condemns banks as instruments of the wealthy. In this passage from his 1833 treatise against banks that circulated their own paper money, Gouge compares them with other interests vilified in the Jacksonian consciousness: corporations, usurers, feudal lords, and English aristocrats. In his critique of the corporation, Gouge draws on revolutionary-era rhetoric, focusing on the evils of privilege and monopoly. How are Appleton and Gouge similar to and different from the Federalists and Antifederalists that we studied in the last chapter?

In Documents 7 and 8, Americans debate the future of a new communications technology: telegraphy. First, a journalist for the *Baltimore Patriot* in 1845 appeals to Washington lawmakers to make the telegraph a public utility. Then, the *New York Journal of Commerce* in 1846 explains why private companies should run the telegraph system. The first author is concerned to see the dissemination of information for the public good; the second wants to restrict the unnecessary extension of government. How does the debate over telegraphy echo the deliberations over the corporation and the banks? How does it anticipate the debates in our own time about the World Wide Web?

1. The Corporation as an Artificial Being, 1809

The jurisdiction of this court being limited, so far as respects the character of the parties in this particular case, "to controversies between citizens of different states," both parties must be citizens, to come within the description.

That invisible, intangible, and artificial being, that mere legal entity, a corporation aggregate, is certainly not a citizen; and, consequently, cannot sue or be sued in the courts of the United States, unless the rights of the members, in this respect, can be exercised in their corporate name. If the corporation be considered as a mere faculty, and not as a company of individuals, who, in transacting their joint concerns, may use a legal name, they must be excluded from the courts of the Union. . . .

The controversy is substantially between aliens, suing by a corporate name, and a citizen, or between citizens of one state, suing by a corporate name, and those of another state. When these are said to be substantially the parties to the controversy, the court does not mean to liken it to the case of a trustee. A trustee is a real person capable of being a citizen or an alien, who has the whole legal estate in himself. At law, he is the real proprietor, and he represents himself, and sues in his own right. But in this case the corporate name represents persons who are members of the corporation.

If the constitution would authorize Congress to give the courts of the Union jurisdiction in this case, in consequence of the character of the members of the corporation, then the judicial act ought to be construed to give it. For the term citizen ought to be understood as it is used in the constitution, and as it is used in other laws. That is, to describe the real persons who come into court, in this case, under their corporate name.

2. Corporations and Contracts, 1819

A corporation is an artificial being, invisible, intangible, and existing only in contemplation of law. Being the mere creature of law, it possesses only those properties which the charter of its creation confers upon it, either expressly or as incidental to its very existence. These are such as are supposed best calculated to effect the object for which it was created. Among the most important are immortality, and, if the expression may be allowed, individuality; properties by which a perpetual succession of many persons are considered as the same, and may act as a single individual. They enable a corporation to manage its own affairs, and to hold property without the perplexing intricacies, the hazardous and endless necessity, of perpetual conveyances for the purpose of transmitting it from hand to hand. It is chiefly for the purpose of clothing bodies of men, in succession, with these qualities and capacities, that corporations were invented, and are in use. By these means, a perpetual succession of individuals are capable of acting for the promotion of the particular object,

---

The Bank of the United States v. Deveaux et al., 5 Cranch 61 (1809), in Joseph P. Cotton, Jr., ed., *The Constitutional Decisions of John Marshall,* vol. 1 (New York: G. P. Putnam's Sons, 1905), pp. 209–210, 215.

The Trustees of Dartmouth College v. Woodward, 4 Wheat 518 (1819), in Joseph P. Cotton, Jr., ed., *The Constitutional Decisions of John Marshall,* vol. 1 (New York: G. P. Putnam's Sons, 1905), pp. 363–366.

like one immortal being. But this being does not share in the civil government of the country, unless that be the purpose for which it was created. Its immortality no more confers on it political power, or a political character, than immortality would confer such power or character on a natural person. It is no more a state instrument than a natural person exercising the same powers would be. If, then, a natural person, employed by individuals in the education of youth, or for the government of a seminary in which youth is educated, would not become a public officer, or be considered as a member of the civil government, how is it that this artificial being, created by law, for the purpose of being employed by the same individuals for the same purposes, should become a part of the civil government of the country? Is it because its existence, its capacities, its powers, are given by law? Because the government has given it the power to take and to hold property in a particular form, and for particular purposes, has the government a consequent right substantially to change that form, or to vary the purposes to which the property is to be applied? This principle has never been asserted or recognized, and is supported by no authority. Can it derive aid from reason?

The objects for which a corporation is created are universally such as the government wishes to promote. They are deemed beneficial to the country; and this benefit constitutes the consideration, and, in most cases, the sole consideration of the grant. In most eleemosynary institutions, the object would be difficult, perhaps unattainable, without the aid of a charter of incorporation. Charitable, or public-spirited individuals, desirous of making permanent appropriations for charitable or other useful purposes, find it impossible to effect their design securely, and certainly, without an incorporating act. They apply to the government, state their beneficent object, and offer to advance the money necessary for its accomplishment, provided the government will confer on the instrument which is to execute their designs the capacity to execute them. The proposition is considered and approved. The benefit to the public is considered as an ample compensation for the faculty it confers, and the corporation is created. If the advantages to the public constitute a full compensation for the faculty it gives, there can be no reason for exacting a further compensation, by claiming a right to exercise over this artificial being a power which changes its nature, and touches the fund, for the security and application of which it was created. There can be no reason for implying in a charter, given for a valuable consideration, a power which is not only not expressed, but is in direct contradiction to its express stipulations.

From the fact, then, that a charter of incorporation has been granted, nothing can be inferred which changes the character of the institution, or transfers to the government any new power over it. The character of civil institutions does not grow out of their incorporation, but out of the manner in which they are formed, and the objects for which they are created. The right to change them is not founded on their being incorporated, but on their being the instruments of government, created for its purposes. The same institutions, created for the same objects, though not incorporated, would be public institutions, and, of course, be controllable by the legislature. The incorporating act neither gives nor prevents this control. Neither, in reason, can the incorporating act change the character of a private eleemosynary institution.

3. Corporations and Bankruptcy, 1840

I do not know, that there are any absolutely insuperable objections to bringing corporations within the reach of a Bankrupt Law; but there are some practical difficulties. The same machinery which would be complete as to individuals, would require many complex provisions in cases of corporations. What would you do as to Railroads, Turnpike, and Bridge Corporations? Should Banks be also entirely subject to the same summary proceedings, as common trading and manufacturing corporations, considering the sudden changes in circulation and markets, which may compel them sometimes to suspend for a short time? What would be the effect of requiring all debtors to a Bank, suddenly to pay all their notes and liabilities? How would you manage with Insurance Companies, when there are many policies of insurance outstanding on long voyages? Here again, you must reach the assets of corporations, not only by examining the officers thereof on oath, but also the stock-holders on oath; otherwise, in many cases, the remedy would be ineffectual. Consider what difficulties would arise in cases of numerous stockholders residing in different States; some infants, some married women, some trustees. I see much practical embarrassment in bringing them compulsorily within a Bankrupt Act. But if they are brought within such an act, I think the stockholders should have the benefit of a discharge, upon surrendering all their stock and the corporation assets, exactly as individuals. Their sacrifices, otherwise, would be enormous, and the future creation of corporations would be greatly discouraged.

But one main difficulty with me, is, that if corporations, now existing, should be brought within a Bankrupt Law, without such a discharge, it would at once shake all confidence in corporation stock, and depreciate it excessively. The corporation capital in New England would at once lose a large part of its present value, and be scarcely marketable. This would be a sad consummation of all our public calamities, and depress us still more.

I confess, too, I have some doubts as to the constitutionality of a Bankrupt Law, which should put corporations upon a different footing from individuals, giving the latter a discharge, and not the former; and providing different rules of bankruptcy in the one case from the other. The act would not be a "uniform act on the subject of bankruptcy," in the sense of the Constitution.

No Bankrupt Law in England, or, indeed, in any other country, as far as I know, ever has reached corporations. Is not this a strong, practical objection? Is it quite certain, that State Rights, as to the creation and dissolution of corporations, are not thus virtually infringed? I confess, that I feel no small doubt, whether Congress can regulate State Corporations by any other laws than the State laws. A State Corporation is entitled to just such rights and powers, as the charter gives it, and I do not well see where Congress can get the power to alter or control them, or to suspend or extinguish them.

These are first, hasty thoughts. Pray consider them.

Joseph Story to Daniel Webster, May 10, 1840, in William W. Story, ed., *Life and Letters of Joseph Story,* vol. 2 (Boston: C. C. Little and J. Brown, 1851), pp. 330–332. This document can also be found in Meyer Weinberg, ed., *America's Economic Heritage: From a Colonial to a Capitalist Economy, 1634–1900,* vol. 1 (Westport, Conn.: Greenwood Press, 1983), pp. 295–296.

4. The Corporation Becomes an Artificial Citizen, 1844

I equally rejoice, that the Supreme Court has at the last come to the conclusion, that a corporation is a citizen, an artificial citizen, I agree, but still a citizen. It gets rid of a great anomaly in our jurisprudence. This was always Judge Washington's opinion. I have held the same opinion for many years, and Mr. Chief Justice Marshall had, before his death, arrived at the conclusion, that our early decisions were wrong.

5. Nathan Appleton Explains How Banks Benefit Everyone, 1831

The business of banking (separate from the issue of bank notes) is a necessary branch of mercantile operations, resulting from a proper division of labor. A bank is employed, by the merchants and traders, to collect and keep safe their moneys, and to make their payments; for which purpose it becomes necessary to build secure vaults, and to employ a number of clerks and faithful officers. It is true, that when a bank keeps the cash of a great number of persons, the payments which are made by one, go frequently to the credit of another, so that the amount held in deposit is not subject to very material variation, nor liable to be called for at once. It is, therefore, agreed between the parties, that the bank is at liberty to loan such portion of their deposits as they think proper, only taking care to be able to furnish to each individual depositor his entire deposit on demand. In this way the bank is enabled to collect, keep, and pay away the money of the merchant without making any charge for the trouble of doing so; in fact, it is frequently the source of very considerable profit.

It may at first sight be thought that this source of profit, the receiving money in deposit, affords a proper subject of taxation; but a slight examination will show, that this ground is not tenable. As an original proposition, nothing would appear more absurd. If banks derive a profit which they are not entitled to, from holding in deposit the property of other persons, it is those other persons, whose money is lying unproductive, who are entitled to the profit, not the State at large. It is an affair between the parties, with which the public have nothing to do. If my banker do[es] not transact my business on as good terms as he can afford to do, it does not give the legislature a right to step in, and claim those extra profits, which in fairness belong to me; much less should the legislature come between us, and claim a *douceur* for allowing us to transact our business together, thus putting it out of the power of the bank to do my business on as good terms as it would otherwise be glad to do. In some parts of England, it is the custom for bankers to allow full interest on balances in their hands, and charge a commission for transacting the business. The Scotch

Joseph Story to James Kent, August 31, 1844, in William W. Story, ed., *Life and Letters of Joseph Story*, vol. 2 (Boston: C. C. Little and J. Brown, 1851), p. 469. This document can also be found in Meyer Weinberg, ed., *America's Economic Heritage: From a Colonial to a Capitalist Economy, 1634–1900*, vol. 1 (Westport, Conn.: Greenwood Press, 1983), p. 297.

Nathan Appleton, *Remarks on Currency and Banking; Having Reference to the Present Derangement of the Circulating Medium in the United States*, 3rd ed. (Boston: J. H. Eastburn's Press, 1857), pp. 46–48, 51–52.

banks allow interest on all deposits, but at a rate one per cent. below that which they charge to their borrowers.

The prohibition of individuals or associations from loaning money or making discounts without paying a tax for the privilege of doing so, is even more objectionable, it being a direct interference with private right, and opposed to every sound principle of political economy, inasmuch as the obvious tendency of such a measure is to drive capital out of the State.

The principle of our government, and of all free governments, is, that all property should contribute equally to the support of the government which affords it protection. The power of taxation, given to the General Court by the Constitution of Massachusetts, is limited by this rule as strictly as language can do it. It may not be possible, in all cases, practically to apply the principle with perfect equality; but it is highly important that the principle itself should never be lost sight of. Every attempt to levy a tax on any class or profession, as such, or on any one description of property, should be resisted as a violation of the free and equal principles of our government. Should any such tax have been adopted, it ought to be abandoned the moment its true character is discovered.

The idea has sometimes been advanced, that a tax might be levied for the privilege of an act of incorporation. This is a dangerous doctrine, and ought to be put down as equally opposed to the spirit of our institutions. Government is established and supported for the common benefit of all. The good of all is made up of the good of each and every one; if the facility arising from an act of incorporation will promote the good of the parties asking for it, who are the only proper judges, and if no improper injury to others is to be apprehended from it, the legislature is bound to grant it; and if granted at all, it should be granted without tax. A contrary practice would lead to the worst evil of the worst governments, a price upon legislation; a price would be paid for monopolies, and monopolies would be granted for a price. . . .

Bank capital consists of money, which the proprietors do not choose to employ themselves, but have established as a fund, to be employed by the active and enterprising classes of society. It is thus placed where those classes can command it, at their pleasure, either in the way of loan, or by discounting their business paper. Abundance of such capital is, in the highest degree, favorable to public prosperity, by exciting industry and extending trade. A tax upon bank capital, as such, is a tax upon the fund destined to pay the wages of labor, and to keep in motion the wheels of commerce; it thus operates unfavorably upon all industry, and upon all trade; in other words, upon all the interests of the Commonwealth. Abundance and cheapness of capital, and high wages of labor, act favorably and reciprocally upon each other, and, when united, are evidence of the happiest condition of political society. High wages stimulate industry, and thus add to the accumulation of comforts and capital; a tax upon bank capital, therefore, is an indirect tax upon the working classes of society. Any mode of raising revenue is preferable to one which touches the vital springs of industry. . . .

The business of banking should be open to as free a competition as any other branch of commercial business; there should be nothing like monopoly, or exclusiveness about it; there should be no restriction upon any amount of capital going into it—the more the better for the public—the better for all trade and for all industry. Banks act merely as convenient brokers between the owners of the capital, and the persons employing it; the cheaper the rate at which they are enabled to transact the business, the better for both parties, and for every body.

It has been sometimes suggested, that large chartered companies, possess a dangerous aristocratic influence; that they are machines liable to be controlled by the rich for their own purposes, and dangerous to our republican institutions. This opinion can only arise from a superficial view of the subject. No more ingenious mode could possibly be invented, to paralyze the power of individual wealth, than the creation of monied corporations, where the property of the retired capitalist is placed at the disposal of the active men of business; for such, from the nature of the case, must compose the directors of these companies. What power does the original owner of the capital possess over it, after he has converted it into bank stock? None, whatever, except as a director; and a board of directors, consisting of mere capitalists, would be wholly unable to manage a bank, in competition with the young and active members of the trading community. A reference to the list of bank directors in Boston, will prove the correctness of this view. There are amongst them, some few men of experience and capital, who have retired from business, but the chief management and direction is always in the hands of those deeply engaged in the bustle of business. All the sympathies of these institutions are with the industrious classes. There is, therefore, no danger in permitting any amount of capital to flow into this channel, under our system of free competition.

A monopoly of banking is the most dangerous of monopolies. Every project, therefore, for placing the banking business exclusively in the hands of great national or state institutions, is bad. The power of compressing or expanding the circulating medium, is too tremendous, and that of dispensing bank favors, too dangerous, to be intrusted to any one body of men.

6. William M. Gouge Decries Banks as Corporations, 1833

Against corporations of every kind, the objection may be brought, that whatever power is given to them, is so much taken from either the Government or the people.

As the object of charters is to give to members of companies powers which they would not possess in their individual capacity, the very existence of monied corporations is incompatible with equality of rights.

Corporations are unfavorable to the progress of national wealth. As the Argus eyes of private interest do not watch over their concerns, their affairs are much more carelessly and much more expensively conducted than those of individuals. What would be the condition of the merchant who should trust every thing to his clerks, or of the farmer who should trust every thing to his laborers? Corporations are obliged to trust every thing to stipendiaries, who are oftentimes less trustworthy than the clerks of the merchant or the laborers of the farmer.

Such are the inherent defects of corporations, that they never can succeed, except when the laws or circumstances give them a monopoly, or advantages partaking of

William M. Gouge, *A Short History of Paper Money and Banking in the United States* (Philadelphia: T. W. Ustick, 1833), pp. 41–44.

the nature of a monopoly. Sometimes they are protected by direct inhibitions to individuals to engage in the same business. Sometimes they are protected by an exemption from liabilities to which individuals are subjected. Sometimes the extent of their capital or of their credit, gives them a control of the market. They cannot, even then, work as cheap as the individual trader, but they can afford to throw away enough money in the contest, to *ruin* the individual trader, and then they have the market to themselves.

If a poor man suffers aggression from a rich man, the disproportion of power is such, that it may be difficult for him to obtain redress; but if a man is aggrieved by a corporation, he may have all its stockholders, all its clerks, and all its proteges for parties against him. Corporations are so powerful, as frequently to bid defiance to Government.

If a man is unjust, or an extortioner, society is, sooner or later, relieved from the burden, by his death. But corporations never die.

What is worst of all, (if worse than what has already been stated be possible,) is that want of moral feeling and responsibility which characterizes corporations. A celebrated English writer expressed the truth, with some roughness, but with great force, when he declared that "corporations have neither bodies to be kicked, nor souls to be damned."

All these objections apply to our American Banks.

They are protected, in most of the States, by direct inhibitions on individuals engaging in the same business.

They are exempted from liabilities to which individuals are subjected. If a poor man cannot pay his debts, his bed is, in some of the States, taken from under him. If that will not satisfy his creditors, his body is imprisoned. The shareholders in a Bank are entitled to all the gain they can make by Banking operations; but if the undertaking chances to be unsuccessful, the loss falls on those who have trusted them. They are responsible only for the amount of stock they may have subscribed.

For the old standard of value, they substitute the new standard of Bank credit. Would Government be willing to trust to corporations the fixing of our standards and measures of length, weight, and capacity? Or are our standards and measures of value of less importance than our standards and measures of other things?

They coin money out of paper. What has always been considered one of the most important prerogatives of Government, has been surrendered to the Banks.

In addition to their own funds, they have the whole of the spare cash of the community to work upon.

The credit of every business man depends on their nod. They have it in their power to ruin any merchant to whom they may become inimical.

We have laws against usury: but if it was the intention of the Legislature to encourage usurious dealings, what more efficient means could be devised than that of establishing incorporated paper money Banks?

Government extends the credit of these institutions, by receiving their paper as an equivalent for specie, and exerts its whole power to protect and cherish them. Whoever infringes any of the chartered privileges of the Banks, is visited with the severest penalties.

Supposing Banking to be a thing good in itself, why should Bankers be exempted from liabilities to which farmers, manufacturers, and merchants are subjected? It will not surely be contended that Banking is more conducive than agriculture, manufactures, and commerce, to the progress of national wealth.

Supposing the subscribers to Banks to be substantial capitalists, why should artificial power be conferred on them by granting them a charter? Does not wealth of itself confer sufficient advantages on the rich man? Why should the competition among capitalists be diminished, by forming them into companies, and uniting their wealth in one mass.

Supposing the subscribers to Banks to be speculators without capital—what is there so praiseworthy in their design of growing rich without labor, that Government should exert all its powers to favor the undertaking?

Why should corporations have greater privileges than simple co-partnerships?

On what principle is it, that, in a professedly republican Government, immunities are conferred on individuals in a collective capacity, that are refused to individuals in their separate capacity?

To test this question fairly, let us suppose that a proposition were made to confer on fourteen individuals in Philadelphia, and three or four hundred individuals in other parts of the country, the exclusive privileges which three or four hundred incorporated Banks now possess. How many citizens would be found who would not regard such a proposition with horror. Yet privileges conferred on corporations are more pernicious, because there is less moral feeling in the management of their concerns. As directors of a company men will sanction actions of which they would scorn to be guilty in their private capacity. A crime which would press heavily on the conscience of one man, becomes quite endurable when divided among many.

We take much pride to ourselves for having abolished entails, and justly, in so far as the principle is concerned: but it seems to be lost sight of by many that entails can prove effective only when the land is of limited extent, as in Great Britain; or where the mass of the population are serfs, as in Russia. In those districts of our country where negro slavery prevails, entails, aided by laws of primogeniture, would have kept estates in a few hands: but in the Middle and Northern States, a hundred ways would have been contrived for breaking the succession. If direct attempts had proved unsuccessful, the land would have been let on leases of 99 or 999 years, which would have been nearly the same in effect as disposing of them in fee simple. The abundance of land prevents its being monopolized. Supposing the whole extent of country, from the Atlantic to the Pacific, and north of the 39th degree of latitude, parcelled out among a few great Feudatories; those Feudatories, in order to derive a revenue from their domains, would be forced to lease them in a manner which would give the tenants the whole usufruct of the terrene; for, the quit rent would be only an annual payment, instead of a payment of the whole in advance.

But the floating capital of the country is limited in amount. This, from the condition of things, may be monopolized. A small portion of the community have already, through the agency of Banking operations, got possession of a great part of this floating capital, and are now in a fair way of getting possession of much of the remainder. Fixed and floating capital must be united to produce income, but he who has certain possession of one of these elements of revenue, will not long remain without the other.

The difference between England and the United States, is simply this: in the former country, exclusive privileges are conferred on individuals who are called

Lords; in the latter, exclusive privileges are conferred on corporations which are called *Banks.* The effect on the people of both countries is the same. In both the many live and labor for the benefit of the few.

7. *Baltimore Patriot* Supports Government Regulation of Telegraphy, 1845

The rapid extension of the magnetic telegraph to all the principal cities of the Union has already given to this means of conveying intelligence an importance that demands the attention of the government. The effect, as we have already seen in the working of the line between this city and Washington, is to annihilate space, so far as the transmission of intelligence is concerned, between all places where the lines extend. Its practical effect must be to supersede, in a general degree, the use of the ordinary mails, and it is scarcely too much to say, that it may ultimately do away with the mails as an agent of commercial intercourse.

In this view we have regretted the neglect of Congress to make the telegraph a government work, to be controlled by its laws, and regulated by its public agents. If it were owned and controlled by the government, it would not be worked for profit, as it of course will be whilst it belongs to private individuals or companies, and as the paying of the expense of operating it would be the only object of the government in making charges for its use, the rate of charge would be so small, that every person might avail of it for sending and receiving communications.

One of the uses to which the telegraph will at once be applied will be the transmission of news for the newspapers. This news is for public use, and not for private advantage, and ought, therefore, as in the case of the exchange papers in the ordinary mail, be sent free. The editor of a paper who receives this news has, and can have, no special advantage in it, and the only use he can make of it is to give the public the benefit of the knowledge of it, as soon as possible after it is received.

These remarks apply as well to Congressional proceedings, as to the general news of the day, and as it fortunately happens, that the telegraphy between Washington and Baltimore is the property of the Government, it has no doubt suggested itself to the Postmaster General, that some provision ought to be made by which the report of the proceedings of Congress could be given, at a cost which would reimburse the Government for the expense it would incur in employing a reporter—or, perhaps it would be better, that the Post-Master General should authorize a report of the proceedings, not exceeding a certain length, to be sent free of expense for the telegraph, the business of employing the Congressional reporter being left to the newspapers.

We make this suggestion because it is in accordance with the policy of the Government from its foundation, to carry news for newspapers free of charge, on the obvious ground that all such news is virtually for public information and public benefit—and that the reason of it is stronger in the case of the telegraph than it was in that of the ordinary mail, as the communications of the former are so much more rapidly made, and can therefore be so much more easily used for private speculation.

"The Magnetic Telegraph," *Baltimore Patriot,* November 14, 1845.

And because, also the expense to a newspaper in paying for the use of the telegraph for the transmission of news, at any thing like the rate of charge now exacted, would be so great as to utterly forbid its use by them for any practical purposes.

We trust the Postmaster General will give this matter his attention, and that the private companies who are constructing telegraphs will also examine the subject, so that a result may be arrived at which will secure the transmission of intelligence, important or interesting to the whole people, free of expense, whilst the cost of the work and whatever profits it may be capable of yielding, will be gathered from those who will use it for *private* benefit or speculation. This will be found, we are sure, to be the true policy of the telegraphs, whether regard be had to their profits or to their use.

8. *New York Journal of Commerce* Presses for the Privatization of Telegraphy, 1846

For once, we agree with the *Albany Eve. Journal.* We are opposed to the purchase of the Magnetic Telegraph by the government. The government monopoly is bad enough already. The proposed purchase would make it worse. Government cannot manage so complicated and subtle a concern, without vast expense, if at all. There is no certainty that [Samuel F. B.] Morse's patent,—which, with the contracts under it, is all that the government can purchase,—will not be superseded by other inventions. The general idea of the transmission of intelligence by means of electricity, is older than Mr. Morse. His invention, and the patent which secures to him the benefits of the same, relates to the mode of carrying the idea into effect. Other modes have been devised—some of them claiming to be equal or superior to his. We do not say that they are so. But they are not, no man can tell how soon a superior method will be devised. Therefore we say it is *not prudent* for the government to pay any considerable sum for a property so uncertain. There is *no need* of it. Private capital has hitherto been sufficient for the purpose, and doubtless will continue so, for all lines which would not be a dead loss if owned by the government. Again, there is no need of such ownership, because the government can avail itself of the telegraph, when owned by private companies, by paying as individuals do. The expense of its communications would be nothing compared with the cost of purchasing, and the expense of managing and repairs. Let the government confine its operations within its own sphere, and not attempt to grasp the business of private companies and citizens. We do not think the telegraph will interfere greatly with the Post Office revenue. Communications by it are expensive, and not always correct. In the vast majority of cases, the time which would be saved by resorting to the telegraph is of no great importance. Business transactions commenced through the telegraph, will commonly lead to a correspondence by mail. If the Government is wise, it will at least wait and see how the experiment works. It will take warning from its own experience, as proprietor of the Washington and Baltimore line. How many dollars has that line cost to the Government, for every dollar earned or saved? Instead of buying more lines, it should sell what it now owns. So at least we think.

"The Magnetic Telegraph," *New York Journal of Commerce,* December 16, 1846.

ESSAYS

First, Naomi R. Lamoreaux, professor of economics and history at the University of California–Los Angeles, examines the forms of business organization available to entrepreneurs in the early 1800s. She looks at the partnership, the limited partnership, and the corporation, explaining how businessmen elected one form or the other based on the degree of "firmness" required by the enterprise. Some elected the partnership, which in part allowed ease of dissolution. Still others preferred the corporation, which offered limited liability, existence in perpetuity, and access to more capital through small investors. Previously, scholars argued that the corporation triumphed as an organization form in the nineteenth century. Lamoreaux debunks this claim, showing that partnerships, limited partnerships, and corporations existed side-by-side.

Next, Cathy Matson, professor of history at the University of Delaware and director of the Library Company's Program in Early American Economy and Society in Philadelphia, surveys the financial history of the new nation from 1790 to 1850. After the American Revolution, citizens had to find institutions and policies that would feed economic growth. Finance counted among the biggest challenges for the national government. Matson's survey shows that debates over incorporation and banks were necessary to the process of "creative destruction" that ultimately stabilized the economy.

Finally, Richard R. John, professor of history at the University of Illinois–Chicago, looks at the electric telegraph in the 1840s and examines debates over control of this high-technology communications medium. Inventor Samuel F. B. Morse advocated a public-private joint venture, while others lobbied for government management. Skeptics of privatization cried "monopoly" and advocated federal regulation to ensure that telegraphy would benefit the public good. Advocates of privatization emphasized Morse's right, as an inventor, to benefit from his patent, laying the foundation for an ideology of "free enterprise."

The Shape of the Firm: Partnerships and Corporations

NAOMI R. LAMOREAUX

The purpose of this essay is to use business history, in particular the history of the contractual choices made by 19th-century entrepreneurs to organize their businesses, as raw material for reflecting on the nature of that entity we call the firm. . . . I argue that businesspeople could choose from a range of contractual forms that offered varying degrees of "firmness," that is, that differed in the extent to which they protected contracting parties against holdup. I also argue that increasing the degree of "firmness" of a contract was not always desirable from the standpoint of entrepreneurs.

The organizational choices available to entrepreneurs varied over the course of the 19th century. During the early part of the century, most businesses were organized as single proprietorships or partnerships. The only way to form a corporation was to secure a special charter from a state legislature, but such charters were usually granted only to projects deemed to be in the public interest. As the century progressed, however, the states gradually liberalized their policies on charters, and by the 1870's

Naomi R. Lamoreaux, "Partnerships, Corporations, and the Theory of the Firm," *American Economic Review* 88 (May 1998): 66–70. Reprinted by permission of American Economic Association.

most had passed general incorporation laws that made the corporate form widely available. Thus by the post–Civil War period, most businesses could organize either as partnerships or corporations.

The choice was an important one. On the most obvious level, partners had unlimited liability for their firm's debts, whereas the liability of members of corporations was limited. But there were other significant differences as well. For example, the partnership form of organization typically had a short time horizon. Partnership agreements either expired after fixed periods of time or included procedures for terminating the arrangement at the will of one of the members. The death of a partner also typically forced the dissolution of a firm. Although corporations could be organized for fixed periods of time, they were more commonly chartered in perpetuity. Moreover, the life of a corporation was independent of that of any of its stockholders. No one stockholder could force a dissolution of the firm, unless he or she owned a majority of the shares.

Another difference between partnerships and corporations, closely related to the issue of longevity, was the structure of governance. Members of a partnership all had the power to act as if they were the sole owners of the enterprise. As long as they were acting within the scope of the firm's normal business, they could enter into obligations that were binding on the firm without the consent of the other partners. Although partnership agreements might impose a hierarchical order on the firm's members and limit the actions that any one partner could take, such agreements did not exempt firms from liabilities assumed by partners contrary to their terms. Members of corporations, on the other hand, did not individually possess authority to bind the firm. The corporate form of organization concentrated management in the hands of officers elected by a vote of the stockholders, and the firm was not liable for debts incurred by members who were not empowered to act on the stockholders' behalf.

It is important to realize that these differences between the partnership and the corporation were not rigidly fixed, but rather varied in magnitude over time. Over the course of the century, as the courts worked through a wide variety of cases involving such matters as bankruptcies and stockholders' rights, they drew upon contending bodies of legal theory regarding corporations. During the early part of the century, the view that corporations were artificial creatures of the state held sway; by the middle it was increasingly common to view corporations as private contracts made by "aggregations" of businessmen; by the end, the courts were moving toward the view that corporations were legal persons in the eye of the law. During the period when aggregation theory dominated, the courts applied many aspects of partnership law to cases involving corporations, and the differences between the two forms narrowed. During the same period, there were various circumstances in which stockholders of corporations might find themselves liable for amounts in excess of their investment. As [Morton J.] Horwitz has written, "the distinction between the liability of the members of a corporation and a partnership, so clear to modern eyes, was still regarded as a matter of degree rather than of kind."

It makes sense, therefore, to conceptualize the differences between partnerships and corporations, not in terms of discrete categories, but rather in terms of continuous variables that could take on different values at different points in time. In particular, the differences between these forms might be arrayed along two dimensions. The first dimension would be liability (the extent to which members of a firm were responsible for the enterprise's debts), with partnerships generally high on liability compared to corporations. The second might be thought of as a measure of the firm's autonomy (the extent to which it had a legal existence beyond that of its members). The ability of a partner acting alone to bind a firm and to dissolve it at will meant that partnerships were low on autonomy compared to corporations. These two dimensions were not, of course, completely independent, but they can be distinguished analytically, and as I will show, it is useful to do so.

The literature on the advantages of the corporate form has focused almost exclusively on the first of these two dimensions, liability. Some scholars have argued that there were no clear benefits to limited liability because whatever savings it permitted in raising equity capital were offset by higher costs in securing loans. Others have countered that limited liability played an important role in lowering transaction costs, for example, those associated with transferring shares on the securities markets. Arguments like the latter imply, however, that the benefits of limited liability were greater for large firms seeking public ownership than for small closely held companies. Although the historical record indicates that large enterprises almost universally adopted the corporate form, the vast majority of businesses choosing to incorporate during the late 19th century were small firms whose stock was closely held. It is important to understand why small as well as large firms made this decision, for the widespread adoption of the corporate form by small firms played a major role in its subsequent history.

In the case of small firms, there appears to be abundant evidence that liability rules in and of themselves did not determine the choice of organizational form. First, firms did not always take advantage of limited liability when it was readily available to them. Many British joint-stock companies, for example, could have obtained limited liability by reorganizing under a general incorporation law passed during the mid-1850's but chose instead to remain as they were. Similarly, in the early 19th-century United States, small firms sometimes voluntarily wrote into their corporate charters clauses that specified unlimited liability. Throughout the century, moreover, it was common for the officers and leading stockholders of small corporations to endorse personally their company's debts in order to secure commercial credit and bank loans.

A second type of evidence, which is perhaps more revealing about the determinants of contractual choice, was small firms' reluctance to adopt an available alternative: the limited partnership. Legislation permitting this type of organization was first passed in New York and Connecticut in 1822 and then adopted by most other states over the next couple of decades—long before the advent of general incorporation laws made the corporate form a widely available alternative—and yet few firms seem to have chosen the new form. This lack of interest is somewhat surprising, because limited partnerships would seem to have had some advantages over ordinary partnerships. The statutes created firms with two types of partners: general partners, who had unlimited liability and whose rights and responsibilities were the same as those of members of ordinary partnerships; and special partners, whose liabilities were limited to their investments and who had no authority over the management of the company. From the standpoint of a general partner, the limited partnership functioned much like a limited-liability corporation in which officers assumed personal responsibility for debts in excess of the firm's capital. From the standpoint of a special partner (i.e., an investor who did not intend to participate in the management of the firm) the form involved the possibility of greater gains than could be obtained from a simple loan contract without the risks that an ordinary partnership entailed. Compared to a corporation, moreover, the arrangement may have reduced principal–agent problems because the firm's general partners not only shared fully in whatever gains or losses their actions generated, but were personally liable for debts in excess of capital. Moreover, investors who were dissatisfied with the quality of the firm's general partners could vote with their feet and refuse to renew the partnership when its term expired. Stockholders of corporations could sell out only if there were willing buyers for their shares; limited partners could force the firm to reimburse them.

This, of course, was the crux of the problem from the standpoint of the general partners. If one adopts an Oliver Williamson type of transaction-cost view of the firm, the reason is apparent. According to Williamson, whenever resources have a significantly greater value in combination than they do in alternative uses, there is a risk of holdup which can only be countered by bringing the assets together within a single firm. In general, however, firms organized as partnerships had much less ability to protect members against holdup than did firms organized as corporations for the simple reason that partnerships were lower in autonomy. The ability of partners to dissolve the firm at will or after the fixed term of the agreement meant that there were circumstances under which one party could use the threat of dissolution to force the others to grant more favorable terms. For example, during the first decade of the 19th century, E. I. Dupont's refusal to allow his partner, Peter Bauduy, to count as capital a note he had endorsed for the enterprise produced much "animadversion on the part of P. Bauduy, who threatened to sue for a dissolution of partnership to stop the factory and could not be pacified, but by the new agreement" in which Bauduy "exacted from the concern some extra compensation and advantages."

Ordinary partnerships were nonetheless an improvement over nonfirm contractual agreements, because they raised the costs that had to be borne by a party that failed at an attempt at holdup. If, instead of better contract terms, the attempt resulted in the dissolution of the firm and the liquidation of its assets, all of the partners stood to lose from the forced sale of resources whose value outside the firm was less than it was within. In the case of limited partnerships, however, this principle of equal pain did not hold. Instead, the claims of the special partners took precedence over those of the general partners. At the end of the term of the limited partnership, the general partners either had to meet the special partners' conditions for renewal or face dissolution. In effect, they were in the position of borrowers who owed a big balloon payment at the end of a fixed period of time. If they could not get another loan, they would have to liquidate assets to pay off their debt. The risk of holdup, moreover, was not borne only by one side. If the firm was unusually successful, the general partners could extract higher payments from the special partners in return for their agreed-upon share of the profits. For example, Aaron Benedict reorganized his Connecticut button manufactory as a limited partnership in 1829. The firm did very well, and when the agreement expired in 1834, Benedict raised the price of the smallest share from $1,000 to $2,500. In 1838 he raised the price again to $5,000. In both 1834 and 1838, small investors who could not come up with the requisite sums were forced to drop out of the company.

In other words, the limited partnership, although lower on the liability dimension than the ordinary partnership, was also lower on the dimension of autonomy. The latter seems to have outweighed the former in the eyes of 19th-century entrepreneurs, and few seem to have organized their enterprises as limited partnerships. The choice between the partnership and the corporate form was very different, however, for corporations were not only lower on the liability dimension, but higher on the autonomy dimension compared to partnerships; that is, corporations also offered greater protection against holdup. The following example helps to explain why.

The case involves the company formed by George Corliss to manufacture the famous steam engine that bore his name. The firm was first organized as a partnership in 1847 and then, ten years later, reorganized as a corporation, with the bulk of the stock evenly divided between Corliss himself and an investor named Edwin J. Nightingale, who served as the firm's treasurer. The two men agreed to admit several additional members to the firm by selling equal amounts of their stock to the new parties, but when Corliss sought to increase the number of shares owned by his brother William, Nightingale refused to reduce his own holdings for this purpose. Perhaps he realized that the two brothers would likely vote as a block and that by selling stock to William he would in effect be giving George control of the company. After repeated attempts to persuade Nightingale to change his mind, George sold William a block of his own stock. But he also determined to force Nightingale to sell out his interest. If the firm had still been organized as a partnership, this action would have been relatively easy to take. Corliss could have unilaterally forced a dissolution of the firm and, at the same time, prevented a mutually disastrous liquidation by offering Nightingale cash for his share. The corporate form of organization made things much more difficult, however, because the two parties had to agree to a dissolution. In this particular case, Corliss had an ace up his sleeve. He retained personal control of the patents on his steam engine and used them to threaten to destroy the company by licensing competitors to make his patented engines. Nightingale was forced to capitulate, but later investors in similar situations would protect themselves against holdup by making the assignment of full patent rights a condition of their participation in the corporation.

If one adopts Williamson's logic and thinks about firms as organizational arrangements that reduced opportunities for holdup, then the Corliss example suggests that it is not very useful to think about firms and nonfirms as either/or categories. Rather it is more useful (again) to think in terms of a continuum of contractual arrangements arrayed according to their degree of "firmness." Some contracts offered parties relatively little protection against holdup; that is, they had relatively little of that attribute I am calling "firmness." Others with more "firmness" offered stronger protection. In general, organizational arrangements that ranked higher on the autonomy dimension had more "firmness" than those that ranked lower.

The Corliss example also suggests that increasing the degree of "firmness" of an organization entailed costs for at least some of the contracting parties that were directly related to the greater protection against holdup. The relatively lower "firmness" of the partnership form of organization would have allowed Corliss to benefit from Nightingale's investment when he needed it and then to take control of the company when he did not. The relatively higher "firmness" of the corporation made this sequence of events much more difficult to effect. The general point I wish to make here is that use of the term "holdup" may have misleadingly negative connotations. What is really at stake is the ability of one party to a contract to use some form of economic muscle against another. Although the exercise of such muscle could have undesirable consequences for one or more parties, so could blocking its use. In other words, from the standpoint of the economic actors involved, there was a trade-off between greater protection against holdup and the ability to use economic power. The corporate form of organization was not always an improvement over the partnership for all of the parties concerned.

Financial Innovation in the New Nation

CATHY MATSON

By 1783 many Americans were beginning to realize that the toll of a long and costly war dampened their hopes for a seamless transition into prosperity. The initial flood of cheap English goods and "easy credit" came to an end quickly, and northern states began to raise taxes on the property of middling property holders just as the money and credit supply contracted; as a result, debts went unpaid and investment in new lands and enterprises diminished. Moreover, Pennsylvania, New York, New Jersey, and Maryland began to pay back, or "assume," large amounts of their state and national debts—debts which nationalists believed should be assumed by Congress in order to attach the loyalties of creditors to the nascent federal government. Most of the states discriminated against each other in commerce; while some port cities such as Wilmington, Delaware, and Hartford, Connecticut, invited more trade by establishing "free ports" that eliminated most import duties, others such as New York and Philadelphia promoted their own commercial and manufacturing independence by tightening import regulations against "outsiders," whether foreign nations or neighboring states. Newspapers printed stinging denunciations of imported "luxuries." After 1784, a deep depression settled on the cities, and within two years the portent of debtor rebellions rose on many rural frontiers. To make matters worse, these frontiers became breeding grounds for contests among Native Americans, French and British troops, and squatters and land speculators, while seven states disputed overlapping land claims beyond their boundaries. Where people on the western edges of settled states became openly rebellious in the face of steep state taxes, justices became hostile to debtors, sheriffs foreclosed on hundreds of farmsteads, and farmers faced declining prices for agricultural goods. Shays' Rebellion in western Massachusetts, a protest movement of "combustibles" who rose up against the economic authority of eastern interests, was just one of the social disturbances that aroused nationalists into more decisive action by 1786.

Once nationalists secured passage of the Constitution, however, the prospects for a more stable economy brightened. The Constitution conferred authority on a new federal government to create a uniform commerce and a steady revenue, two important building blocks for the republic's future economy. The government, said its framers, would protect and extend the mutual interests of citizens whose markets were linked to cooperation in a world of hostile nations. It would sanction a single currency, safeguard contracts and private property, standardize business practices,

Cathy Matson, *Risky Business: Winning and Losing in the Early American Economy, 1780–1850* (Philadelphia: Library Company of Philadelphia, 2003), pp. 4–15. Reprinted by permission of The Library Company of Philadelphia.

patent inventions, and naturalize immigrants. The framers also projected that a strong federal government would hasten the creation of a widespread free labor market alongside expanding slavery, sanction money-lending at interest and validate entrepreneurship, and spread goods into markets as far away as China. Although sales of western land did not add significantly to federal revenues before the Civil War, a national system of import duties begun in 1789 provided about ninety per-cent of the federal government's revenue for many years—a boon to stabilizing the nation, as well as fuel for future regional and sectional quarrels. These were lofty goals, and during the first generation after ratification of the Constitution, an influen-tial contingent of Federalists, including Alexander Hamilton, promoted the institu-tions and social structures that began to fulfill them, touching off widespread public responses—sometimes creative, sometimes destructive—that have become a regular hallmark of economic growth in America.

One of the most important safeguards provided by state and national govern-ments in the early republic was incorporation. Colonial merchants had known for decades that by forming marine insurance companies they could spread the risks of international trade, but these were unincorporated agreements made among trust-ing individuals. In 1752, Benjamin Franklin founded the first fire insurance com-pany, the Philadelphia Contributionship for the Insurance of Houses from Loss by Fire, as a consortium of merchants and public officials who met in local coffee houses to review surveys of properties, issue policies, and share out equally among all policy holders the profits and losses of the Contributionship. By the late 1760s, the Pennsylvania legislature incorporated the company. In 1792 the Insurance Company of North America became the first joint stock insurance company in the country, and by 1800 London insurers were opening branches of insurance providers such as the Phoenix Company in Philadelphia and New York City, using local agents to write policies. By then, states were granting corporate charters to a few local and state banks, and in the next couple of decades corporations for longer roads, deeper canals, and larger ports attracted the small investments of thousands of Americans who collectively poured millions of dollars into projects that otherwise might have languished for want of capital, and who also used these joint stock companies' notes along with bank notes as currency. The New York Stock Exchange, loosely organized in 1792, emerged as an important incorporated institution after 1817. So many interest groups clamored for charters of incorporation that state governments began to pass laws to sidestep the test of whether a corporation served the "public good" and to permit a wide array of would-be investors to seek charters based more simply on the assets and reputation of individuals. By 1828, New York had 39 char-tered banks, 76 insurance companies, 127 manufacturing companies, 74 corpora-tions for scientific and benevolent causes, and scores of canal, steamboat, ferry, road, and bridge companies specially created by the state.

Alexander Hamilton had studied how the Bank of England, created at the end of the seventeenth century to mobilize capital to fund both wars and empire-building, had nevertheless failed to provide central financing for important aspects of the country's industrial revolution. English domestic enterprise, lamented Hamilton, had instead been entrusted to private interests and local resources. He had also gained first-hand experience with Revolutionary credit and currency experiments during his service with George Washington in the field. A first step toward remedying the post-war "imbecility" of the American economy, he and other Federalists argued, was to shore up faltering credit relations and put the country on a sound financial footing. This would mean, in part, eliminating the depreciated state and Congressional currencies in circulation and establishing a reliable fund for repaying the debts of Congressional securities. These debts had assumed great significance to individuals in the inner circles of the financial establishment who accumulated more and more of them into their own hands. Hamilton was determined to connect the financial interests of these individuals to a firmer reputation for the national government, not only by boosting their investments in commerce and landholding, but also—he hoped—by eliminating the most blatant deceits and injustices of an uncertain monetary system riddled with counterfeiting, uneven prices and markets, and absconding debtors.

In January 1790 Hamilton presented his first proposal to begin remedying these ills, his *Report on Public Credit*. The report established the principle of the national government's obligation to repay its debts to foreign countries, states, and private citizens, and went on to design the consolidation of the state debts into one national fund. Congress would reissue new interest-bearing securities that would be "backed" by revenues from import duties and special excise taxes. A prolonged Congressional and newspaper debate ensued, in which Americans wondered how, and how much, to pay the private creditors of the states and the federal government. As Continental currencies had depreciated during the Revolution from their face values to near worthlessness, farmers and soldiers had often found it necessary to sell any payments they received in Congress's wobbly money at low market value in order to get cash for their immediate needs. Over the years, these securities traded hands over and over, and those who had the ability to buy them at deep discounts or speculate accumulated the lion's share of them. These newer holders of the Revolutionary war debt anticipated that a stronger federal government would ensure their payment at reasonable rates. And they were right. Federalists, many of whom owned large amounts of government securities, argued in favor of "assumption and funding" of state and private debts at market values instead of face values, and their argument won out against men such as James Madison who wished for payment of securities at face value to the original holders. Soon, the funded securities were successfully traded in all the major cities, prompting states and corporations to issue local securities to fund special projects.

State banks in Philadelphia, New York, and Boston were already teaching Americans from all walks of life valuable lessons about the benefits of available credit when Hamilton presented his proposal for a central national bank in December 1790. His plan called for the First Bank of the United States to become an integral part of restructuring and enlarging the national debt. The Bank was capitalized at $10 million, $8 million subscribed privately at $400 a share within the first hours of being offered to the public, and $2 million held by the federal government. Its charter permitted this first central Bank to operate for twenty years, headquartered in Philadelphia with branches in other cities.

The Bank, like the assumption and funding of the debt, met with staunch criticism about its necessity and constitutionality. At one extreme, advocates such as Oliver Wolcott of Connecticut imagined that banks would be a greater benefit to an enterprising elite than to middling inhabitants whose economic means, he argued, were circumscribed. Very quickly, Wolcott's view bore little resemblance to the reality of expanding demand for the benefits of banking. At the other extreme, opponents attacked banks as reservoirs of aristocratic privilege that drew international traders into great debt with the lure of excessive commercial credit, or that tempted would-be entrepreneurs into dangerously overextending their economic projects and incurring a mountain of debt. Critics at this time also linked Hamiltonian finance to unjust taxation, pointing to the 1791 excise taxes on the consumption of tea, wine, coffee, and whiskey. The tax on this last item was widely believed to be an egregious imposition on American livelihoods, especially on the frontier where whiskey production flourished, and opposition to it erupted into the Whiskey Rebellion of 1794.

Somewhere between these poles of opinion, many Americans welcomed the credit of state and local banking when it was widely available, even as they continued to fear the periodic failures of banks and the potential for abuse by special economic interests. Even Thomas Jefferson, who argued in 1791 against the constitutionality of the national Bank and who divested the government's roughly 2,000 shares in it after he became President, used the new financial system to double the size of the country when he paid France $11.25 million of just-printed Treasury bonds to purchase Louisiana. Napoleon in turn sold the American bonds primarily to British investors, whose capital was thus indirectly used to fund a war on Britain in 1812. Jefferson admitted in 1805 that it was a good thing for the Bank's notes to continue circulating, especially in larger port cities where merchants needed a steady flow of reliable and widely-accepted currency. Others, especially mid-Atlantic leaders of the Democratic-Republicans, believed that failing to continue the Bank in 1811 when its charter was up for renewal was poor economics. As they noted, state and local banks would have to bear the weight of public pressure for loans and capital funding; there were about 210 such banks by 1815, 41 of them chartered in Pennsylvania in 1814 alone. Each state-chartered bank printed its own notes that circulated far and wide, providing a means of exchange and a backing for investments—provided the notes were accepted where they were offered. When banks issued orders to printers to make vastly more currency than there was specie to back it up they facilitated widespread economic development. State and local banks became forums for scores of bank directors to promote development projects by lending themselves money from bank coffers, and by attracting the deposits of myriad small investors. Banks disbursed paper money, gave liberal credit, and, as a result, expanded public confidence in bold development projects. Foreign investors became eager buyers of securities as well, thereby creating an atmosphere interpreted by some leading Americans as proof of international confidence in the new republic. But over time it became clear that state banks were so popular that they failed to protect the credit of investors by providing adequate specie reserves for their notes, and they could not respond to the demands of wealthier aggressive investors for investment loans. So in 1816 a new group of central bank supporters secured a charter for the Second Bank of the United States.

The Panic of 1819 was not directly linked to the financial system taking shape in America, but this first truly national depression spurred many people to reassess whether they had become overconfident about their still-fragile economic institutions and had created "an extravagant people" who had too much bank credit at hand. The causes of the panic can be traced to Europe. Following the War of 1812, Europeans began to feed themselves again, cutting the demand for American food products. English textile manufacturers, faced with rising cotton prices, looked more to India for cotton. Although in the long run Indian cotton was not a desirable substitute for the tougher fiber of sea island cotton from the Carolinas, the British alterations in markets wreaked havoc on American producers. When these conditions deepened, the overextension of numerous banks in America added to the woes of small farmers and rising entrepreneurs, as well as planters and northern shippers. Easy credit came to a halt, and banks began to call in their loans, some of them demanding that borrowers repay in specie. Beginning in the late summer of 1818, commodity prices declined, businesses failed, unemployment rose, creditors dunned debtors, and widespread foreclosures devastated hundreds of farm families. Indeed, the Panic of 1819 struck the hardest where expansion had been the greatest, in the South and newly settled areas of the West. But even in the mid-Atlantic, many development projects were simply abandoned.

In the midst of widespread economic disarray, Americans entered the 1820s with contradictory assessments of the financial innovations they had embraced earlier. A more widely enfranchised population of urban craftsmen and commercial farmers joined concerned merchants to deeply politicize issues related to financing the nation's business. They demanded more democratic tariff and public land policies, general bankruptcy laws to handle dislocations of small businesses and indebted individuals, and credit and banking institutions that they believed would soften the blows of the depression and open up economic opportunities. Popular hostility toward certain bankers and corporation leaders, especially those bank directors who suspended specie payments on note issues, led to investigations that revealed the speculation and corruption of insiders. It was widely recognized that most small banks, especially on the frontier, lacked adequate capital and specie reserves to back up the loans and currency they issued. Holders of bank notes experienced a repeat of Revolutionary problems when their notes depreciated sharply and they faced foreclosures on their property.

A popular cry for debtors' relief linked the rash of bankruptcies of the early 1820s to banking difficulties. Long understood by Americans as one of the risks merchants regularly faced, business failures began to reach alarming proportions in the commercial farming and rising entrepreneurial population. The Bankruptcy Act of 1800 had a short three-year existence but paved the way for reconsidering who bore the blame for economic crises. In previous generations, the individual accepted moral as well as contractual responsibility for debts. Into the nineteenth century, Americans began to propose that some economic traumas lay outside of debtors' control and should be dealt with by legislators. Little progress was made toward new bankruptcy protections during these years. Eventually, the Bankruptcy Act of 1841, repealed in 1843, moved toward favoring individual risk-takers by allowing them to declare bankruptcy voluntarily and with certain immunities against excessive claims by creditors.

Meanwhile, during the economic hardships and labor radicalism that returned in the late 1820s and 1830s, men such as Langton Byllesby and Thomas Skidmore called for dissolving private property as it existed and redistributing land and manufacturing into the hands of middling Americans. More moderate observers reasoned that economic problems lay with national banking and the elite that controlled it, not with the state and local banks that extended credit to commercial farmers and ambitious urban artisans. By the late 1820s Jacksonians coalesced large numbers of these different dissenters in a campaign against central banking (though often not against all banking in principle) and led a major realignment of national politics. By 1828, when Jacksonian Democrats won the presidency, the many strands of this discussion were focused on a "bank war" between advocates and opponents of rechartering the Second Bank, which was due to expire in 1836.

By 1832, when the Bank's supporters—including Nicholas Biddle, Henry Clay, and Daniel Webster—sought an early recharter of the Bank in an effort to extend its privileges, Jacksonians were in no mood to accommodate central banking interests. The President thundered out a resounding veto message in July 1832, echoing both Jefferson's constitutional arguments against a central bank and popular anxieties about "monster institutions." There was no Congressional authority to create a bank, insisted Jackson, and the present one had attracted dangerous levels of foreign investment. Adding that a central bank was "subversive of the rights of the States," and built on a foundation of special individual privileges for the wealthy, Jackson vowed to terminate its existence. When the Senate failed to override Jackson's veto, the recharter was buried; in 1833, upon his re-election, Jackson told his secretary of the treasury to remove the government's specie reserves—much of it silver that flowed into federal coffers from foreign trade with Mexico—and deposit them into regional "pet" banks of his choosing.

The Second Bank's supporters argued that it had helped check the tendency of state banks to issue too much paper money by periodically calling in state loans and requiring the state banks to have a sufficient supply of specie on hand to cover deposits, which the Bank seemed to be doing successfully until the rampant land and credit speculation after the mid-1820s began to collapse and pinch midwestern and southern farmers and shopkeepers who could not repay loans from banks. Charges that "eastern monopolists" hundreds of miles away had created the crisis rang throughout the countryside. Then two additional events deepened public concerns. First, Nicholas Biddle engineered a tightening of bank credit throughout the northeast in 1834, which threw the country into a sharp recession. Second, the British economy had begun a long-term decline in 1833 that was especially damaging to cotton and textiles markets internationally. By 1836, hard-pressed British merchants and manufacturers curtailed credit to American cotton growers and began to call in debts. Americans in turn dunned debtors throughout the states for payments, which many merchants and numerous southern banks could not provide.

But worse conditions lay ahead. Jackson issued a Specie Circular in 1836 that was intended to curb escalating land speculation and farm start-up loans by requiring borrowers to repay their loans in specie. But loans had so outstripped the specie funds of state banks, price inflation for common necessary food and household items had so steeply risen since 1833, and landowners had so overextended their hunger for cheap land that no single presidential measure could reverse the impending crisis by 1836.

Southern and western banks first tried foreclosing on properties of hundreds of Americans, primarily farmers, but by early 1837 bank doors began to close. Bankruptcies of merchants rose during the spring months, while average consumers and small investors flooded to eastern banks and demanded withdrawals of their savings in silver and gold. Banks could only deny them, and then suspend specie payments altogether. Eventually, people could not pay taxes, and cash was in critically low supply; stores closed and canal and road building projects lay abandoned when states announced that they could not finance bonds earmarked for them.

Depression rocked the country by the fall of 1837. Prices rose steeply, store goods became scarce, unemployment skyrocketed in the cities, and farmers despaired of selling their surpluses to impoverished townspeople at any price. Hundreds of banks closed, thousands of city dwellers lived off their wits in the streets. The depression that lasted until 1842 spurred thousands of families to move west and many more thousands of Americans to join an array of moral and social reform movements. Government resources—whether federal, state, or local—were utterly inadequate to the tasks of meeting immediate needs or longer-term recovery.

But the longer-term lesson of the 1830s was that Jacksonians could not return the nation to "Jeffersonian principles" of an imagined agrarian simplicity—which would have been foolhardy indeed, given the rapid economic change affecting American life in every quarter—and they failed to lead the country toward adoption of a hard-money economy despite their destruction of the Second Bank. Instead, during the mid-1830s, Americans turned ever more toward demanding more state and local banks, more paper currency, and a more sophisticated financial system in general. In effect, although large numbers of Americans agreed with the Jacksonian creed of fearing national and international economic control, and wished to return economic control to local and state levels, they did not support the wholesale destruction of the financial institutions that had furthered their efforts to share in the American capitalist dream.

Building the First Information Highway: The Deregulation of Telegraphy

RICHARD R. JOHN

Electric telegraphy was new in the 1840s, and it was by no means obvious to contemporaries how it was going to be commercialized, or even whether it would promote the public good. These anxieties are worth underscoring, since they are often forgotten. From the outset, newspaper editors, merchants, and public figures from almost every corner of the United States hailed the new technology as the greatest invention of the age. Almost no one questioned the desirability of facilitating high-speed—and, at least in theory, instantaneous—communication between far-flung localities. Accompanying this euphoria, however, was a strong undercurrent of concern. The new technology was so powerful, its critics warned, that were it not properly regulated, it might well prove less of a blessing than a curse.

Richard R. John, "Private Enterprise, Public Good? Communications Deregulation as a National Political Issue, 1839–1851," in Jeffrey L. Pasley, Andrew W. Robertson, and David Waldstreicher, eds., *Beyond the Founders: New Approaches to the Political History of the Early American Republic* (Chapel Hill: University of North Carolina Press, 2004), pp. 339–342, 347–350. Copyright © 2004 by the University of North Carolina Press. Used by permission of the publisher.

The appeal of federal control helps explain why the first telegraph line in the United States to be open to the public—a forty-mile line between Washington and Baltimore—was financed out of general revenue and administered during its first two years by the Post Office Department. Among the most tireless champions of federal control was Samuel F. B. Morse, the painter-turned-inventor whose ownership of a majority share in a key telegraph patent gave him a major voice in the early history of the industry. Morse fervently believed that the federal government should own the rights to his patent—which, with a self-confidence bordering on arrogance, he presumed to cover every important feature of the new technology. In pursuit of this goal, Morse secured federal support for experiments that culminated in 1844 with the successful demonstration of the commercial possibilities of electric telegraphy and in 1845 with the opening of the Washington-Baltimore line.

Morse's faith in federal control antedated by almost a decade the commercialization of the new technology. "It would seem most natural," Morse observed in 1837, to "connect a telegraphic system with the Post Office Department; for, although it does not carry a mail, yet it is another mode of accomplishing the principal object for which the mail is established, to wit: the rapid and regular transmission of intelligence." Morse predicated his postal analogy on the expansive role that the Post Office Department had come to assume since the 1820s in the circulation of time-specific information. Beginning with Postmaster General John McLean, a succession of postal administrators had proclaimed that the federal government had an obligation to transmit information faster than any possible rival. In an age when merchants could make fortunes overnight by running private horse expresses to outpace the mails, this federal guarantee was vital to the thousands of planters and farmers who were dependent on foreign markets for the sale of their crops. Federal control, Morse predicted, would prevent the few from defrauding the many. Should Congress leave telegraphy to speculators to monopolize for themselves, Morse warned, it might easily become the means of enriching a single corporation while causing the "bankruptcy of thousands."

Equally disturbing for Morse was the possibility that the federal government might monopolize the new technology by itself. Such an arrangement, Morse warned, might well work "vast mischief." The optimal form of federal control, instead, was a mixed enterprise in which the federal government retained the exclusive right to the new technology by virtue of its ownership of the key patents—including, of course, Morse's own. Under such a scheme, the federal government could designate a number of lines for its own use. The core of the network, however—the "private telegraphs," as Morse termed them—would be built and maintained by investors upon payment to the federal government of a licensing fee that granted them exclusive rights to specific routes. In this way, the federal government would possess the communication facilities it needed, while encouraging a general competition among investors governed by whatever regulations legislators might think proper. . . .

Similar, though usually less elaborate, plans for federal control had broad support in the press. Early on, many editors regarded a federal buyout of Morse's patent as inevitable, if only because, like the private expresses, private telegraph companies threatened to deprive the Post Office Department of a great deal of revenue. Others looked to federal control as a safeguard against speculative fraud and abuse. Private enterprise, declared James Gordon Bennett of the *New York Herald* in April

1845, was fast erecting telegraph lines in many directions, yet the public interest would be much more securely promoted should the federal government undertake the arrangement. It must be "clear to every one," declared James Watson Webb of the *Morning Courier and New-York Enquirer,* at about the same time, that no private enterprise should be permitted to use the new technology for "private and exclusive purposes." On the contrary, the federal government should control it and make "such a disposition of its vast powers as should most conduce to the public welfare." So enormous were the dangers of speculation, editorialized William M. Swain of the Philadelphia *Public Ledger* the following October, that the federal government might even find it advisable to prohibit anyone other than a government official from transmitting a message over the wires. "Perhaps the best security," Swain speculated, "would be in the prohibition of all private correspondence. Some will say that this would render the telegraph nearly useless. We grant that it would—to speculators, and we add that for mercantile speculations only will it be much used in private correspondence, excepting during elections." . . .

Editorial support for federal control owed a good deal to the uneasiness with which editors contemplated the disruptive effects of telegraphy on their own news-gathering efforts. Some editors worried that private telegraph companies might discriminate against their newspaper in ways that would benefit their rivals. Others worried that the new technology would raise the cost of news gathering. Telegraphic dispatches were expensive, and, at least initially, it was far from self-evident that newspapers would receive favorable rates. At present, observed the editor of the Baltimore *Patriot,* newspaper editors enjoyed under federal law the right to exchange with each other an unlimited number of newspapers free of charge. These exchanges, in turn, provided editors with the bulk of the news that they relied on to fill their columns. Should the Post Office Department retain control of the new technology, this policy would presumably be maintained; if it devolved upon private enterprise, however, it might well be abandoned. In either event, the postmaster general should work with the private telegraph companies to ensure the free circulation of all information "important or interesting to the whole people." The cost of this information, in turn, should be borne by those individuals who used the telegraph for "*private* benefit or speculation"—by analogy with the longstanding presumption that the postage on merchants' letters subsidized the exchanges upon which editors relied for their news: "This will be found, we are sure, to be the true policy of the telegraphs, whether regard be had to their profits or to their use." Should this policy be adopted, editors would continue to receive news broadcasts free of charge "as in the case of the exchange papers in the ordinary mail." . . .

Popular support for federal control never disappeared altogether. With the expansion of the telegraph network, however, several once-potent criticisms of the new technology came to seem overblown. Once the new technology became a mundane reality, rather than a visionary dream, editors discovered it to be less threatening to ordinary commercial transactions than they had feared, and more useful in their daily operations than they had anticipated. It was, for example, by no means incidental that the most searching critiques in the New York press of private enterprise in telegraphy antedated the extension of the first telegraph line to New York City.

Particularly important in legitimating private control of the new technology were the steady stream of public statements that Amos Kendall issued between

1845 and 1847. In these statements, Kendall enunciated the rules and regulations of Morse's Magnetic Telegraph Company and defended the patentees' right to a monopoly of Morse's patent. "Of one kind of monopoly I am in favor," Kendall declared in the Washington *Union* in September 1847, "a monopoly of a man's own property. . . . Patent rights are as much private property as printing presses." To mollify the press, Kendall promised editors special rates for the circulation of news—a promise that Kendall's own long tenure as a newspaper editor rendered especially credible. And to win over merchants, Kendall stressed that his company would guarantee equal access for anyone who could afford the regular fees, and dismiss any employee who manipulated its wires to promote a purely private speculation. To fault the new technology for encouraging insider trading, Kendall believed, was particularly unfair. Prior to the advent of the electric telegraph, Kendall reminded his critics, merchants had long maintained an optical telegraph between New York and Philadelphia for the benefit of *"speculators exclusively"*—and no one had complained. It would be impossible, Kendall added, to devise a set of administrative procedures that would preclude the possibility of speculative abuse. Still, the rules his company had devised would "place all men on equality, in the use of the telegraph"—even though, of course, they could not "make them equal in the sagacity, industry, and enterprise, which enables them to use it profitably to themselves."

Beginning in the summer of 1846, criticisms of federal control began to find their way into the press. Led by *Niles's National Register* and the *Albany Evening Journal,* a small but influential number of journals raised questions about the effectiveness of public administration of the new technology and warned against the political dangers that might accompany federal control. Private enterprise, they agreed, had thus far worked remarkably well. Just as competition had brought about major reforms in mail delivery, editorialized Jeremiah Hughes of *Niles,* so, too, it would spur technical innovation in telegraphy. The commercialization of the new technology by the federal government was likely to prove very costly, warned the *Evening Journal,* and was in any event too complicated for public administrators to coordinate. Furthermore, unless Congress enacted laws as arbitrary as the laws prohibiting private competition in mail delivery, Morse's patent would in all likelihood be quickly superseded, and "individual enterprise" would drive the government into bankruptcy. If any business could be safely left in the hands of the people, predicted the editor of the New York *Evening Mirror*—in articulating the emerging consensus—it was telegraphy: "It is free to all who choose to pay for the use of it, and thus far has been managed with admirable skill and discretion." The case for federal control received a further blow when, shortly thereafter, several state legislatures, led by New York, passed laws to curb the most serious forms of potential abuse. . . .

During the 1840s, large numbers of Americans participated in a broad-ranging discussion of national communications policy, the first such discussion in American history. Political engagement was high and the command of the issues impressive. Though the privatization of the postal system had influential champions, in the end, Congress buttressed the existing regulatory regime. Indeed, in 1851 Congress went so far as to authorize improvements in the level of mail delivery that were independent of their possible impact on postal finance. In an age in which historians have often dismissed governmental institutions as agents of change, here was one policy decision that dramatically broadened the mandate of the federal government.

In telegraphy, in contrast, deregulation prevailed. Notwithstanding the explicit preference of Morse and the misgivings of a leading segment of the press, legislators declined to establish a regulatory regime that was in any way comparable to the regulatory regime that had long existed in mail delivery. Even in telegraphy, however, deregulation had its limits. The industry remained constrained not only by a congeries of state regulations but also by federal court rulings on patent rights, contracts, and eminent domain. Following the Civil War, reformers would once again agitate for federal control, catalyzing a popular movement for "postal telegraphy" that, in the early twentieth century, would shape the regulatory regime in the telephone industry.

The enactment of legislation to promote the public welfare is central to what the founders of the American republic meant by political republicanism and is among the most important of the legacies of the American Revolution. Not until the 1840s would a younger generation move beyond the founders and decisively challenge this shared consensus. For various reasons, these reformers rejected political republicanism and embraced the noninterventionist economic credo that has come to be known as economic liberalism. In transportation, banking, and telegraphy, federal regulation was almost ritualistically disparaged. For the first time in American history, it became common to characterize as private even those enterprises that were the most heavily dependent on the public largesse—such as, for example, the land-grant railroads in the trans-Mississippi West. In the process, the now-familiar idealization of private enterprise emerged. It was a genuinely new idea, an invented tradition popularized by critics of governmental expansion as a reaction to, and critique of, the prior expansion of the early American state. In mail delivery, in contrast, a regulatory regime that dated back to the 1790s retained enough popular support to endure. Postal deregulation was not without its defenders; yet, in the end, this was one market revolution that failed.

 ## FURTHER READING

Appleby, Joyce. *Capitalism and a New Social Order: The Republican Vision of the 1790s* (1984).
Chernow, Ron. *Alexander Hamilton* (2004).
Cochran, Thomas C. *Frontiers of Change: Early Industrialism in America* (1981).
Hall, Kermit L., ed. *The Oxford Guide to United States Supreme Court Decisions* (1999).
Hammond, Bray. *Banks and Politics in America from the Revolution to the Civil War* (1957).
Horwitz, Morton J. *The Transformation of American Law, 1780–1860* (1992).
John, Richard R. *Spreading the News: The American Postal System from Franklin to Morse* (1995).
Kutler, Stanley, Jr. *Privilege and Creative Destruction, the Charles River Bridge Case* (1971).
Lamoreaux, Naomi R. *Insider Lending: Banks, Personal Connections, and Economic Development in Industrial New England* (1994).
———, and Christopher Glaisek. "Vehicles of Privilege or Mobility? Banks in Providence, Rhode Island, during the Age of Jackson." *Business History Review* 65 (Autumn 1991): 502–527.

Larson, John Lauritz. *Internal Improvement: National Public Works and the Promise of Popular Government in the United States* (2001).

Maier, Pauline B. "The Revolutionary Origins of the American Corporation." *William and Mary Quarterly*, 3d ser., 50 (January 1993): 51–84.

Perkins, Edwin J. *American Public Finance and Financial Services, 1700–1815* (1994).

Peskin, Lawrence A. *Manufacturing Revolution: The Intellectual Origins of Early American Industry* (2003).

Rock, Howard B. *Artisans of the New Republic: The Tradesmen of New York City in the Age of Jefferson* (1979).

———, et al., eds. *American Artisans: Crafting Social Identity, 1750–1850* (1995).

Schweikart, Larry. *Banking in the American South from the Age of Jackson to Reconstruction* (1987).

———. "Jacksonian Ideology, Currency Control, and 'Central' Banking: A Reappraisal." *Historian* (November 1988): 78–102.

———. "U.S. Commercial Banking: A Historiographical Survey." *Business History Review* 65 (Autumn 1991): 606–661.

Sellers, Charles. *The Market Revolution: Jacksonian America, 1815–1846* (1991).

Stott, Richard B. "Artisans and Capitalist Development." *Journal of the Early Republic* 16 (1996): 257–271.

Sylla, Richard. "U.S. Securities Markets and the Banking System, 1790–1840." *Federal Reserve Bank of St. Louis* 80, no. 3 (May/June 1998): 83–98.

———, et al. "Banks and State Public Finance in the New Republic: The United States, 1790–1860." *Journal of Economic History* 47 (June 1987): 391–403.

Wright, Robert E. *Hamilton Unbound: Finance and the Creation of the American Republic* (2002).

CHAPTER
5

Doing Business in the Slave South, 1800–1860

In the early nineteenth century, while the North veered toward a diversified industrial economy, the South remained steadfastly agrarian. Agriculture thrived almost to the exclusion of everything else. Industrialization and international trade created an enormous demand for cotton, so that Southern production increased eightfold between 1820 and 1850 to 2.8 million bales, and nearly doubled to 5.4 million bales in 1859. Cotton became America's most important export, turning the largest Southern planters and merchants into an aristocracy whose agricultural and commercial fortunes rivaled those of the wealthiest Northern elites. Cotton went from the plantations to a series of domestic and foreign ports before finding its way to textile mills in Europe and New England. When James Henry Hammond addressed the U.S. Senate in the 1858 deliberations over Kansas, he reiterated the sentiments of many Southern entrepreneurs: "Cotton is King!"

The antebellum South rested on a tripartite foundation in international trade, state sovereignty, and chattel slavery. By the Civil War, a third of the region's 12 million people were slaves. In South Carolina and Mississippi, they constituted a majority. Some slaves worked as domestic helpers, skilled artisans, and industrial laborers. Most worked as field hands on small farms or midsized plantations, growing cotton as a cash crop alongside grain and livestock. About a million lived on large plantations in the deep South, harvesting cotton under regimented systems. Much like Northern factories, plantations used labor-saving devices and other technologies as they saw fit. Horns, bells, whistles, and clocks regulated the workday, while threshing machines and cotton gins sped up production and increased output. All this was buttressed by the state slave codes, which protected the property rights of slave holders.

As the Cotton South expanded, the sectional divide between North and South deepened. In economics, the debate over the tariff epitomized the chasm that widened as the nation moved toward civil war. After the War of 1812, Southern politicians like John C. Calhoun joined Northern industrialists to support protectionism, for the sake of national unity and American solidarity against the British. Southern economic sentiment shifted in the ensuing decades. When President John Quincy Adams raised import duties in 1828, Southern businessmen cried out against the

"Tariff of Abominations." Calhoun captured the cotton lords' feelings, arguing that the new tariff levied unjust taxes on the South. With the volatile price of cotton in international markets and higher cost of imported goods, the South had been dealt a double blow. When President Andrew Jackson signed the 1832 tariff, which modified rather than reduced the earlier rates, Calhoun led a South Carolinian charge to nullify and secede from the union. Both sides compromised in the tariff of 1833, but the wound was fatal. Southern fire-eaters like William Harper pointed to the bigger picture. The tariff, he wrote, was merely a symptom of the disease: the consolidation of federal power that threatened slavery, the very livelihood of the South.

Historians know that the slave system gave a distinctive tenor to the Old South. Some leading scholars of slavery, including Eugene D. Genovese and Peter Kolchin, contend that the South's reliance on unfree labor created a backward economy, more like feudalism than capitalism. Economic historians, such as Stanley L. Engerman and Robert William Fogel, take a different approach, quantifying data from court and plantation records to examine a range of issues, from agricultural productivity to slave culture. A rising wave of scholarship has made the study of slavery one of the most active areas of American history. This chapter builds on that foundation to consider how entrepreneurs did business and negotiated economic matters in the antebellum South.

 D O C U M E N T S

In Document 1, businessman Alexander Telfair of Savannah, Georgia, writes to the overseer at his Thorn Island Plantation, near Augusta, in June 1832. Telfair provides the new plantation manager with instructions on disciplining slaves, maintaining the grounds, tending to the crops, and more. What does Telfair's detailed letter reveal about the job of running a cotton plantation? About the relationship between planter and overseer? Between overseer and slave?

While the South remained agricultural, some entrepreneurs pressed for economic diversification. William Gregg (1800–1867) counted among the South's prominent proponents of industrialization. In the early 1840s, this South Carolina industrialist and politician visited New England, where he toured mill towns and factory cities such as Lowell, Massachusetts, the subject of Chapter 6. In 1844, Gregg described the trip in the Charleston *Courier*, reprinting his articles in a pamphlet, *Essays on Domestic Industry*. Shortly afterward, he built a model mill village in Graniteville, which manufactured cotton fabrics.

Document 2 presents a chapter from Gregg's *Essays*, explaining how manufacturing would benefit South Carolina's economy. Gregg advocates industry as a new source of Southern wealth, an opportunity for capitalists who might otherwise go west, and a potential employer of poor whites. However, enthusiasm for mill building faded whenever cotton prices soared. How does Gregg make a case for the industrialization of South Carolina? How does the proslavery politician John C. Calhoun, who served as the state's U.S. senator for nearly two decades, figure into Gregg's argument?

Historians sometimes turn to narratives by former slaves to learn about slavery from the "bottom up." Among these first-person accounts, the writings of Frederick Douglass (1817–1895) are remarkable for their clarity of detail and eloquent language.

Born into slavery, Douglass escaped to freedom from Baltimore, where he had learned to read and write as a house servant. In the North, the articulate Douglass became an ardent supporter of the antislavery movement, publishing autobiographies, running an abolitionist newspaper, and lecturing widely on slavery, women's suffrage, and industrial education for blacks.

In his childhood, Douglass had seen the slave trade in action, later making it the subject of a public address in Rochester, New York. Document 3 contains an excerpt from this 1852 lecture. How does Douglass describe the slave trade? How can historians determine the accuracy of this reminiscence?

During the antebellum era, Southern legislatures passed laws designed to support the slave economy. The codes varied from state to state, but the overall objective was consistent. To endure, the slave system depended on the subordination of blacks to white authority. The states stripped slaves of most legal rights. They passed legislation limiting slave mobility and literacy, and voted for regulations that banned slaves from trade and commerce.

Document 4 provides a glimpse of the slave laws in Louisiana. Here, Judge John Perkins addresses a jury in 1853, summarizing race relations in his state under the slave codes. What types of slave laws most helped Louisiana businessmen? How did the laws aim to protect slaves as a type of property?

The next document presents a letter from James C. Davis to his father, William W. Davis, who ran the Gibraltar Forge in western Virginia. James describes his efforts to re-cruit bound laborers from neighboring slave holders during the winter of 1855–1856. Two aspects of James's letter provide insight into business practices.

First, among those hired was Garland (Thompson), a skilled artisan who once belonged to James's great uncle, the iron master William Weaver—the subject of Charles B. Dew's essay in this chapter. We know from Dew's research that the slave Garland and his wife Dicey were sold to Mrs. Mary Dickenson, who was James's maternal grandmother. The Dickenson household hired out Garland in 1856. This complex bit of genealogy sheds light on the family and slave networks that buttressed the Southern economy.

Second, while James was pleased with Garland, he had a hard time with other slaves from the Dickensons. James worried when a hired slave named Elick resisted the transfer to Gibraltar Forge: "There is some difficulty, . . . & I hardly know how to act." How did James handle the situation? What does his response tell us about slave management practices?

The last source is an excerpt from a famous speech by planter-politician James Henry Hammond, delivered to the U.S. Senate during the 1858 debates over the admission of Kansas as a slave state under the Lecompton constitution. The Kansas question had been raging since 1854 when Illinois Senator Stephen A. Douglas intro-duced a bill for organizing the Kansas-Nebraska territories, which provided that slavery would be determined by popular sovereignty. After several bloody years of agitation in Kansas, President James Buchanan pressed for a resolution by submitting the slave state constitution to Congress and recommending admission.

As the Senate debates heated up, Hammond addressed his colleagues with a de-fense of the Southern political economy and the slave system. The passages excerpted here showcase Hammond's ideas about the solidarity and power of the South, which rested on the "harmony of her political and social institutions." What are the key points in Hammond's argument? What is his position on the tariff? How does the Cotton South compare to the Bank of England? How does the "mud-sill of society" fit into the economic picture?

1. A Georgia Planter Instructs His Overseer, 1832

Rules and directions for my Thorn Island Plantation by which my overseers are to govern themselves in the management of it.—ALEXANDER TELFAIR.

(The directions in this book are to be strictly attended to.)

1. The allowance for every grown Negro however old and good for nothing, and every young one that works in the field, is a peck of corn each week, and a pint of salt, and a piece of meat, not exceeding fourteen pounds, per month.

2. No Negro to have more than Fifty lashes inflicted for any offence, no matter how great the crime.

3. The sucking children, and all other small ones who do not work in the field, draw a half allowance of corn and salt.

4. You will give tickets to any of the negroes who apply for them, to go any where about the neighborhood, but do not allow them to go off it without, nor suffer any strange negroes to come on it without a pass.

5. The negres [*sic*] to be tasked when the work allows it. I require a reasonable days work, well done—the task to be regulated by the state of the ground and the strength of the negro.

6. The cotton to be weighed every night and the weights set down in the Cotton Book. The product of each field to be set down separately—as also the produce of the different corn fields.

7. You will keep a regular journal of the business of the plantation, setting down the names of the sick; the beginning, progress, and finishing of work; the state of the weather; Births, Deaths, and every thing of importance that takes place on the Plantation.

8. You are responsible for the conduct of all persons who visit you. All others found on the premises who have no business, you will take means to run off.

9. Feed every thing plentifully, but waste nothing.

10. The shade trees in the present clearings are not to be touched; and in taking in new ground, leave a thriving young oak or Hickory Tree to every Five Acres.

11. When picking out cotton, do not allow the hands to pull the Boles off the Stalk.

12. All visiting between this place and the one in Georgia is forbidden, except with Tickets from the respective overseers, and that but very seldom. There are none who have husbands or wives over there, and no connexions of the kind are to be allowed to be formed.

13. No night-meeting and preaching to be allowed on the place, except on Saturday night & Sunday morn.

14. Elsey is allowed to act as midwife, to black and white in the neighborhood, who send for her. One of her daughters to stay with the children and take charge

Alexander Telfair, Instructions to the overseer at Thorn Island Plantation, June 11, 1832, in John R. Commons et al., eds., *A Documentary History of American Industrial Society,* vol. 1: *Plantation and Frontier* (Cleveland, Ohio: Arthur H. Clark Company, 1910), pp. 126–129.

of her business until she returns. She draws a peck of corn a week to feed my poultry with.

15. All the Land which is not planted, you will break up in the month of September. Plough it deep so as to turn in all the grass and weeds which it may be covered with.

16. If there is any fighting on the Plantation, whip all engaged in it—for no matter what the cause may have been, all are in the wrong.

17. Elsey is the Doctoress of the Plantation. In case of extraordinary illness, when she thinks she can do no more for the sick, you will employ a Physician.

18. My Cotton is packed in Four & a half yard Bags, weighing each 300 pounds, and the rise of it.

19. Neither the Cotton nor Corn stalks to be burnt, but threshed and chopped down in every field on the plantation, and suffered to lie until ploughed in in the course of working the land.

20. Billy to do the Blacksmith work.

20. [*sic*] The trash and stuff about the settlement to be gathered in heaps, in broken, wet days to rot; in a word make manure of every thing you can.

21. A Turnip Patch to be planted every year for the use of the Plantation.

22. The Negroes measures for Shoes to be sent down with the name written on each, by my Raft hands, or any other certain conveyance, to me, early in October. All draw shoes, except the children, and those that nurse them.

23. Write me the last day of every month to Savannah, unless otherwise directed. When writing have the Journal before you, and set down in the Letter every thing that has been done, or occurred on the Plantation during the month.

24. Pease to be planted in all the Corn, and plenty sowed for seed.

25. When Picking Cotton in the Hammock and Hickory Ridge, weigh the Tasks in the field, and hawl the Cotton home in the Wagon.

26. The first picking of Cotton to be depended on for seed. Seed sufficient to plant two Crops to be saved, and what is left, not to be thrown out of the Gin House, until you clean it out before beginning to pick out the new Crop.

27. A Beef to be killed for the negroes in July, August and September. The hides to be tanned at home if you understand it, or put out to be tanned on shares.

28. A Lot to be planted in Rye in September, and seed saved every year. The Cow pens to be moved every month to tread the ground for this purpose.

29. When a Beef is killed, the Fifth quarter except the hide to be given to Elsey for the children.

30. Give the negroes nails when building or repairing their houses when you think they need them.

31. My Negroes are not allowed to plant Cotton for themselves. Every thing else they may plant, and you will give them tickets to sell what they make.

32. I have no Driver. You are to task the negroes yourself, and each negro is responsible to you for his own work, and nobodys else.

33. The Cotton Bags to be marked A. T. and numbered.

34. I leave my Plantation Shot Gun with you.

35. The Corn and Cotton stalks to be cut, and threshed down on the land which lies out to rest, the same as if it was to be planted.

2. A Carolina Industrialist Explains Why Factories Are Good for the South, 1845

We want no laws for the protection of those that embark in the manufacture, of such cotton fabrics, as we propose to make in South-Carolina; nor does it follow, as a matter of course, that because we advocate a system which will diversify the pursuits of our people, and enable them to export a portion of one of our valuable staples, in a manufactured state, that we wish manufactures to predominate over other employments. All must admit that, to a certain extent, the system we advocate could not operate otherwise than to produce beneficial results, by regulating prices—by insuring a certain reward to labor—a profitable income to capital, and by infusing health, vigor and durability into every department of industry. It is a well established fact, that capital employed in this State, in the culture of cotton, does not, with ordinary management, yield more than 3 or 4, and in some instances, 2 per cent.; this being the only mode of employing our capital, except in the culture of rice, how can we expect to retain men of *capital* and *enterprise* among us? Those having the first, must be wholly wanting in the last—or they must possess an extraordinary attachment to the land of their nativity, to remain with us under such a state of affairs.

With this fact before us, is it surprising that South-Carolina should remain stationary in population? And let it be remembered that the same cause which has produced this result, will continue to operate hurtfully, in the same ratio, as the price of our great staple declines. In all probability, an additional outlet will soon be opened to drain us of our people and our capital. How much this is to take from us, remains to be seen. Unless we betake ourselves to some more profitable employment than the planting of cotton, what is to prevent our most enterprising planters from moving, with their negro capital, to the South-West? What is to keep our business men and moneyed capital in South-Carolina? Capital will find its way to places that afford the greatest remuneration, and in leaving our State, it will carry with it, its enterprising owner. These are truly unpleasant reflections, but they force themselves upon us. Who can look forward to the future destiny of our State, persisting, as she does, with such pertinacity, in the exclusive and exhausting system of agriculture, without dark forebodings[?] If we listen much longer to the *ultras* in agriculture and *croakers* against mechanical enterprise, it is feared that they will be the only class left, to stir up the indolent sleepers that are indisposed to action, and that are willing to let each day provide for itself.

Since the discovery that cotton would mature in South-Carolina, she has reaped a golden harvest; but it is feared it has proved a curse rather than a blessing, and I believe that she would at this day be in a far better condition, had the discovery never been made. Cotton has been to South-Carolina what the Mines of Mexico were to Spain, it has produced us such an abundant supply of all the luxuries and elegancies of life, with so little exertion on our part, that we have become enervated, unfitted for other and more laborious pursuits, and unprepared to meet the state of

---

William Gregg, *Essays on Domestic Industry: or, An Inquiry into the Expediency of Establishing Cotton Manufactures in South Carolina* (Charleston, S.C., 1845). This document can also be found in Michael Brewster Folsom and Steven D. Lubar, eds., *The Philosophy of Manufactures: Early Debates over Industrialization in the United States* (Cambridge, Mass.: MIT Press, 1982), pp. 433–436.

things, which sooner or later must come about. Is it out of place here to predict, that the day is not far distant, yea, is close at hand, when we shall find that we can no longer *live* by that, which has heretofore yielded us, not only a bountiful and sumptuous living, at home, but has furnished the means for carrying thousands and tens of thousands of our citizens abroad, to squander their gold in other countries—that we have wasted the fruits of a rich, virgin soil, in ease and luxury—that those who have practised sufficient industry and economy to accumulate capital, have left, or are leaving us, to populate other States.

We shall indeed soon be awakened to look about us for other pursuits, and we shall find that our soil has to be renovated—our houses and workshops have to be built—our roads and bridges have to be made, all of which ought to have been done with the rich treasures, that have been transferred to other States. Let us begin at once, before it is too late, to bring about a change in our industrial pursuits—let us set about it before the capital and enterprise of our State has entirely left us—let croakers against enterprise be silenced—let the working men of our State who have, by their industry, accumulated capital, turn out and give a practical lesson to our political leaders, that are opposed to this scheme. Even Mr. Calhoun, our great oracle—a statesman whose purity of character we all revere—whose elevation to the highest office in the gift of the people of the United States, would enlist the undivided vote of South-Carolina—even he is against us in this matter; he will tell you, that no mechanical enterprise will succeed in South-Carolina—that good mechanics will go where their talents are better rewarded—that to thrive in cotton spinning, one should go to Rhode Island—that to undertake it here, will not only lead to loss of capital, but disappointment and ruin to those who engage in it.

If we look at this subject in the abstract only, we shall very naturally come to the above conclusions; it is, however, often the case, that practical results contradict the plainest abstract propositions, and it is hoped, that in the course of these remarks, it will be proved to the satisfaction of at least, some of our men of capital and enterprise, that the spinning of cotton may be undertaken with a certainty of success, in the two Carolinas and Georgia, and that the failures which have taken place, ought not to deter others from embarking in the business, they being the result of unpardonable ignorance, and just such management on the part of those interested, as would prove ruinous in any other undertaking.

There are those who understand some things, as well as, if not better, than other people, who have taken the pains to give this subject a thorough investigation, and who could probably give, even Mr. Calhoun, a practical lesson concerning it. The known zeal with which this distinguished gentleman has always engaged in every thing relating to the interest of South-Carolina, forbids the idea that he is not a friend to domestic manufactures, fairly brought about; and, knowing, as he must know, the influence which he exerts, he should be more guarded in expressing opinions adverse to so good a cause.

Those who project new enterprises, have in all ages and countries had much to contend with, and if it were not that we have such immense advantages, in the cheapness of labor and of the raw material, we might despair of success in the manufacture of cotton in South-Carolina. But we must recollect that those who first embarked in this business in Rhode Island, had the prejudice, of the whole country against them. There were croakers then as well as now, and in addition to all the disadvantages we have to contend with, the wide ocean lay between them and the nations skilled in mechanic arts—the laws of England forbade the export of machinery, and affixed heavy penalties to prevent the emigration of artisans, and it was next to impossible to gain access to her manufacturing establishments; so that these men were completely shut out from knowledge. How is with us? We find no difficulty in obtaining the information, which money could not purchase for them, and which cost them years of toil. The New England people are anxious for us to go to spinning cotton, and they are ready and willing to give us all the requisite information. The workshops of England and America are thrown open to us, and he who has the capital at command may, by a visit to England, or to our Northern machine shops, supply himself with the best machinery that the world affords, and also the best machinists, and most skilful manufacturers to work and keep it in order. With all these advantages, what is to prevent the success of a cotton factory in South-Carolina? It may safely be asserted, that failure will be the result of nothing but the grossest mismanagement.

It will be remembered, that the wise men of the day predicted the failure of *steam navigation,* and also of our own rail road; it was said we were deficient in mechanical skill, and that we could not manage the complicated machinery of a steam engine, yet these works have succeeded—we have found men competent to manage them—they grow up amongst us, and we are not only able to keep such machines in order, but to build and fit them to steamboats, mills, locomotive carriages, &c. and the shops engaged in this sort of manufactures, do away with much of the reproach that attaches to our city—they remove many of the obstacles in erecting cotton factories, for they can furnish steam engines, water wheels, shafting, and all the running gear to put machinery in operation.

3. Frederick Douglass Remembers the Slave Trade, 1852

Behold the practical operation of this internal slave trade, the American slave-trade, sustained by American politics and American religion. Here you will see men and women reared like swine for the market. You know what is a swine-drover? I will show you a man-drover. They inhabit all our southern states. They perambulate the country, and crowd the highways of the nation, with droves of human stock. You will see one of these human flesh jobbers, armed with pistol, whip, and bowie-knife, driving a company of a hundred men, women, and children, from the Potomac to the slave market at New Orleans. These wretched people are to be sold singly, or in lots, to suit purchasers. They are food for the cotton-field and the deadly sugar-mill. Mark the sad procession, as it moves wearily along, and the inhuman wretch who drives them. Hear his savage yells and his blood-curdling oaths, as he hurries on his affrighted captives! There, see the old man with locks thinned and gray. Cast

---

Frederick Douglass, "The Meaning of the Fourth of July for the Negro," speech delivered in Rochester, N.Y., July 5, 1852, in Philip S. Foner, ed., *The Life and Writings of Frederick Douglass,* vol. 2 (New York: International Publishers, 1950), pp. 188–195. This document can also be found in Robert Edgar Conrad, *In the Hands of Strangers: Readings on Foreign and Domestic Slave Trading and the Crisis of the Union* (University Park: Pennsylvania State University Press, 2001), pp. 194–196.

one glance, if you please, upon that young mother, whose shoulders are bare to the scorching sun, her briny tears falling on the brow of the babe in her arms. She, too, that girl of thirteen, weeping, *yes!* weeping, as she thinks of the mother from whom she has been torn! The drove moves tardily. Heat and sorrow have nearly consumed their strength; suddenly you hear a quick snap, like the discharge of a rifle; the fetters clank, and the chain rattles simultaneously; your ears are saluted with a scream, that seems to have torn its way to the centre of your soul! The crack you heard was the sound of the slave-whip; the scream you heard was from the woman you saw with the babe. Her speed had faltered under the weight of her child and her chains! that gash on her shoulders tells her to move on. Follow this drove to New Orleans. Attend the auction; see men examined like horses; see the forms of women rudely and brutally exposed to the shocking gaze of American slave-buyers. See this drove sold and separated forever; and never forget the deep, sad sobs that arose from that scattered multitude. Tell me, citizens, where, under the sun, can you witness a spectacle more fiendish and shocking? Yet this is but a glance at the American slave-trade, as it exists, at this moment, in the ruling part of the United States.

I was born amid such sights and scenes. To me the American slave-trade is a terrible reality. When a child, my soul was often pierced with a sense of its horrors. I lived on Philpot Street, Fell's Point, Baltimore, and have watched from the wharves the slave ships in the Basin, anchored from the shore, with their cargoes of human flesh, waiting for favorable winds to waft them down the Chesapeake. There was, at that time, a grand slave mart kept at the head of Pratt Street, by Austin Woldfolk [*sic*]. His agents were sent into every town and county in Maryland, announcing their arrival, through the papers, and on flaming hand-bills, headed "cash for Negroes." These men were generally well dressed men, and very captivating in their manners; ever ready to drink, to treat, and to gamble. The fate of many a slave has depended upon the turn of a single card; and many a child has been snatched from the arms of its mother by bargains arranged in a state of brutal drunkenness.

The flesh-mongers gather up their victims by dozens, and drive them, chained, to the general depot at Baltimore. When a sufficient number have been collected here, a ship is chartered for the purpose of conveying the forlorn crew to Mobile, or to New Orleans. From the slave prison to the ship, they are usually driven in the darkness of night; for since the anti-slavery agitation, a certain caution is observed.

In the deep, still darkness of midnight, I have been often aroused by the dead, heavy footsteps, and the piteous cries of the chained gangs that passed our door. The anguish of my boyish heart was intense; and I was often consoled, when speaking to my mistress in the morning, to hear her say that the custom was very wicked; that she hated to hear the rattle of the chains, and the heart-rending cries. I was glad to find one who sympathized with me in my horror.

Fellow-citizens, this murderous traffic is, to-day, in active operation in this boasted republic. In the solitude of my spirit I see clouds of dust raised on the highways of the south; I see the bleeding footsteps; I hear the doleful wail of fettered humanity on the way to the slave-markets, where the victims are to be sold like *horses, sheep,* and *swine,* knocked off to the highest bidder. There I see the tenderest ties ruthlessly broken, to gratify the lust, caprice, and rapacity of the buyers and sellers of men. My soul sickens at the sight.

4. Louisiana's Slave Laws Simplified, 1853

In Louisiana we have a population of 517,839 persons. Of these, 255,416 are whites; 244,786 are slaves, and 17,537 are free negroes. The white and black population are very nearly equal. . . . I find that there are more blacks in proportion to the white population in this than in any other judicial district of the state. This district is composed of the parishes of Tensas, Madison and Carroll. In Tensas there are 900 white persons and 8,138 blacks, that is, about nine blacks to one white person. In Madison the proportion is about six blacks to one white person, and in Carroll nearly three blacks to one white person.

This is a great difference, and it imposes upon grand jurors extreme vigilance in seeing that the laws of the police of the parish are properly enforced. . . . We have been born into existing institutions, and assumed with the other obligations those resulting from the existence of slavery in our midst. We must discharge them. . . .

. . . There has been so much unjust abuse of the slaveholder, and such scandalous misrepresentations of the laws of Louisiana with reference to the treatment of slaves, that I can understand how difficult it is for you, as grand jurors, to preserve such feelings of indifference in the midst of denunciation, as to enforce the statutes of our State for the protection of the negro, with the zeal your natural impulses would prompt. You should recollect, however, in the words of a distinguished judge of South Carolina, (Judge O'Neal,) "that the first law of slavery is that of kindness from the master to his slave," and that it is as much your duty to protect the negro from the evil effects of fanaticism, as from anything else. He is our dependent, and looks to us for protection; and interest and humanity both require that kindness be enforced and inculcated by law. So considerate is the law of Louisiana on this point, that it makes it the duty, not only of every judge and grand juror, but of every private citizen to whose knowledge the ill-treatment comes, to report it at once to the nearest magistrate, whose duty it is to keep himself informed of the treatment of the negroes within his district, and enforce, "by every means in his power," the humane provisions of our law. As this court is given especial jurisdiction in much that concerns the police of this class, and is particularly required to bring to your notice certain statutes, I would remind you of that one affixing a penalty to the introduction into the State, or the subsequent sale, or purchase of a "*Statu Liber,*" or one who is entitled to his freedom after a certain period—or of one who has been convicted of a capital crime, or who has ever been accused of insurrection, or who has resided in any county of any State where there has been an insurrection within two years.

Self-protection requires that this statute be rigorously enforced. It was passed at a time when public attention was alarmingly directed to the subject, and a necessity for it still exists.

The first legislature that met in this State passed a law, that negroes should be well fed and clothed, comfortably housed, taken care of in sickness, ("with temporal and spiritual care;") supported in their old age; not brutally punished, nor cut nor mutilated, nor sold away from their children when no longer able to work; nor a mother separated from her child under ten years of age; that they should have their

---

[John Perkins], "Relation of Master and Slave in Louisiana and the South," *De Bow's Review* 15, no. 3 (September 1853): 275–277.

Sundays free or if made to work on that day, be paid for their labor. Nearly half a century has passed, and these provisions are still the law of Louisiana. They have been sanctioned by decisions of our Supreme Court, been enforced by juries, and have become so far incorporated into public sentiment, that scarce a greater reproach can be made a citizen than that of cruelty to his slaves. For although our law regards negroes as property, it also deals with them as human beings; and one of the most beautiful decisions of the late Supreme Court (delivered by Judge Preston) declares the slave to be the property of the master for lawful, "not for immoral or inhuman purposes." In the newspapers of this State, so far back as 1806, there are advertisements of the sale of negroes by public authority, because of ill-treatment from their owners.

To make however the humane provisions of our law effective, it is necessary to enforce rigidly those statutes that require a free man to reside permanently as overseer on every plantation; that permits no one to receive articles for sale or deposit from a slave, or to sell to or buy from him anything without the written consent of the master; nor under any pretence whatever to give or sell him liquor. I call your attention to a most stringent law on this subject passed last year.

There are severe penalties in our law against the hiring of a runaway, or the concealing, or aiding to conceal a negro from his master; against the persuading or carrying off a negro, or the aiding or advising another person to carry one off; against any one who shall, by word or action, or in any way whatever, encourage or advise a slave to insurrection against his master or the government; or who shall write or distribute anything tending to discontent among the free colored people, or insubordination among the slaves; or who shall in public, from the bench, the pulpit, or the bar, or in conversation, public or private, use language, signs or actions having this tendency; or shall knowingly be instrumental in bringing into this State any papers, pamphlets, or books, incendiary in their character; or who shall teach, or permit or cause to be taught, any slave in this State to read or write.

5. A Virginia Iron Master Hires
a Slave Workforce, 1856

James C. Davis to William W. Davis.

Seclusion Jan 5th 1856

Dear Father:

Yours of the 2nd Inst came to the P.O. day before yesterday. I answer by John because, he, starting tomorrow, will take it to you Monday which will be as quick as the mail will carry it. It came too late to mail anything with reference to that matter for Bryan started back the day before I received it. Hands are hiring a little higher this year than last; the cause of it is the high price of the produce of farms & the consequent demand for their labor in that direction. I have hired 11, the same as last

James C. Davis to William W. Davis, January 5, 1856, William W. Davis Manuscripts, Alderman Library, University of Virginia, Charlottesville, Va. This document can also be found in Willie Lee Rose, ed., *A Documentary History of Slavery in North America* (New York: Oxford University Press, 1976), pp. 370–372.

year except Jim & Ben; the one besides is a wagoner belonging to old Mr. Nunn near the C[our]t House. I want to get one more. I could not get as many *such* hands as I wanted because there were very few for hire at the Ct House which was the only place I went to—there were plenty of half way hands, but them I did not want. The hiring came off the same days at the Ct House as at Waller's & Mt Pleasant & I, hiring most of last year's hands at the Ct House, went there. It seems that somebody has just put Massie up to the idea of charging extra prices for Bob & Mose on account of their being a wagoner & colier; he asked me $360 for the three & would not put them a cent lower. Dickenson's two Elick & Minor cost me $215; Nester's $190, same as last year; old Mr Nunn's boy $125: he is said to be a first rate wagoner, & has been driving at B[uena] Vista Furnace for the last 6 or 7 years. Blacksmith John $100; & Garland $75. The old Lady put him at that this year but would not knock off a single cent for last year. I was on my way to Orange Ct. House to hire Blacksmith John when John Jordan told me at L[ouisa?] Ct H[ouse] that he had hired him to go back to us & also asked whether we were going to hire them Nelson again. You can do as you please about it, but I think that if we do not hire more than 12 hands we will need him at home. If you do hire him you ought to get at least $100. Uncle Keefer gets that from B & W. N. Jordan for his boy, William, who is about the same age,—& that too on condition that he shall work in the shop and be taught the trade. I haven't heard anything from or about Coleman. I have'nt [*sic*] been in Spottsylvania at all as I had to be at the Ct House on the days that there was hiring in that county. From what I can hear I think I got my hands cheaper than the most of Iron masters; they gave about $120 for common hands, i.e. hands without any particular vocation, except it be wood chopping.

I hear that old Mr McCormack gave Norrell Trice $150 a piece for 7, and, that the Jordans gave Capt Jim Trice $130 a piece for 12. There is some difficulty about Dickenson's hands & I hardly know how to act. When they came from over the mountains they wished to go back: & under the impression that they still wished so I hired them of Dickenson at the Ct House Tuesday. Shortly after I hired them he came & told me that Elick did not wish to go, that a railroad man had offered him five dollars cash in his hands to go with him & that tickled his fancy, but says "I believe he will get over that & be willing to go with you & if he doesn't I will not ask him any odds but send them on" and the subject dropped. But yesterday I re-cieved [*sic*] a letter from him saying that his boys had come to him & avowed they would not go, & if they did go they would run off after they got there. Now I believe that this is nothing but an empty threat for the purpose of scaring their master & that it only requires decisive measures to bring them straight. But even if they were in earnest they would be apt to run before they got there & not after they crossed the blue [*sic*] Ridge, for they know that they dont understand the country well enough to start when so far from home. Should they do this they will come down in Dicken-son's neighborhood & he will be perfectly willing to take them back & so no harm will result in that case. But should they on the other hand run off after they get there, which I dont believe they will do, they, not being used to the country, nor skilled in the wiles of running away, will be taken before they get far. All this is on the hypothesis that Elick goes with them. If he is cooled down & kept in Jail until I choose to let him off & the others sent on I dont apprehend any difficulty whatever: because he is the ringleader and has persuaded the other's [*sic*] (I mean Hester's too for I have no doubt but he has infected them too) who are willing to go back up to last Monday when I saw them at the Ct House. Should I let these hands off it is now too late to get others in their places, for the hands through the country are hired: else I would not care so much to let them off. Moreover I got them cheaper than I could get hands again even if I could find any for hire. In consideration of all these things I wrote to Mr Dickinson by this morning's mail that I could not let them off, but for him to take them to the Ct House Monday morning, put Elick in Jail before the eyes of the others without saying a word as to the meaning of it, then take the others & send them on the cars for Staunton with a pass to Gibralter: and after they are gone to take Elick out of Jail & hire him out there at the Ct House by the day, letting on to him that he [Dickinson] will hire him where he wishes to go when he finds a place which he might do if I found I could make it suit to let him off; if not, I would take him over when I went. I think this plan will work. The boys, if he sends them Monday as I wrote to him to do, ought to get there Tuesday night & will get there (at the farthest) [in] time enough on wednesday for you to write me by that day's mail, which do & if they have not come give me your views: or, if they have, tell me what you think about keeping Elick if I cannot get another hand.

This negro's perversity is but another instance of the [assimilation?] of the negro to the dog. In order to make a dog like and follow you you must whip him occasionally & be sparing of favors, or he will turn at last & bite the hand that feeds him. So with this boy. Of all those five negroes he was the only one that escaped the lash: & frequently recieved [*sic*] favors that I would have denied the others. Now he not only turns from me, but tries to lead them away likewise. I have not been able to come across an old man for hire yet. I think it would be best to employ Wright even if you have to pay him 37½ cts cash for every cord; but you can get him for less cash than that, for when I saw him at the Forge that day he only asked half money at 37½ cts & the rest trade at 40 cts. I believe that will [be?] equally as cheap if not cheaper than black labor. We are all well down here; but the weather is mighty bad. There has been a sleet on the ground for more than a week, & it is now snowing very fast & has been ever since day[light] this morning—the snow is now about a foot deep. My love to all. Your affectionate Son

Jas C Davis

6. Senator James Henry Hammond Declares "Cotton Is King," 1858

If we never acquire another foot of territory for the South, look at her. Eight hundred and fifty thousand square miles. As large as Great Britain, France, Austria, Prussia, and Spain. Is not that territory enough to make an empire that shall rule the world? With the finest soil, the most delightful climate, whose staple productions none of those great countries can grow, we have three thousand miles of continental shore line, so indented with bays and crowded with islands, that, when their shore lines are added, we have twelve thousand miles. Through the heart of our country

James Henry Hammond, Speech on the Kansas-Lecompton Constitution, U.S. Senate, March 4, 1858. In *Congressional Globe,* 35th Cong., 1st sess., Appendix, pp. 70–71.

runs the great Mississippi, the father of waters, into whose bosom are poured thirty-six thousand miles of tributary streams; and beyond we have the desert prairie wastes, to protect us in our rear. Can you hem in such a territory as that? You talk of putting up a wall of fire around eight hundred and fifty thousand square miles so situated! How absurd.

But in this Territory lies the great valley of the Mississippi, now the real, and soon to be the acknowledged seat of the empire of the world. The sway of that valley will be as great as ever the Nile knew in the earlier ages of mankind. We own the most of it. The most valuable part of it belongs to us now; and although those who have settled above us are now opposed to us, another generation will tell a different tale. They are ours by all the laws of nature; slave labor will go over every foot of this great valley where it will be found profitable to use it, and some of those who may not use it are soon to be united with us by such ties as will make us one and insepa-rable. The iron horse will soon be clattering over the sunny plains of the South to bear the products of its upper tributaries to our Atlantic ports, as it now does through the ice-bound North. There is the great Mississippi, a bond of union made by Nature herself. She will maintain it forever.

On this fine territory we have a population four times as large as that with which these colonies separated from the mother country, and a hundred, I might say a thousand fold, stronger. Our population is now sixty per cent. greater than that of the whole United States when we entered into the second war of independence. It is as large as the whole population of the United States was ten years after the con-clusion of that war, and our exports are three times as great as those of the whole United States then. Upon our muster-rolls we have a million of militia. In a defen-sive war, upon an emergency, every one of them would be available. At any time, the South can raise, equip, and maintain in the field, a larger army than any Power of the earth can send against her, and an army of soldiers—men brought up on horse-back, with guns in their hands.

If we take the North, even when the two large States of Kansas and Minnesota shall be admitted, her territory will be one hundred thousand square miles less than ours. I do not speak of California and Oregon; there is no antagonism between the South and those countries, and never will be. The population of the North is fifty per cent. greater than ours. I have nothing to say in disparagement either of the soil of the North, or the people of the North, who are a brave and an energetic race, full of intellect, but they produce no great staple that the South does not produce; while we produce two or three, and those the very greatest, that she can never produce. As to her men, I may be allowed to say they have never proved themselves to be superior to those of the South, either in the field or in the Senate.

But the strength of a nation depends in a great measure upon its wealth; and the wealth of a nation, like that of a man, is to be estimated by its surplus production. You may go to your trashy census books, full of falsehood and nonsense. They will tell you, for example, that in the State of Tennessee, the whole number of house-servants is not equal to that of those in my own house, and such things as that. You may estimate what is made throughout the country from these census books, but it is no matter how much is made if it is all consumed. If a man possess millions of dollars and consume his income, is he rich? Is he competent to embark in any new enter-prise? Can he build ships or railroads? And could a people in that condition build ships and roads, or go to war? All the enterprises of peace and war depend upon the surplus productions of a people. They may be happy, they may be comfortable, they may enjoy themselves in consuming what they make; but they are not rich, they are not strong. It appears, by going to the reports of the Secretary of the Treasury, which are authentic, that last year the United States exported in round numbers $279,000,000 worth of domestic produce, excluding gold and foreign merchandise reëxported. Of this amount $158,000,000 worth is the clear produce of the South; articles that are not and cannot be made at the North. There are then $80,000,000 worth of exports of products of the forest, provisions, and breadstuffs. If we assume that the South made but one third of these, and I think that is a low calculation, our exports were $185,000,000, leaving to the North less than $95,000,000.

In addition to this, we sent to the North $30,000,000 worth of cotton, which is not counted in the exports. We sent to her seven or eight million dollars' worth of tobacco, which is not counted in the exports. We sent naval stores, lumber, rice, and many other minor articles. There is no doubt that we sent to the North $40,000,000 in addition; but suppose the amount to be $35,000,000; it will give us a surplus production of $220,000,000. The *recorded* exports of the South now are greater than the whole exports of the United States in any year before 1856. They are greater than the whole average exports of the United States for the last twelve years, including the two extraordinary years of 1856 and 1857. They are nearly double the amount of the average exports of the twelve preceding years. If I am right in my calculations as to $220,000,000 of surplus produce, there is not a nation on the face of the earth, with any numerous population, that can compete with us in produce *per capita*. It amounts to $16 66 per head, supposing that we have twelve million people. England, with all her accumulated wealth, with her concentrated and educated energy, makes under $16 50 of surplus production per head.

I have not made a calculation as to the North, with her $95,000,000 surplus. Admitting that she exports as much as we do, with her eighteen millions of population it would be but little over twelve dollars a head. But she cannot export to us and abroad exceeding ten dollars a head against our sixteen dollars. I know well enough that the North sends to the South a vast amount of the productions of her industry. I take it for granted that she, at least, pays us in that way for the thirty or forty million dollars' worth of cotton and other articles we send her. I am willing to admit that she pays us considerably more; but to bring her up to our amount of surplus production, to bring her up to $220,000,000, a year, the South must take from her $125,000,000; and this, in addition to our share of the consumption of the $333,000,000 worth introduced into the country from abroad, and paid for chiefly by our own exports. The thing is absurd; it is impossible; it can never appear anywhere but in a book of statistics.

With an export of $220,000,000 under the present tariff, the South organized separately would have $40,000,000 of revenue. With one fourth the present tariff she would have a revenue adequate to all her wants, for the South would never go to war; she would never need an army or a navy, beyond a few garrisons on the frontiers and a few revenue cutters. It is commerce that breeds war. It is manufactures that require to be hawked about the world, and give rise to navies and commerce. But we have nothing to do but to take off restrictions on foreign merchandise and open our ports, and the whole world will come to us to trade. They will be too glad to bring and carry for us, and we never shall dream of a war. Why the South has never yet had a just cause of war. Every time she has drawn her sword it has been on the point of honor, and that point of honor has been mainly loyalty to her sister colonies and sister States, who have ever since plundered and calumniated her.

But if there were no other reason why we should never have war, would any sane nation make war on cotton? Without firing a gun, without drawing a sword, should they make war on us we can bring the whole world to our feet. The South is perfectly competent to go on, one, two, or three years without planting a seed of cotton. I believe that if she was to plant but half her cotton for three years to come, it would be an immense advantage to her. I am not so sure but that after three total years' abstinence she would come out stronger than ever she was before and better prepared to enter afresh upon her great career of enterprise. What would happen if no cotton was furnished for three years? I will not stop to depict what every one can imagine, but this is certain: England would topple headlong and carry the whole civilized world with her, save the South. No, you dare not make war on cotton. No power on earth dares to make war upon it. Cotton *is* king. Until lately the Bank of England was king, but she tried to put her screws as usual, the fall before last, upon the cotton crop, and was utterly vanquished. The last power has been conquered. Who can doubt, that has looked at recent events, that cotton is supreme? When the abuse of credit had destroyed credit and annihilated confidence, when thousands of the strongest commercial houses in the world were coming down, and hundreds of millions of dollars of supposed property evaporating in thin air, when you came to a dead lock, and revolutions were threatened, what brought you up? Fortunately for you it was the commencement of the cotton season, and we have poured in upon you one million six hundred thousand bales of cotton just at the crisis to save you from destruction. That cotton, but for the bursting of your speculative bubbles in the North, which produced the whole of this convulsion, would have brought us $100,000,000. We have sold it for $65,000,000, and saved you. Thirty-five million dollars we, the slaveholders of the South, have put into the charity-box for your magnificent financiers, your cotton lords, your merchant princes.

But, sir, the greatest strength of the South arises from the harmony of her political and social institutions. This harmony gives her a frame of society, the best in the world, and an extent of political freedom, combined with entire security, such as no other people ever enjoyed upon the face of the earth. Society precedes government; creates it, and ought to control it; but as far as we can look back in historic times we find the case different; for government is no sooner created than it becomes too strong for society, and shapes and molds, as well as controls it. In later centuries the progress of civilization and of intelligence has made the divergence so great as to produce civil wars and revolutions; and it is nothing now but the want of harmony between governments and societies which occasions all the uneasiness and trouble and terror that we see abroad. It was this that brought on the American Revolution. We threw off a Government not adapted to our social system, and made one for ourselves. The question is, how far have we succeeded? The South, so far as that is concerned, is satisfied, harmonious, and prosperous.

In all social systems there must be a class to do the menial duties, to perform the drudgery of life. That is, a class requiring but a low order of intellect and but little skill. Its requisites are vigor, docility, fidelity. Such a class you must have, or you would not have that other class which leads progress, civilization, and refinement. It constitutes the very mud-sill of society and of political government; and you might as well attempt to build a house in the air, as to build either the one or the other, except on this mud-sill. Fortunately for the South, she found a race adapted to that purpose to her hand—a race inferior to her own, but eminently qualified in temper, in vigor, in docility, in capacity to stand the climate, to answer all her purposes. We use them for our purpose, and call them slaves. We found them slaves by the "common consent of mankind," which, according to Cicero, "*lex naturæ est;*" the highest proof of what is Nature's law. We are old-fashioned at the South yet; it is a word discarded now by "ears polite." I will not characterize that class at the North by that term; but you have it; it is there; it is everywhere; it is eternal.

The Senator from New York said yesterday that the whole world had abolished slavery. Ay, the *name,* but not the *thing;* all the powers of the earth cannot abolish it. God only can do it when he repeals the *fiat,* "the poor ye always have with you;" for the man who lives by daily labor, and scarcely lives at that, and who has to put out his labor in the market and take the best he can get for it; in short, your whole hireling class of manual laborers and "operatives," as you call them, are essentially slaves. The difference between us is, that our slaves are hired for life and well compensated; there is no starvation, no begging, no want of employment among our people, and not too much employment either. Yours are hired by the day, not cared for, and scantily compensated, which may be proved in the most painful manner, at any hour, in any street in any of your large towns. Why, you meet more beggars in one day, in any single street of the city of New York, than you would meet in a lifetime in the whole South. We do not think that whites should be slaves, either by law or necessity. Our slaves are black, of another and inferior race. The *status* in which we have placed them is an elevation. They are elevated from the condition in which God first created them, by being made our slaves. None of that race on the whole face of the globe can be compared with the slaves of the South. They are happy, content, unaspiring, and utterly incapable, from intellectual weakness, ever to give us any trouble by their aspirations. Yours are white, of your own race; you are brothers of one blood. They are your equals in natural endowment of intellect, and they feel galled by their degradation. Our slaves do not vote. We give them no political power. Yours do vote; and being the majority, they are the depositaries of all your political power. If they knew the tremendous secret, that the ballot-box is stronger than "an army with banners," and could combine, where would you be? Your society would be reconstructed, your government overthrown, your property divided, not as they have mistakenly attempted to initiate such proceedings by meeting in parks, with arms in their hands, but by the quiet process of the ballot-box. You have been making war upon us to our very hearth-stones. How would you like for us to send lecturers and agitators North, to teach these people this, to aid in combining, and to lead them? . . .

You say, send them along. There is no need of that. Your people are awaking. They are coming here. They are thundering at our doors for homesteads, one hundred and sixty acres of land for nothing, and southern Senators are supporting them. Nay, they are assembling, as I have said, with arms in their hands, and demanding work at $1,000 a year for six hours a day. Have you heard that the ghosts of Mendoza and Torquemada are stalking in the streets of your great cities; that the inquisition is at hand? There is afloat a fearful rumor that there have been consultations for vigilance committees. You know what that means.

Transient and temporary causes have thus far been your preservation. The great West has been open to your surplus population, and your hordes of semi-barbarian immigrants, who are crowding in year by year. They make a great movement, and you call it progress. Whither? It is progress; but it is progress towards vigilance committees. The South have sustained you in a great measure. You are our factors. You bring and carry for us. One hundred and fifty million dollars of our money passes annually through your hands. Much of it sticks; all of it assists to keep your machinery together and in motion. Suppose we were to discharge you; suppose we were to take our business out of your hands: we should consign you to anarchy and poverty.

You complain of the rule of the South: that has been another cause that has preserved you. We have kept the Government conservative to the great purposes of government. We have placed her, and kept her, upon the Constitution; and that has been the cause of your peace and prosperity. The Senator from New York says that that is about to be at an end; that you intend to take the Government from us; that it will pass from our hands. Perhaps what he says is true; it may be; but do not forget—it can never be forgotten; it is written on the brightest page of human history—that we, the slaveholders of the South, took our country in her infancy; and, after ruling her for sixty out of the seventy years of her existence, we shall surrender her to you without a stain upon her honor, boundless in prosperity, incalculable in her strength, the wonder and the admiration of the world. Time will show what you will make of her; but no time can ever diminish our glory or your responsibility.

E S S A Y S

In the first essay, Walter Johnson, associate professor of history at New York University and author of *Soul by Soul: Life Inside the Antebellum Slave Market* (1999), looks at the New Orleans slave market in the 1840s and 1850s. As the South's largest city, New Orleans attracted traders, brokers, and planters from all directions. During the antebellum era, its auction blocks sold some 100,000 men, women, and children. Johnson surveys the network of businesses, from the slave pens and auction houses to the hotels and saloons, that supported the city's trade in human beings. What does Johnson's essay tell us about Southern entrepreneurs?

Next, Charles B. Dew, the Ephraim Williams Professor of American History at Williams College and author of *Bond of Iron: Master and Slave at Buffalo Forge* (1994), examines industrial slavery on the eve of the Civil War. In his case study, Dew focuses on William Weaver, the master of two iron-making facilities in Virginia's Shenandoah Valley: Buffalo Forge and Etna Furnace. At Buffalo Forge, Weaver engaged nearly seventy slaves. Many worked in highly skilled jobs, having apprenticed alongside other family members at Weaver's forges. How would you characterize the relationship between Weaver and his slaves? What role did the "overwork" system play in furnace management? How did Weaver's experience with his slaves differ from that of his grand nephew, James C. Davis, described in Document 5?

Finally, Drew Gilpin Faust, dean of the Radcliffe Institute and the Lincoln Professor of History at Harvard University, probes the business operations of James Henry Hammond, a prominent South Carolina planter, outspoken advocate for slavery, and

U.S. senator. Faust sees Hammond as arrogant, self-centered, and greedy, while present-ing a sophisticated portrait of him as a paternalistic slaveholder. How do Hammond's business practices compare with Weaver's? As you read Faust's sketch in tandem with Document 6, consider what factors shaped Hammond's views on slavery and the Southern political economy.

The Slave Traders of New Orleans

WALTER JOHNSON

The seasonality of the slave trade was tied to the cycles of the larger agricultural economy. In the upper South, exportation had to wait until after harvest, because hands were needed in the summer and fall to tend the crops; in the lower South, buying was delayed until after harvest because that was when buyers had money available to pay for slaves. The rhythm of the trade marks its centrality to the econ-omy of slavery; the historic role of the slave trade in binding the diverging fortunes of the upper and lower South into mutual interest was yearly recapitulated in the seasonal cycle of interregional trade. In New Orleans, at least, there was an even deeper seasonality to trade of all kinds. Less of everything was done there in the summertime, when the stifling heat turned the air pestilent and those who could afford to do so left town to avoid malaria.

After the traders had gathered their slaves, they started them south. The traders' coffles, lined out along rural roads or packed onto the decks of ships, were part of the landscape of the antebellum South, especially in the late summer and early fall. . . .

Like those who traveled on foot, slaves shipped through the trade seemed re-markable to onlookers—real-life manifestations of an aspect of slavery they had heard about but not seen. When Samuel Page discovered that a trader with about twenty slaves was aboard the schooner *Orleans,* for example, he immediately went to look at them. As he later explained, he did so out of "curiosity": "he had never been in the South and he had never seen a drove of Negroes for sale."

The duration of the journey south depended upon the route and means of trans-port. The inland journey could take as long as seven or eight weeks on foot, with the slaves covering about twenty miles a day; shipboard around the coast from Norfolk to New Orleans the trip required only about three weeks; and down the Mississippi from St. Louis, it might only take a few days by the 1850s. Some inter-state traders traveled south with the slaves they sold; some hired employees to make the journey; and some simply wrote out a bill of lading and shipped the slaves as they would any other commodity. Though their business was centered in large urban markets like New Orleans, the large interstate traders made occasional journeys to outlying markets—Donaldsonville or Cheneyville or Alexandria in Louisiana—where they sold slaves. . . .

Walter Johnson, *Soul by Soul: Life Inside the Antebellum Slave Market* (Cambridge, Mass.: Harvard University Press, 1999), pp. 49–52, 54–57. Copyright © 1999 by the President and Fellows of Harvard College. Reprinted by permission of the publisher.

Large traders . . . superintended slave yards in New Orleans. The City Treasurer's Census of Merchants listed nineteen such yards in 1854. These yards provided room and board for out-of-town traders and their slaves for a fixed daily cost (around twenty-five cents per day per person) and a cut (usually two and a half percent) of the business done in the pens. Many of the slaves in these men's yards were being sold by the traders on behalf of people who would not have considered themselves professional slave traders. Interested sellers often contracted to have their slaves sold out of the pens, and interested buyers often contacted brokers to help them find slaves. When they were recorded by a notary public, these transactions bore only the name of the legal titleholders, seller and buyer, not the broker. It is a crucial omission, and one that has led historians to underestimate the extent of the business done in the pens. John Farmer to Francis Fisk, Louis Shelton to Mary Ann Cornish, Daniel Twogood to David Winn, César Martin to Joaquin Brabo, Antonio Costa to Mrs. Bonhomme Cohn: none of these sales were recorded as if a slave trader was involved, and thus they have been passed over by those who have tried to tabulate the traders' share of the broader market in slaves by counting out the numbers of traders' names on registered Acts of Sale. And yet it became apparent in the trials that emerged from these sales that every one of them had been arranged by a man described in court as a slave dealer or broker—Samuel Hite, Thomas Foster, Robert Wright, Réné Salain, Louis Caretta. What appear on the surface of the commercial record to have been sales between neighbors or acquaintances often turn out to have been professionally brokered sales.

In fact, it sometimes must have seemed as if slave traders were everywhere in antebellum New Orleans. Charles Prince, whose occupation was "buying and selling Negroes and apprehending runaway slaves," for example, had no office but was "every morning" and "most of the day on the Levee." Similarly, during the selling season Samuel Hite boarded in the slave yard owned by New Orleans trader Theophilus Freeman, but he spent his days making connections on the street, pitching the slaves in Freeman's yard to prospective buyers and sending a messenger to the pens to retrieve the slaves when negotiation reached the point of inspection. Hite, however, was more than a middleman for Freeman, for he apparently controlled his own information-gathering network of brokers. It was, for example, D. W. Bowles who initiated one of the sales Hite eventually sealed on the street. Bowles, who described himself as a "hotel keeper, bar keeper, and restaurant keeper who has also acted as a Broker in slaves, and has traded in slaves for his own account," had run into an old friend, discovered the man was in town to sell a slave, and steered him to Hite. For Bowles's trouble, Hite paid him five dollars. Later that night, after Hite had made the sale and pocketed the commission, another broker, Michael Glasgow, confronted Bowles at the bar of the St. Charles Hotel, demanding "why the hell he had not brought the Negro to him," and adding that "he would have given twenty-five dollars Brokerage." Bowles later maintained that he had not known that Glasgow was a slave trader until that moment. He had known the man only as a bar keeper at the Planter's Hotel, where Glasgow had been employed by none other than Samuel Hite.

The tenor of Glasgow's remarks to Bowles suggests that the erstwhile bartender might have been making a play to control the slave-selling network of which he had once been a part. But even if the specific character of the business relation between Hite and Glasgow is unclear (indeed, it was at issue in the courtroom in which Bowles told his story), its geography is revealing. Bowles's testimony outlines a pyramidal network of information gathering and slave selling that stretched from the slave pens through the city's hotels and barrooms—a network in which every bartender was a potential broker and every broker tried to control every bartender. The lively traffic in information and influence that joined the slave traders to the hotels and bars where travelers and traders gathered and discussed their business suggests that the practice of trading slaves far outreached the cluster of pens publicly identified as "the slave market." . . .

In addition to the interstate traders, the local traders, the landlords, the brokers, and the employees, there were auctioneers who made a living selling slaves. State business, such as succession and debt sales, made up the bulk of the auctioneers' work and accounted for most of the slaves they sold. But the auctioneers also sold slaves for the "ordinary" slaveholders so carefully distinguished from the traders by Daniel Hundley, and, in exceptional circumstances, for slave dealers who could not sell their slaves in the pens. In effect, these men were licensed brokers for slaves and other sorts of property. In Louisiana their numbers were limited by state law, and they received a standard commission on the property they sold, one percent for state business and the standard two and a half percent for private business. Their offices—where, in the style of the traders' pens, slaves were available for inspection before a sale—were just south of the uptown slave market. Their auctions, held every Saturday, drew large crowds of onlookers. Beneath the rotundas of the city's luxury hotels, slaves were publicly exposed, cried, and sold along with all manner of other goods—furniture, cotton, livestock, and so on.

The large trading firms were often family businesses, passed from one generation to another, and their principals were men of means: they lived in large houses, attended fine dinner parties, and held public offices. There was apparently little stigma attached to the trade for those who were successful at it (Daniel Hundley's claims notwithstanding). At one point John Hagan was planning a New Orleans suburb that would bear his name; John White was known by one of the honorifics common to the antebellum ruling class, Colonel White; Joseph A. Beard, New Orleans' most prominent auctioneer, was known as Major Beard. Some of these men—Isaac Franklin, for instance—had worked their way to prominence through the trade. The son of a Tennessee long hunter, Franklin parlayed the trade into six Louisiana plantations and six hundred slaves of his own. (On the land of one of his plantations, called then as now Angola, the state of Louisiana later built a prison.) J. W. Boazman's success story was more modest. A one-time slave-pen employee, Boazman eventually got together enough money to trade on his own account. The gains others made out of the trade were more fleeting. Theophilus Freeman, who owned a New Orleans pen in the 1840s, ended his life on the run from the law, having been accused of stealing slaves and defrauding his creditors.

Trying to make their way upwards through the trade, many of the smaller interstate traders spent long periods away from home, sleeping out, traveling over muddy roads, or in close quarters on ships. Interstate trading was associated with young and single men—"until they find wives" was the way that one woman characterized the duration of the traders' careers. Or, as recently married Harriet Jarratt wrote to her slave trader husband, "I am afraid Dear Husband that you and Carson will keep up Negro trading as long as you can get a Negro to trade, and when you can't buy through the Country you will carry off al you can pirade at home, but one good thing Mr. Carson has no wife to leave behind when he is gone." Jarratt's response was to rework his wife's critique of his immediate failings as a husband into evidence of his deeper virtue: "The Negroes at home I never will take from you unless you wish it. So long as you are pleased with them I will try to be and when you wish them sold I will sell them . . . I have no disposition to continue Negro trading and hope to engage in something else by which I can accumulate a little and remain with my family." In closing, Jarratt underlined his incongruous paternalism with the phrase "*Howdy to the Negroes.*" . . .

During the selling season the traders lived with one another. In New Orleans both interstate and local traders boarded at the houses of other traders, sold one another's slaves, served as witnesses for one another's sales, and executors for one another's wills. The company the traders kept was almost exclusively male, as were many of the spaces in which they entertained themselves. The traders usually took their meals in the pens, grouped around a single table, and socialized with one another, some spending their evenings, as ex-slave John Brown remembered of Theophilus Freeman and Thomas McCargo, going to saloons and gambling. The transactions that John White recorded in his day book began each morning in the pens, where he prepared his slaves for sale, settled accounts with other traders, and sold slaves. During the day White ventured out of the pens for "marketing" and to purchase the supplies that he used to prepare his slaves for sale. And at the end of most days there is a notation for "whisky" or "brandy and oisters" or "oister dinner with Mitchell."

Some of the traders established close emotional ties. Before Michael Glasgow disappeared with Theophilus Freeman's money, there was, according to one trader, "great intimacy existing between Glasgow and Samuel Hite." The same phrase was used to describe the relations between William Cotton and Thomas Coot before business between them soured: they were "on terms of great intimacy," one witness remembered. Cotton paid for Coot's clothes and the house where they lived together, and when they were apart, Cotton signed his letters to Coot "your friend until death." When it became clear that Coot had spent the trader's money on liquor and gambling, Cotton apparently tried to salvage a relationship that was both personal and professional. As a witness heard it, he told Coot, "I will give you a thousand dollars, and do you come and spend your days with me, and when I die you shall have what I have got." Cotton wanted to put an end to his personal problems by purchasing his companion—truly a slave trader's solution.

The traders' letters to one another are full of phrases like "the traders tell me" or "the traders say," and if the recountings that follow are any indication, in the time they spent together the men in the slave trade talked mostly about business. There was plenty to talk about: bank loans had to be repaid and the interstate money market considered; the prices of sugar and cotton had to be tracked; debts had to be collected and overhead costs reckoned. The records left behind by the traders are full of predictions, obligations, collections, and daily accounts. They were experts at imagining the economy: interest rates, crop yields, and slave sales interacted in their heads, suggesting the revealed principles of a wider market whose mysterious workings they tried to map and predict. More than anything, the records of traders, like those of John White, are filled with prices given and gained for slaves in the market.

Running Buffalo Forge: Master, Slaves, and the Overwork System

CHARLES B. DEW

By 1860, William Weaver owned sixty-six slaves: twenty-eight adult men, fifteen women, fourteen boys, and nine girls. His core forge crew in that year had all grown to manhood at Buffalo Forge: Sam Williams, master refiner; Henry Towles, refinery underhand; Tooler, Jr., chaffery hammerman; Harry Hunt, Jr., chaffery underhand; and Henry Matthews, forge carpenter. All these men had served their apprenticeship at Buffalo Forge, and often they had trained alongside their own fathers. All belonged to families that had an impressive history of turning out highly skilled artisans.

Assembling a full crew of skilled forgemen and maintaining their number as death and injury thinned the ranks of his original force were formidable challenges for Weaver. These were not, however, the ultimate challenges he faced as a southern ironmaster. Even more imposing was the task of motivating these slaves to work, and work well, at the art—for that is what it was—of ironmaking.

Weaver, of course, had considerable coercive power at his disposal. He could punish any recalcitrant or troublesome slave, but if he had relied on the whip to achieve satisfactory levels of production, his career as a Virginia ironmaker would have been very short-lived indeed. Excessive use of force certainly would have backfired, and a whipping administered to a skilled slave would, at minimum, leave the man sore and incapable of work. It would probably leave him seething with anger as well and looking for ways to get back at the master. Acts of industrial sabotage could be accomplished with relative ease around a forge. . . . The slaves, in short, were in a position to do considerable physical and financial damage to Weaver's interests, even if they limited their activities to passive forms of resistance like work slowdowns or slipshod performance of their duties. Not surprisingly, there is no indication that Weaver ever whipped one of his slave forge workers at any time during his forty years in the Valley.

A far greater threat to the slaves was the possibility of sale. Even skilled slaves who tried to run away or who carried their resistance beyond Weaver's level of toleration could be turned over to slave traders and readily sold. Yet no ironmaster would want to part with a trained slave ironworker. . . . Buying or training an immediate replacement would be difficult, if not impossible, and trying to hire skilled slave forge workers was, as Weaver well knew, both uncertain and expensive. It was far better, from Weaver's point of view, to avoid the use of physical coercion to the fullest extent possible and to turn to a weapon like the sale of a slave only in the most extreme circumstances.

The alternative to force was positive incentive. From his earliest days in Virginia, Weaver paid slaves who did extra work. Weaver's artisans had a daily or weekly task to perform, but he compensated them, either in cash or in goods from his store at Buffalo Forge, for anything they turned out over and above the required amount. Payment for "overwork," as this system was called, was a common practice

---

at slave-manned manufacturing establishments throughout the antebellum South, and it was a feature of the labor regimen at southern ironworks as early as the mid-eighteenth century. The task for slave refiners at Buffalo Forge, and everywhere else in the Valley, was a ton and a half of anchonies per week for a forge worked in the customary fashion—two-handed by a master refiner and his underhand. Chaffery forge hammermen throughout the Virginia iron district were required to draw two "journeys" of 560 pounds of bar per day. For a two-handed forge, again the usual method of operation, this meant a total daily task of 1,120 pounds. Choppers cutting wood for charcoal pits had a task of 1½ cords per day—9 cords for a six-day work-week. All these tasks had been the customary quotas for years in the Valley, and they did not change during the forty years Weaver lived at Buffalo Forge. They were in place when he arrived, they were there when he died, and he never, as far as we know, made any attempt to alter them.

The unchanging nature of these tasks over time suggests that both master and slave regarded them as a traditional standard, and these quotas seem to have been set at levels that an average worker could reach by putting in a day, or week, of steady labor. They were not pegged at an excessively high point for good reason: The whole intent of the task system was to encourage slaves to produce a set amount of output in a given time and then to work beyond that minimum point in order to earn compensation for themselves.

Pay for slave overwork was identical to the pay given free artisans for doing the same job. In the 1830s and 1840s, for example, the rate for refining anchonies with free labor was $8 per ton in Virginia, for drawing bar iron $6 per ton. Thus, a slave master refiner and his helper would start earning overwork, at the rate of $8 per ton, for all the iron they produced after they had met their weekly task of 1½ tons of anchonies. The $8 would be divided between the refiner and his underhand on the basis of the level of skill the helper possessed. The same thing held true for the two slaves working at the chaffery forge. The hammerman and his assistant would split the overwork payment of $6 per ton for any iron they made over and above their combined task of 1,120 pounds of bar per day. . . .

The overwork system was absolutely crucial to the functioning of Weaver's ironmaking enterprise and slave-manned industrial establishments throughout the antebellum South. Weaver's need to both discipline and motivate his slave workers required that a rather delicate balance be worked out between the demands of the master and the wishes of the slave. The words "delicate" and "balance" are not often used to describe any aspect of the slave regime, and the chances for misunderstanding and misinterpretation here are obviously legion. No sane person would deny that the scales were weighted far more heavily on the side of the party that possessed the power to inflict brutal punishment on, or put on the auction block and sell, a recalcitrant worker. But it still seems fair to say that southern ironworks employing slave artisans had to develop a labor system that brought the requirements of both master and slave into some sort of harmony. The long-standing traditions of a reasonable task for each worker and the practice of paying all slaves who exceeded their tasks or performed any sort of extra labor were critical elements in achieving this balance of needs and wills, however rough and inherently unequal it might be.

Entries in the Buffalo Forge "Negro Books," as the overwork ledgers were called, indicate that most of the slave hands, both skilled and unskilled, used the system to earn compensation for themselves. Traditional practice allowed slaves to choose whether they would take payment in cash or in goods from the ironmaster's store. If they chose cash, they could use the money to shop at other country stores, and this seems to have afforded the slaves a measure of protection against price gouging by the local storekeeper. . . .

If the slaves did opt for payment in merchandise, they could draw on their over-work immediately for things like coffee, sugar, tobacco, molasses, cloth, or articles of clothing. The one item conspicuous by its absence in the list of slave purchases was alcohol. Weaver tried, not always successfully, to keep whiskey out of the hands of his slaves. Only on special occasions would he issue a whiskey ration to slaves who had performed difficult work under arduous circumstances, such as cutting ice from the frigid waters of Buffalo Creek or dam building.

Admittedly, in the process of earning overwork compensation, the slaves were in one sense doing the master's bidding: They finished their required tasks before they began working for themselves and thus responded positively to Weaver's attempt to motivate them. But on another level the slaves were being very much their own men. They could do extra work if they wished, or they could take their time off as leisure. Even in the simple act of accepting or rejecting the overwork system they were achieving, in at least one small phase of their existence, some measure of self-choice. If they did choose to do additional labor, the sums they earned were theirs to control, and they gained an even greater measure of personal initiative.

One of the most significant things about the overwork accounts is the way in which they suggest how a sizable number of Weaver's slaves took advantage of the system to carve out something of a private and individual life for themselves. Opening these ledgers and turning page after page with the names of slaves written across the top is very much a process of opening a window into a hidden past. The "Negro Books" afford a rare glimpse into the lives of antebellum southern slaves because they tell us what slaves chose to do with resources they themselves controlled. They worked exceedingly hard to accumulate the sums recorded on the credit side of these ledgers. The debit side reveals how they spent these precious resources, and by tracing their expenditures we can learn a surprising amount about their values and priorities, about what was important to them and, frequently, to their families.

For example, Phill Easton, one of Weaver's master refiners at Buffalo Forge, built up impressive amounts of overwork earnings from 1839 to 1840. His account opened on April 1, 1830, with a transfer of $65.27 to his credit from an earlier "Negro Book" (which unfortunately has not survived) against a debit account of only $40.34. Phill regularly bypassed Weaver's annual clothing allotment for both himself and his wife, Betsy, and for each year that he did so he was credited with $15 (except for 1834, when the figure was $13.50) on the books as a payment in lieu of clothing. He raised a calf every year, which he sold to Weaver for $2 through 1834 and for $3 thereafter, and he made extra tonnages of iron over and above his weekly task of 1½ tons of anchonies.

Weaver, like all ironmasters in the Valley, paid $8 per ton for iron refined by free labor or by slaves as part of their overwork, and Phill received either $4 or $5 per ton for his extra iron; the rate depended on whether he worked two-handed at his forge with a skilled or less skilled helper. When fully trained refiners like John Baxter or Billy Hunt assisted him, the $8 fee was split evenly.

By his ironworking and calf raising and by choosing to forgo his annual issue of new clothing, Phill regularly put between $20 and $30 in overwork credit on Weaver's books each year during the 1830s. On February 29, 1840, when his account was totaled up, he showed a balance in his favor of $100.28½. Included in this sum were two exceptionally interesting items. One, dated August 18, 1837, was for 44¾ cents "By Wm. Empy for Cooking for him." Bill Empy, a free Negro forgeman who occasionally worked for Weaver, had apparently taken meals with the Eastons and was paying Betsy for the cooking she had done on his behalf. The other was dated February 29, 1840, the date Phill's account was balanced. This entry read: "By 14 months Interest your former Duebill . . . $6.72." Phill apparently held Weaver's I.O.U. for a substantial amount of overwork credit and was drawing interest on this note.

The debit side of the ledger is even more revealing. Phill Easton's most frequent use of his overwork credit was for the purchase of coffee and sugar, for which he clearly had a taste, as did, in all probability, his wife. Phill regularly bought cloth, such as "6 yds Fancy Calico for Betsy $3.00" in September 1831, "3 yds Jeans $1.87½" in December 1833, "8 yds Flax linen $3.00" in June 1834, and "3½ yds. Casanet $3.50" in January 1838. He occasionally bought items like handkerchiefs and new shoes, and there are a number of small charges for mending shoes for both himself and his wife, a reflection of his decision to opt for the clothing credit instead of new clothing each year.

In addition to his regular purchases of sugar and coffee, he occasionally used his overwork to acquire a gallon of molasses or a barrel of fine flour. He also bought items for the home: "1 sifter 1 Sett knives & forks $3.00" on June 4, 1830, and "1 Sett cups & saucer .50¢" on August 13, 1831. He sometimes drew cash from his account, sums ranging from as little as 50 cents to as much as $5. There is an intriguing entry dated August 11, 1838, debiting his account 25 cents for "postage on letter from Columbus" (a black hammerman named Columbus worked for a time at Buffalo Forge in the mid-1830s). And there are almost always Christmas entries: for coffee, sugar, shoes, and withdrawals of cash, which he, or Betsy, could use to shop at one or more of the stores that dotted the countryside around Buffalo Forge. After Phill left the forge, probably as a result of infirmities brought on by old age, he continued to earn money by raising and selling calves to Weaver, who by the early 1850s was paying $5 for each calf.

It does not take a great leap of the historical imagination to grasp the importance of the overwork system to Phill Easton. He clearly used his earnings to improve the quality of life which he and his wife were able to enjoy, but he also seems to have used his overwork to stake out some precious independence—some psychological breathing space—in the midst of a system that theoretically held him totally bound to the will of his owner. Phill's decision to take primary responsibility for clothing himself and his wife is particularly telling in this regard, since it broke with a traditional form of slave dependence and substituted his own work, sweat, and skill for the master's beneficence, such as it was. The clothes on his back he put there himself, and the same held true for his wife. The fact that his purchases included expensive fabrics like fine calico and cassinette also meant that Betsy Easton would be wearing something other than coarse "Negro cloth" as the result of his efforts. . . .

The overwork system was only one of the techniques Weaver employed to make Buffalo Forge a profitable enterprise. . . . By systematically building up his crew of skilled slave artisans by purchase and by allowing younger slaves to apprentice alongside his experienced operatives, Weaver eliminated his dependence on free forge labor and placed himself in an advantageous competitive position in the Valley iron trade. Reliance on overwork as a principal means of motivating his forge workers allowed both Weaver and his forgemen to find that elusive middle ground where at least the minimal demands of both the master and the slaves could be brought into some sort of balance.

Weaver generally got what he most wanted and needed from his slave force—a sufficient quantity of high-quality iron produced at a cost that allowed him to earn a profit on his sizable investment in land, ironworks, and labor in Virginia. Weaver could have been a slaveowner without the extensive use of the overwork system, but he could not have been the successful ironmaster that he was—the master of Buffalo Forge—without it.

James Henry Hammond and the Plantation as a Business Enterprise

DREW GILPIN FAUST

Plantation management, Hammond once ruefully observed, was like "war without the glory." For three decades he battled with his slaves, as both master and bondsmen implemented ingenious strategies of tactical advances, surprises, and retreats. But Hammond's struggles in his role as planter were not restricted to conflicts with his black laborers. He was determined to rationalize and regularize as much of the operation of his plantation as managerial efficiency and the existing state of agricultural science would permit. . . . Like a general preparing for battle, Hammond set out to mobilize all his resources in the pursuit of victory over his slaves, over the vicissitudes of markets and weather, over the low fertility of much of his land. His ambition made him an aggressive and interventionist master; it similarly transformed him into an innovator in farming methods and a leading advocate of scientific agriculture.

James Henry Hammond never forgot his father's exhortation that "Knowledge is power." On the plantation, he recognized, knowledge meant control—and in due course prosperity. Knowledge could transform Silver Bluff into a shining exemplar for all to admire; agricultural success could distinguish the ambitious Carolinian among all the planters of the South.

When Hammond took possession of his new property in 1831, he estimated the value of land, slaves, and other plantation assets at $90,240. He had become one of the wealthiest men and largest slaveholders not only in the surrounding area but in the entire state. Yet the average net income from the Bluff over the preceding four years, he reported in disgust, had been only $775. Such a paltry sum, representing a return on investment of less than 1 percent, seemed a clear indictment

Drew Gilpin Faust, *James Henry Hammond and the Old South: A Design for Mastery* (Baton Rouge: Louisiana State University Press, 1982), pp. 105–108, 111–120, 123–125, 129–131, 133–134.

of the Fitzsimons family management. The new owner was determined to increase this profit margin substantially. Always jealous of his independence, Hammond struggled to earn the right to call the plantation his own: he would always consider the increased value of Silver Bluff under his administration as evidence for the legitimacy of his ownership. He had not simply married a great plantation, he would insist, but had in good part created it.

Hammond did not wait long to introduce changes in agricultural operations at the Bluff. He at once set out to create a "business appearance," and he increased the acreage under cultivation by 16 percent in an effort to produce a more remunerative crop. On the very date of his first wedding anniversary the first cotton bolls symbolically opened, promising a rich yield for his new property. . . .

The harvest fully lived up to these preliminary expectations. With characteristic meticulousness Hammond calculated his receipts from the sale of cotton, corn, lumber, and other plantation products during his first year of management to be $11,292.99. Expenses of only $2,754.34, which included such costs as the overseer's $350 salary, cloth for slave garments, shoes and blankets, doctors' fees, and some new tools and equipment, left a profit of $8,538.65—$113.85 per full working hand. By his own calculations, this represented a return of 9.5 percent on his capital. . . .

But Hammond soon learned that he could not entirely regulate plantation productivity. Severe storms during his second year of management destroyed much of the crop, dashing his plans for a corn surplus. In 1835 a drought defeated his calculations, and three years later weather again so diminished his cotton crop that he harvested only half what he had expected. Despite these setbacks and despite Hammond's complaints that his economic goals seemed all but unattainable, his balance sheets showed a remarkable overall growth in income throughout the 1830s. Profits per hand increased to $215.49 by 1836, and Hammond estimated in 1841 that "Exclusive of this year my income has averaged about $12,500 clear of plantation . . . expenses." At the end of a decade of ownership, Hammond reckoned that he had increased the value of his property by 50 percent. But, he remarked with the dissatisfaction he characteristically exhibited about even the most impressive of his achievements, "I should have doubled it."

Hammond remained unhappy with his profits and grew increasingly aware of the inherent shortcomings of his land. Too much of it, he complained, was sandy and sterile; the rest lacked adequate drainage. . . . Hammond had good reason to feel discouraged about his plantation's prospects. The decision to increase income by expanding the percentage of land under cultivation could be at best only a partial solution to the agricultural and entrepreneurial dilemma posed by the qualities of such soils. . . .

By the end of the decade, Hammond had . . . diversified his landholdings through the purchase of Texas and Fairfield District land, and had also begun to vary his investments more generally by acquiring $5,500 worth of railroad and bank stock. These and other nonagricultural investments in which he dabbled throughout the antebellum years had several purposes. Most such ventures were designed to provide a degree of liquidity lacking in land and slaves. Railroad stock, Hammond explained, always served as "a sort of deposit in which I can realize money in a pinch." He searched eagerly as well for opportunities in South Carolina's manufacturing sector. He invested in cotton mills as early as the 1830s, and his emerging ideological commitment to economic diversification reinforced a later interest in purchasing a share in the successful mill ventures of William Gregg at nearby Graniteville. Others of Hammond's financial schemes were more hazardous speculations, often made in cooperation with friends who, Hammond complained, seemed always to lead him to disaster. The Texas land investment company ultimately failed entirely, as did an $8,500 gold mine gamble Hammond made with one of his neighbors in the late 1850s. . . .

But in spite of these ventures, Hammond retained the bulk of his wealth in his plantations. . . . Temperamentally, Hammond preferred the "despotic sway" that a planter could at least aspire to establish over his landed investments. Yet his drive for a modern, rationalized system of management, for a plantation that would be like a factory, created important underlying tensions in view of Hammond's decidedly prebourgeois notions of lordlike mastery. There could be no genuine delegation of authority or division of responsibility at Silver Bluff; the idea of bureaucracy was entirely inconsistent with Hammond's understanding of his power. "I only succeed," he explained, "when everything is under my control."

By the late 1830s, agricultural operations at Silver Bluff were indeed coming more tightly under Hammond's control. He had increased the value of the property by rationalizing acreage and by making a variety of improvements, clearing additional arable land, and building a new dwelling for himself, as well as new slave cabins, a ginhouse, and a slave hospital. Hammond had worked carefully to make the plantation both efficient and self-sufficient, ensuring that it produced enough corn to feed the slaves and sufficient fodder to fatten the livestock that were slaughtered as the plantation meat supply. Not only cotton production but every detail of plantation output was to be included in his entrepreneurial design.

But like businessmen and investors throughout the nation, Hammond was deeply worried about financial prospects in the early 1840s. Despite the many indications of his wealth, Hammond was well aware of the troubling economic conditions North and South that had followed the nationwide financial panic of 1837. These forces exerted their fullest impact on the Carolina cotton market in 1840 and inaugurated a period of hard times that plagued the state throughout the decade. Charleston cotton prices fell from a high of $0.168 per pound in 1836 to $0.129 in 1839, to just $0.084 in 1840. By the middle of the decade, they lingered between six and seven cents per pound. Hammond estimated that he was unable to cultivate cotton profitably for less than ten cents per pound, and thus the 1840s drove him to a searching reassessment of his financial condition and options. "If prices do not improve," he told the Barnwell Agricultural Society in November, 1840, "most of us will become compelled to abandon cotton." . . .

. . . [I]n order to remain in Carolina, he would be compelled . . . to extend the arable portion of his land. As early as 1838, a friend had urged Hammond to consider revivifying his Silver Bluff property rather than abandoning it entirely. . . . "I am confident," he had written, "you have Marl not far from you & if you have, you will do better to get it & improve your old lands." Marl is a kind of clay rich in calcium carbonate that is used even today on acidic soils to increase their friability and their receptivity to the enriching effects of animal manures. . . . In the third and fourth decades of the nineteenth century, marl was the watchword of the agricultural reform crusade Edmund Ruffin launched in hopes of reversing the declining fertility of Virginia's tired lands. But in the early forties, the "gospel of marl" had only just begun to win converts in the Old Dominion and was almost unknown in South Carolina. . . .

Twelve miles downriver from his plantation, Hammond located a bluff composed largely of marl that he was able to rent for one hundred dollars per year. During the next twelve months, eleven slaves manned a boat that made eighty-five trips to haul nearly a hundred thousand bushels of the fertilizer. Estimating that a prime hand could marl an acre a day, Hammond applied the material in varying proportions to land carefully laid out in experimental squares. . . .

In the first year of his experiment, Hammond recorded increases in productivity as high as 50 percent in cotton and approximately 25 percent in fodder and corn. By the end of 1841 he had become an evangelist for scientific agriculture in the South. Invited to deliver the anniversary oration to the State Agricultural Society, Hammond publicly announced his conversion. "It will be perceived that the means I recommend . . . involve an important change in our system of Agriculture, & a resort to manuring, contracted planting & drainage to an extent which I confess I have not heretofore advocated." As he confided to his diary in early 1842, he was amazed that only a year before he had been considering abandoning Carolina altogether. "Since then," he observed, "important changes have taken place in consequence of turning my attention to marl & succeeding in procuring it at a reasonable cost. All my calculations are now based on this experiment in which at this time I have the utmost confidence." . . .

The adoption of marling, however, marked an important change in Hammond's overall attitude about his agricultural endeavors, one that quickly involved him in a whole series of experimental projects at the Bluff. From his initial days as a planter, he explained to a friend, he had "carried on my business" with "systematic *energy and forethought.*" But now these analyses and plans would be directed not simply toward maximizing profit. Hammond would begin to regard his plantation activities as part of a wider world of southern agriculture upon which not just the prosperity but the survival of his region and its peculiar institutions depended. Reading voraciously in agricultural literature, Hammond began to generalize, to experiment, to philosophize about the practice of husbandry, and to disseminate his views in essays and orations. Silver Bluff became a source not just of profits but of pride; it would be, he hoped, a kind of plantation on a hill, a beacon guiding agriculturists throughout the South. But Hammond's conversion meant that plantation administration had of necessity to become more complex. He could no longer struggle just for financial gain; now he had to transform agricultural theory into daily practice. As in his management of slaves, Hammond established idealized standards and goals and was inevitably frustrated in his efforts to conduct every detail of plantation operations in accordance with "scientific principles." . . .

The plantation self-sufficiency Hammond sought was a basic principle of the South's agricultural reform movement. Twentieth-century scholars have argued heatedly about whether or not the antebellum South so concentrated on cotton production as to become dependent on other regions for food. While the balance of historical opinion at present lies on the side of regional self-sufficiency, nineteenth-century southern agricultural writers clearly viewed the situation differently, endlessly berating their compatriots for their dependence on western livestock and grain. "It is the true policy of the cotton planters," a local South Carolina agricultural convention resolved in 1843, "to curtail the cotton crop and increase the provision crop—so as to supply all the breadstuffs and raise all the different kinds of stock . . . which may be necessary for family and plantation use." . . .

Closely related to the goal of self-sufficiency, a second cardinal tenet of the agricultural reform movement in the South was the diversification of plantation production to render the region less dependent upon the fluctuation of the world cotton market. During the 1840s, low prices made this a particularly pressing appeal. In an 1841 address to the State Agricultural Society Hammond himself called for a drastic curtailment of the cotton crop, and his own actions at Silver Bluff indicated his attention to these economic necessities. His plantation records include the details of his crop selection at the Bluff through 1855. Until 1853, when he gathered the first harvest at his newly established Cowden Plantation just downriver from Silver Bluff, these data provide a comprehensive portrait of his decisions about the proper ratio between cotton and corn. . . .

Hammond's initial response to what he judged to be a 33 percent drop in prices and values in 1839 was to decrease total acreage planted by nearly half. Yet the next year he increased both cotton and provision crops, possibly to compensate for the drop in price by raising output. In 1842 he shifted toward corn for the first time, but reversed his priorities again in 1843 to return to his concentration on cotton for two more seasons. At last in 1845, when cotton prices had been below an average of eight cents for three consecutive years, he turned decisively toward corn. Through the rest of the decade, Hammond maintained a predominance of corn acreage at the Bluff, but the rise in cotton prices to $0.084 in 1849 seems to have prompted him to shift the balance once again. The South's restored confidence in its economy and its staple crop was reflected in Hammond's own choices, for in 1850, 1851, and 1852 he reestablished the dominance of cotton on his plantation. The pessimism he had expressed in 1841 about the future of cotton was forgotten; Hammond's actions at Silver Bluff seemed to embody the conviction he would later display to the United States Senate when he proclaimed in 1858 that "Cotton is King." . . .

In addition to self-sufficiency and crop diversification, the South's agricultural reform movement preached managerial efficiency. Too many southerners, its advocates warned, were neglectful of the details of plantation administration, if not absent from their lands entirely. Too much of the responsibility for plantation management had been left to overseers, and ignorance had thus been enshrined as the directing force in agricultural affairs.

Hammond himself regarded the upgrading of overseers and their work as central to the advancement of southern agriculture. In the *Carolina Planter,* he bluntly declared that "it would be as much to the interest of planters to improve them, as to improve their lands, stock or manner of planting. In fact, more; for, without improving them, it is very difficult to effect any other improvement." Hammond spoke from direct experience, for overseers at Silver Bluff seemed a constant hindrance to his grand designs. The "first requisite of a *good overseer*" was, in Hammond's view, very like the primary requirement for being a slave: "to OBEY Orders." At times he had to exert considerable self-restraint not to treat his white deputies as if they were indeed his bondsmen. When one overseer especially enraged him, Hammond reported that he could "hardly keep my hands off him." But if blacks were resistant to Hammond's desires for total control, whites, free and equal before the law, were even more unwilling to submit to his demands. . . .

Hammond's conversion to scientific agriculture in the 1840s further increased the demands upon his deputies. One "Smart & . . . high tempered" applicant for the job at Silver Bluff declined at the last moment to take the position. "On reading my rules," Hammond explained, "he said they were to [*sic*] strict. I told [him] I could not alter them & declined his services." More than once during the forties Hammond dismissed unsatisfactory overseers at the height of the growing season. In 1845 he explained to fellow reformer Edmund Ruffin that he had fired John Barnes in late July "because he would not weigh measure & attend properly to the details of my affairs—experiments particularly. . . . Damn the overseers." Although Barnes was admittedly "the best I have ever had if left to himself . . . he would not keep the track in *executing* orders, & as I have some dozens of nice experiments in all the branches of farming and stock raising going on, he worried me beyond endurance & continually thwarted all my views in detail. The present race of Overseers are far the greatest curse under which our agriculture labours." Hammond's hierarchical view of the world included a very precise place for these intractable white superintendents who seemed determined to frustrate his resolution to make the plantation as efficient as a factory. "An overseer," he explained, "cant conform to routine more than twice, a piney woods man once & a negro never again." . . .

Hammond's capital resources and great wealth left him relatively unharmed by the economic depression that raged about him, and he was even able to take advantage of hard times. While most other southerners were suffering from shortage of funds, Hammond had an apparent surplus. Low stock prices prompted him to buy thirteen thousand dollars' worth of railroad shares; yet he still had enough cash to increase his plantation investment. The decreased cost of slaves enabled him to accelerate his plans for improvement. Similarly, he acted to acquire land on favorable terms. In the mid-forties he made a series of purchases that added 337 acres to the Silver Bluff property. And between 1848 and 1852, he at last realized his dream of establishing a second plantation. Through ten judicious purchases—including one bargain of 300 acres for five dollars—he secured 2,789 acres in the Savannah River swamps below Silver Bluff. Wild, marshy, and overgrown, this tract, called Cowden after the livestock that roamed unbridled through it, stood as the ultimate challenge to Hammond's reformist creed. If he could subdue this land, if he could conquer the vines, brambles, gum, bay, and poplar trees, he would prove himself a most extraordinary agriculturist indeed.

Hammond's interest in Cowden arose from his conviction that Savannah swamp soils contained untold mineral and vegetable riches. From the time of his arrival at Silver Bluff, he had transported what he called "peat" from the marshes to spread on upland soil. On reflection, he decided it would be far more efficient to cultivate the swamps themselves. But the lands of Cowden required a level of preparation, clearing, and draining that would entail a major engineering commitment. In the agricultural literature and in Edmund Ruffin's own efforts on his farm near Richmond, Hammond found the model for his drainage schemes, even though the scale of the operation he contemplated far exceeded that undertaken by Ruffin at Marlbourne. Hammond's bold ambitions were exceeded only by his expectations. His success at Cowden, he was sure, would "revolutionize agriculture in this district at least & quadruple its profits."

In his first attempt, Hammond succeeded in clearing and draining 170 acres of swamp with eighteen hundred man-days of labor. Delighted by the five feet of rich black topsoil he had uncovered, Hammond was certain he could improve his rate of reclamation. Because South Carolina contained "hundreds of thousands of acres" of such swamp, Hammond hoped his efforts would serve as a model for transforming the agriculture of his native state. But the project was so enormous Hammond did not think he could complete it even with his expanded slave force, and he feared the effects of the swamp environment on the health of his slaves. . . .

During the initial years of cultivation, Cowden produced enormous yields. But like most swamp soils, these lands were soon exhausted of the organic matter that had rendered them temporarily so productive. Modern soil scientists estimate that under cultivation swamp topsoil would be depleted at a rate of approximately one to two inches a year in moderate temperatures, and perhaps more rapidly in South Carolina's hot and humid conditions. Hammond's five feet of black Cowden earth would at this rate last less than thirty years. In fact, after the Civil War, Hammond's sons found Cowden almost worthless agriculturally.

During Hammond's lifetime, however, Cowden's yields were often extraordinary. He decided the marsh environment would suit corn better than cotton, and in 1853 he was astounded by the crop's success. One acre produced fifty-one bushels, almost four times the thirteen-bushel-per-acre yield recorded up to that time at Silver Bluff. Throughout the fifties, harvests continued to be highly satisfactory, and in 1857 Hammond noted the statistics for the year's crop with pride. "If anyone can beat that let them try it." The difficulties of the drainage and reclamation project made Hammond all the more delighted with his achievement. As ever, he seemed most comfortable when faced by obstacles others would consider all but insurmountable. His efforts at Cowden, he reported, gave him "all the emotions of a Discoverer & a Conquerer.[" "]I am Columbus! Cortez!" he wrote exuberantly. In agricultural reform and improvement lay a power and a control at least as real as that he exercised over his slaves. Not only did these activities increase his wealth—and by the 1850s he was reporting annual profits between thirty and forty thousand dollars—but his attainments contributed as well to a more general enhancement of his status. "If I have been active & industrious," he explained in reference to his plantation undertakings, "it has always been for higher purposes than to accumulate. . . . I delight to accomplish."

Hammond relished the sense of achievement he derived from extending rational control over operations at Cowden and Silver Bluff. But he thrived too on the wider influence he knew his role entailed; a master's power had necessarily to be forged at home, but it then stretched well beyond the immediate boundaries of his plantation; effective dominance over land and slaves led naturally to authority over other whites in the immediate locality and could even reach throughout the state and the nation at large. A wealthy and distinguished planter was a natural focus of power in his neighborhood, and it was this local preeminence that served as the foundation and legitimation of wider public ambitions. Through their economic and social functions, plantations were integrated into a web of social relationships within the surrounding community. Hammond served variously as banker, doctor, and employer, offering to hold money, prescribe drugs, gin cotton, educate children, and market crops of neighbors fortunate enough to attract his interest and beneficent attention. "Once a year," a guest at Redcliffe recounted, "like a great feudal landlord," Hammond "gave a fete or grand dinner to all the country people about, at which . . . every neighbour, poor or rich, for miles about was present." The interactions between the planter and his less-privileged neighbors had a profound influence upon class relations within the society as a whole. Lacking less-personal structures for social and economic welfare and education, the South left the relationships of plantation paternalism to fill these institutional roles. Within the microcosm of a plantation and its neighborhood originated the complex ties of interdependence that assured white solidarity in the antebellum South. . . .

Temperamentally, Hammond found the loosely defined ties of patronage and privilege between himself and his neighbors difficult to manage. As always, he was most comfortable with unchallenged and undiluted omnipotence. But if there existed unspoken limits on his absolute power over blacks, there were even more stringent restrictions on his coercive rights over whites. Indeed, the ambiguities of the master-slave relationship seemed almost simple in comparison to the complexities of power relations among whites in South Carolina's "aristocratical democracy." Yet Hammond was well aware that his culture expected the forms of benevolent paternalism to extend beyond the boundaries of the plantation to encompass a larger "family white and black" within its framework of obligation and manipulative control.

For James Henry Hammond, the plantation was in one sense a world unto itself, a "little kingdom" in which he could at least seek to satisfy his yearnings for "despotic sway." But the plantation had broader significance as well, for it served at the same time as a foundation upon which to erect his ambitions in the wider world, a base from which to reach out to a more extensive domain of achievement and control. From the first, Hammond recognized that ownership of a plantation and slaves was the surest means of acquiring the status prerequisite to political advancement. Planting, he knew, was "in this country . . . the *only* independent & really honorable occupation. The planters here are essentially what the nobility are in other countries. They stand at the head of society & politics." Yet the ways in which the plantation provided access to power were more complex than simply bestowing the honorific title of "planter" upon the ambitious Hammond. The young Carolinian found at Silver Bluff the financial basis to ensure that "independence" enshrined in republican ideology, as well as funds to support a life-style befitting his aspirations for gentility. In his planting efforts, he discovered a new arena for personal accomplishment and public eminence, and his agricultural leadership encouraged and reinforced his emerging political authority as a defender of the South and its institutions. The assumption of social and economic ascendancy within his Barnwell and Edgefield community served as a first step in the extension of Hammond's dominion beyond Silver Bluff into South Carolina and the nation. The world, he hoped, might become his plantation writ large.

 # *F U R T H E R   R E A D I N G*

Carlton, David L., and Peter A. Coclanis. *The South, the Nation, and the World: Perspectives on Southern Economic Development* (2003).

Conrad, Alfred, and John Meyer. "The Economics of Slavery in the Antebellum South." *Journal of Political Economy* (April 1958): 95–130.

Dew, Charles B. *Ironmaker to the Confederacy: Joseph R. Anderson and the Tredegar Iron Works*, rev. ed. (1999).

Dunn, Richard S. "After Tobacco: The Slave Labor Pattern on a Large Chesapeake Grain-and-Livestock Plantation in the Early Nineteenth Century." In John J. McCusker and Kenneth Morgan, eds., *The Early Modern Atlantic Economy* (2000).

Egerton, Douglas R. "Markets Without a Market Revolution: Southern Planters and Capitalism." *Journal of the Early Republic* 16 (Summer 1996): 207–221.

Fogel, Robert William. *Without Consent or Contract: The Rise and Fall of American Slavery* (1989).

———, and Stanley L. Engerman. *Time on the Cross: The Economics of American Negro Slavery* (1974).

Foner, Eric. *Reconstruction: America's Unfinished Revolution, 1863–1877* (1988).

Genovese, Eugene D. *The Political Economy of Slavery: Studies in the Economy and Society of the Slave South* (1965).

———. *The World the Slaveholders Made: Two Essays in Interpretation* (1969).

Goldin, Claudia Dale. *Urban Slavery in the American South, 1820–1860: A Quantitative History* (1976).

Gudmestad, Robert H. *A Troublesome Commerce: The Transformation of the Interstate Slave Trade* (2003).

Kolchin, Peter. *American Slavery, 1619–1877,* rev. ed. (2003).

———. *A Sphinx on the American Land: The Nineteenth-Century South in Comparative Perspective* (2003).

Lakwete, Angela. *Inventing the Cotton Gin: Machine and Myth in Antebellum America* (2003).

Oakes, James. *The Ruling Race: A History of American Slaveholders* (1998).

———. *Slavery and Freedom: An Interpretation of the Old South* (1990).

Scarborough, William K. *The Overseer: Plantation Management in the Old South* (1984).

Shore, Lawrence. *Southern Capitalists: The Ideological Leadership of an Elite, 1832–1885* (1986).

Smith, Mark M. *Mastered by the Clock: Time, Slavery, and Freedom in the Antebellum South* (1997).

Tadman, Michael. *Speculators and Slaves: Masters, Traders, and Slaves in the Old South* (1989).

Wright, Gavin. *The Political Economy of the Cotton South: Households, Markets, and Wealth in the Nineteenth Century* (1978).

C H A P T E R
6

Inventing American Industry,

1810–1890

As Americans debated democracy, states rights, and slavery in the political arena, entrepreneurs took advantage of the stabilizing financial system and turned to the business of making the Northern economy work. In the early 1800s, international trade had propelled steady economic growth. Transportation innovations had reduced shipping costs, cut travel time, and opened up the west. By the 1820s, manufacturing facilities—factories, craft shops, flour and grist mills, iron furnaces, and publishers—responded to the growing demand for capital goods and consumer products. By midcentury, much in this picture was novel: the steamboat and the railroad, the smokestack and the mill worker, the cheap periodicals, ready-made clothing, and colorful advertisements.

In the past, historians called this transformation the industrial revolution and credited it to farsighted entrepreneurs with technological and organizational wizardry. The prime movers in this heroic saga were Samuel Slater and Francis Cabot Lowell, who had established highly publicized, water-powered textile factories in Rhode Island and Massachusetts, respectively. After his 1817 death, Lowell's business partners so revered his achievements that they memorialized him by developing model manufacturing cities at Lowell, Lawrence, Holyoke, and Manchester. Everything was cutting-edge. In Lowell, they adopted the corporate form, installed power canals, built factories and boardinghouses, engaged resident managers, hired country girls as operatives, and promoted the experience as new. The city became a tourist destination for eminent Victorians such as Charles Dickens, whose visits contributed to the excitement. Although conditions declined by midcentury, Lowell's "Golden Age" lingered in the historical consciousness for generations. Francis Cabot Lowell and his cohorts were celebrated as the geniuses responsible for launching American industry.

Scholars now understand that the story of nineteenth-century industry is more complicated and compelling. While the city of Lowell may have been New England's flagship, hundreds of sites, from New York to Chicago, participated in the process of industrialization. Throughout the Northeast and the Midwest, there certainly was a shift from handicraft to assembly-line production, a greater separation of capital and labor, and a heightened interest in new technologies. But traditions *persisted, and craftsmen adapted their methods to new circumstances. Skilled artisans turned into technical innovators, while small businessmen learned to use their spheres of influence differently. In Philadelphia, mechanics custom built locomotives at the Baldwin works, and in Trenton, potters modified craft traditions to create innovative production networks. There were great successes, but there were even more failures, which provided learning opportunities. Pockets of industry bubbled up in the countryside, market towns, and great urban centers. When viewed in this light, we can see that the rise of American industry was not really a revolution, but a process combining the old and new. American industrialization was evolutionary, progressive, and risky.*

Industry became a subject of celebration and an object of contemplation. This effort more fully integrated business into American culture. The emphasis on personal industry encouraged the entrepreneurial spirit and deflected critiques of manufacturing. By the late 1800s, "industry" had multiple meanings, referring to commerce, manufacturing, and individual perseverance.

 D O C U M E N T S

The city of Lowell was the brainchild of Nathan Appleton, who appeared in Chapter 4's discussion of banks. Appleton belonged to a group of wealthy businessmen known by historians as the "Boston Associates," who promoted economic development in Massachusetts. An astute capitalist, Appleton never missed a chance to make money, and he saw a great future in high-technology manufacturing. In the 1810s, he, Francis Cabot Lowell, and others had built a textile factory in Waltham. Subsequently, Appleton spearheaded the planned community of Lowell, twenty-five miles north. He knew about impoverished laborers in the British cotton mills, and wanted no such thing in America. The Boston Associates envisioned Lowell as an experiment in large-scale production and social engineering.

In Document 1, Kirk Boott, one of Appleton's partners, describes Lowell in 1827. Boott's letter was addressed to Mathew Carey, a renowned advocate of American industry, who published it in his Philadelphia newspaper, *United States Gazette*. The Lowell experiment gained wide attention through such publications.

From the 1820s to the 1840s, the Boston Associates recruited New England farm women to work in Lowell's state-of-the-art factories. The Boston elites resolved to create a model labor force that embodied Yankee ideals: virtue, thrift, simplicity, hard work, and doing good. Young women steeped in Protestant religion and family values seemed the perfect fit. To guard against moral deterioration, Lowell's founders provided everything: boardinghouses, churches, libraries, night schools, evening lectures, literary clubs, a savings bank, and a shopping street.

In Document 2, "Lowell girl" Josephine L. Baker takes an imaginary visitor on a tour of her adopted city in 1845. Her description considers the pros and cons of the Lowell system from the worker's perspective. It appeared in *The Lowell Offering* (1840–1845), a magazine edited and written by "factory girls," which captivated the American, English, and French literati, whose admiration fed the Lowell fanfare.

In the long run, the great experiment at Lowell decayed. Heightened competition resulted in price cuts, speed-ups, and longer working hours. The Boston Associates took umbrage when the mill girls went on strike in 1834 and 1836, and managers started hiring Irish immigrants. By the Civil War, Lowell was far removed from its idyllic origins.

Lowell's heyday coincided with an ongoing debate over the factory system that harked back to Hamilton and Jefferson. This national discussion pitted the proponents of industrial growth and national expansion against the advocates of agriculture and international trade. The promanufacturing selection in Document 3 comes from George S. White's biography of Samuel Slater, the pioneer Rhode Island textile manufacturer, published during the turbulent era of the Lowell strikes. White combats the widespread suspicion of factories and factory owners with moral arguments. He emphasizes the community benefits of manufacturing, the economies of labor-saving machinery, and the merits of industrial virtues: diligence, discipline, and sobriety.

During the antebellum era, North and South embraced opposing views on the tariff. As we saw in Chapter 5, many Southern businessmen advocated free trade, while Northern industrialists lobbied for protection. On the eve of the Civil War, Congress passed the Morrill Tariff Act, launching a protectionist era that lasted until the post–World War II years. In Document 4, the *New York Times* weighs in on protectionism during congressional debates over the Morrill Tariff.

Document 5 shifts to Pittsburgh after the Civil War. When journalist James Parton visited the Iron City in 1868, it was well established as a major manufacturing center, thanks to the conjunction of natural resources and markets. With general readers in mind, *Atlantic Monthly* catalogs Pittsburgh's assets: the sublime landscape, the range of manufactories, and the industrious businessmen and workforce. With its diversified manufacturing base, Pittsburgh epitomized the Northern economy more than single-industry Lowell.

In the face of economic change, businessmen turned to self-reflection, assessing the cultural meanings of ambition and industry. In the next two documents, accomplished businessmen give advice on failure and success. In Document 6, Freeman Hunt, editor of *Hunt's Merchants' Magazine* in New York, reminds his readers in 1856 that 75 percent of tradesmen will fail at least once, blaming "the haste to be rich." Three decades later, steel millionaire Andrew Carnegie shares his recipe for success with students at a Pittsburgh commercial college (Document 7). What values and character traits do Hunt and Carnegie stress? How do their ideas differ from White's? Historians know that Carnegie admired Herbert Spencer, the British social theorist who applied Darwin's theory of evolution to human civilizations. How are evolutionary ideas reflected in Carnegie's talk?

During the late nineteenth century, businesses began identifying themselves as industrious through the use of visual symbols. In Document 8, Jacob Estey promotes his Vermont parlor organ factory in an advertising poster. What motifs convey the idea of progress? How do these visual images relate to the narratives by Parton and Carnegie?

1. Industrialist Kirk Boott Chronicles the Great Achievements at Lowell, 1827

There are now in full operation, at Lowell, six cotton mills, four stories high, 155 feet by 44, containing 25,000 spindles, and about 150 looms; in which were made, the last year, 5,042,408 yards of cloth, weighing 1,045,386 pounds, from 1,176,082 pounds of raw cotton. The numbers of yarn, 22, 26, 30, and 40. Two mills for twilled and four for plain goods. Three other mills are covered in; the first will be started in

Kirk Boott to Mathew Carey, October 25, 1827, in George S. White, *Memoir of Samuel Slater, The Father of American Manufactures, Connected with a History of the Rise and Progress of the Cotton Manufacture in England and America* (Philadelphia, 1836), pp. 252–255.

January, and the other two in July and January following. There are now employed 1200 persons in the mills; nine tenths of whom are females, 20 of whom are from 12 to 14 years of age. Adjoining the mills of the Merrimack Manufacturing Company, are their bleach and print shops, covering more ground, but equal in capacity to two mills; something over a hundred are here employed, about one fifth females, and one fifth boys. None are taken under 12. Apprentices are taken at 14 to 16, until 21; receiving for the first year, including board, $125, and $25 in addition, each succeeding year. Except in the print works, there are no foreigners, and there exceed not one quarter part. Daily wages would perhaps average 50 cents, the minimum being 37½, and the maximum $2 00. At present about 2,500,000 yards are printed, the residue are sold bleached. The average value of the prints is about 18 cents, of the bleached goods 12 to 13 cents. The foundation of the first mill was laid in 1822, and the first return of cloth, November 1823. Belonging to the mills and print works, and in their immediate vicinity, are 130 tenements, about 24 by 36 feet, which rent from $60 to $100 per annum.

The machine shop is of the same dimensions as the mills, and gives employment to about 1,800 machinists; average wages about ninety cents; but as a large portion of the work is by contract, and done by the apprentices, many of them earn from four to six dollars per day. There are 20 tenements attached to the shops; the rent of each of which is about $90 per annum. The cast iron is furnished from Gen. Heach's furnace, about four miles above: consumption averages a ton daily.

The company to whom the machine shop belongs, have a large tract of land and an immense water power, and are prepared to furnish machinery of all descriptions at short notice, and erect the necessary buildings. They have lately contracted to erect two mills, 155 by 44, near the same, and furnish the machinery capable of making 3,000,000 of yards of cloth, yard wide, of No. 14 yarn, per annum,—to build thirty three-story brick tenements, agent's house, and out buildings,—to furnish eight acres of land, and ample water power, and to put the same in operation for about $300,000.

Besides those steadily employed in the mills, about 150 mechanics, such as masons, carpenters, &c., find constant work. The amount of capital actually invested is $2,400,000, viz:

Merrimack Manufacturing Company,	-	-	-	$1,200,000
Proprietors of Land and Canals,	-	-	-	- 600,000
Hamilton Manufacturing Company,	-	-	-	- 600,000

With respect to the appropriation of land, I will mention a fact. I purchased, in 1822, nine tenths, undivided, of a farm of 110 acres, for $1,800. The owner of the other one tenth had agreed to convey it for $200, but dying, suddenly, insolvent, it was sold by order of the court, and I gave, for seven and a half tenths of his one tenth, upwards of $3,000. All his debts being satisfied the remainder was sold, a year afterwards, for the benefit of minor children, for nearly $5,000.

Land favourably situated is worth fifteen cents a foot, and there are a few spots that would command fifty. In 1822, the whole population of that part of Chelmsford which now constitutes Lowell, did not, exclusive of Mr. Hurd's mill, exceed 100; it is now probably 5,000.

The solitary storekeeper of 1822, is now surrounded by numerous rivals; and there are few luxuries, and no necessaries, that sharp competition among the dealers does not enable the consumer to purchase as cheap in Lowell as in Boston.

Lowell is situated 25 miles northwest of Boston, on the Merrimack river, and is divided from Tewksbury by the Concord, which here falls into the Merrimack. Middlesex canal empties into the Merrimack, a mile above Lowell, and furnishes a cheap conveyance for heavy articles. At present no manufactured goods are conveyed by this channel to Boston, there being no suitable boats. And indeed, if there were, unless the tolls were considerably lower, there would be little saving. Teaming is done low, and the goods carried to any point. The canal terminating in Charles's River, trucking would be necessary, and the expense would thus very nearly equal teaming.

The consumption of foreign articles, in Lowell, such as madder, sumac, indigo, &c., gives employment to far more tons of shipping than would be required to bring the manufactured goods from abroad; and at the same time furnishes to our own coasters an immense increase of freight, by its steady demand for the products of the other states of the Union, such as quercitron bark, flour, starch, copperas, lime, &c. Were this subject actually examined it would be found to exceed the belief of even those most favourable to the American system.

There is a branch of manufactures rapidly increasing, (and in which there is still great room for improvement,) that owes much of its progress to the establishment of print works. I allude to chemical works; many articles are imported from abroad that can be made full as well at home, and which I have no doubt soon will be. Trusting that the present duties will not be abated for some years, we shall go on building two mills a year; and while we hope to reap a reasonable return, I am sure we are benefiting our country, in at least an equal degree.

2. A Factory Girl Leads a Tour of the Lowell Mills, 1845

There is an old saying, that "When we are with the Romans, we must do as the Romans do." And now, kind friend, as we are about to renew our walk, I beg that you will give heed to it, and do as factory girls do. After this preliminary, we will proceed to the factory.

There is the "counting-room," a long, low, brick building, and opposite is the "store-house," built of the same material, after the same model. Between them, swings the ponderous gate that shuts the mills in from the world without. But, stop; we must get "a pass," ere we go through, or "the watchman will be after us." Having obtained this, we will stop on the slight elevation by the gate, and view the mills. The one to the left rears high its huge sides of brick and mortar, and the belfry, towering far above the rest, stands out in bold relief against the rosy sky. The almost innumerable windows glitter, like gems, in the morning sunlight. It is six and a half stories high, and, like the fabled monster of old, who guarded the sacred waters of Mars, it seems to guard its less aspiring sister to the right; that is five and a half stories high, and to it is attached the repair-shop. If you please, we will pass to the larger factory,—but be careful, or you will get lost in the mud, for this yard is not laid out in such beautiful order, as some of the factory yards are, nor can it be.

Josephine L. Baker, "A Second Peep at Factory Life," *The Lowell Offering* 5 (1845): 97–100. This document can also be found in Benita Eisler, ed., *The Lowell Offering: Writings by New England Mill Women, 1840–1845* (New York: J. B. Lippincott, 1977), pp. 77–78, 80–82.

We will just look into the first room. It is used for cleaning cloth. You see the scrubbing and scouring machines are in full operation, and gigging and fulling are going on in full perfection. As it is very damp, and the labor is performed by the other half of creation, we will pass on, for fear of incurring their jealousy. But the very appearance might indicate that there are, occasionally, *fogs* and *clouds;* and not only fogs and clouds, but sometimes plentiful showers. In the second room the cloth is *"finished,"* going through the various operations of burling, shearing, brushing, inking, fine-drawing, pressing, and packing for market. This is the pleasantest room on the corporation, and consequently they are never in want of help. The shearing, brushing, pressing and packing is done by males, while the burling, inking, marking and fine-drawing is performed by females. We will pass to the third room, called the "cassimere weaving-room," where all kinds of cloths are woven, from plain to the most exquisite fancy. There are between eighty and ninety looms, and part of the dressing is also done here. The fourth is the "broad weaving-room," and contains between thirty and forty looms; and broad sure enough they are. Just see how lazily the lathe drags backward and forward, and the shuttle—how spitefully it hops from one end of it to the other. But we must not stop longer, or perchance it will hop at us. You look weary; but, never mind! there was an end to Jacob's ladder, and *so* there is a termination to these stairs. Now if you please we will go up to the next room, where the spinning is done. Here we have spinning jacks or jennies that dance merrily along whizzing and singing, as they spin out their "long yarns," and it seems but pleasure to watch their movements; but it is hard work, and requires good health and much strength. Do not go too near, as we shall find that they do not understand the established rules of *etiquette,* and might unceremoniously knock us over. We must not stop here longer, for it is twelve o'clock, and we have the "carding-room" to visit before dinner. There are between twenty and thirty set of cards located closely together, and I beg of you to be careful as we go amongst them, or you will get caught in the machinery. You walk as though you were afraid of getting blue. Please excuse me, if I ask you not to be afraid. 'Tis a wholesome color, and soap and water will wash it off. The girls, you see, are partially guarded against it, by over-skirts and sleeves; but as it is not *fashionable* to wear masks, they cannot keep it from their faces. You appear surprised at the hurry and bustle now going on in the room, but your attention has been so engaged that you have forgotten the hour. Just look at the clock, and you will find that it wants but five minutes to "bell time." We will go to the door, and be ready to start when the others do; and now, while we are waiting, just cast your eyes to the stair-way, and you will see another flight of stairs, leading to another spinning-room; a picker is located somewhere in that region, but I cannot give you a description of it, as I have never had the courage to ascend more than five flight of stairs at a time. And—but the bell rings. . . .

You ask, if there are so many things objectionable, why we work in the mill. Well, simply for this reason,—every situation in life, has its trials which must be borne, and factory life has no more than any other. There are many things we do not like; many occurrences that send the warm blood mantling to the cheek when they must be borne in silence, and many harsh words and acts that are not called for. There are objections also to the number of hours we work, to the length of time allotted to our meals, and to the low wages allowed for labor; objections that must and will be answered; for the time has come when something, besides the clothing and feeding of the body is to be thought of; when the mind is to be clothed and fed; and this cannot be as it should be, with the present system of labor. Who, let me ask, can find that pleasure in life which they should, when it is spent in this way. Without time for the laborer's own work, and the improvement of the mind, save the few evening hours; and even then if the mind is enriched and stored with useful knowledge, it must be at the expense of health. And the feeling[,] too, that comes over us (there is no use in denying it) when we hear the bell calling us away from repose that tired nature loudly claims—the feeling, that we are *obliged to go*. And these few hours, of which we have spoken, are far too short, three at the most at the close of day. Surely, methinks, every heart that lays claim to humanity will feel 'tis not enough. But this, we hope will, ere long, be done away with, and labor made what it should be; pleasant and inviting to every son and daughter of the human family.

There is a brighter side to this picture, over which we would not willingly pass without notice, and an answer to the question, why we work here? The time we *do* have is our own. The money we earn comes promptly; more so than in any other situation; and our work, though laborious is the same from day to day; we know what it is, and when finished we feel perfectly free, till it is time to commence it again.

Besides this, there are many pleasant associations connected with factory life, that are not to be found elsewhere.

There are lectures, evening schools and libraries, to which all may have access. The one thing needful here, is the time to improve them as we ought.

There is a class, of whom I would speak, that work in the mills, and will while they continue in operation. Namely, the many who have no home, and who come here to seek, in this busy, bustling "City of Spindles," a competency that shall enable them in after life, to live without being a burden to society,—the many who toil on, without a murmur, for the support of an aged mother or orphaned brother and sister. For the sake of them, we earnestly hope labor may be reformed; that the miserable, selfish spirit of competition, now in our midst, may be thrust from us and consigned to eternal oblivion.

There is one other thing that must be mentioned ere we part, that is the practice of sending agents through the country to decoy girls away from their homes with the promise of high wages, when the market is already stocked to overflowing. This is certainly wrong, for it lessens the value of labor, which should be ever held in high estimation, as the path marked out by the right hand of GOD, in which man should walk with dignity.

3. George S. White, The Moral Influence of Industry, 1836

We have already seen that manufacturing establishments exert a powerful and permanent influence in their immediate neighbourhoods, and time, if not already, will teach the lesson, that they will stamp indelible traits upon our moral and national character. Evidences abound, wherever man exists, that his character is modified by localities, by a diversity of pursuits, by a facility of acquiring a living, by the

George S. White, *Memoir of Samuel Slater, the Father of American Manufactures, Connected with a History of the Rise and Progress of the Cotton Manufacture in England and America* (Philadelphia, 1836), pp. 113–118, 120.

quality and fashion of the living itself, by a restrained or free exercise of his rational powers, and by restraint on the enjoyment of liberty. Different climates and different countries produce indelible peculiarities. In the same climate and in the same country similar changes appear, from the effects of immoral habits, and from what may be termed artificial or mechanical causes. The effects of immoral habits are well known to all observers of human nature. . . .

Manufacturing establishments become a blessing or a curse according to the facilities which they create for acquiring a living, to the necessary articles which they provide, and the general character which they produce. To set up and encourage the manufacturing of such articles, the use and demand of which produces no immoral tendency, is one of the best and most moral uses which can be made of capital. The moral manufacturer, without the power or disposition to overreach, is in reality a benefactor. The acquisition of wealth in this way, is the most laudable. In point of benevolence and real worth of character, it claims a decided advantage over the cent per cent. process of accumulation. Some have not the requisite ability to carry on manufacturing establishments; capital, then, with great propriety is loaned to those who have. The moral influence of a community is not promoted by creating or submitting to a manufacturing, or any other aristocracy, solely in the pursuit of interest, in which selfishness is wont to predominate.

The manufacturing interest, in a flourishing state, naturally creates power and wealth. The value of labour and the value of money are then at his disposal; but, in this free country, there is a sufficient counteracting influence to keep up the price of labour and to equalise the prices of their commodities with the value of the products of the earth. Without such a resisting power, a few would abound in wealth and influence, while the multitude would be in poverty and reduced to servitude. But there always exists a counteracting influence in the rival establishments, and the general spirit of enterprise. . . .

Our day has witnessed the surprising effects of the ingenuity of man, in calling into existence and putting in operation labour-saving machinery. . . .

. . . To be moral and desirable, labour-saving machinery must bring along with it some particular benefit to the community, as well as to individuals. . . .

The first introduction of Hargreaves' and of Arkwright's machinery into England, was not only met with objections, but with popular vengeance. It threatened a speedy destruction to every jenny and water-frame in England, and so in appearance carried in its motions frightful evils. The anticipated evils actually happened; hand spinning met with a speedy overthrow, and those who had earned a few pence per day in following it, were compelled to resort to other employments, and perhaps to be employed in manufacturing on the new plan which they had laboured to oppose.

Similar feelings and similar consequences have happened and are still happening in America. Manufacturing, instead of going on quietly and single-handed in private families, with immense labour, grows into large establishments, which employ and bring into association, masses of population. . . .

Industry, directed by honest and intelligent views in moral pursuits, and honourably rewarded, holds a very high rank among moral causes. To maintain good order and sound government it is more efficient than the sword or bayonet. . . . So far as manufacturing establishments have promoted industry, and furnished means for an honest livelihood, thus far they have exerted a salutary influence on the character of those who have been employed. Multitudes of women and children have been kept out of vice, simply by being employed, and instead of being destitute, provided with an abundance for a comfortable subsistence. . . .

On the score of employment, manufacturing establishments have done much to support the best interests of society. It appears also, at the present time, that they have done so by their improvements. On the supposition that one or a few individuals, by the invention of labour-saving machinery, succeed, so as to furnish any particular article much cheaper than it could be done in the ordinary way, in this country where it deprives no one of a living, and goes to forward and hasten the general improvement, it cannot fail to be a benefit to the community. The diminution of price in the articles has been such, that the people have been doubly paid for all the protection granted; and commerce has been benefited by the opening of a foreign market. The failures and fluctuations in the manufacturing establishments have arisen from their weak and incipient state, and the competition of European fabrics. This cause appears greater than want of management and calculation, for the same men have alternately succeeded and failed on the same ground. . . .

In the present happy condition of the manufacturing districts, there are no advantages enjoyed by the rich, that are not reciprocated with the poor. Labour was never better paid, and the labourer more respected, at any period, or in any part of the world, than it is at present among us. And that man is not a friend to the poor who endeavours to make those dissatisfied with their present condition, who cannot hope, by any possibility of circumstances, to be bettered by a change.

4. *New York Times* Discusses the Morrill Tariff and American Industry, 1861

The Morrill Tariff

Congress, at the very instant the country is threatened with dismemberment, which may involve a recasting of all our foreign and domestic relations, and the adoption of an entirely new chart for the future, presents the singular spectacle of seeking to inaugurate a line of policy which cannot be changed or modified in any of its important features for many years, without most disastrous consequences. It is now proposed to reënact a highly protective tariff, both for revenue and protection. To the adoption at this crisis of such a measure, there are certainly very grave objections.

No act of the kind should become a law, unless it is to be the *permanent* policy of the country; for immediately upon its adoption capital will rush into manufactures, which would necessarily be sacrificed by its repeal. But are we in a position to cast the horoscope for the future, or determine the policy it may be our interest to adopt, under circumstances which we cannot by any means foresee? All admit the breaking up of the Confederacy to be possible. Suppose it to happen; is it not almost certain that we must adapt our import duties to our altered relations? Suppose the

---

"The Morrill Tariff," *New York Times,* February 14, 1861, p. 4.

Cotton States to maintain even a form of government; they will certainly leave no stone unturned to draw off the Border States. One of the strongest arguments they could address to these would be furnished by a highly protective tariff on the part of our Government, toward which they cherish the deepest aversion, except, perhaps, Maryland and Kentucky. While efforts at reconciliation are still pending, both in and out of Congress, is it wise to divest ourselves of the power of offering similar arguments, and throw an additional firebrand among the present causes of difference?

Another reason for letting things remain as they are, is found in our foreign relations. The tendency of all leading commercial nations, is unmistakably toward *free trade.* If the Southern States go off, we shall immediately come in conflict with them in every court of Europe, if not on our own soil. They will, by appealing to the popular sentiment in all commercial circles, make every effort to secure favorable recognition and relations at our expense. We should be in a pretty fix, with free trade at every Southern port, and a prohibitory tariff at New-York, Philadelphia and Boston. Instead of settling down upon such a policy, we should hold ourselves in a position in which we can readily adjust ourselves to the contingencies that may arise, abroad as well as at home. If we are to have a foreign commerce, it must be a reciprocal one. We must have something to offer as a means of obtaining favorable terms from others. To tie our hands, when, if ever, they should be free, by adopting a policy which we cannot, without a great loss, abandon, is most unwise and unstatesmanlike.

A still stronger reason is drawn from the effect of the proposed measure upon our *internal* trade. In the present crisis we are striking for a trade which has been previously monopolized by the Gulf ports. The action of the seceding States will, to a very considerable extent, close these ports, on account of the dangers to which property in them is exposed. Enough has been seen to prove this. Already are all the highways leading to the Northeastern States crowded with freights that, but for secession, would be going down the Mississippi. Is it not for our interest to draw this trade to us by every means in our power? Once secured it will be retained, compensating in some degree the losses sustained by the present disturbances. With proper measures we can draw to our own harbor no small part of the cotton trade of the Southwestern States, adding the staple, which is the great figure in our foreign commerce, as one of our leading exports. Is it wise in the present emergency to meet this stream of trade by the passage of a law most odious to those turning it to us? Such a course would be commercial suicide.

The modification of the Tariff should not be attempted till we see more clearly the policy we may desire, or be compelled to adopt, especially as it is almost certain that the one proposed will *diminish* instead of increasing the revenue. Such is the opinion of every person who has any familiarity with the subject. The bill was apparently framed with such an object. It virtually sweeps away at a blow the warehouse system, which has recently done more to build up the trade of New-York, than almost any other agency. This was mainly copied from the English system, and is an essential feature in that of any great commercial people. United with our unrivaled means for distribution, this system renders the City of New-York the dépôt for the whole country. People come here to buy for the reason that they know that in the warehouse they can find the genuine foreign manufactured article, not adulterated or imitated by some cunning trickster. . . . The warehouse in effect, makes our City instead of Paris, London, or Liverpool, the dépôt for foreign merchandise. To abolish it, or to limit the time for retaining merchandise in it, would be to send abroad for their goods, merchants who now flock to us from every part of the United States. Its passage would be a blow to our trade quite as fatal and disastrous as secession:—the two coming together would inflict upon us injuries which twenty years could not repair.

The proposed bill is most objectionable both in its principle and in its details, uniting the specific and *ad valorem* duties with such minuteness of subdivision and detail as to give rise to endless misunderstandings and disputes, and rendering necessary, with our present imports, a force at least treble that now employed. Unbleached cottons, for example, having not over *one hundred threads* to the square inch, warp and filling, and not exceeding five ounces in weight, pay one cent duty. Such as have *one hundred and forty threads* to the square inch, and weighing over five ounces, pay two cents; over one hundred and forty threads three cents. If the cottons are bleached the duty is increased in ratio to the number of *threads* per square inch, and weight. The duty on prints is levied in the same way with ten per cent. *ad valorem* added. The first thing appraisers will have to be fitted out with after the law goes into effect, will be magnifying glasses of great power, and scales of exquisite sensitiveness. For the appraisement of what [the great N.Y. store of A. T.] Stewart daily sells, an army of office-holders would be required. In fact, the amount of business now daily transacted at the Customhouse would be impossible; and importations would be necessarily greatly curtailed, because the goods could not be got through the Customhouse. The duty upon manufactures of iron is framed upon a principle often as complicated as upon cottons, and is in most cases entirely prohibitory. On wooden screws, a specific duty, varying from five to eight cents, is laid, equaling 60 per cent. *ad valorem,* and is entirely prohibitory. Bar iron pays $15 per ton. Railway tires pay two cents per pound, and 15 per cent. *ad valorem;* rails, $12 per ton; pig iron, $6. The duty on table blade steel is 136 per cent.; on hoe and fork steel, 167 per cent.; on German machinery steel, 216 per cent.; on round machinery steel, 154 per cent.; on blistered steel, 211 per cent. In fact, the Morrill Tariff is nearly, if not quite, prohibitory upon all manufactures of iron. This is a sop thrown to Pennsylvania. Upon silks, that we can neither produce, nor to any considerable extent manufacture, a duty of 30 per cent. is imposed upon the greater part of the list.

Such are some of the features of this ill-timed, ill-advised, and if carried into effect, disastrous measure. It ties our hands when they should be free. It will destroy our commerce at the very instant our whole care should be directed toward its cultivation and development. It alienates extensive sections of the country we seek to retain. It will tend directly to destroy our credit, by showing to the world that the great source from which we have derived our revenues is no longer available. It is unjust to the manufacturer, because it cannot be maintained. Under these circumstances, we ask Congress to act in view of the circumstances by which it is surrounded, not by the light of tradition, or party affiliations. Otherwise they will deal a deadly blow at the trade and commerce of the country, at the measures now in progress to heal our political differences, and particularly at the party now about to assume the reins of Government, which, by the measures now proposed, will find itself greatly weakened, if not defeated and destroyed.

5. *Atlantic Monthly* Visits Pittsburg, the Workshop of the West, 1868

It is chiefly at Pittsburg that the products of the Pennsylvania hills and mountains are converted into wealth and distributed over the world. The wonder is, not that Pittsburg is an assemblage of flourishing towns of 230,000 inhabitants, but that, placed at such a commanding point, it is not the *most* flourishing and the *most* populous city in America. . . .

Pittsburg announces its peculiar character from afar off. Those who approach it in the night see before them, first of all, a black hill, in the side of which are six round flaming fires, in a row, like six fiery eyes. Then other black hills loom dimly up, with other rows of fires half-way up their sides; and there are similar fiery dots in the gloom as far as the eye can reach. This is wonderfully picturesque, and excites the curiosity of the traveller to the highest point. He thinks that Pittsburg must be at work behind those fires, naked to the waist, with hairy chest and brawny arms, doing tremendous things with molten iron, or forging huge masses white-hot, amid showers of sparks. No such thing. These rows of fires, of which scores can be counted from a favorable point, are merely the chimneys of coke-ovens, quietly doing their duty during the night, unattended. That duty is to convert the waste coal-dust at the mouths of the mines, where it has been accumulating for a century, into serviceable coke. These are almost the only fires about Pittsburg that are always burning, night and day, Sundays and holidays. . . .

There is one evening scene in Pittsburg which no visitor should miss. Owing to the abruptness of the hill behind the town, there is a street along the edge of a bluff, from which you can look directly down upon all that part of the city which lies low, near the level of the rivers. On the evening of this dark day, we were conducted to the edge of the abyss, and looked over the iron railing upon the most striking spectacle we ever beheld. The entire space lying between the hills was filled with blackest smoke, from out of which the hidden chimneys sent forth tongues of flame, while from the depths of the abyss came up the noise of hundreds of steam-hammers. There would be moments when no flames were visible; but soon the wind would force the smoky curtains aside, and the whole black expanse would be dimly lighted with dull wreaths of fire. It is an unprofitable business, view-hunting; but if any one would enjoy a spectacle as striking as Niagara, he may do so by simply walking up a long hill to Cliff Street in Pittsburg, and looking over into—hell with the lid taken off.

Such is the kind of day of which Pittsburg boasts. The first feeling of the stranger is one of compassion for the people who are compelled to live in such an atmosphere. . . . It is interesting to hear a Pittsburgher discourse on this subject; and it much relieves the mind of a visitor to be told, and to have the assertion proved, that the smoke, so far from being an evil, is a blessing. The really pernicious atmospheres, say the Pittsburg philosophers, convey to man no intimation of the poison with which they are laden, and we inhale death while enjoying every breath we draw;

James Parton, "Pittsburg," *Atlantic Monthly* 21 (January 1868): 17–18, 21–22, 25–26, 28, 30–32, 34–35. Another edited version of this document can be found in Roy Lubove, ed., *Pittsburgh* (New York: New Viewpoints, 1976), pp. 8–16. The nineteenth-century spelling of Pittsburg has been preserved in this document.

but this smoke is an evil only to the imagination, and it destroys every property of the atmosphere which is hostile to life. In proof of which the traveller is referred to the tables of mortality, which show that Pittsburg is the most favorable city in the world to longevity. . . .

The "great fact" of Pittsburg is coal. Iron and copper can better afford to come to coal to be melted, than send for coal to come and melt them. All those hills that frown down upon Pittsburg, and those that rise from the rivers back of Pittsburg, have a stratum of coal in them from four to twelve feet thick. . . . The mere quantity of coal in this region is sufficiently staggering. All the foundries and iron-works on earth could find ample room in this region, at the edge of a navigable stream, and have a coal mine at their back doors. . . . [T]here are fifteen thousand square miles of "this sort of thing." The "great Pittsburg coal seam," as it is called, which consists of bituminous coal only, is put down in the books as covering eight and a half millions of acres. . . .

. . . There are in the congregation of towns which the outside world knows only by the name of Pittsburg, five hundred manufactories and "works." Fifty of these are glass-works, in which one half of all our glass-ware is made, and which employ three thousand persons. . . .

Oil Creek is a branch of the Alleghany River, and empties into it one hundred miles above Pittsburg. Pittsburg is, consequently, the great petroleum mart of the world. It is but five years ago that this material became important; and yet there were received at Pittsburg during the year 1866 more than sixteen hundred thousand barrels of it. The Alleghany River is one of the swiftest of navigable streams; but there is never a moment when its surface at Pittsburg is not streaked with petroleum. It would not require remarkable talent in an inhabitant of this place to "set the river on fire." The crude oil is floated down this impetuous river in the slightest-built barges . . . into which the oil is poured as into an enormous trough. . . . It needs but a slight accident to knock a hole in one of these thin barges. When such an accident has occurred, . . . the petroleum lies all spread out upon the swift river, making its way toward Pittsburg, while the barge is filled with water and sunk. . . .

Down by the swift and turbid Alleghany, close to the river, as all the great foundries are, we discovered with difficulty, on a very dark morning, the celebrated Fort Pitt Foundry, where twenty-five hundred of the great guns were cast that blew the late "So-Called" out of water. In this establishment may be seen the sublime of the mechanic arts. Only here, on the continent of America, have there ever been cast those monsters of artillery which are called by the ridiculous diminutive of "the twenty-inch gun." . . .

From seeing one of these enormous guns cast, the visitor at Pittsburg may go, if he chooses, to an establishment where they make tacks so minute that it takes a thousand of them to weigh an ounce. We went thither, having long had an imbecile curiosity to know how nails and tacks are made. How startling the contrast between the slow movements, and tranquil, gloomy vastness of the cannon foundry, and the animation of the great rattling, roaring, crowded nail-works of Chess, Smyth, & Co., all glaring and flashing with light, with many tall chimneys pouring out black smoke and red blaze into the December evening! Noise? There is only one place in this world as noisy as a large nail-factory in full operation, and that is under the sheet at Niagara Falls. How should it be otherwise, when the factory is making many thousand nails a minute, and when every single nail, spike, brad, and tack is *cut* from a strip of cold iron, and headed by a blow upon cold iron? We saw one machine there pouring out shoemakers' brads at the rate of three thousand a minute, and it required the attendance of only one boy. They came rattling down a tin gutter as fast as meal comes from a mill. But to see this wonderful machine astonishes the stranger less than to see a girl in the packing-room who *weighs* and packs two thousand papers of tacks in nine hours. . . .

The crowning glory of Pittsburg is the "American Iron-Works" of Messrs. Jones and Laughlins. This establishment, which employs twenty-five hundred men, which has a coal mine at its back door and an iron mine on Lake Superior, which makes almost every large and difficult iron thing the country requires, which usually has "on hand" seven hundred thousand dollars' worth of finished work, is such a world of wonder that this whole magazine would not contain an adequate account of it. Here are machines ponderous and exact; here are a thousand ingenuities; here is the net result of all that man has done in iron masses during the whole period of his residence upon earth. What should there be here, too, but a specimen of what man can *undo* in iron, in the form of a great heap of rusty twisted rails from Georgia, so completely spoiled by General Sherman's troops that there was nothing to be done with them but sell them for old iron! . . .

We cannot linger among these wondrous "works" of the strong men of Pittsburg. The men themselves have claims upon our notice.

The masters of Pittsburg are mostly of the Scotch-Irish race, Presbyterians, keen and steady in the prosecution of their affairs, indifferent to pleasure, singularly devoid of the usual vanities and ostentations, proud to possess a solid and spacious factory, and to live in an insignificant house. There are no men of leisure in the town. Mr. George H. Thurston, President of the Pacific and Atlantic Telegraph Company, . . . assured us positively that there were not, in all the region which we call Pittsburg, three persons out of business who were physically capable of conducting business. The old men never think of "retiring," nor is there anything for them to retire to. The family tie being powerful in this race, the great firms are usually composed of near relatives, and generally survive the generation that founded them. Thus, the Fort Pitt Foundry, founded in 1803, has cast cannon for every war in which the United States has been engaged, and is now conducted by the worthy and talented nephews of the Charles Knap who made the establishment what it is. In the American Iron-Works, we find six partners, namely, the two chiefs, Messrs. Jones and Laughlin, two sons of one of these chiefs, and two brothers of the other,—a nice family party. Hence, there are few hired clerks in Pittsburg. These mighty "works" are managed with the minimum of expense. The visitor generally finds "the old man" bustling about the "works" in his cap and fustian jacket; while perhaps his eldest son is keeping the books, a son-in-law or nephew is making up the wages accounts, and a younger son is in the warehouse.

The conservative elements here are powerful, as they are in all communities in which families *endure.* Until very recently, in Pittsburg, it would have boded ill for a man to build a handsome house a few miles out of the smoke; and to this day it is said that a Pittsburg man of business who should publish a poem would find his "paper" doubted at the bank. "A good man, sir, but not practical." These excellent and strenuous men accuse themselves vehemently of a want of public spirit, and it is evident the charge is just. For the last few years, business has rushed in upon them like a torrent; and all their force having been expended in doing this business, they now awake to the fact, that a GREAT CITY is upon their hands, to be consolidated, organized, paved, policed, parked, purified, and adorned. They now feel that some of those iron kings, those great men of glass, oil, coal, salt, and clay, must leave business to their sons and nephews, and take hold of Pittsburg. . . .

Nothing in the life of Pittsburg is more striking to a visitor than the completeness of the cessation from labor at the close of the week. The Scotch-Irish race are strict Sabbatarians, and nothing goes on in Pittsburg on Sundays which it is possible to stop. Of all those five hundred tall chimneys, there will not usually be more than two that smoke on Sundays. During the week the town gets under such a headway of industry, that it takes all Saturday afternoon for it to come to a stand. The regular work ceases at noon, but the afternoon is spent in paying wages, grinding tools, cleaning up, making repairs, and getting ready for a fair start on Monday morning. By seven in the evening, the principal streets of Pittsburg are densely filled with washed men. They stroll about; they stand conversing in groups; they gather, in thick semicircles, about every shop-window that has a picture in it, or any bright or curious object; especially do they haunt the news-stands, which provide a free picture-gallery for them of Illustrated News, Comic Monthlies, and Funny Fellows. The men are so numerous, that the whole width of some of the streets is filled with them; and there is not a woman to be seen! Not a single petticoat among thousands of other coats! Yet no crowd could be more orderly and quiet. These men, after a week of intense monotony,—gazing at dull objects and doing the same dull act ten hours a day,—how hungry they seemed for some brightness to flash into their lives! How we longed to usher them all into some gorgeous scene, and give them a banquet of splendors! Mere brilliancy of color and light is transport, we should suppose, to a man who has been making nails or digging coal from Monday morning until Saturday noon.

6. Freeman Hunt, The Ups and Downs of Business, 1856

All men are liable to the ups and downs of business, and those who are engaged in commerce or trade, though they may be cautious and prudent, are sometimes caught in a tight place and are obliged to stop. It has been stated that considerably over seventy-five per cent of those engaged in trade, fail in the course of their career. It must be very disagreeable to be obliged to call a meeting of creditors; but when circumstances render it necessary, it should be done ere it is too late to retrieve one's failing fortunes. No honest creditor will ever treat an honest debtor hardly, who is frank and open[;] the community at large, have respect for that man, who shows his hand fairly and makes a truthful statement.

Recent occurrences show the folly which some men will resort to, in order to retrieve their position,—and who, in hopes of avoiding a failure, commit a thousand times greater evil, and not only sacrifice their credit, but their honor. How often do we hear on 'change, of this or that man failing, who, the day previous, victimized

Freeman Hunt, *Worth and Wealth: A Collection of Maxims, Morals and Miscellanies for Merchants and Men of Business* (New York: Stringer & Townsend, 1856), pp. 78–80.

an intimate friend by exchanging checks, or borrowing a few thousand dollars. This robbing Peter to pay Paul, is a greater sin by far, than allowing a note to be protested, which has been given in exchange for goods. It is not a rare case either, to find that a merchant will sometimes enter into rash speculations, to raise money to relieve himself from embarrassments, which proves only temporary, and only tends to bury him deeper in the mire. We are aware that some men commit these errors, in the hope of better times dawning, but where one is favored by a freak of fortune, twenty find themselves more involved than before.

These evils arise in a great measure from the fear that some men have of facing trouble. To put off from to-day, that which must inevitably happen to-morrow, the vilest schemes are resorted to, and men raise money at a sacrifice of principle, integrity and character. If such a prolongation of misery brought relief, it could not be wondered at, but it is an exception, rather than a rule, that it only renders more certain, that ruin which stares them in the face. Instead of standing on the brink of the precipice, and saying, "Here, gentlemen, are my books, here is my statement, such and such causes have brought me here," and commencing anew, they plunge into the vortex, and, having lost the confidence of their fellow men, find it impossible to rise again.

The haste to be rich, is urged as the primary cause of half the failures. A resort to speculation will probably take the balance. A desire to be considered smart, induces many young men to dabble in stocks, but the chances are about equal to the faro table. A legitimate business closely attended to rarely fails to secure a profit. It will rarely fail to secure wealth, if that profit is not wasted by extravagance or profligacy. It is in Boston as elsewhere, that young merchants live up to their incomes so closely that they have nothing to fall back upon, and thus barter years of happiness for a few years of mistaken gentility.

7. Andrew Carnegie, How Young Men Can Succeed, 1885

It is well that young men should begin at the beginning and occupy the most subordinate positions. Many of the leading businessmen of Pittsburg had a serious responsibility thrust upon them at the very threshold of their career. They were introduced to the broom, and spent the first hours of their business lives sweeping out the office. I notice we have janitors and janitresses now in offices, and our young men unfortunately miss that salutary branch of a business education. But if by chance the professional sweeper is absent any morning the boy who has the genius of the future partner in him will not hesitate to try his hand at the broom. . . . I was one of those sweepers myself, and who do you suppose were my fellow sweepers? David McCargo, now superintendent of the Alleghany Valley Railroad; Robert Pitcairn, Superintendent of the Pennsylvania Railroad, and Mr. Moreland, City Attorney. We all took turns, two each morning did the sweeping; and now I remember Davie

Andrew Carnegie, "The Road to Business Success: A Talk to Young Men," address at Curry Commercial College, Pittsburgh, Pa., June 23, 1885, in Joseph Frazier Wall, ed., *The Andrew Carnegie Reader* (Pittsburgh: University of Pittsburgh Press, 1992), pp. 42–50. The nineteenth-century spelling of Pittsburg has been preserved in this document.

was so proud of his clean white shirt bosom that he used to spread over it an old silk bandana handkerchief which he kept for the purpose, and we other boys thought he was putting on airs. So he was. None of us had a silk handkerchief.

Assuming that you have all obtained employment and are fairly started, my advice to you is "aim high." I would not give a fig for the young man who does not already see himself the partner or the head of an important firm. Do not rest content for a moment in your thoughts as head clerk, or foreman, or general manager in any concern, no matter how extensive. Say each to yourself, "My place is at the top." *Be king in your dreams.* . . .

Let me indicate two or three conditions essential to success. Do not be afraid that I am going to moralize, or inflict a homily upon you. I speak upon the subject only from the view of a man of the world, desirous of aiding you to become successful businessmen. You all know that there is no genuine, praiseworthy success in life if you are not honest, truthful, fair-dealing. . . . I hope you will not take it amiss if I warn you against three of the gravest dangers which will beset you in your upward path.

The first and most seductive, and the destroyer of most young men, is the drinking of liquor. I am no temperance lecturer in disguise, but a man who knows and tells you what observation has proved to him; and I say to you that you are more likely to fail in your career from acquiring the habit of drinking liquor than from any, or all, the other temptations likely to assail you. . . .

The next greatest danger to a young business man in this community I believe to be that of speculation. When I was a telegraph operator here we had no Exchanges in the City, but the men or firms who speculated upon the Eastern Exchanges were necessarily known to the operators. They could be counted on the fingers of one hand. These men were not our citizens of first repute: they were regarded with suspicion. I have lived to see all of these speculators irreparably ruined men, bankrupt in money and bankrupt in character. There is scarcely an instance of a man who has made a fortune by speculation and kept it. Gamesters die poor, and there is certainly not an instance of a speculator who has lived a life creditable to himself, or advantageous to the community. . . .

The third and last danger against which I shall warn you is one which has wrecked many a fair craft which started well and gave promise of a prosperous voyage. It is the perilous habit of indorsing—all the more dangerous, inasmuch as it assails one generally in the garb of friendship. . . . You will as businessmen now and then probably become security for friends. Now, here is the line at which regard for the success of friends should cease and regard for your own honour begin. . . .

Assuming you are safe in regard to these your gravest dangers, the question now is how to rise from the subordinate position we have imagined you in, through the successive grades to the position for which you are, in my opinion, and, I trust, in your own, evidently intended. I can give you the secret. It lies mainly in this. Instead of the question, "What must I do for my employer?" substitute "What can I do?" Faithful and conscientious discharge of the duties assigned you is all very well, but the verdict in such cases generally is that you perform your present duties so well that you had better continue performing them. Now, young gentlemen, this will not do. It will not do for the coming partners. There must be something beyond this. We make Clerks, Bookkeepers, Treasurers, Bank Tellers of this class, and there they remain to the end of the chapter. The rising man must do something exceptional, and beyond the range of his special department. HE MUST ATTRACT ATTENTION. A shipping clerk, he may do so by discovering in an invoice an error with which he has nothing to do, and which has escaped the attention of the proper party. If a weighing clerk, he may save for the firm by doubting the adjustment of the scales and having them corrected, even if this be the province of the master mechanic. If a messenger boy, even he can lay the seed of promotion by going beyond the letter of his instructions in order to secure the desired reply. . . . Such an employee must perforce be thought of, and thought of kindly and well. It will not be long before his advice is asked in his special branch, and if the advice given be sound, it will soon be asked and taken upon questions of broader bearing. This means partnership; if not with present employers then with others. Your foot, in such a case, is upon the ladder; the amount of climbing done depends entirely upon yourself. . . .

There is one sure mark of the coming partner, the future millionnaire; his revenues always exceed his expenditures. He begins to save early, almost as soon as he begins to earn. No matter how little it may be possible to save, save that little. Invest it securely, not necessarily in bonds, but in anything which you have good reason to believe will be profitable, but no gambling with it, remember. A rare chance will soon present itself for investment. The little you have saved will prove the basis for an amount of credit utterly surprising to you. Capitalists trust the saving young man. . . .

You may grow important, or become discouraged when year by year you float on in subordinate positions. There is no doubt that it is becoming harder and harder as business gravitates more and more to immense concerns, for a young man without capital to get a start for himself, and in this city especially, where large capital is essential, it is unusually difficult. Still, let me tell you for your encouragement that there is no country in the world where able and energetic young men can so readily rise as this, nor any city where there is more room at the top. It has been impossible to meet the demand for capable, first-class bookkeepers (mark the adjectives), the supply has *never* been equal to the demand. . . .

And here is the prime condition of success, the great secret: concentrate your energy, thought, and capital exclusively upon the business in which you are engaged. Having begun in one line, resolve to fight it out on that line, to lead in it; adopt every improvement, have the best machinery, and know the most about it.

The concerns which fail are those which have scattered their capital, which means that they have scattered their brains also. They have investments in this, or that, or the other, here, there and everywhere. "Don't put all your eggs in one basket" is all wrong. I tell you "put all your eggs in one basket, and then watch that basket." Look round you and take notice; men who do that do not often fail. It is easy to watch and carry the one basket. It is trying to carry too many baskets that breaks most eggs in this country. He who carries three baskets must put one on his head, which is apt to tumble and trip him up. One fault of the American businessman is lack of concentration.

To summarize what I have said: Aim for the highest; never enter a barroom; do not touch liquor, or if at all only at meals; never speculate; never indorse beyond your surplus cash fund; make the firm's interest yours; break orders always to save owners; concentrate; put all your eggs in one basket, and watch that basket; expenditure always within revenue; lastly, be not impatient, for, as Emerson says, "no one can cheat you out of ultimate success but yourselves."

8. Picturing Progress: An Estey Organ Company Advertising Poster, ca. 1890

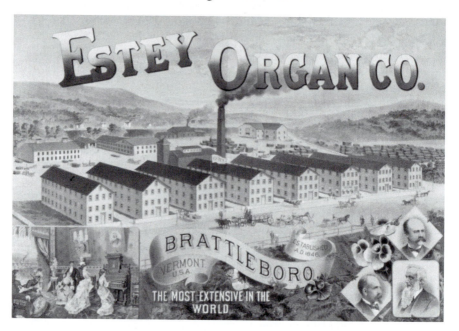

 E S S A Y S

In the first essay, John N. Ingham, professor of history at the University of Toronto, looks at the history of Pittsburgh's iron and steel industry. At midcentury, an old aristocracy of iron makers was challenged by upstart steelmakers, including Andrew Carnegie and Henry Clay Frick. Some members of the old order tried to compete on Carnegie's terms, while more independent manufacturers remained committed to the small-scale production of specialty goods. By the 1880s, Pittsburgh was home to a regional iron and steel industry that produced a range of products for many types of applications. How does this depiction of Pittsburgh compare with the image of Lowell?

Next, Pamela Walker Laird, a historian of business and culture at the University of Colorado at Denver and author of *Advertising Progress: American Business and the Rise of Consumer Marketing* (1998), examines the meaning of ideas such as progress, success, and industry. As the nation industrialized, these celebratory notions achieved wide currency through advertisements, newspapers, periodicals, and books. Such images and narratives provided businessmen with guideposts as they sought to establish, operate, and expand all types of enterprise. What do Laird's conclusions tell us about nineteenth-century attitudes toward business? Who read the prescriptive literature about business opportunities? Did these stories about individual industriousness defuse some of the antagonism toward business?

Show card, Estey Organ Company, Brattleboro, Vt., ca. 1890. Collection of Pamela Laird. This document can also be found in Pamela Walker Laird, *Advertising Progress: American Business and the Rise of Consumer Marketing* (Baltimore, Md.: Johns Hopkins University Press, 1998), opposite p. 256.

Finally, Sven Beckert, the Dunwalke Professor of History at Harvard University and author of *The Monied Metropolis: New York City and the Consolidation of the American Bourgeoisie, 1850–1896* (2003), considers how the Civil War reshaped industry, finance, and trade in Manhattan. How did the Civil War affect business-government relations? How does Beckert's analysis relate to Laird's discussion of industry?

Clash of the Titans: Andrew Carnegie and Pittsburgh's Old Iron Masters

JOHN N. INGHAM

If Pittsburgh's mercantile aristocracy was confronted by a sizable challenge with the emergence of the iron industry during the antebellum years, it faced an unbelievably awesome encounter with the rise of Andrew Carnegie and the Bessemer steel industry in the years after the war. The stable, contented, almost smug Presbyterian local elite watched massive steel mills rise from dusty fields and observed the emergence of new men who commanded these enterprises—men who were sometimes from divergent social, economic, and cultural origins but who also brought radically new ideas about the way business should be conducted in the city. This new group, most dramatically presented in the person of Andrew Carnegie, bid fair to be a plutocracy in the young industrial city, one that would supplant the older mercantile and small industry iron and steel elite. Within this context, then, a class war of enormous proportions ensued during the last years of the nineteenth century.

That class war had its origins in Braddock's Field, about twelve miles from downtown Pittsburgh on the Monongahela River. There, in 1875, Andrew Carnegie was building a massive Bessemer steel complex, one larger, more integrated, and more complete than existed anywhere in the world. Since the nation was caught in the grip of its first modern depression, most sensible businessmen were cutting back, waiting out the hard times before expanding their operations. Not the impetuous Carnegie. Like Henry Clay Frick, his future partner, Carnegie viewed hard times as ideal for expansion, since costs were so much lower. Nonetheless, the depression caused him much trouble, as several of his business associates were bankrupted and Carnegie's own resources were stretched to the limit. All of this was characteristic of the man and his technique. It was a method that would frustrate, awe, and alienate many members of the older Pittsburgh aristocracy.

But what a wonder Carnegie constructed at Braddock's Field! Soon to be known as the Edgar Thomson Works (significantly and not coincidentally named for the president of the Pennsylvania Railroad), it was a technological and organizational marvel of the modern world. Located at the junction of three railroads (the Pennsylvania, the Baltimore & Ohio, and the Pittsburgh & Lake Erie), it was a sprawling series of buildings, switchyards, engines, sheds, and smokestacks. The crowning glory of the mill was a wonder of the industrial world: a screaming, belching series

John N. Ingham, *Making Iron and Steel: Independent Mills in Pittsburgh, 1820–1920* (Columbus: Ohio State University Press, 1991), pp. 47–49, 74–75, 77–80, 84, 94–95. Reprinted by permission of Ohio State University Press.

of Bessemer converters, capable of making steel in vast quantities. This new company was a model of modern integration. . . .

When the Edgar Thomson Works reached its production peak later in the century, it was capable of producing three thousand tons of steel rails daily, as much as a typical Pittsburgh puddling mill of the 1830s could produce in an entire year. This greatly increased velocity of flow through the works placed increased demands on the managers. As a result, Carnegie hired William P. Shinn, formerly a railroad accountant, to install railroad accounting techniques in his new steel plant. . . . Shinn and Carnegie revolutionized manufacturing practice and the traditions of accountability in American business. Carnegie's dictum had always been "Watch the costs, and the profits will take care of themselves," and his accounting system, a revolutionary change from traditional lump accounting techniques in the iron industry, allowed him to fulfill his ideals. Carnegie used Shinn's cost sheets to give him control over the entire operation, even from New York City, where he had already moved by this time. All of this was an enormous departure from the hovering, personal, idiosyncratic rule-of-thumb methods practiced by most Pittsburgh iron masters.

As a result, Carnegie and his massive steel complexes have naturally dominated our view of the late nineteenth-century iron and steel industry. He was, after all, the most dynamic element on the Pittsburgh industrial scene. And his techniques of mass production, high throughput, accountability, control, and professional bureaucratic management came to characterize large-scale American industries increasingly in the twentieth century. Carnegie was a harbinger of what Chandler has called "the managerial revolution in American business." Yet, the unspoken assumption seems to be that the rest of the iron and steel industry, especially in Pittsburgh, the very cockpit of America's industrial transformation, either followed suit or, more likely, was bludgeoned to death by the massively efficient Carnegie mills. Nothing could be further from the truth. . . .

Most of Pittsburgh's independent iron and steel makers never directly challenged Carnegie or became involved in the large-batch rail market. And even those who did quickly learned their lesson, a deceptively simple one that has resurfaced in recent years as a maxim for businessmen: "Stick to your knitting." In this case, sticking to their knitting often meant staying with familiar markets and technologies. If they did branch out into new markets and technologies, these old-line steel men made sure these endeavors suited their temperaments and abilities. As a result, the independent iron and steel manufacturers at the turn of the century in Pittsburgh engaged in a quest that has become the hallmark of small business, the search for a specialized market niche in which they could survive and prosper and, at the same time, be shielded from the economies of scale and cost efficiencies of large-scale operators like Andrew Carnegie.

It is difficult to make broad general statements about specialized niche marketing. It is, after all, by its very nature rather small, unique, and resistant to generalization. It was precisely those characteristics that made it difficult for the large-scale producers to enter these markets. If the markets had been amenable to generalization, products and market strategies could have been standardized and large-scale producers would have conquered them. Nonetheless, it is possible to isolate certain essential features of the market strategies and technological responses employed by Pittsburgh's independent iron and steel manufacturers during these years. . . .

. . . In 1894, . . . Pittsburgh was still in many respects Iron City. Of the sixty-three iron and steel plants in Pittsburgh and the surrounding area, thirty (48 percent) made wrought iron. At a time when the number of puddling furnaces had declined to 4,700 nationally, there were still 1,050 single puddling furnaces in Pittsburgh, representing 22 percent of the national total. These furnaces produced about 808,000 tons of wrought iron annually. At the same time, there were just eight Bessemer plants in the city, eighteen open hearth plants, and ten crucible operations. Wrought iron was still king in Pittsburgh in the mid-1890s, even though the output of the Carnegie works alone exceeded that of all thirty-one iron mills combined.

By 1901, the number of plants producing wrought iron in the Pittsburgh area had dwindled significantly. In that year, there were just nineteen such plants, containing 573 puddling furnaces with a capacity for about 605,000 tons of wrought iron. Of these, only a dozen remained independent entities, with production capacity of 363,000 tons. At this time, there were sixty-three steel plants and rolling mills in Pittsburgh and Allegheny County, seven producing Bessemer steel, twenty-two making open hearth steel, ten producing crucible, and four making blister steel. Pittsburgh was no longer Iron City, but wrought iron production was not quite dead, and, in fact, manufacturers still found lucrative markets for its products. We shall examine a few of those firms and their market strategies, better to understand the complex operation of the iron and steel industry at the turn of the century.

Most of the iron firms that managed to operate successfully in the late nineteenth century were not exciting or spectacular. As a result, there has been a tendency to dismiss them as unimportant. That is a mistake, because although they were certainly less dramatic than the Carnegie operations, they were far more typical of the iron and steel industry in Pittsburgh, and of American manufacturing generally, at the turn of the century. One such firm was the Sable Rolling Mill. One of the oldest and most conservative merchant iron firms in the city, it was run by Christopher Zug and his son Charles. The plant had been built in 1845 in partnership with the Graff family. When the Graffs erected their blast furnace in Pittsburgh in 1859, it gave the Zug and Graff iron firm an informally integrated structure. During the Civil War, the Sable mill emerged as one of the strongest and wealthiest in the city; by 1874 it had thirty-four puddling furnaces with an annual capacity of fifteen thousand tons of merchant iron, along with a nail factory in the city's Ninth Ward. . . . [I]t was worth $1 million by this time.

The Sable mill was crippled by a combination of factors in the mid-1870s. Partly, it was caused by the depression of the time, but even more by a dispute between Charles H. Zug and his sisters over the distribution of their father's estate. The result was that the firm, with assets of between $800,000 and $900,000 and liabilities of only $400,000 to $600,000, was forced to file for bankruptcy. It is quite clear that on the business side, Sable was still doing well, but the family feud over inheritance rights caused great problems. The firm was reorganized in 1877, with Charles Zug and his son still running it, but with a number of new partners who brought in additional capital. By 1880, Sable mill was in good financial condition, and the company continued to prosper despite the vicissitudes of the 1880s and 1890s. By the turn of the century, Sable Iron was a small- to moderate-size iron mill (they made no steel) with an annual capacity for 22,500 tons of merchant bar iron. Their one concession to finding new markets and new products was the erection of a sheet mill, which produced 14,000 tons of sheet per year. Like many other small Pittsburgh iron firms, the Sable mill marketed its products with its own sales force, seldom relying on the services of metals or hardware brokers. It was a business that depended on a reputation for high-quality products and personal service. Sable mill, as one of the old-line iron firms in the city, was steeped in reputation and rectitude, and this fact was of great benefit to the company in terms of its economic survival at the turn of the century. The quiet, conservative Sable Rolling Mill continued to be run profitably and successfully by the Zug family until it was dismantled around the time of World War I. Like many other Pittsburgh iron families, the Zugs found a safe and profitable market niche in the late 1870s and 1880s and never tried to produce steel or to challenge any of the larger firms in areas where their economies of scale gave them an advantage. Quiet, cautious Sable Iron and the Zug family did not make headlines and were seldom noticed. All they did was survive and make money.

Vesuvius Iron was similar to Sable Iron in many respects. Built in 1846, it was run for years by the Lewis, Dalzell, O'Hara, and Bailey families. By 1868, . . . it was worth between $500,000 and $600,000. Six years later, it had twenty-four single puddling furnaces and produced twelve thousand tons of bar and sheet iron, rods, hoops, and nails. As it was for Sable Iron, the depression of the 1870s was hard on Vesuvius, and the plant sat idle for two years, until it was taken over by John Moorhead, Jr., member of another wealthy pre–Civil War . . . upper-class iron family.

Moorhead, who had just graduated from Yale, ran Vesuvius for nearly fifty years until his death in 1927. During these years, although Vesuvius increased its output slightly, it never changed its basic structure of operation. In 1884, the plant had twenty-eight single puddling furnaces and could produce 12,000 tons of iron, along with 105,000 kegs of cut nails. By 1894, it produced 22,500 tons of iron annually and no longer made cut nails, which had been rendered largely obsolete by wire nails. In 1901, still only puddling wrought iron, Vesuvius had forty single puddling furnaces with an annual capacity for 100,000 tons. No steel of any kind was ever produced in the works. Like Sable and other independent iron and steel firms, Moorhead marketed Vesuvius's products in traditional markets, using his own contacts and in-house sales force to pursue them. There was nothing fancy or innovative here, just old-line basic business enterprise, a business system inherited from the nineteenth century that lasted well into the twentieth.

The A. M. Byers Pipe Works was perhaps the most successful of the old Pittsburgh iron firms that stuck to their knitting. Taking as its motto "Wrought iron pipe or bust," Byers Pipe profitably pursued rather traditional technologies and markets until the 1960s. Much of the market for Byers's product came from the burgeoning oil and gas industry during the first half of the twentieth century. Its pipe was also used for irrigation systems and hydraulic mining. It was a market that the Byers family executives began exploiting when the oil and gas industry was located in western Pennsylvania, and when the industry began migrating west and south, they used their contacts with industry executives, especially the Mellon-and-Guffey-owned Gulf Oil, to enhance their network of personal contacts.

Just as it is inaccurate to assume that Pittsburgh's wrought iron firms were all dying out at the turn of the century, it is wrong to conclude that all of them were able to find the elusive secret of success. A stark example of failure was the Pittsburgh Iron Mill, one of the oldest and most prestigious merchant iron firms in the city. Owned by the Painter family, it was worth over $1 million in the mid-1870s and as late as 1879 was the second-largest iron mill in the city, producing twenty-seven thousand tons annually. But although Pittsburgh iron underwent some linear expansion, it did not move successfully into profitable market areas. As a result, the Painters sold the plant to American Steel & Wire in 1898, turning their attention to the lucrative banking field. If Pittsburgh Iron did not survive, the Painters did, simply transferring their wealth and social connections to banking. Other old iron mills, such as Sligo Iron, Pennsylvania Iron, Kensington Iron, and Keystone Rolling Mill, had varied experiences during the later years of the nineteenth century. Sligo, like Sable, continued running profitably until it was sold in 1903, but Kensington Iron, Pennsylvania Iron, and Keystone Rolling Mill were dismantled in the late 1890s. . . .

Andrew Carnegie was the least typical of all of Pittsburgh's iron and steel manufacturers; rather it was men and firms like the Zugs at Sable Iron and John Moorhead at Vesuvius who constituted the archetype. Normally cautious and conservative, they were successful in finding profitable markets and adopting the proper technologies. Attaining great wealth and esteemed social status, few were willing to risk them. . . . These men were determined to run their mills, and to run them in their own way, so they chose a quieter and safer path of survival.

For most Pittsburgh iron and steel manufacturers in the late nineteenth century, the route to survival and profitability lay neither with breathtaking expansion and innovation nor with steadfast refusal to produce anything but wrought iron. . . . They continually sought out new markets, markets of a more specialized nature that could be serviced by small production runs of specialty iron and steel. A majority of the older Pittsburgh iron and steel men followed this path. . . .

. . . [T]he independent iron and steel makers in Pittsburgh were hardly an aberration. If literature on the American scene has tended to glorify the large and the dynamic, to thrust forward images of Andrew Carnegie and the large-scale integrated organization with its armies of professional managers and bureaucrats, it is useful to recall that all of the world was not America. Not even all of America was America, or at least the standard textbook version of the country. America, despite the Carnegies and Rockefellers, was still largely dominated by small business at the turn of the century.

The same was true of the iron and steel industry, of which Pittsburgh was the largest and most important center in the country. Long before Carnegie made his first Bessemer steel at the Edgar Thomson Works in 1875, Pittsburgh's mills dominated the industrial scene in the city, state, and nation. The dazzling brilliance of the Carnegie works obscured their role and accomplishments in the last quarter of the nineteenth century. But they did not fail, or even cease to grow and change. They continued as a strong backbone of more traditional segments of the wrought iron and crucible steel production. . . . With their more traditional methods on the shop floor and in the office, these iron and steel masters were not simply a forgotten remnant of the past. They continued to grow and prosper until at least the outbreak of World War II and represented an American equivalent to the smaller, traditional family-dominated iron and steel firms in Britain and France.

Progress and the Double Meaning of Industry

PAMELA WALKER LAIRD

The fiercest battles in the West's perpetual war between spiritual and material values may well have been fought in nineteenth-century America, and they very much colored the popular culture, including the advertisements, of that period. Never before had such material opportunities presented themselves to so many, and never since has outspoken religious morality had such a hold on those same people. The tensions between these two powerful attractions pulled at everyone. The decisions about how to balance the opposing attractions dominated some people's public lives, pushing them to take strong positions—a few ascetics at one extreme and the most ostentatious of the robber barons and their families at the other. Most people who had the option found a more even balance comfortable, and their compromise contributed to the formation of the Victorian-era American middle class and its bourgeois cultural style. . . .

Businesspeople often operate in the center of the battle between materialism and moralism, the targets of proselytizing from all sides, receiving both praise and criticism. Nineteenth-century entrepreneurs experienced the lures of materialism in part because money measured their business success, yet they also carried the still-strong traces of a deeply rooted tradition of wrestling with materialism. . . . In this context, those who took on the task of advising people with ambitions in business always addressed the problem of balancing the tensions between materialism and moralism. For instance, in Haines's *Worth and Wealth: Or the Art of Getting, Saving and Using Money,* the chapter on "Money-Getting" began with the assertion that "Money-getting is the aim, the paramount end, of business." The 1884 tome described in tantalizing detail the merits of money and "its secret charm" for meeting practical and social needs, despite the "intonation of contempt [with which] the word is sometimes uttered." But then the author joined ranks with thousands of others in print and pulpit who warned the ambitious of the difficulties of seeking both money and salvation, for "Money is king; and here lies the danger. . . . For money is hardening to the heart. . . . [Every] true business man . . . [must] feel . . . that while he is laboring for the increase and distribution of wealth, he is working for the elevation and civilization of the masses." If men followed the commandments "to be diligent in business, to be active, to contrive, to invent, to waken up intellect, to render the material world tributary and subservient, and to accumulate the products of art and nature," then they would be able "to accumulate money to enhance their own and others' happiness." . . .

Most nineteenth-century writers offering this kind of advice identified their own balances as "success." Thousands of missives, including trade journals, proclaimed the Victorian compromise that exalted character as the sure road to success. *One Hundred Lessons in Business,* 1887, preached typically, "Let a young man *fear God, be industrious, know his business, spend a little less than he earns,* and success is

Pamela Walker Laird, *Advertising Progress: American Business and the Rise of Consumer Marketing* (Baltimore, Md.: Johns Hopkins University Press, 1998), pp. 102–106, 108–110, 113–117. Copyright © 1998. Reprinted with permission of The Johns Hopkins University Press.

sure." The popularity of the Victorian compromise did not reside only in print. In 1867, Horace Greeley spoke to thousands of young men on at least two occasions at the behest of S. S. Packard, the president of Bryant & Stratton Business College in New York. Indeed, people were turned away for lack of space when Greeley gave his "Address on Success in Business." Inspired by the opportunities for success in an America that was destined "to bound forward on a career of prosperous activity such as the world has not known," Greeley extolled his audiences to "believe that success in life is within the reach of every one who will truly and nobly seek it." Reciting the usual list of characteristics that ensured success, Greeley emphasized "that thrift, within reasonable limits, is the moral obligation of every man; that he should endeavor and aspire to be a little better off at the close of each year."

Yet wealth alone could not serve as the measurement of success for Victorian businesspeople in the United States. An 1891 trade journal article with advice to young men began: "Being an American, you are ambitious. If that ambition is of the right kind, you are striving for two things: first of all, reputation, and second, money. Success in these two things will make you an example of what is every American young man's ideal—'The successful business man.'" Moral character, in turn, determined the success or failure of a person's business career. Thus, young people were extolled to piety, industry, honesty, frugality, punctuality, and like virtues—the standards of middle-class respectability—plus the virtues of masculine, middle-class heroics, such as initiative and competitiveness, all entirely within the range of any young man's potential. By this logic, success implied that a person must have followed the path of rectitude. . . .

Linking Business and Personal Industry

The intimate association between owner-managers and their businesses linked the industrialists' sense of personal worth with that of their firms. The owner-manager represented more than the typical mode of operating the American firm before 1890: the owner-manager also exemplified the ideal of the businessperson for the century. Owning and managing well one's own business was everywhere cited as how one could elevate oneself above anonymity without artistic or literary genius, but with the steadfast application of good character. Within this context that so prized self-employment, one's business and its reputation became an extension of one's self and personal reputation. . . . Andrew Carnegie declared that for business men, "Your firm is your monument." Similarly, Cyrus Hall McCormick frequently made it known that he was, according to his biographer William Hutchinson, "proud of his industry, and to have his name synonymous with harvesting machinery the world over was the chief ambition of his life." McCormick's grandson accorded the inventor the accolade that "the reaper was his life." . . .

The ethos of work pervaded popular literature of that century, and the businesspeople of whom we have direct reports seem to have gloried in their never-ending labors. Particularly the materially successful employers of others, or those who sought their patronage, praised the virtues of discipline and work in a marketplace allegedly teeming with opportunities for the diligent. The multitudinous nineteenth-century declarations on the virtues of work include *Triumphant Democracy,* throughout which Carnegie proclaims that work is the mark of the Republic. Of all the character traits that the advice literature of the period expounded upon to guide ambitious young people, willingness to work was the most central. The messages typically followed this pattern: "Accordingly, labor has ever been the indispensable condition of success in any and all departments of life. We are now pointing out to you, reader, an imperial highway to fortune, but we do most earnestly assure you that this highway can never be built without the most unremitting and indefatigable exertion on your part. . . . Industry is the price of excellence in everything." A firm's success, therefore, indicated the hard-working, good character of its owner-manager.

Embedded within this ethos of work was the importance of productiveness, as both an extension of the Protestant ethos of calling and as a major component of the traditional middle-class critique of nonproductive elements in society, both upper- and lower-class. The impulse to measure success in some way that transcended wealth derived in part from industrialists' desire to distinguish themselves from the traditional elites, the mercantile, financial, or idle rich. . . . [A]fter the Civil War "the title of 'producer' had taken on the lustre formerly inherent in the word 'merchant.' " Increasing employment and the stocks of available goods, in addition to lowering costs, were grand accomplishments for innovative producers. Under the title of "The Greatest Wealth Producers," the lead editorial in an 1893 issue of the *Iron Age* praised those whose work created more wealth than they consumed. . . . The double meanings of *industry*—more widely applied then than now—as a production activity and as diligence in personal character, also indicates these linkages. . . .

Progress as the Measure of Legitimacy

The productivity on which the nineteenth-century industrialists prided themselves required not only their own diligent labors but also their employment of the period's newest technologies of production, transportation, and communication. The larger cultural context within which manufacturers operated was a century of phenomenally dramatic changes in people's material and cultural experiences. . . .

Once American industrialization was under way, debates abounded about what sort of changes might best move society closer to perfection, but only the hopeless and rare skeptics did not adopt some version of progress. Even working-class people generally hoped that their children would someday share in the abundance that their exploited labor produced. The artisans whose shops were outmoded by mechanization tended to displace their distress, blaming immigrants or other minorities, including women factory workers. . . . Although some scientists and philosophers held more sophisticated interpretations of progress, many shared the popular views that "the growth of free-enterprise commercialism as the driving force of progress paved the way for a social evolutionism in which the attainment of middle-class values was the last step in the ascent of a linear hierarchy of developmental stages." At the core of this process was "the individual's effort to conquer his environment through the exploitation of better technology." . . .

Virtually every writer in the late nineteenth century who addressed contemporary issues included references to achieved progress, hopes for more, programs to ensure it, or concerns for its inequities. In fact, the concept was so ubiquitous that it is almost meaningless to refer to a separate literature of progress. Rather, the themes of improvement on personal, national, and world levels pervaded the century's writing and iconography. In particular, the vast majority of writers favorably associated technological developments with positive change and, hence, progress. Horace Greeley wrote in 1872 that industrial growth "is in the line of progress, in the direction of securing to each individual the largest liberty for his personal endeavors, and for society at large the greatest amount of material for its collective comfort and well-being." Even those who criticized the destructive and exploitative aspects of American development generally believed that industrialization itself was not the source of problems. Both Henry George in *Poverty and Progress* and Edward Bellamy in *Looking Backward* firmly believed that a positive progress through the advances of technology and industry could be had, although it required significant redirection of the nation's patterns of power and distribution. Most writers did not debate the merits of contemporary progress as generally defined, but simply accepted the changes as natural and appropriate. For example, a reference manual of "facts and figures" on American development was entitled *The National Hand-Book of American Progress,* expressing the connection between quantitative development and the author's notions of progress.

The industrialist class was prominent among the many Americans "convinced" . . . of both the reality and the merits of progress, as they experienced it. Indeed, as important actors in the material developments of their era, industrialists . . . helped to define progress by their enterprise both in production and in marketing. Their industries made available new and increasingly abundant material goods; their messages to the public about the desirability of those goods helped to set the direction and pace of America's sense of progress. Yet they also experienced great anxieties about their status as a new class as well as tensions when their materialism challenged their traditional values. They were, therefore, of all Americans, particularly likely to find attractive the notions of industrialization as progress. For them, participation in the developments of the era became an important indication of success because it combined control over technological power and acquiring wealth from it with a transcendent value, namely, the betterment of humankind. Such notions of progress resolved their internal tensions between spiritual and worldly ambitions; they gave industrialists a measure of their successes and thereby legitimated their agency in the century's transformations. Of the various transcendent values that industrialists could have adapted to project their successful enterprises, such as piety, charity, family devotion, and so on, progress offered the most powerful explanation and legitimation for the revolution in which they participated.

Yet material progress was not an unmixed blessing, then any more than now. The transformations entailed enormous costs, and some of those costs have been accounted extensively. From our vantage point, we are recently sensitive to the environmental costs. Other costs included the greatest mass dislocation—still ongoing—in history, as wave after wave of rural and village peoples subjected themselves to industry's regimentation of time and behavior. City living eliminated cheap, fresh food from most people's diets, even during harvest season, as it also did away with traditional communities and quiet. The exploitation and degradation of the laboring classes have been well documented, as have myriad other tragic consequences.

Such lists of the costs of the industrial, urban transformation typically focus on the people who suffered most obviously and who had the least control over the conditions under which they struggled. Other Americans seemed to have gained more than they had lost in the transformation. The Victorian bourgeois, for example, and those close enough to aspire to join that dominant stratum, were generally reckoned the successes of the era. Certainly in terms of material goods, they had opportunities to partake of the new profusion of goods from industry and world trade that marked material progress. Yet there were costs for these successful people, too. Indeed, the dislocations and stresses of "modern" living generated new ailments for Victorian women and men, such as neurasthenia and varieties of depression and anxiety. Furthermore, explosive urbanization and industrialization threatened and often destroyed the spaces people had known and trusted. Confrontations with the new technological systems, living conditions, and multicultural melange that were intrinsic parts of the changes at every level created tensions even as they fascinated and challenged people, individually and collectively. . . .

Why, then, did Victorian Americans subject themselves to such stresses and dislocations? Unlike the laboring classes, who mainly sought modest improvements in their meager standards of living through their decisions, the middle and upper classes had to have been driven by ambitions beyond subsistence. To a great extent, a desire to keep up with the processes of industrial, urban transformation propelled many people; they did not want to be left behind by either their peers or the abstract standards of success that signified participation in the progress of the time. Their cultural inheritance also attributed spiritual as well as worldly value to work as the means to success and progress. In 1883, *The Golden Gems of Life* typified how the Victorian compromise tied together the work ethos with success and progress. "Labor may be a burden and a chastisement, but it is also an honor and a glory. Without it nothing can be accomplished. All that to man is great and precious is acquired only through labor. . . . It is by labor that mankind have risen from a state of barbarism to the light of the present. It is only by labor that progression can continue. Labor [is] the grand measure of progress." In a complex and powerfully motivating spiral, the very people whose access to the means of production made them the prime actors in the era's transformations, themselves felt a compelling need to keep step with the processes that they and their peers drove forward. . . .

This ideology of progress linked material and social improvements. Its power to justify and to motivate enterprise helps explain why industrialization and urbanization dominated the American nineteenth century despite their disruptions and costs. Although these processes have appeared so vast and profound that both contemporary and later observers have been inclined to declare them inevitable, even deterministic processes, they were not. Like any other historical process, they resulted from countless decisions by countless individuals driven by their personal needs, ambitions, and expectations. There were, of course, different orders of self-determination in people's decision making; investors generally had more freedom of choice than did unskilled laborers, for example. Whatever their circumstances, people generally tried—as they do now—to weigh as well as possible the consequences of alternative decisions. The sum total of infinite numbers of individual decisions determined the nature of the industrial and urban transformations the nation experienced. In this context, Victorian beliefs about progress dominated a worldview that could explain what people experienced, while motivating them and providing some direction for their efforts. Attributing changes to progress, with its positive connotations, legitimized, even glorified, both the changes and their consequences, however unfortunate or disruptive they appeared in the short run. As Lewis Mumford has written of the American nineteenth century, "Life was judged by the extent to which it ministered to progress, progress was not judged by the extent to which it ministered to life." Successful participation in the new order could also validate an individual's activities and values by placing them into the perspective of this grand historical sweep. Since the products of material progress themselves defined the rewards of participating in modern times, producing as well as acquiring and using modern manufactured and marketed goods became a primary measure of one's successes, and hence one's worth in the new order.

Competition and Progress

Besides self-justification, why might nineteenth-century industrialists try to project a public image of themselves as progressive producers? Without question, a fiercely competitive experience dominated businesspeople's activities and thoughts. In a collection of biographies, *Men of Business,* written for Scribner's Men of Achievement series in 1893, William O. Stoddard compared business with the "ancient idea that war is the normal condition of the human race." In the "warlike rivalry" of business, "there is perpetual conflict. Business men of all occupations still speak of the season before them as 'the campaign.' In it they expect to meet with competition, and . . . enemies in the field." Accounts and trade were, and are still, *won* in the business world. Some commentators even attributed the intensification of competition to the very technological developments also responsible for material progress. "With the introduction of such forces as steam, machinery and electricity, the laws which prevailed fifty years ago no longer avail. This is aptly shown in the remark of the French economist, who said: 'In ancient days, when fortunes were made by war, war was a business; in these later days, when fortunes are made by business, business is war.'" Exacerbating this sense of competition were business owners' very realistic fears for the survival of their firms and the personal finances and commitments tied up in them. [The historian Edward Chase] Kirkland indicates that "contemporary observers were prone to assert that ninety-five per cent of all capitalists, 'men carrying on business,' failed." As a result, fears and anxieties about "hazardous" and "perilous" businesses and times filled their letters and conversations, including those of highly successful figures such as Andrew Carnegie and John D. Rockefeller. Furthermore, entrepreneurs ever "tend to seek novel ventures in the context of an environment of uncertainty" and to operate during rapidly changing times, and these conditions also add to their sense of insecurity. In light of the industrialists' perceptions of the world as dominated by risky competition, imperiling business survival, Social Darwinism gained adherents much more as a reflection than a cause of their worldviews, including racism. It provided a discourse to explain and communicate their experiences in terms of "the survival of the fittest" and a "struggle for success." It also allowed the successful to discount the suffering of others whose failures allegedly evinced their inferiority. Participation in progress could validate their efforts and investments, and demonstrating that participation to others argued for the merits of their activities as well as their wares.

Industrialists of this period also experienced competition outside of the marketplace. . . . An intense competition for cultural authority determined whose ideas and whose values would direct the nation's course in the throes of unprecedented change. Writers and speakers of innumerable persuasions proselytized avidly and prolifically, competing to influence the populace or portions thereof. The American industrialists figured as important actors in the dominant changes that some people praised, some questioned, and yet others decried. As a prospering and highly visible new class, the industrialists often felt uneasy about their status and identity relative to the ambient value systems. Even the Boston patricians who founded and profited from the Merrimack River's industrialization experienced this source of concern in the first half of the nineteenth century, when factories were a new and alien phenomenon in the United States. As a study of later American business attitudes theorized, "the content of the business ideology can best be explained in terms of the *strains* to which men in the business role are almost inevitably subject." They respond to "the emotional conflicts, the anxieties, and the doubts engendered by [their] actions" and the "conflicting demands of other social roles which they must play in family and community." Within the constraints of their cultural contexts, businesspeople shape their ideology "to resolve these conflicts, alleviate these anxieties, overcome these doubts." In the nineteenth-century competition for cultural hegemony, the industrialists had investments of time and financial resources, family security and status, and personal reputation to enhance as well as to protect. The ideologies of the American Victorian compromise and progress through increased productivity served these functions in their time.

New York Business Elites and the Civil War

SVEN BECKERT

Paying for and equipping the war effort increased the dependence of the state on New York's bourgeoisie and the bourgeoisie's dependence on the state. Their important material role and their assumption of governmental functions during the first months of the crisis strengthened their relationship to the federal government; the relatively weak American state became, to a large extent, dependent on the material support of those who controlled capital. At the crux of the modern American state thus stood upper-class northerners, particularly those of New York City. As a result, private investment decisions became more and more entangled with the fate of the nation, and the defeat of the South became a question of economic survival. "[W]e uphold the Government in order that the institutes of commerce may be sustained," explained Abiel Abbot Low to the members of the Chamber of Commerce. Financial support for the government, confirmed the *American Railroad Journal,* was "dictated by a wise regard to their own interests, [because the] first condition of property is a stable government."

The mutual dependence of state and economic elite enabled "a vast realignment of forces in the national economy." The war presented the federal government with an opportunity to forge a new and different kind of political economy, including

---

Sven Beckert, *The Monied Metropolis: New York City and the Consolidation of the American Bourgeoisie, 1850–1896* (New York: Cambridge University Press, 2003), pp. 119–125. Reprinted by permission of Cambridge University Press.

strengthened forms of state intervention—from tariffs to immigration laws, from land grants to banking regulations. Though the federal government needed to bargain with all segments of New York City's upper class to gain access to the resources necessary to equip huge armies, the influence of these different segments varied widely. The power of the merchants who invested in trade with southern agricultural commodities and in the import of manufactured goods from Europe declined vis-à-vis the central state because their most important political allies, the southern slaveholders, had disappeared from the halls of power in Washington. Industrialists and some bankers, however, strengthened by a political coalition with western farmers, gained considerable influence to help shape the newly emerging political economy. If the war provided the federal government with new opportunities to intervene in existing economic arrangements, it also gave important segments of the upper class substantial bargaining power to influence this political economy.

Manufacturers in particular benefited tremendously from the mobilization for war, while at the same time, the government's new economic policy linked them solidly to the state. Demands for military equipment led many manufacturers, in particular makers of iron, textiles, and boots, to produce at capacity. At the same time, the newly enacted Morrill Tariff Act of 1861, as well as subsequent tariff increases (which by 1864 had doubled the 1857 duties on a wide range of goods), protected American industrialists from foreign competition. Homestead laws and land grants to railroads, moreover, benefited commercial agriculture in the West and increased demands for agricultural implements produced by domestic industries. Joseph Seligman, mindful of these connections, concluded in September of 1864 that if the Republicans would win the November elections, "I would be in favor of investing in manufacturing as in that case the tariff would hardly be lowered during nearly 5 years." The *American Railroad Journal* went even further, and predicted that the government's need for revenue would keep the tariff in place for at least twenty years.

Industrialists, indeed, saw the war early on as a decisive and irreversible break with the antebellum political economy. The war "has released us from the bondage to cotton," opined the *American Railroad Journal,* "which for generations has hung over us like a spell, destroying all freedom of commercial or political action, and rendering us slaves to the most absurd delusions." With "the old channels of business" gone, trade with the West, in combination with high tariffs and the provision of an abundant labor supply through immigration, spelled a bright "future of our manufacturing interests." And these new arrangements, forged by war, were to last, since "[t]emporary war measures," such as higher tariffs, have "brought into existence business interests largely dependent on the continuance of" them. Many industrialists were clearly aware that the war had the potential for revolutionizing not only the South but also the political economy of the North, and they welcomed this revolution.

Bankers, however, saw the new political economy emerging in the war years with considerably more ambivalence. Their business activities had traditionally focused on financing trade as well as the transfer of foreign capital to the United States, and both these activities were now disrupted by the conflict. Moreover, their tight economic and social links to the city's merchant community made it difficult for them to embrace wholeheartedly the newly arising economic policy of the federal government, which impeded the developmental trajectory of Atlantic trade. As if this was not enough, the war also endangered the delicate balance of state regulation and self-policing that had given a semblance of stability to the nation's monetary and banking system. Indeed, the war years decisively recast the nation's banking system, and New York's bankers could not help but feel ambivalent about such rapid change.

Ambivalence about change, however, did not equal unforgiving hostility to the newly emerging political economy. For bankers, winning the war and forcefully re-uniting the nation was of tantamount importance, since the stability of the nation's monetary and banking systems, and therefore, the stability of their enterprises, rested on subjugating the South. More immediately, the federal government owed huge and ever-growing amounts of money to them, and its ability to serve on principal and interest depended on victory in the war. Because their business interests, in effect, depended on capturing the Confederacy, they provided the government with ever more resources, making a victory in war ever more urgent. The federal government, in turn, desperately sought the resources of New York's banks, giving the bankers enormous influence over central areas of government policy.

The federal government hence depended on New York City's bankers, and vice versa. It was a dependence fraught with tensions. At their core was the question of how to restructure the nation's monetary and banking systems. The rapid mobilization for war put the old institutional framework under such tremendous strains that it effectively broke down. As early as December 1861, New York banks had suspended specie payment because of high demand for gold from the government and speculators. In obvious ways, the old system was not capable of sustaining the necessary war mobilizations.

Open conflict surfaced as early as February 1862, when Congress responded to the banks' suspension of specie payment by issuing legal tender notes worth $150 million. Many, but not all, of the city's bankers opposed this bold new assertion of federal powers. George S. Coe of the American Exchange Bank, Jacob D. Vermilye of the Merchants' Bank, David R. Martin of the Ocean Bank, and James Gallatin of the National Bank all spoke out against the bill. As creditors and old-fashioned merchant bankers, they feared the inflationary impact of such a move. Other bankers, however, supported the measure, among them Moses H. Grinnell, Moses Taylor of City Bank, and the president of the Bank of Commerce, John A. Stevens. Their move was certainly politically motivated, as both Stevens and Grinnell were leading Republicans in New York, but they also expressed willingness to experiment with new forms of monetary policy to advance the Union's military position.

The split in the city's banking community on monetary politics allowed Lincoln and Congress to proceed with the planned issuance of greenbacks. However, when New York's bankers stood as a phalanx against reform, the federal government lacked the power to effect change. This effective veto power of New York's bankers came into sharp focus in the winter of 1862/63 when [U.S. Treasury Secretary Salmon P.] Chase pushed for the creation of national banks, which, regulated by the federal government, would create a secure market for federal bonds and integrate the new greenbacks into the financial system. The measure promised to revolutionize the United States banking system, creating the position of Comptroller of the Currency, who could charter "national" banks. In return, these banks would receive national bank notes in the amount of 90 percent of the market value of the bonds. These national banks would have to keep reserves of greenbacks and specie of at least 25 percent of their outstanding notes and deposits.

New York's bankers opposed this reform unequivocally. Distrusting federal regulation, they feared that the reserve requirements would keep a larger share of very profitable funds away from New York City banks. This would effectively strengthen non–New York banks. As a result, by November 1863, only three national banks had organized in New York City. Yet without national banks organizing in sufficient numbers in New York, national banks in other states could not keep some of their reserves as bankers' balances in the city, thus undercutting the viability of the system as a whole. In fact, New York's bankers opposed the new law to such a degree that they collectively decided to resist its implementation. In September 1863, banker Augustus Ely Silliman went as far as to call upon members of the New York City Clearing House to refuse cooperation with the federal government.

The pressure of the city's bankers, undercutting the aims of the banking bill, was so powerful that by November, Comptroller of the Currency Hugh McCulloch proposed changing the law in order to accommodate the protesting banks. The new banking act reduced reserve requirements from 25 percent, as legislated in the first bill, to 15 percent, of which three-fifths could be kept as bankers' balances in eighteen designated redemption cities, including New York. Banks in these eighteen cities were then required "to redeem their notes in New York; in return, these banks were permitted to keep one-half of their twenty-five percent required reserves on deposit in New York City banks." The upshot of these complicated regulations was that the city's banks would be able to draw the very profitable bankers' balances into their vaults. Moreover, a special provision in the act was made solely for Stevens's Bank of Commerce, exempting it from the double liability rule, thus inducing a political friend of the Republican administration to convert to the national system. According to Charles Russell, who at that time was a director of the Bank of Commerce, "the administration and the leaders of the majority in Congress were anxious to meet the wishes of the Bank of Commerce."

The revised act was now successful; by October 12, 1864, twelve national banks were doing business in New York City, and by mid-November, the important Bank of Commerce had become a national bank. Through their determined struggle, New York City's bankers had influenced the nation's new banking structure and succeeded in concentrating ever more financial resources in the city. Most remarkably, even in times of war, the United States had opted against creating a central bank, and though for the next forty years conflicts over monetary politics would focus on the relative importance of the state vis-à-vis the market, it was the latter that remained dominant.

As a further result of this twisted path toward reform, the war catapulted bankers into the center of the newly emerging political economy. Bankers had pledged a good deal of their future on the survival of the Union, and they eventually agreed to a strong role for the federal government in financial policy making. They also agreed to and paid for a vast expansion of the state apparatus. These attachments to the nation would bring them into close contact with the federal government and its particular developmental vision for many decades to come. The institutionalization of national bank regulations, and the issue of a national currency, in particular, linked the city's bankers to the state to a degree before unknown, while simultaneously emancipating them as a group from the tight grip of the traders in southern agricultural commodities. By virtue of their importance to the war, their eventual openness to change, and their ability to shape financial policy, bankers were among the greatest beneficiaries of the conflict.

The emancipation of many of the city's bankers from the city's merchant community and its developmental vision was made all the easier because of the ever more prominent role played by a generation of bankers who only came into their own during the Civil War. It was the Morgans and Seligmans, linked to the national government and the newly emerging industries, not the Belmonts and Wards, who became the most powerful bankers of the postbellum United States. Indeed, some bankers got their start only as a result of the war. George F. Baker, as we have seen, was one of them, and Levi Parson Morton another. The Seligmans also began their career in finance during the Civil War when they sold treasury bonds in the European market, eventually giving up their clothing business and turning themselves into important international bankers. By 1865, as a result, the makeup of New York's banking community, its links to the state, and its developmental vision had all changed dramatically.

Even more ambiguous than the position of the bankers was the relationship of the city's merchants to the war. Although they profited from the conflict, their position was weakened relative to other segments of New York's upper class. Many of their trade links were disrupted, and attacks by the Confederate navy on 150 Union merchant vessels during the first three years of the war alone damaged the United States shipping industry severely, as insurance premiums skyrocketed. Rising tariffs, a cornerstone of Republican economic policy, further threatened to undermine the merchants' foreign trade. Although the Chamber of Commerce opposed the passage of new tariff laws, it did so largely without success, drawing into stark relief the merchants' weakened political power.

A minority of merchants, however, began to adjust themselves to the dynamics of the new age, and it was these who blossomed most during the war. Their trade and other business activities moved them away from dependence on the South. Republican William E. Dodge, for example, with his investments in railroads and metals rooting him firmly in the country's newly emerging political economy, ran successfully for Congress in 1864, mostly with the help of his constituents in the wealthy Murray Hill section of Manhattan. Seeing himself as the representative of the "commercial interests of the city," he still embraced the high tariffs of his Republican colleagues, envisioning a political economy in which merchants would flourish, "promoted by the prosperity of the agricultural and manufacturing interests, and by the ability of the country, which alone can come from that prosperity, to buy and pay for the vast amounts of import."

Like merchants, builders and contractors showed ambivalence about the effects of the war on the nation's political economy. Because they did not forge strong links to the federal government, and because they depended on local political connections for public construction projects, they remained sensitive to the concerns of working-class voters and politicians who fought for local autonomy, an allegiance which would come into sharp focus during the conflict over conscription in 1863.

Still, for these local capitalists, as for the merchants, bankers, and manufacturers, the importance of the federal government increased tremendously, not least because it was only through a strong state that the Union could be reunited. Never before in United States history had the federal government played such an important role in domestic economic life, and never before had upper-class Americans been so thoroughly linked to this government. As a result, the economic elites' stakes in the war increased as the fighting continued. By 1863, the Chamber of Commerce had added to its reasons to "unite in putting the rebellion down" the "vast pecuniary obligation" that the war itself had created.

 F U R T H E R   R E A D I N G

Brown, John K. *The Baldwin Locomotive Works, 1831–1915: A Study in American Industrial Practice* (1995).

Dalzell, Robert F., Jr. *Enterprising Elite: The Boston Associates and the World They Made* (1987).

Dublin, Thomas. *Women at Work: The Transformation of Work and Community in Lowell, Massachusetts, 1826–1860*, 2d ed. (1993).

Eno, Arthur L., Jr., ed. *Cotton Was King: A History of Lowell, Massachusetts* (1976).

Folsom, Michael Brewster, and Steven D. Lubar, eds. *The Philosophy of Manufactures: Early Debates over Industrialization in the United States* (1982).

Hindle, Brooke, and Steven D. Lubar *Engines of Change: The American Industrial Revolution, 1780–1860* (1986).

Kulik, Gary, et al., eds. *The New England Mill Village, 1790–1860* (1982).

Licht, Walter. *Industrializing America: The Nineteenth Century* (1995).

McGaw, Judith A. *Most Wonderful Machine: Mechanization and Social Change in Berkshire Paper Making, 1801–1885* (1987).

Porter, Glenn, and Harold C. Livesay. *Merchants and Manufacturers: Studies in the Changing Nature of Nineteenth-Century Marketing* (1971).

Scranton, Philip B. *Endless Novelty: Specialty Production and American Industrialization, 1865–1925* (1997).

———. *Figured Tapestry: Production, Markets, and Power in Philadelphia Textiles, 1885–1941* (1989).

———. *Proprietary Capitalism: The Textile Manufacture at Philadelphia, 1800–1885* (1983).

Steinberg, Theodore. *Nature Incorporated: Industrialization and the Waters of New England* (1991).

Stern, Marc J. *The Pottery Industry of Trenton: A Skilled Trade in Transition, 1850–1929* (1994).

Temin, Peter. *The Jacksonian Economy* (1969).

Wall, Joseph Frazier. *Andrew Carnegie* (1970).

Wallace, Anthony F. C. *Rockdale: The Growth of an American Village in the Early Industrial Revolution* (1978).

Zakim, Michael. *Ready-Made Democracy: A History of Men's Dress in the American Republic, 1760–1860* (2003).

Zonderman, David A. *Aspirations and Anxieties: New England Workers and the Mechanized Factory System, 1815–1850* (1992).

CHAPTER

7

Technology in the Age of

Big Business, 1870–1920

Between the Civil War and World War I, the United States joined England, France, and Germany as world-class industrial powers. While agricultural productivity increased, industrial output expanded by leaps and bounds. By 1900, manufacturing, construction, and mining accounted for two-thirds of the economy. Small and mid-sized businesses persisted, specializing in manufacturing, wholesaling, construction, banking, retailing, and other services. A new type of enterprise appeared in this era. These large companies operated multiple factories, controlled their own procurement and distribution channels, and served a national market. In 1905, McClure's Magazine *gave them a new name: big business.*

Writing in the postwar years, the prominent business historian Alfred D. Chandler, Jr., whose work appears in Chapter 1, examined the rise of big business with reference to the railroads. According to Chandler, railroad managers took advantage of new technologies—steam-powered locomotives, steel rails, and explosives—to build a transportation system that integrated local and regional economies into a transcontinental market. System expansion forced railroad men to develop techniques for managing large companies. Business strategies such as horizontal consolidation and vertical integration facilitated expansion, while modifications to organizational hierarchies encouraged specialization and eased managerial burdens.

Chandler's account of the railroads as the first big businesses is powerful. By fostering a national market, the railroads had an immense impact on the economy. Some enterprises emulated the railroads' approach to technology and corporate organization as they also grew into big businesses. According to Chandler, meat packing, steel manufacturing, and petroleum processing demonstrated this trend.

Over the past few decades, historians have built on the Chandler thesis to develop a deeper understanding of the age of big business. We now know that railroad managers may have emulated organizational innovations developed by merchants and publishers in the early nineteenth century. We now acknowledge that networks of small and midsized firms, scattered throughout the country, contributed much to the economy. Most important, we now also know that the story of big business and technological change was fraught with controversy. In

Chandler's view, new technologies and technical opportunities served as driving forces that shaped management decisions, corporate strategies, and organizational structures. The documents and essays in this section explore this thesis and its alternatives by using examples from information processing, railroading, and telephony. In particular, the materials on railroads and telephones suggest that technology could limit as well as foster innovation.

 D O C U M E N T S

Many Americans critiqued the factory system and aspects of industrialization, even as they responded positively to the many new technologies that appeared in the late nineteenth century. For the nation's hundredth birthday, Americans celebrated their country's technological prowess with a gigantic world's fair, the United States Centennial International Exhibition of 1876, in Philadelphia. The 10 million visitors saw new foods, rare minerals, and consumer goods. Yet nothing excited more attention than the technology. Document 1, taken from a souvenir guidebook, describes some of the popular technological displays, including the sewing machines and the world's largest steam engine, the great Corliss, the fair's most celebrated symbol. How does the guidebook convey the excitement about these new technologies? Why did these machines attract so much attention? How does the guidebook describe the businesses producing them?

Today, Americans equate office technology with computers and other electronic devices, but office equipment has a long history. Whether the product was insurance or transportation, many businesses of the 1800s had to manage ever-growing amounts of information. Dating from 1897, the circulars in Documents 2 and 3 advertise office equipment: the Rapid Roller Copier and the Globe Routing System. How did the manufacturers of these devices use visual images and language to promote these office technologies to other businesses?

As the railroads grew after the Civil War, they recruited thousands of well-educated workers to process information and manage operations. Many of the new white-collar jobs provided job security, a degree of upward mobility, and decent salaries, enabling many American households to enter the middle class. Writing for *Cosmopolitan* magazine, William J. Wilgus, vice president of the New York Central & Hudson River Railroad, urges the educated young man searching for a profession to consider a railroad career. How does Wilgus make railroad management sound appealing? Why does he only address men?

While the railroads managed the nation's transportation network, telegraph companies dominated high-speed communications. In Document 5, social worker Elizabeth Beardsley Butler describes working conditions in a Pittsburgh telegraph office. Her 1908 visit came on the heels of a major strike initiated by female telegraph operators over wage discrimination. How did Victorian gender conventions shape work in the telegraph industry? What role did gender stereotyping play in the adoption of typewriters by this telegraph office?

By World War I, the American Telephone and Telegraphy Company (AT&T) ran the nation's largest communications network. This firm had grown through vertical integration, combining units that manufactured equipment and provided telephone service under one umbrella, the Bell system. In Document 6, AT&T president Theodore N. Vail describes the company's operations in his 1909 annual report to stockholders, emphasizing the national interconnectedness of the entire system.

1. Technology Enshrined at the World's Fair, 1876

Mechanism is the grand and leading science of the world. For centuries, nations, held in ignorance, were only ruled by force; the will of the ruler compelling obedience and controlling the lives and actions of the multitude. Freedom of action was denied, and freedom of conscience bound with an iron rod. Men were the machines of kings and princes. . . .

. . . But peoples were not always to be thus ruled. When the world was ready for intellectual advancement, He who governs nations raised the curtain of the earth and called man to a higher destiny. In the midst of superstition, the printing press burst upon the darkness, and the light of letters flashed out upon the bewildered world. Knowledge spread. Men compared thoughts and joined action. Ignorance was driven from her wonted haunts, while educated intelligence assumed the mastery. Letters commanded attention, and the hidden genius of the world wore a bold front, claimed its right, and forced the despots of the day to acknowledge its strength and its ability. Brains had always force, but they were never aggregated and marched in a body upon ignorance until the invention of letters.

Immediately mechanism began to develop its suppressed powers; and though its progress was slow at first, it continued to advance in its career of usefulness. The closing years of the 18th century found the scientist, philosopher, and mechanic blending ideas and preparing the grand march of the present century. And now, turn where we may, we find machinery providing for the wants of the peoples, and ruling the future of nations. The mighty powers of the forge and furnace are riveting the bonds of peace.

Men think. Machines are automatic, and almost think. Nations think, and so do armies. The advance of the last seventy years has been more than that of previous hundreds. The world is thrown forward a thousand years, and mechanism takes its place among the first sciences.

As we enter Machinery Hall, we hear the hum of thousands of machines, from the tiniest hand-power to the mighty steam-engine. The clamor interrupts conversation, but eyes are not idle. Every wheel and pulley is scrutinized. We are in the largest and grandest machine shop that the world has ever seen. All the expositions of the world heretofore, have failed to concentrate so much strength and usefulness—so much thought and intelligence. Most prominent of all are the machines made in the United States; and, taken as a whole at the present day, they can not be surpassed. The mechanics have sent here their best efforts; and being, as it were, at home, they have spared no exertions to make the Hall attractive in all its features.

. . . More than four-fifths of the space are occupied with machines of this country, and near the center of all we find the—

Corliss Engine

This engine stands as a great double-armed giant, quietly—almost noiselessly—and yet effectively throwing its exhaustless powers upon the heavy beltings, and thence to the innumerable shaftings—main and auxiliary—that speed ten thousand machines

---

Samuel J. Burr, *Memorial of the International Exhibition* (Hartford, Conn.: L. Stebbins, 1877), pp. 37–38, 43, 90–92.

from 9 A.M. to 5 P.M. daily. We can not be minute in our description of this mighty motor, but will give a few prominent features that we trust will interest our readers. The engine is placed in the transept near the center of the Hall, and where the building is 70 feet from the floor to the top of the ventilator. . . . The main belts, instead of being an eye-sore and in the way, as is too often the case, pass through the Hall in out of the way places, and are inclosed in glass apartments eight by six feet in size, so as to make a proper exhibit of the belts.

The engines are what are known as "beam engines" of the Corliss improved pattern, with all the latest improvements, and nominally of 700 horse-power each, or 1,400 horse-power in both, though this can be increased even to 2,500 horse-power should occasion require. The cylinders are forty inches in diameter, with ten feet stroke. The engines are provided with air-pumps and condensing apparatus, and are intended to work with from fifteen to eighty pounds of steam, according to the requirements of the exhibition.

The gear fly-wheel is thirty feet in diameter, two feet across the face, and has 216 teeth, the wheel makes thirty-six revolutions per minute, and the periphery moves at the rate of about thirty-eight miles an hour. . . .

The large gear with which the gear fly-wheel connects is ten feet in diameter, and is a solid casting of 17,000 pounds. The height of the engine from the floor is thirty-nine feet, and every part is accessible by means of iron staircases and balconies, which add much to the artistic beauty of the design. The weight of the engine and its appurtenances amounts to 1,383,264 pounds, making sixty-one car loads of 22,676 pounds each. . . .

It has now been running for five months, and shows not the least imperfection, and without the slightest interruption. It is the design and construction of Geo. H. Corliss, engineer; and is his individual property, furnished by him free of all expenses and generously run at his individual cost. When the exhibition closes, he will take it back to Rhode Island and hold it until an improved condition of manufacturing business shall create a demand for such a power. . . .

The extent and capacity of the Corliss Steam-Engine Works can be best appreciated by considering the fact, that the Centennial engine was constructed from the crude materials—transported—set up, and put in operation in the short space of nine months and twenty-six days. . . .

Sewing Machines

The sewing machine is, comparatively, a recent invention; and can hardly be said to have reached perfection. There are many very excellent devices; and great ingenuity, deep thought, and mints of money have been expended in order to render them complete. The contest still rages, and every year we encounter improvements more and more valuable. . . .

HOWE'S SEWING MACHINE CO., New York; Factories, Bridgeport, Conn.; Peru, Ind., and Glasgow, Scot.—The exhibit embraces many machines, and several cases containing elegantly dressed dolls, the work, embroidery, and braiding having been done on the Howe machine. One case has a lady's saddle beautifully adorned on this machine, showing its adaptability to piercing heavy leather as well as fine fabrics.

After devoting years of thought to the perfecting of a sewing machine, Mr. Howe conceived the idea of placing the eye near the point of the needle—a plan that is now used in all machines; and which eventually made a fortune for the inventor. The following year he sewed the first seam ever made by machinery. The machine is now on exhibition at the pavilion of the Howe company in Machinery Hall. . . . His patent was issued September 10, 1846. The model accompanying the application for this patent may now be seen in the Government Building, Centennial Grounds. His brother, Amasa, was sent to England the same year; and sold the English right to Wm. Thomas for $1,000; and he (Thomas) realized therefrom over $1,000,000. Mr. Howe went to England in 1847, and after various trials, returned to the United States in 1849, penniless. To secure passage home, he was obliged to pawn his first machine and also his letters patent. Again he was compelled to pursue his trade as a machinist in order to obtain a living.

Many began to infringe upon his patent; suits were commenced; and to prosecute these, his father mortgaged a valuable farm. It was not until 1854 that a decision was obtained in his favor. In pronouncing the opinion of the Court, Judge Sprague, of Massachusetts, used the following emphatic language:—"There is no evidence in this case that leaves a shadow of doubt that for all the benefits conferred by the introduction of sewing machines, the public are indebted to Elias Howe, Jr." Upon the rendition of this opinion, the various manufacturers formed a combination to protect each other against infringements, and all agreed to pay Mr. Howe a royalty upon every machine made. In 1869 Mr. Howe exhibited his machine at the Paris Exposition, where he was awarded a gold medal, the highest premium; and was decorated by the Emperor with the Cross of the Legion of Honor. Shortly after his return home he died.

A bronze statue of Mr. Howe has been erected on the border of the lake in the park, opposite the main entrance of Machinery Hall. It is of heroic size, nine feet six inches in height. It was designed by Robert Wood & Co., at a cost of $20,000; and at the close of the present exhibition, is to be placed in Central Park, New York. We give the particulars of the trial of this remarkable man for the encouragement of young inventors, to whom we say never be discouraged by difficulties in introducing new inventions. Trials always await genius, and the moment of success may be the hour of the greatest peril. It was so with him, but his determined will overcame all, and placed him eventually upon the pinnacle of fortune. No less than thirty-two companies have been formed, with an aggregate capital of $30,000,000, and producing 400,000 machines annually. More than 12,000 men are engaged in the various factories, and nearly an equal number in the sales and agencies.

The exhibit of this company has cost $38,000; $12,000 of which have been expended for pamphlets and catalogues. The [Howe] factories give employment to 3,500 people, and cover a space of over twelve acres.

2. Duplicating Before Xerox: The Rapid Roller Copier, 1897

THE RAPID ✦ ✦ ✦ ✦
ROLLER COPIER ⚜ ⚜ ⚜ ⚜

Instantaneous damp-leaf copies of any writing can be secured by merely turning a crank. This Copier is invaluable, not only in mercantile and public offices, but also in banks, insurance and real estate agencies, and in hotels for the convenience of commercial patrons.

THE ONLY PERFECT COPYING MACHINE.

SAVES TIME AND MONEY.

IT IS TWENTY-FIVE YEARS IN ADVANCE

OF THE SCREW LETTER-PRESS.

NO DELAY.
NO INCONVENIENCE.
ALWAYS RELIABLE.

The SHANNON FILING CABINET and RAPID ROLLER COPIER when used together afford the most perfect system of filing correspondence. Copies can be filed with the letters to which they are answers and the entire correspondence of an individual thus kept together.

Office Specialty Manufacturing Company (Rochester, N.Y.: Office Specialty Manufacturing Company, 1897), n.p. Trade catalog collection, Hagley Museum and Library, Wilmington, Del. Courtesy Hagley Museum and Library.

3. An Office Supply Company Advertises the Globe Routing System, 1897

For many years the serious problem to manufacturers, jobbers, in fact to all commercial houses has been to systematically keep track of their traveling salesmen, agents, inquiries, exclusive territory, reports, mortgages, etc. The old system of hanging maps on the wall and using different colored pencils, strings, pin tags, etc., for indicators, whenever a change was necessary, scratching or erasing the old mark and adding the new, caused these maps at the end of a very short time not only to have the appearance of a "Chinese puzzle," but to be discarded as utterly worthless.

The Globe Company offers to the commercial world its "Globe Routing System" for keeping track of their traveling salesmen, agencies, exclusive territory, etc. . . .

A Brief Description Of How The Routing System Can Be Used

The plan which is embodied in The Globe Routing System employs maps mounted in drawers and built in cabinets of sizes to suit any class or size of business. The whole, or any part of the country, can be included in the system, as the requirements of the business may determine. The drawers contain maps 21 × 28 inches in size, with certain smaller States combined, making single maps of 21 × 14 inches, and properly labeled. The maps themselves vary, for a single map may cover any territory desired—for example, the whole United States, or a single State, or a single county, or even a single city. This feature demonstrates the elasticity of the system. To cover the entire United States and Canada, using a single drawer for each of the larger states, a 44 drawer cabinet is employed.

Different colored silk headed tacks are employed as indicators. In some cases these indicators are numbered from 1 to 12, and designate the different months. For example, if a traveling man visits a city in February, and his color is yellow, a yellow tack numbered 2, is used, indicating that the city was last visited in February. Similar variations and combinations are used in the matter of mortgages and collections, indicating the month due, and, in some cases, the man in charge of that particular piece of business.

We will first consider its application in managing traveling men. In laying out the route for a traveling salesman named Jones, we select some color for him, we will say green. Using the green indicators, we stick one on the map at every city to be visited. After Jones has started on his trip, we follow the route with a white indicator, thus showing at all times the city in which Jones is at the present time. Or, we may vary the plan by replacing the green indicators with numbered ones, showing the month the city was visited, the last numbered indicator showing the city in which Jones is at the present time.

Let us next consider the system in the matter of agents. We would select a number of colors among the indicators to be known as agent's indicators. Or, we may choose a single color, but with different numbers for different values. Upon the latter

Office Appliances (New York: Globe Company, 1897), pp. 38, 40. Trade catalog collection, Hagley Museum and Library, Wilmington, Del.

plan we will take yellow as the agents' indicator. Number 1 of the yellow is to indicate exclusive territory; number 2 to indicate that the house is represented in that territory, but no exclusive rights have been given. Number 3 would be still another variation in these particulars, and so on. By placing these indicators over the territory, there is at once revealed to the managing man who glances at the map the exact condition at any given point.

Still another colored indicator may refer to collections, for example, denoting bad debts or slow accounts. Wherever a debt of this kind exists, one of these indicators is placed. When in making up the route of traveling men, glancing at the map for information, these indicators call attention to the fact that an account at a certain place is to be collected or looked up. Still other variations and adaptations are possible, for the system is sufficiently elastic to meet every requirement made in the conduct of business. A key is, of course, necessary in order to maintain proper system in the use of the indicators. In a corner of the drawer, as shown in cut of drawer, a key can be placed, showing what the different indicators represent, as for example, travelers: Jones, green; Hopkins, blue; Smith, black and Kelly, red. Collections may be indicated by orange, agents by yellow, and so on. Instead of writing the names of the colors on the key slip it is best to put after the heading an indicator of the color used, thus appealing to the eye by means of color and form, as well as to the brain by name.

In this account only a few uses of the system have been given, for as previously indicated, the users find new adaptations constantly, and the utility grows as familiarity is acquired. Any record of a geographical nature can be kept by this system, and the records read at a glance, thereby doing away with memorandas, tedious reference to correspondence, and taxing the memory with details that are hard to retain. The Routing System may be very properly supplemented by an adaptation of a Card System, so that one becomes the key to the other. The cards may be arranged alphabetically by state and city, or by salesmen's routes. Changes and alterations are made without interfering with the index arrangement.

The advantages of a system of this kind to the progressive business house of the present day when every point must be counted, are obvious.

4. A Vice President at the New York Central Railroad Describes Railroad Management as a Manly Profession, 1903

The avenues open to the young man contemplating entering railroading are many— all leading to the common goal, the presidency of the company. The principal grand divisions are engineering, motive power and rolling-stock, transportation, traffic, law, finance and accounting. Each of these in turn splits up into many specialties. The selection among these departments depends entirely on the natural bent and tastes of the young man.

William J. Wilgus, "Making a Choice of a Profession, VIII—Railroading," *Cosmopolitan* 35 (1903): 462–464.

Engineering embraces the duties of constructing and maintaining the fixed or stationary property of the company, as distinguished from the movable motive power or rolling-stock. The results attained by this department determine the degree of safety and economy with which the railroad can be operated. Therefore, it will be realized that the engineering officer bears a heavy responsibility. His mistakes, when made, are not of a temporary character, buried and soon forgotten, but they stand out so that all can see them, irremediable except at great expense. The successful engineer has not only a technical training in his own profession, but also a suitable knowledge of the details of the other departments, in order properly to design, construct and maintain for their needs. In other words, the modern railway engineer must be a broad-gauge man of the strictest integrity and common sense.

The construction side of engineering has jurisdiction over new work of magnitude, such as the reconnoissance, location, and construction of new lines of railway, double-tracking, new bridges, tunnels and important buildings, signals, terminals, grade-reductions, heat-, light- and power-plants, water-supply, the elimination of grade-crossings, electrification of traffic; and also of the real estate of the company, and of standard plans and specifications. Construction engineering usually calls for men with a technical education, studious tendencies and a taste for scheming, planning, designing and executing new work.

Maintenance of way comprises what may be termed the executive branch of engineering. It includes all forces engaged in the maintenance of the company's existing physical property in accordance with standards fixed by the chief engineer of the construction department. Supervisors or roadmasters, trackmen, signalmen, wreckers, carpenters, masons, bridgemen and other mechanics and laborers report to this department, and on the larger systems aggregate from ten to twenty thousand men. This large force is subdivided and organized so as to maintain the property in a safe condition for operation under all conditions of weather. The direction of such forces requires men possessing executive ability of the first quality, physical strength and practical experience. An engineering training, either technical or acquired, is a great aid to success. Storms, washouts, wrecks, and emergencies of all kinds call for constant watchfulness day and night, frequent long-continued exposure to the elements, with little sleep, and require the ability to anticipate and prevent trouble. The experience in this department is an excellent education for entrance into the transportation department, with its opportunities for continued advancement.

The motive-power and rolling-stock department has jurisdiction over the building and maintenance of locomotives, cars and other rolling-stock. The forces include the foremen and mechanics in the shops and engine-houses, and in some instances the enginemen and firemen. Usually, however, the motive-power department is responsible only for the mechanical fitness of the latter two classes of employees, and the transportation department passes on their knowledge and observance of operating rules. The department of motive-power and rolling-stock appeals to mechanically inclined men who are either educated in technical schools or who have learned the trade. Such men should have inventive skill, careful habits, physical endurance and keen intelligence.

Transportation claims the most numerous and varied class of employees in the service, and is the closest in contact with the general public. It uses the facilities given by the engineering and motive-power departments to transport the freight and passengers delivered to it by the traffic department. The proper administration of this department is of the first importance to the company. Trains must run safely and on time; freight must be promptly handled without friction with shippers; ingenuity and resourcefulness are always demanded to meet unexpected conditions, such as moving business despite blockades, accidents, washouts and snow-storms; and the maximum tonnage must be moved with a minimum of cost. The men in the transportation department are, above all others, expected to render faithful, loyal service. Enginemen and firemen, conductors, baggagemen and trainmen carry the safety and comfort of the train service in their hands; agents, clerks, telegraphers and their assistants serve the public in stations and depots; signal-operators man the towers; flagmen guard the highway-crossings; yardmasters and switchmen operate the terminals, which are the digestive organs of a railroad; the medical staff renders aid to the injured; and the superintendents, car-accountants, trainmasters and despatchers oversee and direct the movements of the entire transportation machine.

Traffic covers the securing of passenger and freight business, and its success is vital to the prosperity of the company. In competitive territory where many railroads are striving for business the traffic official is required to have the highest grade of tact and diplomacy to hold and increase the shipments over his line.

The passenger traffic officer taxes his ingenuity to attract the attention of the public to his line by unique advertisements, timetables, maps and notices.

Law commands an important place in railroading, as it is the bulwark against which all kinds of claimants, of varying degrees of honesty, surge to mulct the company. The railroad lawyer is required to have a keen knowledge of human nature, ready wit, and the mental characteristics of the judge, in order to distinguish between the just and the unjust claim. On one hand, he can save the company from unnecessary lawsuits, and deserving claimants from injustice; and, on the other hand, he protects his client from extortion and robbery. All contracts, deeds, bonds and mortgages pass under his scrutiny, and must have his approval. Legislative acts require his watchfulness to see that laws that would be unjust to the company as well as to the general public do not pass surreptitiously.

Finance comprises supervision over the receipts and expenditures of the railroad. The payments of interest on the securities of the company, the issuance and recording of new securities, pay-rolls, vouchers, and all matters affecting the financial obligations are handled by this department.

Accounting watches and checks the results of operation, and feels the pulse of business to quickly detect variations in the financial health of the company. The comptroller or auditor is the first to know what the railroad is earning from month to month. All vouchers for expenditures approved by heads of departments are first compared with formal contracts or authorities, and must have the endorsement of the comptroller or auditor before payment by the treasurer. All bills for collection of revenue, and all receipts from passenger and freight traffic are checked by this department. Monthly statistics that illustrate the operative efficiency of the various departments, the total receipts and expenditures and the net revenue, are issued monthly or oftener for the information of the president, the general officers, and of the investing public. A mass of data is tabulated that enables the executive to know exactly what each department is doing, and, if necessary, institute changes or reforms before the interests of the company might suffer.

Thus it will be seen that the young man considering the choice of a profession has a wide range of selection in railroading. His decision should be guided, not by the immediate gain that one branch may offer over the others, but rather by the class of work that best suits his talents, and that can hold enthusiastic and undivided affection. Promotion step by step widens the knowledge until, upon reaching the top of the ladder of one of the specialties, without effort the climber passes over to the next ladder, mounting higher, and this, repeated, gradually leads to the climax.

5. Male and Female Telegraph Operators Go on Strike, 1907

The main office of a telegraph company impresses the uninitiated observer but does not enlighten him. All that electricity implies of the miraculous seems expressed in the keys of the Morse instruments and in the wizardry of control that connects the operator at the board with his co-worker a thousand miles away. You see men and women, row back of row, receiving, sending, writing messages. You hear the intermittent click of the telegraph keys, the banging of typewriters, and you are conscious of a steady undercurrent of haste, concentration, quick efficiency.

The main and branch offices of the two telegraph companies in Pittsburgh employ 90 women and 198 men. Men and women do the same kind of work, which they learn for the most part through apprenticeship as floor messengers and gradual promotion to manipulation of the keys. If there is a difference in the grade of work assigned, it is that the women are employed more generally at branch offices and at the lighter wires.

Yet although the work done by men and by women in telegraph offices is apparently the same, conditions growing out of the employment of women proved to be the pivot about which swung the strike of the summer of 1907 against one of the Pittsburgh companies. . . .

In Pittsburgh 38 women and about 150 men were in the union, together making up 75 per cent of the operating force. When the strike was ordered, the union asked that typewriters be furnished by the company, that the sliding scale of wages be abolished, and that a shorter working day be arranged. The typewriter is part of the operator's equipment. When it was first introduced, a special bonus was offered to employes who would learn to use it, and as its use became general, it proved as valuable to the employes as to the company. Many whose handwriting was poor, and who on this account had been classed below first-class, were able to draw higher pay. Operators, however, are required to buy and to keep in repair their own machines, which is a heavy initial expense.

The demand for a shorter working day grew out of the fact that the telegraph service is continuous through the twenty-four hours. Shifts and relays have to be arranged for among the operating force. The schedule provided for a nine-hour day with overtime service to fill the places of absentees or in cases of emergency, and

Elizabeth Beardsley Butler, *Women and the Trades: Pittsburgh, 1907–1908.* The Pittsburgh Survey, ed. Paul Underwood Kellogg (New York: Charities Publication Committee, 1909), pp. 292–294.

different turns were assigned to the operators in rotation. The night work schedule was shorter, seven hours and a half; and the "split trick," planned to accommodate the period of heaviest traffic, was eight hours,—ten to two, and five to nine. Once at the key-board, relief was granted for no cause, without specific permission from the traffic chief; and operators complained that at times they would have to stay at their posts all day without being relieved, and when relieved would frequently be allowed only twenty minutes at noon. Sunday work was assigned to different members of the force as extra work with pay based on seven hours as a full day.

But important as these points were, abolition of the sliding scale was the cardinal demand. The grievance referred to as the "sliding scale" was the outcome of alleged differences in the work done by men and by women, and of resultant unfair discrimination. Managers and operators as a rule agree that the lesser physical strength of women tells against them after several years of light wrist and finger motions; that because of this lesser strength, women have neither the speed nor the accuracy of men; and that they get "glass arm," a nervous inability to work, more frequently. On the other hand, both managers and operators agree that although women work for the most part on light wires, the quantity of work done by given operators is fairly well equalized, and that the difference between a light and a heavy wire is less than would be supposed. Whereas an operator on a heavy wire does sending only, or receiving only, the operator on a light wire does both sending and receiving, or else works by a system of "floats" whereby three wires are handled by two operators. Yet the potential ability of men operators to do heavier work than women is reflected in the differences in wages. One company paid $30, $35, and $44 a month to women in branch offices, and $62 to women in the main office. The other company paid two-thirds of its women employes $30 to $55 a month, and one-third of its women employes from $55 to $75 a month. It was charged that the former company paid its salaries on the basis of individual bargaining, and not on the basis of kind or quantity of work done; that a man who had earned $82.50 on a heavy wire would be superseded by a woman at $75; and that a man who had been receiving $75 would be superseded by a woman at $62. By this system, the rates of payment for given wires were being lowered. Although the work might tell on women sooner than on men, and although they might in some cases be less efficient than men, they were yet sufficiently capable to supersede men at a lower rate of pay. They were lending themselves to a scheme for cutting wages.

The strike was broken in the fall, in part through the agency of unorganized women. Most of the women went out when the men went out, but a few of them stayed in, and others who had formerly been in the employ of the company were impressed for the occasion. In one point, however, the strike was not without effect. Conditions in the company against which the strike was chiefly directed remained unchanged, but the other company granted a 10 per cent increase in wages by which some of the women operators are now earning as much as the men can earn at the heavy wires. Two-thirds of the women employes of this company now earn from $33 to $60.50 a month; and one-third of the women earn from $60.50 to $82.50 a month. This scale would seem to show that this company does not discriminate against women nor force competition between women and men, but pays equally for equal work.

6. AT&T President Theodore N. Vail Celebrates the Bell System, 1909

The Bell system is one system telephonically interconnected, intercommunicating and interdependent. This is such a system that any one of over 4,000,000 subscribers can talk with any other one within carrying power of the voice over wires, the only exception being that the Pacific Coast and the Middle Rocky Mountain region are not yet connected.

This system was built up under this policy and its continuance as a system depends on the continuance of the policy.

In the telephone business development is continuous. As conditions enlarge and change, new methods develop. The whole business suggests changes and stimulates inventions, and opportunities for improvements are frequent.

If each separate exchange or group of exchanges had not been assisted and directed in the development and introduction of these new ideas, methods and inventions, there would now be as many systems, as many methods of operating as there are separate companies. This would have made impossible the organization which now gives the Bell system that universality and preponderance on account of which no matter how many other systems may exist, every one of any commercial or social importance must have connection with the Bell system.

The same generalization runs through many departments. The companies are so organized, or fast becoming so, that every department continues through the local administration to the central administration of the American Telephone and Telegraph Company.

The American Telephone and Telegraph Company owns and maintains all telephones. It also owns either directly or through the Western Electric Company all patents.

It has a department which was organized at the very beginning of the business and has continued since, where is to be found practically everything known about inventions pertaining to the telephone or kindred subjects. Every new idea is there examined, and its value determined so far as the patent features are concerned.

The Engineering Department takes all new ideas, suggestions and inventions, and studies, develops, and passes upon them.

It has under continuous observation and study all traffic methods and troubles, improving or remedying them.

It studies all construction, present and future development or extension schemes, makes plans and specifications for the same, and gives when desired general supervision and advice. It has a corps of experts which, in addition to the above work, is at all times at the service of any or all of the separate companies.

When it is considered that some of these questions involve the permanency, duration and usefulness of a telephone plant costing millions of dollars, and changes

---

Theodore N. Vail, "American Telephone and Telegraph Company's Relations to Associated Companies," Annual Report of the American Telephone and Telegraph Company, March 1909, in *Views on Public Questions: A Collection of Papers and Addresses of Theodore Newton Vail, 1907–1917* (New York: Privately Printed, 1917), pp. 13–18.

costing hundreds of thousands, some idea of its importance can be formed. To give an illustration: One group of patents covering inventions which seemed likely to be useful and economical in the service was purchased by the company. These inventions were developed into operating apparatus and put into use. While this cost hundreds of thousands of dollars, placing it beyond the scope of one operating company, the saving already accomplished to the associated companies runs into the millions.

A large staff has been and is continuously engaged in the consideration of disturbances arising from transmission and other lines carrying heavy currents, and in many cases that any telephone system can even exist in the vicinity of such lines is due to the constant and continued attention given this subject.

Every new trouble, and there are many, comes before this department. When settled there, it is settled for all. This has established a commercial, operating and plant practice not only for our own associated companies, but for others of high standing throughout the world.

All devices or inventions submitted receive the most thorough and painstaking investigation, and it [is] safe to say that there has as yet been no instance where any invention, system or method, rejected by the Patent and Engineering Departments of the American Telephone and Telegraph Company has ever had any permanent success when used elsewhere.

The Manufacturing Department creates and builds the equipment and apparatus which have been adopted. In this way throughout the whole grand system will be found standardization and uniformity. This is not any handicap on improvement or development of the art, for, on the contrary, every suggestion or idea, and there are many, has abundant opportunity to be tested, which would not be possible otherwise. No one of the companies could by itself maintain such an organization, and it would be fatal to any service to introduce or try out undeveloped ideas in actual service.

In the Legal Department all the big and general questions are looked after. It forms a clearing house in all legal matters for all the legal departments of the separate companies to which assistance and advice are given on all questions of general scope.

In the administration all questions which affect all companies, all questions between the associated companies, and the general policy and the general conduct of the business, are considered and close touch and relationship maintained with all parts of the system. Experts on every subject connected with this business are continually at work on old or new subjects and ready at call to go to the assistance of any of the companies. In short, the great work and substantially all the expense of the American Telephone and Telegraph Company are involved in this "Centralized General Administration," taking care of all those matters which are common to all companies, or which if taken care of by each company would mean multiplication of work, effort, expense without corresponding advantage or efficiency.

To sum up, quoting the words of the representative of a large stockholding interest in one of the associated companies: "The contract relation with the American Telephone and Telegraph Company is the biggest asset this company has."

In submitting this report, we wish to call your attention to two things which indicate the stability of the company and property.

One is the wide dispersion and small average holding of the shares—including the shareholders in the associated and connected companies, there are over 70,000 shareholders in the Bell system. From January 1 to March 2, the date of bond conversion, the shareholders increased about one hundred per week.

Another is the stability of the business, year after year shows an increase, no matter what the prevailing business conditions. There has, it is true, been a slight decline in the rate of increase in exchange earnings, and the toll line business has given some indication that conditions were not normal, but even in that there was an increase in earnings.

This stability and the position that the Bell system holds is due very largely to the policy and conditions under which it was developed, not alone to the telephone.

A telephone—without a connection at the other end of the line—is not even a toy or a scientific instrument. It is one of the most useless things in the world. Its value depends on the connection with the other telephone—and increases with the number of connections.

The Bell system under an intelligent control and broad policy has developed until it has assimilated itself into and in fact become the nervous system of the business and social organization of the country.

This is the result of the centralized general control exercised by the company, the combination of all local systems into one combined system developed as a whole.

Nor could the development have been made in any other way. If the business had been developed by different organizations—each absolutely independent of and unrelated to the others—each little system would have been independent and self-contained without benefit to any other. No one has use for two telephone connections if he can reach all with whom he desires connection through one. Through the development of the Bell system, the relation and benefit as a whole have been considered. The policy has been to bring together all units which contribute to the value of the whole. The demand for facilities is seldom found waiting in these days for the facilities to come. The demand is created by the existence of the facilities. This is particularly true of the telephone service. It took courage to build the first toll line—short as it was—and it took more to build the first long-distance line to Chicago. . . .

There are no other countries where the telephone service occupies the same relation to the public. Elsewhere narrow control and a policy of restriction have prevented its full development. Whatever is good in those systems has been adopted from the practice in this country. . . .

Promptness and certainty therefore mean that each message, connection or other unit of actual service availed of must bear the expense of a number of unused possible units not availed of. If, instead of the immediate or prompt service of this country, the service as it exists in most other countries were in vogue, the cost would be reduced, but to a much greater extent would the value be reduced. Delayed service—service which keeps a line of customers waiting, so that there need be no loss of units of service, would reduce to a minimum the number of operators and given facilities, and all that creates cost.

Instead of waiting and idle operators and facilities, there would be waiting, idle and patient, customers.

We do not think the American public desires this kind of service.

E S S A Y S

In the first essay, JoAnne Yates, the Sloan Distinguished Professor of Management at the MIT Sloan School of Management, examines the history of the typewriter. Originally sold to court reporters and telegraph companies, the typewriter eventually displaced the pen as the primary tool for creating business correspondence. Along the way, it transformed the craft of producing letters from a respected "white-collar" occupation for male clerks into series of routinized tasks handled by "pink-collar" labor: female stenographers, typists, and secretaries. Yates echoes Chandler to argue that technology was the driving force behind an information revolution that transformed office work.

The next two essays provide counterpoints to Chandler's account of technology as an agent of change in the business world. Steven W. Usselman, associate professor at the School of History, Technology, and Science at the Georgia Institute of Technology and author of the prize-winning book, *Regulating Railroad Innovation: Business, Technology, and Politics in America, 1840–1920* (2002), examines the testing laboratory at the Pennsylvania Railroad, one of the nation's largest railroads. Established in the 1870s, this department determined quality standards for materials and equipment. Usselman reveals the railroad's conservative position on technology, which emphasized reliability rather than novelty. Kenneth J. Lipartito, a professor of history at Florida International University and author of *The Bell System and Regional Business: The Telephone in the South, 1877–1920* (1989), looks at technology and labor in the telecommunications business. In Lipartito's account, executives at the American Telephone and Telegraph Company (AT&T) relied on female switchboard operators long after the invention of automatic switching equipment. This case study shows how culture—in the form of gender conventions about women's proper roles—influenced managers as they made choices about labor and technology.

How the Business World Adopted the Typewriter

JoANNE YATES

The physical creation of correspondence had always been a laborious and time-consuming process. In the second half of the nineteenth century, when so much else was speeding up, it was natural that people should look for ways of speeding up the production of documents. The typewriter, which appeared in the final quarter of the century during the period of most rapid firm growth and transformation, provided the necessary speed.

Attempts to mechanize the production of documents had begun as early as 1714, but for a century and a half none of them progressed beyond the experimental stages to a saleable product. Some succeeded in making machines that produced printlike writing, but because none of the machines worked faster than handwriting, they were not attractive to those who might have bought them. Consequently, these machines never even approached commercial viability. Finally, in 1868, Christopher Latham Sholes, along with Carlos Glidden and Samuel W. Soulé, registered the first of a series of U.S. patents that would at last produce a commercially viable product.

JoAnne Yates, *Control Through Communication: The Rise of System in American Management* (Baltimore, Md.: Johns Hopkins University Press, 1989), pp. 39–45. Copyright © 1993. Reprinted with permission of The Johns Hopkins University Press.

That first patent was only a beginning, and the typewriter progressed slowly toward commercial success. The machine underwent four more years of development under the direction of James Densmore before it first came to market. During this period Sholes settled on the current keyboard configuration, beginning with an alphabetical arrangement and rearranging keys to minimize their clashing. The first twenty-five nonexperimental machines were manufactured in a makeshift private factory in 1871–72. Although these machines were eventually sold, it soon became clear that production expertise was needed to produce a typewriter of acceptable quality in large quantities. At this point the developers approached the Remingtons, whose factory, one of the largest of the time, manufactured firearms and sewing machines. An agreement was reached, and the first machines from the Remington factory reached the market in 1874.

Ironically, Sholes and Densmore, unlike the developers of the telegraph and telephone, did not immediately target the business world as their major market. They originally looked to a much smaller and more specialized user: the court reporter. The first typewriter Sholes sold, an early experimental model, was bought by a court reporter named Charles E. Weller for use in his work. Indeed, most of the first small batch of pre-Remington typewriters went to court reporters and telegraphers, not to "ordinary business firms." An advertising brochure issued for the first Remington-made machines put court reporters at the top of the list of prospective users, followed by lawyers, editors, authors, clergymen, and others. Only in its last sentence does it suggest that "the merchant, the banker, ALL men of business can perform the labor of letter writing with much saving of valuable time."

Sales were slow in the late 1870s but increased rapidly in the 1880s. In the first five years on the market, 1874–78, only four thousand of the Remington typewriters were sold. Meanwhile, a few improvements, including the shift key to allow upper and lower case, made them more appealing to buyers. By 1880, a second company entered the market.

The business world's discovery of the typewriter in the 1880s undoubtedly accounts for the rapid sales growth, competition, and further technological innovation of that decade. From 1881 to 1884, the two companies sold a total of almost eighteen thousand machines, over four times as many as were sold in the first five years. As the market grew, more competition entered it and soon spurred more improvements and more sales. By 1886, according to the *Scientific American*'s estimate at that time, a total of fifty thousand typewriters of all makes had been manufactured. "'Five years ago the type writer was simply a mechanical curiosity,'" noted one observer in 1887. "'Today its monotonous click can be heard in almost every well regulated business establishment in the country. A great revolution is taking place, and the type writer is at the bottom of it.'" Annual capacity of all companies in 1886 was about fifteen thousand, but by 1888 the Remington Standard Typewriter Company (now a separate company bought from the Remingtons in 1886) made more than that in one year. In the 1890s, Underwood introduced the first successful "visible typewriter," which allowed the typist to see what was being typed. Soon all typewriters had this feature, and more were being sold than ever. In 1900, according to the 12th Census, 144,873 typewriters were sold. After a slow start, perhaps partly attributable to the developers' initial misreading of the market, the typewriter rapidly became a familiar part of office life.

Sholes's typewriter undoubtedly owed its success in business in part to the fact that it, unlike its predecessors, was faster than the pen. In the late 1870s the *Typewriter Magazine,* started by a Remington sales agent, pointed out that the typewriter could type seventy-five words per minute, while the pen typically produced only about twenty-four words per minute. After the development of touch typing in the 1880s, typing became even faster: typing speed contests in the early twentieth century produced speeds of around one hundred twenty net words per minute. Although the average typist did not approach this speed, a normal typing rate of eighty words per minute was more than three times faster than the normal handwriting rate. This improvement in efficiency appealed to the expanding businesses of the late 1870s and the 1880s.

The typewriter also opened the way for another change in the procedure by which documents came into being in business establishments: creation was completely separated from final production. Before the typewriter, the writer sometimes drafted a document (or even, in a few cases, dictated it to a stenographer) and turned it over to a clerk to copy it out in final form. But such separation was by no means universal. An owner or manager might compose and produce his own correspondence some or all of the time. Conversely a clerk, who frequently was in training for advancement in the firm, might compose as well as produce many routine letters. But the almost universal separation of those functions only occurred in conjunction with the typewriter. A whole new class of clerical workers arose to operate the new machines, as well as to take dictation and perform other clerical functions related to the handling of written documents.

The statistics on typists, stenographers (who typed up their shorthand notes), and secretaries during the period following business adoption of the typewriter suggest how rapidly the severance of composing from producing took place. In 1890, there were already 33,000 people employed as stenographers and typists. By 1900, the U.S. Census showed 134,000 in the broader occupational category including stenographers, typists, and secretaries. Such workers continued to flood into business and government in increasing numbers. By 1910 that occupational category had almost tripled to 387,000, and by 1920 it had doubled again to 786,000.

The almost universal separation of composing from typing had both technological and social roots. It reflected the skill needed for rapid typing, a technological factor, as well as the systematizers' conscious search for efficiency at all levels in business. Increasing subdivision of tasks and specialization of jobs, with the techniques of systematic management to coordinate the various specialized elements, helped achieve this efficiency. The typewriter provided an obvious opportunity to extend this principle to office work.

Although the earliest typists (often referred to as "typewriters") were trained primarily by the manufacturers, the private commercial schools that taught penmanship and bookkeeping soon began training typists. As early as the mid-1870s, before the typewriter became popular, one major commercial school magnate began to hold special classes in shorthand and typing. Soon it became clear that stenography and typing could be linked to achieve rapid production of documents, and the two skills began to feed on each other. In 1888 the U.S. Commissioner of Education noted the spread of departments and even whole schools of stenography and typing. By 1900 the amanuensis course, which included both skills, accounted for 36 percent of the enrollment in commercial schools. By the end of the century, public high schools had also begun to offer typing and other business skills. The commercial and public schools together trained an ever-growing workforce to operate typewriters.

Of those learning to type, an increasing proportion were women. The commercial schools had welcomed women long before the coming of the typewriter; nevertheless, in 1871 only 4 percent of total commercial school enrollment was female. The popularization of the typewriter, however, brought women pouring into the commercial schools and business offices. The proportion of women in commercial schools increased to 10 percent by 1880, 28 percent in 1890, and 36 percent in 1900. The employment statistics are even more revealing: as early as 1890[,] 64 percent of all stenographers and typists were women, and by 1900 the figure stood at 77 percent. The composition of the office workforce had changed radically.

The typewriter and those who used it also transformed the production and use of documents. By taking physical production out of the hands of those who composed the messages, stenographers and typists reduced the amount of time the highly paid executive spent on correspondence. The typewriter itself decreased the amount of less expensive clerical time taken to transcribe correspondence from dictation or from a handwritten draft. Moreover, by replacing illegible scrawls with neat, print-like text, the typewriter reduced both the time needed to read the document initially and the time needed to locate a given document in the files later. Finally, the large workforce of trained typists and secretaries helped standardize the formats and conventions for . . . new genres of internal written communication. . . .

Typewriters and related innovations accelerating the production of documents both fed on and facilitated enormous growth in external and internal written communication. The expanding market for these devices encouraged competition and continued technological evolution, while the reductions in time and cost associated with the typewriter increased the attractiveness of written communication as a managerial tool. Finally, the typewriter opened up the way for new methods of duplicating and filing documents that made certain types and uses of internal communication practical for the first time.

Mastering Technology, Channeling Change: The Testing Laboratory at the Pennsylvania Railroad

STEVEN W. USSELMAN

Over the course of the late nineteenth century, railroad managers . . . developed a powerful set of tools for evaluating technology and monitoring the course of innovation in their industry. By establishing testing facilities and creating staffs of technical advisors linked by a technical press, trade associations, and engineering societies, railroads mobilized a large community of highly trained technical experts who had no responsibilities other than assessing the condition of railroad technology. At a time when rapid growth made traditional methods of personal exchange difficult to

Steven W. Usselman, *Regulating Railroad Innovation: Business, Technology, and Politics in America, 1840–1920* (New York: Cambridge University Press, 2002), pp. 211–213, 199, 201–210, 213–214. Reprinted by permission of Cambridge University Press.

sustain even at individual lines, the language and analytical methods of engineering lifted discussions of technology to a more abstract plane, free from the peculiarities of particular devices and locales. Managers could readily exchange information about techniques gathered from across their industry, and they could implement desired changes in technology quickly throughout their sprawling enterprises. "The professionalization of the railroad manager increased the productivity of the American transportation system," states esteemed business historian Alfred Chandler [in *The Visible Hand*] unequivocally after pointing out the increasing prominence of engineers in railroad management. "Repeated discussions by the salaried managers of both organizational and technological innovations permitted their quick development and rapid adoption by American railroads."

These benefits resulted not so much from a vast effort aimed at generating and promoting technical novelty but from attempts to focus technical efforts on a few areas of particular importance. Managers charged with responsibility for operating highly developed systems of great complexity had little interest in revolutionary change that might seriously disrupt established operations. They sought to gain small economies by incorporating minor innovations and refinements as smoothly and as fully as possible. This desire to optimize performance in the context of a fixed system and established practices drew railroads readily into alliance with the growing body of academically trained scientists and engineers and with the educational institutions that trained them. Engineers and scientists possessed just the sort of knowledge and orientation to problems that railroads needed. Their novel methods of analysis sought not to generate significant departures in technology but to evaluate existing practices and materials and to establish standards of performance. Laboratory facilities and testing equipment subjected materials to routine evaluation along well-established criteria. . . . To the extent high-level managers perceived the laboratories as centers of experiment and novelty, they deemed them suspect. Faced with a particularly acute financial crisis during the early 1890s, Charles Perkins [of the Chicago, Quincy, and Burlington Railroad based in Illinois] advised a subordinate who proposed a test that "we cannot be experimenting" and suggested that "our policy is to let our richer neighbors in the East point the way for us." Even at progressive lines such as the Pennsylvania [Railroad], laboratories rarely assumed new responsibilities outside their established realm of standards-setting. No railroad turned to research and testing of new products as a possible avenue of escape from the woes of the depression. . . .

New testing equipment . . . figured prominently in perhaps the most significant development in railroad research: the founding of formal laboratories for physical and chemical analysis staffed by professionally trained experts. The Pennsylvania initiated this movement in the early 1870s when it consolidated its study of mechanical engineering problems in a new bureau of experiments located at its Altoona shops. The company replaced the bureau in 1874 with a Department of Physical Tests, which though located at Altoona fell directly under the authority of Superintendent of Motive Power Theodore N. Ely. Soon Ely bypassed the master mechanic at Altoona entirely and placed this facility under John W. Cloud, a formally trained mechanical engineer who assumed the title "mechanical engineer." . . . In November of the following year, Charles B. Dudley joined the small staff in the testing department. A

Ph.D. chemist recently graduated from Yale's Sheffield Scientific School, Dudley organized a chemical laboratory to supplement the new mechanical engineering facility.

Ely, who by all accounts originated the idea, apparently launched these ventures with no clear idea of what they would accomplish. Looking back years later, he characterized the decision to create the test department as an "experiment" and stressed that the company had authorized "an engineering laboratory in its broadest sense." The choice of Dudley—a general experimentalist fresh out of college with no direct experience in railroad affairs—reflected the unspecified character of the new testing facility. . . .

While undeniably modest and perhaps lacking a clear sense of purpose, these pioneering laboratories did not take shape out of thin air. In several respects, they fit squarely within emergent trends that garnered considerable attention in American industry at the time. The U.S. Government Testing Board, which had responsibility for assessing materials purchased by the navy and other federal agencies, had with the cooperation of Robert Thurston of Stevens Institute of Technology just opened a laboratory containing machines designed by Thurston and a few other engineers. Ely appeared to mimic this widely publicized venture when outfitting his lab. . . .

. . . The foundry at Altoona had begun casting steel car wheels shortly before Cloud arrived, and he devoted a great deal of his time to testing samples of the material that went into them. Gradually, Cloud came to perform similar bending and breaking tests on metals used in items such as boilers, springs, axles, brake chains, and crank pins. Such analyses rapidly became the bread-and-butter activity of the physical laboratory. . . .

Dudley took a bit longer to establish a niche for his chemical laboratory but ultimately traced a similar course toward routine analysis of purchased materials and supplies. During his first few years at the Pennsylvania, Dudley acted something like an in-house consultant, bringing his techniques of chemical analysis to bear upon a number of technical problems that arose in the course of running the railroad. He spent much of his first eighteen months, for instance, attempting to determine why the valves on locomotive boilers clogged so frequently. Toward the end of the 1870s, . . . he undertook a study intended to reveal why some steel rails wore more rapidly than others. Trained in the basic methods of scientific experiment, Dudley collected random samples of any materials that might contribute to these problems and performed chemical analyses of them, then correlated his findings to the observed performance. When seeking an answer to the problems with clogged boiler valves, for instance, he analyzed the mineral content of water from various sources used in the boilers and also determined the amounts of impurities in the tallows used to lubricate the valves. In the case of rails, he looked for possible variations between the chemical constituents of rails that wore more or less rapidly. In similar fashion, Dudley analyzed the contents of oils the Pennsylvania used in its lamps, searching for clues to why some burned cleaner than others.

The sort of knowledge Dudley accumulated through these early studies soon drew him into alliance with the purchasing agent, whose authority the Pennsylvania bolstered in late 1878. In another example of the intensified drive for uniformity that pervaded the railroad at the time, this officer would coordinate all purchasing activities of the various departments and geographical divisions of the entire system. Dudley's work dovetailed readily with this mission. In several cases, his investigations revealed that supplies such as lubricants and lighting oil contained adulterants that lay at the roots of the problems. By prescribing a preferred formula and analyzing samples from purchased lots, the Pennsylvania could identify such potential sources of difficulty in advance. As this practice grew routine, the purchasing agent began publishing the formulae as official specifications and letting suppliers know that the railroad would reject any lots that deviated from the stipulated amounts.

In addition to providing a check against unscrupulous suppliers, such specifications provided the purchasing agent with an important tool in his struggle to impose uniformity throughout the Pennsylvania system. Under the old, decentralized system of purchasing, individual managers had grown accustomed to selecting supplies and products based largely on their personal preferences. Dudley and his chemical analyses, like the apparatus for testing metals in the physical laboratory, in effect functioned as a neutral arbiter. They provided the purchasing agent with independent and impersonal assessments he could easily invoke when managers disagreed with his choice of material for a certain purpose. . . . [T]he goal was not to produce the most accurate analyses possible, but to provide consistent assessments from one time to the next.

During the remaining years of the 1880s—his most productive period—Dudley set out to extend the practice of purchasing according to specifications to as many products as possible. Though operational problems generally still first drew him to a topic, Dudley consistently expanded his inquiries into exhaustive studies covering all varieties of materials that might have contributed to the problem. He would then suggest detailed guidelines for an entire line of products, and the purchasing agent would issue specifications based on his advice. When shock-absorbing springs on railroad cars began to break with alarming frequency, for example, Dudley analyzed the steel used in the springs and recommended a certain type of steel for that application. This work, which flowed in part out of Dudley's investigations of steel rails, in turn prompted him to devise specifications for all steel and cast-iron products purchased by the railroad. . . .

By proceeding in this fashion, Dudley had by 1889 secured a well-defined role for the chemical laboratory in the management of the Pennsylvania Railroad. The established character of the lab emerged clearly in a series of articles Dudley and his assistant, F. N. Pease, wrote for the *Railroad and Engineering Journal.* Naming their series "Chemistry Applied to Railroads," Dudley and Pease described in detail the work done in their laboratory at the Pennsylvania. They portrayed the facility as an established institution built firmly on the foundation of making and enforcing specifications. By 1889, they reported, the Pennsylvania regularly purchased twenty-five products according to chemical specifications drawn up by Dudley in collaboration with the purchasing agent. To enforce these specifications the company maintained an expanded laboratory facility and employed several additional personnel. Under Dudley's supervision this staff performed over 25,000 chemical analyses each year, making it perhaps the largest analytical chemistry laboratory in the country.

Informed observers had long since detected the benefits of the facilities at the Pennsylvania and begun to emulate them. An 1880 article in the *Railroad Gazette* described activities at the test department in glowing terms, and another published two years later concluded that the laboratory "proves that science, as a method of investigation, is fully recognized as having a place in railroad affairs." Such facilities, its author confidently declared, would soon become standard in the railroad industry. The Burlington, in characteristic fashion, followed the Pennsylvania nearly from the start. In October 1876 it hired a mechanical engineer and a chemist and set up laboratory facilities for both in its main shops at Aurora, Illinois. . . . By 1883, the practice of purchasing materials based on specifications had become so established that the Burlington extended the work of Higginson and the laboratory to cover purchases by its branch lines. Several more railroads followed suit during the 1880s, as assistants trained in the laboratories of the two pioneers moved on to set up testing facilities and laboratories at other companies. . . .

While routine analyses performed in connection with purchasing materials rapidly became the raison d'etre of most railroad laboratories, the chemists and mechanical engineers also contributed to the developing tradition of testing when they assisted in occasional tests of new technology. By the mid-1880s, Dudley had established ongoing programs for examining products such as storage batteries, fire extinguishers, paints, greases, and a variety of lighting systems used to illuminate cars, tracks, and buildings. . . .

Executives at the Pennsylvania and many other lines identified the laboratories and testing departments as important drawing cards in the recruitment of young scientists and engineers. As early as 1880, *Railroad Gazette* noted that the experimental department usually "becomes a training school for subordinate officers." New graduates of scientific and technical schools were offered jobs as "special apprentices" in the labs, where they would find a familiar environment and perhaps work on the same problems and with the same equipment they had used in college laboratories. Applicants requested these positions even though they paid little. "There is now such a large and increasing class of educated young men, many of whom can afford to spend from one to five years in practical training with little or no compensation," observed the *Gazette,* "that the salaries of assistants in such a department are a very small item."

Over time, railroads came to view the laboratories as ideal entry points on the path to careers in management. New graduates refined their drafting and analytical techniques in the laboratories and test facilities while beginning to familiarize themselves with all aspects of railroading. Within months of arriving at the railroad, the young recruits would move from the lab to some mechanical or even commercial department. Both the Pennsylvania and the Burlington relied heavily on such men for their managerial talent. By the 1890s, most Pennsylvania division superintendents and master mechanics had served as special apprentices, and many executives not directly involved with machinery had spent time in the testing facilities and laboratory as well. The laboratory became so important to recruitment and training at the Burlington that when an economizing Perkins threatened to cut back the facility during the depression of the 1890s, Superintendent of Motive Power Godfrey Rhodes objected on the grounds that it would harm the Burlington's technical reputation and undermine efforts in these areas. "The CBQ RR would never hold its present position in motive power matters among railroads were it not for the information it has gathered through its laboratory," Rhodes wrote. "It would be better to abandon the practice of starting young men in the mechanical department if they are to be discharged at every falling off in business."

While testing facilities at several lines came under similar scrutiny from economizing executives during the financial crises of the 1890s, they generally survived the cutbacks and came back stronger than ever. Though Perkins in reviewing possible areas to make cuts had inquired "whether we might not cut off entirely or materially curtail the laboratory at Aurora," Rhodes and Higginson managed to nurse the facility through the crisis until the tide turned in 1896. The Burlington then expanded its standards-setting activities, adding a physical laboratory to its chemical facility. Testing activities at the Pennsylvania slumped a bit with the onset of depression, but in 1896 the line completed improvements that tripled the size of its chemical laboratory. Dudley and Pease curtailed their experimental work slightly but continued to develop new standard analytical techniques for use in connection with specifications. By 1903, the Pennsylvania employed a laboratory staff of approximately twenty-five people and enforced forty-seven sets of chemical specifications. Top executives at the Reading, besieged by a second bankruptcy, repeatedly turned down requests from the chemist for a higher salary and an expanded facility but did not eliminate them altogether. Other companies, accepting specifications as a routine component of railroad operations, built their first separate laboratory facilities during the decade. . . .

While the turn toward engineering methods shifted analysis of railroad technology onto terms that transcended conditions at particular firms and in many respects depersonalized choices regarding technology, the institutional and organizational changes worked in some ways to centralize technical decision-making and to concentrate it in the hands of a few individuals. Matthias Forney, through his dual position as editor of *Railroad Gazette* and secretary of the Master Car Builders Association, exerted a strong influence over the flow of information and attitudes pertaining to innovation. The Pennsylvania Railroad and, in particular, General Superintendent of Motive Power Theodore N. Ely, assumed a position as the foremost expert in technical matters. Burlington President Charles Perkins described Ely as "the highest authority," and the CB&Q, along with nearly every other railroad, kept an eye turned to practices deployed by the Pennsylvania. The Burlington itself became the leader in technical matters among the many Chicago roads. By cooperating freely and allowing this informal hierarchy of expertise to develop, railroads avoided unnecessary duplication of research and kept the costs of evaluating and selecting techniques low. Railroads obtained similar benefits by concentrating their purchases of equipment and supplies in a handful of manufacturers. Executives looking for novel technology no longer scoured a diffuse market, but instead entrusted established firms such as Baldwin and Westinghouse with the task of finding and marketing the best available devices. In entering into such established relationships, railroads looked for reliability more than novelty. Producers and consumers of railroad technology engaged in sustained collaboration that encouraged ongoing refinement but perhaps placed less emphasis on radical departures from routine.

. . . [T]hese policies may have led managers to overlook innovations that would have been tried and used widely in an earlier era. Relying on the judgment of experts at a few railroads and suppliers was a cheap and efficient way to evaluate innovation across a narrow spectrum; it was not a policy designed to ensure that the best ideas came to fruition. Rather than many inventions being tried and some ultimately surviving and becoming common, most inventions never received a trial. But in the competitive conditions of the late nineteenth century, managers were willing to risk missing the benefits of a dramatic innovation if they could incorporate minor changes without difficulty while maintaining efficient operations.

Switchboard Operators or Girl-Free Automation? Gender Stereotypes and Managerial Choice in the Bell Telephone System

KENNETH J. LIPARTITO

Before the invention of automatic equipment, female operators carried out the crucial task of connecting telephone subscribers. In simplest form, the work of the operator involved receiving verbal requests for connections and physically plugging one line into another at the switchboard. But the rudiments of the work belied a complex labor process built on a number of related factors: the economics of networks, the strategies of telephone firms, evolving switchboard hardware, and the culture of the workers.

Early in the history of telephony, managers had recognized the importance of the operator's task. At large urban telephone exchanges, managers quickly perceived switching to be a potentially serious bottleneck. As telephone networks grew, the number of possible calls to be switched increased geometrically. Mathematics indicated that at some point demand for switching might exceed capacity. The problem was not a purely technical one. It related to the strategy of the Bell Telephone Company, a sprawling monopoly composed of dozens of regional firms that dominated telephony in America from 1880 until 1894. Bell had built its strategy around the promotion of urban telecommunications. Its prime concern was cultivating telephone use in big city markets, rather than in less densely populated rural areas. Urban telephone networks quickly reached the size at which switching became a problem. Managers avoided a breakdown in the networks by organizing a techno-labor system that employed human operators carefully selected by class, race, and sex. A complex of women and machines solved the critical problem of switching.

Multiple switchboards were the crucial hardware of this techno-labor system. To overcome capacity constraints in cities such as New York, telephone engineers designed a three-panel board containing jacks for every subscriber line—up to 10,000 lines. Operators sat before one panel but, by stretching to the right or left, were able to reach all the other subscriber jacks in the exchange. Each operator was responsible for only a small number of incoming lines but could complete her calls to any other line in the exchange. Multiplying this triptych arrangement, firms engaged dozens of operators working together to handle the heavy load of large central offices.

Manual switching had a gender, and here we can see how cultural categories combined with strategy and technology to form a labor process. The social construction of telephone technology created an entirely new group of skilled workers—telephone operators. Since the 1880s, the telephone companies had employed women almost exclusively in this position, a practice also followed in other nations. The origins of this sexual division of labor remain obscure, but two things stand out. Women, male telephone managers believed, possessed the inherent qualities needed in a manual system; and they were available in large numbers.

Kenneth J. Lipartito, "When Women Were Switches: Technology, Work, and Gender in the Telephone Industry, 1890–1920," *American Historical Review* 99, no. 4 (October 1994): 1074–1111 (excerpt, pp. 1081–1082, 1084–1085, 1087–1088, 1091, 1093, 1095–1097, 1099–1110). Reprinted by permission of American Historical Association and the author.

Many historians have speculated about the link between the feminization of occupations such as telephone operator and management's drive to cut costs and control its labor force. Here we have to distinguish carefully between entrepreneurial strategies aimed at reaching new markets and labor strategies designed to increase worker effort and compliance. The nature of the operator's task reflected telephone managers' entrepreneurial strategy for differentiating telephone service from rival forms of communications such as the telegraph. Telegraph firms employed male operators, who received and transmitted coded information but who did not speak with customers. The job required mastery of Morse code, facility with the telegraph key, and a quick and neat pen. But telegraphy was not a switched form of communications, as was telephony. Telephone companies stressed the interactive quality of their service, which allowed users to speak directly with each other. Fast, accurate switching was vital to this more complex method of communications. Switching required new specialized forms of labor utilizing different skills.

Since manual technology required operators to speak with subscribers, if only briefly, telephone firms wanted employees who would project a comfortable and genteel image to their customers. Applicants for the job were expected to have at least a grammar school education. Policy in both the North and South was "whites only," and companies sought native-born workers, rejecting those with strong ethnic accents. By hiring employees of "good character," telephone firms were seeking workers who could deal with customers "on an equal plane," as one manager put it. Telephones in the early twentieth century remained a luxury even for the middle class. A prime category of user—who made expensive and profitable long distance calls—was the businessman.

The job requirements quickly took on a gender, for telephone managers believed that women possessed the qualities they sought. Respectable deportment, accuracy, attention to detail, good hearing, and good speech were commonly held to be female more than male traits. They characterized traditional female occupations such as teaching and women's jobs in such industries as textiles and paper making. Astute companies were not above exploiting male solicitude for the weaker sex, reminding subscribers that operators were "entitled to the same consideration and courtesy that is extended to women in our everyday business and social activities and that we expect for our wives, sisters or daughters." When dealing with cranky and irritable customers, women's purportedly more patient nature—formed, no doubt, from their maternal instincts—was seen to be especially valuable. Early trials with male operators did not pan out because young men had neither the discipline nor deportment desired. By 1900, over 80 percent of operators were single, white, native-born females. . . .

Telecommunications provides an extreme example of how technology and innovation could contribute to the construction of new female occupations while at the same time confirming old ideas about female work. Women's contributions were crucial to the success of the complex technology of manual switching. While scanning ten thousand tiny jacks, keeping an eye open for lights indicating new calls, and sweeping the board of old connections, operators had to complete several hundred calls per hour during peak times. Months of practice were required before they mastered the "overlaps," or the knack of performing multiple tasks simultaneously. Managers recognized that "the attainment of service standards necessarily involves a good grade of well-trained operator." The good operator, however, became the female operator, a definition that carried with it many old assumptions about women's work. Operators were expected to be young and unmarried. They were restricted to repetitive tasks that could be monitored and controlled by male engineers. And they were not allowed to advance outside their own separate employment track. . . .

Unlike other women workers in the age of mechanization, telephone operators were engaged with the latest technology of a complex technological system. Companies improved the switching process by incremental adjustments that substantially raised operator productivity. They invested in worker training and accommodations, although, of course, they also profited from the discrimination that limited women's job options. Telephone operating, however, was a new source of employment for women. By bringing together technology and women, telephone companies created a highly successful techno-labor system. . . . Redesigning the labor process proved far more difficult than simple models of technological change would suppose. By turning to issues beyond cost and control, we can understand why this process was so stable and what caused it to change.

By the mid-1880s, Bell was well on its way to building telephone systems in the nation's major urban centers. Secure with a virtual monopoly, the corporation embarked on another path that it would follow for more than half a century—construction of a national long distance network. . . .

Although the new strategy followed in the footsteps of the old, it placed even more pressure on the switching bottleneck. The larger the total system, the more calls that flowed through a given point. Building an interconnected network, moreover, demanded a high degree of standardization, since each part interacted with the others. Accordingly, Bell centralized research, development, and manufacturing. It limited the range of options available to consumers, keeping research on a narrow path. Innovation focused on incremental rather than radical improvements in individual components such as switching.

Fixed firmly on its course, Bell ran into some heavy seas after 1894. The firm's telephone patents expired, and numerous new competitors entered the industry. No longer able to maintain monopoly prices, Bell saw its revenues plummet. As prices fell, telephones became more widely available. Even more people gained telephones for the first time when so-called independent firms rushed to serve towns and cities neglected during the monopoly years. Flourishing between 1898 and 1907, they took almost half the market from the senior firm.

Competition altered the mode of innovation in the industry. Upstart firms experimented with different combinations of equipment to produce novel services for new markets. . . . One new contribution was the automatic switch. In 1891, a Kansas City undertaker named Almon Strowger patented a device that switched telephone calls mechanically. . . . In a society that had long believed labor-saving technology meant progress, many predicted that the day of the human operator was over. But events did not unfold so predictably. Invention was only the start of a long course of change.

Strowger was neither a capitalist faced with an intractable work force nor a rational engineer carefully weighing the price of labor and capital. . . . Invention, the creation of the first model of a new technology, remains a mysterious and poorly understood practice, and Strowger's story does little to clear up the picture. Exactly why he devoted himself to making a telephone switch is unknown, although one legend suggests a motivation related to labor problems. Apparently, Strowger believed that the local telephone operators were sending calls intended for his undertaking business to rivals. This dissatisfied consumer of telephone services made a dramatic and unexpected contribution to the art. . . .

Transforming this raw invention into a component of a giant technological system fell to the many telephone firms now competing sharply for business. An outsider to the industry, Strowger was ill equipped for the task. The newly competitive market, however, seemed to promise a great opportunity to promote his infant invention. But the largest firm of the industry, American Bell, greeted it with suspicion. Bell patent expert Thomas Lockwood asserted that "both experience and observation have united to show us that an operation so complex as that of uniting two telephone subscribers' lines . . . can never efficiently or satisfactorily be performed by automatic apparatus, dependent on the volition and intelligent action of the subscriber." "The telephone girl has come to stay," predicted another observer, more succinctly. The Bell corporation declined to either purchase or license Strowger's breakthrough. . . .

Conceiving of technology as a system helps to explain why Bell resisted automation despite . . . potential savings. After invention of the Strowger switch, telephone companies had a choice: either invest in the new technology or continue to improve their existing techno-labor methods. Although costs and benefits are clear in hindsight, the alteration of a complex technical system to make room for a radical new device involves much uncertainty about whether the change will yield sufficient returns to justify its expense. . . . Savings offered by mechanization also had to be weighed against the advantages of human operators. They served as a point of personal contact between subscribers and telephone companies, helped to locate trouble, and assisted users with an unfamiliar technology.

For a corporation dedicated to a competitive strategy that emphasized long distance service, standardization of components, and vertical and horizontal integration, the uncertainty of the new technology made it especially risky. Bell engineers and managers had long focused their attention on the "critical problems" that threatened to block system growth. Manual technology embodied this substantial experience and expertise. Automatic switching, however, introduced an entirely new set of considerations. It served only for local telephone calls, offering no means of switching long distance calls. At the very least, Bell engineers observed, more work was needed on the link between manual long distance and automatic local switching. Modifying the device to fit the firm's strategy became more difficult, however, when Strowger sold his patent to a new manufacturing concern, the Automatic Electric Company. Bell firms would have to purchase or license the switches from a competing organization if they wanted to use them. Either move ran counter to the corporation's pursuit of vertical control and standardization of technology.

Given the risks of radical change, it seemed more expedient to continue investing in manual switching. . . . Centralized power . . . permitted new features at the switchboard. Lights now signaled operators to answer or disconnect calls, replacing noisy and confusing mechanical drops, which had to be reset by hand. Switchboards were also wired for "automatic ringing," so that merely plugging the connecting line into the jack rang the telephone of the called party.

These and other improvements allowed the female labor force to handle the growth in telephone calls between 1900 and 1910. Company engineers modified and redesigned the switching process to take full advantage of its new potential for raising labor productivity. . . . [S]witching capacity expanded without resort to automation. . . .

. . . Only by increasing switching capacity could the corporation achieve its goal of expanding telephone service nationally. Incremental improvements in existing technology seemed a less risky means of doing so than investing in a radical new mechanism. At the time, competition was driving down profits, which created financial pressures on the company to reduce all unnecessary capital expenditures.

The position of top management on these matters was summed up concisely by Chief Engineer J. J. Carty in 1910. The system, he maintained, not any one component, should be the focus of concern. Improved switching, Carty went on, depended more on the overall design of the switching process than on any one machine. Not explicitly addressed to issues of labor, the statement nonetheless had implications for how AT&T should handle labor conflict. So long as it did not substantially interfere with the operational requirements of the system, it could be dealt with by incremental adjustments. Worker culture and resistance could be important issues, as we shall see. But unless managers perceived labor conflict as a critical problem of system growth or as a challenge to their basic strategy, they did not replace workers with machines. . . .

With the industry's largest player content with manual switching methods, it fell to others to promote automation. Non-Bell firms turned to the Strowger switch as a means of challenging their corporate rival for control of the telephone market. Some of them saw it as a means of reducing costs and bringing service to new areas. To new entrants without preexisting commitments to technology, savings that the incumbent could afford to ignore mattered greatly. Even among these firms, however, labor costs did not wholly determine behavior. These companies tended to operate in smaller towns and cities, where switching capacity and labor conflict were not great problems. Market share was their prime concern, and automatic switching proved an effective marketing tool. Heartened by an impression that customers liked dialing, independents appealed to the belief that the mechanical was modern and efficient, the human quaint and slightly out-of-date. Advertisements explained that machines kept their secrets and "never gossiped." They did not require customers to speak with operators, who could be "surly" or "saucy" (and who often received the blame when calls went awry). As one sales brochure exclaimed, the day of the "cussless, waitless, out-of-orderless, girlless telephone" was now at hand. . . .

Despite creative campaigns, the independents made only limited headway with automation. By 1915, only about 4 percent of the market was served by mechanical switches. Some urban telephone concerns had prospered through automation—Los Angeles had the largest system, with 60,000 subscribers. Many independents, however, served places too small to reap substantial savings by eliminating workers. Others had customers to whom "girlless" telephones were a mixed blessing. Though often decried as the town gossip, the telephone operator was also appreciated as a source of information. She located missing parties, took messages, provided wake-up calls, and gave out the correct time. With automatic switching, it was impossible to provide such services.

The failure of automation to catch on was less a result of its technical and economic shortcomings than of structural weaknesses in markets and organizations. These institutional factors hampered the spread of this technology. Almost all the independent telephone enterprises were beset by organizational problems. Equipment manufacturers such as Automatic Electric were not integrated into the operating end of the business. Independent operating companies themselves remained largely separate and either uninterested in or incapable of effective cooperation. Unlike the vertically integrated Bell System, manufacturers and operating companies of the independent sector lacked the means to coordinate research, production, and operations. It was difficult for them to adjust technology to customers' needs or to upgrade local facilities so that they were compatible with new equipment.

Most significant, independents did not achieve the integration needed to provide a telephone service competitive with AT&T's long distance network. Without this competitive asset, they were largely unable to penetrate the big city market, where the advantages of automatic switches were greatest. . . . Their market share shrank steadily, and Bell was able to recapture its dominant position. With market dominance came the ability to shape telecommunications technology. The fate of automatic switching rested largely in the hands of one giant corporation.

When AT&T regained control of the telephone market in 1913, it still showed little interest in automatic switching. Yet, within a few years, the corporation reversed course and was deploying the machines in its exchanges. This change of heart reflected the intersection of technology, business strategy, and politics with new labor issues. After 1913, a series of developments threw automatic technology into a more favorable light. Years of speculation, experimentation, and field trials finally convinced skeptics that there were indeed places where automation saved money. In the conjectural realm of innovation, such knowledge was important. Nonetheless, like a big ship in the water, the corporation was turning slowly. It was still unclear precisely where and when to automate, how fast and how far to go. Strong internal dissension was still brewing over the technology. Crucial to erasing these doubts and determining policy was a growing perception that the manual techno-labor process was nearing a maximum. When the existing system seemed to be in crisis, the will to change was forthcoming. . . .

[First,] system growth, the cornerstone of the Bell strategy, was falling victim to its own success. Bell companies were forced to continually build new exchanges as old ones reached the limit of manual switchboards. By 1920, New York City had nearly two hundred exchanges. Ninety percent of all calls in Manhattan terminated at an exchange other than the one of the calling party. Requiring many more steps to complete, these trunk calls lowered switching speed and efficiency. . . .

Even though virtually a monopolist, AT&T could not afford to meet this crisis by either allowing service to deteriorate or raising prices. Politics limited its room to maneuver. Under the threat of an antitrust suit, company president Theodore Vail had compromised with the remaining independent firms in 1913. Bell would serve as the senior partner and "manager" of the nation's telecommunications network, dominating the large urban areas and long distance transmission but allowing non-Bell firms to operate on the periphery as "sub-licensees" and permitting them access to its toll lines. To seal the bargain, Vail launched a massive public relations campaign, portraying his firm as progressive and socially responsible. He emphasized the speed, quality, and availability of Bell service. He pronounced monopoly superior to competition in building the telephone network that the nation needed. After such statements, for the company to appear technologically backward was to invite government intervention. . . .

. . . [Second,] changes taking place in the labor market suddenly increased the power of the formerly docile female operator corps. . . . During World War I, . . . labor problems arose that threatened manual switching and pushed AT&T to embrace automation more rapidly and more thoroughly than it otherwise would have. Between 1917 and 1920, a sudden jump in government demand for female clerks, plus generally high levels of employment, cut into the supply of operators. The decrease in operators coincided with the increase in telephone demand brought on by system growth and led to rapid wage escalation. Wages as a percentage of total costs in the Bell System reached a high of 58 percent in 1920, when top operators in large cities were earning up to $900 per year.

Despite higher wages, telephone operators were lured away by opportunities in the military and in booming wartime industries. . . . "The greater demand for women in the trades," one Bell executive wrote, "is making it difficult to secure enough operators." By 1920, yearly operator turnover averaged 93 percent nationwide, rising to as much as 120 percent in some cities. . . . Lack of experienced personnel placed additional burdens on those who remained, particularly in the vulnerable urban exchanges. Problems pyramided, and absenteeism more than doubled. . . .

The war years also brought to the surface some deeper labor issues. The strata of society that AT&T managers believed made the best operators constituted only about 5 percent of the population, less when those of "questionable character" were eliminated. "In most parts of the country," one manager noted, "we are requiring a larger and larger proportion of the available female labor." In the nation's fifty-eight largest cities, about 8 percent of the female labor force was already employed as operators. In some places, it was as high as 20 percent. Even when the war ended, the group of women on which telephone companies traditionally drew was likely to have more and more options for employment, while the need for skilled operators to meet the requirements of a growing, increasingly complex telephone system continued to rise.

In the tightening labor market, power shifted in favor of workers. Bell System employees grew restive and militant, ready to organize their own unions rather than take hand-outs from management. . . . Operator strikes swept through towns and cities in New England, the Pacific Coast, and the Southwest between 1917 and 1919. . . .

The sudden expression of independence among the operators unsettled Bell management. As one member of the corporation observed, unions instilled in operators a "lack of respect for authority" and resulted in "independence of action by the individual." . . . [T]he same order and purpose that made for efficient switching could be turned against the company. Because manual switching required machine-like discipline, independence of mind endangered the entire telephone network. Strikes, stoppages, and slowdowns resulted in "a continual fight to maintain orderliness and efficiency of service." Service was the watchword of the re-monopolized industry. President Vail remarked, "The service which [the Bell System] furnishes is of the first importance in the business and family life of the nation . . . [it] must be prompt, reliable and accessible." In providing such service, Vail continued, "the importance of having an intelligent, interested, satisfied and loyal body of employees cannot be overestimated." . . .

. . . [T]he experience between 1918 and 1919 had revealed some of the other weaknesses of the manual switching system. AT&T was particularly concerned about its shrinking pool of "appropriate" women. Having defined the job as women's work, the corporation did not believe it would be appealing to men, and it refused to recruit from the lower end of the socioeconomic scale. AT&T hired some immigrants, notably Irish women, whose accents, it felt, were not offensive to middle-class subscribers. But it did not employ working-class men, black women, or other immigrants. . . . AT&T had configured manual switching to rely on the skills, deportment, and dedication of a certain group of women, whose numbers were dwindling. Changing the hardware of the techno-labor process—something management could fully control—proved easier than changing the gender and culture of the work force, which it could only partially influence.

The system nature of technology . . . means that even capitalists who are ever on the search for profits engage in a complex series of decisions before they determine to substitute capital for labor. One cannot assume that the effects of technology—skill-destroying or labor-saving—also explain its origins and path of development. In telecommunications, firms could choose from several methods to deal with labor. Different firms made different choices at different times. Some took the plunge into automatic switching without experiencing any labor problems; others, such as AT&T, continued to invest in manual switching. Only the convergence of a number of factors—strategic managerial objectives, system bottlenecks, government telecommunications policy, and shifts in the labor market—led to the automation of telephone operating.

 F U R T H E R   R E A D I N G

Berk, Gerald. *Alternative Tracks: The Constitution of American Industrial Order, 1865–1917* (1994).

Chandler, Alfred D., Jr. *The Visible Hand: The Managerial Revolution in American Business* (1977).

Cowan, Ruth Schwartz. *A Social History of American Technology* (1997).

Cronon, William. *Nature's Metropolis: Chicago and the Great West* (1991).

Dunlavy, Colleen A. *Politics and Industrialization: Early Railroads in the United States and Prussia* (1994).

Fishlow, Albert. *American Railroads and the Transformation of the Antebellum Economy* (1965).

Fogel, Robert William. *Railroads and American Economic Growth: Essays in Econometric History* (1964).

Hounshell, David A. *From the American System to Mass Production, 1800–1932: The Development of Manufacturing Technology in the United States* (1984).

Hughes, Thomas P. *American Genesis: A Century of Invention and Technological Enthusiasm, 1870–1970* (1989).

———. *Networks of Power: Electrification in Western Society, 1880–1930* (1983).

Licht, Walter. *Working for the Railroad: The Organization of Work in the Nineteenth Century* (1983).

Lipartito, Kenneth J. *The Bell System and Regional Business: The Telephone in the South, 1877–1920* (1989).

Misa, Thomas J. *A Nation of Steel: The Making of Modern America, 1865–1925* (1995).

Nye, David E. *American Technological Sublime* (1994).

Porter, Glenn. *The Rise of Big Business, 1860–1920,* 2d ed. (1992).

Taylor, George Rogers. *The Transportation Revolution, 1815–1860* (1951).

CHAPTER
8

The Age of the Octopus:
Business and the Reform
Impulse, 1876–1920

By the early twentieth century, Americans concerned with the ramifications of rapid change—industrialization, urbanization, mass immigration, and business consolidation—rallied around a loosely organized reform movement that historians call "progressivism." Between 1876 and 1920, much of this impulse concentrated on industry and big business. To be sure, reformers understood that industrial capitalism had created a prosperous economy and a cornucopia of consumer products. They also saw that it generated urban blight, political corruption, plundered natural resources, and social discontent. Moral decay seemed rampant, as exemplified by the spread of saloons and prostitution. Since the nation's hundredth birthday in 1876, recurrent business depressions resulted in widespread unemployment and violent strikes. Ordinary citizens suffered while giant corporations profited. Something had to be done to tame the "octopus" known as big business, and concerned progressive reformers took on the challenge.

Reformers' efforts to end the abuses of power had roots in the Jeffersonian and Jacksonian critiques of centralization. The progressives intensified the crusade against corporate giantism and fought battles on the city, state, and national levels. They turned trust-busting, good government, and moral reform into issues that drove presidential politics under Theodore Roosevelt, William Howard Taft, and Woodrow Wilson. Ironically, some progressives, such as Roosevelt and social worker Jane Addams, came from the leisure class created by corporate expansion. Other reformers, such as Boston retailer Edward A. Filene and Pennsylvania Railroad executive Alexander Cassatt, were men of business. Given such ties, progressives often sought to apply management techniques to controlling the social order. The regulatory state that emerged from progressive deliberations—the effort of big government to use legislation to dampen immorality and to monitor big business—owed much to corporate practices.

Noting these connections, Marxist historian Gabriel Kolko in The Triumph of Conservatism *(1963) argued that corporate greed, rather than altruistic reform,*

240

inspired the progressive movement toward business regulation. In Kolko's view, corporate interests used their influence to shape progressive reform for their own ends. More recently, business historians such as Christine Meisner Rosen, whose work appears in Chapter 1, have examined the local connections between business-men and reform, formulating a more subtle analysis. Rosen's research on Chicago business groups shows how concerned executives tried to battle air pollution long before any watch-dog agencies mandated emission controls. In her account, Chicago businessmen espoused self-regulation for the greater good, and they tried to implement those controls without government intervention. Rosen's work shows that the relationship between business and society is more ambiguous than Kolko suggested. The documents and essays in this chapter explore that gray territory.

 D O C U M E N T S

As industrialization accelerated and big business grew, the status of labor underwent a dramatic shift. Small workshops, run by sole proprietors and a few helpers, remained important. In many industries, however, factories and assembly-line production re-placed hand labor and separated owners from workers. Employees responded in part by establishing unions to represent their interests. Founded in 1869 by Philadelphia's skilled garment workers, the Knights of Labor soon attracted workers from other trades and included women, blacks, immigrants, and unskilled workers. Before col-lapsing after the 1886 Haymarket Affair, the Knights had 750,000 members, making it the largest union in nineteenth-century America. Document 1 is from the preamble to the Knights' constitution, written during the depression of 1873–1878 and in the wake of the Great Railroad Strike of 1877. What do the workers demand as their natural rights? Why do they use the symbol * * * * * instead of the union's name?

In Document 2, the journalist Henry Demarest Lloyd (1847–1903) exposes the monopolistic practices of John D. Rockefeller's Standard Oil Company. Writing for *Atlantic Monthly,* Lloyd aims to shock the 40 million Americans who use kerosene but know little about Rockefeller's cut-throat practices. His description of Standard Oil as an "octopus" captured the American imagination. As the critique of big business grew, the media popularized the octopus as a symbol of monopoly. How did Rockefeller gain control of the oil business? Why did his arrangements with the railroads upset critics like Lloyd?

Alerted to horrible working conditions, state governments passed laws regulating factories and established agencies to monitor them. Document 3 is an excerpt from a factory inspector's report describing conditions in Philadelphia's garment district in 1894. What does this report tell us about small industries in the age of big business? About sweatshops? About the middle-class values of the factory inspector? Why would garment manufacturers claim that they could not improve conditions?

Document 4 presents an executive's view of labor-management conflict during the depression of 1893–1894. In spring 1894, workers at the Chicago-area Pullman Palace Car Works, led by Eugene V. Debs of the American Railway Union, went on strike to protest wage cuts and layoffs. Workers condemned George M. Pullman's paternalistic practices: "We are born in a Pullman house, fed from the Pullman shop, taught in the Pullman school, catechized in the Pullman church, and when we die we shall be buried in the Pullman cemetery and go to the Pullman hell." When other workers in the American Railway Union boycotted trains hauling Pullman cars, the U.S. attorney general obtained a court order to prevent them from obstructing mail deliveries, and President Grover Cleveland ordered troops to crush the strike, which had attracted national attention. In his annual report, Pullman gives his perspective on these events. How does he justify the wage cuts and interpret the workers' demands?

By the 1890s, progressive reformers came to see corporate consolidation through the legal mechanisms of the trust and the holding company as great evils. Eventually, "trust" became synonymous with monopoly, and it was used to describe all types of big businesses. The question before lawmakers was whether to break up the trusts or to regulate them. Documents 5 to 7 present views on this subject.

In Document 5, Henry O. Havemeyer, president of the American Sugar Refining Company in New York, testifies at the U.S. Industrial Commission's 1899 hearings on monopolies. Ironically, the head of the "Sugar Trust" critiques the protective tariff, which "plunders the people" by encouraging corporate consolidation. Colleen A. Dunlavy explains Havemeyer's position in essay one. Next, President Theodore Roosevelt delivers his opinion on big business and the trusts in his first annual message to Congress (Document 6). Roosevelt argues that corporate growth is inevitable, and he urges lawmakers to control big businesses through regulation. This position was challenged in the 1912 presidential campaign by Woodrow Wilson, who believed that trusts were inimical to free competition. In Document 7, Louis D. Brandeis offers an incisive critique of the "Money Trust" in an article for *Harper's Weekly*, later included in his book, *Other People's Money: and How the Bankers Use It* (1914). A graduate of Harvard Law School and a Jew shunned by Boston WASPs, he accumulated a fortune as counsel to small and midsized manufacturers and Jewish merchants. Once financially secure, Brandeis built a career as the "people's attorney," using his legal skills to assail "corporate tyrants" in oil, steel, railroading, and banking. His critique of banking built on hearings about the Money Trust, conducted by U.S. Congressman Arsène Pujo for the House Committee on Banking and Currency in 1912–1913. Why does Brandeis target J. P. Morgan & Co. and other New York banks?

Businesses like the Pullman Palace Car Works tried to defuse criticism in numerous ways, including corporate paternalism. Later companies, such as the Goodyear Tire & Rubber Company, the world's largest manufacturer of motor vehicle tires, modified Pullman's approach to deal with the "Labor-Capital problem." In a 1920 public relations pamphlet (Document 8), Goodyear explains the extensive welfare program at its factories in Akron, Ohio. How does the Goodyear program compare with the Kodak effort described in Sanford M. Jacoby's essay?

1. Unionized Workers in the Knights of Labor Demand a Fair Share of American Wealth, 1878

The recent alarming development and aggression of aggregated wealth, which, unless checked, will invariably lead to the pauperization and hopeless degradation of the toiling masses, render it imperative, if we desire to enjoy the blessings of life, that a check should be placed upon its power and upon unjust accumulation, and a system adopted which will secure to the laborer the fruits of his toil; and as this much desired object can only be accomplished by the thorough unification of

Preamble to the constitution of the Knights of Labor, 1878, in Timothy Patrick McCarthy and John McMillan, eds., *The Radical Reader: A Documentary History of the American Radical Tradition* (New York: Free Press, 2003), pp. 244–245.

labor, and the united effort of those who obey the divine injunction that "In the sweat of thy brow shalt thou eat bread," we have formed the * * * * * with a view of securing the organization and direction, by co-operative effort, of the power of the industrial classes; and we submit to the world the object sought to be accomplished by our organization, calling upon all who believe in securing "the greatest good to the greatest number" to aid and assist us:—

I. To bring within the folds of organization every department of productive industry, making knowledge a standpoint for action, and industrial and moral worth, not wealth, the true standard of individual and national greatness.

II. To secure to the toilers a proper share of the wealth that they create; more of the leisure that rightfully belongs to them; more societary advantages; more of the benefits, privileges, and emoluments of the world, all those rights and privileges necessary to make them capable of enjoying, appreciating, defending, and perpetuating the blessings of good government.

III. To arrive at the true condition of the producing masses in their educational, moral, and financial condition, by demanding from the various governments the establishment of bureaus of Labor Statistics.

IV. The establishment of co-operative institutions, productive and distributive.

V. The reserving of the public lands—the heritage of the people—for the actual settler;—not another acre for railroads or settlers.

VI. The abrogation of all laws that do not bear equally upon capital and labor, the removal of unjust technicalities, delays, and discriminations in the administration of justice, and the adopting of measures providing for the health and safety of those engaged in mining, manufacturing, or building pursuits.

VII. The enactment of laws to compel chartered corporations to pay their employes weekly, in full, for labor performed during the preceding week, in the lawful money of the country.

VIII. The enactment of laws giving mechanics and laborers a first lien on their work for full wages.

IX. The abolishment of the contract system on national, state, and municipal work.

X. The substitution of arbitration for strikes, whenever and wherever employers and employes are willing to meet on equitable grounds.

XI. The prohibition of the employment of children in workshops, mines, and factories before attaining their fourteenth year.

XII. To abolish the system of letting out by contract the labor of convicts in our prisons and reformatory institutions.

XIII. To secure for both sexes equal pay for equal work.

XIV. The reduction of the hours of labor to eight per day, so that the laborers may have more time for social enjoyment and intellectual improvement, and be enabled to reap the advantages conferred by the labor-saving machinery which their brains have created.

XV. To prevail upon governments to establish a purely national circulating medium, based upon the faith and resources of the nation, and issued directly to the people, without the intervention of any system of banking corporations, which money shall be a legal tender in payment of all debts, public or private.

2. Journalist Henry Demarest Lloyd Exposes
the Standard Oil Monopoly, 1881

Kerosene has become, by its cheapness, the people's light the world over. In the United States we used 220,000,000 gallons of petroleum last year. It has come into such demand abroad that our exports of its increased from 79,458,888 gallons in 1868, to 417,648,544 in 1879. It goes all over Europe, and to the far East. . . . After articles of food, this country has but one export, cotton, more valuable than petroleum. It was worth $61,789,438 in our foreign trade in 1877; $46,574,974 in 1878; and $18,546,642 in the five months ending November 30, 1879. In the United States, in the cities as well as the country, petroleum is the general illuminator. We use more kerosene lamps than Bibles.

The raw material of this world's light is produced in a territory beginning with Cattaraugus County in New York, and extending southwesterly through eight or nine counties of Pennsylvania, making a belt about one hundred and fifty miles long, and twelve or fifteen miles wide, and then, with an interval, running into West Virginia, Kentucky, and Tennessee, where the yield is unimportant. The bulk of the oil comes from two counties, Cattaraugus in New York, and McKean in Pennsylvania. . . .

Very few of the forty millions of people in the United States who burn kerosene know that its production, manufacture, and export, its price at home and abroad, have been controlled for years by a single corporation,—the Standard Oil Company. This company began in a partnership, in the early years of the civil war, between Samuel Andrews and John Rockefeller in Cleveland. Rockefeller had been a bookkeeper in some interior town in Ohio, and had afterwards made a few thousand dollars by keeping a flour store in Cleveland. Andrews had been a day laborer in refineries, and so poor that his wife took in sewing. He found a way of refining by which more kerosene could be got out of a barrel of petroleum than by any other method, and set up for himself a ten-barrel still in Cleveland, by which he cleared $500 in six months.

Andrews' still and Rockefeller's savings have grown into the Standard Oil Company. It has a capital, nominally $3,500,000, but really much more, on which it divides among it stockholders every year millions of dollars of profits. It has refineries at Cleveland, Baltimore, and New York. Its own acid works, glue factories, hardware stores, and barrel shops supply it with all the accessories it needs in its business. It has bought land at Indianapolis on which to erect the largest barrel factory in the country. . . . It buys 30,000 to 40,000 barrels of crude oil a day, at a price fixed by itself, and makes special contracts with the railroads for the transportation of 13,000,000 to 14,000,000 barrels of oil a year. . . .

The Standard produces only one fiftieth or sixtieth of our petroleum, but dictates the price of all, and refines nine tenths. Circulars are issued at intervals by which the price of oil is fixed for all the cities of the country, except New York, where a little competition survives. . . . There is not to-day a merchant in Chicago, or in any other

Henry Demarest Lloyd, "Story of a Great Monopoly," *Atlantic Monthly* 47 (March 1881): 320–323, 327–330.

city in the New England, Western, or Southern States, dealing in kerosene, whose prices are not fixed for him by the Standard. . . .

This corporation has driven into bankruptcy, or out of business, or into union with itself, all the petroleum refineries of the country except five in New York, and a few of little consequence in Western Pennsylvania. . . .

Their great business capacity would have insured the managers of the Standard success, but the means by which they achieved monopoly was by conspiracy with the railroads. . . . The Standard killed its rivals, in brief, by getting the great trunk lines to refuse to give them transportation. Commodore Vanderbilt is reported to have said that there was but one man—Rockefeller—who could dictate to him. . . .

. . . [T]he Pennsylvania Railroad agreed with the Standard, under the name of the South Improvement Company, to double the freights on oil to everybody, but to repay the Standard one dollar for every barrel of oil it shipped, and one dollar for every barrel any of its competitors shipped. . . . Ostensibly this contract was given up, in deference to the whirlwind of indignation it excited. But Rockefeller, the manager of the Standard, was a man who could learn from defeat. He made no more tell-tale contracts that could be printed. He effected secret arrangements with the Pennsylvania, the New York Central, the Erie, and the Atlantic and Great Western. . . . The Standard succeeded in getting from Mr. Vanderbilt [of the New York Central Railroad] free transportation for its crude oil from the wells in Pennsylvania, one hundred and fifty miles, to the refineries at Cleveland, and back. This stamped out competing refineries at Pittsburg, and created much of the raw material of the riots of July, 1877. Vanderbilt signed an agreement, March 25, 1872, that "all agreements for the transportation of oil after this date shall be upon a basis of perfect equality," and ever since has given the Standard special rates and privileges. He has paid it back in rebates millions of dollars, which have enabled it to crush out all competitors. . . . He united with the Erie [Railroad] in a war on the Pennsylvania Railroad, to force it to sell to the Standard all its refineries, and the great pipe lines by which the oil . . . was carried from the wells to the railroads. He then joined with the Erie and the Pennsylvania in a similar attack on the Baltimore and Ohio, which had to sell out to the Standard. So the Standard obtained the control of all the pipe lines and of the transportation, of everything. . . . Mr. Vanderbilt began, as did the Erie and Pennsylvania railroad kings, with paying back to the Standard, but to no other shipper, ten per cent of its freight bills. He continued making one concession after another, till when he was doing the business for other shippers at $1.40 and $1.25 a barrel, he charged the Standard only eighty and eighty-one cents, and this was afterwards reduced to sixty cents a barrel. During the war against the Pennsylvania road to make it sell out to the Standard, the New York Central carried oil for less than nothing. Besides the other allowances, Mr. Vanderbilt paid the Standard through its alias, the American Transfer Company, a rebate of thirty-five cents a barrel on all the crude oil shipped by it or its competitors. . . .

So closely had the Standard octopus gripped itself about Mr. Vanderbilt that . . . its competitors could not get transportation from him. He allowed the Standard to become the owner of all the oil cars run over his road, and of all his terminal facilities for oil. As the Standard owned all but 200 of the oil cars run on the Erie, and leased all that road's terminal facilities, it could charge its rivals anything it pleased for the privileges of New York harbor. . . .

If we turn to the experience of the refiners we find they fared as badly as the producers. The handful of New York refiners who survived the conspiracy against them . . . had to keep their capacity limited and to do as little as they could. They did not dare to build large refineries, because they would not be able to get oil enough carried to them to keep them going. Mr. Alexander, of Cleveland, tells how he was informed by Rockefeller, of the Standard, that if he would not sell out he should be crushed out. . . . Refiner after refiner in Pittsburg, buying his crude oil in the open market, manufacturing it at his works, shipping it to the seaboard, met with a continued succession of losses, and was forced into bankruptcy or a sale of his works to the Standard, who always had a buyer on the spot at the right time. The great majority of these refineries, when bought by the Standard, were dismantled. . . .

Its genius for monopoly has given the Standard control of more than the product of oil and its manufacture. Wholesale merchants in all the cities of the country, except New York, have to buy and sell at the prices it makes. Merchants who buy oil of the Standard are not allowed to sell to dealers who buy of its few competitors. Some who have done so have been warned not to repeat the offense, and have been informed that, if they did so, the Standard, though under contract to supply them with oil, would cut them off, and would fight any suit they might bring through all the courts without regard to expense. . . .

To-day, in every part of the United States, people who burn kerosene are paying the Standard Oil Company a tax on every gallon amounting to several times its original cost to that concern. The average price of crude oil at the wells or at Cleveland, as the railroads carry the crude free to the Standard's refineries, was in December last about three cents a gallon. The price of refined at Cleveland was seventeen cents a gallon. Oil that the Standard sells in New York at a profit, at ten and one half cents a gallon, they charge nineteen and three fourths cents for in Chicago. The average cost, last December, of the one and a third barrels of petroleum needed to make a barrel of kerosene was $2.05 at Cleveland. The cost of refining, barreling, and all expenses, including a refiner's profit of half a dollar a barrel, is . . . $2.75 a barrel. To bring it by rail to Chicago costs seventy cents, making the total cost $5.50 for a barrel of fifty gallons, or eleven cents a gallon. The price the Standard charges in Chicago is nineteen and three fourths cents a gallon, in which, as the difference between eleven and nineteen and three fourths cents, there is a tax on the public of eight and three fourths cents. This tax is transmitted by the middle-men, jobbers, and retailers to the consumer. When at twenty-five cents a gallon the workingman buys kerosene because it is cheaper than gas, or the student because it is better, each pays the Standard this tax of eight and three fourths cents a gallon. A family that uses a gallon of kerosene a day pays a yearly tribute to the Standard of $32, the income from $800 in the four per cents. . . .

[T]he Standard pays dividends of $1,000,000 a month. It can do this, and have millions left to pay the suits of refineries it has leased and keeps idle, its backsheesh [payback] to railroad men, the bribes it has had to give judges, state legislatures, and state inspectors, and its salaries of hundreds of thousands of dollars a month to men whom it has turned out of the business, and who are acting as its paid agents. To-day the only visible hope of cheap light for the people of this country is the discovery, announced by the Atlantic cable on January 28th, that in the Hanover petroleum district in Germany a basin has been found, which is thought by experts to be, beyond doubt, as large and rich as the one in Pennsylvania. In Europe, such alliances between the railroads and the refiners as created the Standard monopoly are impossible. German oil wells, German refineries, and the Canadian canals may yet give the people of the interior of this continent what the American Standard and the American railroads have denied them,—cheap light.

3. Sweatshop Conditions Horrify a Factory Inspector, 1893

[T]he sweating industry is carried on principally in the south-east part of Philadelphia; . . . at least 90 per cent. of the whole of this work in the sewing line is done right here; a close count shows from 3,500 to 4,000 people engaged, with a few exceptions, at work in tenement houses or a combination if you choose; the living apartments, cooking, eating and sleeping are on the first, and part second floors, the remaining part second and all of the third is used for work rooms. The nationalities represented are Russian Jews, Poles, Huns, Slavs and Italians, and their general temperament is of a most avaricious kind.

The matter of hours seemingly do not count. It is simply this; If a contractor wants a coat, pants, or vest as the case may be, the person who sub-contracts for the work has no choice of hours or aught else, but hastens to accomplish the task, being sure to get back at the given time or forfeit his chance for getting more work, so that after all the whole system is the effort of an industrial evil, which is being fostered by our American people through their very indifference to actual surroundings, and the sooner the whole people get on their thinking cap the better, and adopt such means (radical though they may seem) as will prohibit entirely, work of this kind being done in the home. Then and then only, will contractors provide proper work rooms subject to proper shop discipline, and regulated by a full enforcement of the Factory Law. For the conditions that surround this class of people is outrivaled by no other. Actual filth contributing largely to their immediate surroundings, and any attempt on my part to describe my actual findings, would mean a shock to the pride of our much boasted prosperity in this, our city of homes.

Speaking to a sub-contractor recently of the condition of trade, he said in answer to my query, "Why, the coat I used to get $3 for making two years ago, I now get $1.50 for. Then I was treated with some consideration, some respect, but since the invasion . . . of the tenement house workers I am glad to take just what I can get without making a remark, lest I be subject to insult and deprived of all work. It is a tremendous odds to be competing against, and the few of us who strive to keep shops would gladly hail the enactment of a law compelling all to do likewise." I will cite just a few instances that you may get a faint idea of some of the prevailing conditions.

In visiting what I can only describe as an old tinder box a few days since, I found three different contractors with men, women and boys amounting in the aggregate upwards of sixty. The drinking water was drawn in buckets and filled into a tin boiler, each day's sediment going to the bottom (for it was never cleaned,) only to be rolled

Fourth Annual Report of the Factory Inspector of the Commonwealth of Pennsylvania. For the Year 1893 (n.p.: Clarence M. Busch, 1894), pp. 38–39.

and raised by each day's filling. Cigarettes were being smoked at such a rate as to make the air blue; confusion reigned supreme; coal ashes were strewn all over the floor; this coupled with scraps of basting threads, clippings of cloth, etc., went to make up a most trying picture. In the midst of it all sat a young man who was temporarily disengaged from his work, eating a dark colored piece of bread with mustard. Out of the rooms and in the hallway was one water closet in a vile condition, and the stairway gave evidence of mistaken use too disgusting to mention.

Another was a building three stories high in which rag sorting was the main occupation. On the ground floor I discovered the wife of the proprietor and three of her children, aged 3, 5 and 8 respectively, the mother was acting as purchaser and sorter in the absence of the man. The children naturally were close beside her; when she sorted, they tried to help her; when she weighed they stood around the scales looking worldly wise. On I went to the second story and there discovered a number of old women working, who, from all appearances, were closing in on their three score years, they were surrounded by rags of the filthiest kind. After a general survey of this room I ascended still higher only to find more old women on the third floor, occupied in like manner as those on the floor below. The odor that pervaded this room was vile in the extreme. I immediately set to work to fathom the cause, when, lo and behold, there in a corner was a bin which was used as a receptacle for dog manure. I could scarcely believe my eyes, but there it was, and there it had been for the best part of the summer months, so the women told me. This is but a brief account of much more that could be enumerated by me, for this is the dark side of our darkest Philadelphia, and when I discover the reckless spirit manifest among those people, their total disregard for any law, only that which (as they themselves tell me) will bring them dollars and cents, I fear for the future.

4. Industrialist George M. Pullman Explains the Strike at Pullman Palace Car Works, 1894

The depression in the car-building business, which began in 1893, manifested itself not only in a falling off in the prices for cars, averaging in all classes 24%, but in such stagnation that the force in the Pullman shops on November 1st, 1893, was less than 1,100, while the average number employed in the fiscal year ending July 31st, 1893, was 4,497. In the months of August and September, 1893, we had an opportunity of making only six bids for work, of which but three were accepted.

In order to procure car-building contracts a reduction of the wages of April, 1893, of the car shop employes, averaging 19% was made, to make them correspond with those paid by other car manufacturers, and by making bids at shop cost and less, we secured work aggregating about $1,500,000, and were underbid on bids for nearly the same amount. On the accepted bids our net loss was over $50,000. By taking this course we had been able by last May to secure work enough to raise the number having employment to nearly 3,300.

"President Pullman's Statement at the Stockholders' Annual Meeting, October 18, 1894," in *The Strike at Pullman* (Pullman, Ill.: Pullman Company, 1894), pp. 39–42.

Although these conditions were carefully explained to a large committee of the shop employes, three-fourths of them were persuaded to enter upon the strike, because the company declined to restore wages to the scale of the prosperous times of the early part of 1893. Several suggestions were made to the company that it should consent to arbitration as a means of ending the strike, but it declined to do so upon the ground that it being an ascertained fact that even at the existing rates of wages, car building contracts could only be procured for execution at actual and serious losses, the company could not possibly submit to the discretion of any person, not responsible to its shareholders, the question whether or not it should increase its manufacturing losses by any increase of wages, or even whether or not it should continue the manufacturing of cars at current prices, at the wages complained of. . . .

There has been no substantial change in the condition of the car building business, and the contracts taken by us before the strike, and those taken since the strike, are being executed at prices which give no profit, and such contracts are taken because the shops are being kept in operation for the repairing of the company's own cars, and to give as much employment as is possible in the present condition of business.

I have learned in various ways that a good many persons during the strike lost sight of its true origin, and gained the impression that it was influenced by the house rents at Pullman not being lowered when wages were reduced from the high scale of the spring of 1893. That this is not true is shown by the fact that more than two-thirds of the employes who began the strike, were not tenants of the company; indeed, between 500 and 600 of them owned their own homes. . . .

The real cause of complaint during the autumn of 1893 and the succeeding winter was not altogether on account of the scale of wages, but largely because there was not enough work to give an opportunity for anything like full earnings by all the men. . . .

I may observe also, that there have been indications of a feeling in some quarters that this company ought to have maintained the scale of wages existing in the car manufacturing department in April, 1893, without regard to the current selling prices for cars, paying the consequent increased losses in the car-building business out of the company's earnings in the independent business of operating sleeping cars. . . . At what point did a principle take effect that the latter business must be kept going by the former, regardless of their independence or of the discrepancy between the cost and selling price of cars? At the time of the strike 227 of the shop employes had been in the employment of the company for less than a year, and more than half the entire force had been with the company less than five years. Had all of them earned a guaranty of uninterrupted, undiminished wages? . . .

Of the present force at the car shops only about 300 are new employes, and the remainder have returned to their former work with, I believe, a widely prevailing feeling, that they have learned by experience that this company was earnest in befriending them in seeking work for them when little was to be had, and in giving them work at wages which the selling prices of their product did not justify, and that the genuineness of the interest of this company in their welfare is far more to be trusted than the promises of the agitators who misled them.

5. Sugar King Henry O. Havemeyer Declares the Customs Tariff as the Mother of All Trusts, 1899

The mother of all trusts is the customs tariff bill. The existing bill and the preceding ones have been the occasion of the formation of all the large trusts, with very few exceptions, inasmuch as they provide for an *inordinate* protection to all the interests of the country, sugar refining excepted. Economic advantages incident to the consolidation of large interests in the same line of business are a great incentive to their formation, but these bear a very insignificant proportion to the advantages granted in the way of protection under the customs tariff.

There probably is not an industry that requires a protection of more than 10 per cent ad valorem, and it is to obtain what is provided over such percentage in the tariff that leads to the formation of what are commonly spoken of as "trusts."

With a protection to an industry not exceeding 10 per cent, all menace to the community from trusts would cease. This 10 per cent would represent the difference in cost of production, and likewise act as a protection against surplus products of foreign countries being dumped in our local markets, thereby intefering with the regular and economic working of our industries. Any advantage that might then accrue to such combinations, they would be fully entitled to, and the public would not be damaged thereby, as any expansion of price would be met by foreign competition and relief. . . .

The Government Plunders the People.

I repeat that all this agitation against trusts is against merely the business machinery employed to take from the public what the Government in its tariff laws says it is proper and suitable they should have. It is the Government, through its tariff laws, which plunders the people, and the trusts, etc., are merely the machinery for doing it. . . .

Capital and Labor.

All I have to say about trade organizations and strikes is that, without violence, they are natural. They have one objection, however—their tendency to reduce all labor to a low level.

Business is not philanthropy. Capital and labor will adjust their own relations if they are let alone. Interference always operates against one or the other; that means to the disadvantage of both. . . .

The true "communism of pelf" is the customs tariff bill. It says to the people, "Here is the law we have enacted for your robbery. Do not complain of it, but do your utmost to attack and injure the machinery engaged in extracting from you what we legislate shall be taken from you.

"Testimony of Henry O. Havemeyer," in U.S. Industrial Commission, *Preliminary Report on Trusts and Industrial Combinations, Together with Testimony, Review of Evidence, Charts Showing Effects of Prices, and Topical Digest, Vol. 1 of the Commission's Reports* (Washington, D.C.: GPO, 1900), pp. 101–102, 104–106.

"Keep up the clatter while the voters on the tariff bill take advantage of the noise to enact laws that cause your impoverishment and thus contribute to the greed and avarice of the few." . . .

Only Two Forms of Monopoly To-day.

In these days there are two forms, and only two forms, of monopoly:

One, that which results from a patent and copyright. It is universally recognized that this is in the interest of, not against, the public.

The other, that which comes from unfair tariff discrimination.

Tariff for revenue need not be considered. The expenses of the Government must, of course, be provided for. Tariff for the purpose of equalizing against foreign bounties or foreign discrimination does not need to be justified. Beyond that there is no excuse for giving to one industry a protection of 100 per cent as against 4 per cent to another. The result is that the Government fleeces the community at large in the interest of some favored industry.

6. President Theodore Roosevelt Advocates Regulation, 1901

The tremendous and highly complex industrial development which went on with ever accelerated rapidity during the latter half of the nineteenth century brings us face to face, at the beginning of the twentieth, with very serious social problems. The old laws, and the old customs which had almost the binding force of law, were once quite sufficient to regulate the accumulation and distribution of wealth. Since the industrial changes which have so enormously increased the productive power of mankind, they are no longer sufficient.

The growth of cities has gone on beyond comparison faster than the growth of the country, and the upbuilding of the great industrial centers has meant a startling increase, not merely in the aggregate of wealth, but in the number of very large individual, and especially of very large corporate, fortunes. The creation of these great corporate fortunes has not been due to the tariff nor to any other governmental action, but to natural causes in the business world, operating in other countries as they operate in our own.

The process has aroused much antagonism, a great part of which is wholly without warrant. . . . The captains of industry who have driven the railway systems across this continent, who have built up our commerce, who have developed our manufactures, have on the whole done great good to our people. Without them the material development of which we are so justly proud could never have taken place. . . . The slightest study of business conditions will satisfy anyone capable of forming a judgment that the personal equation is the most important factor in a business operation; that the business ability of the man at the head of any business,

Theodore Roosevelt, First annual address to Congress, December 3, 1901, in James D. Richardson, ed., *A Compilation of the Messages and Papers of the Presidents,* vol. 16 (New York: Bureau of National Literature, 1897–1914), pp. 6643–6647. This document can also be found in Richard Hofstadter, ed., *The Progressive Movement, 1900–1915* (Englewood Cliffs, N.J.: Prentice-Hall, 1963), pp. 141–144.

big or little, is usually the factor which fixes the gulf between striking success and hopeless failure.

An additional reason for caution in dealing with corporations is to be found in the international commercial conditions of today. . . . Business concerns which have the largest means at their disposal and are managed by the ablest men are naturally those which take the lead in the strife for commercial supremacy among the nations of the world. America has only just begun to assume the commanding position in the international business world which we believe will more and more be hers. It is of the utmost importance that this position be not jeoparded, especially at a time when the overflowing abundance of our own natural resources and the skill, business energy, and mechanical aptitude of our people make foreign markets essential. Under such conditions it would be most unwise to cramp or to fetter the youthful strength of our Nation.

Moreover, it cannot too often be pointed out that to strike with ignorant violence at the interests of one set of men almost inevitably endangers the interests of all. The fundamental rule in our national life—the rule which underlies all others—is that, on the whole, and in the long run, we shall go up or down together. . . .

The mechanism of modern business is so delicate that extreme care must be taken not to interfere with it in a spirit of rashness or ignorance. Many of those who have made it their vocation to denounce the great industrial combinations which are popularly, although with technical inaccuracy, known as "trusts," appeal especially to hatred and fear. These are precisely the two emotions, particularly when combined with ignorance, which unfit men for the exercise of cool and steady judgment. In facing new industrial conditions, the whole history of the world shows that legislation will generally be both unwise and ineffective unless undertaken after calm inquiry. . . .

All this is true; and yet it is also true that there are real and grave evils, one of the chief being over-capitalization, because of its many baleful consequences; and a resolute and practical effort must be made to correct these evils.

There is a widespread conviction . . . that the great corporations known as trusts are in certain of their features and tendencies hurtful to the general welfare. This . . . is based upon sincere conviction that combination and concentration should be, not prohibited, but supervised and within reasonable limits controlled; and in my judgment this conviction is right.

It is no limitation upon property rights or freedom of contract to require that when men receive from government the privilege of doing business under corporate form, which frees them from individual responsibility, and enables them to call into their enterprises the capital of the public, they shall do so upon absolutely truthful representations as to the value of the property in which the capital is to be invested. Corporations engaged in interstate commerce should be regulated if they are found to exercise a license working to the public injury. It should be as much the aim of those who seek for social betterment to rid the business world of crimes of cunning as to rid the entire body politic of crimes of violence. Great corporations exist only because they are created and safe-guarded by our institutions; and it is therefore our right and our duty to see that they work in harmony with these institutions.

The first essential in determining how to deal with the great industrial combinations is knowledge of the facts—publicity. In the interest of the public, the

Government should have the right to inspect and examine the workings of the great corporations engaged in interstate business. Publicity is the only sure remedy which we can now invoke. What further remedies are needed in the way of governmental regulation, or taxation, can only be determined after publicity has been obtained. . . . The first requisite is knowledge, full and complete. . . .

The large corporations, commonly called trusts, though organized in one State, always do business in many States, often doing very little business in the State where they are incorporated. There is utter lack of uniformity in the State laws about them; and as no State has any exclusive interest in or power over their acts, it has in practice proved impossible to get adequate regulation through State action. Therefore, in the interest of the whole people, the Nation should, without interfering with the power of the States in the matter itself, also assume power of supervision and regulation over all corporations doing an interstate business. This is especially true where the corporation derives a portion of its wealth from the existence of some monopolistic element or tendency in its business. There would be no hardship in such supervision; banks are subject to it, and in their case it is now accepted as a simple matter of course. Indeed, it is now probable that supervision of corporations by the National Government need not go so far as is now the case with the supervision exercised over them by so conservative a State as Massachusetts, in order to produce excellent results.

When the Constitution was adopted . . . no human wisdom could foretell the sweeping changes, alike in industrial and political conditions, which were to take place by the beginning of the twentieth century. At that time it was accepted as a matter of course that the several States were the proper authorities to regulate, so far as it was then necessary, the comparatively insignificant and strictly localized corporate bodies of the day. The conditions are now wholly different and wholly different action is called for. I believe that a law can be framed which will enable the National Government to exercise control along the lines above indicated; profiting by the experience gained through the passage and administration of the Interstate Commerce Act. If, however, the judgment of the Congress is that it lacks the constitutional power to pass such an act, then a constitutional amendment should be submitted to confer this power.

7. "People's Attorney" Louis D. Brandeis Lashes Out Against the Money Trust, 1913

The dominant element in our financial oligarchy is the investment banker. Associated banks, trust companies and life insurance companies are his tools. Controlled railroads, public service and industrial corporations are his subjects. Though properly but middlemen, these bankers bestride as masters America's business world, so that practically no large enterprise can be undertaken successfully without their participation or approval. These bankers are, of course, able men possessed of large fortunes; but the most potent factor in their control of business is not the possession

Louis D. Brandeis, "Breaking the Money Trust: Part 1—Our Financial Oligarchy," *Harper's Weekly* 58 (November 22, 1913): 10.

of extraordinary ability or huge wealth. The key to their power is Combination—concentration intensive and comprehensive—advancing on three distinct lines:

First: There is the obvious consolidation of banks and trust companies; the less obvious affiliations,—through stockholdings, voting trusts and interlocking directorates,—of banking institutions which are not legally connected; and the joint transactions, gentlemen's agreements, and "banking ethics" which eliminate competition among the investment bankers.

Second: There is the consolidation of railroads into huge systems, the large combinations of public service corporations and the formation of industrial trusts, which, by making businesses so "big" that local, independent banking concerns cannot alone supply the necessary funds, has created dependence upon the associated New York bankers.

But combination, however intensive, along these lines only, could not have produced the Money Trust—another and more potent factor of combination was added.

Third: Investment bankers, like J. P. Morgan & Co., dealers in bonds, stocks and notes, encroached upon the functions of the three other classes of corporations with which their business brought them into contact. They became the directing power in railroads, public service and industrial companies through which our great business operations are conducted—the makers of bonds and stocks. They became the directing power in the life insurance companies, and other corporate reservoirs of the people's savings—the buyers of bonds and stocks. They became the directing power also in banks and trust companies—the depositaries of the quick capital of the country—the life blood of business, with which they and others carried on their operations. Thus . . . distinct functions, each essential to business, and each exercised, originally, by a distinct set of men, became united in the investment banker. It is to this union of business functions that the existence of the Money Trust is mainly due.

8. Goodyear Tire & Rubber Company Applies Human Engineering to the Labor-Capital Problem, 1920

Business Building Is Man Building

Too often there has been a wide chasm separating industrial management and workers and an atmosphere of autocratic discipline has come between executives and the men of their shops and factories. In this atmosphere the will and ideal of the management, no matter how just or equitable, is always marred in transmission. The iron rule of the distant and "military" management is all that is felt by the worker. Dread broods over all, and employees fear to exercise their own initiative, since they lack incentive, kindly encouragement and the sense of common interests which puts men "on their toes."

Goodyear Tire & Rubber Company, *The Work of the Labor Division* (Akron, Ohio: Goodyear Tire & Rubber Company, 1920), pp. 7, 9, 11, 13, 15, 17–18, 31–32, 34, 59. Pamphlet Collection, Hagley Museum and Library, Wilmington, Del.

The happy industrial institution that reaps the reward of steady, fearless service is the one where a very different "spirit of the organization" is found—anxious to adopt policies consonant in the industrial field with American political liberties, and open-minded to suggestions for the good of the institution, let them come from what source they may.

Perceiving that many possibilities for building a permanent organization lay in the field of "human engineering," The Goodyear Tire & Rubber Company early emphasized conceptions of justice and fraternity as the first step toward a solution of the so-called Labor-Capital problem. Conscious that people do not give their best to a collective enterprise until they believe—head and heart and hand—in its rightness, Goodyear aimed to choose correct ideals of labor administration at the outset, reaping her reward in the firm allegiance and loyalty which have carried her safely through every crisis of her history. . . .

The Work of the Labor Division

The Labor Division of The Goodyear Tire & Rubber Company might be called "the tie that binds." It was founded early in 1912—over seven years ago—and ever since has devoted its entire time to promoting in a very large organization the same understanding, goodwill and justice, as between men and management, which exist in small factories. It aims to see that everyone associated with the Company gets "the square deal." All its many activities . . . are but the embodiment of a single Goodyear policy, viz.: *That the success of The Goodyear Tire & Rubber Company has been, and in the future will be, due to the ability, loyalty and aggressiveness of Goodyear men and women, and that to make conditions as nearly right as possible for its great community of workers is a natural obligation which is owed to men and management alike.*

On a Business Basis   The Labor Division of The Goodyear Tire & Rubber Company is governed by no paternalistic "welfare" motive. All its activities are devised on businesslike, self-supporting bases, the idea being to help those who help themselves, make industrial life interesting to capable and thoughtful people, and to attract only persons of character and judgment to become associated with Goodyear.

The Goodyear Factories

. . . The Goodyear Tire & Rubber Company is the world's largest manufacturer of rubber tires for motor vehicles—trucks and automobiles. Goodyear also manufactures mechanical goods, belting, hose, and shoe soles and heels.

Goodyear has its two main factories at Akron, comprising 80 buildings, most of them five to eight stories high, with a total floor space for manufacturing purposes of nearly 4,500,000 square feet—the equivalent of over 100 acres. About 25,000 men and women are employed.

A subsidiary Goodyear rubber factory employing about 400 people is located at Bowmanville, Ontario, Canada; another, employing nearly 800, is located at Toronto. A cotton plantation near Phoenix, Arizona, supplies an exceptionally fine long-staple cotton exclusively for Goodyear, while a Goodyear weaving factory in Connecticut employing approximately 800 persons provides the excellent fabric which enters into Goodyear products. In addition to these a 20,000-acre rubber plantation in Sumatra brings nearly 8,000 more people into the "Goodyear Family" and makes the sphere of Goodyear influence well-nigh world-wide. . . .

Labor Administration at the Akron Plant

Construction and Sanitation   All buildings are well lighted and ventilated, and comfortably heated in winter time. Where dust or dirt are involved in the manufacturing processes, vacuum systems for removing the fine particles before they get into the air have been installed. A plentiful supply of the most modern and sanitary toilets have been installed in all parts of the factory, together with wash basins, and certain departments have been supplied with shower baths. All are kept scrupulously clean at all times by special janitor service. Steel lockers for clothing are supplied to every worker, while cooled and sterilized drinking water is supplied to the entire plant through sanitary bubbler fountains.

A Growing Concern   At the present time, January, 1920, nearly 25,000 workers are employed at Goodyear. The factory works in three eight-hour shifts, six days a week. No Sunday work, except such as is absolutely necessary, is the policy of Goodyear. . . .

Management of Plant   The changes of the last hundred years in American political or religious life, great though they have been, sink into insignificance beside the tremendous evolution which has taken place in the realm of industry.

In abolishing autocracy, Big Business has itself come to recognize, as never before, the benefits of contact with its people.

Desiring to formulate a more representative form of Factory government than existed heretofore, the Factory Manager of the Goodyear Company created an Industrial Relations Council for the purpose of drawing up an Industrial Representation Plan. This council was composed of executives, foremen and wage earners. The executives were appointed, the foremen were elected by the foremen and the wage earners' representatives were elected by the workers of the Factory. This council sat together and discussed other existing forms of Industrial Representation and finally drew up a plan for the Goodyear Factory, which plan was presented to the workers of the Factory and to the management of the Factory for ratification.

The Industrial Representation plan as finally worked out and ratified by all includes a House of Representatives and a Senate, quite similar to our national government and, although all executive power is in the hands of the management, legislative power to curb or check improper action or to suggest improved conditions rests with the Industrial Assembly. Joint conferences are frequently held and a spirit of fairness and mutual cooperation exists which bids fair to establish all the people of Goodyear on a firm and successful working basis for a long period to come. . . .

In order to protect the Goodyear organization and the Goodyear industry, it is necessary before a person may participate in the plan of representation, that he must meet certain qualifications and when he has met these qualifications, he is called a Goodyear INDUSTRIAN and is entitled to vote. . . .

To become a Goodyear INDUSTRIAN, it is necessary that he (or she) be eighteen years of age, that they be American citizens, that they understand the English language, and that they have six months' continuous service record with the Goodyear Factory. . . .

Restaurant Service   A working force as vast as Goodyear's cannot all live in the near vicinity of the plant; dependence upon outside restaurants is precarious; modern ideals of efficiency require well-fed workmen; so that the installation of adequate dining facilities was one of the first tasks of the Labor Division.

The Goodyear Restaurants, two in the factory and one in the General Office, are designed to serve a daily total of at least 10,000 people, and are generally operating at full capacity. No Goodyearite need ever go hungry or lack a warm meal at noon, and the beneficial effect of "inside" restaurant service upon industries in general could hardly be overestimated. . . .

The health of a great organization will quickly show, in statistical fashion, the effects of rational feeding, and in the Labor Division's restaurants, food effects are constantly studied and every effort made to insure the gastronomic well-being and satisfaction of Goodyearites. . . .

Teaching Thrift   Without inculcating the essential habits of thrift and economic foresight, liberal pay is no check on industrial discontent. The increasing prosperity that enabled Goodyearites to earn high wages revealed much improvidence so that a Bureau to promote thrift and to provide financial advice was considered advisable. This Bureau will confer with anyone seeking advice concerning investments, and will in every case try to provide the maximum of returns with the maximum of safety. Beyond this it endeavors to show all interested how homes, wearing apparel, and all other necessities may be purchased most economically and how the savings thus made can advantageously be invested in real estate, stocks, bonds and other securities. No charge is made for this service. The Bureau also handles "Hard Luck" cases and tries to manage affairs so as to get Goodyearites out of debt. A few practical instances of the work of the Thrift Subdivision are the selling of coal at wholesale prices, approximately 200 cars being sold during the season of 1917–1918, the making of arrangements with local merchants to supply Goodyearites with certain necessities at reduced rates, Thrift Stamp and Liberty Loan campaigns, the sale of Goodyear stock and the opening of savings accounts with local banks through a payroll deduction plan. . . .

Americanization   There are three distinct phases of work carried on by Goodyear Labor Division among alien employees—(a) courses to teach foreigners to read, write, speak, and thus to think in the English language; (b) the assisting of aliens to become naturalized and in the taking out of their second papers; and (c) the handling of all affairs relating to foreign employees through an interpreter who speaks the important languages.

This interpreter promotes a more complete understanding between the alien employee and Goodyear, and the interpreter has also the handling of all the grievances of alien workers.

About 300 men received the instruction for aliens during the past year, which is about 20 per cent of the 1,500 foreign employees of the Company, based on the year's average employment.

E S S A Y S

In the first essay, Colleen A. Dunlavy, a professor of history at the University of Wisconsin–Madison, examines the growth of big business from a new angle. While Chandler argued that the market and technology impelled the expansion of industrial enterprise, Dunlavy offers an alternative thesis: government policies encouraged some businesses to get big. She draws on testimony from two investigative bodies, the U.S. Industrial Commission and the Chicago Conference on Trusts, created to explore the monopoly problem during the great merger movement (1895–1904). At these hearings, reform-minded business executives announced, loud and clear: "The heart of the trust problem is in our tariff system." Many believed that high tariffs—a component of the Republican national agenda since the Civil War—encouraged protected manufacturers to consolidate operations in a single holding company or trust.

Next, Sanford M. Jacoby, a professor of history, management, and public policy at the University of California, Los Angeles, examines welfare capitalism at the Eastman Kodak Company, a successful family firm that produced cameras and film in upstate New York. By the Progressive Era, Kodak and dozens of other manufacturing companies established programs for guarding the well-being of their employees. By providing social stability and security, these companies aimed to remedy what *they* perceived as the ills of industrial society: employee discontent, labor activism, and government intervention. Kodak's welfare plan focused on ensuring employees' financial security through such mechanisms as profit sharing, retirement benefits, and life insurance. While the Great Depression ended many corporate welfare programs, the Kodak program survived, providing a model for modern employee relations practices.

Why Did Some American Businesses Get So Big?

COLLEEN A. DUNLAVY

Why did big business in the United States become so big that in the late nineteenth century Americans came to demand antitrust legislation? Historians, by and large, have agreed that pure economic forces brought on concentration. But in taking this view they have neglected a strikingly different explanation that was widely propounded at the time it was all happening. This alternative view saw the bigness of some American business as the result of government policies—in particular, protectionism in the form of high tariffs. Because they believed that protective tariffs had encouraged excessive concentration, a number of them viewed free trade as one of the best remedies against the trusts.

Colleen A. Dunlavy, "Why Did American Business Get So Big?" *Audacity, The Magazine of Business Experience* 2 (Spring 1994): 43, 45–47, 49. Reprinted by permission of American Heritage.

The accepted view among business historians, strongly influenced by the work of Alfred D. Chandler, Jr., is that the extraordinary bigness of American business grew naturally from the workings of the market and the demands of modern, capital-intensive technology. The United States, already world-renowned for giant enterprise by the turn of the century, possessed both the world's largest domestic market and entrepreneurs capable of perceiving, exploiting, and expanding that market. In doing so, some built mass production enterprises of impressive proportions and then went on to integrate forward and backward, producing even larger firms, while others joined forces with their competitors, combining horizontally during the great merger movement (1895–1904). The two paths often intertwined, but the result in every case was enterprises of truly enormous proportions. U.S. Steel, formed in 1901, epitomized the process of concentration.

In 1898 Congress created the United States Industrial Commission. It immediately began investigating the trusts, and from April 1899 through early January 1900 it heard testimony from a broad array of public figures. Among the witnesses was the New York attorney John R. Dos Passos.

In testimony that filled nearly forty pages, Dos Passos defended economic concentration as a natural development that legislation should not—and could not—inhibit. History makes abundantly clear, he declared, the futility of legislation to block combinations, whether of manufacturers, distributors, or labor. "And the simple reason," he maintained, "is that the laws of trade, the natural laws of commercial relations, defy human legislation; and that is all there is in it. Wherever the two clash the statute law must go down before the operations of those natural laws."

John D. Rockefeller, the head of what was popularly termed the Standard Oil Trust, echoed this view in a written response to the commission in 1899. "It is too late to argue about advantages of industrial combinations," he flatly asserted. "They are a necessity."

Halfway across the country, Chicago's Civic Federation convened the Chicago Conference on Trusts in September 1899. "Some months since," the federation president, Franklin H. Head, explained, "no topic seemed so widely discussed as what was designated by the general title of 'Trusts,'—and . . . upon no current topic was there so widespread and general an ignorance and confusion of ideas." So the federation invited hundreds of men to Chicago for "a conference in search of truth and light." They included governors, attorneys general, state delegates, academics, congressmen, state and federal officials, representatives of chambers of commerce and boards of trade, and delegates from a large number of associations that represented agricultural, labor, and other interests.

Many speakers at the Chicago conference also concurred with the economic view. "Consolidations are the outgrowth and the symptom of the advancing civilization of to-day, and the inevitable tendency of its complex trade conditions," maintained a Pennsylvania lawyer, A. Leo Weil. David Ross of the Illinois Bureau of Labor Statistics observed, "Men talk of destroying such combinations by legal enactment, on the supposition, presumably, that it is possible and desirable to return to the simpler systems of the past." But it would do no good, he thought: "Our development as an industrial state is the result of trade conditions and opportunities which no legislative power could anticipate or control." Even the labor leader Samuel Gompers adhered to the economic view. "For our part, we are convinced," he explained, "that the state is not capable of preventing the legitimate development or natural concentration of industry." Instead Gompers merely wanted the right for his men to organize on a scale comparable to the level of organization achieved in industry.

Two years later a Chicago lawyer and the author of a two-volume tract on the law of combinations put the economic view succinctly. The legal world had not yet come to grips with combinations, Arthur J. Eddy observed; "the lack of harmony is only too apparent." But eventually the law would be brought in line: "Combination as an economic factor in the industrial and commercial world is a fact with which courts and legislatures may struggle, and struggle in vain, until they frankly recognize that, like all other conditions, it is a result of evolution to be conserved, regulated and made use of, but not suppressed."

The economic interpretation of the concentration movement then under way thrived in business circles in the ensuing years. "The business world generally," Francis Walker reported in 1912, "regards great combinations . . . as the natural and necessary development of trade, and declares in picturesque metaphor that 'natural laws can not be repealed by statute.'"

This is the view that has come down to us as a consensus, but it was nothing of the kind. On the contrary, out of the diversity of views expressed before the Industrial Commission, at the Chicago Conference on Trusts, and in print, a broadly opposing view emerged, one that saw dangerous economic concentration as a political phenomenon. The Industrial Commission recognized this broad dichotomy of views on the trust problem, and it concluded its hearings with testimony from both camps. Two men were called to speak on "general aspects" of the problem. One was Dos Passos; the other was the St. Louis lawyer Charles Claflin Allen, whose testimony filled another thirty pages and who took issue with Dos Passos on nearly every point.

Allen did not deny that *some* consolidations in the merger movement then under way "followed a natural normal tendency under economic laws," as the economic view maintained, but like others who endorsed a political view of trusts, he saw the bigness of American business as a product of the nation's industrial policy.

We usually associate the term *industrial policy* with direct intervention or "industrial targeting" of specific industries. But Chalmers Johnson, much acclaimed for his 1982 study of Japan's Ministry of International Trade and Industry (MITI) and Japanese policy, sees this as only one kind of industrial policy—what he terms *microindustrial policy.* More broadly, he argues, "industrial policy" also encompasses "all government measures [that] . . . have a significant impact on the well-being or ill-health of whole sectors, industries, and enterprises in a market economy." Thus what he terms *macroindustrial policy* comprises the array of policies (e.g., fiscal, monetary, trade, or labor policies) that subtly shape the broad environment in which business operates. Macroindustrial policies, in effect, create what Germans call the *Wirtschaftsordnung* (economic order).

Adherents of the political view of big business did not like the direction in which the American economic order was moving at the turn of the century, but it would be wrong to assume (as their contemporaries often did and as historians frequently do) that these critics opposed economic development or did not understand the value of large-scale enterprise. Their quarrel was with the form that economic change was taking. Those who saw economic change as fundamentally political in origin, as the historian Victoria Hattam suggests in *Labor, Visions, and State Power,* preferred a decentralized pattern of growth that would be devoid of concentrations of power. Seeing government policies at the root of the problem, they sought to revamp those policies to promote economic development along more decentralized lines. Therefore, they drew special attention to two aspects of late-nineteenth-century industrial policy: tariffs and railroad-rate regulation.

"The mother of all trusts is the customs tariff bill," Henry O. Havemeyer, the president of the American Sugar Refining Company, declared before the Industrial Commission in June 1899. Since he headed what was popularly known as the Sugar Trust, Havemeyer's statement generated a good deal of excitement. The potential benefits of horizontal combination, he argued, "bear a very insignificant proportion to the advantages granted in the way of protection under the customs tariff." He at first testified that tariff protection had helped the leaders of the iron and steel industries; but under questioning he admitted that his own sugar industry was affected too, conceding, as the commission's summary of evidence noted, "that had it not been for the high protective tariff existing at the time the original Sugar Trust was formed he would probably not have taken the risk of putting his refineries into the trust."

At the Chicago Conference on Trusts three months later, Havemeyer's opinions stirred considerable interest. Byron W. Holt, of the New England Free Trade League, applauded his comments. Havemeyer's views had "startled the country," Holt reported, but they ought not to have: "That the tariff, by shielding our manufacturers from foreign competition, makes it easy for them to combine, to restrict production, and to fix prices—up to the tariff limit—ought to be evident to every intelligent man." Among protected industries, he named "glass, furniture, leather, iron and steel, paper, coal, woolen goods, and silk goods"—not to mention Havemeyer's refined sugar—and he singled out for lengthy discussion the tinplate industry. "The heart of the trust problem is in our tariff system of plunder," Holt concluded. "The quickest and most certain way of reaching the evils of trusts is not by direct legislation against them, or by constitutional amendment, but by the abolition of tariff duties."

In *The Tariff and the Trusts,* a book published in 1907, the New York lawyer Franklin Pierce also laid the problem at the feet of Congress: "Our protective tariff is the genesis of the trust. The trust comes out of it as naturally as fruit from blossom. Obviously the control of a market by a combination or trust is facilitated where the field of competition is artificially limited to one country since it is easier to combine the producers of one country than those of all countries, and to that extent all must concede that the tariff encourages trusts."

The McKinley tariff of 1890 had raised rates to levels not seen since the Civil War, and the Dingley tariff of 1897 had pushed them even higher. Events in the business world since then, Pierce maintained, left little doubt about how the process worked.

But in one sense Pierce endorsed the economic view of American "bigness." He too saw the nation's large domestic market as essential to the rise of the trusts: "When the trust is established the very largeness of our country results in the largeness and success of the trust." But only market size and tariff protection working in tandem produced giant enterprise: "So vast a field secured to them from outside competition is tempting enough to invoke the energies of immense capital for its exploitation, and as a result gigantic trusts protected by the tariff come into existence with a power for evil in trade and politics which would be impossible in a small country, however high might be the tariff sheltering them from competition."

Although pessimistic, Pierce knew what should be done: "The true remedy against our trusts is to seek out the cause of a trust and remove that cause." He meant lower tariff levels: "Throw down the tariff wall which encircles every trust . . . and let the trust contend with the full stream of international commerce. If it continues to exist, it will be because it sells its products at home for cheaper prices than the cost of the imported foreign product."

But the necessary political action, Pierce thought, would demand "a rebirth of patriotism." His words sound oddly contemporary to the late-twentieth-century ear: "Let the people come together, not as Republicans nor as Democrats but as Americans loving their country and ready to join battle against the interests which corruptly rule it. There is no other question of importance before the country. It is simply a fight at close quarters between the people and this mighty system of wrong and corruption." In the late twentieth century his words would have rallied support for NAFTA—provided, of course, that *it* would not be surrounded by a new wall of protection.

Turn-of-the-century proponents of the political view also perceived another kind of tacit industrial policy promoting combination: railroad rate regulation, or more precisely the failure of regulation to eliminate discriminatory rates. "Numerous witnesses," according to the Industrial Commission's summary of evidence, "attribute the growth of combinations primarily to discriminating rates or other advantages given by railways."

Independent oil producers, for example, argued before the Commission that Standard Oil's market control depended on the special low rail rates that it enjoyed, even after creation of the Interstate Commerce Commission. M. L. Lockwood, the president of the American Anti-Trust League and an oil producer in Pennsylvania since 1865, maintained that the roots of the problem extended back to his first years in business: "Away back in the latter part of the sixties some of the refinery men in the oil regions who did not have the ear of the railway managers were unable to get a freight rate over the railroads that would enable them to sell their oil in New York and the export cities at a profit. They were obliged to sell the refined oil to the men who afterwards helped to create the Standard Oil Company, for these men even at that early date seemed to have an advantage in freight rates that enabled them to market oil at a profit when no one else could." He wanted it understood that his testimony was directed not at the Standard Oil men themselves but "against an accursed system of railway discriminations which has made this great curse, the Standard Oil Trust monopoly, a possibility. . . ."

Lockwood proposed three measures to combat monopoly: government ownership of the railroads, a policy of equal rates, and "a law forcing the great trusts and monopolistic combinations to fix a price upon their goods which, freights considered, will be the same in every township and hamlet of the land." Lockwood, like others at the time, saw capital-intensive industry in a class with natural monopolies and wanted to see pro rata principles applied to the mass production industries as well as to the railroads. A committee member interrupted to clarify Lockwood's views: Did he consider rate discrimination "the mother of all the great trusts of this country?"

Lockwood replied: "I do, largely, yes; that is really the foundation; a trust must be protected in some way; the brains of the country are not in the heads of a few men. The protection which has created the Standard Oil Company, the Big Four Beef Combine, and trusts and monopolies of that class, is that of discrimination in freights."

In these views Lockwood had the support not only of other independent oil producers but also of men outside the industry. Charles Claflin Allen concurred with and elaborated on Lockwood's views. "It is in the railroad companies that the greatest danger lies," he declared, for their discriminatory rates, contrary to law, formed the basis on which "the large trusts or combinations" accumulated "their wealth and power." At the Chicago conference testimony ran along similar lines, although with interesting variations. S. H. Greeley, of the National Grain Growers' Association, viewed railroads as "the very mainspring of many of the combinations and trusts, which are now crushing out the middle class in the United States." The "skillfully managed combinations" that controlled the grain trade of the Mississippi Valley, he said, had been "created by secret rates and special privileges, granted them by railroads." His solution was government ownership of the railroads.

Others at the Chicago conference went further, however, stressing the interplay of tariffs and discriminatory railroad rates. J. G. Schonfarber, a member of the Executive Committee of the Knights of Labor, neatly tied trusts to railroads [and] to tariffs, and he advocated political action to cut the knots that bound them: "Corporate ownership of railroads is the backbone of the trust and a protective tariff its right arm. It is within the limit of possibilities for the government, by the right of eminent domain, to come into the ownership and control of the railroad, and also to repeal the tariff tax upon every article controlled by a trust. Do both these things, and it is scarcely probable that trusts could exist at all." Implicitly, his words denied that concentration was a natural economic process. In his view, a trust problem created by government policy could be cured by government policy.

But not all those who adhered to the political view of big business agreed. The Democratic presidential candidate William Jennings Bryan also spoke to the Chicago conference, creating a great stir among the public. Although Bryan maintained "that the primary cause of monopoly is the love of money and the desire to secure the fruits of monopoly," he also allowed that high tariffs and discriminatory rates were contributing factors. "No question about it," he said of rate discrimination. But he did not think that lowering tariffs and equalizing rates would suffice. "The great trouble has been," he noted, "that, while our platforms denounce corporations, corporations control the elections and place the men who are elected to enforce the law under obligations to them." Thus he proposed that antitrust law be made uniform at the state and national levels and that it be made "a penal offense for any corporation to contribute to the campaign fund of any political party."

Such differences in strategy aside, these men clearly brought to bear a broader analysis than business historians and economists have employed in understanding how American business became so big. Viewing the world through the lens of a different political economy, they saw a de facto industrial policy at the root of the trust problem—and at least a partial remedy in free trade.

Welfare Capitalism at Kodak

SANFORD M. JACOBY

In March 1932, the industrial world was stunned by news that George Eastman, founder and chairman of the Eastman Kodak Company, had committed suicide at the age of seventy-seven. The event occurred at the nadir of the Depression, a time when magazine cartoons depicted managers leaping from Wall Street ledges. Yet Eastman's suicide was prompted by his own poor health, not that of the company he left behind. Under his leadership, Kodak had grown from a small factory employing six people in 1881 to one of the largest and most profitable firms in the United States. In 1929, it ranked sixtieth in assets among American industrial companies and employed nearly 24,000 people worldwide. The year of Eastman's death, Kodak reported profits of $6 million, while two-thirds of all U.S. firms showed losses.

Kodak's early growth was propelled by a marriage of mass production to mass distribution. Whereas photography had once been a difficult and cumbersome process, George Eastman simplified it in the 1880s by introducing roll film and lightweight roll-film cameras. Both were manufactured in large quantity but with careful attention to quality, thus providing inexpensive and accurate photographic equipment to the amateur market. Kodak's chief distribution outlets were the drugstores found in every American city and town. Low prices and clever advertising ("You press the button. We do the rest.") formed the link between production and consumption.

Kodak was a highly integrated company—horizontally, vertically, and spatially. During the 1890s and 1900s, Eastman acquired various firms in the film, paper, and camera industries to protect and expand Kodak's patents. At the same time, Kodak expanded vertically through purchase or construction of its own supply sources. In an antitrust era, this was less controversial than horizontal integration and it gave Kodak control over quality and costs. A small chemical plant was opened in 1898, followed by a box factory, printing facility, gelatin plant, lens factory, and distillation-chemicals factory (the Tennessee Eastman division, purchased from the government in 1920). Except for Tennessee Eastman, Kodak's domestic facilities were concentrated in Rochester, which by the early 1900s had become the center of the nation's photographic industry. From 1900 to 1930, over 80 percent of Kodak's domestic employees worked in Rochester.

The company's flagship was its giant Kodak Park facility, opened in 1891. The plant was a behemoth of capital-intensive mass production. It made all Kodak's photosensitive products, including film and paper. Kodak Park covered 230 acres and employed about 7,000 people. Nearby were Kodak's Camera Works (employing more than 2,000 workers) and the small Hawk-Eye lens factory. By 1896, the company had made its hundred thousandth Kodak camera and was churning out miles of film and paper each month. . . .

Kodak had a centralized management structure in these years. Eastman, said historian Blake McKelvey, "kept a tight hand on his firm. He had little patience with

Sanford M. Jacoby, *Modern Manors: Welfare Capitalism Since the New Deal* (Princeton: Princeton University Press, 1997), pp. 58–70. Copyright © 1997 by Princeton University Press. Reprinted by permission of Princeton University Press.

directors' meetings and made most decisions himself." Although Henry A. Strong, one of Eastman's early backers, was the company president from 1884 to 1919, Eastman retained for himself a more powerful position as president of Kodak's holding company. As late as 1913, Eastman still owned 25 percent of the company's stock. Gradually he loosened his grip, giving vast quantities of stock to employees and various philanthropies. Other changes followed a 1919 Price Waterhouse report that recommended a reduction in presidential control as well as greater staff involvement and autonomy for Kodak's factories. Around this time, Eastman handed over the reins to a group of younger managers headed by Frank W. Lovejoy. In charge of Kodak Park since 1903, Lovejoy became vice president in 1919 and general manager in 1925. The three main Rochester facilities and Tennessee Eastman were given considerable independence—from each other and from Kodak's head office.

Kodak occasionally found itself charged with patent infringement and related offenses. By purchasing other film and camera companies, it avoided such problems and availed itself of its competitors' trade secrets. And Kodak's dominance in photographic film and its soaring profits made a tempting target for antitrust prosecution. The government focused on the lack of competition in Kodak's photographic markets and on the company's distribution methods, which included exclusive dealerships and fixed prices. In 1911, a complex antitrust suit was filed against Kodak. The charges were dropped when Kodak signed a consent decree in 1921.

Yet antitrust remained an abiding concern. Because an unfavorable ruling could have decimated Kodak, legal strategies permeated Kodak's business decisions. To protect against being broken down into smaller units, Kodak was prepared to claim that, for technical reasons, production of photographic goods required close physical and administrative coordination of its various operations. The claim was probably true of sensitive goods like film and paper, where there existed economies of scope and scale, but it made less sense for products like chemicals and cameras. Nevertheless, by keeping most facilities in Rochester, Kodak protected itself from government efforts to split it up.

By the early 1920s, Kodak was far and away the city's largest employer, with 20 percent of Rochester's work force on its payroll, so involvement in local affairs was motivated by self-interest as well as civic duty. Eastman believed that what he gave to the community ultimately would redound to Kodak's benefit. Speaking of his gifts to the University of Rochester, Eastman said, "From the Kodak point of view I consider it a very highly desirable thing to have a good college here, not only to help train good men but also to make Rochester an attractive place for Kodak men to live and bring up their families." Though Rochester was too large to be called a company town, Kodak was the city's center of gravity. . . .

Eastman was an ascetic, taciturn, and distant man, but his philanthropy enhanced his reputation. With the exception of some enormous gifts to the Massachusetts Institute of Technology, most of his money went to the University of Rochester and other local projects such as the Eastman Theater, the Mechanics Institute, Rochester City Hospital, and the Children's Dental Clinic. After 1915, he took an increasingly active role in Rochester civic affairs.

The local community—including the trade unions—respected Eastman for his rectitude. Although rarely active in partisan politics, he was a staunch Republican and conservative. He called antitrust laws "socialistic" and inserted a codicil in his will cutting off the local YMCA because a socialist once gave a speech in its auditorium. Like many others, Eastman saw socialism as an alien and un-American philosophy. This view was reinforced by his observations of Rochester's clothing companies—the city's second-largest industry—whose unionized workers were mostly Italians and Jews and included socialists. Eastman was discomfited by foreigners who could not speak English, and in the 1920s he became a supporter of the National Eugenics League.

Yet Eastman stressed to Kodak managers the importance of treating employees fairly and avoiding personal favorites. This opinion had its roots in Eastman's own experience as a bank clerk, a job he took at age fourteen and held for ten years. When his immediate superior resigned, Eastman expected a promotion, but he was passed over in favor of a bank director's relative. Years later Eastman recalled, "It wasn't right. It wasn't fair. It was against every principle of justice." The experience sensitized Eastman to the importance of making employees "feel that the fair thing was being done."

When Kodak Park began hiring workers in 1891, there was nothing unusual about its employment policies, but by the 1920s Kodak had become a prominent member of welfare capitalism's vanguard. The first step in this direction came in 1897, when Eastman set up an employee suggestion system after hearing a speech by John Patterson of National Cash Register, a pioneer in the industrial welfare field. Monthly prizes were awarded to the best employee proposals. Kodak later introduced a slew of traditional welfare activities for men and women—dining halls, smoking rooms, reading rooms, recreation programs, and an assembly hall for concerts and dances. Eastman, a lover of classical music, had string quartets come out to Kodak Park and serenade employees at lunch. In 1910 Kodak established the Athletic Association, which elected its own officers and charged a membership fee of only one dollar. In return, members could use the company's tennis courts, baseball diamonds, cinder track, and basketball gymnasium. Activities were hierarchically inclusive: production workers sang and played alongside foremen and managers.

Although its facilities and the funding for them were impressively lavish, Kodak was best known for its copious financial benefits. On three occasions—in 1899, 1911, and 1919—Eastman gave large amounts of his own wealth to company employees. The 1899 "divvy" came when Eastman made a fortune on the London stock market after launching Kodak Ltd., the firm's British subsidiary. Twelve years later, Eastman endowed an employee welfare fund by donating stock worth over $1 million, an enormous sum. The fund compensated sick and injured workers and offered emergency loans to employees in need. In 1919, Eastman sold to employees another chunk of stock priced substantially below market value.

Each of these gifts solidified Eastman's reputation as a model employer. The 1919 stock sale brought him accolades from the national press, including a laudatory article in the *New York Times*. By the early 1920s, the Kodak Employees' Association (KEA) ran one of the nation's most comprehensive private welfare programs, including retirement bonuses in the amount of one week's pay per year of service; disability and accident insurance; and sickness benefits.

On top of this, in 1912 Kodak started a profit-sharing plan covering all employees. Payments were based on Kodak's stock dividends, hence the name

Wage Dividend Plan. Tying the plan to stock dividends prevented erratic swings in bonus payments, because dividends fluctuated less than profits. Also, the link to dividends reminded employees that they had a stake in the company similar to the shareholders'. . . .

The amount a worker received was based on earnings and tenure, with the maximum reached after five years. Annual payments were large, averaging about a month's wages for employees with five years' service. Instead of saving their dividends, most Kodak workers spent the money on major consumer goods like automobiles and appliances. On dividend payment day, auto dealers lined the streets in front of Kodak Park selling new cars for cash. That workers treated the dividend like regular income was attributed by one manager to "the fact that [the plan] has paid cash since 1912 without interruption." As a result, "most employees look upon its payment as practically assured, the only question being the rate." Kodak did not try to force workers to save the wage dividend by investing it in company stock or holding it until they had been with the firm for ten years or more, both common features of other profit-sharing plans. This policy stemmed from Eastman's reluctance to "put any string on the money. The employee is either entitled to it or not."

International Harvester, National Cash Register, and other large companies designed their welfare programs to weaken existing craft unions, but this was not a primary motive in Kodak's case, since almost none of its craft workers were union members. . . .

Although unions were a distant threat, Kodak nevertheless had reason to be concerned about them. Despite the growth of overseas production during the 1920s, in 1930 Rochester still accounted for more than half of the company's employees worldwide. Of these, the vast majority worked at one facility—Kodak Park. . . . Were a labor dispute ever to have shut down the plant, it could have inflicted serious damage to Kodak's revenues and profits. Further, Kodak's production technology made the firm vulnerable to sabotage on the part of disgruntled employees. At Kodak Park, "much of the work was done in dark rooms where there could be no direct supervision. An employee could spoil in a day materials worth what was paid him in salary over an entire year. There was no way to inspect the results of the individual employee's work."

These factors led Kodak to spend substantial sums to secure its workers' loyalty. The company's generous financial benefits, particularly the wage dividend, were supposed to demonstrate that Kodak was fairly dividing the huge surplus that flowed to it. The benefits were also intended to foster a sense of obligation and reciprocity. Eastman made a point of telling employees that the 1899 divvy was not a gift but "extra pay for extra work." Twenty years later, much the same was said about the stock plan, which, declared Eastman, proved "that those who have shown their fidelity to the Company will be fully warranted." Finally, Kodak's wage dividend and other cash bonuses raised the potential cost to employees of losing their jobs. By being munificent, Kodak deterred disloyalty and indiscipline, an effect that was useful in situations where workers could not be monitored directly by management. . . .

Kodak's welfare programs were also a reaction to external economic pressures. Financial houses were reluctant to recommend Kodak stock because Eastman owned so much of it. Investors worried that if anything happened to Eastman, it would hurt Kodak's share value. By giving stock to employees, Eastman reduced his personal holdings and eased these concerns. Putting large chunks of stock on the market also held share prices down and kept the antitrust lawyers at bay: high stock prices were sure to attract the lawyers' attention, as were large earnings, which the wage dividend plan helped reduce. Two years before starting the plan, when Kodak profits had reached record levels, Eastman wrote Henry Strong, "I am sorry we had to declare the extra dividend. It seems necessary on account of the accumulation of ready money." The following year, the U.S. Supreme Court ruled against Standard Oil's holding-company structure and ordered the dissolution of the American Tobacco trust. Kodak already had been investigated by New York's attorney general, and Eastman worried that the firm might soon come under federal scrutiny. "The power of this popular uprising against trusts," he wrote, "is a thing that has to be now taken into calculations by anyone whose business comprises any large part of the total output in any given line." His fears were well founded: the Justice Department launched an investigation of Kodak in 1912, the same year that Kodak paid out its first wage dividends.

By emphasizing cash benefits instead of in-kind services, Kodak's welfare programs were less manipulative and moralistic than those at other companies. The pecuniary approach can be traced to Eastman, who, like Frederick W. Taylor, thought that what mattered most to industrial workers was money. "You can talk about cooperation and good feeling and friendliness from morn to midnight," said Eastman, "but the thing the worker appreciates is the same thing the man at the helm appreciates—dollars and cents." . . .

Kodak also had less need of aggressively paternalistic programs because it employed relatively few immigrants. Hardly any Italians, Jews, or Poles worked at Kodak Park. . . . Most Kodak workers were either native white Protestants (often from farm villages near Rochester) or German-Americans from Rochester's sizable German community. By hiring only high school graduates, Kodak Park's employment department kept out most immigrants and nonwhites. A Kodak manager wrote approvingly of "the high average intelligence of [Kodak] workers. Their native-born tastes and conservative habits of thought have been highly favorable to economic experiment and to the development of the company's ideals."

Kodak's family hiring system reinforced these attitudes. It was common for two or three generations to be employed at Kodak, with mothers and daughters or fathers and sons often working side by side. Not only did family hiring literally make Kodak workers a clan, it also was a subtle way of maintaining discipline and avoiding workers from union-loyal families.

On a more philosophical level, Kodak's hiring practices corresponded with Eastman's larger vision of the company as an industrial community. The company's "ideals" (today these would be called its "culture") harked back to nineteenth-century republicanism, marked by small-town virtues, communal solidarity, and ethnic homogeneity. Yet Kodak was hardly a hamlet of yeoman smallholders; most of the company was owned by Eastman. Hence producerist rather than property-owning values infused this updated version of republicanism. Eastman liked to describe himself as an inventor rather than a marketing genius, and he wanted the company run by engineers rather than financiers. This was a scientized sort of producerism in which engineers made key decisions that clean-clothed workers carried out in return for stable jobs and a high standard of living.

Eastman enjoyed working with his hands and respected men like Thomas Edison and Henry Ford who could combine tinkering with scientific knowledge. . . . The men Eastman hired from schools such as MIT shared his infatuation with rational, systematic methods of administration. Eastman's technocratic orientation fueled his interest in such things as eugenics. . . . It also attracted him to psychological testing, which was supposed to enhance social efficiency by directing individuals to the jobs that best suited them. During the First World War, Kodak began giving aptitude tests to prospective clerical employees and to people (mostly women) being considered for jobs in the film-finishing department. The results were so promising that in the early 1920s testing was extended to all factory applicants and to prospective supervisors as well. Kodak was one of eight corporate sponsors (along with Western Electric and AT&T) of the Personnel Research Federation, established in the 1920s to promote the application of psychology to industrial management. . . .

. . . [T]he management literature touted Kodak for being among the nation's first companies to offer career employment to its manual workers. Along with year-round jobs, Kodak promised to promote from within whenever possible. In 1920, it adopted a formal system by which workers could be "interchanged between departments and promotions made for higher positions within the organization." Kodak's career policies made it easier for the firm to move workers around. In addition, as Lovejoy told Eastman, the policies gave Kodak "the whole-hearted interest and cooperation of the worker . . . [and] a satisfied, contented, and permanent body of employees."

When describing these policies, Kodak relied on the same family metaphors used by other practitioners of welfare capitalism—including upstate New York firms like Endicott Johnson, IBM, and Solvay Process. But unlike its neighbors, Kodak worried about being excessively paternalistic. It warned managers that workers were "suspicious of 'welfare' benefits," changed the name of the Welfare Fund to the Kodak Employees' Association, and began to use the term "clan" instead of "family." The changes were, in part, a cosmetic response to a postwar surge in worker assertiveness, but they also connoted the kind of organization Kodak was striving for: a stable industrial community held together not by loyalty to George Eastman but by a common commitment to corporate growth. The ends were those of welfare capitalism; the means were supplied by scientific management. If workers were offered the same incentives as managers, they would start thinking like them.

George Eastman abhorred the strikes that hit Rochester and other cities in 1919, seeing in them the beginnings of "Bolshevism or Anarchy, born twins, just the same." An August strike at Bausch and Lomb, a neighbor of Kodak with similarly progressive policies, touched off rumors that the Sheetmetal Workers were trying to organize Kodak's Camera Works. In response, Kodak launched the Anti-Bolshevistic Program, which included mass meetings of Kodak workers, posting of "anti-Bolshevistic bulletins," and distribution to all employees of a letter from Eastman. The letter warned that professional agitators were ready "to fasten the poisoned talons of anarchy upon the whole community." It urged employees to "see to it that the disciples of anarchy do not influence the foolish and the thoughtless." After all, Eastman reminded them, "your comfort and prosperity and the growth and prosperity of the company are inter-dependent."

Although nothing came of the purported drive, Eastman was sufficiently shaken that he approved some immediate changes in Kodak's personnel program. One was the stock sale, proceeds from which were deposited in the Welfare Fund. Another was the creation in 1919 of a corporate industrial relations department. Although Kodak had employment departments at each plant, these were responsible for little more than hiring and record keeping. The new department administered company-wide welfare programs and provided staff assistance to the plants. . . .

Under [Harry D.] Haight, the industrial relations department introduced . . . power-balancing reforms of a . . . lasting nature, particularly those limiting foreman discretion. Among its changes, the department prohibited foremen from directly firing workers. Instead, workers were to be sent to the employment manager with a written disciplinary report. The manager was allowed to rescind the discharge and reassign workers to other jobs. The department also initiated a complaint system by which, said Lovejoy, "the employee can freely state and discuss any complaints or grievances and whereby same can receive considerate, unprejudiced, and prompt attention." Workers were encouraged to bring complaints to the plant manager or the industrial relations department. . . .

Haight also expanded Kodak's welfare benefits during the 1920s. As before, these benefits focused on the employees' financial security instead of their moral fiber. A new sickness plan insured against illness or accident off the job, and also enlarged Kodak's medical department to include four full-time doctors, ten visiting nurses, and eye and dental clinics. Housing needs were met through two new institutions: the Eastman Savings and Loan Association, which provided mortgages to employees, and the Kodak Employees' Realty Corporation, which sold vacant lots to Kodak workers. The Realty Corporation built several housing developments in and around Rochester that were keyed to different corporate strata—from the inexpensive homes of the Koda-Vista subdivision near Kodak Park to the more elaborate homes in suburban Meadowbrook. Eastman told Haight that "employees should be encouraged to buy their own homes. Nothing stabilizes a working force like having them own real estate."

By the late 1920s, Kodak was, if anything, too successful at stabilizing its work force. Good pay, benefits, and steady work made Kodak a "sticky" company, with turnover rates well below the U.S. average. But in solving one set of problems related to security and motivation, Kodak unwittingly created another: older workers, who received the highest relative pay, were reluctant to retire. This raised costs while blocking promotions for younger workers. Kodak managers were reluctant to dismiss older workers even though they privately complained of "privileged senility" and "deadweight." Compounding the problem was the absence of a formal pension plan. Eastman opposed the idea of pensions, believing that workers should fend for themselves with funds saved from profit sharing. "Set [the money] aside for a rainy day or for your old age," he told them. Few did so, however. In 1927, [Kodak statistician Marion B.] Folsom . . . investigated corporate pension plans and went to Europe to study social insurance policy. Upon returning, he and an insurance executive designed a pension plan for Kodak, which they persuaded Eastman to accept because it would "retire workers after . . . their period of usefulness and replace them with more efficient workers." It went into effect in January 1929.

Along with retirement annuities, the plan included disability and life insurance. The annuities were the most innovative and costly part of the plan. Although pension plan details are not usually of much interest today, matters were quite different in the 1920s. Of the roughly four hundred pension plans then in existence, the vast majority were discretionary and unfunded. Even before the stock market crash, some firms abandoned their plans because of financial problems. Kodak caught the industrial world's attention by being the first major employer to adopt a pension plan that was contractual, nondiscretionary, and fully insured. Other features included vesting after twenty years and careful actuarial projections. The plan was featured in the *New York Times* and analyzed at a special session of the American Management Association. Folsom was proud that it placed Kodak "in the vanguard of the leading American corporations."

 F U R T H E R   R E A D I N G

Becker, William H. *The Dynamics of Business-Government Relations: Industry & Exports, 1893–1921* (1982).

Buder, Stanley. *Pullman: An Experiment in Industrial Order and Community Planning, 1880–1930* (1967).

Chernow, Ron. *The House of Morgan: An American Banking Dynasty and the Rise of Modern Finance* (1990).

———. *Titan: The Life of John D. Rockefeller, Sr.* (1998).

Crawford, Margaret. *Building the Workingman's Paradise: The Design of American Company Towns* (1995).

Cuff, Robert D. *The War Industries Board: Business-Government Relations During World War I* (1973).

Haber, Samuel. *Efficiency and Uplift: Scientific Management in the Progressive Era, 1890–1920* (1964).

Hays, Samuel P. *The Response to Industrialism, 1885–1914* (1957).

Hirsch, Susan Eleanor. *After the Strike: A Century of Labor Struggle at Pullman* (2003).

Kolko, Gabriel. *The Triumph of Conservatism: A Re-interpretation of American History, 1900–1916* (1963).

Lamoreaux, Naomi R. *The Great Merger Movement in American Business, 1895–1904* (1995).

Lustig, R. Jeffrey. *Corporate Liberalism: The Origins of Modern American Political Theory, 1890–1920* (1982).

Mandell, Nikki. *The Corporation as Family: The Gendering of Corporate Welfare, 1890–1930* (2002).

McCraw, Thomas K. *Prophets of Regulation: Charles Francis Adams, Louis D. Brandeis, James M. Landis, Alfred E. Kahn* (1984).

McQuaid, Kim. *A Response to Industrialism: Liberal Businessmen and the Evolving Spectrum of Capitalist Reform, 1886–1960* (2003).

Nelson, Daniel. *Managers and Workers: Origins of the Twentieth-Century Factory System in the United States, 1880–1920*, 2d ed. (1995).

Rosen, Christine Meisner. "Businessmen Against Pollution in Late Nineteenth Century Chicago." *Business History Review* 71 (Fall 1995): 351–397.

Sklar, Martin J. *The Corporate Reorganization of American Capitalism, 1890–1916: The Market, the Law, and Politics* (1988).

Strouse, Jean. *Morgan: American Financier* (1999).

Tone, Andrea. *The Business of Benevolence: Industrial Paternalism in Progressive America* (1997).

Wiebe, Robert H. *Businessmen and Reform: A Study of the Progressive Movement* (1962).

CHAPTER
9

The Many Faces of Entrepreneurship, 1840–1930

Over the past four centuries, small business has been vital to the American economy. In our own time, local businesses—truck farms and grocery stands, pizza parlors and sub shops, convenience and dollar stores, savings banks, nonprofits, and dot-coms—produce important goods and services while sustaining families, neighborhoods, and regions. In the past as now, small business opened the door to social mobility for many Americans on the margins: immigrants, blacks, and women. Success was never guaranteed. Many small businesses failed after a few years, as the proprietors or partners died, disagreed, went bankrupt, or simply moved on. Yet others endured for decades, remaining indispensable to local and regional economies or growing into larger concerns with a broader reach.

Entrepreneurial business prospered in the years surrounding the rise of big business as studied in Chapters 7 and 8. In A History of Small Business in America *(2003), Mansel G. Blackford describes many of these small enterprises in manufacturing, farming, sales, and services. He recounts the experiences of Ohio native Lewis D. McMillen, who operated a midsized, 125-acre family farm between 1891 and 1926, raising wheat, corn, fruit, eggs, milk, chickens, sheep, and cattle for personal use and commercial sale. McMillen typified the self-employed businessman from the turn of the century. He purchased his property on credit, embraced the latest management methods, sold his products in the national market—and fiercely valued the independence imparted by his business. Toward the end of McMillen's life, the expansion of agribusiness—thousand-acre farms organized as corporations—eroded the profitability of midsized family farmsteads. After World War II, American agriculture divided into two spheres, with agribusiness dominating and "small" farms filling in. This reduced the options for people like McMillen because the minimum profitable acreage for family farms rose sharply.*

Elsewhere, the competition continuously shifted, but there was always a place for new entrants. Women, minorities, and immigrants found niches. To be sure, social prejudice—sometimes sanctioned by the law—limited their choices, channeling Asians

272

into laundries and restaurants, Irish into construction and saloon-keeping, Jews into retailing and banking, African Americans into various types of segregated services, and women into discretely feminine occupations. Many famous brands—from Heinz pickles to Chanel fashions—were pioneered by entrepreneurs on the fringes. The documents and essays in this chapter examine some of their experiences.

D O C U M E N T S

Document 1 is an excerpt from the diary of twenty-three-year-old immigrant Abraham Kohn (1819–1870), a Bavarian Jew who turned to peddling in New England after failing to secure a retail job in New York. Following his stint as a peddler in 1842–1843, Kohn moved to Chicago, where he set up a small store. In 1860, he successfully ran for city clerk of Chicago, ardently supporting Abraham Lincoln's Republican Party.

As a New England peddler, Kohn laments his lot: "Is such a life not slavery rather than liberty? Is this condition not misery rather than happiness?" Why is Kohn disappointed with America and the life of a peddler? What frustrates him the most? What factors might have influenced his decision to move west?

In the mid-nineteenth century, the national market put great distances between different types of businesses—materials suppliers and manufacturers, wholesalers and retailers—and created the need for specialized brokers to compile confidential data about creditworthiness. Based in New York, the Mercantile Agency (1841–1859) and R. G. Dun & Company (1859–1933), predecessors to Dun & Bradstreet, relied on correspondents throughout the country to monitor local businesses. Document 2 presents six entries taken from the master ledgers kept at the credit agency's headquarters. What type of language do the agents use to describe businesses that are stable and creditworthy? Shaky and untrustworthy? What do the entries reveal about reputation, risk, and resilience? What do they tell us about the culture of nineteenth-century business?

Next, an African American newspaper celebrates the grand opening of the Peoples' Drug Company in Cleveland, Ohio. Established in 1906, this pharmacy epitomized black enterprise of the Progressive Era, when African Americans joined immigrants to pursue business opportunities in the service sector. This flurry has led historian Juliet E. K. Walker to call the years 1900–1930, "the golden age of black business." How does the *Cleveland Journal* portray the Peoples' Drug Company? How might this establishment have compared with other pharmacies, including those in immigrant neighborhoods?

The nineteenth-century publishing industry gave birth to a new literary form that survives today: the "how-to" book. Rapid economic change made many Americans uneasy about their proper place in society, and they looked to books and magazines for tips. Some prescriptive literature told Americans how to dress, decorate their homes, and use the correct fork at a formal dinner. Other sources, like *The Autobiography of Andrew Carnegie* and Horatio Alger's *Ragged Dick* novels, advised young men on the ins-and-outs of business. Building on this model, female writers began to publish career advice for women, who by the 1880s were entering offices and factories in growing numbers. In *What Can a Woman Do*, Mrs. M. L. Rayne guides young women in pursuit of jobs (Document 4). What does Rayne see as the great strengths and weaknesses of the businesswoman? How is her book shaped by Victorian conventions?

By the early 1900s, female college graduates pioneered new professions geared toward using women's special talents and training. The rise of social work, fashion design, retail management, and home economics demonstrate this trend. The first generation of professional home economists included Christine Frederick, who built a lucrative consulting business as an expert on the "woman's viewpoint." Writing for the trade journal *Hardware Age* in 1920, Frederick implores hardware stores to sell small electrical appliances, explaining why these devices would appeal to housewives. How could these silent servants make "more work for mother"? How does Frederick convey her knowledge of the "woman's viewpoint" in Document 5? Why does this expertise have market value?

1. Jewish Immigrant Abraham Kohn Laments His Wanderings as a Peddler, 1842–1843

At nine we saw from afar the city of New York, and at eleven we anchored some two hours' distance from the city, where we were kept in quarantine. I was allowed to go by boat to the islands which extend in front of New York, but only after I had been examined by a doctor and found well. From there we took a steamboat to the city itself. I enjoyed my first sight of the city immensely, but, as I proceeded through the crowded streets on my way to see my brother, I felt somewhat uncomfortable. The frantic hurry of the people, the hundreds of cabs, wagons, and carts—the noise is indescribable. Even one who has seen Germany's largest cities can hardly believe his eyes and ears. Feeling quite dizzy, I passed through Grand Street where, to my great joy, I met my old friend Friedmann, who has changed greatly since he left Fürth. He was taking a walk with his sister and guided me immediately to my brother's residence. The latter was out looking for me, having heard of the arrival of our ship. He soon returned home to embrace me, and at that moment I wished only that my mother could have been present. It is impossible to describe our feelings. It is enough to say that, with the Lord's help, we were together and happy. . . .

4. Sunday, New Year's Day. On the eve of the New Year I found myself with a new career before me. What kind of career? "I don't know"—the American's customary reply to every difficult question. . . .

7–29. During this period I was in New York, trying in vain to find a job as clerk in a store. But business was too slow, and I had to do as all the others; with a bundle on my back I had to go out into the country, peddling various articles. This, then, is the vaunted luck of the immigrants from Bavaria! O misguided fools, led astray by avarice and cupidity! You have left your friends and acquaintances, your relatives and your parents, your home and your fatherland, your language and your customs, your faith and your religion—only to sell your wares in the wild places of America, in isolated farmhouses and tiny hamlets.

Only rarely do you succeed, and then only in the smallest way. Is this fate worth the losses you have suffered, the dangers you have met on land and sea? Is this an equal exchange for the parents and kinsmen you have given up? Is this the celebrated freedom of America's soil? Is it liberty of thought and action when, in order to do business in a single state, one has to buy a license for a hundred dollars? When one must profane the holy Sabbath, observing Sunday instead? In such matters are life and thought more or less confined than in the fatherland? True, one does hear

Abram Vossen Goodman, "A Jewish Peddler's Diary, 1842–1843," *American Jewish Archives* 3, no. 3 (June 1951). This document can also be found in Abram Vossen Goodman, "A Jewish Peddler's Diary, 1842–1843," *Critical Studies in American Jewish History: Selected Articles from American Jewish Archives,* vol. 1 (Cincinnati, Ohio: American Jewish Archives, 1971), pp. 58–65, 70.

the name "Jew," but only because one does not utter it. Can a man, in fact, be said to be "living" as he plods through the vast, remote country, uncertain even as to which farmer will provide him shelter for the coming night?

In such an existence the single man gets along far better than the father of a family. Such fools as are married not only suffer themselves, but bring suffering to their women. How must an educated woman feel when, after a brief stay at home, her supporter and shelterer leaves with his pack on his back, not knowing where he will find lodging on the next night or the night after? On how many winter evenings must such a woman sit forlornly with her children at the fireplace, like a widow, wondering where this night finds the head of her family, which homestead in the forests of Ohio will offer him a poor night's shelter? O, that I had never seen this land, but had remained in Germany, apprenticed to a humble country craftsman! Though oppressed by taxes and discriminated against as a Jew, I should still be happier than in the great capital of America, free from royal taxes and every man's religious equal though I am! . . .

There is woe—threefold woe—in this fortune which appears so glamorous to those in Europe. Dreaming of such a fortune leads a man to depart from his home. But when he awakens from his dreams, he finds himself in the cold and icy night, treading his lonely way in America. . . .

But leading such a life, none of us is able to observe the smallest commandment. Thousands of peddlers wander about America; young, strong men, they waste their strength by carrying heavy loads in the summer's heat; they lose their health in the icy cold of winter. And thus they forget completely their Creator. They no longer put on the phylacteries; they pray neither on working day nor on the Sabbath. In truth, they have given up their religion for the pack which is on their backs. Is such a life not slavery rather than liberty? Is this condition not misery rather than happiness? . . .

It is the inherent instinct for trade which leads one to this way of living. Could not this instinct be suppressed and our strength employed in other and better ways? Could not each of us, instead of carrying a burden on his back, cultivate the soil of Mother Nature? Would not such labor be more profitable? . . .

These were my thoughts on the first Sunday I spent in Dorchester, a village near Boston. These were the doubts I felt, O dear, good mother, feelings you cannot share with your son, who wanders through America with his bundle on his back. . . .

Peddling in New England

Last week in the vicinity of Plymouth I met two peddlers, Lehman and Marx. Marx knew me from Fürth, and that night we stayed together at a farmer's house. After supper we started singing, and I sat at the fireplace, thinking of all my past and of my family. . . .

Today, Sunday, October 16th, we are here in North Bridgewater, and I am not so downcast as I was two weeks ago. The devil has settled 20,000 shoemakers here, who do not have a cent of money. Suppose, after all, I were a soldier in Bavaria; that would have been a bad lot. I will accept three years in America instead. But I could not stand it any longer.

As far as the language is concerned, I am getting along pretty well. But I don't like to be alone. The Americans are funny people. Although they sit together by the dozen in taverns, they turn their backs to each other, and no one talks to anybody else. Is this supposed to be the custom of a republic? I don't like it. Is this supposed to be the fashion of the nineteenth century? I don't like it either. "Wait a little! There will be more things you won't like." Thus I can hear my brother talking.

The week from the 16th to the 22nd of October found me feeling pretty cheerful, for I expected to meet my brother. Ah, it is wonderful to have a brother in this land of hypocrisy, guile, and fraud! How glad I was to meet my two brothers in Boston on Saturday, the 22nd! Now I was not alone in this strange country. . . .

This week I went, together with my brother Juda, from Boston to Worcester. We were both delighted, for the trip was a welcome change from our daily heavy work. Together we sat in the grass for hours, recalling the wonderful years of our youth. And in bed, too, we spent many hours in talking.

Today, the 30th of October, we are here in Northborough, and I feel happier than I have for a fortnight. Moses is in New York, and we will meet him, God willing, at Worcester on Tuesday. The sky is clear and cloudless, and nature is so lovely and romantic, the air so fresh and wholesome, that I praise God, who has created this beautiful country.

Yet, at the same time, I regret that the people here are so cold and that their watchword seems to be "Help yourself; that's the best help." I cannot believe that a man who adapts himself to the language, customs, and character of America can ever quite forget his home in the European countries. Having been here so short a time, I should be very arrogant if I were to set down at this time my judgments on America. The whole country, however, with its extensive domestic and foreign trade, its railroads, canals and factories, looks to me like an adolescent youth. He is a part of society, talking like a man and pretending to be a man. Yet he is truly only a boy. That is America! . . .

On Monday night, October 31st, we came to Worcester in order to meet Moses. However, he was prevented from leaving New York. On Wednesday night we received a letter from him, asking that I come to New York to get my case out of the customs house. I therefore took a steamboat for New York, arriving there on Thursday, November 3rd, and returning to Worcester on Saturday. On Wednesday, November 9th, Moses and I went to Holden, where we stayed until Sunday with Mr. How. On Monday we went on, arriving on Tuesday at Rutland. In the morning our packs seemed very heavy, and we had to rest every half-mile. In the afternoon a buggy was offered to us and, thank Heaven, it was within our means. We took off our bundles and anticipated thriving business. Wednesday we proceeded to Barre by horse and carriage, and on Thursday went to Worcester to meet Juda. Here we stayed together until Friday, November 25th, when we left for West Boylston, staying for the night at Mr. Stuart's, two miles from Sterling. We stayed on Saturday night and over Sunday at the home of Mr. Blaube where I met the most beautiful girl I have ever seen. Her name is Helena Brown and she is from Boston. But despite this girl, I do not yet like America as well as I might wish. But if Heaven causes us to prosper we may yet be entirely satisfied. . . .

Winter has come. . . . We were at Sterling and Leominster on Monday, November 28th, and went from there to Lunenburg.

Not far from here we were forced to stop on Wednesday because of the heavy snow. We sought to spend the night with a cooper, a Mr. Spaulding, but his wife did not wish to take us in. She was afraid of strangers, she might not sleep well; we should go our way. And outside there raged the worst blizzard I have ever seen. O God, I thought, is this the land of liberty and hospitality and tolerance? Why have I been led here? After we had talked to this woman for half an hour, after repeatedly pointing out that to turn us forth into the blizzard would be sinful, we were allowed to stay. She became friendlier, indeed, after a few hours, and at night she even joined us in singing. But how often I remembered during that evening how my poor mother treated strangers at all times. Every poor man, every traveler who entered the house, was welcomed hospitably and given the best at our table. Her motto, even for strangers, was, "Who throws stones at me shall be, in turn, pelted by me with bread." Now her own children beg for shelter in a foreign land. . . .

Thursday was a day of inactivity owing to twelve inches of snow. On Friday and Saturday business was very poor, and we did not take in two dollars during the two days. . . .

On Thursday I went on to Enfield and then continued so as to arrive at Amherst on Saturday, the 18th. Here I spent Sunday. I expected mail from my brothers, but there was none. Monday, the 20th, to Hadley; Tuesday, Hatfield; Wednesday, Northampton; Thursday, Williamsburg; Friday, Goshen. On Saturday, the 25th, I came to Cummington, where I stayed on Sunday. I am sometimes depressed by poor trade and bad weather, yet God leads me always to good lodging and at night, sitting by the fireplace, I thank Him that I have finished another day of servitude.

Here in the land of the free, where every child, every human being, preaches and enjoys liberty, it is I who am compelled to follow such a trade, to devote myself to so heavy and difficult a life. Each day I must ask and importune some farmer's wife to buy my wares, a few pennies' worth. Accursed desire for money, it is you that have driven the Bavarian immigrants to this wretched kind of trade! No, I must stop this business, the sooner the better.

The great Lord will help me that I come in a fortnight to Worcester & I hope to meet there my two brothers healthy & after that good-bye peddling.

2. A Credit Agency Monitors Businesses Nationwide, 1850s–1880s

James Rorke, glassware, 102 John Street, New York City

Nov. 1, 1850. An Irishman by birth, formerly in Boston, commenced there by peddling and while doing so, his sons learned the glass trade, making vials, etc. He came to NY about six years since. Commenced here in a very small way and gradually worked himself into a fair trade. Profitable business, no doubt made money. Buys a good deal for cash and has good credit with glass manufacturers. Business not extensive. Buys in his own name, no endorsers.

R. G. Dun & Company Collection, Baker Library, Harvard University Graduate School of Business Administration, Boston, Mass. Ledger N.Y. 191, p. 431 (James Rorke); Ledger N.Y. 191, p. 480 (John Ryan); Ledger Mass. 72, p. 294 (George Burnham); Ledger Mass. 75, p. 106 (Mrs. Emaline H. Torrey); Ledger Mass. 68, p. 460 (S. E. Kendall & Company); Ledger Ohio 33 (Columbiana County 2): 671 (Gaston & Brother).

John Ryan, crockery, 577 Eighth Avenue, New York City

Aug. 25, 1856. Began this business some years ago, kept a small stock of crockery on the sidewalk, which he still continues. Is of steady, industrious habits and good character. Has made some money, all invested in his stock, surplus of which he keeps in this cellar. Thought honest, doing well, worth of small credit. . . . July 21, 1863. Has his stock still in the cellar, his stand on the sidewalk; failed three years ago and compromised at 30 cents on dollar; making several hundred by the operation, under very small expenses and has no occasion to ask for credit. Should buy for cash. Is miserly and estimated worth $3,000 to $4,000.

George P. Burnham, Boston, Mass.

Aug. 7, 1855. Is author of the "hen book" [*The History of the Hen Fever: A Humorous Record* (Boston: James French and Co., 1855)]. Said to be worth $20,000 to $25,000. Owns some real estate in Melrose, uninsured. Has an interest in a stock of refreshments and books at the Fitchburg railroad station and pays $1,800 rent. Is of the "Barnum" order of men, but said to be good though an unwilling and tardy paymaster. . . . Nov. 24, 1857. Lately of Burnham, Federhen & Co. Is about 40 years of age and has a family. Lives at Melrose. Has been connected with various newspapers and held government offices. Was the chief promoter of the "hen fever" a few years ago, by which he made considerable money; has been author and publisher. . . . July 25, 1859 . . . Appointed by Gov. Banks, State Liquor Commissioner, the most lucrative office under the state administration; his income is variously estimated at from $10,000 to $30,000. He lives like a prince, giving frequent and large parties to his political and personal friends, procures his liquors in this market through one house . . . and with it is prompt in payment; not generally regarded as a scrupulous man but his interest doubtless will make him safe while holding his present position.

Mrs. Emaline H. Torrey, dry goods, South Boston, Mass.

Sept. 12, 1860. A sister of Edwin Tilden . . . and a widow, has a small property which she has put into a dry goods stock and deals in a most quiet way. An exemplary woman, who will not thoroughly go beyond her ability to respond. . . . Oct. 29, 1861. A respectable widow with no family, lives with her mother, been in business some 2 years, and sells a fair amount of goods. Pays her rent promptly. Means small, but considered a fair risk for such modest credit as she would be likely to ask. Aug. 22, 1862. No change. Does a modest business, pays in 30 days, and considered safe for her modest wants. . . . July 20, 1864. Deceased.

S. E. Kendall & Company, eating house, 8 Congress Square, Boston, Mass.

Nov. 12, 1862. Kendall failed and went through insolvency four years ago. Owed $6,000 or $7,000 and had $250 assets, paid no dividend. Has since taken in a partner, D. W. Powers, who formerly worked for him and who had $1,000 or $1,500, it is said. Do considerable in their lines and make a living but not much more. We understand they don't ask credit at all now and ought not to. A friend . . . says he would trust them $100 to $300 on 30 days if asked. . . . Jan. 14, 1865. S. E. Kendall and John W. Dearborn mortgaged furniture, etc., in restaurant, 8 Congress Square, to Merrill Frost for $2,000.

Gaston & Brother, drugs and hardware, East Liverpool, Ohio

June 1879. In business under style Gaston & Brother, $8,000 to $10,000. George and Ephriam Gaston. George owns a farm, $5,000, and a nice residence, $6,000, think clear. Ephriam owns farm worth $3,000 and the firm owns store building worth $3,000 or $4,000, think clear. Ephriam's property is well mortgaged, . . . estimated worth all told $15,000. Are close, saving men, "but not the best accountants," and sometimes slow pay more from want of ability in management than means. Ephriam is a tolerably honest fellow, but George very close and mean. Are quite responsible for the requirements of the business. It does them no harm to "Dun" them keenly as they do not appreciate the necessity of promptness. Jan. 26. 1880. Slow pay, but responsible for their debts. Not much danger of their contracting debts beyond their ability to pay. April 8, 1880. Dissolved. George Gaston taking the hardware and Ephriam taking the drugs. George is worth in real estate, $5,000, and worth all told about $10,000, but rather slow pay. May 1881. Owns farm and residence and ½ interest in store property and is estimated worth all told $10,000. Very close and mean and not pleasant in his business manners. Quite responsible but better have contracts well defined.

3. A Cleveland Newspaper Heralds the Peoples' Drug Company as an Achievement for the Negro Race, 1906

Success often comes through failure. More than a year ago two young men of our race agreed to jointly enter the drug business. But failing to perfect arrangements and carry out their plans, they gave up their proposed enterprise and the present drug company was formed.

A number of citizens became interested in having a drug store established and did organize a drug company, with two thousand shares of one dollar each. A sufficient amount of money being subscribed, the company secured their present locality at the corner of Central avenue and Thirty-third street. The building was occupied for business February 1, 1906. A lease of five years was secured for the store and rooms occupied by the drug company; also a cottage in the rear, 42 Thirty-third street, now occupied by Dr. E. A. Dale, a practicing physician.

Hence we have a thriving industry known as The Peoples' Drug Co., of Cleveland, Ohio.

The first months' proceeds from sale of goods was $800[?]. Since then the receipts have shown a monthly increase, which amounts are constantly used for the further equipment of the store to increase the business. The location of the store is

---

Martha A. Sissle, "New Drug Store Spells Success—Big Business Within the Year—Credit to the Community—Shows the Possibilities of Our Race in the Business World," *Cleveland Journal,* December 15, 1906.

good, being on Central avenue, which is a thoroughfare, and being surrounded by a condensed mixed population.

A pharmacist and two clerks are regularly employed. A business manager and five members of the company constituting the board of directors, manage and control the store.

Hon. H. T. Eubanks, ex-member of the Ohio legislature, president; Welcome T. Blue, real estate agent, contractor and builder, vice president[;] J. Walter Wills, of the Gee & Wills undertakers' firm, treasurer; O. W. Ferguson, secretary; C. C. Johnson, registered pharmacist, a graduate of the Ohio State university of pharmacy, Columbus, Ohio; O. W. Ferguson, B. S. C., drug clerk, also a graudate [*sic*] of the Ohio university of agricultural chemistry.

Much credit is due the promoters and organizers of the company. Considering their capital the store is well equipped and is a great credit to the community. The store commands the respect and patronage of all classes of people, having in their employ men who are thoroughly competent, always courteous and obliging. That the store meets all requirements of the business, is shown by the number of prescriptions filled coming from some of the leading physicians.

This enterprise shows to a great extent the possibilities of our race in the business world, and is thereby making a higher status for the Negro.

4. Mrs. M. L. Rayne Highlights Proper Business Ventures for Victorian Women, 1893

As a forceful illustration of the extent to which women are now invading the fields of labor which have hitherto been occupied in the main by men, we append the following list which offers an interesting study. There are a great many branches not included in this list into which women are making their way, and to which reference is made elsewhere in the book.

Bankers and brokers, clergy, teachers, lawyers, physicians and surgeons, dentists, nurses, poets, dramatists, artists, journalists, editors, reporters, printers and type-setters, proof-readers, stenographers and type-writers, telegraphers, musicians, elocutionists, piano tuners, teachers of dancing, photographers, retouchers of photographs, government clerks and officials, dressmakers, professional cooks, hotel and boarding-house keepers, restaurateurs, inventors, electricians, lecturers, pilots, bookkeepers, commercial travelers, canvassers, engravers, wood turners and carvers, carriage trimmers, bell foundry operators, brass founders, gun and locksmiths, tinners, architects, auctioneers, clockmakers, agricultural laborers, gardeners, bee-keepers, poultry raisers, stock herders and stock raisers, barbers and hair dressers, cigarmakers, brewers, fishers, distillers, curriers and tanners, weavers.

It is now almost impossible to find any business in which a woman is not engaged, if not as principal, as assistant; in which position she pays the penalty of a lack of business knowledge and experience, by receiving a lower rate of remuneration

Martha Louise Rayne, *What Can a Woman Do; or, Her Position in the Business and Literary World* (Petersburgh, N.Y.: Eagle Publishing Co., 1893), pp. 22–24.

than a man would for doing exactly the same work; but she must patiently bide her time and learn what it is that she can do best, and not be spasmodic in her work or in her business relations.

False Pride.

When a young girl selects some money-making business she will naturally aspire to one of the professions, such as teaching, because of the desirable associations which surround it. School influences are all good, and a teacher is fitted to appear in the best society, as the result of association with the cultured and refined educators of youth. But all can not be teachers, nor are they adapted to the work if they could secure situations. What then? The shop, cashiers, bookkeepers or clerks? The training for any of these positions must be such that they can compete with the male clerk who began by sweeping out the store, and not only learned to cast up accounts with accuracy and precision, but to understand and take an interest in the fundamental laws upon which business is based. The girl who was playing with dolls when her fellow-clerk began his apprenticeship expects to pick it up in a few months, and earn as much as he! She will learn in a few lessons that she is mistaken, and if she is wise will pocket her pride and go down to the bottom of things as he did, learning the science as well as the routine of what she is doing. She need not abate a particle of her dignity of character, or grow hard and commonplace through the service of life, any more than she need ape the manners or don the garb of her male co-worker. It is not necessary that she lose that essential charm of womanhood, which is her natural heritage, because she turns the pages of a ledger. The whole tendency of her being is to grow in womanly strength, not to develop into some kind of a masculine nondescript.

5. Christine Frederick Advises Retailers on Selling to Women, 1920

Up to just recent times most electrical utilities, especially those of small size, were regarded generally as toys, gifts, something pretty and attractive, but not at all necessary. The point of view was something like this: These electrical things are very nice, and make good gifts, but we don't need them, and they are useless expense. We might give a chafing dish to a college friend or a toaster to mother, but we did not look on this large class of cooking, heating, comforting and accessory devices as serious!

But to-day there has come about a marked change in public opinion on the whole matter. And for the following reasons:

1. Women now understand electric operation better, and no longer fear it.
2. More and more homes installed with current, especially the isolated country home with its independent lighting plant.

Christine Frederick, "Selling Servants Who Never Leave: The Electrical Solution of the Servant Problem—As Many Maids as You Want and No 'Cops' in the Kitchen, Either," *Hardware Age* 105 (January 1, 1920), pp. 80–81, 83.

3. Higher standards of comfort, well-being, health, etc., among all classes.
4. Widespread education on things electrical due to shows, demonstrations, trade magazines and retailer co-operation with electric manufacturer.
5. Changed conditions and prices paid household workers of all kinds.
6. Very high-grade present manufacture and improved quality of all electric equipment.

I think this last and important point will bear explanation: If formerly we could secure a general houseworker for $25 and board monthly, who would do every kind of task, why should we then pay $5 to $25 additional for electric utilities which she might misuse, to help her, since it cost the same for her wage, even though she did have these devices to aid her? But to-day the matter stands, that we can't secure a worker for even $25 a week and board, so that, therefore, it is well worth while to pay from $10 to $100 and more to save our own labor, and replace the servant. For-merly the human worker was cheaper than any machinery which could do the same work—to-day machinery is far cheaper than the human worker.

I sincerely feel that not even the trade and the hardware retailer appreciate the enormous difference this changed public opinion makes in selling electric utilities to the consumer. At this very moment conditions are so serious, especially in suburbs and country places, that there is no limit to the price which the household woman is willing to pay for any device, for every device, which she can get to replace the servant who has vanished so completely. Indeed, I think it safe to say that unless women in the home do buy and learn to use intelligently the many household electric utilities, that they will have to shut up their homes altogether!

The Logical Electrical Dealer

Probably the Central Station which sold current to its subscribers was the first agent to increase the sale of electric utilities. Naturally the more utilities it sold the more current to be paid for on the bills, and it could afford to give time payments, and make other attractive offers to its customers who wished to purchase electric irons, cooking devices, etc. Then the department store, keen to sense profit, added this to its other lines, and it must be admitted that many of the largest stores in big cities do have complete displays, and are a potent selling outlet for things electrical.

But why do I sincerely think that the hardware retailer is the one man to push electrical household goods to the home? First, because he has (or should have!) a better trained selling force. Compare, for a moment, the average, cheap department store clerk with the salesman in a good hardware store. I could write pages on my experiences in purposely questioning girl clerks in the electric ware department of department stores. "What is the voltage?" I would ask, but I might as well have said, "What is Voltaire?" for all they knew! "How much current is used by this disk stove per hour?" "Are the parts easy to renew?" But the chewing girl, with padded pompadour, answered not!

I surely do not need to prove that men clerks, trained in selling other mechani-cal tools, appliances and familiar with metals, electrical terms and information, as trained hardware clerks should be, must be better salesmen than the department store offers. And better and more intelligent salesmen, make better buyers, buyers who will come back for other utilities from time to time, once their confidence is gained in the first purchase.

My second reason why the hardware retailer is the logical dealer is because of the reputation he has gained along mechanical lines. Wouldn't you rather buy an electric iron from a store which had sold you a dependable wrench than buy an iron from a store which had sold you a blanket? The fact that the hardware retailer has built up over a number of years a reputation as to his excellence and standards in tool and mechanical selling in general is the very reason why the consumer wishes to trust him to also sell her the dependable electric tool. The hardware dealer has behind him a reputation in tool selling, on which he can most easily cash in, with the added "velvet" of selling electric small wares.

I repeat, electric devices for the household are tools, every one of them. They are not toys, or fancy stock, or anything of the kind. They help the woman in the home accomplish in her duties, what other kinds of tools help men to accomplish in their particular lines of work. Take, for example, an ovenette. It enables the woman to cook a small meal more efficiently, with less odor, smoke, time and labor than any other kind of cooking equipment. It is a tool, therefore, to the woman's cooking trade. Or take the electric iron—it certainly is the tool par excellence of the laundry. Just as a man worker must have a saw and a plane and a level to change rough lumber into a smooth board, so the woman worker must have ironing tools to change tough dried materials into smooth wearing apparel. I say again, let the hardware retailers think of all electric household helps as tools—and bring this idea out in their selling plans. . . .

In closing, Mr. Hardware Retailer, I say again that electrical household equipments are tools for the woman's trades, and that you are the right and best man to sell her those tools. Selah!

 # E S S A Y S

In the first essay, Rowena Olegario, assistant professor of history at Vanderbilt University, compares the culture of Jewish merchants with that of the wider business world in nineteenth-century America. Drawing on records from the Mercantile Agency and other credit reporting firms, she finds Jewish entrepreneurs valuing secrecy and mobility. This emphasis contrasted sharply with American commerce at large, which stressed transparency and stability, and frustrated wholesalers, who wanted information about the trustworthiness of their distant customers. Olegario's case study shows how cultural differences reinforced ethnic stereotyping and deepened the separation between ethnic and Anglo-American businesses.

Next, Angel Kwolek-Folland, associate dean in the College of Liberal Arts and Sciences at the University of Florida–Gainesville and author of *Incorporating Women: A History of Women and Business in the United States* (1998), examines women's business ventures in early-twentieth-century America. Industrialization and big business provided women with new opportunities, while ultimately limiting their choices. Kwolek-Folland contrasts the careers of millionaires such as Madame C. J. Walker and Mary Pickford, who built national beauty and movie empires, respectively, with those of ordinary women like Edith McConnell, who ran a small catering and confectionary company. In Kwolek-Folland's account, what happened between 1880 and 1930 to limit the trajectory of women in business?

Jewish Merchants, Creditworthiness, and Business Culture

ROWENA OLEGARIO

Mid-nineteenth century Americans found much to respect about Jewish ways of doing business. Jewish merchants were perceived to be thrifty, orderly, "wide-awake" go-getters in a country that had come to embrace the values of the market and the ideal of the self-made man. American elites could afford to be indulgent. The number of Jews in the United States was small, and they were deemed less threatening than were the "disorderly" and "intemperate" Irish (and to a lesser extent Germans) who immigrated to the United States in large numbers beginning in the 1840s. The absence in Judaism of a central political-religious authority further distinguished Jews from Catholic immigrants ("papists"), whose mass arrival inflamed nativist sentiments and fundamentally altered the American political party system.

Nevertheless, specific Jewish practices clashed with the assumptions that increasingly underlay the business culture of the United States during these decades. . . . Arguably, much of what we term "business culture" revolves around the question of what constitutes creditworthiness: Who deserves credit? Should lenders extend it only to family and close associates? What are the specific traits that render an individual or firm creditworthy, and can these traits be assessed with accuracy? Such decisions are made within a framework that encompasses far more than narrow economic calculations. Formally or not, creditors also consider the country's current business and political conditions, the efficacy of its banking and legal institutions, their own past experiences, and prevailing ideas about specific groups.

Credit reporters' criticisms of Jewish businesses fell into two interrelated patterns, both important for understanding the development of American business culture. . . . First, although Jews were highly visible in their communities, their business ownership and financing structures were opaque and heavily dependent on a distribution network that was unusually close-knit and secretive. In effect, American Jews presented an alternative way of doing business, and one that posed problems for credit reporters whose clients operated in a dynamic and increasingly competitive environment. . . .

Second, the credit reporters perceived Jewish merchants to have a lower level of commitment to the communities in which they operated. . . . Jewish migratory patterns ran afoul of the ambitions of local elites who had a stake in their communities' future prosperity. Jews were accused of being, in the words of some credit reporters, mere "birds of passage," who settled in communities only to make money before moving on.

The perceptions were so generally shared among American credit reporters that "Jew" or "Israelite" became a shorthand for these specific business risks. Yet although the stereotypes were widely accepted, credit reports displayed no systematic

Rowena Olegario, "'That Mysterious People': Jewish Merchants, Transparency, and Community in Mid-Nineteenth Century America," *Business History Review* 73 (Summer 1999): 161–165, 173–176, 178–181, 188–189. Reprinted by permission of the *Business History Review*. Copyright © 1999 by the President and Fellows of Harvard College; all rights reserved.

discrimination against Jewish merchants. Intense competition for new business . . . combined with a genuine ideology of openness and opportunity to work against exclusion. The credit reports are therefore intensely paradoxical. They are, simultaneously, a record of the antisemitism that for centuries has been a part of the Christian world and . . . evidence of the inclusivity and fluidity that characterized the competitive and expanding commercial society of the United States. . . .

Jewish settlement and occupational patterns in the United States resembled those that had evolved in Europe. . . . Jews exhibited distinctive characteristics, including a much stronger preference for settling in urban areas and a greater tendency to engage in commercial rather than agricultural activities. Single male migrants predominated among Jews, whereas German Gentiles were more likely to travel in family groups. . . . [S]ubstantial Jewish communities emerged in only a small number of cities and towns. New York was their most likely destination, and the city's Jewish population grew exponentially, from approximately 500 in 1825 to 40,000 (out of an overall population of 805,000) in 1860. That year, two-thirds of all Jewish Americans lived in only fifteen cities. By 1880 New York contained a full 35 percent of the country's 280,000 Jews, and Philadelphia, Baltimore, Boston, and New Jersey combined accounted for an additional 19 percent.

Alongside this concentration occurred a wide dispersion. Compared to German Gentiles, Jews were more likely to head west, and by 1880 they made up 1.5 percent of the populations of California, Oregon, and Washington, versus only 0.5 percent of the American population as a whole. In 1870 nearly 900 small towns throughout the United States had at least some Jewish residents. These places had fewer . . . than a hundred Jews, who almost always worked in a retailing capacity. Commercial districts in small towns consisted of only a few downtown blocks, and Jews typically sited businesses in the same neighborhood, with many owners living in or near their stores. Their heavy concentration in the retail sector obliged them to interact extensively with non-Jews, who made up the bulk of their customers. So although the overall number of Jewish immigrants during this period was small, they were a highly visible minority. Substantial Jewish communities existed in the country's largest cities, and the Jewish clothing or dry goods dealer became a familiar figure in many small towns and villages. Even isolated farm households were likely to have encountered Jews, who made up a large proportion of the country's peddlers beginning in the 1840s. . . .

The distinctive migratory and occupational patterns that evolved among Jewish merchants ran headlong into . . . American anxieties. Old stereotypes of the "wandering Jew" which had long been prevalent in the Christian world were exacerbated by the peculiar pressures inherent in . . . new American towns. During the nineteenth century, towns in the United States were not established by monopolistic state and corporate bodies. Instead they were essentially private business start-ups forced to contend with others for people and capital. As the boosterist town histories produced during this period attest, communities' reputations in the larger market played an important role in attracting resources. A town's economic base and its general reputation for stability, enterprise, and good business practices affected the creditworthiness of its individual members and the amount of capital likely to flow in its direction. . . .

The exaggerated optimism of boosterist writings masked a starkly different reality, consisting not of orderly growth but of feverish speculation, frequent bankruptcies, and the disturbing evidence of failure at every turn. The conventional wisdom was that some 95 percent of all businesses either failed outright or were forced to make arrangements with their creditors. In this environment, communities came to serve several economic functions, all of which had important consequences for American Jewish merchants.

For one, outside creditors considered local knowledge to be the best, most accurate information for making their decisions. In its 1851 article on the Mercantile Agency, *Hunt's Merchants' Magazine* wrote: "Information of this character can, in general, be satisfactorily obtained only at the *home of* the trader." Lewis Tappan, the successful merchant and social reformer who founded the agency in 1841, regarded its system of local correspondents as a distinct advantage. The local agent, he wrote, "having his eye upon every trader of importance in his county, and noting it down, as it occurs, every circumstance affecting his credit, favorably or unfavorably, becomes better acquainted with his actual condition than any stranger can be." Nearly all of the information in the credit reports originated from local sources, especially attorneys, merchants, government officials, and banks. . . . The phrasing of the credit reports leaves no doubt that an individual merchant's local standing was considered a key index of trustworthiness. Clothing dealer Samuel Rosenwald, the agency reported in 1868, "[s]tands well in the community for fair dealing and integrity." In 1867 the agency wrote that "[b]usiness men of the community have little confidence in" clothing dealer Sigmund Benjamin. The importance of local knowledge tended to work against traders who had only recently moved into the community or who showed few signs of intending to stay.

Jews were sometimes praised for making positive contributions to their communities, perhaps in implied contrast to the Irish and German laborers who were perceived by town elites to be less orderly and therefore less manageable. . . . But even so, the pattern of Jewish economic mobility which emerged during the antebellum period fed the anxieties of residents who had a stake in their towns' success. Town boosters, allied with local newspapers, tried not only to encourage migrants to settle in their communities but also attempted to promote an image of stability, especially of their towns' local businesses. . . . For many Jewish business owners, however, economic mobility was linked to geographic mobility: they progressed up the economic ladder in stages, beginning with a kind of apprenticeship period in smaller towns and, ideally, ending up in a large manufacturing and wholesaling center. . . .

Jewish merchants' disinclination to own real estate in the community caused further suspicion and resentment. . . . From a creditor's point of view, land was an excellent gauge of an individual's worth because its dollar value could be verified in the public records, and it could also be mortgaged to pay for goods. In contrast, inventory was difficult to value with any certainty and, depending on shelf life, could depreciate rapidly. But Jewish merchants planning to move on to a larger town preferred to keep their money in inventory, not land, and that preference injured their creditworthiness. . . .

The demographic make-up of early Jewish immigrants reinforced their migratory patterns. . . . Later migrants were more likely to be part of a family group consisting of a married couple and children, but during the antebellum period large numbers were single young men or unmarried siblings traveling together. . . .

Peddling was a popular occupation for early Jewish immigrants, and it further contributed to the negative stereotype. Beginning in the 1840s, Jews took over the role that New Englanders had performed in the eighteenth and early nineteenth centuries. Many Jews engaged in peddling for only a short time, or during certain times of the year. Available statistics confirm that peddling was an important occupation for Jewish men. In the 1860s, 23 percent of Nashville Jews worked as peddlers, as did one-quarter of Boston Jews in the years 1845–61, four-fifths of the Jewish residents in Iowa in the 1850s, and two-thirds of all Jews in Syracuse. Jewish peddlers continued to work in large cities and in underdeveloped rural areas until well into the twentieth century.

Peddling attracted recent Jewish immigrants because it required only a small amount of capital to start and could be accomplished extensively on credit. The trade was particularly well suited to the young unmarried men who made up a large proportion of immigrants. Merchants such as Cincinnati's Kuhn family regularly hired Jewish males between the ages of fifteen and twenty to peddle shirts; Levi Strauss, who began as a peddler in San Francisco, was supplied initially by members of his family. Ambitious peddlers moved up the career ladder as they accumulated capital: pack peddlers graduated to wagon peddlers and then to store owners, who sometimes also continued to peddle during certain times of the year. Being highly mobile, peddlers were perceived as less committed than were stationary merchants to the communities that served as their home base.

Whether Jewish or otherwise, peddlers were regarded with ambivalence. They were welcomed in isolated hamlets as distributors of the manufactured goods that people craved. But in more settled areas peddlers were regarded with resentment by local dealers. In 1852 one newspaper explicitly linked these itinerant sellers to a popular Jewish stereotype: "One of these wandering Jews stept into a counting room a few days since," began the story, which related how the peddler took advantage of a gullible buyer. After the experience, the buyer "resolved never to patronize a peddler, but to extend his patronage to those good tax paying citizens who have a local habitation and a name." Public pressure led Massachusetts and other New England states to allow peddlers to sell their wares, but established merchants complained. The backlash resulted in a number of new state licensing laws, including the Massachusetts Hawkers and Peddlers Act of 1846, which "established a graded level of licenses based on 'morals and citizenship,'" extending from "town licenses for general merchandise peddlers . . . to state licenses for wholesale peddlers."

Distrust of strangers and peddlers predated the arrival of large numbers of Jewish immigrants and transcended ethnicity or religious affiliation. . . . [T]he appearance in new towns of drifters, consisting largely of unmarried males looking for work, alarmed community leaders and contributed to the fury of the religious revivals that occurred in the region during the 1820s and 1830s. . . . In 1835, several years before Jews began arriving in larger numbers, the established merchants of Ludlow, Massachusetts, declared that their town was "overrun with Hawkers and Pedlars," who were "carrying on a temporary and irregular business in towns and neighborhoods, where they are unknown, and to which they never expect to return." The

Ludlow merchants argued that, unlike themselves, peddlers were outsiders who had no interest in the community's welfare. . . .

Other sources upheld these views. . . . In 1869, the business writer Samuel Terry advised retailers to be careful about extending credit to certain types of individuals. In addition to speculators, criminals, and drunks, Terry listed the following as high-risk debtors: "Men without families, whose attachments to any one locality are not firm, and who find no trouble in making a change of location, when even small obligations become pressing. . . . Strangers either with or without families, who drop down into a community without any one being able to learn who they are, what they are, what they have done or are doing, or what are their resources for a livelihood." Inevitably, Terry's warning encompassed the ambitious Jewish merchants whose patterns of geographic mobility often prevented them from participating in the social life of communities, and who were therefore regarded as lying outside of these communities' collective scrutiny.

The role that communities played in an increasingly national market is a . . . facet of the business culture that the American Jewish experience places in stark relief. In a speculative environment that was characterized by high failure rates, communities provided the local knowledge that bolstered the confidence of outside creditors. Despite their impulse to boost their towns to outsiders, locals appear to have provided fairly accurate information on their resident merchants; indeed, credit-reporting firms such as R. G. Dun & Co. and the Bradstreet Agency . . . could hardly have prospered if creditors had not deemed their locally gathered information to be reliable. As the credit manuals published at the beginning of the twentieth century reveal, the role of communities in determining individuals' creditworthiness became entrenched in American business culture. One typical manual, first published in 1917 and reissued for several decades thereafter, advised out-of-state suppliers to contact local attorneys for information on individual business owners. Attorneys, the manual explained, were "frequently acquainted with the personal and family history of local merchants from the time of their youth; and what the attorney does not know from this acquaintance, he knows from the gossip of other members of the community."

The economic functions that communities came to assume worked to the disadvantage of many Jewish merchants, especially those who spent substantial amounts of time peddling away from home, or whose business networks allowed them to migrate to progressively larger towns. Although praised for their orderliness and business success, the behavior of Jewish merchants provoked concern about their commitment to their communities' prosperity and well-being. At a time when towns competed energetically for migrants, capital, and transportation facilities, and when residents felt threatened by the large number of "strangers" within their midst, the migratory and aloof behavior that came to be associated with Jewish merchants caused resentment and distrust.

David Gerber writes that the image of "Shylock" was widespread in American culture during this period. If that is true, the broad inclusion of Jews and the careful scrutiny of their businesses in the credit reports seem even more intriguing. The disapproval that Jewish business practices provoked did not result in rigid or systematic discrimination; in general, Jews continued to be judged using criteria that applied to all potential borrowers. These included not only the appraisal of these merchants' resources and assets but also of their willingness to provide information on their businesses' ownership and financial structures. The criteria involved, too, a specific set of character traits, including the borrower's honesty, punctuality, economy, temperance, and energy as determined by individuals in his community.

Judgments were colored by the perception, long widespread in Europe before migrating to America, that Jews were close-fisted, secretive, and prone to dishonest dealings. But prejudices were contingent upon new information, reflecting a dynamic and ongoing reassessment of individuals and their particular circumstances rather than an inflexible attitude based solely on widely held stereotypes. Competitive pressures and the complementarity that developed between the wholesale and retail sectors made creditors receptive to the information: it made no sense to ignore potential customers solely because they were Jewish, especially in cases where these individuals' own communities vouched for their creditworthiness. Thus the allegedly "impersonal" market of the nineteenth century was in reality mediated by the highly personalized and fluid perceptions that individuals had of one another. As the credit reports on American Jewish merchants reveal, constructing individual merchants' reputations involved a process of continual negotiation among all the players, including the subjects of the reports themselves, their communities, outside suppliers, and the credit-reporting agencies.

Women's Businesses, New and Old

ANGEL KWOLEK-FOLLAND

Women's engagement in various aspects of business at the turn of the century was a decisive element in creating the modern business world. Conversely, business developments were important to the lives of women. In almost no other area, besides perhaps politics, can we see so clearly the changed nature of women's lives in the early twentieth century. Understanding women's involvement in business requires a closer look at several issues. Women in general, and women in the business world particularly, heard conflicting messages about their latent chances for individual entrepreneurial success and career or job fulfillment and their capabilities for negotiating the public economy. Adjustments in divorce, inheritance, labor, and citizenship laws affected women's economic status. The ascent of big business and professionalism opened up some arenas such as the so-called women's professions even as they blocked others. New technologies diversified women's relationship to entrepreneurship, professionalism, and even housework. Finally, the federal government's response to the increased presence of women in the workforce highlighted women's role on the national economic stage. . . .

Ethnicity operated as both a bar and an opportunity for many women in the business world. Social and economic segregation of ethnic groups had long been a part of American life, but it took on renewed vigor with the end of slavery and the

Angel Kwolek-Folland, *Incorporating Women: A History of Women and Business in the United States* (New York: Twayne Publishers, 1998), pp. 87–88, 116–122, 124–129. Reproduced with permission of Palgrave Macmillan.

appearance of scientific and racial justifications for ethnic differences. For African-Americans released from slavery, economic viability quickly became a vital issue. Its importance was widely discussed, beginning with the economic demands of politicians and black leaders during Reconstruction. Booker T. Washington's articulation of a philosophy of self-help and segregation as a necessary temporary stage on the way to full assimilation merely framed in new form what many African-Americans had long known. Without meaningful economic autonomy, social and political power and "racial uplift"—the improvement of the social and economic status of all American blacks—would be impossible.

Throughout the major cities of the South, where most black Americans lived, local leaders and entrepreneurs began in the 1880s to build an economic infrastructure of African-American businesses—banks, barber shops, restaurants, and insurance companies—that would undergird autonomy. . . . The presence of black consumers, the growth of black businesses, the segregation of occupations that reserved certain types of businesses and jobs to blacks, and the traditional business niches afforded women allowed black businesswomen to operate hairdressing, confectionery, and catering establishments, as well as restaurants, laundries, and taverns. . . .

One of the most spectacular success stories of this era was that of Madame C. J. Walker, . . . who started a traditional type of women's business—beauty aids—by identifying the particular needs of African-Americans and building on the existing support networks for black businesses. She was among the first women in the United States to become a millionaire through her own efforts. . . . Walker (1867–1919) was born to former slaves. Her life began in absolute poverty and was marred by the early death of her parents and physical abuse by her brother-in-law. She was married at 14 and widowed at 16 with a two-year-old daughter to raise. She moved in with relatives in St. Louis, Missouri, and earned a precarious living doing laundry. Then, in 1904, Walker began marketing a hair-care preparation, the recipe for which she claimed to have learned in a dream. Along with her daughter, sister, and nieces, Walker bottled her home remedy, which was designed to meet the unique needs of African-American women, many of whom did not have access to running water and struggled with products designed for a different type of hair. The product found an eager public, and Walker's business expanded quickly, in large part because of her shrewd entrepreneurship.

In 1910 Walker had more than 5,000 African-American women selling on commission her hair preparation and a hot comb she had invented. By 1919 Walker agents numbered 25,000. She founded several beauty schools to teach the Walker hair-care method, developed a real estate complex in Indianapolis, built a personal mansion on the Hudson River, and contributed to numerous educational and philanthropic charities. Illiterate, she hired tutors to teach her reading and writing. . . . Madame Walker was profoundly interested in the fate of black women and consciously aimed both her products and her self-help message at them. "The girls and women of our race," she observed, "must not be afraid to take hold of business endeavors. . . . I have made it possible for many colored women to abandon the washtub for a more pleasant and profitable occupation." Like many progressive blacks of her day, Walker saw economic development and business entrepreneurship as an avenue to racial uplift. She also believed, like many reformers, in the importance of women's financial autonomy.

Ethnic businesses also embodied many of the contradictions of negotiating ethnicity in a nation that reserved its largest rewards for the assimilated. Madame Walker's hair preparations, for example, generated intense controversy because the tonics and hot combs she sold were designed to straighten and smooth African-American hair, making it appear more like that of whites. Some black newspaper editors and community leaders deplored the use of such products, arguing instead for maintaining the physical markers of ethnic identity. However, the popularity of Walker's products suggests that African-American consumers saw advantages in adopting white standards of beauty and self-presentation, advantages that probably ranged from passing for white to merely striving to emulate the mainstream white ideal. The tensions between assimilation and ethnic assertion could be found in many products that catered to ethnic groups.

Ethnicity also affected whether women went into business at all. Recent immigrants since at least the mid-nineteenth century have consistently found small businesses attractive. These entrepreneurial ventures draw on family and kin networks as well as voluntary associations and mutual aid groups and require less capitalization. The more than 2 million immigrants from southern and eastern Europe between 1870 and 1910 included a large contingent of Jews. Eastern European Jewish culture afforded women—who handled household finances and often participated actively in family businesses—importance as economic actors within the family. Consequently, urban Jewish women were among the most active entrepreneurial women in the United States at the turn of the century. Usually these businesses were small, such as corner groceries. Sometimes they could be spectacular successes. A case in point is Lena Himmelstein Bryant (1879–1951), who came to the United States in 1895 and took work in a lingerie factory until she married. When she found herself a widow with a small child in 1906, she pawned earrings her husband had given her and bought a sewing machine and went back to making lingerie. She was particularly skilled in designing clothing that hid figure flaws, and her attractive creations sold well. Her biggest marketing innovation was to address the ready-made clothing needs of women who were ignored by other companies. She designed and produced clothes that pregnant women could wear on the street, and maternity wear became the basis of the Lane Bryant Company's fortune. After World War I, Bryant began production of a line of clothing for larger women. By 1923 the company had several stores in major cities and an annual sales volume of $5 million. Lena Bryant continued to run the business until her death.

New technologies—particularly the development of film at the turn of the century—radically altered the world of popular entertainment and generally opened important business avenues to women. Moving pictures went from a curiosity at their inception in 1895 to the status of a full-fledged industry by the 1920s. . . .

. . . The history of women's involvement in the film industry is in many ways a scenario typical of women's opportunities and limitations in any new industry. In its earliest years, making films was a seat-of-the-pants process. Most films were "written" as they were being filmed, the actors often contributing ideas, direction, and even production money. Since virtually all of the tasks involved in filmmaking were new, there was little previous gender typing with which to contend. Film's antecedent, the theater, traditionally had made room for women. . . . [T]he work culture of filmmaking—the set of behaviors and expectations generated within this community of workers—emphasized the sort of individualized, even masculinized, behavior connected with the image of the modern "new woman." These new women, like the settlement house founders, Progressive reformers, and professionals of all types, were committed to their careers and believed in the importance of economic independence for women. Finally, in its earliest years, the industry was financed mostly from internal sources, and investors were willing to take a chance on an unknown director, actor, or writer. This generally more open and unrationalized climate allowed women full participation in the growth of the industry, and women took advantage of these factors.

The most common avenue for women entering the fledgling industry before about 1920 was as screenwriters. Women made up about 50 percent of all screenwriters in the silent era. However, women could be found in every aspect of filmmaking, from props and cameras to acting, producing, and directing. In fact, acting and writing often led to producing and directing. The most famous actress of her day, Mary Pickford (1893–1979) was also the first person to make a million dollars from acting. Her on-screen image as a fragile and helpless orphan was belied by her firm control over her career and her steely business acumen. In her early career, she insisted on and got the same pay scale as comparable male stars. Unable to get the extravagant terms that she wanted from two major production companies in 1919—essentially complete control of the product—she created her own studio with her second husband, Douglas Fairbanks, and Charlie Chaplin. As studio owner, star, executive producer, and director of United Artists, Pickford gave herself the gross proceeds of her films.

The theater also provided women an avenue into filmmaking. Mae West (1893–1980), who went on to become the second-highest-salaried individual in the United States in the mid-1930s (after William Randolph Hearst), started her entertainment career in vaudeville, achieved renown as a Broadway playwright, and entered motion pictures at the relatively late age of 40 in 1933. That year, Paramount Studios asked her to convert her 1928 hit Broadway play, *Diamond Lil,* into her first motion picture, *She Done Him Wrong.* The unique ability of motion pictures to bring fame to a few recognizable faces worked to many stars' advantage, as it did for Mary Pickford and Mae West, among others. To get West and her play in 1933, Paramount had to concede to her absolute creative control over the script, casting, production values, and directorial choices.

The best-known woman director of the early twentieth century started as a typist in 1919 at Famous Players-Lasky and went on to a 24-year career in film. Dorothy Arzner (1900–1979) directed or codirected 21 attributed films and worked as first or second director on countless others. Arzner's career spanned the shake-ups brought to the industry by the advent of talking pictures and job specialization, the creation of the star system, and the corporate mergers that created the major studios after 1920. She survived, in fact, as the only woman director in the major studios by 1930. . . . She always attributed her staying power in Hollywood to her ability to bring films in on time and under budget—an efficiency expert in a risky and often decidedly inefficient business.

The film industry underwent profound changes after World War I. Various developments increased the complexity of filmmaking, and the marketing, production, distribution, and exhibition of films became more expensive. As the capitalization needs of production companies increased, it became more difficult for independent companies to compete. Larger production budgets were needed to cover the swelling costs of new technologies. The conversion to multiple-reel films after 1910 and the advent of indoor filming between 1910 and 1920 and sound after 1929 all required larger capital investment. Popular stars demanded heftier salaries, and the sheer numbers of people necessary to the complex production process swelled expenses. All of these costs led production companies to search for capital sources from banks, investment companies, and stockholders. The resulting corporatization of the film industry created a much more conservative investment atmosphere—and sometimes the intrusion of powerful outside investors into artistic decisions. In this environment actors, directors, writers, and editors became more like laborers, and even the most popular stars found themselves bound to salaries and exclusive contracts. These changes in the industry made it less open to women in positions of power, such as producers, directors, and studio heads. Not until the 1980s would women again attain the important institutional presence they had in the earliest years of the film industry.

A uniquely twentieth-century phenomenon—the celebrity—allowed some women with special talents or abilities to achieve not only fame but also a measure of financial independence. The celebrity, in effect, is a person who makes himself or herself into a business by selling an image, persona, or talent. . . . Although fame is not a modern invention, the intense public scrutiny and familiarity that fed celebrity-hood was made possible by the mass media of the twentieth century: radio, film, and sound recording. It became possible, for the first time in history, for anyone to hear and see individuals performing in their own living rooms or the corner theater.

Probably one of the best-known Americans in the early twentieth century was Amelia Earhart, the aviatrix whose flights across the Atlantic and Pacific Oceans made her a household name. "Earhart the Aviatrix" was the product. In addition, Earhart started and oversaw her own line of casual clothing for women. As was typical of women celebrities who were independent of a film studio or other institution, Earhart was "managed" by her husband. He sought out contacts and funding for her flights, handled publicity, arranged scheduling, and supervised their domestic arrangements. She flew at a time when both flying and women pilots were highly unusual and fascinating. Her widely publicized transoceanic and cross-country flights, as well as her clothing business, brought in enough money to support Earhart, some of her family members, and her husband and to allow her to continue flying. . . .

. . . [M]ost women continued to inhabit the business world in much more traditional ways, even as the environment in which those traditional forms operated changed, sometimes dramatically. New technologies in farming and agriculture, for example, influenced women's involvement in this type of business. In many ways women's farming tasks in 1930 were the same as those of 100 or 200 years earlier. They raised poultry, prepared butter, preserved food, sewed, cleaned, and cooked. By 1900, however, agriculture had changed radically. Farming had become oriented almost completely to a mass-production market. Cash crops had also become increasingly specialized. Farmers grew wheat but not rye, celery but not tomatoes. Processing companies interposed themselves between farmers and ranchers and their markets. The railroads transported crops to market, canneries processed them, and chain stores sold them. The nation's farmers and ranchers were almost completely integrated into the national market economy.

The gap between men's and women's experience within the family farming business widened. New machines and other products that could simplify both household tasks and general farm chores such as plowing, reaping, and milking became available. Among these products were washing machines, the telephone, self-feeders for animals, mechanical corn shredders, indoor plumbing and running water, modern cookstoves, and home canning equipment. But whether a farm woman had access to these new items involved a complex set of equations. Farm families made their economic decisions on much the same basis as any other business: where to place resources so that they would generate the most return. Since about the late eighteenth century, generating the most return meant putting financial and human resources back into major cash crops, the province of men, rather than into improvements that would assist or simplify women's contribution to the household economy. Many farm women were faced with continuing to operate their part of the family business in an almost preindustrial environment while men's farming tasks were mechanized and rationalized—in short, modernized. The economic decision-making process that was part of farming as a family business widened the gap between men's and women's work and thus their contribution to the household economy, which further devalued women's labor. . . .

Other traditional business venues remained for women as well. Women continued to operate family businesses and businesses in typically feminized areas such as catering, confectionery shops, hairdressing, and boardinghouses. In 1900 85 percent of all boardinghouses were owned and operated by women. About 30 percent of confectioners and 99 percent of dressmakers, seamstresses, and milliners were women. These numbers remained relatively unchanged from 1890. In Wilmington, Delaware, Edith McConnell took over the D. B. Jones catering and confectionery company in 1921 and ran it successfully until about 1957. The complexities of the catering business had increased from a similar type of business 100 years earlier. McConnell was typical of small-business owners in doing most of the work herself, including bookkeeping, dealing with a variety of vendors, hiring waiters and maids for large public functions, and—after the passage of the federal income tax amendment in 1913—paying federal as well as local and state taxes. As was also true historically, running a boardinghouse, making baked goods or liquor for neighborhood sale, and taking in laundry were often the province of widows or female-headed households with few other options. . . .

The bright prospects that seemed attainable in 1880 seemed less possible 50 years later. New types of businesses and technologies, as in motion pictures, provided new opportunities for women but also followed the familiar process of narrowed opportunities as industries matured, requiring more capital, adopting professional management, and addressing larger markets. Although early in this period women's access to professional training in areas such as medicine and the law increased, by the 1920s those opportunities had shrunk, and instead a series of "women's professions" had developed in social work, librarianship, teaching, and nursing. These professions were less well paid than related professions for men. Patterns of gender segregation first noticeable in the early nineteenth century continued on into the twentieth, even as new jobs appeared in various white-collar industries. . . .

Some fabulous success stories came out of the years between 1880 and 1930. There is no question that this 50-year period witnessed more profound growth in women's waged labor than any previous time. What is equally important, however, is the fact that traditional models of women's business role continued to hold such force for so many. Women developed a managerial role for themselves, but it was a role justified and shaped by domesticity. During the depression in the 1930s, women's business and professional opportunities would shrink even further as the economy contracted and state and federal agencies stepped in to regulate business in a variety of ways.

F U R T H E R   R E A D I N G

Blackford, Mansel G. *A History of Small Business in America,* 2d ed. (2003).

Bristol, Douglas, Jr. "From Outposts to Enclaves: A Social History of Black Barbers, 1750–1915." Ph.D. dissertation, University of Maryland–College Park, 2002.

Bundles, A'Leila. *On Her Own Ground: The Life and Times of Madam C. J. Walker* (2001).

Cowan, Ruth Schwartz. *More Work for Mother: The Ironies of Household Technology from the Open Hearth to the Microwave* (1983).

Drachman, Virginia G. *Enterprising Women: 250 Years of American Business* (2002).

Gamber, Wendy. *The Female Economy: The Millinery and Dressmaking Trades, 1860–1930* (1997).

Gill, Tiffany M. "Civic Beauty: Beauty Culturalists and the Politics of African American Female Entrepreneurship, 1900–1965." Ph.D. dissertation, Rutgers, The State University of New Jersey, 2003.

Godley, Andrew. *Jewish Immigrant Entrepreneurship in New York and London, 1880–1914: Enterprise and Culture* (2001).

Hughes, Jonathan R. T. *The Vital Few: The Entrepreneur and American Economic Progress* (1986).

Ingham, John. "African American Business Leaders in the South, 1810–1945: Business Success, Community Leadership and Racial Protest." *Business and Economic History* 22 (Fall 1993): 262–272.

Mohun, Arwen. *Steam Laundries: Gender, Technology, and Work in the United States and Great Britain, 1880–1940* (1999).

Norris, James D. *R. G. Dun & Co., 1841–1900: The Development of Credit Reporting in the Nineteenth Century* (1978).

Peiss, Kathy. *Hope in a Jar: The Making of America's Beauty Culture* (1998).

Schweninger, Loren. "Black-Owned Businesses in the South, 1790–1880." *Business History Review* 63 (Spring 1989): 22–60.

Strasser, Susan. *Waste and Want: A Social History of Trash* (1999).

Wadhwani, Rohit Daniel. "Citizen Savers: The Family Economy, Financial Institutions, and Social Policy in the Northeastern U.S. from the Market Revolution to the Great Depression." Ph.D. dissertation, University of Pennsylvania, 2002.

Walker, Juliet E. K., ed. *Encyclopedia of African American Business History* (1999).

———. *The History of Black Business in America: Capitalism, Race, Entrepreneurship* (1998).

Weems, Robert E., Jr. *Black Business in the Black Metropolis: The Chicago Metropolitan Assurance Company, 1925–1985* (1996).

Wyatt-Brown, Bertram. "God and Dun and Bradstreet, 1841–1851." *Business History Review* 40 (1966).

CHAPTER
10

Satisfaction Guaranteed?
American Business and the Rise
of Consumer Society, 1900–1940

In November 1924, Atlantic Monthly *published a review of the nation's mass-production economy. Assessing current living standards, journalist Samuel Strauss noted, "The American citizen has more comforts and conveniences than kings had two hundred years ago." In Strauss's eyes, the 1920s saw a "stream of automobiles and radios, buildings and bathrooms, furs and furniture, liners, hotels, bridges, vacuum cleaners, cameras, bus lines, electric toasters, moving-pictures, railway cars, package foods, telephones, pianos, novels, comic supplements"—and more. As the flip side of mass production, mass consumption had become a "new necessity" and a "new science."*

In the late twentieth century, scholars such as Stuart Ewen and T. J. Jackson Lears critiqued mass consumption, blaming business for encouraging a culture of waste and profligacy. Since then, business historians have probed the relationship between business, consumers, and culture more deeply. Most recently, scholars like Regina Lee Blaszczyk, Richard Butsch, Sally H. Clarke, and André Millard have shown that successful businesses labored to imagine the wants, needs, and desires of consumers, rather than trying to manipulate them. Firms and consumers were engaged in a protracted courtship, with businessmen trying to figure out consumers' tastes.

This elaborate dance took place against a backdrop of major institutional change. The rise of consumer society owed much to the mechanization of countless industries, from housewares to jewelry, which benefited from government policies in the form of protective tariffs. It accelerated with increased access to internal markets provided by the automobile, the telephone, and the radio. Easy credit—the installment plan—introduced by companies making furniture, appliances, and automobiles contributed as well. Most important, it also stemmed from the phenomenon that Alfred D. Chandler, Jr., described as the "retailing revolution."

The retailing revolution began in the mid-1800s, when dry-goods dealers diversified to create the nation's first department stores. Department stores first

*appeared in big cities like Paris, London, and New York, but midsized U.S. cities,
from Lowell to Seattle, had smaller versions by the early twentieth century. Con-
currently, chain stores became a salient feature of the retailing scene. Pioneers
included the Great Atlantic and Pacific Tea Company (A&P), which sold coffee, tea,
and pantry staples at discount, and F. W. Woolworth and other "five-and-tens,"
which offered household necessities and personal products at low, fixed prices. Here,
immigrant shoppers could buy into the American dream, purchasing china teacups
or lace doilies to brighten up their lives. Finally, mail-order houses took advantage of
the expanding railroad network and rural free delivery to reach remote territories.
By the early 1900s, Sears, Roebuck and Company, Montgomery Ward, and other
mail-order catalogs were bringing a staggering array of mass-market goods to
families in small towns and isolated farmsteads.*

*The documents and essays in this chapter explore the relationship between
business and consumer society between 1900 and 1940. They examine the rise of
mass retailing, advertising, and marketing, as described by the businesspeople who
pioneered these fields. What are the pros and cons of studying consumer society from
this perspective? Where do the voices of consumers fit into this type of analysis?*

 D O C U M E N T S

By the turn of the century, a new type of mass merchandiser—the department store—
came to dominate the shopping districts of many large cities: Boston, New York, Philadelphia, and Chicago. These large stores thrived by appealing to newly prosperous middle-
class shoppers and the wealthy. They were the first retailers to offer one-stop shopping,
selling clothing, food, jewelry, furs, furniture, and housewares under one roof. Some of
these luxurious "palaces of consumption" had amenities such as restaurants, powder
rooms, and lounges, designed to make shopping more comfortable for female customers.

In Document 1, an advertisement by department store pioneer John Wanamaker lists
the strategies that made his Philadelphia emporium competitive starting in the 1870s.
Why are Wanamaker's "four cardinal points" of mass retailing important? How have the
strategies and tactics pioneered by Wanamaker influenced retailing in our own time?

In the nineteenth century, businesses advertised their products by hiring printers
to design eye-catching labels, trade cards, billboards, and placards, such as the Estey
Organ Company poster in Chapter 6. By the early 1900s, professional advertising
agencies—firms dedicated primarily to the creation and dissemination of magazine
advertisements—had established themselves. Documents 2 and 3 explore this
business environment.

With national manufacturers as their clients, professional advertising agencies
created imaginative campaigns for the mass-circulation magazines that proliferated
beginning in the 1890s. Many early-twentieth-century magazine campaigns focused on
the "reason why" a consumer should buy a product, as illustrated by the 1913 advertisement for the Victor Talking Machine Company of Camden, N.J., celebrating the classical
repertoire (Document 2). World War I transformed the advertising world. Writing in 1918,
the advertising director for E. I. du Pont de Nemours & Company explains how this happened. What lessons did he learn from wartime propaganda? How might these lessons
have shaped advertising campaigns in the 1920s? What role did government play?

In the prosperous 1920s, market research emerged as a business tool along with
mass advertising and industrial design. Documents 3 and 4 focus on two marketing
pioneers: the J. Walter Thompson advertising agency in New York and the General
Motors Corporation (GM) in Detroit. In Document 3, Paul T. Cherington, research

director for Thompson, stresses the importance of "putting the American market under the microscope" in a 1924 issue of the trade journal *Advertising and Selling Fortnightly*. In this prescient article, Cherington acknowledges that the United States is a multi-cultural society, and he urges businesses to target particular ethnic groups and social classes. In Document 4, GM president Alfred P. Sloan, Jr., describes how his firm uses its dealer network to get "the facts" about car purchasers. Sloan also writes about GM's research facilities, accounting practices, decentralized organization, and competition with the Ford Motor Company's new car, the Model A. In the second essay on Corning Glass Works, Regina Lee Blaszczyk explains how these seemingly opposing objectives—the imperative to create new markets through advertising and the desire to gather the hard facts about consumer needs—could play out within a particular company.

While businesses pioneered new practices, the Republican Party guarded corporate interests with a hands-off policy toward consolidation, rebuking the trust-busting prac-tices of the prewar years in favor of business-government collaboration. In a 1928 campaign speech, presidential candidate Herbert Hoover, who had served as secretary of commerce since 1921, explains the party's position on the mass-production economy (Document 6). He celebrates the American standard of living, fostered by industrial-ization and big business, while urging agriculture and industry to pursue global markets. Hoover advocates international trade while promoting the protective tariff, a long-established component of the Republican platform. How does Hoover reconcile his commitments to foreign trade and protectionism?

Documents 7 and 8 present two opposing opinions on chain stores, taken from 1930 congressional hearings on the subject. First, J. C. Penney, founder and chairman of J. C. Penney Stores—a mass retailer targeting small communities—explains how chain stores benefit rural consumers. Next, the National Wholesale Grocers' Association decries the chain store as the destroyer of democracy and individuality, drawing on language used by earlier generations to criticize the corporation, the factory system, and the trusts, and foreshadowing later critiques of Wal-Mart. The essay by Jonathan J. Bean puts this debate in historical context.

1. John Wanamaker, The Four Cardinal Points of the Department Store, 1911

FOUR CARDINAL POINTS
**By which we will hereafter
steer our craft**

FULL GUARANTEE   **CASH PAYMENT**
ONE PRICE   **CASH RETURNED**

Explanation and Elaboration of the New Plan

FIRST POINT—"CASH"—Houses doing a credit business must provide for losses on bad debts, interest on long-standing accounts, capital locked up, etc. To bear such losses themselves would drive them out of business. Therefore a per cent. is added to the price of each article sold to cover this leakage, and cash buyers, whether they know it or not, really pay the bad debts and the interest on the long credits of the

---

Golden Book of the Wanamaker Stores, Jubilee Year, 1861–1911 ([Philadelphia]: John Wanamaker, 1911), pp. 152–154. This advertisement was originally published in 1874.

other customers. Under the cash payment system one pays only for what he gets, and contributes nothing to a "Sinking Fund."

By this radical change we shall lose some of our customers, no doubt, but we will gain ten where we lose one, the advantages being so great to all who can avail themselves of them. So we say CASH THROUGHOUT. Bring money for Clothing and we will supply it at prices possible under no other plan.

SECOND POINT—"ONE PRICE"—The fairness of this feature of our plan all will praise. It is simply treating all alike—exacting nothing from indisposition to bargain or ignorance, and, at the same time, conceding all that shrewdness on the shrewdest customer's part could possibly extort, because the "One Price" which we mark on our goods shall invariably be

Not the "First" Price, but the Last and Lowest Price.

Not the "Top" Price, but the Very Bottom Price.

THIRD POINT—"FULL GUARANTEE"—A printed guarantee, bearing the signature of our firm will accompany each garment as a warrantee. This binds us in every sense, and will be honored as quickly as a good draft of the Government of the United States. This is a sample of the full guarantee, and tells its own story—

Guarantee.

WE HEREBY GUARANTEE—

First—That the prices of our goods shall be as low as the same quality of material and manufacture are sold anywhere in the United States.

Second—That prices are precisely the same to everybody for same quality, on same day of purchase.

Third—That the quality of goods is as represented on printed labels.

Fourth—That the full amount of cash paid will be refunded, if customers find the articles unsatisfactory, and return them unworn and uninjured within ten days of date of purchase.

FOURTH POINT—"CASH RETURNED"—This is simply a concession on our part to our customers, to secure them full confidence in dealing for goods they know very little about, and we thus prevent any occasion for dissatisfaction from any and every cause whatsoever. If the garment is not exactly what you thought, if your taste changes, if the "home folks" prefer another color or another shape, if you find you can buy the same material and style elsewhere for less money, if you conclude you don't need it after you get home, if the season changes suddenly and you wish you had not bought it, bring it back unworn and uninjured, and the full amount of money you paid will be returned on the spot. What more can we do for our customers than this, when we make our clothing so that they can draw the money value with it equally as well as with a check on the banks?

THE ADVANTAGES incident to a system having for its cardinal points these which we have now explained, are simply innumerable. Saving of time and temper, perfect security, absence of all huckstering, etc., etc.

But above all this, . . .

All of these "By-ways" lead direct to CHEAPNESS; and this without lowering the quality or style of our celebrated make of MEN'S AND BOY'S CLOTHING.

2. Victor Talking Machine Company
Advertises the Victrola, 1913

Victor Talking Machine Company, "Victor Exclusive Talent: Victor-Victrola," advertisement, *Collier's* (April 11, 1913): back cover. Collection of Regina Lee Blaszczyk. Courtesy of Regina Lee Blaszczyk.

3. Du Pont's Advertising Director Describes the Impact of World War I, 1918

The effect of the war on advertising is a large subject. We cannot consider it in detail, but only in fundamentals.

We cannot state it maturely because we are still at war. But we can be guided by history and by knowledge of human nature in estimating the probable effect of the war on the world at large, which is the field of advertising, and on the civilized peoples of the earth, who are the subjects of advertising.

Tremendous as is the present war, it is no larger in proportion to the size of the civilized world than other great wars have been. World dominion has been attempted heretofore and almost attained. Each succeeding century makes its attainment more nearly impossible.

This line of argument bears on the first effect of the war on advertising, namely, an atmosphere of hesitation and uncertainty which is fatal to the success of any project that demands clarity and fixity of purpose and constant, aggressive action.

No one can advisedly question the wisdom of hesitation and just cause for uncertainty on the part of the advertiser seeking chiefly temporary results. But the business man who realizes that the chief value of advertising is its institutional rather than its merchandising effect, does not halt his constant effort to build for his concern and its products that enduring structure of which each selling appeal may be likened to one of the myriads of bricks that compose a towering building.

This type of advertiser—he who is always building a commercial structure, rather than making temporary sales is one of the great steadying factors that sustain the business morale of a nation during periods of stress.

An important effect of war on advertising is to disclose who are the structural and who the tentative advertisers. This classification is of importance not only to those chiefly interested in advertising, but also to all devoted to the progress of America.

Preparedness Taught by the War

In the commercial war that will follow the cessation of military activity, the big guns that America will have for her peace armament are the institutional advertisers who have the foresight, resolution and courage to "carry on" whether the way be plain and easy or dark and difficult.

The war has surely taught the necessity for and value of preparedness for any great undertaking. We have always known, as we know now, that America had within itself all the spiritual, physical, and financial powers to protect itself and to help other nations needing protection.

But we were like the manufacturer who has all the materials, machinery, money, and workers to produce an important necessity, but no organization to market it. Our lack of preparedness or national organization has cost us and our allies a lot of trouble, losses, and expense.

George Frank Lord, "War Will Make Us Plan Advertising Further Ahead: The Advertiser Will Dig Deeper and Build Bigger," *Printer's Ink* 102, no. 10 (March 7, 1918): 25–26.

Germany's half-century of preparedness has enabled her to terrorize the world and stay in the fight against odds that in theory should have overwhelmed her two years ago.

The thoughtful advertiser must see the moral of preparedness as applied to advertising. He will dig deeper and build bigger. He will forsake tentative policies for long plans, catch-penny schemes for sound constructive effort. He will wisely plan ten years ahead and stick to that plan and all the experience thus far recorded in advertising tells us he will succeed.

The business man who has never advertised must have noted the tremendous strength of educational publicity as employed by all the nations concerned in the war. Propaganda is a mixture of promotion and advertising. It is operated on the theory that the way to achieve any great public undertaking is to influence public opinion in favor of it.

Germany, through domestic propaganda, has held her people together through three years of suffering, sorrow, and near-starvation. By the same means she has put Russia out of action, seriously checked Italy and delayed for months important American activities. France, England, and America have, through propaganda, secured patriotic support, induced their peoples to undertake tremendous financial burdens and make heroic sacrifices.

These campaigns are based on the same principles on which commercial advertising campaigns depend for success. Undoubtedly the war is creating, and to a greater extent will create, new advertisers and they will be of the enduring, constructive type.

Finally, the effect of war on advertising in America has been to nationalize it, in the sense that it is no longer conducted solely along the narrow line of individual advantage to the advertiser.

Every big business man, and every man with the capacity for bigness, realizes that his business and his efforts are American in origin and American in effect. The patriotic note runs through all important advertising messages. We advertise to-day along lines that will advantage our concerns because they strengthen and promote the development of our country, which must prosper as a whole, if we hope to prosper as individual advertisers.

At least one of the products we are advertising is being advertised because of the effect of the war, and that is Ivory Pyralin [a plastic used to make hair ornaments, combs, and brushes]. The most serious competition we have for this class of goods is with imported goods sold at low prices. We started to advertise this product when we couldn't fill orders and when it looked as though we couldn't catch up with orders. There was every apparent reason for us to stop advertising.

We started on the theory that it is necessary for us to entrench our brand before the war should end and we were subjected to cheap competition. There must be lots of other manufacturers in the same boat who either hesitate or have stopped advertising. If they started now they would be in a far stronger position to meet after-war competition.

We have found it necessary greatly to expand manufacture, and have a large cash surplus. We're trying to build up a shock absorber for an eventual drop in war sales. The further we go in building up a strong sales organization for peace goods, the readier we will be to absorb the shock of the transformation to a peace basis.

4. Paul T. Cherington, Putting American Consumers Under the Microscope, 1924

The field of market research is a relatively new one, but with the changes in industry the methods of marketing cannot longer serve. Revolutionary changes in the conduct of commerce are in progress before our very eyes. In many ways the overthrow of the principles and practices of merchandise distribution now going on is not less momentous than that series of changes in industrial organization and operation running through the nineteenth century, commonly referred to as the Industrial Revolution. Just as the shift from household to factory production involved many collateral social and economic adjustments, so the change from personal selling on a small scale to impersonal selling on a large scale necessarily is accompanied by new and difficult problems. It is with an appreciation of the revolutionary nature of the present condition in commerce that market study in the United States has been undertaken.

The United States is not a single market. It is rather a collection of markets which have certain factors in common. With 110 million people spread over three million square miles of territory, the country is the most populous area on the planet, having no customs tariff or serious commercial barriers between its parts. There is a common business language, there is a uniform currency and a single monetary system. The states are closely knit by transportation facilities and by telegraph, telephone and radio communication; interstate trade is under uniform legal jurisdiction, and the state legal systems have a certain degree of similarity. Throughout the country commercial customs are, in the main, similar, and there is a fairly well unified distributing mechanism in every important trade.

But, notwithstanding these common factors, the country cannot safely be treated as a unit in market studies. There are few studies in this field which are not obliged to take into account one or more of the non-political bases for subdivision of population. These are as numerous as the whims of human impulse, but often they are more powerful commercial influences than nationality. The markets for some products are determined by the economic status of the people. Silk underwear, for instance, may be ever so much desired, but for most people, under present circumstances, it is a luxury not practical for general use. Other markets rest on habits and customs, as, for example, market preferences for brown eggs in Boston and for white eggs in New York. Others are dependent on prejudices, such as those which account for the difficulty of selling certain cuts of meat.

Climatic conditions are another factor: mufflers and ear tabs sell briskly in New England and not at all in certain other sections of the country. Racial influences are among the strongest factors determining markets. The 978 foreign language newspapers published in the United States bear evidence of the importance of racial cleavages.

The composite nature of the population is illustrated by this as it is also by the more familiar facts that in New York City there are more Irish people than in Dublin, more Jews than in Jerusalem, and more Italians than in Rome. Over one-tenth of all

Paul T. Cherington, "Putting the American Market Under the Microscope," *Advertising and Selling Fortnightly* 3 (July 16, 1924): 15, 60–61.

the Jews in the world live in New York City (1,600,000 out of 14,000,000). The total populations of Buffalo, San Francisco, and Pittsburgh combined about equal this racial group in New York City. This group is almost as large as the whole city of Philadelphia and twice the size of Boston or St. Louis. The Italians in New York (over 800,000) outnumber those in Rome, and are served by 1,933 grocery stores and 204 drug stores, more than all the stores of those classes in some entire states. Buffalo has 218,000 Polish people, which is nearly a quarter of the population of Warsaw. The foreign-born population of the United States is one-fourth of the total, and in New York state the foreign born is one half. Over 70 percent of the population of New York is either foreign-born or of foreign parentage.

The United States has about one-quarter as great a population as Europe in an area approximately equal. The chief contrast is that our races are mixed together in forty-nine states while those of Europe are held separate by language and other factors in forty-one countries.

A relatively short time ago almost any manufacturer could sell goods up to the capacity of his plant by appealing to any convenient portion of the possible market. But with the growth of plants, in both size and number, the sharpened competition with other producers of similar products, substitute competition, and the increased scattering of response due to multiplied pressure it is no longer possible to depend on getting adequate results from efforts to reach a market without a factual background.

All modern business enterprises recognize this side of the sales problem in one form or another as a result of competition. Quotas commonly are set for the sales force, based not merely on the total number of inhabitants, but with due regard for the variations in habits, or other qualitative factors. For many years, the National Cash Register Company could base its sales quotas on the ratio of 1 to every 4,000 inhabitants. But such rough approximations no longer suffice in highly competitive markets.

Similarly, advertising plans and their corresponding selling operations involve an increasing use of qualitative studies of markets and the means for reaching them. A short time ago an advertising agency made an analysis of the circulation of 44 magazines in a western city of about 500,000 inhabitants. By classifying the income groups and checking the subscription lists by occupations as ascertained from local directories, it was possible to get an idea of the subscriptions by occupational groups and by approximate economic status. The figures thus obtained have proved to quite closely parallel actual figures for national circulations in instances where these were available. By such methods the qualitative factors in circulations may be gauged in buying magazine advertising space.

There is scarcely an advertising campaign or a selling plan of first magnitude now operating which has not back of it at some stage a study of the market to determine not only the number of actual or potential customers, but to get as good an idea as is possible of who they are, what their economic status is, what their buying habits and practices are, and what control their purchases of the goods to be sold. When advertising is involved, these data are supplemented by studies of the means of putting before these people in the most effective way those ideas about the merchandise best designed to convince them of the merits of the merchandise and its adaptability to their use. In this way, not only has advertising become an activity far more constructive than mere "puffing," but the whole process of marketing with which it is allied has been freed from many wasteful elements of chance.

5. Alfred P. Sloan, Jr., How GM Gets the Facts on Car Buyers and Competes with Ford, 1927

There is a very fundamental principle, the importance of which I am continually trying to impress upon our direct organization as well as our dealers; viz.: Get the Facts.

I would like to tell you some of the things we do in General Motors to get the facts:—

First, let me tell you about what we call our field trips. It may surprise you to know that I personally have visited, with many of my associates, practically every city in the United States from the Atlantic to the Pacific and from the Gulf of Mexico to the Canadian border. In these trips I visit from five to ten dealers per day. I meet them in their own places of business, talk with them across their own desks and solicit from them suggestions and criticisms as to their relations with the corporation; the character of the product; the corporation's policies; the trend of the consumer demand; their viewpoint as to the future, and many other things that such a contact makes possible. I solicit criticism of anything and everything.

I make careful notes of all the points that come up that are worth while and when I get back home I study and develop these points and capitalize them so far as possible. The reason for all this is, that irrespective of how efficient our contact through our regular organizations may be, our men in the field are charged with doing specific things and that takes all their time and effort. I go out from the standpoint of general policies and get the facts in a very personal way without the intermediary of an organization which is apt to overlook the most important points and inject their own personal viewpoint on such points as they do get. I believe that this work that we have done has contributed much more than any of us appreciate, to the progress that General Motors has made.

Our research laboratories are no different from our field trips in principle. We are searching for the facts that we may know more about the fundamentals and be able to add value to the performance and effectiveness of our products, just the same as in the field work we are trying to learn more about the distribution of our products. We send representatives abroad to study foreign methods and foreign cars. We have an engineering office in London with representatives in the other countries to keep us advised at all times as to what progress there may be along European lines that General Motors can capitalize. Again, we are seeking the facts.

The Proving Ground is also dedicated to the principle of getting the facts. As you see, we not only operate our own cars, but all competitive cars, both those made at home and abroad. We are seeking the facts about all these cars to the end that General Motors cars are better cars. We are seeking in our sales activity here at the proving ground to impress upon our dealers the facts about our cars so that they may more intelligently present the facts to the consumer.

I want to outline to you what I believe to be a great weakness in the automotive industry today and what General Motors is trying to do to correct that weakness.

I have stated frankly to General Motors dealers, in almost every city in the United States, that I was deeply concerned with the fact that many of them, even

---

"'Getting the Facts' Is Keystone of General Motors' Success," *Automotive Industries* 57 (October 8, 1927): 550–551.

those that were carrying on in a reasonably efficient manner, were not making the return on their capital that they should. Right here let me say that so far as General Motors dealers are concerned, from what facts I have—I realize there has been much improvement during the past two or three years, but interested as the management of General Motors must be in every step, from the raw material to the ultimate consumer, and recognizing that this chain of circumstances is no stronger than its weakest link—I feel a great deal of uncertainty as to the operating position of our dealer organization as a whole. I hope that this feeling of uncertainty is unwarranted. I am sure that with a responsibility so great, all elements of uncertainty must be eliminated and that our dealers should know the facts about their operating position as clearly and as scientifically as we feel that we know the facts about General Motors operating position.

This brings us to *proper accounting*. Many of our dealers, and the same thing applies to dealers of other organizations, have good accounting systems. Many of them have indifferent ones and I regret to say that too large a percentage of them have practically no accounting system at all. Many of those who have accounting systems, through lack of their being properly developed, are not able to effectively use them. In other words, they are not so developed that they give the dealer the facts about his business; where the leaks are; what he should do to improve his position. As I said before, uncertainty must be eliminated. Uncertainty and efficiency are as far apart as the North Pole is from the South. If I could wave a magic wand over our dealer organization, with the result that every dealer could have a proper accounting system, could know the facts about his business and could intelligently deal with the many details incident to his business in an intelligent manner as a result thereof, I would be willing to pay for that accomplishment an enormous sum and I would be fully justified in doing so. It would be the best investment General Motors ever made.

We consider our dealers partners in our business. It is true they operate on their own account, but they are, nevertheless, partners in the sense that their prosperity is linked up with our prosperity and all good partners should recognize the necessities of each other and should cooperate so that all weaknesses can be eliminated. This is exactly what General Motors is doing in this connection.

We have organized a subsidiary whose sole functions will be to establish proper accounting systems wherever desired by our dealers. We will audit such accounts periodically in order that our dealers may have the assurance that their records are properly established and that the facts that come to them are facts rather than fiction. We feel that with the great amount of specific knowledge we have, involving all phases of the automotive business, and with an organization that specializes in this particular branch of accounting, with nothing else to think of, that we can, through evolution and with the cooperation of our dealers, place before them facts and figures that will indicate to them very clearly what they should do and what they should not do.

I do not think there is anything that will contribute more to our complete stabilization than an accomplishment of this kind. I do not think there is anything that will establish greater confidence in the minds of the banking interests whose cooperation we must have in carrying on. Some time ago I saw it stated, and I believe it is absolutely correct, that if business, using that term in its broadest sense, was equipped with proper accounting, a very large percentage of the failures and losses incident to same, could be eliminated. We hope to be able, in due course of time, to place before our dealers "bogeys" I might say, showing the proper relationship of each expense item to the business as a whole with the result that if a dealer will conduct his affairs along the lines that we can ultimately outline to him, he will, in a sense, take the straight and direct course to a reasonable and fair profit.

I have told my associates time and time again, that with this program of ours accomplished to the degree that I am hopeful that it can be accomplished, that it will be the greatest achievement of General Motors.

A few words about our organization itself. We operate on the principle of what I might term a "decentralized organization," I mean by that, each one of our operations is self-contained, is headed up by an executive who has full authority and is responsible for his individual operation. We, naturally, think that this is the best scheme of organization or we would not adopt it. Our responsibilities are so great, the necessity of quick action and prompt decision is so great and contributes so much increased efficiency and effectiveness that it is about the only way a business of magnitude of General Motors could be conducted. It also, I think, has the very great advantage of developing executive ability and initiative on the part of a greater number of individuals.

Each member of our organization appreciates what is absolutely true—that he has a real function to perform and that upon their initiative, their industry and the constructiveness of their decisions as a whole, depends the success of the institution as a whole. Coordination is effected through what we call Inter-Divisional Relations Committees where those interested in the same functions of the important divisions meet together and discuss their own problems as well as the same problems from the standpoint of corporation policy. For instance, our Purchasing Agents meet together in the form of a General Purchasing Committee, presided over by a Vice President of the Corporation. If it is found that one or more of the Divisions can profit by purchasing as one unit, then we purchase as General Motors and all profit. If it is found that there is nothing gained, we do not do so. In that event the purchase is by the individual operations as their judgment may determine. In that way we get individual initiative and at the same time we do not overlook anything from the Corporation standpoint.

In addition to this, the Corporation maintains an organization in Detroit as an advisory service for the benefit of all. The Research activity acts in a consulting capacity for the Engineering Departments of all the divisions, and in addition to this, is constantly searching for new principles and ideas of a more fundamental and scientific character than would be possible for any of the individual Engineering Departments, which must be more concerned with immediate production problems.

Legal and patent problems, as well as accounting and financial control, are handled in a similar manner.

Speaking of General Motors' position in the industry, I am reminded of the fact that many of our newspapers and magazines seem to be devoting more or less space to a discussion of the relative position of General Motors and Ford as important factors in the automotive industry, their present relation and their future relation.

Now, I have tried to consider the question from all sides, and it seems to me it is not such a complicated problem as it is made out to be. If the past is any indication of the future, the new Ford car will be a car that will appeal to a great mass of people.

Naturally, that car must meet present conditions, but the basic idea is likely to be the same. General Motors is in quite a different position. General Motors' idea is to make a car of greater luxury than the Ford—a car that properly belongs to the next higher price class. With every price car there is a definite market.

This applies to the Cadillac as well as it does the Ford. Any manufacturer that will give to the public a definite number of dollars' worth of value and do it constructively and honestly, will get a certain proportion of the market that belongs to that number of dollars. It is purely a question of giving the public honest value.

There is plenty of opportunity in the world today for Mr. Ford to give the public honest value, which of course he will do, with the result that he will sell an enormous number of cars per year, and there is an equal opportunity for General Motors to give the public honest value at a higher price and, likewise, sell a very large number of cars per year. To make a long story short, it seems to me that both Ford and General Motors are governed by the same economic principle, viz., to give the greatest possible value in their respective price classes. There is absolutely no reason why General Motors cannot today give a greater per dollar value than anyone in the world. That is why I say, upon analysis, the problem does not look so complicated.

6. Herbert Hoover Explains How World Trade and Protective Tariffs Ensure American Prosperity, 1928

Economic questions have over the past 50 years grown to a larger and larger proportion of our national issues. Today these questions are more dominant than ever. Upon their sound solution depend our prosperity, our standards of living, and the opportunities for a fuller life to every home. I make no apologies, therefore, for speaking to you tonight on economic questions, as they are affected by the tariff and our foreign trade. . . .

. . . [T]oday the whole Nation has more profound reasons for solicitude in the promotion of our foreign trade than ever before. As the result of our inventive genius and the pressure of high wages, we have led the world in substituting machines for hand labor. This, together with able leadership and skilled workers, enables us to produce goods much in excess of our own needs. Taking together our agriculture and our manufactures and our mining, we have increased our production approximately 30 percent during the last 8 years, while our population has increased only about 10 percent. Much of this increase of production has been absorbed in higher standards of living, but the surplus grows with this unceasing improvement. To insure continuous employment and maintain our wages we must find a profitable market for these surpluses.

Nor is this the only reason for lending high importance to our foreign trade. . . . Our business ideal must be stability—that is, regularity of production and regularity of employment. We attain stability in production, whether it be in the individual factory or in the whole industry, or whether it is in the Nation at large, by the number

Herbert Hoover, Address delivered in Boston, Mass., October 15, 1928, *Public Papers of the Presidents of the United States: Herbert Hoover, 1929, Supplement II: Addresses During the Campaign* (Washington, D.C.: GPO, 1974), pp. 557–561, 564, 567–569.

of different customers we supply. The shock of decreased demand from a single customer can be absorbed by the increase from another, if distribution be diffused. Consequently our industries will gain in stability, the wider we spread our trade with foreign countries. This additional security reflects itself in the home of every worker and every farmer in our country.

The expansion of export trade has a vital importance in still another direction. The goods which we export contribute to the purchase from foreign countries of the goods and raw materials which we cannot ourselves produce. We might survive as a nation, though, on lower living standards and wages, if we had to suppress the 9 percent or 10 percent of our total production which is now sold abroad. But our whole standard of life would be paralyzed and much of the joy of living destroyed if we were denied sufficient imports. Without continued interchange of tropical products with those of the temperate zone, whole sections of the world, including our own country, must stagnate and degenerate in civilization. We could not run an automobile, we could not operate a dynamo or use a telephone, were we without imported raw materials from the tropics. In fact, the whole structure of our advancing civilization would crumble and the great mass of mankind would travel backwards if the foreign trade of the world were to cease. The Great War brought into bold relief the utter dependence of nations upon foreign trade. One of the major strategies of that hour was to crush the enemy by depriving him of foreign trade and therefore of supplies of material and foodstuffs vital to his existence.

Trade in its true sense is not commercial war; it is a vital mutual service. The volume of world trade depends upon prosperity. In fact, it grows from prosperity. Every nation loses by the poverty of another. Every nation gains by the prosperity of another. Our prosperity in the United States has enabled us in 8 years to make enormous increases in the purchase of goods from other nations. These increasing purchases have added prosperity and livelihood to millions of people abroad. And their prosperity in turn has enabled them to increase the amount of goods they can buy from us.

Realizing these essentials, one of the first acts of the Republican administration when we came into power 7½ years ago—confronted as we were by millions of unemployed—was to devise measures to vigorously restore and expand our foreign trade. It was evident that we must sell more products abroad if we would restore jobs, maintain steady employment for labor and activity for our industries. It was clear that we must dispose of the farmer's surplus abroad if he was to recover stability and an ability to buy the products of our labor. As an aftermath of the war we were confronted with a total disorganization of our export trade. Our exports of war materials had been brought suddenly to an end. But, more than this, the trade of the entire world was demoralized to the extent that the actual movement of commodities between nations was less than before the war. We set out on a definitely organized campaign to build up the export of our products. To accomplish this we reorganized the Department of Commerce on a greater scale than has ever been attempted or achieved by any government in the world. We mobilized our manufacturers and exporters, and cooperated with them in laying out and executing strategic plans for expanding our foreign trade with all nations and in all directions.

The Republican administration by this action introduced a new basis in government relation with business and, in fact, a new relationship of the Government with its citizens. That basis was definitely organized cooperation. The method was not dictation nor domination. It was not regulation, nor subsidies, nor other artificial stimulants such as were adopted by foreign nations in similar plight. It was the Government, with all its prestige, interested solely in public welfare, acting through trained specialists in voluntary cooperation with committees of businessmen to promote the interest of the whole country in expansion of its trade and its ultimate expression, which is increased and stable employment. . . .

In the year 1922 our foreign trade upon a quantitative basis was almost the same as it was before the war, that is, if we reduce the values by the amount of inflation of the dollar. Since that time our trade has increased steadily year by year until in the year 1927 our exports amounted to the gigantic sum of $4,865 million—or a billion dollars increase under Republican rule. Our imports increased in the past 7 years by over $1,675 million to a total of $4,185 million. There never have been such increases in a similar period before in our history. Today we are the largest importers and the second largest exporters of goods in the world. Our exports show on a quantitative basis an increase of 58 percent over prewar, while our imports are 80 percent above prewar. The other combatant nations are only now barely recovering their prewar basis. All this has a very human interpretation. Our total volume of exports translates itself into employment for 2,400,000 families, while its increase in the last 7 years has interpreted itself into livelihood for 500,000 additional families in the United States. And in addition to this, millions more families find employment in the manufacture of imported raw materials. The farmer has a better market for his produce by reason of their employment. . . .

One of the most important economic issues of this campaign is the protective tariff. The Republican Party has for 70 years supported a tariff designed to give adequate protection to American labor, American industry, and the American farm against foreign competition. . . .

During this campaign some of our opponents have asserted that it is inconsistent to support the protective tariff and at the same time expect a greater expansion of our foreign trade. Their presentation of this theory at least indicates that some of them have not departed from their long-held free trade theories.

Their theory is that if by a tariff wall against competitive goods we reduce the sales of goods to us from foreign countries, we thereby diminish the resources of those foreign countries with which to buy goods from us and thus in turn our sales abroad are decreased. It is still further asserted that if we by the tariff reduce the shipment of goods into our markets, then we diminish the ability of foreign countries to pay principal and interest on the debts which they owe us. This theory was sound enough in the old days of direct barter of goods between nations. The trouble with it is that it has lost most of its practical application in a modern world and especially as applied to the American situation. . . .

One primary fault of this economic theory is that foreign trade is no longer a direct barter between one single nation and another. World trade has become more of the nature of a common pool into which all nations pour goods or credit and from which they retake goods and credit. Let me give you an example: We ship more goods to Great Britain than we receive from her. But we buy vast quantities of tropical goods and she in turn supplies the tropical countries with her manufactures. In this way the settlement of international balances and obligations is lifted entirely out of the category of direct barter. . . .

. . . Our domestic prosperity has been greatly increased by the building up of wages and standards of living, to which the protective tariff has greatly contributed. By the very result of the tariff we have been able vastly to increase our imports of luxuries, raw materials, and things we do not produce. With our domestic prosperity we require more raw materials, and by that same prosperity we have the resources with which to buy them. By our prosperity we have been able to go abroad as tourists and also to remit to our relatives in Europe. This I believe finally extinguishes the already depleted importance of this theory that our tariff seriously damages the buying power of foreign countries and thus diminishes our export trade.

But if any more answers are needed to this theory there is that of actual practical experience. I have already observed that we have increased our imports during the last 7½ years under the present tariff act by over $1,675 million annually, or to an amount at least 80 percent above prewar average after allowing for the higher prices. The exports of five leading manufacturing nations of Europe to the United States have increased 75 percent since 1913, whereas the sales of these same nations to the rest of the world have only increased 27 percent. Certainly that does not indicate any great destruction of their ability to sell us something despite our tariff. In short, there is no practical force in the contention that we cannot have a protective tariff and a growing foreign trade. We have both today.

7. J. C. Penney, How Chain Stores Benefit Farmers, 1930

Wherever general business conditions have been carefully studied before and after the advent of chain stores in a town, it has nearly always been found that more money came into the town subsequent to the opening of the chain store than was the case previously.

This expansion in retail sales volume is usually due to the fact that the chain stores bring an extension of the lines offered by local merchants. A greater range of selection is offered customers and, because the chain stores usually handle items adapted to widespread distribution and on the basis of mass production and volume purchases, more attractive prices are presented.

Chain store managers and employees in general are trained in service, in rapid turn-over of stock, in rigid control of operating expense. Profit margins on single items are low and savings in expenses of operation are passed on to the customers.

These facts are known to purchasers all over the country. They are attracted to cities and towns where they can get the values offered by chain stores, and they bring their money with them instead of sending it to other localities where they had previously done their buying, oftentimes largely by mail.

The largest buying group in the United States is that group represented by the American farmer. A visit to any community on Saturday night will substantiate this fact. In every street in the business section of the town automobiles are parked against the curb in solid lines. Saturday's business in many stores accounts for from fifty to

---

"Do Chain Stores Benefit the Farmer? Pro: J. C. Penney, Chairman, Board of J. C. Penney Stores," *Congressional Digest* 9, no. 8–9 (August–September 1930): 212, 222.

sixty per cent of the total sales for the week. And a large percentage of Saturday's business is done by people from the farming districts.

During the past twenty years, great changes have taken place in living conditions on the farm—greater even than those which have taken place in the cities. Electric power lines, or individual electric power plants, have materially added to the comfort of living on the farm. Telephone connections have brought the farm home in instant touch with the trading towns.

With fewer organizations handling a line of merchandise—because of direct shipment through the central buying organization to the retail store—it becomes possible for new styles and new qualities to be placed before customers within a few days after they come on to the market.

Instead of being restricted in her choice as heretofore, the woman from the farm can obtain what she wants from a range of stock equivalent to that previously carried only in larger stores located in distant cities. In short, she can get what she wants and not be obliged to accept what the storekeeper has to sell.

Furthermore, chain stores will be found to offer not only opportunity for the individual farmer to spend his dollar for needed merchandise to his own advantage; but, keenly analyzed, they will be found to further the interest of the farmer in a way that does not occur to the casual thinker, i.e.: If the chain store can, through systematic savings in costs, offer a twenty per cent saving to retail customers in cotton, wool or leather goods, and other commodities, it automatically builds up a twenty per cent greater buying capacity on the part of the public. If the chain grocery store can offer an equivalent saving in fruits, vegetables, meats, or bakery products, it automatically builds up a correspondingly increasing purchasing power for the dollar spent for food.

Chain store savings are made not in reductions in prices paid for raw products but in intermediate costs which benefit neither producer nor consumer—those costs that levy the unfair tax on prices because of too many operations in handling between the producer and consumer.

8. National Wholesale Grocers' Association, Why Chain Stores Threaten the Nation's Welfare, 1930

Is it better for America that retail business be in the hands of a vast number of individuals or in the control of a few gigantic corporations? The system that contributes the greater net benefit to the welfare of America should prosper and prevail.

The burden of proof rests clearly upon the chain store. The manufacturer-wholesaler-retailer method, representing local ownership and local operation, is a natural economic and social product of the ages. Twenty to thirty millions of America's population depend upon wholesale and retail business for their livelihood. The chain system received its impetus after the dislocation of mercantile and social conditions following the World War. It is the challenger.

"Does the Chain Store System Threaten the Nation's Welfare? Pro: The National Wholesale Grocers' Association of the United States," *Congressional Digest* 9 (August–September 1930): 213–214.

Its proponents must establish the alleged efficiency of the chain stores and offer more than their own opinions as proof. They must compare the costs of their services with the costs of similar services offered by the independent merchant. The typical chain store asks cash terms, does not deliver, offers severely restricted stocks of standard quality, urges rigorous buying policies on manufacturers, converters and farmers, practices shrewd and varying pricing methods, avoids the responsibility of community citizenship and holds down local expenses to the minimum. The typical independent merchant grants credit, delivers, offers complete stocks according to the demands of his individual community, is not so adept at modern tricks of merchandising and must be, in the nature of things, a full-time citizen. When costs of doing business are compared all these factors must be considered.

When the friends of the chain store insist that they are not anti-social, they may not advance the economic argument as representing the complete answer. They must explain how and why absentee ownership of local enterprises is more desirable socially; how and why the itinerant store manager system is superior to the independent business men and permanent citizen system; how and why the system of drawing off the net cash surpluses to the great centers is more beneficial to the community and the nation; how and why America should encourage further concentration of power and wealth in the hands of a few and if so, why America should submit to a growing commercial despotism even if it might be benevolent and not predatory.

And all arguments should be carefully sifted not only as to their accuracy, but as to their authority. A huge prize is at stake.

It has been said by economists for many years that manufacturing processes have been improved more than have those of distribution and it is generally admitted that mass production has brought about some benefits both economic and social. Those of an economic character are generally more evident and those of a social nature more indirect and more difficult to prove. But for the time being, admitting without question the advantages of mass production, it is fair to question whether the same principle can be applied to distribution.

Is there not something inherent in retailing that is not true in manufacturing? Is there not something lost of individual initiative, responsibility, self-reliance, citizenship and relations between the individual and his community that after all is essential to America? Even if all that can be said in favor of mass manufacturing is true, does it apply to retailing, agriculture and the professions?

If the chain theory is right, why should it not be carried to its logical conclusions and be applied to religious institutions? It can easily be argued that having half a dozen religious establishments in every community is a waste. Why not abolish local small churches and have a central radio preaching station in the larger cities and broadcast sermons over the country? Efficiency can be carried too far. Sooner or later it comes into conflict with humanity. Already there are signs that there is a general reaction.

But even in the boasted efficiency of chain stores we must rely principally on the testimony of the chains themselves. We have little impartial authority for the degrees of their efficiency.

Then, too, the social side of the question is more important than the economic. Even if chain stores do save pennies for consumers, does that offset their social disadvantages?

Main Street was lined with the stores of small individual merchants a few years ago. Then came a chain store and soon others followed. After all the small retailers had been displaced and their places were taken by chain stores the question of the savings came up at a woman's meeting. The wife of an ousted retail merchant told the story of her husband being forced out of business. Was it better for the women of that town to save a few cents or to have the breadwinners of their families deprived of their means of livelihood?

There is another tendency that is worth watching. In the last few years many of the medium size chain stores companies have merged or have been absorbed by others to form larger and larger corporations. It has been predicted that in a few years there will be only three or four large chain companies in the great food industry of the country. Remember that food represents one of the largest expenditures in the family budget. It is only fair to agree with chain store men that food monopoly is impossible, but if there are only three or four large corporations in the grocery trade they may become so large as to be dominant price factors; affecting what the producer receives and what the consumer pays.

But how about women? We have been told by marketing experts that the women make more than nine-tenths of the purchases of all goods bought at retail. Do women want farmers, doctors and churches standardized and machinized? Will women throughout the country submit to dictation of the headquarters of great chain organizations in a few large cities about what they shall eat, what they shall wear and what they shall have in their homes? They see quickly enough that chain stores mean the greater and greater growth of large cities and the further and further shrinking of other towns.

 E S S A Y S

In the first essay, André Millard, a professor of history and American studies at the University of Alabama at Birmingham and a specialist in recorded sound, examines the international music business during the heyday of the talking machine. From 1900 to 1920, three firms—the Edison, Victor, and Columbia companies—formed an oligopoly in the talking machine and record business. By the mid-1910s, new entrants forced prices down and eroded profits. Millard demonstrates how the Big Three tried to compete by developing new products and markets. The companies that succeeded did so by paying attention to consumer desire, rather than trying to shape it.

Next, Regina Lee Blaszczyk, coeditor of this volume and author of *Imagining Consumers: Design and Innovation from Wedgwood to Corning* (2000), examines the early history of Pyrex Ovenware in regard to new practices in advertising and marketing that emerged during the 1920s. Introduced by Corning Glass Works during World War I, Pyrex baking glass failed to sell in the roaring twenties, despite an expensive national advertising campaign. Perplexed managers turned to marketing experts at J. Walter Thompson to figure out why. In the end, Corning learned that it had failed to identify the desires of the women who bought kitchen utensils. This case study shows that advertising does not measure corporate success.

Finally, Jonathan J. Bean, a professor of history at Southern Illinois University and author of *Beyond the Broker State: Federal Policies Toward Small Business, 1936–1961* (1996), surveys the transformation of retailing in the late 1800s and early

1900s. Sequentially, mass retailers displaced family-run stores and undermined the face-to-face commercial relationships valued in small towns and urban ethnic enclaves. By the 1920s, the economic contest reached the political arena, where businesses, consumers, and politicians deliberated the future of American retailing. The battle culminated in the 1936 passage of the Robinson-Patman Act, designed to control the spread of chain stores. Ultimately, Robinson-Patman failed, permitting the rise of deep-discount retailers like Kmart, Target, and Wal-Mart—the subject of Chapter 14.

The International Industry of Recorded Sound

ANDRÉ MILLARD

The period from 1900 to 1920 marked the high point in the fortunes of the talking machine. With a small interruption caused by the depression of 1907, each succeeding year of the twentieth century brought higher sales. A record player stood proudly in the sitting rooms of millions of Americans, and there was little to challenge its position as the leading form of home entertainment. Where once only the upper classes could enjoy fine music, usually in the form of a piano, now everybody could afford it. The phonograph had ushered in the age of mechanical entertainment in America, and it was to prepare the ground for many other high-tech entertainers in the future.

The Big Three—[the Edison, Victor, and Columbia companies]—had succeeded in the daunting task of mass-producing complex machines and pressing millions of exact duplicates of recordings. They had built massive industrial plants. Their interests ranged from stockpiles of chemicals used in their records to contracts with well-known musicians and singers. They had recorded some of the world's greatest musical figures and made a permanent record of their art.

Each of the Big Three did millions of dollars of business each year. In 1914 the U.S. census found that there were eighteen manufacturing establishments in the industry with a total value of output that exceeded $27 million. Of this total $4 million was accounted for by Edison and $16 million by Victor. . . .

The large companies lived in an atmosphere of friendly rivalry that came far short of the all-out trade war which had erupted at the turn of the century. They discussed forming a cartel to fix prices and adjudicate patent disputes but failed to bring it into being. . . . [T]he Big Three managed to maintain their prices. Profits were high enough to tolerate the numerous small competitors who made inferior machines and nondescript records.

The Big Three perfectly represented the "Age of Big Business" in America. All were committed to high-volume, low-cost production, and all managed a national network of dealers. They were all vertically integrated operations, like many of the large industrial concerns at that time. Businessmen such as Andrew Carnegie, John D. Rockefeller, and Henry Ford had assembled vast enterprises in which they controlled every aspect of manufacture from the provision of raw materials to the marketing of the final product. The advantages of this strategy were the elimination of the

André Millard, *America on Record: A History of Recorded Sound* (New York: Cambridge University Press, 1995), pp. 65–79. Reprinted by permission of Cambridge University Press.

middleman and complete control over production. The large talking-machine companies also followed this strategy, supervising the process from recording studio to record store.

Edison, Easton, and Johnson [the men who ran the Big Three] were no different from Carnegie or Rockefeller, but the challenges confronting them were more complex than those facing makers of steel or refiners of petroleum. In the talking-machine business, the raw materials were not only metal and chemicals but also the musical talents of those who sang into the recording horns. Each of the Big Three operated recording studios and maintained long-term contractual relationships with performers. As the first large-scale entertainment business, they had to be closely connected to the world of music. They had to keep abreast of technological advance[s] and the changing tastes of the audience for music: two disparate and volatile factors in the economic equation.

The technology and the music were part of an international movement of people and ideas. The technology had emerged from the intercourse between the United States and other developed industrial nations in Western Europe. . . . The mature industry of recorded sound continued to draw upon this international dialogue of technology.

While the technology of sound recording was formed in the United States and then diffused to Europe, musical styles and performers moved in the opposite direction. Europe was the center of the world of music: Milan, London, and Paris were the undisputed leaders of fashion and culture, both high and low. The great opera houses, leading concert halls, and trend-setting vaudeville acts were all to be found in Europe.

For these reasons the talking-machine companies had to operate internationally. They were first established in the United States and then in Europe. Edison formed a phonograph company in London in 1878 right after he invented the phonograph to promote the tinfoil machine. After the new "perfected" phonograph was unveiled at the West Orange laboratory in 1888, it was immediately despatched to England in the care of Col. George Gouraud, Edison's English agent and the proprietor of the Edison Phonograph Company of the British Isles. This company placed a large order for the new machines and set about marketing them in Europe. From the outset, the business relationship of England and the United States was critical in the international diffusion of recorded sound.

Emile Berliner followed Edison's practice of selling the rights of his inventions to foreign investors. He visited Germany in 1889 and arranged for some of his machines and records to be manufactured by a toy company. His gramophones were imported directly into England. . . . Berliner built a record-pressing factory in Hanover, Germany, to supply the requirements of several new European affiliates. . . .

The third member of the Big Three soon established itself in the European market. The Columbia Graphophone Company set up branches in Paris and London in 1899; these offices supervised its overseas operations. . . .

The production of [the opera singer Enrico] Caruso's historic recordings illustrates the international character of the industry. The records were made in Italy by an American in the pay of the English branch of the gramophone company. An executive of the Russian branch of the organization is said to have had the idea of specially marked celebrity records. Caruso's masters were delivered to the German company's pressing plant in Hanover, which provided duplicates for the European market on the HMV (His Master's Voice) label. They went to the United States to be duplicated at Victor's Camden [N.J.] plant. From this point they were marketed not only in the United States but in South America and the Far East.

Once the American companies had successfully established themselves in Europe, they began to extend their operations farther afield. Edison, Columbia, and Victor were soon operating in South America and the Pacific. The Japanese Victor Company (JVC) was formed to bring gramophones to the Far East. The British Gramophone Company looked to the Indian subcontinent as a vast new market for recorded sound. Australia was next to hear the music of imported talking machines. In 1907 the British and American gramophone companies refined their trading relationship in an ambitious agreement which divided the globe between them.

The outbreak of war in Europe in 1914 severely disrupted these international operations. . . . Although the United States remained neutral when hostilities broke out in 1914, the interruptions in world trade had an immediate effect on the American economy. The Royal Navy began a blockade of Germany, which cut off the supplies of chemicals to the United States, especially phenol, which was an important ingredient in making records. In 1914 Edison's factories were the largest importer of phenols in the United States. The German answer to the British blockade was to send their submarines into the North Atlantic to sink ships heading for the British Isles or France. This discouraged transatlantic travel, and soon the flow of master recordings from all points of Europe to the pressing plants in West Orange and Camden dried up. . . .

Although the companies had been claiming for years that the talking machine was an indispensable part of modern life, it took a world war to bring this fact home to their customers. With cabarets and music halls closed, and many entertainers enlisted, the public was now making its own music by playing the piano or by listening to the phonograph at home. The companies could now claim with some justification that "we are no longer manufacturing a specialty but a standard product of such importance in home comfort as to be a necessity."

While growing ever more popular at home, the talking machine became an essential part of military life. The record companies had tried to persuade customers that music could evoke all sorts of pleasurable sensations and rekindle fond memories. The war proved that nothing could remind a soldier of home better than music. Sales of machines boomed. Every billet and army camp had one, and even in the front lines one could hear the refrain of a popular song coming from a tin horn.

At war's end there was a surge of consumer spending, and sales of records and players rose encouragingly. The 1920 sales year was the best ever for the Edison organization, which sold goods amounting to $22 million. Yet Edison was not optimistic about the future and warned his executives to prepare for a harsh, competitive business environment in the coming years. His gloomy expectations were not far wrong, for after a brilliant beginning, the decade of the 1920s proved to be a nightmare for the talking-machine industry.

The basic problem was that there were too many companies competing in a market that was already showing signs of saturation. The dominance of the Big Three and the atmosphere of calm stability came to an end when many new ventures crowded into what had become a very profitable business. In 1914 there had been 18 companies in the industry of recorded sound, but by 1918 this number had increased to an astounding 166. The attraction of this business is not hard to find; the value of its products had shot up from $27 million in 1914 to $158 million in 1918, an increase of over 500 percent in 4 years. The boom in sales and profits was not the only factor enticing entrepreneurs. Most of the basic patents for phonographs and gramophones had expired by 1917, which removed a serious barrier to new entrants. . . .

The foreign market for American machines and records had provided an important outlet for excess production, but this dried up when European products were made to compete with American exports. It did not take too long until the leading European concerns began to look to the United States as a market. The Carl Lindstrom group of companies operated in Central Europe, and it owned important labels such as Odeon and Parlophone. . . . It offered a full line of models, from $15 to $175, and a record catalogue strong in the classics.

The typical new entrant was a small company whose products—machine, records, or both—were priced low. They usually depended on the recording and manufacturing facilities of other companies. Many bought masters from recording studios and paid for them to be pressed in record factories. For example, the Regal and Cameo companies had their 50¢ records pressed by a private record maker, the Scranton Button Works, and sold them through Macy's and other chain stores. Oriole's 25¢ records were pressed from masters acquired from Emerson.

The Big Three were not directly challenged by any of the new entrants. . . . Yet the sheer number of competitors continually forced down prices and eroded profit lines. When department and general stores added cheap records to their shelves, the trade of the Big Three's retail networks was reduced. Edison's predictions about cut-price competition turned out to be true, and by 1921 prices had slumped. The Big Three saw their sales decline precipitously: Edison went from 140,000 disc players sold in 1920 to 32,343 in 1921; Victor from 560,000 to 320,000; and Columbia went bankrupt.

The normally optimistic *Talking Machine World* now had to admit that the market for machines was saturated. Over 20 years of mass-producing and marketing basically the same product—the spring-motor disc player—had put a phonograph or gramophone in every American home, but what then? The only hope for the industry was the continuing sale of records. In the period up to 1914, the focus had been on perfecting mass production and improving the technology of recorded sound, but after 1919 the emphasis was on pushing sales, especially sales of records. Companies large and small now staked their survival on a record catalogue that kept pace with the changing taste in popular music. The challenge of mass-producing complex machines had now evolved into the problem of accurately predicting the public's musical needs and recording music to suit it. The manager of Edison's Phonograph Division concluded that "the company who correctly solves these problems will dominate the trade." He was absolutely right.

The small companies suffered an initial disadvantage in this struggle, because the Big Three had signed up most of the well-known classical singers and musicians and had exclusive contracts with the stars of vaudeville. It was simple necessity that pushed the independent companies into recording new types of music and exploiting new audiences for recorded sound. Although their recordings had none of the prestige of the Big Three's classical records, they did bring important new music such as blues and jazz to the American public.

In the nineteenth century, when the phonograph was still a novelty the market for recordings was ill defined. Records were a generic product sold by quantity and not by musical type. The introduction of the high-priced celebrity record at the turn of the century created the market for "good music" and helped to focus marketing efforts onto the middle classes. But as competition in the business increased in the 1920s, companies were forced to seek customers at both ends of the social ladder.

A changing economy at the time of World War I created new audiences for recorded sound. The United States became the arsenal of democracy. Those who stayed at home enjoyed prosperity and high incomes, especially the people at the lower end of the social scale. The business strategy of "a phonograph in every home" naturally led manufacturers to exploit every segment of the market, including minorities and the working classes—even the low-paid immigrants who toiled in their factories.

In order to gain access to the minority markets in American cities, the companies began a program of recording music for narrowly defined ethnic groups—hoping that such specialized recordings would encourage these groups to purchase players and, sooner or later, regular records. "How Recognition of the Pride of Race Will Increase Record Sales" was the title of an article in *Talking Machine World.*

Although every minority audience in the cities was addressed by record companies, rural dwellers had been largely ignored by them. The rise in prices of agricultural commodities during the war boosted personal incomes in the South and brought a talking machine within the budget of many more people. New industrial jobs in Southern cities and ports also made this market more attractive to the record companies, who now began to cultivate the custom of rural blacks and what they called "the cheaper white trade" in the South and West. A talking machine was a highly desirable luxury good in many of these homes. As one commentator noted, "In the delta of Mississippi it was not unusual to find a ramshackle carpetless darky shanty boasting a bright red mahogany $250 Victrola."

Until World War I, African Americans were concentrated in the rural South and several Southern cities and therefore not considered to constitute much of a market by the record companies, who were all based in the Northeast. The "Great Migration" of over a million African Americans from the South changed this situation. Hundreds of thousands of them moved to cities like Chicago and Detroit. At the same time the flood of European immigrants was reduced to a trickle by the war. Not only were there large concentrations of black customers in large cities but also their incomes had risen as a result of the war—the lack of white labor gave them a rare opportunity for high-paying factory work. The long lines outside record stores on Friday nights was evidence of the importance of this segment of the market.

In February 1920 the recording director of the OKeh Company of New York agreed to record a young black singer called Mamie Smith. Her initial release sold well enough in Harlem music stores to bring her back to the studio to make some more masters. Her recording of "Crazy Blues" was an instant success. It sold at the unprecedented rate of about 7,500 records a week and achieved total sales in excess of 70,000.

"Crazy Blues" began a musical fad in America which encompassed recordings of all sorts of female singers and all types of musical styles gathered together under the loose title of "blues," which had first been introduced as commercial music by W. C. Handy. Although the initial audience for this music was black, it soon crossed over into the white mainstream popular market, where the really high sales were. The record companies scrambled to sign up female blues artists. Records of love lost and faithless lovers poured out from their presses as fast as they could record them. The leading artists of this genre were Ma Rainey, Bessie Smith, Ida Cox, and Alberta Hunter, but there were hundreds more, and most of them are now forgotten. . . .

Many record companies and manufacturers of talking machines went out of business in the 1920s. . . . Those who remained in the record business had to adjust to bitter competition and the changing musical tastes of the 1920s. As the Victor recording manager had said about "jass" records back in 1917: "This dance music changes from day to day and this [jazz] might be something entirely new which we should get after at once." Failure to respond quickly to new fads could result in a precipitous drop in sales.

The downfall of the Edison company proved beyond any doubt that artistic considerations now outweighed technology in the talking machine business. It was entirely appropriate that the company founded by the great inventor should focus on the machine and not the music on the records. In 1913 Edison finally deserted the cylinder format and introduced the Edison Diamond Disc player. Announced as Edison's "greatest triumph" and his "masterpiece," it was the final culmination of years of experiments to perfect the recording of sound. The reproduction was so good, it was claimed, that it was superior to listening to live music in the imperfect acoustic environment of the opera house. The Diamond Discs themselves were marketed not as mere recordings but "re-creations" of the original sounds.

The selling point of this machine was its diamond-tipped stylus, but the real innovation was in the composition of the Edison discs, which were made of a new material based on phenol resins. It was called *condensite* and was similar to Bakelite. A hard, easily molded plastic, it provided the best recording surface to date. The first releases were plagued with an annoying surface noise, but the improved discs introduced after World War I had superior reproduction. The sound of the human voice was so well reproduced by an Edison Diamond Disc that the company sponsored a series of "tone tests" to illustrate how close a recording could come to the real thing. Although there was a great deal of showmanship involved in the "experiment," and the singers were practiced in duplicating the sound of the phonograph, audiences did find it difficult to distinguish the sound of a machine from that of the human voice. Edison had proved his point.

Although the "phonograph with a soul" marked a brilliant innovation, it was hampered by the limited selection of records. Edison insisted on personally approving every recording issued on a Diamond Disc. His opinionated views about music were probably more serious a handicap in this task than his partial deafness. He disliked modern dance music, and this was an enormous disadvantage in the popular music market. When his sales staff carried out customer surveys, they found that their listeners liked the sound quality of the Diamond Discs but would not buy them because of the unappealing musical selections. This was the main reason why Edison's sales dropped throughout the 1920s.

Back in the 1880s the content of the recording counted for nothing. The little experience gained in selling records indicated that the public would buy whatever they could get. By the time of World War I, the type of music recorded was an important consideration; by the 1920s it had become the main factor in the success or failure of a phonograph company.

Marketing Pyrex Ovenware

REGINA LEE BLASZCZYK

In 1925, marketing experts at the J. Walter Thompson (JWT) advertising agency met with managers from Corning Glass Works to discuss the future of Pyrex Ovenware. Much to Corning's dismay, American consumers had lost interest in the company's miraculous glass cooking ware. Introduced in 1915 with fanfare, Pyrex initially sold well, due to its novelty as the only glass baking ware on the market. By the mid-1920s, Pyrex Ovenware foundered. Perplexed, Corning managers hoped to learn why with JWT's help.

The JWT-Corning liaison was fitting to the historical moment. Both companies had mastered new businesses to thrive in the prosperous, consumption-oriented 1920s. One of the nation's top advertising agencies, JWT billed itself as a full-service firm versed in copywriting, layout, package design, and market research. From its headquarters on Lexington Avenue in New York City, JWT served an impressive national portfolio of clients that included such leading manufacturers as Aunt Jemima Mills; Andrew Jergens; Lever Brothers; Libby, McNeill & Libby; and Swift & Company. JWT president Stanley B. Resor loved to boast about his clients' sales figures when touting his firm's accomplishments. The Andrew Jergens account was a case in point. To resuscitate faltering sales of a moisturizer, JWT had helped this Cincinnati manufacturer to rename, repackage, reprice, and readvertise the product as Jergens Lotion. In magazine advertisements, the agency had depicted this utilitarian hand cream as a magical potion that could turn a housewife's harsh paws into smooth hands fit for a Vanderbilt heiress or a Hollywood movie star. In essence, JWT's marketing and advertising effort had turned a functional line into a product with transformative powers. As a result, sales increased significantly.

Achievements like Jergens Lotion stemmed from Resor's pluck and behind-the-scenes work by JWT's staff of experts. Anxious to gain competitive advantage in the cutthroat advertising world, Resor filled the upper echelons of his agency with specialists from various disciplines. By mid-decade, JWT's all-star cast included three art directors, several commercial photographers, a slew of copywriters versed in the "woman's viewpoint," a top-notch behavioral psychologist, and a director of consumer research. With this cadre of college and university graduates, by the mid-1920s JWT was uniquely positioned to serve clients like Corning Glass Works.

Written for this volume by Regina Lee Blaszczyk. For more on the history of Pyrex, see Regina Lee Blaszczyk, *Imagining Consumers: Design and Innovation from Wedgwood to Corning* (Baltimore, Md.: Johns Hopkins University Press, 2000), pp. 208–248.

Located in upstate New York, Corning was one of the nation's few high-technology glass manufacturers; its fate was inexorably linked to other high-tech companies. Pyrex Ovenware was the only consumer line in Corning's product portfolio. Since the late nineteenth century, Corning had focused on making producers' goods; it profited by making custom signal glass for the railroads and light bulb envelopes and filament for the electrical manufacturers. As the U.S. chemicals industry took off in the 1920s, companies such as E. I. du Pont de Nemours & Company turned to Corning for steady supplies of heat-resistant laboratory glassware. Orders rolled in intermittently and unpredictably; enormous retorts, bizarre beakers, spiral tubing, and other strange forms could only be made by craftsmen using traditional production techniques. To fill demand in this lucrative niche market, Corning needed to maintain a workforce of skilled glassblowers. When orders for laboratory ware were low, glassblowers needed something to do. With Pyrex Ovenware, a foreman could keep them busy making pie plates, custard cups, cake pans, and other baking dishes. In short, Pyrex Ovenware filled out the product ensemble necessary for full employment and constituted a tiny but critical component of Corning's product line. Corning's managers needed Pyrex Ovenware.

In their eyes, Pyrex Ovenware was a miracle of modern industrial science, created for up-to-date consumers concerned with efficiency and cleanliness. Made from the same formulas used for chemical beakers, Pyrex cookware was the first household glass that baked in the oven and went from there to the cold refrigerator without breaking. For generations, cooks had used unsightly metal, ceramic, or enamel pans for baking meats, breads, casseroles, souffles, pies, and cakes. Pyrex Ovenware could cook more evenly, thoroughly, and quickly. Impervious to foods, it was clean and sanitary. Smooth and transparent, Pyrex even looked nicer than conventional utensils, which tarnished, chipped, and rusted.

Consumers, however, were not impressed. Corning managers had tried several tactics to stimulate interest in the product: they consulted home economists on what women liked, hired salesmen knowledgeable about the hardware stores that sold Pyrex, and sponsored window display contests for retailers. Still, women refused to buy Pyrex Ovenware, sticking by conventional utensils. By the mid-1920s, Pyrex Ovenware was a thorn in Corning's side. To tackle the problem, Corning turned to JWT.

As a pioneer in market research, JWT was well equipped to help Corning's managers learn more about the wants, needs, and desires of Pyrex Ovenware consumers. JWT could boast of its dedication to "sound" research techniques for getting "the facts from the real consumer" largely due to the presence of research director Paul T. Cherington. Formerly with the Harvard Business School, Cherington had helped to found its Bureau of Business Research, a think tank that pioneered the study of industry's marketing problems, and had served as president of the American Marketing Association. At JWT from 1922 to 1931, Cherington supervised a staff that investigated consumers' attitudes toward household goods, including cereal, spices, makeup, toilet paper, mattresses, silverware, and rugs. The aim was to gather information about purchasing habits that firms could use to improve product performance, augment ad copy, and design better artwork. Cherington's approach appealed to Corning's executives, who hoped the new mechanism of market research could establish a dialogue between the factory and household consumers.

Cherington's past research had convinced him of the independence, resilience, and power of the consumer. He had thought long and hard about key issues that pre-occupied the advertising profession, and his ideas about demand, taste, and fashion are especially pertinent to the Pyrex story. Cherington believed that demand stemmed from the "fussy and troublesome ideas" that people had about particular products. These preferences emanated from the basic human need to express individuality or taste through the careful selection, display, and use of objects. Cherington admitted that forces large and small engaged people's imaginations and ultimately reshaped fashion. The challenge before the nation's new experts on consumption—its product designers, department-store stylists, and advertising executives—was not to manipu-late desire but "to please and satisfy the public." From his perspective, the "balance of power" in the marketplace rested with the "buying side," and "the measure of the manufacturer's or merchant's skill" was the degree to which the firm responded to consumers. Persuasively, Cherington spoke about consumer sovereignty, whether the product was packaged food or ready-to-wear and whether his audience was statisti-cians or retailers.

By the mid-1920s, Cherington's strong convictions situated him squarely in the middle of two fiery debates that preoccupied the advertising business. Few advertis-ing executives disagreed with the journalist for *Nation's Business* who declared that "fact finding" constituted a new "economic necessity," but they hotly debated two best-way issues: how to get the right facts about consumers and how to use those facts to design advertising campaigns.

The first disagreement pitted advocates of the "man-on-the-street" school of imagining consumers against proponents of the new field of market research, includ-ing Cherington. To learn about potential consumers, practitioners of the first approach visited stores, spoke to shoppers, and formulated generalizations about tastes based on observations. While these observers claimed the ability to judge a woman's social class from her clothing, hairstyle, makeup, and manners, market research advocates pointed to flaws in this tactic. From their perspective, the growth of an impersonal retailing system made it difficult to engage consumers in friendly, truthful conver-sation on the selling floor. Just as important, rising living standards had allowed more people to step through the portal of consumer society. Economic prosperity meant that women could easily dress beyond their means, introducing the trouble-some possibility of misreading the selected shopper.

To guard against these problems, market researchers advocated a more scientific approach: the audience survey. By the 1920s, big businesses like Procter and Gamble Company depended on this method to collect measurable data about the potential purchasers of packaged foods. These early audience surveys consisted of practices like canvassing neighborhoods on a door-to-door basis, tallying return coupons, interviewing shoppers, and compiling demographic statistics. Cherington relied on these techniques.

Under his guidance, JWT's research department developed a consumer classifi-cation system that shaped the agency's work on the Pyrex account. Cherington's ABCD system categorized households by income, occupation, and education, so as to determine what different groups wanted. Cherington was one of the first mar-ket researchers to classify consumers by social classes. Under his model, Class A referred to homes with live-in servants and $10,000-plus incomes; Class B, middle-class houses "personally directed by intelligent women"; Class C, the "industrial classes," including mechanics, mill operators, and tradesmen; and Class D, unskilled laborers, immigrants, and blacks earning less than $2,000. Cherington aimed to get the facts about those Americans with the greatest purchasing power. In his view, the consumers that mattered to products like Pyrex Ovenware belonged to the A category, representing the [high] "class" audience for luxury goods, and the B-C groups, constituting a larger "mass" market.

Once researchers had accumulated consumer feedback on particular products, JWT executives debated the best way to use that data in advertising campaigns. Cherington supported the truth-in-advertising movement, introduced by *Printers' Ink* in 1911, endorsed by the Associated Advertising Clubs of the World in 1912, and invigorated by the efficiency drives of the Great War. To him, corporate attempts to mislead consumers were unethical; responsible advertising agencies must present the hard facts in a straightforward and truthful manner.

Ideologically, Cherington's commitment to truth-based, or "reason why," advertising placed him in direct opposition to fellow JWT executive John B. Watson, father of the newer practice of psychological advertising. Watson, who had joined JWT in 1920, had previously been a nationally known behavioral psychologist on the faculty of The Johns Hopkins University. Like Cherington, he believed that experts could dissect desire: "The consumer is to the manufacturer, the department stores, and the advertising agencies," he told managerial trainees at R. H. Macy & Company in 1922, "what the green frog is to the physiologist." Beyond this point, Watson parted ways with Cherington, for he disagreed with the research director's belief in consumer sovereignty. At Johns Hopkins, Watson had studied the effects of conditioning on humans, concluding that environment more than heredity influenced behavior. Watson's experiments had startling implications for advertising practitioners. If external factors alone kindled response, those who understood psychological principles could manipulate the innate emotions—fear, rage, and love—that drove all behavior. Based on emotional appeals, Watson's exploitative strategy suited disposable goods such as Jergens Lotion, which promised to alleviate consumers' fears of inadequacy by improving personal appearance. Resor so admired the results of Watson's stimulus-response campaigns that the psychologist, by the middle of the decade, found himself a vice president at JWT.

While Watson studied human emotions, Cherington focused on gathering the facts about Pyrex Ovenware and its consumers. At first glance, it may seem odd to find two men with such different ideas working for the same company. In the 1920s, the advertising agency was a novel form of business, tracing its origins back only to the turn of the century. This relatively new environment encouraged experimentation. As agencies searched for best practices, they tried different approaches to campaign development. JWT found that Watson's psychological theories worked best for health and hygiene products, such as cosmetics, deodorant, or mouthwash. The "reason why" approach was more suited to consumer durables, such as Pyrex Ovenware. When buying throwaway goods on impulse, consumers willingly indulged in a bit of fantasy. When purchasing more costly items they meant to keep, consumers wanted the truth about price, utility, and durability. Watson and Cherington were flip sides of a coin; JWT could show either side, depending on the client.

In quest of the truth, Cherington and his staff collected the "trustworthy facts" about Pyrex consumers. Between 1925 and 1937, they completed forty-plus surveys of Pyrex retailers and users, seeking to ascertain how retailers and consumers viewed and used Pyrex. Almost immediately, the surveyors discovered that Pyrex's problems stemmed from Corning's disregard for consumer habits, tastes, and expectations. Efficient baking ware appealed most to middle- and upper-class women. By the mid-1920s, 75 percent of consumers surveyed in Class A and Class B homes in Ohio, New York, and New England owned some Pyrex dishes, acquired as gifts for weddings, birthdays, holidays, and anniversaries. In contrast, Pyrex had barely penetrated Class C households. Some ten years after its introduction, baking ware remained a gift item for the "class" market rather than a staple for the "mass" market.

Cherington's research team found that price constituted the greatest barrier to Pyrex sales. Even consumers at the upper ends of the economic pyramid found ovenware too expensive to buy for themselves. Those making personal purchases of glass cookware ordered items from mail-order houses, which stocked competitively priced mock Pyrex. Although they willingly splurged on inexpensive household accents like colorful spatulas, buckets, and brooms, women clung to their cash rather than spend it on Pyrex Ovenware. They banked dollars for larger products like radios, record players, and refrigerators. Pyrex Ovenware was a novelty, and so it would remain as long as the price was high.

Starting in 1926, JWT executives applied what they learned from Cherington's audience surveys to an advertising campaign geared toward eroding consumer resistance to the high price of Pyrex. Ovenware fans reported that they preferred Corning glassware over metal utensils for three major reasons: 61 percent thought Pyrex baked better, 40 percent found it easier to clean, and 33 percent appreciated the oven-to-table concept. Five forms—pie plates, casseroles, bread pans, baking dishes, and custard cups—constituted 81 percent of the Pyrex in use. Armed with these data, JWT's copywriters applied their so-called fail-safe formula for giving "new expression" to "old desires" and created a series of fact-based campaigns. While they encouraged women's fantasies about romance with every purchase of Jergens Lotion, advertising executives saw little point in trying to scare, entice, or anger potential Pyrex purchasers. Surveys revealed that women appreciated Pyrex Ovenware as a vehicle for improving their families' culinary habits and a solution to burdensome chores—and not a winning weapon in the game of love. Everything about Pyrex baking ware, including its durability, efficiency, sturdiness, suggested the antithesis of Watson's stimulus-response model. Women did not buy glass baking dishes on impulse. Consumers splurged on Jergens Lotion, but they invested in Pyrex Ovenware.

The JWT Pyrex campaigns focused on "reason why" themes—good baking, economy, speed, and versatility—cast in an upbeat, modern mode that would appeal to Jazz Age consumers up and down the social scale. Typically, a large headline dominated each advertisement; the remaining space featured a dense narrative, a mail-in coupon, and several ovenware photographs in black and white. The text described the workmanship, appearance, price, and material of the product; generalized about the item's high performance standards; and testified to the line's unique qualities, especially its value. The realist-style photographs focused on the product, conveying an objective appearance, a look that suited Corning's self-image as a technological leader and Pyrex's identity as an efficient product for both the "class" and the "mass" markets. Masters of realism, JWT's photographers arranged Pyrex Ovenware in asymmetrical groups, positioned their cameras at oblique angles, and focused their lenses tightly and sharply to portray baking ware as a smart product. The JWT ad campaign transformed Pyrex Ovenware into a stylish consumer line, fitting for the fashion-conscious 1920s.

With the JWT Pyrex campaign, Corning became one of the nation's leading national advertisers of cooking utensils—to no avail. In 1927 and 1928, the glass-works' new advertisements appeared in six major mass-circulation magazines—*Woman's Home Companion, Ladies' Home Journal, Good Housekeeping, McCall's, Better Homes and Gardens,* and *Farmer's Wife*—read by women in Class A, B, and C homes. Although coupon returns suggested that women enjoyed reading the adver-tisements, sales figures demonstrated that the campaign was a failure. As consumers, women still refused to buy products they did not want even when bombarded by appealing, stylish images. Between 1926 and 1929, sales of Pyrex Ovenware hovered at around $1.5 million, much as they had earlier in the decade.

When the new advertising campaign failed to stimulate sales, JWT executives delved deeper into audience research. Additional audience surveys found two new factors circumscribing consumer appreciation. First, customers were disappointed with Pyrex's performance in the oven. Although it was the most sophisticated con-sumer glassware around, Pyrex Ovenware was not without technical flaws. The glassware could shatter in the oven if it chipped or cracked through ordinary use. Pyrex Ovenware came with a two-year money-back guarantee, but cooks who opened their stoves and found "glass and potatoes splattered all over" declined to return the dishes. Instead, they tossed the broken glass in the trash and turned their backs, exclaiming, "Thumbs down on Pyrex!"

Second, style-conscious shoppers reported boredom with Pyrex's standardized appearance, with "the same old thing year after year." Acclimated to the varieties of visual modernism that gained momentum in the 1920s, these women longed for fashionable cooking utensils. JWT's art department had tried to hit the style button with its smart advertising campaign, complete with modernistic photographs. Al-though Pyrex looked modern in the new advertisements, it was a disappointment in the stores. Costly and plain, Pyrex was a dowdy cousin of the fashionable consumer products that flooded the home-furnishings trade in the 1920s. Taking additional cues from the automobile industry, consumers reported that they wanted more shapes, colors, and even annual model changes in the Pyrex line.

By 1929, JWT experts grew frustrated by consumers' resistance to its forceful advertising campaigns. The hard lessons of the Pyrex experience were not wasted on JWT. The agency took consumers' stubbornness as verification of Cherington's theories about consumer sovereignty. In certain product categories, manufacturers could use advertising only to deepen existing markets, rather than build entirely new ones. The Pyrex effort showed that household durable goods fell into this category.

In the long run, JWT and Corning came to understand that the "best solution" to the Pyrex predicament lay in manufacturing rather than advertising. With both "class" and "mass" markets in mind, JWT proposed a two-part "manufacturing solution" to the Pyrex Ovenware problem. First, if Corning were to find new ways to please more Class A consumers, the look of ovenware had to change. The line needed "new features, new colors, [and] lighter-weight articles." With these factory solu-tions, baking glass could take its rightful place among discerning consumers in the "class" market. Second, if Corning hoped to sell Pyrex to Class B and C consumers, the price had to be lower. Pyrex Ovenware was simply too expensive to become a kitchen staple in Class B and C homes. To reach this "mass" market, Corning needed to revamp Pyrex production to lower the retail price.

Ultimately, Corning managers achieved success in the mass market by pursuing a range of manufacturing solutions. Although scientifically advanced, Corning was nevertheless limited by the technical knowledge available to the glass industry at large. In the mid-1920s, Corning's engineers had succeeded in mechanizing the job of making light bulb envelopes. It took them another decade to build a cutting-edge factory that put Pyrex Ovenware on "straight-line production." Meanwhile, the firm in 1929 established the American glass industry's first test kitchen, where professional home economists versed in the "woman's viewpoint" collaborated with scientists, engineers, and designers to improve the look and performance of Pyrex. During the 1930s, Corning's home economists drew on feedback in JWT's consumer surveys and customer letters to redesign Pyrex Ovenware and create a new line of kitchen utensils, Top-of-Stove Ware. At the same time, Corning's accountants streamlined the ovenware line and made significant cuts to wholesale prices.

When the new Pyrex factory opened in 1937, Corning's managers had fully implemented the manufacturing solution proposed by JWT. A pie plate that retailed for a dollar in 1920 sold for twenty-five cents in 1938; a two-dollar casserole was sixty-five cents, and so on. The road to success had by no means been straight and narrow. By the late 1930s, Pyrex Ovenware was on its way to reaching the "mass" market.

Mass Marketing Meets Main Street: Department Stores, Mail Order, and the Chain Store Menace

JONATHAN J. BEAN

In the years after 1914, small business advocates called for new antitrust legislation to counter the rise of big business in retailing. This concern with preserving the market share of small retailers had its roots in the late nineteenth century, when merchants faced competition from department stores and mail-order firms. However, a more serious threat to small business emerged in the 1920s and 1930s, with the spread of chain stores. This chain store "menace" sparked a national movement that resulted in the passage of state and federal legislation regulating mass-marketers.

Until the late nineteenth century, small businesses handled nearly all of the nation's retail trade. Markets were small, and merchants frequently enjoyed a local monopoly within their line of trade. This situation changed with the birth of department stores in America's largest cities. Alexander T. Stewart constructed the first large department store in 1846 in New York City. Other department stores—including Marshall Field's, Lazarus, and Macy's—appeared after the Civil War. Urbanization had created large, concentrated markets served by new means of mass transit, including electric trolleys and subways. Department stores took advantage of this mass market by selling a high volume of goods at low prices. These stores also broke with tradition by adopting fixed prices, relying heavily on advertising, carrying a variety of goods, and offering a satisfaction guarantee. Elegant displays turned department stores into "palaces of consumption" that dazzled the American consumer.

Department stores provoked fear and outrage among small merchants and among newspaper editors, who depended on the advertising revenues of small business owners. Apocalyptic articles attacking this "colossus of trade" appeared in big-city newspapers. In 1889, the author of one such article in the *Chicago Tribune* complained that "when each fresh department was added to Marshall Field store it was like a cyclone had gone forth among the smaller houses which were in the same line of business. . . . Against such a power . . . nothing could stand." The *Philadelphia Gazette* provided a forum for another merchant, who attacked the "greedy, grasping and godless spirit" that led department stores to destroy smaller businesses. This merchant traced the origins of the menace to Alexander Stewart, whom he described as "one of the meanest merchants that ever lived."

Small merchants did more than complain. Trade associations representing small druggists and booksellers boycotted manufacturers who sold to department stores, but without much success. In the 1880s and 1890s, small retailers convinced state legislators to introduce bills banning the construction of new department stores and imposing special taxes on existing ones. These bills never became law, in part because small retailers in the largest cities were the only ones concerned with the issue, and they simply lacked the votes needed to secure passage of state legislation discriminating against department stores.

They were no more successful at the federal level. The Industrial Commission, a body created by Congress in 1898 to study the "trust question," investigated the impact of department stores on small retailers and concluded that this new form of retailing benefited consumers. The investigation also revealed that many small retailers had imitated department store methods, leading the commission to conclude that "the growth of the department store must be regarded as being a benefit to the small retailer who has profited by incorporation of many of its techniques." . . . Furthermore, in the early twentieth century, the competitive pressure on independent merchants eased when department stores began specializing in luxury items, leaving the market for other goods to smaller retailers.

Unlike their urban cousins, small-town merchants faced very little direct competition from department stores. Railroads offered excursion trips to big cities, but the inconvenience of having to travel far from home discouraged most residents from making the trip. But small-town merchants did encounter competition from the mail-order firm, another new form of mass marketing. Aaron Montgomery Ward created the first national mail-order firm in 1872, and his firm was soon joined by Sears, Roebuck, and Company. Ward and Sears took advantage of the nation's newly constructed railway net to ship goods to small towns across America. Later, the creation of Rural Free Delivery (1896) and parcel post (1913) enabled these companies to mail goods to the customer's doorstep. By buying in bulk and eliminating the middleman, these mail-order companies undercut small-town merchants. Mail-order firms sold an enormous variety of goods (Sears carried 100,000 items in 1908) and backed them up with a liberal return policy ("Satisfaction Guaranteed or Your

Money Back"). The guarantee transformed the way American merchants did business: to remain competitive with department stores and mail-order firms, smaller merchants had to abandon the old philosophy of *caveat emptor* ("buyer beware") in favor of *caveat venditor* ("seller beware"). The notion that "the customer is always right" became part of the new way of doing business. Meanwhile, farmers, who had long resented the high prices and limited selection of goods offered by small merchants, eagerly sent away for the catalogs of Montgomery Ward and Sears, Roebuck. (The latter became known as "the Farmer's Bible.")

Consumers might have benefited, but small merchants felt threatened by mail order. Many merchants refused to call the companies by name; they referred to them as "Shears and Rawbuck" and "Monkey Ward." Southern merchants played on racism by spreading rumors that Sears, Ward, and other mail-order magnates were black. Newspaper editors alleged that mail order was "making commercial graveyards of once prosperous towns," while local chambers of commerce organized "trade at home" campaigns encouraging residents to shop in town rather than through the mail. . . .

The verbal heat generated by the controversy over department stores and mail-order catalogs was out of all proportion to the amount of market share that small retailers lost to these mass-marketers. As late as 1920, department stores and mail-order firms accounted for less than 10 percent of total retail sales. But small merchants soon faced an even greater threat in the form of the chain store, which extended the "visible hand" into retailing and into America's small towns. The chain store's advantage lay in its low operating costs and in the discounts it received for quantity purchases. Chain stores eliminated services offered by traditional merchants, including credit and home delivery, but offered lower prices to attract customers.

This form of mass marketing spread rapidly in the 1920s, as the automobile connected small towns to the larger urban markets. Almost overnight, the rise of the chain store upset the world of the independent merchant, destroying the local monopolies enjoyed by many small business owners. Between 1919 and 1929, the chains increased their share of retail sales from 4 percent to 20 percent, and the nation's first modern chain, The Great Atlantic & Pacific Tea Company (A&P), increased its number of stores from 4,600 to nearly 16,000. The total number of chain-store units in the country rose from 300 in 1900 to over 100,000 in 1930. Chain-store sales continued to increase during the cost-conscious depression years; by 1935, the chains handled 23 percent of all retail sales. The "Chain-Store Age" had dawned on America.

Many small retailers responded to chain-store competition by improving their service and selection of goods. Some merchants imitated chain-store methods by cutting costs and increasing turnover, while others formed voluntary chains to secure quantity discounts. . . .

Independent retailers also engaged in public relations efforts aimed at diminishing the appeal of the chain store. For example, local store owners sponsored advertising campaigns encouraging Americans to "trade at home" and joined together to boycott manufacturers who sold to chain stores. Organized merchants promoted "fair trade" by urging the government to amend the antitrust laws to allow manufacturers to fix minimum retail prices in an attempt to overcome the chain stores' competitive advantage. However, these attempts at persuasion failed to change the attitudes of consumers or manufacturers. Most manufacturers continued to sell discount goods, and Americans continued to buy them.

This economic contest soon played itself out in the political arena, as ambitious politicians seized upon anti-chain-store sentiment and used the issue to attract the votes of independent merchants and others critical of big business. Although the United States had been urbanizing for nearly a century, most Americans still lived on farms or in towns with a population of less than 10,000, and many of these small-town Americans viewed the chain store as a menace to their way of life. . . .

. . . The critics claimed that the young men who worked in chain stores could not earn enough to support a family and that "girls are employed at wages so low that the moral status of this country is in danger." Thus, in their view, the chain store threatened the most basic unit of society, the family. The anti-chain-store movement also gained particular momentum in the South and West, where politicians played on the long-standing populist fear of outside corporations' controlling the local economy. In this area of the country, critics propagated the notion that chain stores were part of a Wall Street conspiracy aimed at making small-town workers and consumers dependent on the absentee owners of large corporations.

Despite all this hubbub, the chain store did have its defenders. Government statistics showed that chain stores paid higher wages and provided better working conditions for their employees than did their smaller competitors. The chains also responded to the torrent of criticism by hiring managers from the local communities and encouraging them to act as civic leaders. Supporters of the chain stores considered their lower prices a community asset, since the savings remained with local residents. Finally, business writers noted that many small retailers had learned to survive in an economic world inhabited by large chain stores, and they predicted that there would be room enough for both big and small business.

These positive arguments failed to sway those Americans who feared that the rapid rise of the chain store might mean the end of a cherished way of life. This fear first found expression in a Maryland state law, passed in 1927, that prohibited the expansion of chain stores and imposed a progressive tax on the chains based on the number of units they owned. A circuit court judge struck the law down, however, on the grounds that it denied chain stores the equal protection of the laws under the Fourteenth Amendment. Consequently, between 1927 and 1930, few states considered chain tax legislation, because lawyers assumed that the courts would nullify such laws. Then, in 1931, the U.S. Supreme Court upheld the legality of chain taxes imposed in Indiana and North Carolina. The Court ruled that the larger size of chain stores made them qualitatively different from their single-store competitors, and, therefore, that state legislatures could discriminate between the two types of retailers. This decision opened the floodgate to anti-chain-store legislation: other states, desperate for sources of revenue during the depression, passed similar measures, and by 1939, twenty-seven states had enacted some form of chain tax legislation.

These taxes did not impose much of a burden on most chain stores, but they did squeeze grocery chains and filling stations. Operating on exceptionally narrow profit margins, grocery chains could not pass the cost on to the consumer, and they lost market share in the late 1930s. Chain taxes also affected the distribution of gasoline through filling stations, another chain that operated on a thin profit margin. This taxation encouraged petroleum refiners to convert their wholly owned outlets into franchises. Franchising motivated dealers to increase sales and benefited both the oil companies and their franchisees. Thus, this anti-chain-store legislation helped give birth to the "franchise revolution" that would later transform retailing in America. . . .

During the Great Depression, disgruntled small business owners also urged the federal government to adopt measures aimed at restricting the buying power of the chain store. Thus, under the National Recovery Administration, independent wholesalers and retailers tried unsuccessfully to limit quantity discounts. At the same time, small business people sought judicial relief from price discrimination by bringing cases under Section 2 of the Clayton Antitrust Act. This law offered inadequate protection, however, because while it prohibited price discrimination, it permitted discounts made because of differences in the quantity or quality of the goods sold (manufacturers did not have to relate the size of their discount to actual cost savings). In their interpretations of the law, the courts ruled that a manufacturer had the right to freely determine discount schedules. This interpretation restricted the scope of FTC action, and the agency hesitated to use the law against chain stores. . . .

[Along with tire dealers who faced competition from Sears' new retail stores,] wholesale grocers led the drive to limit quantity discounts. Like independent retailers, wholesalers had lost market share to the chain stores. Chain stores acted as wholesalers by performing the functions of distribution (shipping, warehousing, etc.), and like wholesalers, they received "functional" discounts from manufacturers. Organized wholesalers sought legislation to eliminate this competition. Thus, in May 1935, a lawyer for the United States Wholesale Grocers' Association (USWGA) drafted a bill to amend Section 2 of the Clayton Act. The proposed amendment protected the functional discounts of wholesalers while requiring manufacturers to cost-justify their discounts to chain stores. The bill offered a narrow definition of allowable cost savings; chain stores would have to pay a share of the manufacturer's total cost even if they did not use all of the services reflected in these costs. The authors of the bill still feared that discounts, even if they were justified, might be so large as to foster monopoly. . . .

The wholesalers brought their bill to the attention of Representative Wright Patman (D.-Tex.), a fiery populist known for his hatred of big business. In April 1935, a Texarkana grocer approached Patman with the USWGA proposal in hand. The grocer told Patman that the wholesale grocers had chosen him to introduce this legislation because he was "an untiring worker and never know[s] defeat." Moreover, as chairman of a special committee investigating the lobbying activities of chain stores, Patman seemed the perfect vehicle for this legislation. Patman relished the opportunity to lead the anti-chain-store fight in Congress, and on 5 June 1935 he introduced the bill in the House.

The measure also attracted the support of Democratic leaders in Congress and the approval of the Roosevelt administration. On June 23, Senate Majority Leader Joseph T. Robinson (D.-Ark.) offered a companion bill in the Senate. Robinson's endorsement reflected the popularity of the issue in the South. During the next year, other prominent southern politicians, including Representatives Millard Tydings (D.-Md.) and John E. Miller (D.-Ark.), helped push the bills through Congress. Popular support for anti-chain-store legislation was reaching its peak in the South, and these congressmen hoped to exploit the political potential of the issue. . . .

Although it began as a piece of special-interest legislation, the bill's sponsors offered the Robinson-Patman Act as a panacea for the ills afflicting small business and the nation at large. In the first place, Patman's bill gave expression to anti-chain-store sentiment. Like many of his rural constituents, the Texas congressman saw the chain store as part of a Wall Street conspiracy aimed at controlling the retail trade of the nation. Yet Patman and Robinson insisted that they did not seek the death of the chain store; they claimed that their legislation simply promoted "fairness" by making the same discounts available to all purchasers. Thus Patman stated that his bill would instill "the Golden Rule in business." . . .

This view did not go unchallenged, however. As Robinson and Patman gathered support for their legislation, Representative Emanuel Celler (D.-N.Y.) led the opposition. Celler considered himself an advocate of small business but believed that the blatantly anticompetitive nature of the Patman bill violated the spirit of antitrust legislation. Celler dismissed the threat of a "chain store monopoly," noting that chains accounted for only a quarter of all retail sales. He cited the testimony of economists who predicted that the act would increase prices by preventing manufacturers from passing cost savings on to the consumer. Finally, Celler argued that Patman's bill would hurt small businesses because it would force the largest manufacturers to avoid price discrimination altogether by dealing with a few mass-distributors on a flat-price basis. Celler summarized his arguments by describing Patman's bill as "an antimanufacturers bill . . . an anticonsumer bill . . . an antifarmers bill. . . . It is an anti-almost everything" bill.

Celler had the support of chain stores, manufacturers, consumer advocates, and nearly all economists. Initially, these groups reacted slowly to the threat of the Robinson-Patman Act; but once it became clear that Congress would pass Patman's bill, they quickly organized, and over the course of a year they succeeded in watering down the proposed legislation. Passed in June 1936, the final act allowed manufacturers to grant functional discounts to chain stores as well as wholesalers. Sellers still had to justify their quantity discounts, but Congress broadened the definition of allowable cost savings. The act also included a "good faith" defense to charges of illegal price discrimination (i.e., discounts were legal if made in good faith to meet the price of a competitor). . . . Violations of the act were a criminal offense.

Like earlier antitrust legislation, the Robinson-Patman Act embodied a compromise among competing interests: it promised to preserve small business, enhance consumer welfare, and give due process to large chain stores and manufacturers. The act also applied a "rule of reason" by allowing manufacturers to make "reasonable" (i.e., cost-justified) discounts available to chain stores. The vague and ambiguous wording of the act meant that the Federal Trade Commission and the courts would have to define "reasonableness"; but congressional small business advocates did not intend to remain on the sidelines. In the coming years, they would encourage the FTC to vigorously enforce the law and, when necessary, to take sides with small business.

F U R T H E R   R E A D I N G

Benson, Susan Porter. *Counter Cultures: Saleswomen, Managers, and Customers in American Department Stores, 1890–1940* (1986).

Blaszczyk, Regina Lee. "No Place Like Home: Herbert Hoover and the American Standard of Living." In *Uncommon Americans: The Lives and Legacies of Herbert and Lou Henry Hoover,* ed. Timothy Walch (2003).

Butsch, Richard, ed. *For Fun and Profit: The Transformation of Leisure into Consumption* (1990).

Calder, Lendol Glen. *Financing the American Dream: A Cultural History of Consumer Credit* (1999).

Clarke, Sally H. "Consumer Negotiations." *Business and Economic History* 26 (1997): 101–122.

Cohen, Lizabeth. *Making a New Deal: Industrial Workers in Chicago, 1919–1939* (1990).

Deutsch, Tracey. "Making Change at the Grocery Store: Government, Grocers, and the Problem of Women's Autonomy in the Creation of Chicago's Supermarkets." Ph.D. dissertation, University of Wisconsin–Madison, 2001.

Elvins, Sarah. *Sales and Celebrations: Retailing and Regional Identity in Western New York State, 1920–1940* (2004).

Emmet, Boris, and John E. Jeuck. *Catalogues and Counters: A History of Sears, Roebuck and Company* (1950).

Ershkowitz, Herbert. *John Wanamaker: Philadelphia Merchant* (1999).

Ewen, Stuart. *Captains of Consciousness: Advertising and the Social Roots of the Consumer Culture* (1976).

Friedman, Walter A. *Birth of a Salesman: The Transformation of Selling in America* (2004).

Gudis, Catherine. *Buyways: Billboards, Automobiles, and the American Landscape* (2004).

Horowitz, Roger. *Putting Meat on the American Table: Taste, Technology, Transformation* (2006).

———, and Arwen P. Mohun, eds. *His and Hers: Gender, Consumption, and Technology* (1998).

Hower, Ralph M. *History of Macy's of New York, 1858–1919: Chapters in the Evolution of the Department Store* (1943).

Jacobs, Meg. *Pocketbook Politics: Economic Citizenship in Twentieth-Century America* (2005).

Jacobson, Lisa. *Raising Consumers: Children and the American Mass Market in the Early Twentieth Century* (2004).

Koehn, Nancy F. *Brand New: How Entrepreneurs Built Consumers' Trust from Wedgwood to Dell* (2001).

Leach, William. *Land of Desire: Merchants, Power, and the Rise of a New American Culture* (1993).

Lears, T. J. Jackson. *Fables of Abundance: A Cultural History of Advertising in America* (1994).

Marchand, Roland. *Advertising the American Dream: Making Way for Modernity, 1920–1940* (1985).

McNair, Malcolm P., and Eleanor G. May. *The American Department Store, 1920–1960* (1963).

Moskowitz, Marina. *Standard of Living: The Measure of the Middle Class in America* (2004).

Parr, Joy. *Domestic Goods: The Material, the Moral, and the Economic in the Postwar Years* (1999).

Strasser, Susan. *Satisfaction Guaranteed: The Making of the American Mass Market* (1995).

Tedlow, Richard S. *New and Improved: The Story of Mass Marketing in America* (1996).

Thomas, Bernice L. *America's 5 & 10 Cent Stores: The Kress Legacy* (1997).

Walsh, William I. *The Rise and Decline of the Great Atlantic and Pacific Tea Company* (1986).

Winkler, John K. *Five and Ten: The Fabulous Life of F. W. Woolworth* (1970).

CHAPTER
11

Times of Crisis:
From the Stock Market Crash
Through World War II,
1929–1945

In the presidential campaign of 1932, Democratic candidate Franklin D. Roosevelt (FDR) promised a "New Deal" to Americans who had experienced the 1929 stock market crash and three years of the worst depression in a generation. For business, FDR's New Deal signaled a retreat from the hands-off policies of the 1920s Republican administrations and a return to the activist government of the Progressive Era and World War I. Yet business soon learned that FDR's New Deal differed from Theodore Roosevelt's Square Deal in dramatic ways.

During the First New Deal, FDR asked business, labor, and consumer groups to collaborate under the guidance of the National Recovery Administration (NRA) to write "codes of fair competition" that limited output, so as to increase prices and wages. Such cooperation drew heavily on the associational strategies promoted by Republican Herbert Hoover during his commerce secretariat and presidency. Industries were accustomed to this approach, modeled after the interfirm collaborations characteristic of many trade associations. In his first term, FDR also tackled the financial crisis, initiating legislation to reorganize the banking system, reform the stock market, and insure bank deposits. Initially, many businessmen embraced the First New Deal, which seemed to put industrial and economic interests at the center of its recovery plan.

By 1934, criticism of the New Deal emerged, with some businesses sounding the loudest protests. Whereas businesses had once displayed the NRA's "Blue Eagle" to show solidarity, many ripped down their New Deal banners in disgust. Small companies took issue with the NRA's seeming favoritism toward large corporations, while others complained about the New Deal's welfare handouts, which they believed squelched the entrepreneurial spirit at the core of the American economic system.

When the U.S. Supreme Court unanimously struck down the National Industrial Recovery Act (NIRA) in Schechter Poultry Corporation v. United States *(1935), conservative business organizations such as the American Liberty League cheered. Like the justices, League members believed that the NIRA had violated the U.S. Constitution by establishing codes to regulate intrastate commerce and by vesting too much legislative power in the office of the president. FDR retaliated with a turn to the left, initiating antitrust suits, utilities regulation, heavy taxes on corporations and the rich, and labor legislation. Despite all of this, many businessmen continued to support the New Deal. The business response was just as varied as the business world.*

To some degree, business-government antagonism temporarily subsided as the nation entered World War II. Mobilization required the talents and know-how of executives to manage the agencies that coordinated the flow of materials, supplies, equipment, and personnel. To guard their interests, big businessmen continued to mediate with FDR through the Business Advisory Council for the Department of Commerce, helping to establish wartime policies that ensured corporate autonomy, tax breaks, and profits. The strategy worked for them. By 1943, 70 percent of manufacturing output was controlled by the hundred largest American corporations. FDR's secretary of war, Henry Stimson, summed it all up: "If you are going to go to war . . . in a capitalist country, you have to let business make money out of the process or business won't work." The nation had come a long way from the stock market crash of 1929.

 # D O C U M E N T S

In Document 1, financier Arthur A. Robertson speaks to interviewer Studs Terkel about his experience on Wall Street in the 1920s and 1930s. Reminiscing in the 1960s, Robertson recalls the stock market in the heady days before the crash, and the scrambling to pick up the pieces afterward. Robertson's interview provides a colorful, highly personalized view of the Great Depression. What are the advantages and disadvantages of relying on oral history interviews to document economic events like the stock market crash?

Documents 2 and 3 examine two business responses to the New Deal. First, the photograph showing a "Blue Eagle" banner in a neighborhood restaurant speaks to FDR's popularity among small concerns. In contrast, businessmen belonging to the American Liberty League, the exclusive club organized in 1934 by Irénée du Pont for the purpose of defending the Constitution, staunchly opposed FDR. Using the business press, the League launched a bitter anti–New Deal campaign. The 1936 League pamphlet (Document 3) lists twenty-eight complaints against the New Deal. How would you assess the accuracy of these charges?

No industrial interest group felt the impact of the New Deal more than American labor. The New Deal was highly sympathetic to industrial workers, giving legal sanction to the formation of independent unions and the right to collective bargaining in Section 7a of the National Industrial Recovery Act (1933) and again in the National Labor Relations (Wagner) Act (1935), which created the National Labor Relations Board (NLRB). On December 30, 1936, General Motors workers—organized by the United Auto Workers (UAW)—initiated a major strike at the Fisher Body plant in Flint, Michigan. Known as the GM Sit-Down Strike, this forty-four-day work stoppage eventually involved 40,000 employees directly and some 110,000 more indirectly. Documents 4 and 5 present two perspectives on labor conflict and big business from the time of the strike. First, in an address on NBC radio, John L. Lewis, chairman of the Committee for Industrial Organization—the umbrella union for the UAW—issues a warning to business leaders, demanding a "new deal in America's great industries." As workers launched the Flint strike, GM executives worked behind the scenes to formulate a strategy for dealing with the unions. Next, in an internal GM memorandum, company labor economist Stephen M. Du Brul outlines the automaker's position on FDR, the New Deal, and labor unions. He compares FDR to William Jennings Bryan, leader of the 1890s populist revolt against big business, while warning GM executives about the dangers of the Popular Front surrounding Roosevelt.

While banks, farmers, small retailers, and family manufacturing firms suffered during the Great Depression, many big businesses survived the stock market crash to earn profits. One investors' periodical, *The Magazine of Wall Street*, kept tabs on corporate performance for its readers. In a 1938 article (Document 6), it recommends that investors consider equities from the Monsanto Chemical Company and International Business Machines (IBM), while cautioning them against investing in the Kroger Grocery & Baking Company and the Lambert Company, makers of Listerine mouthwash. Why did certain types of businesses perform well during the depression?

As the country emerged from the Great Depression, American business celebrated by participating in the 1939 New York World's Fair. The nation's largest corporations—General Motors, General Electric, Du Pont, and others—mounted exhibits depicting the future as a technological wonderland, filled with new products such as nylon and television. In a pavilion devoted to chemistry, E. I. du Pont de Nemours & Company—by then the nation's largest chemical firm—displayed a mural celebrating big business. Found on the cover of this book, the 13' × 16' mural depicts an impoverished world that has been transformed into a consumer paradise by Du Pont's research and development laboratories. It is labeled with the slogan, "Better Things for Better Living Through Chemistry," created for Du Pont by Bruce Barton's public relations firm. In 1935, Du Pont had hired Batten, Barton, Durstine, and Osborn (BBDO) to revamp its corporate image during the U.S. Senate Munitions Investigating Committee's 1934–1936 hearings on wartime profiteering ["Nye Committee"], which had probed Du Pont's activities as a major gunpowder and explosives manufacturer.

Documents 7 to 9 focus on American business during World War II. In Document 7, banker John W. Snyder, who served as President Harry S. Truman's treasury secretary from 1946 to 1953, recollects his wartime career in Washington. As head of the Defense Plant Corporation (DPC) from 1940 to 1944, Snyder directed the key government agency that helped private enterprise to fund, build, and equip manufacturing plants for war production. How might Snyder's experience in banking have been an asset to the DPC?

In 1936, Henry Luce, cofounder of Time Inc., had added a new photojournalistic magazine to his company: *Life*. Luce was a stalwart Republican and anticommunist who distrusted the New Deal but supported FDR's decision to involve the United States in World War II. Throughout the conflict, Luce's gigantic news machine—*Time, Fortune, Life*, and The March of Time documentaries—lionized the American political and economic system to generate support for the battle against fascism.

In Document 8, a journalist for *Life* describes the career of entrepreneur Henry J. Kaiser, a California-based general contractor who built dams for the U.S. government during the Great Depression and converted to shipbuilding in World War II. This 1942 profile spotlights Kaiser's efforts to construct Liberty Ships on a mass-production basis, borrowing assembly-line techniques from the automobile industry. What journalistic techniques are used to present Kaiser as a patriotic businessman? What messages did *Life* hope to impart?

Finally, the trade journal *Mill and Factory* looks at industry's efforts to recruit women for wartime jobs, surveying factories from the Carolinas to California (Document 9). How did industry attract a female labor force?

1. A Wall Street Broker Remembers 1929

In 1929, it was strictly a gambling casino with loaded dice. The few sharks taking advantage of the multitude of suckers. It was exchanging expensive dogs for expensive cats. There had been a recession in 1921. We came out of it about 1924. Then began the climb, the spurt, with no limit stakes. Frenzied finance that made Ponzi look like an amateur. I saw shoeshine boys buying $50,000 worth of stock with $500 down. Everything was bought on hope.

Today, if you want to buy $100 worth of stock, you have to put up $80 and the broker will put up $20. In those days, you could put up $8 or $10. That was really responsible for the collapse. The slightest shake-up caused calamity because people didn't have the money required to cover the other $90 or so. There were not the controls you have today. They just sold you out: an unwilling seller to an unwilling buyer.

A cigar stock at the time was selling for $115 a share. The market collapsed. I got a call from the company president. Could I loan him $200 million? I refused, because at the time I had to protect my own fences, including those of my closest friends. His $115 stock dropped to $2 and he jumped out of the window of his Wall Street office.

There was a man who headed a company that had $17 million in cash. He was one of the leaders of his industry and controlled three or four situations that are today household words. When his stock began to drop, he began to protect it. When he came out of the second drop, the man was completely wiped out. He owed three banks a million dollars each.

The banks were in the same position he was, except that the government came to their aid and saved them. Suddenly they became holier than thou, and took over the businesses of the companies that owed them money. They discharged the experts, who had built the businesses, and put in their own men. I bought one of these companies from the banks. They sold it to me in order to stop their losses.

The worst day-to-day operators of businesses are bankers. They are great when it comes to scrutinizing a balance sheet. By training they're conservative, because they're loaning you other people's money. Consequently, they do not take the calculated risks operating businesses requires. They were losing so much money that they were tickled to get it off their backs. I recently sold it for $2 million. I bought it in 1933 for $33,000.

In the early Thirties, I was known as a scavenger. I used to buy broken-down businesses that banks took over. That was one of my best eras of prosperity. The whole period was characterized by men who were legends. When you talked about $1 million you were talking about loose change. Three or four of these men would get together, run up a stock to ridiculous prices and unload it on the unsuspecting public. The minute you heard of a man like [William C.] Durant or Jesse Livermore buying stock, everybody followed. They knew it was going to go up. The only problem was to get out before they dumped it.

Durant owned General Motors twice and lost it twice . . . was worth way in excess of a billion dollars on paper, by present standards, four or five billion. He started

Studs Terkel, *Hard Times: An Oral History of the Great Depression* (New York: Pantheon Books, 1970), pp. 72–76. Copyright © 2000 Studs Terkel. Reprinted by permission of Donadio & Olson, Inc.

his own automobile company, and it went under. When the Crash came, he caved in, like the rest of 'em. The last I heard of him I was told he ended up running a bowling alley. It was all on paper. Everybody in those days expected the sun to shine forever.

October 29, 1929, yeah. A frenzy. I must have gotten calls from a dozen and a half friends who were desperate. In each case, there was no sense in loaning them the money that they would give the broker. Tomorrow they'd be worse off than yesterday. Suicides, left and right, made a terrific impression on me, of course. People I knew. It was heartbreaking. One day you saw the prices at a hundred, the next day at $20, at $15.

On Wall Street, the people walked around like zombies. It was like *Death Takes A Holiday*. It was very dark. You saw people who yesterday rode around in Cadillacs lucky now to have carfare.

One of my friends said to me, "If things keep on as they are, we'll all have to go begging." I asked, "Who from?"

Many brokers did not lose money. They made fortunes on commissions while their customers went broke. The only brokers that got hurt badly were those that gambled on their own—or failed to sell out in time customers' accounts that were underwater. Of course, the brokerage business fell off badly, and practically all pulled in their belts, closed down offices and threw people out of work.

Banks used to get eighteen percent for call money—money with which to buy stock that paid perhaps one or two-percent dividends. They figured the price would continue to rise. Everybody was banking on it. I used to receive as much as twenty-two percent from brokers who borrowed from me. Twenty-two percent for money!

Men who built empires in utilities, would buy a small utility, add a big profit to it for themselves and sell it back to their own public company. That's how some like Samuel Insull became immensely wealthy. The thing that caused the Insull crash is the same that caused all these frenzied financiers to go broke. No matter how much they had, they'd pyramid it for more.

I had a great friend, John Hertz. At one time he owned ninety percent of the Yellow Cab stock. John also owned the Checker Cab. He also owned the Surface Line buses of Chicago. He was reputed to be worth $400 to $500 million. He asked me one day to join him on a yacht. There I met two men of such stature that I was in awe: Durant and Jesse Livermore.

We talked of all their holdings. Livermore said: "I own what I believe to be the controlling stock of IBM and Philip Morris." So I asked, "Why do you bother with anything else?" He answered, "I only understand stock. I can't bother with businesses." So I asked, "Do men of your kind put away $10 million where nobody can ever touch it?" He looked at me and answered, "Young man, what's the use of having ten million if you can't have big money?"

In 1934—after he went through two bankruptcies in succession—my accountant asked if I'd back Livermore. He was broke and wanted to make a comeback in the market. He always made a comeback and paid everybody off with interest. I agreed to do it. I put up $400,000. By 1939, we made enough money so that each of us could have $1,300,000 profit after taxes. Jesse was by this time in the late sixties, having gone through two bankruptcies. "Wouldn't it be wise to cash in?" I asked him. In those days, you could live like a king for $50,000 a year. He said he could just never get along on a pittance.

So I sold out, took my profits, and left Jesse on his own. He kept telling me he was going to make the killing of the century. Ben Smith, known as "Sell 'Em Short Ben," was in Europe and told him there was not going to be a war. Believing in Smith, Livermore went short on grain. For every dollar he owned, plus everything he could pyramid.

When I arrived in Argentina, I learned that Germany invaded Poland. Poor Jesse was on the phone. "Art, you have to save me." I refused to do anything, being so far away. I knew it would be throwing good money after bad.

A couple of months later, I was back in New York, with Jesse waiting for me in my office. The poor fellow had lost everything he could lay his hands on. He asked for a $5,000 loan, which, of course, I gave him. Three days later, Jesse had gone to eat breakfast in the Sherry-Netherlands, went to the lavatory and shot himself. They found a note made out to me for $5,000. This was the man who said, "What's the use having ten million if you can't have big money?" Jesse was one of the most brilliant minds in the trading world. He knew the crops of every area where grain grew. He was a great student, but always overoptimistic.

2. NRA's Blue Eagle Displayed in a Restaurant Window, 1934

Photograph of a woman hanging an NRA poster in the window of a restaurant, ca. 1934, in Public Domain Photographs, 1882–1962, ARC Identifier: 196519, Franklin D. Roosevelt Presidential Library & Museum, Hyde Park, N.Y. Courtesy of Franklin D. Roosevelt Presidential Library & Museum.

3. American Liberty League Vigorously Opposes the New Deal, 1936

28 Facts about The New Deal

1. IT DELIBERATELY has increased the cost of living.
2. IT SPENDS $1.74 for every dollar it receives.
3. IT HAS SOUGHT to give the President the powers of a dictator.
4. IT HAS ADDED more than $10,000,000,000 to the public debt.
5. IT HAS MADE no effort to keep outgo within income.
6. IT REPUDIATED the Nation's contracts to pay off bonds in gold.
7. IT MADE a scrap of paper of the 1932 platform, after a solemn pledge to up-hold it.
8. IT HAS SOUGHT to create class prejudice.
9. IT HAS USED WPA as a political football.
10. IT HAS ASSASSINATED the merit system and built up the most flagrant spoils system in history.
11. IT HAS BROKEN all peace-time records in collecting taxes, but at the same time has spent more, thus creating new deficits.
12. IT WITHHOLDS from the people the truth about the tremendous tax burden made necessary by its orgy of extravagance.
13. IT HAS SOUGHT to conceal huge increases in the "regular" costs of Government by the pretense that they have been due to relief costs.
14. IT HAS ILLEGALLY taxed groups of citizens to raise "benefit funds" for other groups.
15. IT HAS REDUCED Congress to the status of a servile instrument of the Executive department.
16. IT HAS FORCED enactment of legislation violative of the rights of the people as guaranteed in five of the ten articles of the Bill of Rights.
17. IT HAS PARADED its contempt of the Constitution.
18. IT HAS MADE vicious charges against the Supreme Court, meanwhile forcing through Congress legislation admittedly of doubtful legality.
19. ITS STANDARD BEARER has publicly boasted that he has centralized the powers of the Government in Washington, in contempt of the 48 States and their sovereign rights.
20. ITS STANDARD BEARER has publicly boasted that he has "built up new instruments of power," which would be—in his opinion—dangerous to the liberties of the people if placed in the hands of some one other than the present New Deal leader.
21. IT HAS REDUCED production of food while millions are in want.
22. IT HAS SPENT billions for work-relief, but, after three years, there are still more than 12,000,000 persons unemployed.

American Liberty League, *28 Facts About the New Deal*, page titled "American Liberty League Vigorously Oppose the New Deal," Leaflet No. 11 (Washington, D.C.: American Liberty League, [1936]), box 1, series A: American Liberty League, 1934–1939, accession 228: Irénée du Pont Papers, Hagley Museum and Library, Wilmington, Del. Reprinted by permission of Hagley Museum and Library.

23. IT HAS INVENTED boondoggling as a method of making it easy for political payrollers to spend the taxpayers' money.
24. IT HAS PLOWED under the Constitutional right and duty of the United States Senate to give advice and consent to the Executive on international treaties.
25. IT HAS MADE a tragic joke of the national budget, confusing ordinary and emergency items in such manner as to obscure the true financial situation of the country.
26. IT HAS ADDED more than 225,000 loyal New Dealers to the Executive payroll on the plea of emergency. While claiming the emergency has passed, the New Deal refuses to break up this giant political bureaucracy.
27. IT HAS CLIMAXED its monetary policy by a disastrous experiment in buying huge stores of silver.
28. ITS FOUR-YEAR SPENDING PROGRAM is costing more than the entire costs of Federal Government from the administration of President Washington to the administration of President Taft, inclusive—a period of 125 years.

4. CIO Leader John L. Lewis Issues a Forceful Warning to Industry, 1936

The Committee for Industrial Organization is carrying its plans forward. Extensive unions have been promoted and expanded in the steel, automotive, glass, ship-building, electrical manufacturing, oil, and by-product coke industries. Tremendous enrollment of the workers is under way. Unabashed by employer opposition, they are joining the unions of their industries literally by the thousands.

The year 1936 has witnessed the beginning of this great movement in the mass production industries. The year 1937 will witness an unparalleled growth in the numerical strength of labor in the heretofore unorganized industries, and the definite achievement of modern collective bargaining on a wide front where it heretofore has not existed. Not only the workers, but our nation and its entire population will be the beneficiaries of this great movement. Labor demands collective bargaining and greater participation by the individual worker, whether by hand or brain, in the bountiful resources of the nation and the fruits of the genius of its inventors and technicians.

Employers talk about possible labor trouble interfering with continued expansion and progress of industry. They ignore the fact that unless people have money with which to buy, the wheels of industry slow down, and profits and likewise capital disappear. It would be more fitting and accurate to talk about "employer trouble"—that is something from which wage earners are suffering. I refer you to the refusal of some of the largest and most powerful corporations in this country to follow modern labor practice or to obey the law of the land. They deny the entirely reasonable and just demands of their employees for legitimate collective bargaining, decent incomes, shorter hours, and for protection against a destructive speed-up system.

It is the refusal of employers to grant such reasonable conditions and to deal with their employees through collective bargaining that leads to wide-spread labor

John L. Lewis, "I Solemnly Warn the Leaders of Industry," Speech delivered on the Red Network, National Broadcasting Company, Washington, D.C., December 31, 1936. Copyright © 2005 NBC Universal, Inc. All rights reserved. Used by permission. This speech also appears in *Vital Speeches of the Day* 3, no. 7 (January 15, 1937): 201–204.

unrest. The strikes which have broken out in the last few weeks, especially in the automotive industry, are due to such "employer trouble." Modern collective bargaining, involving negotiations between organized workers and organized employers on an industry basis, would regularize and stabilize industry relations and reduce the economic losses occasioned by management stupidity. The sit-down strike is the fruit of mismanagement and bad policy towards labor. Employers who tyrannize over the employees, with the aid of labor spies, company guards, and the threat of discharge, need not be surprised if their production lines are suddenly halted.

Mr. Alfred P. Sloan, Jr., President of General Motors Corporation, in his published year-end summary, refers to the possibilities of industrial strife in industry. Is it possible that Mr. Sloan is predicting continued hostility on the part of his corporation towards the demands of its employees for fair consideration? The giant General Motors Corporation is at present pursuing the dangerous course of refusing to answer the request of the United Automobile Workers for a national conference for collective bargaining purposes. The Union has repeatedly requested such a conference, but was told by a vice-president that any grievances should be taken up with plant managers or general managers in the various localities. It is absurd for such a corporation to pretend that its policies are settled locally. Every one knows that decisions as to wages, hours, and other conditions of employment are made at a central point for all the plants controlled by General Motors. General Motors is, indeed, a DuPont-controlled organization, and it is the DuPonts, and not the plant managers, who lay out the broad lines of labor policies. The United Automobile Workers' representatives have already been told by various plant managers that their reasonable demands must be referred to higher company officials before an answer can be given. The Union will continue its demand for a conference with persons who have the power to negotiate. Any other arrangement would be a perversion of collective bargaining and is an evasion of definite industry obligations.

The steel corporations are likewise trying to avoid collective bargaining with their employees. They have tried, by fostering and subsidizing company unions, to get around the law. Instead, they have transgressed the law. The steel companies, themselves, are organized, and they appreciate and exploit the value of organization in the conduct of their business enterprises. The United States Steel Corporation is trying to enforce upon its two hundred and twenty thousand employees the outmoded labor policy adopted by its Board of Directors in 1901, a policy which denies the right of self-organization to any employee of that Corporation or its subsidiaries. At the same time the United States Steel Corporation associates itself with an organization, known as the American Iron and Steel Institute, which on July 1st, 1936, in an advertisement published in three hundred and seventy-five newspapers, presumed to speak for the iron and steel industry and denied the right of the steel workers to similar organization in their own interests. . . .

Huge corporations, such as United States Steel and General Motors, have a moral and public responsibility. They have neither the moral nor the legal right to rule as autocrats over the hundreds of thousands of employees. They have no right to transgress the law which gives to the worker the right of self-organization and collective bargaining. They have no right in a political democracy to withhold the rights of a free people.

The workers in the steel industry are organizing; the workers in the automotive industry are organizing; the workers in other industries are organizing; any sane concept of industrial relations would indicate that the labor problems of these industries should be settled across the council table. . . .

Labor now demands the right to organize and the right to bargain. Labor demands a new deal in America's great industries. Labor holds in contempt those who for mercenary reasons would restrict human privileges. Labor demands legislative enactments, making realistic the principles of industrial democracy. It demands that Congress exercise its constitutional powers and brush aside the negative autocracy of the Federal Judiciary, exemplified by a Supreme Court which exalts property above human values. Either by constitutional amendment or statutory enactment, the right of Congress to legislate for the welfare of the people and the perpetuity of the Republic must be assured. The court has overstepped the bounds of its own authority and has gratuitously offended over two-thirds of the nation's citizens. Labor will support the elected representatives of the Republic in any attempt to restore to the Federal Congress the legislative powers of which it has gradually been stripped by the judicial encroachment and arbitrary decrees of the Supreme Court. . . .

Labor desires a peaceful solution of the problems of its relationships in the mass production industries. The organizations associated with the Committee for Industrial Organization are not promoting industrial strife—they are hoping for industrial peace on a basis that recognizes the rights of the workers as well as the employers. Peace, however, cannot be achieved by employers' denial of the right to organize; by denial of conferences for bargaining purposes; by the purchase and use of arms, ammunition, and tear gas; by a continued policy of arrogance and repression.

The time has passed in America when the workers can be either clubbed, gassed, or shot down with impunity. I solemnly warn the leaders of industry that labor will not tolerate such policies or tactics. Labor will also expect the protection of the agencies of the Federal Government in the pursuit of its lawful objectives.

5. GM Managers Work Behind Closed Doors on a Collective Bargaining Policy, 1936

So far we have taken a firm position, at least in private if not in public, that we will enter into no union agreements. It is the purpose of this memorandum to analyze this position and to suggest a possible compromise with it if we find that it has become untenable, in the light of actual public relations and political developments.

Background of Present Situation

It goes without saying that our present labor difficulties must be appraised and handled in the light of present political trends. The following points seem clear—

1. Roosevelt has received a sweeping personal approval of himself and his leadership and has no commitments. The public has said "Carry On."
2. The public are convinced that Government is all-powerful and can and should remedy all of our social and economic ills.

S. M. Du Brul, "The Question of Written Agreements," December 31, 1936, Vertical File: General Motors, Walter P. Reuther Library, College of Urban, Labor, and Metropolitan Affairs, Wayne State University, Detroit, Mich.

3. The temper of the people and Congress is Popular, in the political sense. The New Deal is now a Popular Front movement similar to the Bryan campaign in the nineties, which failed, and the present Popular Front in France, which is succeeding in establishing the rule of the masses.
4. Therefore, we can be sure that—

    (a) Mr. Roosevelt will be a "Popular" leader, and thus will be "for the masses," for "organized labor," against the "economic royalists," and will generally support any group which appears to be championing "the cause of the workingman."

    (b) General Motors is peculiarly vulnerable under these circumstances, as a result of the fact that we are successful, we are very large, we are currently making a lot of money, and the position of most of our executives in the recent campaign was against the present administration, so that politically General Motors will make a very good "whipping boy."

As a result, it seems to follow that—

    (a) Any Corporation-wide or industry-wide strike is a national issue because of the very large number of employes who will be put out of work, directly or indirectly.

    (b) We must be extremely careful to handle our situation so that the public are sympathetic to our cause, and so that the Administration and Congress cannot take sides against us. This means that *we must be so fair in every position we take that the Union is on the defensive both with the public and the Administration.*

The Position of the Union

John Lewis and his followers are playing for large stakes. Lewis himself is probably the keenest labor strategist in the country today. He has a large following, plenty of money, great political power and support both in and out of Congress, and a great deal of experience. We may be sure that he will play a very astute game and it will be hard to put him on the defensive. Unless we do, however, his chances are greatly improved and ours correspondingly suffer.

If he can make us come to terms, he will have won a victory which will enormously increase his power and many other industries will then fall before his onslaught. If he fails to bring us to terms which establish an unquestioned victory for him, his power will be seriously weakened. The only way by which we can put him on the defensive with the public and through it, with the politicians, is by taking a position which the bulk of people will grant is so fair that he becomes an obstructionist and the consequences for the unemployment resulting from any Corporation-wide strike may be blamed on him or his followers.

Once our plants are closed, the real problem will be to get them open again. It appears that it will be easier for the unions to keep them closed than to have closed them in the first place, that is, a weak union may hesitate to strike a plant, but once it is closed, it is much easier to recruit members and form picket lines, so that a union which could be ignored while the plant was running cannot be ignored in any effort to get it operating again. It is at this juncture that our strategy must be planned so carefully that even Senator Wagner will have no proper cause for criticism of our conduct and the failure of negotiations to produce results can be blamed upon the unreasonable demands of the unions themselves rather than on us.

This question then arises—What positions should be taken which

(a) Will be those which a majority of our workers and the public will probably approve, and

(b) Cannot be fairly attacked by the Administration and thus give them an excuse to side with the unions against us?

Collective Bargaining

Our position on this seems satisfactory. Actions speak louder than words. So long as we actually meet with representatives of our men and attempt to reach a settlement of specific issues, we can say that we are bargaining collectively and the union cannot attack us for refusing to do so. So long as the issues are "bargainable," that is, are issues on which there can be a reasonable difference of opinion, such as hours and wages, seniority, shop rules, etc., the public will not blame us for the failure to settle it. Since our wages are already very high and our hours reasonable, we are in a good position to argue this part of our case in public. It is on questions of principle over which our negotiations may become dead-locked that we must be very cautious. . . .

Union Recognition

We should insist that this is no issue, since meeting with the Union representatives is de facto recognition. The Union may counter by saying that the issue is that of recognition of them as the *sole* representative organization of our workers. This will raise the issue of—

Majority Rule

The majority-rule issue will be much more difficult to handle since it has been carefully misrepresented to the public by its proponents as a parallel to our political system and has been written into law in the Wagner Act. Therefore, a careful presentation of our position on this must be prepared and the publicity must be handled very effectively. . . .

The Union will probably demand that the National Labor Relations Board conduct a Corporation-wide vote to determine which organization shall represent all employes. The National Labor Relations Board will no doubt move into our situation on the slightest excuse in order to dramatize our position and itself and help to make the issue a critical one. Of course, since there is no Corporation-wide opposition organization, the results of any elections are a foregone conclusion, so that if we ever capitulated our position on this issue, we might just as well grant the Union sole bargaining power and save the trouble of an election.

I presume, however, there is no thought of compromise of our position on this, regardless of consequences, even though the President backs the Union and the National Labor Relations Board in their demand which, in my opinion, he will do if he finds that it is politically the expedient course to take.

We have no accurate knowledge of the public's sympathies on this question, but if the President does back the majority rule, we may be sure that he is certain a majority of the public will support him in it.

Signing a Union Agreement

It is very questionable if we can defend ourselves successfully before the public if we take a flat position that we will not make any agreements with unions. . . . Obviously we have no intentions of making any agreements unless and until the question of a written agreement is the only remaining barrier to a settlement which we conclude must be achieved as soon as possible. If, under these circumstances, we were to take a public position that we will not make any agreements at all, it seems to me that not only would a majority of the public be against us but *it would immediately give the politicians favorable to the "labor front" the very issue they need to throw their full political strength behind the unions and to pillory us with the public.*

Therefore, we should be very careful not to take any public position that we will not sign any agreements. . . .

The history of labor agreements themselves is that unless they provide a closed shop or at least preferential union hiring, most unions cannot survive under them because the bulk of the men stop paying dues as soon as they find it no longer necessary to do so, either as an investment to improve wages or working conditions, or as an insurance policy against violence by the union against themselves.

In short, our position at all times must be that of a reasonable employer who is unfortunately being victimized by irresponsible professional agitators whose demands exceed all reasonable limits. Any other attitude at this time would place our whole case in jeopardy, regardless of the basic merits of our side, and would be politically about as stupid a blunder as we can commit. We must not forget that there has been an election.

6. *Magazine of Wall Street* Assesses Corporate Performance for Investors, 1929–1938

Of all factors that must be considered in the selection of common stocks for investment or longer-range speculation, the prospective earnings trend is by far the most important. With few exceptions corporate earnings are subject to wide cyclical fluctuations, in line with the general business trend, so that wise timing is the first investment or speculative problem. . . .

In selecting uptrend stocks we apply two simple tests. The company must have shown a more than cyclical growth of earnings in the 1933–1937 recovery. The influences making such progress possible must, in our opinion, be continuing influences, likely to produce above average expansion of profits in the next period of general business expansion. In recent issues of THE MAGAZINE OF WALL STREET we have recommended various such issues, including International Nickel, Eastman Kodak,

---

Ward Gates, "Uptrend Stocks to Buy; Downtrend Stocks to Avoid," *Magazine of Wall Street* 61, no. 8 (January 29, 1938): 508–511, 540.

du Pont, Union Carbide, Boeing Airplane, Minneapolis-Honeywell, Masonite, Caterpillar Tractor, Allis-Chalmers and Food Machinery. Herewith we are presenting three additional issues that we regard as longer-term uptrend stocks—Monsanto Chemical, Black & Decker Manufacturing Co., and International Business Machines Corp.; and by contrast, as an added service feature, we are briefly analyzing four issues—Gillette Safety Razor, Lambert Co., Kroger Grocery and National Dairy Products—as samples of downtrend stocks to be avoided.

Monsanto Chemical Co.

For the nine months ended last September 30 earnings of Monsanto Chemical amounted to $3,999,758. It is probable that the company's forthcoming annual report will show full year profit not far from $5,000,000. This would be approximately three times the net income shown in 1929. That is, of course, a far greater expansion of earning power than can be accounted for by anything in the business cycle. Had all American business in 1937 been proportionate to Monsanto's business the national income would not have been the 68 billions of dollars estimated by the Department of Commerce, but something on the order of 200 billions! Moreover, comparing the 1933–1937 recovery cycle with that of 1923–1929, one will note that Monsanto's progress in sales and earnings has been superior to that of the chemical industry as a whole.

This record has been made possible by successful emphasis on research, aggressive product diversification and efficient merchandising. But since these methods are common also to the much larger chemical companies, such as du Pont and Union Carbide, they do not fully explain the greater percentage growth of Monsanto sales and earnings in recent years. The other answer is simple arithmetic. In the growth of the largest corporations there is a law of diminishing returns. The bigger your business, the smaller the percentage gains in sales and profits tend to become. Relative to such giants as du Pont and Union Carbide, Monsanto is a small company—small

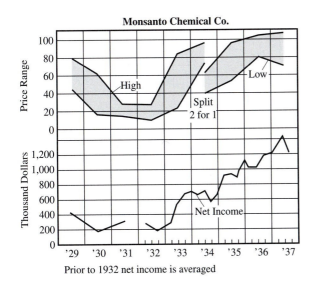

Monsanto Chemical Co.

Price Range

Thousand Dollars

Prior to 1932 net income is averaged

enough to avoid the penalties of bigness; but large enough—sales top $30,000,000 a year and total assets some $53,000,000—and capable enough to give an excellent account of itself in competition with all-comers.

Monsanto manufactures more than 200 chemicals serving fifty diversified industries, with its laboratory exploration of every field of chemistry adding at least several new products to the list each year. It operates four American plants—at St. Louis, Mo., Monsanto, Ill., Everett, Mass., and Nitro, West Virginia,—as well as two plants in England. About 15 per cent of its sales are to the foodstuff industries and 11 per cent to the pharmaceutical industry, with no other field taking more than 10 per cent of sales. This reflects a wide diversification and absence of major dependence on any single market. . . .

International Business Machines Corp.

In International Business Machines we present the Blue Chip of the business equipment industry, a strong company whose sales and profits reached a new all-time high last year and whose stock is of a caliber appealing to the conservative investor. For the nine months ended last September 30 net profit was $6,572,666, including net of foreign subsidiaries. This was equal to $8.47 per share on the 775,880 shares of no-par stock outstanding, and compared with $5,738,406, or $7.76 on 738,934 shares for the first nine months of 1936. On November 23 President T. J. Watson publicly stated that the company had more unfilled orders on its books than ever before. On the basis of that statement there is no reason to assume that the fourth quarter, however drab for many industries, saw any important shrinkage in the earnings of this company. Hence, we may estimate 1937 profit as around $8,500,000 or close to $11 per share.

Previous peak year was not 1929 but 1931, in which year net income was $7,697,000. The company's lowest year of the depression was 1933, with net of $5,736,425 and that figure topped the 1928 net income and was some 50 per cent above the average earnings of the years 1925–1927. That the earnings trend has varied

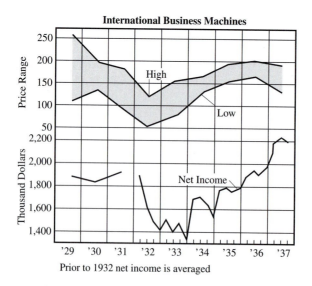

International Business Machines

Prior to 1932 net income is averaged

so strikingly from that of American industry generally is not so strange when it is noted that large revenues from rental of equipment exercise a stabilizing influence on profits, and that foreign sales—not always conforming to the American business trend—are of vital importance. Indeed, revenue from rental of equipment is the most important single source of income. As for foreign business, it has been officially stated that volume increased 50 per cent during the first nine months of last year; and the company expects such business to equal its American volume in the near future.

The company is the leading manufacturer of specialized tabulating and sorting equipment and of the necessary cards and forms used with such equipment. Other products include time-recording machines, weighing equipment, electric typewriters, traffic recorders, alphabetical printing punches, time stamps, machines for sorting, listing and totalling bank checks, etc. Sales are made in seventy-nine countries. The three domestic factories are at Rochester and Endicott, N.Y., and Washington, D.C.; while foreign plants are owned at London, Paris, Milan, and Berlin and Sindelfingen in Germany. . . .

Kroger Grocery & Baking Co.

This company is one of the largest and best managed grocery chains, has long earned substantial profits and paid satisfactory dividends—and yet its stock must be considered a downtrend issue without appeal to conservative investor or to specu-lator under present conditions. Sales have been maintained fairly well, amounting to $248,442,000 for the year recently ended, a gain of 2.5 per cent or $6,168,000. This compares with record high 1929 dollar volume of approximately $286,000,000 and, with allowance for difference in price level, represents a physical volume of business not importantly under former best levels.

But Kroger has thus far fought a losing battle with rising costs, especially as to labor and taxes. While the official report has not yet been issued, an estimate of $3,000,000 for 1937 net income probably will not prove far from the mark. This

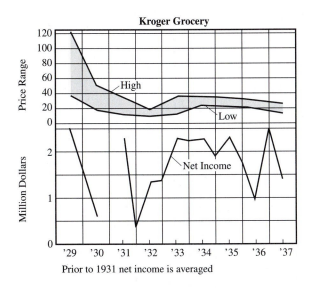

Prior to 1931 net income is averaged

compares with peak of $5,919,000 in 1929. More pertinent to the present position of the stock, however, is the fact that net income has now shown a decline for the fourth successive year, despite considerable rise in sales. Thus $4,546,000 was earned in 1933 on sales of only $205,000,000. Comparing the company's 1933 performance with that of 1937, sales were up nearly 20 per cent and profits were down roughly 33 per cent.

Aggressive adjustments have been made in closing unprofitable or least profitable stores in an effort both to lower overhead expenses and increase dollar volume per store. During the past year 98 stores were closed. During 1936[,] 66 were eliminated. Starting this year [the] number in operation was 4,118, which compares with 5,575 at the top of the expansion which culminated in 1929.

The difficulties confronting this enterprise are common to the chain grocery field and are not peculiar to Kroger. In the recent market slump most equities in this group went down to and in some instances below the lowest prices recorded at the bear market bottoms of the summer of 1932 and March, 1933. To an even greater extent than the regulated rails and the utilities, they proved to be friendless orphans in the New Deal recovery.

It is possible that Kroger has seen the worst impact of rising labor costs and of punitive chain store taxation, but assured forecast to this effect is without factual basis. . . .

Lambert Company

To justify ranking this issue as a downtrend stock, one need only note that earnings available for the stock established a peak of $7,132,000 in 1930 and that every year since then has recorded a shrinkage. By 1932 net income had fallen to $3,788,000. By 1934 it had dropped to $2,206,000. By 1936 it had slid down to $1,272,000. For the nine months ended last September 30, profit was $1,082,000, equal to $1.45 per common share. This was a small gain over the $1,023,000 or $1.37 per share

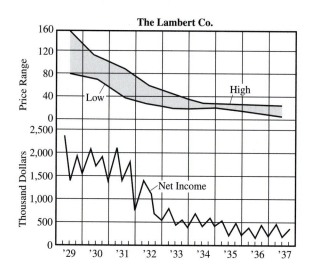

The Lambert Co.

shown for the first nine months of 1936. That it represented a significant turn for the better in the company's position is to be doubted, since the third quarter showing was a bit under that in the third quarter of 1936 and since the fourth quarter—which brought a general economic slump—is yet to be heard from.

The former $8 dividend has been repeatedly reduced, even though surplus was drawn upon in recent years in maintaining relatively generous distributions. Total payments last year amounted to $2 and most recent quarterly dividend was 37½ cents or at annual rate of $1.50.

The company's major product is "Listerine," extensively advertised as a mouth wash and hair dressing. Under the same trademark it sells tooth paste, tooth powder and shaving cream; and under other trademarks sells a line of shaving, tooth and other brushes. Promotional costs are high and competition is intensive both from other trademarked products in the same field and from private brands which are successfully stressing economy. The stock is devoid of appeal.

7. St. Louis Banker Heads the Defense Plant Corporation, 1940–1944

I was about ready to go [from the Reconstruction Finance Corporation back] to the bank [First National Bank of St. Louis] again in 1940 when Mr. [Jesse] Jones [at the RFC] asked me to come down to Washington to help out in some financing for World War II—a great number of pressures being put on manufacturers to manufacture things—airplanes, guns, etc.—for use of the Allies in the European war which had developed into World War II. At that time, of course—this was in July, 1940, about a year and a half before the United States actually got into the war. During our discussions and studies and everything, we came upon the idea of setting up several subsidiaries in the RFC such as the Defense Plant Corporation, Defense Supplies, the Rubber Reserve, and a number of other auxiliary financing groups that would help the Defense Program, as we called it then, because at that time we were only trying to build up our own defenses and to help those that were engaged in actual war, who were our Allies. With that, of course, came the end of going back to St. Louis anytime soon, because I was made head of the Defense Plant Corporation as the executive vice president and ran the organization for nearly four years.

During that time we developed a most unusual way of financing, construct[ing] and equipping large manufacturing plants. The Government would furnish the money and would own the property. We would, upon recommendation of the War Production Board or the War Department or the Navy—we didn't have the Air Force at that time, the Air Corps was under the Army operation—upon their recommendation that a certain firm have financing to build a plant to enable them to build things that were needed for the defense or war effort, the Defense Plant Corporation undertook to supply that money through lease agreements, and then assigned engineers, lawyers and bookkeepers to see that the plant was built according to plans approved.

John W. Snyder, interview by Jerry N. Hess, Washington, D.C., November 8, 1967, pp. 12–15, Harry S. Truman Presidential Library & Museum, Independence, Mo. Accessed at http://www.trumanlibrary .org/oralhist/snyder1.htm (January 2005).

The lease agreement with the manufacturer who was to manufacture items for defense and to [have] use of that facility as long as the emergency existed was a unique legal instrument. I am very proud of those leases because we exercised considerable forethought in drawing up the principles under which they were drawn. Among other things, we put a proviso into the lease agreement which gave the manufacturer—the lessee—an option to buy the plant, after the emergency period was over, at an agreed on formula that was written right into his contract. This, of course, was of tremendous value in later years in our swing from war back into peace operations because these very fine, modern plants could be quickly put back into an expanded usage of production for the great demands for commodities that followed the war. We, of course, at that time had no idea how long the war was going to last, but we just took that precaution to work out a transition from war to peace in light of the experience of many of us of what happened following World War I. After the problem of the financing had pretty well been solved—incidentally, we advanced over eleven billions of dollars to build plants under the Defense Plant Program. When this was finished, I went back to the bank in 1944.

8. *Life* Celebrates Henry J. Kaiser and the U.S. Wartime Shipbuilding Program, 1942

One evening late in November last year, Henry J. Kaiser, a general contractor of Oakland, Calif., gave a talk on the subject of light metals. His audience was a group of enlightened bankers and industrialists, members of the Newcomen Society in New York, who gather to ponder the past and future of industrial progress. Light metals, Mr. Kaiser declared, are about to bring a technological revolution that will end the age of steel. Stirred by this vision, the Newcomen fellows elected him to membership by acclaim. Mr. "Pete" Newell, the Bath, Me. shipbuilder, was simultaneously moved to reveal to Mr. Kaiser the plans for his dream ship, which he had tried and failed to sell to the U.S. Navy. It was a destroyer to be made entirely, except for engines and guns, of the light metal, aluminum.

Mr. Kaiser took the aluminum-destroyer plans to Washington 48 hours later. At the Navy Department he started in on a commander in the Bureau of Ships. By sundown, the Navy had drawn up a preliminary letter of intent. For Henry Kaiser the age of light metals was at hand. Unhappily, within the week the Japs attacked Pearl Harbor and there is now hardly enough aluminum for airplanes. The aluminum destroyer of course must wait. Mr. Kaiser, however, cannot wait.

Because he wants to get to work on the light-metals revolution, Henry Kaiser is in a hurry to win the war. At a tempo worthy of his impatience he is busy doing it. From his six shipyards at San Francisco, Portland, Ore. and Vancouver, Wash. he is rushing shoals of 10,500-ton Liberty ships. To feed his yards with plates and shapes he is in the act of setting up the first vertical steel operation, from mine to rolling mill, in California. To supply California's aircraft factories, and with an eye on the

---

Gerard Piel, "No. 1 Shipbuilder: Henry J. Kaiser Applies Dam-Construction Methods to Launch a Third of the U.S. Shipbuilding Program and Set the Pace for the Rest of It," *Life* 12, no. 26 (June 29, 1942): 81, 88–89. Copyright © 1942 *Time* Inc. Reprinted by permission.

future, Kaiser has built a plant near San Francisco which he hopes will shortly be producing yearly 40,000,000 lb. of the light metal, magnesium. As operator of the world's biggest single cement plant, Kaiser is contributing heavily to the war-construction program all over the map.

Under the heading of ships, it is easy to demonstrate that Henry Kaiser's operations may have something to do with the length and outcome of the war. During the last 18 months he has been assigned one-third of the U.S. shipbuilding program. This assignment, calling for 679 Liberty ships (whose simple design promotes speedy construction), 56 tankers and 30 transports, with more orders to come, makes Henry Kaiser the world's No. 1 shipbuilder. He signed his first contract for the building of 30 "Plain Jane" cargo vessels on Dec. 20, 1940. Into a mud-flat yard site at Richmond, across the bay from San Francisco, on Jan. 20, 1941, he sent his first heavy battalion of bulldozers, dredges and pile drivers. On April 14, 85 working days later, with seven finished ways riding on 20,000 piles driven through to bedrock, he laid his first keel. Since then he has built five more yards, and launched 82 ships of which all but ten have been delivered. Last month, his yards delivered 5 Plain Janes and 16 Liberties, while all the other non-Kaiser yards engaged in the same program on the West, Gulf and East coasts together delivered only 30.

Kaiser's importance as a shipbuilder cannot be measured adequately by the production figures of his own yards alone. He is also the pacesetter of the whole shipbuilding program, the club with which the U.S. Maritime Commission's two admirals, Land and Vickery, belabor other yard operators. From 194 days on his first ship, Kaiser has cut the time between keel-laying and delivery to a spectacular low of 46 days on a ship delivered this June. In May, against a national average of 150 days for delivery of Liberty ships, Kaiser's Oregon yard established a keel-to-delivery average of 72 days. The Maritime Commission has translated each new record into a schedule increase for all yards, from two ships per way per year to six. By August, Henry Kaiser's yards should be launching a ship or more a day. If the rest of the nation's shipyards together can produce two a day, the Maritime Commission will be well on its way to the schedule that will produce 2,300 ships by Dec. 31, 1943.

Kaiser's debut in the steel business, an incidental consequence of his shipbuilding operations, has brought to California a full-dress industrial revolution. He did his best, with a team of "expediters" chasing his orders through every plant, to get his plates and shapes from the established Eastern centers and proved that the East could not satisfy his shipyard appetite for 600 tons of steel per way per week. He thereupon got the blessings of Donald Nelson and $50,000,000 from Jesse Jones to set up his own capacity in California. That was in mid-February. Today, the foundations of his plant near San Bernardino, Calif. are in concrete, and the pot-bellied blast furnace is already shaping up in firebrick and steel plate.

The raw-material needs of California's aircraft plants provided the equally urgent occasion for Kaiser to get his light-metals revolution under way. Its beginning is his Permanente Metals Corp. magnesium plant at San Jose. In magnesium he has a metal lighter, and in some alloys stronger, than aluminum. But the technology of magnesium is not very far on this side of the frontiers of pure research and the Permanente process, just getting into production, is strictly a piece of pioneering. For the present, Kaiser will be happy to see Permanente's projected 40,000,000-lb. capacity go into bombs and bombers. . . .

To Henry Kaiser, who still speaks of the "front end" of a ship, 679 merchant ships have about the heft of Boulder Dam's 3,250,000 yards of concrete. It is another job for facilities. In his yards the word facilities means, first of all, space—a lot more space than is confined in the falsework around the narrow way. His ways are only a final assembly point. The ship is cut up, spread out and built in sections, in fabrication shops, in open lots and on big steel-floored subassembly platforms, where there is room for hundreds of welders and cutters to work without getting in each other's way. The limit to the size of the erection sections that can thus be built is the capacity of a shipyard's cranes. Kaiser has the biggest ones, to lift 100-ton prefabricated double bottoms, bulkheads, side walls, forepeaks and after sections onto the ways.

At the yards on San Francisco Bay he is building a vast fabrication shop through which, on trailers the size of hockey rinks, the superstructures of ships will move down an assembly line. Cut up in four vertical sections, they will emerge with plumbing, wiring, binnacle, wheel, radio transmitter and galley stove installed. With a few swift passes of the welding stinger, the completely furnished deck-house will be sewn on the hull before it leaves the ways.

Because, in peace and war, the Federal Government has always been his biggest client, Henry Kaiser has been called "the New Deal's businessman." In some circles he is also suspect because he makes a practice of signing closed-shop contracts with labor unions. From Mr. Kaiser's point of view this puts the burden of good behavior on the workers, and, to his satisfaction, his operations have never been interrupted by a strike. Apart from this deviation, his political opinions are orthodox enough to have made him a Willkie voter.

There is some confirmation for his anomalous title in the warmth with which Henry Kaiser is regarded in Washington. This admiration, however, cuts across all lines, from Harold Ickes, whose Reclamation Bureau was party of the first part on the dam contracts, to Donald Nelson who set him up in steel. His eminence is such that he was widely discussed, during Admiral Land's recent ordeal, as a possible chief for the whole shipbuilding program. A few industrialists, it is said, are growing tired of having Henry Kaiser held up to them in Washington as an example for their study and emulation.

Mr. Kaiser takes his role as an object lesson seriously. He was distressed by his recent discovery that some industrialists are inhibited, not spurred, to enterprise by the profit motive. On these men he urges his conviction that the avalanche of production now rolling out of U.S. plants will never and can never stop. "When you think of China and all those countries," he says, "our business is to rebuild the world."

It is for the world after the war that Henry Kaiser wants to get his magnesium plant into production. Permanente Metals Corp. is in all respects his most extraordinary enterprise. The Hansgirg patents, on which the Permanente process is based, involve delicate reactions between this incendiary metal and a series of explosive gases. The dam-building approach to the frontiers of technology is symbolized at Permanente by the presence of a Grand Coulee hammerhead crane which will handle the glowing retort bottles when the plant gets under way.

In Permanente's laboratory, Henry Kaiser has a crew of scientists and technicians engaged in fundamental research toward the development of high-strength magnesium alloys. Certain of these researches, watched with interest by West Coast aircraft plants, may revolutionize plane production. On the lightness, strength and durability of magnesium, Mr. Kaiser has projected an era of air transport when freight will be hauled at 2¢ per mile per ton, by trains of gliders pulled by locomotive planes. Light metals in planes, cars, railroad trains and ships, in Henry Kaiser's dreams, will usher in an age of transportation that will call for the redesign of our whole civilization. He has some of its details, in the design of planes, airports and super-highways, in sharper focus than most of our more imaginative industrial designers.

In March, Henry Kaiser was talking to Jesse Jones about another technology that enthralls him—the cracking and synthesizing of fuels, rubber and other strategic materials out of petroleum. Mr. Kaiser likes to speak of planes as made with petroleum and magnesium as their only raw materials. Mr. Jones, perceiving the gleam of another enterprise in Mr. Kaiser's eyes, said, "Henry, you're no longer a young man. I am not accustomed to putting all my eggs in one basket. What would happen to us if you were to go and die?"

"My boys would finish all your contracts, Mr. Jones," said Henry Kaiser, "I would just be sorry not to be here asking for more work to do."

9. *Mill and Factory* Explains How the Aircraft Industry Recruits Women, 1942

The aircraft factories, who made history by training women for jobs long before industry in general realized that we would have a man-power shortage in 1942, are now stealing another march.

They are setting about removing the bottleneck which exists in the full employment of women, who have babies and young children, needing home care. The aircraft industry is establishing day nurseries to take care of youngsters of women they want to hire. By doing this they are freeing "the hand that rocks the cradle" to rock an overhead crane or to keep wheels turning.

Douglas Aircraft has led off in the movement by building these nursery establishments half a mile or more from the main buildings. Because of their foresight, an enemy bomb intended for the plant proper, isn't likely to hit a Douglas mother's baby. These buildings will be open at night to take care of nocturnal lady riveters' young families, while mother goes to work for eight hours on the MacArthur shift. The industrial nursery of the future will keep open all around the clock.

To many plant owners this reaching into a private crib and taking out an infant is something to shy away from.

"Too many angles!" they say.

One of these was that we had not yet drained off our usable manpower. But now with industry needing to go into the home and remove one out of every three housewives between the ages of 18 and 44, to work on War contracts, we must sing a different tune.

Another thing that deterred many employers was wondering what the unions might say. Some union opinion was that nurseries in the plant would "marry" the worker to that establishment and produce in her a blind spot, so that she would think first of what was being done for her child and second about union membership. Now, we have the unions publicly asking for management's help in providing asylums

Elsie Johns, "Industry Minds the Baby—While Mom Minds the Machine," *Mill and Factory* 36 (December 1942): 90–91, 134–136.

for tots who might have to be left out in the street, or at least, left under inferior management than that provided in scientifically built, equipped and maintained day nurseries, such as the Douglas Aircraft Company now provides. . . .

So here we are, with a problem on our hands, and our national objective, (the recruiting of 5,000,000 women acknowledged to be needed for War work by the end of 1943,) with a nice chance of not being met, unless private industry steps in and does something about this.

Thirty-six states which have already set up nursery school programs as a function of Civilian Defense, have been listed in the office of James M. Landis, Director of Civilian Defense.

Some industrialists are conferring with the Boards of Education in their cities and getting help there. The factories have money to contribute toward a budget; the schools have teachers and administrative assistants who can be lent to nursery school projects. Every city has a list of former teachers, now married and retired from teaching, who might be lured back, if it were represented as a patriotic duty and the project had high professional standing.

Among the cities where the Board of Education has already done brilliant work in setting up these projects are Newark, Hartford and Bristol (Conn.), Cleveland and Dayton, Detroit and Los Angeles. This hive of activity in Southern California has had nineteen day nurseries in operation for a number of years as part of the Board of Education's program and now, with War contracts almost breaking its back, is seeking some part of the $6,000,000 which Congress has set aside to handle just such needs. Southern California has asked for 120 units for a kindergarten-nursery fund, with one-half of these going to the Los Angeles area. The Board of Education here is already sponsoring 10 units of WPA nursery schools upon which mothers working in Aviation are drawing heavily. Los Angeles opened three nursery schools during September in three of its new Defense Housing areas. . . .

North American Aviation makes its own approach to the problem by employing a registered nurse and former welfare worker, as women's industrial relations counsellor. She is Mrs. Dorothy Lewis and her job is to help women employed at North American to find reputable day nurseries in Inglewood or in Los Angeles. Mrs. Lewis also volunteers to help women workers find housekeepers. . . .

Curtiss-Wright at one of their plants now has available a modern 8-room nursery, surrounded by a wide lawn, sand-piles and swings. It accommodates 50 children, each of whom is vaccinated and inoculated before admittance. Hot lunches, mid-meal snacks and supervised play are part of the program. Mothers, not employed making Curtiss-Wright "Warhawk" fighter planes, leave their youngsters here before reporting for duty. They pick their children up each night on their way home.

E S S A Y S

In the first essay, Michael A. Bernstein, a professor of history and economics at the University of California–San Diego, analyzes the reasons for the 1929 stock market crash and the Great Depression. Bernstein reviews theories about the interwar slump before offering his own explanation. In his account, the consumption patterns of the 1920s set the stage for the 1930s, favoring the expansion of new industries, such as aircraft and chemicals, and generating slower rates of growth for older ones, including textiles and lumber. World War II did not end the Great Depression. It temporarily pulled industry out of the doldrums, laying the groundwork for economic vitalization in the postwar era.

Next, Howell John Harris, a professor of history at the University of Durham in the United Kingdom and author of *The Right to Manage: Industrial Relations Policies of American Business in the 1940s* (1982), examines how some big businesses dealt with unionization following the National Labor Relations (Wagner) Act. General Motors took a "realistic" approach to labor activism, accepting that unions would "be around for the foreseeable future" and that they should be managed in ways that preserved industrial efficiency. In doing so, GM chose one of several options in labor-management relations, ranging from stubborn resistance to persistent paternalism. Why did GM select the middle ground? What route did Chrysler follow?

Finally, public historian Joel Davidson surveys the role of business during World War II in an essay for an exhibition catalog, *World War II and the American Dream: How Wartime Building Changed a Nation* (1995). Davidson casts a broad net, showing how wartime mobilization set the stage for the birth of the military-industrial complex in the postwar era. How do Davidson's conclusions dovetail with Bernstein's arguments?

Why the Great Depression Was Great

MICHAEL A. BERNSTEIN

Although the American economy has suffered several financial panics in its history, none has had the legacy of the panic of 1929. It was not until the outbreak of war in Europe that industrial production reached its precrash peak levels and the unemployment rate fell below a decennial average of 18 percent. There is no greater puzzle in American economic history than the persistent failure of investment activity during the depression of the 1930s to generate a full recovery. Most economic theorists have tried to solve this puzzle by focusing on what they conceive to be a variety of mechanisms that interfered with the establishment of equilibrium in product, labor, and capital markets after the trough was reached in 1932–33. In particular, it has been argued that obstacles to the appropriate adjustment of prices and wages upset the nation's marketplace, causing unprecedented levels of idle capacity and unemployment. These obstacles have been identified as ranging from "sticky prices" administered by highly concentrated and powerful firms, to excessively high wages maintained by union pressure, political rhetoric, and the provisions of section 7a of the National Industrial Recovery Act. In short, the prevailing view is that the persistence of the slump was the direct outgrowth of distortions in price mechanisms imposed by large firms, government, and labor unions.

A price-theoretic approach to understanding the interwar slump in general, and interwar unemployment in particular, has a great many adherents and a not inconsiderable amount of intellectual appeal. But it is not beyond empirical criticism and refutation. Prices fell by almost one-third in the early thirties. The extent

Michael A. Bernstein, "Why the Great Depression Was Great: Toward a New Understanding of the Interwar Economic Crisis in the United States," in Steve Fraser and Gary Gerstle, eds., *The Rise and Fall of the New Deal Order, 1930–1980* (Princeton, N.J.: Princeton University Press, 1989), pp. 33–37, 46, 48. Copyright © 1989 by Princeton University Press. Reprinted by permission of Princeton University Press.

of so-called administered pricing in producers' and consumers' markets in interwar America has never been shown to be very large. The proportion of the American labor force that was organized in the interwar period, while high by historical standards, was not as high as in other industrialized nations where recovery obtained sooner. These facts leave one unpersuaded that price (and wage) inflexibility explains the longest depression in American economic history.

An older tradition in the literature, first formulated during the depression itself, argued that modern capitalist economies inevitably reached a stage of slow growth and ultimate stagnation. In particular, some economic theorists and historians looked on the interwar period of American economic development as the final stage of internally generated accumulation. They argued that the American economy was moribund by the 1930s, and was revived only by the impact of wars, state expenditures, and the penetration of foreign markets. What the stagnation theorists focused on were those characteristics of the early-twentieth-century economy which seemed to presage an end to the endogenous growth of the system. By the interwar period the geographic expansion of the United States had ceased, and so had the dramatic rates of increase in infrastructural and heavy investment. Population growth had also slowed, along with the rate of immigration. The opportunities offered by foreign markets were reduced by increasingly protectionist policies, and an unequal distribution of income in the nation generated tendencies toward underconsumption.

The stagnation theorists were right to root the Great Depression in secular (that is, long-term) changes in the American economy. But the crucial secular change was not the permanent exhaustion of capitalism's capacity for investment and accumulation—a theory obviously belied by the performance of world capitalism since 1945—but rather a new structure of consumer demand that had triggered profound shifts in the composition of investment and industrial output. By the 1920s, the structure of demand in the interwar American economy reflected a long-term transition to what might be called high-income spending behavior: from 1923 to 1929, for example, consumer spending on clothing, housing, and utilities all fell while spending on food, tobacco, household appliances, medical care, and recreation rose. As a consequence, patterns of investment changed, encouraging a shift in both the composition of national output and in the distribution of employment opportunities from the old to the new sectors. But the financial crash "caught" the secular transition at a very early and vulnerable point. In 1929 and 1930, those firms located in the dynamic sectors of the economy were simply not present in sufficient numbers to lead a general economic recovery. It was this interaction of business cycle and secular trend that accounted for the length of the Great Depression, not the cycle or the trend alone. Had there been no financial disruption in 1929, the secular transition to a consumer economy would have proceeded relatively smoothly. Had the crash occurred at a later point in the long-term trend of development, when the newer industries were more fully established, the length of the disruption would have been significantly shortened. Profitable new enterprises would have been more resilient to cyclic setbacks. Their surplus funds would have been ample, and eventually they would have been able to finance their own recovery. Most important, perhaps, business expectations would have been less depressed, and net investment commitments would have increased at an earlier date.

As a direct result of a secular rise in national income, new, more affluent consumer markets emerged during the interwar period—markets that showed greater potential and faster rates of growth than others that had figured prominently in the past in total consumption expenditures. In a certain sense, this changing pattern of consumer demand was the result of the kind of behavior originally described by Ernst Engel in his now classic studies of demand. Engel found that as people grew richer, they spent proportionately less on basic foods, clothing, and housing and more on manufactures and, as they grew still more affluent, on services. These shifts in consumer demand in the interwar period had important macroeconomic consequences. The new pattern of consumer demand differentially affected industries—benefiting some, harming others. The result was that an uneven growth of industrial sectors became apparent even before 1929. Certain major industries such as textiles, iron and steel, and lumber saw their markets weaken; others, notably appliances, chemicals, and processed foods, faced a new set of opportunities, but were not yet sufficiently strong to sustain a high rate of macroeconomic growth.

Compounding the difficulty posed by the emergence of new consumption patterns, interwar changes in the distribution of income and the impact on the distribution of buying power occasioned by the rapid deflation after the crash in 1929 played an important role in hampering the recovery process. The lower 93 percent of the non-farm population saw their per capita disposable income fall during the boom of the later twenties. The evidence suggests that the interwar years offered relatively limited opportunities for the rapid development of new mass markets. Not until the 1940s and after was the distribution of income sufficiently broad to allow for the full emergence of the markets and firms that were beginning to grow during the interwar era. Although the high-income environment of the 1920s spawned a new composition of aggregate demand—due to changes in middle-class spending behavior—it also created a demand constraint on the growth of new markets in the form of a highly skewed distribution of income. The severe cyclic reduction in disposable income after 1929 only magnified this obstacle to the transformation of the structures of economic growth.

The distribution of buying power, distorted as it was by the postcrash fall in the price level, also played a role in hampering the timely growth of the dynamic sectors. By 1932 the purchasing power of those still employed had risen greatly because of rapid deflation. Insofar as these income recipients tended to be businessmen and professionals, the demand for luxury items, high-priced durables such as large cars, and nonessential services such as entertainment and tourism, rose. Deflation did not, of course, bolster the purchasing power of those who had lost their jobs, except to the extent that they owned assets, borrowed funds, or received relief payments. Thus, a falling price level did not strengthen consumption as a whole; rather, it redirected consumer expenditures toward product markets geared mainly to high-income recipients. This shift in demand patterns intensified the difficulties of the industries most damaged by the depression. Their markets shrank as the number of inactive workers rose. In more dynamic sectors, the demand emanating from those still employed was not large enough, nor was it sufficiently dispersed among a broad spectrum of commodities, to generate a large advance in revenues and thereby a robust recovery.

The divergent growth potentials of American industries during the interwar period can be broadly discerned from the changing pattern of demand for capital goods by major manufacturing sectors. Movements in the demand for capital goods indicate which industries were expanding and which were contracting during the interwar years. As the composition of final consumer demand changed during the period, so the derived demand for investment inputs was altered. The consumption patterns of the twenties favored the emergence and expansion of certain industries and generated a slower rate of growth, if not actual contraction, for others.

For example, an average of 2.1 percent of the total real expenditures on productive facilities in the American economy during the twenties was made in the processed foods sector. That average rose to 2.5 percent during the decade of depression, paralleling the change in the share of consumer spending going to processed foods. By contrast, in the textile industry the mean was 1.54 percent during the twenties and 1.2 percent during the thirties. The same shrinkage occurred in the lumber industry, where the relevant figures are 0.8 percent in the 1920s and 0.4 percent in the 1930s. In the petroleum sector there was expansion as the average share rose from 0.6 percent in the twenties to 1 percent during the thirties. Certain relatively new industries expanded quickly during the interwar years. Aircraft production and chemicals manufacturing were two sectors where the rate of investment in new productive facilities was high. There was also a rise in investment in the manufacture of office machinery and related equipment, absorbing an average of 3.3 percent of real total domestic investment during the twenties and 3.9 percent in the thirties. In iron and steel production there was also a moderate increase in the investment share, but this expansion was limited to firms producing for appliance, food container, and other new markets. The automobile sector experienced a slight rise in its investment share, but again such expansion was limited to firms producing newer styles of cars equipped with what had previously been regarded as luxury items. . . .

The changing composition of consumer and investment demand, combined with the cyclic problems of the early thirties, generated a severe structural unemployment problem. The limited size of the dynamic sectors made the absorption of the unemployed exceedingly difficult. The net result was a continuation of the unpropitious demand conditions facing the economy as a whole. Any large increase in employment had to come from a general revival of all sectors.

A comparison of net investment data for the 1930s with the interwar ranking of industries with respect to their share of national employment and value of output provides further demonstration of the uneven development of major industries that interfered with recovery. . . . [T]he evidence shows that sectors where net investment recovered relatively quickly after the trough of 1932 had low shares of national employment and national value-product. Conversely, those industries that in the interwar period accounted for large shares of employment and output engaged in little if any net expansion in the immediate wake of the crash. Notable examples of the former are food products, tobacco products, chemicals, and petroleum products—precisely those sectors most stimulated by the new patterns of consumer spending at the time. Of the latter, the best demonstrations are afforded by textile mill products, lumber products, primary metal industries, and transportation equipment.

Thus, a massive structural unemployment problem emerged during the thirties that in the absence of an exogenous shock like war would have taken some time to solve. But this problem, which began to emerge prior to 1929, was not derived from interferences with the price mechanism of labor markets. Rather, it was one of mobilizing the necessary capital, information, and confidence to retrain and reallocate the labor force in conformity with prevailing employment trends and opportunities. Indeed, there had been a steady decline since the early twenties in the percentage of national employment accounted for by the manufacturing and construction sectors. The same decline took place in agriculture and mining. In the service industries, such as transportation, trade, finance, selected services, and government operations, there was a rise. Even if there had been no financial crash in 1929, these trends show that structural unemployment would have been a recurrent problem in the interwar period.

The Great Depression must be viewed as an event triggered by random historical and institutional circumstances, but prolonged by the timing of the process of long-term industrial development in the United States—in particular, by a transition in the structure of consumer and investment demand in the interwar period. The financial machinery of the American economy, caught in heavy deflation, was not equal to the task of pushing open the doors to the patterns of growth characteristic of the postwar era.

The problem of delayed recovery and the peculiar difficulties created by the incipient reordering of America's industrial structure in the 1930s were quickly overcome by World War II. The war provided a twofold stimulus. The more mature industries of the interwar period were brought out of their doldrums by the particular demands of making war. The new industries were pulled along by government orders, both through their contribution to a general increase in economic activity and through their particular demands on sectors such as petroleum, chemicals, electronics, and aviation. Indeed, the war itself spawned the development of other new industries, products, and processes. Thus, the 1940s helped to lay the foundation of prosperity in the 1950s and 1960s. Indeed, it has been suggested that wartime production and military procurement during the Korean conflict, cold war, and Vietnam War have been responsible for the prosperity of the American economy in the entire postwar era.

GM, Chrysler, and Unionization

HOWELL JOHN HARRIS

A majority of American center firms were compelled to accept unionism as a fact, often after strong opposition. There was no welcome for unions: they were accepted reluctantly, under pressure, and with ill grace. Contractual improvements and increased security for the union as an organization were both strongly resisted, in the hope that, some day, the union might wither away. Managements were acutely conscious of the union as an infringement upon their power, and supported political action to amend public policy, and propaganda to reorient public opinion. General Motors is probably the best example of a large firm compelled to recognize and deal with a militant industrial union, despite its management's wishes.

Howell John Harris, *The Right to Manage: Industrial Relations Policies of American Business in the 1940s* (Madison: University of Wisconsin Press, 1982), pp. 26–32. © 1982. Reprinted by permission of The University of Wisconsin Press.

Managements had little choice but to be "realistic" in their dealings with labor, once their opposition had been overcome. Management's decision on when to abandon a posture of out-and-out antiunionism was determined by the intersection of two complex and variable forces: the union's bargaining power, and the management's determination to resist. The union's strength was affected by the economic condition of the firm or industry with which it had to deal, and by the state of opinion of the workers and of the communities where they lived. The size and militancy of a union's membership were partly determined by the success of industry's opposition, and in turn affected management's calculation of the costs and benefits of particular courses of action. Continued resistance might very well mean a strike, or serious, repeated interruption of production by workers on the job. Signing a contract promised some stability and continuity. Dealing with a union, either for its members only, or on behalf of all workers in the bargaining unit, signing a contract, and adjusting grievances by formal negotiation, were objectionable practices. But the law seemed to require them, and the costs of managerial obduracy, in terms of loss of control over the workforce, could be very high.

But two firms could very easily be faced with apparently similar circumstances —workers with power and unity, collective consciousness and purpose; the threat or actuality of a costly strike; local media, public opinion, and law enforcement agencies either prolabor or neutral—and *still* reach different conclusions about the proper, "realistic" course of action management should follow. This is because of the other determinant of the course of action any particular firm pursued in response to the challenge of labor: the basic outlook on industrial relations matters of its management. . . .

Managers are people, not calculating machines. They are influenced by more than cost factors in making industrial relations policy. Unionization and conflicts for control were very sensitive issues. Reactions to them were not necessarily "rational." To many businessmen, antiunionism was a matter of principle. Realism, practicality, problem-solving activism, and a readiness to try new approaches are important elements in the self-image of American management, and affect its behavior. But so does a deeply rooted, consistently conservative system of beliefs. The labor problems of the 1930s produced conflicting reactions from business, but certainly indicated that managers were far from being a "purely neutral technocracy." On the contrary, they had a large stake in a system of power and status which was under serious threat and which they had been brought up to consider natural and almost God-ordained. They found themselves living in "a nightmare world where the laws of capitalism, if they operated at all, worked the way the laws of gravity do in a dream." Some saw in industrial conflict and legislated social change the portents of a revolutionary conspiracy against American freedoms. Cool counsel to "get wise" and face realities could hardly prevail where issues were emotion-charged and value-laden. . . .

But no major American firm was willing to continue the fight into the last ditch, though some threatened to. The most antiunion employers, resisting weak unions, could evade the NLRB and the labor movement for years, but for even the stubbornest corporations in the steel, automotive, electrical equipment, rubber, farm equipment, and meat-packing industries, "realism" became a distasteful, if (it was hoped) temporary necessity, in the late 1930s or the war years. The traditional armament of belligerency had been effectively depleted by law and public opinion, and countered by the organization of strong, relatively militant unions. Unions were present as a disruptive force, and were not going to go away soon. It was no use waiting for Congress to make a new law, or for a strong conservative shift in public opinion. Business was very actively in pursuit of both these objectives, but recognized that they were unlikely to bring immediate relief, whereas the labor problem had to be dealt with in the here-and-now, within the plant. Even if the power of labor should be reduced at a later date, there would still be important new operating problems in labor relations. What could be done about them? Once a corporation had rejected, or been forced to abandon, belligerency or stubborn evasion of the Wagner Act, what course was open to it?

. . . The answer was to use corporate resources and available expertise to get the better of the union in orderly, institutionalized confrontations. General Motors and Allis-Chalmers typified this approach, developing a combative, hard-nosed, but fundamentally legal labor relations strategy. They put great efforts into managerial organization for contract negotiation and administration, with the aim of confining the union's intrusions into management's domain. "Management prerogatives"—the traditional authority of the employer to determine the conditions of work unilaterally—were defended, in principle and in daily practice, even at the cost of "taking a strike." The union was denied prestige, security, and legitimacy. Such a course was open and natural to a company faced with a militant union and having large reserves of strength and determination to carry on the fight against it, even after the question of recognition and collective bargaining was settled.

In GM's case, the company was brought to its position of narrow and legalistic acceptance of the union by bitter experience. The great sitdown strike of 1937, which forced the corporation to recognize the UAW, was followed by a turmoil of wildcat strikes over unresolved grievances from 1937 until 1939, as the corporation refused to recognize the necessity of day-to-day negotiations over grievances, or to accept the UAW's shop steward system. Finally, in the "Strategy Strike" of 1939, a weak and divided union compelled the corporation to continue dealing with it. At last, GM management understood that it was going to be troubled by the UAW for a long time, and decided to follow a "tough but fair" labor policy of not interfering with (or supporting in any way) the UAW's drive for members. GM insisted upon the protection of management's right to manage and put pressure upon the union leadership to discipline its own members or not interfere with managerial discipline of them. GM "put its house in order": industrial relations became a top management function; contracts were negotiated, and their local administration was controlled, by a strong central staff; the wage structure was rationalized. As a result of these policies, GM, alone of all major automobile manufacturers, managed to stabilize its labor relations on more or less acceptable terms before the outbreak of the war. GM's strategy of "realism" was what came to be known, after the war, as the establishment of an "armed truce" relationship with the union. But few companies matched the speed and thoroughness of GM's adoption of this course: General Motors was a corporation with immense resources, a tradition of technical progressivism and managerial excellence, and an ingrained habit of "management by policy"—the development of a program of considered action—to handle all important problems.

In contrast, the Chrysler Corporation's management, which was ideologically antiunion and politically reactionary, as were most top GM men, never translated its attitudes into organization, policies, and procedures calculated to secure the common objective of uninterrupted production and unimpaired control. Chrysler handed its labor relations problems over to the corporate attorney in New York. At the plant level, there was lasting chaos. Chrysler continued to be afflicted, into the 1950s, by unofficial workers' actions which were often successful in securing informal adjustments by production supervisors and plant management over such critical issues as discipline and workloads. The "policy," if it can be called that, which Chrysler represented was one of half-hearted defensiveness against the union, in which the avoidance of labor trouble by making expedient concessions got the better of the aim of defending managerial authority. GM adopted some of the techniques of progressive personnel administration at the same time as it developed its basic labor relations policy, trying to reduce the sources of employee dissatisfaction by unilateral management action. Chrysler did little or nothing until "labor problems" became acute, with an organizing drive or a strike. In consequence, in the 1940s, Chrysler was particularly troubled when the frontier of organization advanced from the rank-and-file into the automobile industry's white-collar and supervisory forces. As a result of its considered preemptive action, GM was relatively untouched by this new problem.

Most managements which were compelled to follow the path of realism and deal with unions were evidently not as thoughtful or articulate about it as GM, and did not put as much corporate energy into the fight. Many simply tried to change as little as possible in the aftermath of unionization; to carry on as before, confining union penetration to the very minimum and granting as little recognition as possible. In the late 1930s, such a course was relatively easy to follow. It would become much more difficult once the economy got moving again. But few corporations had the foresight, time, and resources to follow GM's example and put their labor relations on a "sound business footing" before the war broke out.

This was because unions were still in the process of completing the organization of all the important units of mass-production industry when the defense period began in 1940, and their successful extension of organization into many smaller companies and smaller cities had to await favorable wartime conditions. For many corporations, then, the time of decision on strategy and tactics for living with rather than holding off a union was delayed until the peculiar strains of wartime made it impossible for management to choose freely or act to secure its desired objectives. Even for corporations unionized in 1935–37, the time of decision was often deferred until too late.

It is easy to appreciate why this was so. The constitutionality of the Wagner Act was still undecided until 1937 was half over. The short, sharp recession of 1937–38 faced companies with more immediate and severe problems even than the labor movement. And, as unemployment ravaged the new unions and industrial conflict declined, the challenge with which business had to deal appeared less serious. The formation of a conservative coalition in Congress, and its strengthening in the 1938 elections, offered new hope of a legislative solution to the labor problem. The NLRB's interpretation of the Wagner Act developed quickly in 1937–39, but judicial confirmation of such crucial issues as the necessity of reaching written agreement had to wait until the defense period. The code of practice of which an employer had to be aware, even if he was intent on breaking it, was only in the process of being formed. Contracts and the machinery of collective bargaining were similarly in flux. Faced as corporations were with the speed and complexity of change, and the temptation to wait for Congress to turn up with a panacea, it is understandable that GM's self-critical, self-reliant approach to its industrial relations problems was untypical.

In addition, the resources out of which a tough, successful approach to labor relations problems might have been fashioned were scarce. Only a minority of firms had been organized to deal systematically with personnel problems in the 1920s, and many personnel departments had been scrapped in the cost-cutting disorganization of the Depression. Those which survived had neither relevant experience, the correct outlook, nor adequate staff to handle the problems posed by the organization of labor and the burden of new legislative requirements; and then the shock of transition to the new age of strong unions was great, even for such an unusually well-constructed personnel department as International Harvester's. There was a shortage of knowledge and expertise to apply to new labor relations problems, and in any case managements had other, often more important preoccupations as they searched for strategies for corporate survival. Companies were going through the throes of expansion and contraction of personnel and operations, centralization and decentralization of management structures, and the problems of managerial succession (of which Ford provides the best example). In these circumstances, adoption of new policies and structures for the handling of industrial relations problems was inevitably difficult, even where it did command a high priority.

Where progress was made, it was generally taking place in an atmosphere of crisis, as managements reacted to immediate pressures. There was little time for strategic thinking. Rather, companies were adopting what came to be called a "fire-fighting" approach, looking for ways to comply with increased governmental regulation and new personnel record-keeping requirements, and having to recruit or train staff, and then organize them into departments, to handle these tasks and cope with contract negotiation and administration in recently unionized plants.

So it is not surprising that General Motors provided a rare example of a corporation that was able to get over the turmoil of 1935–37 before the war. GM was giving a lead many other corporations would follow in time. But most large and medium-sized firms had reached some of the same "realistic" conclusions: that unions were going to be around for the foreseeable future, and that they must be dealt with, within the law, in such a way as to preserve as much order, efficiency, and control as possible. Unfortunately, developing policy and procedures to make "living with the union" tolerable was a difficult matter which many firms were only beginning in the years 1937–40.

The policy of "armed truce," though the most important, was not the only strategy for living with unionism that existed in the late 1930s. For the most liberal and constructive response to the problems of unionization, we must look to some of the heirs of 1920s-style managerial progressivism. Not all progressive firms by any means accepted change gracefully. Many, like Special Conference firms Bethlehem Steel, Standard Oil of New Jersey, Du Pont, Goodyear Tire and Rubber, and International Harvester, practiced a sophisticated antiunionism, in the later 1930s as throughout the 1920s; some, notably Westinghouse Electric, General Motors, and U.S. Steel, followed the course of realism. But a few, notably U.S. Rubber and General Electric, accepted the labor movement with little hesitation or apparent regret.

World War II and the Birth of the
Military-Industrial Complex

JOEL DAVIDSON

On September 1, 1939, when German forces marched into Poland and war broke out in Europe, the United States was psychologically and physically ill-prepared to play a major military role. The U.S. Army could field just over a quarter of a million men, a far cry from the eight-million-man force that eventually helped spread American power from Okinawa to the Elbe. The Navy, though large, had yet to acknowledge that aircraft carriers had eclipsed big-gun surface ships in military significance, and the Army Air Corps was just beginning to emerge as an independent branch of the armed forces. Perhaps most alarming, however, was the near total absence of a modern arms industry. During World War I, the United States had relied on its allies for much of the Army's planes, weapons, and ammunition. During the 1920s and 1930s, the Army maintained just six arsenals dedicated to weapons manufacture—capable of producing less than a tenth of the armaments required for a major war.

The German blitz across France in May and June of 1940 shattered the assumption that the war could be confined to Europe. With France defeated and Britain in jeopardy, the United States began a crash program to arm itself. Unimpeded by blockade, bombing, or invasion, American war industries expanded with amazing rapidity. In many cases, existing factories, some of which had been idle during the Depression, could be converted to war production with the proper machine tools. The automotive industry, the country's largest, included over a thousand plants. After Pearl Harbor the government banned private automobile production, and almost all of these plants converted to war work. The industry eventually accounted for more than half the national output of tanks and aircraft engines, in addition to millions of military trucks.

However widespread and successful, conversion of plants from civilian to war production could not meet American defense needs, and the Federal government undertook to create a wide range of new industrial facilities. In 1940, Congress approved funding techniques that involved government to an unprecedented degree in industrial finance. Before 1940 Federal funding provided less than five percent of the nation's capital investment; from 1940 to 1943 this contribution jumped to sixty-seven percent. The government agency largely responsible for industrial construction was the Defense Plant Corporation (DPC). By 1945, the DPC had funded over a thousand industrial facilities worth almost $7 billion, mostly aircraft factories and shipyards. Major corporations, motivated by patriotism, increased wartime profits, and new tax laws, invested a nearly equal amount. With a "certificate of necessity" issued by the armed forces, factory owners could deduct the entire cost of new construction over five years rather than the usual twenty.

Joel Davidson, "Building for War, Preparing for Peace: World War II and the Military-Industrial Complex," in Donald Albrecht, ed., *World War II and the American Dream: How Wartime Building Changed a Nation* (Washington, D.C.: National Building Museum, and Cambridge, Mass.: MIT Press, 1995), pp. 186, 189–190, 192, 196–197, 202, 206, 208–209, 212–213, 217–218. Reprinted by permission of The MIT Press.

The third major funding source for industrial expansion was the military. With annual appropriations reaching billions of dollars, the Army and Navy built their own manufacturing base for arms, explosives, and other specialized defense items. Many new plants were operated by the armed services, employing the military for the first time in mass industrial production and plant management. Most, however, were run under special management contracts by major corporations such as E. I. du Pont de Nemours and Remington Arms. Plants operated under contract were known as GOCO—government-owned, contractor-operated—factories. In both cases, the new facilities gave the armed forces direct control over a large and modern weapons industry. . . .

Aircraft Facilities

Without a doubt the most spectacular and far-reaching wartime industrial growth occurred in the field of aircraft production. The aircraft industry received a major boost following the fall of France. President Roosevelt made a nationally broadcast speech calling for manufacturers to increase production from thirteen thousand to fifty thousand planes a year, which the government estimated would require tripling existing factory space. Once the United States entered the war, production targets rose even higher; in early 1942 Roosevelt demanded that plane makers build sixty thousand aircraft in 1942 and one hundred twenty-five thousand in 1943.

In response to these demands, the government and industry launched a major building program. A prime example was Douglas Aircraft Company's Long Beach, California, assembly plant, located across town from Douglas's existing facilities at El Segundo and Santa Monica. Built with Federal money in 1940–41, the one-point-four-million-square-foot factory was one of the most advanced aircraft plants in the world. Forty-three thousand workers labored around-the-clock at Long Beach to produce over nine thousand military aircraft, including Douglas C-47 transports and B-17 heavy bombers built under license from Boeing. . . .

. . . Even as aircraft producers struggled to deal with rapidly changing production goals, military planners acted on the alarming fact that almost all major aircraft plants were concentrated in a few areas along the East and West Coasts. Fears that air raids could cripple key production facilities prompted the War Department to locate new plants in the nation's heartland, thereby giving the industry some strategic depth. In 1941 the Army Corps of Engineers oversaw the construction of large bomber assembly plants in Tulsa, Oklahoma; Omaha, Nebraska; Fort Worth, Texas; and Kansas City, Kansas. By war's end, the Army Air Forces had sponsored one hundred ninety facility projects including fifty-seven airframe plants, eight engine plants, one hundred seven parts plants, and eighteen modification centers. Most of these new factories were built throughout the South and Midwest, completely altering the geographic spread of aircraft manufacturing. By 1944, when industry expansion was nearly complete, almost half of all aircraft plants were located far from prewar production centers.

Typical of this new wave was the Tulsa plant, which Douglas Aircraft operated under contract, assembling Consolidated Aircraft B-24 Liberator heavy bombers and later their own A-26 light bombers. Parts for the B-24s were to be shipped from the Willow Run plant being built in Michigan by Ford Motor Company. To handle these large four-motor planes, the main assembly building was a single open bay nearly a mile long. The Tulsa factory, like most war plants, operated twenty-four hours a day. . . .

As the war progressed, ever-larger plants were created. The six-point-five-million-square-foot Dodge engine factory in Chicago had nearly half as much floor space as the entire industry contained in 1940; the main assembly building itself covered eighty acres. Dodge-Chicago eventually turned out over eighteen thousand high-powered Wright radial engines for Boeing B-29 Superfortress heavy bombers. These advanced aircraft played a key role in the closing stages of the Pacific war, leading an air campaign against Japan that culminated in the dropping of the atomic bomb.

By mid-1945, almost $4 billion had been invested in new aircraft factories and equipment, nearly ninety percent of which came from Federal coffers. The $1.5 billion in new structures, together with converted factories, increased industry floor space to one hundred sixty-seven million square feet. At the height of production in 1944, these new facilities allowed the industry to build ninety-six thousand planes. The war had built up a giant industry from a series of mostly small shops—an industry that depended almost entirely on military sales and government-owned manufacturing facilities.

The government also intervened in industries that supported aircraft production and operation. Almost half the total output of aluminum, the basic structural material for modern aircraft, was produced in government-funded plants, and aluminum production increased nearly fourfold. Magnesium was another primary ingredient in light structural alloys used for aircraft, and in the manufacture of incendiary bombs. By 1941, aircraft and bomb plants were using over four hundred million pounds of magnesium per year, over sixty times prewar levels, and the government ordered construction of fourteen new magnesium plants. The largest of these was the Basic Magnesium plant, located in the Nevada desert near Las Vegas. Basic Magnesium could produce one hundred twelve million pounds of processed metal per year, more than the entire world output prior to the war. . . .

The steel industry also benefited from Federal funding. Nearly $1 billion in government money accounted for just under half of the newly created steel ingot capacity. More significantly, the government made a conscious effort to diversify the eastern-based industry by funding new plants in Utah and California, thereby freeing western shipbuilders from dependence on eastern steel sources. In a speech dedicating the new government-funded steel mill in Fontana, California, master industrialist Henry Kaiser observed, "For the first time on this side of the Rockies we begin the manufacture of iron, the fundamental element in modern industry, from ore mined in our own mountains. . . . The westward movement which began so long ago has not come to an end on the Pacific Slope. It is poised now for the next great thrust. The day of the West is at hand."

While increased industrial muscle helped integrate the Far West into the American economy, additions to the nation's air transportation system ensured that political and cultural integration would soon follow. With planes pouring off the assembly lines, the growing U.S. air forces required thousands of new airfields to train pilots. In 1939, the Army and Navy together had only twenty-eight air stations. During the war, the Army built more than one thousand air bases, while the Navy built over sixty major air stations, including a flight-testing facility at Patuxent, Maryland. . . .

Patuxent and hundreds of new flying fields like it confirmed the ascendancy of military aviation in the postwar world, but the true revolution occurred in the nation's civilian air transportation system. Many existing civilian airports such as Denver, Colorado's, Municipal Airport were expanded and upgraded by the military, and areas that had never been near commercial air transportation routes suddenly became homes to busy modern airports. After the war, over five hundred surplus military airfields were transferred to municipal authorities, making possible a truly national system of air travel. One example is Windsor Locks Army Air Base in Connecticut, built in early 1941 as a fighter station to defend southern New England. State authorities took over the base in 1946 and began laying the groundwork for Bradley International Airport, the region's principal air transportation facility. . . .

Continual improvements and refinements of military aircraft designs prompted the industry to fund sophisticated structures for research and testing. Wartime profits allowed aircraft companies to finance installations that would previously have been beyond their reach. In 1942, four large California aircraft producers—Douglas, Consolidated Vultee, Lockheed, and North American—agreed to cooperatively finance construction of the nation's most technologically advanced wind tunnel. The Southern California Cooperative Wind Tunnel was built in Pasadena, California, and operated by the California Institute of Technology. Clark B. Milliken of Caltech, who became director of the project, had actively lobbied for the wind tunnel, seeking first government and then corporate funding. . . . Updated and improved, the Southern California Cooperative Wind Tunnel continued to serve the aerospace industry for a decade and a half after the war, linking the academic community and the military by performing vital testing on major military and civilian aircraft designs.

The wartime building boom in aircraft plants and related facilities created a large, integrated industry out of what had been a collection of small specialized producers. The war not only enhanced the status of airframe and engine companies, the latter now including giant General Electric for jet turbines; it also fostered the growth of specialized interests that relied on continued aircraft production for their survival. Plants that made parts and instruments, high-octane gasoline and jet fuel, or specialized lightweight forgings had as much at stake in the aircraft industry's survival as the aircraft producers themselves. In some areas, entire communities depended on the aircraft industry for their economic well-being. In Los Angeles, for example, local governments tried to sustain the industry's postwar health by encouraging airport construction and civilian air travel. Corporate and civic interests allied with bureaucratic forces in the government attempted to influence policy decisions that would help maintain a large and modern Air Force.

Munitions Plants

The German victories of 1940 spurred the hurried construction of ordnance plants of all kinds. By early 1941, the Army had thirty-four new munitions factories under construction, and by 1944 U.S. factories led the world in armaments production. Typical of the new munitions facilities was the Radford Ordnance Works, a four-thousand-acre explosive-powder plant begun in rural Virginia in 1940. The first of the new armaments factories to enter service, Radford could turn out three hundred thousand pounds of explosive powder a day. Pursuant to a typical GOCO plant agreement, Radford was designed, built, and operated by the Hercules Powder Company under a cost-plus-fee contract. From 1941 through 1944, the plant produced over three hundred million pounds of smokeless powder for the Army. . . .

The wartime ordnance plants were conceived and created as part of an integrated munitions industry. The Radford factory, for example, was served by an ammunition-loading facility at the nearby New River plant. Explosive powder produced at Radford was loaded into live ammunition and stored for shipment at New River. . . . In addition to powder and shell plants, the Army built factories for tanks, cannons, and machine guns, as well as proving grounds and storage depots. By the war's end, the military owned over $5.5 billion worth of munitions plants and supporting facilities, most of which were operated by private contractors. These plants represented a quantum leap in munitions production capacity, and gave the armed services a degree of independence and control that military leaders would be loathe to relinquish.

Research and Testing Facilities

World War II was the first war for which basic scientific research was harnessed to produce war-winning weapons. By far the most advanced and far-reaching research project was the massive, secret, and science-intensive industry devoted to developing a nuclear weapon. The Manhattan Project helped turn scientific investigation into a national security endeavor that blurred the lines between industry, universities, and the armed forces. At its peak, the Manhattan Project employed over two hundred thousand workers at thirty-seven installations in the United States and Canada. Some of these installations contained specialized structures never before built or even imagined. At Oak Ridge, Tennessee, for example, scientists and architects designed a gaseous diffusion plant that would collect U-235 by pumping uranium-enriched gas through a series of microscopic filters. The main diffusion building, built by J. A. Jones Construction Company, measured nearly half a mile long; its series of precisely engineered and aligned pumps, filters, and instruments made it the most technologically sophisticated factory of its time.

The atomic bomb was only the most impressive of many scientific-military ventures launched during the war. Advances in radar and electronics revolutionized warfare, and the military financed laboratories at leading universities to continually refine this new technology. Government contracts financed new construction at the Massachusetts Institute of Technology, where the secret Radiation Laboratory perfected military radar and guidance systems. At Harvard, the Radio Research Laboratory searched for ways to confuse enemy radars.

Not all government research work could be farmed out to universities and private industry. Federal dollars were also used to create or expand sophisticated government testing facilities that would supplement academic and corporate resources. The David Taylor Model Basin, for example, built in 1938–39 just outside Washington, D.C., tested warship designs by running scale models through an artificial ocean created in a large tank. . . . The basin continues to serve as the nation's premier nautical test facility.

Postwar Conversion

In September 1945, the termination of hostilities brought significant dislocation to these aerospace, ordnance, and defense research facilities. In each case, however, initial cutbacks were followed by a period of continued government intervention. Government interest in creating a permanent defense-production establishment was reflected in the measures taken to maintain the industrial base created during the war. While many war plants were retained by the military, other government-financed defense plants not directly under military control continued to be used for national security purposes. Although certain plants were sold outright after the war, Congress designated over two hundred surplus plants as vital to national security in the event of a future conflict. These factories could be sold to private firms, but only on the condition that they be available for military production in an emergency. Approximately one hundred plants that did not find buyers were retained as a national industrial reserve. These and other government-controlled plants formed the physical basis for the military-industrial cooperative that thrived during the cold war.

FURTHER READING

Adams, Stephen B. *Mr. Kaiser Goes to War: The Rise of a Government Entrepreneur* (1997).

Bernstein, Michael A. *The Great Depression: Delayed Recovery and Economic Change in America, 1929–1939* (1987).

Blum, John Morton. *V Was for Victory: Politics and American Culture During World War II* (1976).

Bordo, Michael D., et al., eds. *The Defining Moment: The Great Depression and the American Economy in the Twentieth Century* (1998).

Childs, William R. *Texas Railroad Commission: Understanding Regulation in America to the Mid-Twentieth Century* (2005).

————. *Trucking and the Public Interest: The Emergence of Federal Regulation, 1914–1940* (1985).

Edsforth, Ronald. *The New Deal: America's Response to the Great Depression* (2000).

Fearon, Peter. *War, Prosperity, and Depression: The U.S. Economy, 1917–45* (1987).

Foster, Mark S. *Henry J. Kaiser: Builder in the Modern American West* (1989).

Hawley, Ellis W. *The New Deal and the Problem of Monopoly: A Study in Economic Ambivalence* (1966).

Higgs, Robert. "Regime Uncertainty: Why the Great Depression Lasted So Long and Why Prosperity Resumed After the War." *Independent Review* 1 (Spring 1997): 561–590.

Koistinen, Paul A. C. *Arsenal of World War II: The Political Economy of American Warfare, 1940–1945* (2004).

Marchand, Roland. *Creating the Corporate Soul: The Rise of Public Relations and Corporate Imagery in American Big Business* (1998).

McElvaine, Robert S. *The Great Depression: America, 1929–1941* (1984).

McQuaid, Kim. *Big Business and Presidential Power: From FDR to Reagan* (1982).

O'Neill, William L. *A Democracy at War: America's Fight at Home and Abroad in World War II* (1993).

Rothbard, Murray N. *America's Great Depression*, 5th ed. (2000).

Temin, Peter. *Did Monetary Forces Cause the Great Depression?* (1976).

Vatter, Harold G. *The U.S. Economy in World War II* (1985).

Wolfskill, George. *The Revolt of the Conservatives: A History of the American Liberty League, 1934–1940* (1974).

Postwar Challenges and Opportunities: The Culture of Affluence and the Cold War, 1945–1980

In the twenty-five years after World War II, American business focused on increasing output and efficiency, enhancing living standards, solidifying best practices, and exporting U.S. products and management techniques. At home, military and cultural imperatives became entwined as the Cold War competed with mass consumption for center stage. Millions of veterans benefited from the Serviceman's Readjustment Act, using federal funds from this "G.I. Bill of Rights" to attend college, buy suburban homes, and start businesses. Some women began to climb the corporate ladder, demonstrating executive acumen that inspired Business Week *to spotlight their achievements. In 1954, Tupperware vice president and general manager Brownie Wise, a marketing wizard, became the first woman featured on the magazine's cover, confirming the consumer economy's significance. During the postwar era, the demand for both military and consumer goods soared, driving the national economic boom.*

In the 1920s and 1930s, American industry had revved up its research and development (R&D) machine and launched a massive public relations campaign to promote industrial science as the great fountain of prosperity. This effort accelerated as industrial research continued to flourish in the postwar era. The accomplishments of corporate research laboratories were touted in print advertisements, television shows, Hollywood movies, educational newsreels, and magazine articles. A miraculous new world was dawning, thanks to plastics and synthetic fibers, antibiotics and vaccines, television and electronic computers. Executives delivered speeches celebrating the triumph of big business and democracy over depression, poverty, war, and tyranny.

The superiority of American science and technology owed much to U.S. globalism and the Cold War. The Soviets and the Americans faced off on several fronts: ideology, military might, nuclear prowess, space technology, and consumer comfort. The showdown cost the United States billions of dollars annually in the name of national security. The Cold War deepened the belief that federal funding for industrial research was a key element in national defense. Vannevar Bush, the physicist who had headed scientific mobilization in World War II, advocated this position and secured major federal dollars for basic science. The party line went something like this: government-sponsored industrial research stimulates progress in science and technology, providing corporations with cutting-edge knowledge leading to innovations for consumer markets. During the Cold War, there was nothing more patriotic, more American, or more businesslike than supporting this linear connection between research and innovation.

To be sure, high levels of defense spending buoyed the postwar economy. In 1975, the U.S. Bureau of the Census reported that the gross national product (GNP) rose from $212 billion in 1945 to $977 billion in 1970, while unemployment remained low. Yet national statistics can hide a lot. As the Cold War heated up in the early 1960s, some Washington lawmakers concerned with the health of American enterprise began to evaluate the effect of the national security state on the country. Minnesota Democrat Hubert H. Humphrey (1911–1978) headed the U.S. Senate Select Committee on Small Business, which investigated the impact of defense spending on the civilian economy. Raised as a New Deal liberal, Humphrey struggled to understand shifting priorities: from the Frost Belt to the Sunbelt, from social welfare to national security, from privately funded research to federally subsidized R&D. Without a doubt, Humphrey understood the fundamental principles that buttressed the military-industrial-academic complex. Still, he represented a region that had been adversely affected by changing patterns of government and corporate spending, and these changes troubled him. Humphrey's observations were farsighted, as other Americans learned, beginning in the 1960s.

 # D O C U M E N T S

In Document 1 from 1944, the National Association of Manufacturers (NAM), a trade association for industrial concerns, outlines its plan for stimulating the American economy after World War II. Targeting factory workers, the NAM pamphlet outlines a "sound program" that emphasizes "*more* jobs and *more* earnings for all." Why did the NAM think that such a program was necessary? How does the NAM program resemble the welfare efforts at Kodak and Goodyear during the Progressive Era (Chapter 8)?

Real estate agents contributed to the excitement about suburbia by promoting commercial development outside of the cities. In 1948, Chicago realtor Philip Levit targeted John Wanamaker, Philadelphia's premier department store, as the potential anchor for a new Illinois shopping center (Document 2). Ultimately, Wanamaker expanded its operations in the East rather than opening Midwestern branches. How does Levit try to make the Chicago-area opportunity appealing to store president J. E. Raasch?

As big business promoted the products of industrial research, consumers like J. H. Green of Lombard, Illinois, took notice—and reflected on the contradictions. If science-based corporations were eradicating what Franklin Delano Roosevelt in 1941 had called the "freedom from want," why did a nylon shirt cost $7.95 when a cotton one was only $3.50? In 1950, Green wrote to E. I. du Pont de Nemours & Company, the inventors of nylon, asking that very question. Document 3 contains the correspondence between Green and Du Pont president Crawford H. Greenewalt. How does the Du Pont executive account for the price of a nylon shirt?

In Document 4, *U.S. News and World Report,* a conservative weekly for businessmen, examines the ramifications of the postwar "baby boom." The magazine looks at the yearly "crop of 4 million babies" as "the customers of the future," presenting a detailed analysis of their potential wants and needs. Which types of businesses were most likely to profit from the population explosion? How accurate was the prediction? What is the relationship between this forecast and the NAM's plan for prosperity in Document 1?

During the postwar years, Time Inc. continued to celebrate American civilization as humane, American business as modern and progressive. In 1930, media magnate Henry R. Luce had launched *Fortune,* a superbly researched and lavishly produced magazine for American executives. By the 1950s, it was the nation's leading business monthly, distinguished for its in-depth coverage and Cold War liberal perspective. In Document 5, a 1959 *Fortune* article describes the recent growth of grand motels and resort destinations such as Atlantic City, Phoenix, Las Vegas, and Miami Beach. What types of evidence does *Fortune* use to explain these developments? What does this story tell us about business-government relations during the Eisenhower years?

The next two documents are primary sources that question the underpinnings of the military-industrial-academic complex. In Document 6, Hubert H. Humphrey, speaking before his Senate committee on small business, compares the American emphasis on federally sponsored R&D to the situation in Europe and Japan, speculating on the long-term implications.

Humphrey and his Senate cohorts were not the only ones to reevaluate the priorities of the Cold War state. In 1971, the journal of opinion, *The Nation,* published an exposé on the Vietnam War, revealing the unpopularity of the conflict in the business community (Document 7). What types of business oppose the war, and why? How do businessmen differentiate between federal spending for Vietnam versus R&D?

1. National Association of Manufacturers Outlines a Plan for Postwar Prosperity, 1944

What's the First Step?

Both right- and left-wing economists agree that a high degree of prosperity cannot be achieved in the country without a high rate of production. They also agree that the problem now facing us is not one of learning *how* to produce but, rather, of seeing to it that there is sufficient consumption—for without sufficient consumption, the things we make will gather dust and rot in warehouses.

This, then, is the *key* to postwar prosperity—maintaining a high rate of production by stimulating a high rate of consumption.

Right now we have the greatest productive capacity in all history. Some of it was built for war and will have to be rebuilt for peace. That can and will be done—in the shortest possible space of time.

In rebuilding it, however, steps must somehow be taken to make sure we shall be able to buy the many things our farms and our factories produce.

Some people feel that this can be done through government spending—and the fact is, that it *can* be, temporarily. The trouble is that such spending would only lead

"National Association of Manufacturers Links Production and Consumption in Plans for Postwar Prosperity, 1944," in National Association of Manufacturers, *How America Can Earn More, Buy More, Have More: A Practical Guide to Postwar Prosperity* (New York: National Association of Manufacturers, 1944), 3–12. Pamphlet in folder: Campaign documents, 1943–45, box 843, series III: NIIC Records, acc. 1411, National Association of Manufacturers Archives, Hagley Museum and Library, Wilmington, Del. Reprinted by permission of Hagley Museum and Library.

us further into debt—at a time when further debt would put the most severe strain on our economy.

Such spending can only be accomplished through further borrowing, and borrowed money has to be paid back through taxes—taxes that eventually would eat into every pay envelope and so actually *reduce* purchasing power. As President Roosevelt has said, "Taxes are paid in the sweat of everyone who labors."

Obviously, therefore, it must be done on a more practical basis—and *can be done* on a basis of far-sighted business policy.

It can be done by using our productive capacity to provide us with *more for our money* in the things we buy, so that we can buy more—and so create *more* jobs and *more* earnings for all.

Under such a policy, continuing prosperity and a constantly increasing standard of living can be achieved and maintained for everyone in our economy.

A Sound Program for Postwar Prosperity

The program which American industry proposes to put into effect is aimed at accomplishing two things:

1. Increasing the opportunities for all to *earn*
2. Increasing the opportunities for all to *buy*

Business's reasons for selecting these two objectives are obvious. As people earn more, they buy more. As they buy more, the need for more production is created and new jobs and better earnings are built. This is the "process of prosperity."

How does business propose *specifically* to increase the opportunities for all to *earn* and to *buy* and so put into operation this "process of prosperity"—without which we can look forward only to more complications and more difficulties in our economic life and, many economists warn us, to an eventual loss of political rights?

Increasing the Opportunities for All to EARN

Business's program is based on fundamental economic facts. It is obvious to anyone that increasing the opportunities for all to *earn* must be accomplished in one or all of three ways: through more jobs, through better pay, through worker advancement to higher-paying positions.

To provide more jobs, business proposes *bold risk-taking in starting new businesses and expanding old,* in order that the services of more people will be called for.

Business plans to proceed immediately, once victory has been attained, with the production of new products and with general expansion programs. This action will automatically create more jobs for more people—directly in business and industry and indirectly in many other fields—thus adding to the national income, so that the products which business manufactures will find money waiting to buy them. . . .

Just and Enlightened Wage Policies

In addition to creating jobs, industry plans to see that those jobs are good-paying jobs. To this end, it proposes to *follow liberal wage policies which pay the worker every last penny his production justifies and to put into his hands the most efficient tools available in order that he can improve his own production.*

Industry cannot sell its products to workers who earn only starvation wages. Consequently, it intends to pay its workers just as much as it possibly can for the work they perform.

Only visionaries would propose that workers be paid more than they are worth—an uneconomic and disastrous process. What industry *does* propose is to establish just and enlightened wage policies—and to provide employees with tools and working conditions which enable them to produce more with the same amount of effort, and so earn more—a wholly sound and practicable process. . . .

Helping Workers Up

The third way by which business proposes to increase earning opportunities is *by opening all possible avenues of advancement for its workers*—by upgrading them as quickly as possible in order that, by exercising increased skill, they can add still further to their incomes.

In the postwar program of industry, such advancement is not only desirable but essential. For, as we expand production, we will automatically need more men for more responsible positions.

That this *can* be done more rapidly than was ever believed possible was demonstrated by industry in its war program—where it had to take special steps and establish special programs to uncover previously unsuspected talents among its workers.

So successful have such programs proved, that industry is carrying its search for talent even further and is actively taking steps, right now, *to put returning servicemen in better jobs than the ones they left.*

The Selective Service Act requires only that a company give a serviceman his *old* job back—but such companies as Carrier Corporation, General Foods, General Motors, Westinghouse and many others have already set up special departments which analyze the new abilities developed in their workers through military experience and see to it that those abilities are utilized fully to the company's and the worker's benefit.

This practice will be continued as a permanent part of peacetime operations. . . .

Increasing the Opportunities for All to BUY

It means little for wages to go up if prices also go up as much, or even more—for then a worker's earnings buy no more than they did previously, his lot is unimproved, and additional markets for new products never materialize.

To increase the opportunities for all to *buy,* business proposes three definite steps. The first of these is *to put on the market the finest products that can be made at the lowest prices for which they can be sold.* Business intends to do this without penalizing wage rates, but accomplishing it through the full utilization of its technological know-how, which has increased tremendously during the war.

The output of goods per worker, for example, increased, up to the war, about two per cent a year. It is expected that workers' output can be expanded at a much greater rate after the war. This means that the cost of production can be brought down if taxes and other costs beyond industry's control do not rise too high. The savings thus effected, business proposes to pass along to consumers in the form of better goods at lower prices.

Engineering Better Values

It will not be enough, however, to satisfy ourselves only with the lower prices made possible through *present* technological know-how. We must lay long-range plans for achieving still lower and lower prices *over the years,* so that the consumer's dollar buys more and more and thus the general standard of living *never ceases to rise.*

This will be done by making *low price* part of the original planning in producing merchandise or setting up services. Better value will be engineered into products *from the beginning.* Industry will employ constant research into the means of both production and distribution, in order to keep prices on a constant downward trend and value constantly upward.

The first results of such "value engineering" are already evident. The companies that intend to make television sets, for example, have already found (by asking consumers) the price at which the greatest number of people can afford to buy television sets. Individually, these manufacturers are making their plans accordingly. About a year after civilian radio production can be resumed, each of them expects to produce a practical television receiver to sell, at the beginning, under $200. Deliberate planning of mass production in advance is expected to make further price reductions possible and to produce 300,000 new jobs in the radio industry within five years after the introduction of the low-priced receivers.

The air lines' postwar plans also show the results of such thinking—in announcements of the cost of postwar air-line travel. The major companies are planning trips to London at the same price one formerly paid to fly from New York to Chicago.

Keeping Industry on Its Toes

While the great majority of manufacturers today are sympathetic to a low price policy, it would be fatuous to assume that *all* are. Manufacturers are no different from any other group of human beings—some are farsighted, some shortsighted. Not all can be expected to demonstrate economic statesmanship in the solution of our problems—just as it would be expecting too much to hope for the same type of statesmanship from all Congressmen or all labor leaders.

There is a way, however, to *force* a low price policy—and that is through strong and vigorous competition. When competition is permitted to flourish, all manufacturers of a given commodity must either improve the quality of their product, lower its price, or both, in order to survive in the market.

Therefore, American business proposes to encourage widespread competition in order to protect its own low price policy.

These are the steps—the only steps—by which sound and continuing prosperity can be built in our country. Business is generally pledged to put them into effect at the earliest moment that war production permits, for it realizes that if it does not undertake such steps its own life as well as the political rights of everyone in the nation will be threatened with extinction. In addition, if the United States of America fails to solve its own economic problems under democratic processes, the long and hard war we are now fighting—with casualties which will exceed those in any of our previous wars—will have been fought completely in vain. This time we must not fail in our position as the economic keystone of world progress. It is the only hope for the future well-being of ourselves and our children and for world peace.

2. Real Estate Developers Lure Business
to the Suburbs, 1948

Dear Mr. Raasch:

H. & E. Balaban Corporation, operators of a chain of very fine theatres in and around Chicago, own two separate parcels of property in the Chicago area for which they are completing plans for the erection of various types of commercial and amusement buildings with a parking area for a minimum of 2,000 cars.

A number of chain store tenants are interested in locating in these "City and Towns Shopping Areas" and we are desirous of having your type of store in this group of merchandising units on a rental basis.

Raymond Loewy Associates have completed a trade area survey of these two locations and I quote the data on one of these locations:

POPULATION	
Within 10 minute driving zone	279,498
" 20 " " "	653,388
" 25 " " "	773,837

WEALTH BY INCOME	
Within 10 minute driving zone	$188,590,000.
" 20 " " "	514,630,000.
" 25 " " "	638,720,000.

PER CAPITA WEALTH BY INCOME	
Within 10 minute driving zone	$675.00
" 20 " " "	810.00
" 25 " " "	825.00

BUYING POWER			
	10 MINUTE	20 MINUTE	25 MINUTE
Food	$ 45,370,000.	$120,943,000.	$151,143,000.
Clothing	36,897,000.	96,692,000.	123,276,000.
Operating	17,225,000.	45,391,000.	55,311,000.
Recreation	6,331,000.	19,062,000.	22,939,000.
	$105,823,000.	$282,088,000.	$352,669,000.

AUTOMOBILE TRAFFIC

14,000 cars in 12 hours

Philip Levit, Chicago, to J. E. Raasch, President, John Wanamaker, Philadelphia, Pa., September 15, 1948, folder 6, box 26, acc. 2188: John Wanamaker Papers, Historical Society of Pennsylvania, Philadelphia, Pa. Reprinted by permission of The Historical Society of Pennsylvania.

PER CAPITA AUTO REGISTRATIONS

Within 10 minute driving zone	1 to 4.5
" 20 " " "	1 to 4.8
" 25 " " "	1 to 4.7

AUTO REGISTRATIONS

Within 10 minute driving zone	61,751
" 20 " " "	137,817
" 25 " " "	163,836

The above are a few of the details which will give you a "birds eye view" of one of the locations we are submitting.

We will be pleased to present in more detail the type of unit we recommend for a department store, also the designs of the surrounding buildings.

We can either arrange to meet you in Chicago or Philadelphia for further presentation.

The writer will be pleased to know of your interest in this submission.

Yours very truly,

PHILIP LEVIT

3. A Concerned Consumer Asks a Big Businessman About the Price of a Nylon Shirt, 1950

October 9, 1950

Mr. Crawford H. Greenewalt, President
E. I. Du Pont de Nemours & Co.
Wilmington, Delaware

Dear Mr. Greenewalt:

I have been reading with interest your many speeches defending "big business," and I can agree with your reasoning that Du Pont's size enables it to spend millions of dollars on chance-taking research which has developed such benefits to humanity, as celophane [*sic*], rayon, nylon, etc.

I agree also that business should have a minimum of control by Government, and certainly I am no New Dealer. However, there is one particular situation in the textile industry that poses a serious question in my mind as to whether certain factors are sincere in their campaigning for the American "competitive" system.

J. H. Green, Lombard, Ill., to Crawford H. Greenewalt, President, E. I. du Pont de Nemours & Company, Wilmington, Del., October 9, 1950; Greenewalt to Green, October 20, 1950, about the price of a nylon shirt, box 26, acc. 1814: Textile Fibers Department, E. I. du Pont de Nemours & Company Archives, Hagley Museum and Library, Wilmington, Del. Reprinted by permission of Hagley Museum and Library.

I recently bought a nylon shirt (tailored by McCoy) for which I had to pay $7.95. I am in the habit of paying $3.50 for a well-tailored cotton shirt. Now I read in your October 6 speech at Camden, South Carolina, that the nylon yarn in a $1.50 pair of stockings represents only 10 cents and that the nylon yarn in a $50 dress represents only $2.04.

I have no quarrel with these figures because I have no knowledge of what the other costs are in a pair of stockings or a dress. But, I do know that there is a terrific spread in the price of a cotton shirt and a nylon one; and since both require the same weaving, cutting, needling, etc.—why this big spread? According to the figures in your Camden speech, there cannot be more than about $1.50 worth of nylon yarn in the shirt, so it can't be the nylon that causes the entire spread.

And why is every nylon shirt priced at $7.95 regardless of maker or retail outlet?

On the face of it, it would seem there is collusion among some factors of the industry and that a price is set at what the traffic will bear. If this is the case, that is not my idea of public benefaction; nor does it bear out your theme of big business operating in the best interests of society in general. It would seem to the average citizen that perhaps there is need of some sort of watch-dog action on the part of Government; and that if left completely uncontrolled, big business could not be trusted to conduct itself in the best interests of society.

I am not accusing you or Du Pont, but I would like to know why nylon shirts are selling at such a margin over cotton shirts; and since you are a well-known exponent of big business in general, and nylon in particular, I am directing my question to you. I would sincerely appreciate an answer.

I believe in the so-called American Way of Life—not as a perfect system, but as the best in existence—and I believe business should publicize its story in the fight against Communism. But, before it starts thumping the tub, it should clean up its own skirts or such publicity will backfire.

Yours truly,

J. H. Green
Lombard, Illinois

October 20, 1950.

Mr. J. H. Green
Lombard, Illinois

Dear Mr. Green:

This is to acknowledge your October 9 letter, which I have read with interest.

Despite the fact that you have directed your questions to me as an exponent of "big business," I am still somewhat puzzled as to just why this was done since the questions you ask concern the business of others. Under the circumstances it is scarcely appropriate for me to comment one way or the other on business practices that are obviously the private affairs of those other companies and concerning which we actually know very little. However, our Nylon Division has provided me with certain information which may serve to give you a better understanding of the situation.

In brief, it appears that the reason for the price differential between average cotton and nylon shirts is the higher cost all along the line in the case of nylon. A typical nylon shirt contains about 90¢ worth of nylon yarn as we sell it in what may be termed a "raw" state. The cotton yarn at a comparable stage would be considerably less. After our customer receives the yarn he processes it further including the dyeing, which is far more difficult and costly than in the case of cotton. The yarn is then woven, and because nylon is much lighter the weave is finer and more expensive than cotton. Following the weaving, nylon fabric must be finished and heat set before going to the cutter. I am informed further that the making of a nylon shirt demands special skills which differ from cotton and, as far as we know at the present time, the nylon article requires more time and labor.

Beyond that are the distribution costs which, as we understand the trade practice, would be greater for the more expensive items because the markup is done on a percentage basis. Right here I should like to clear up the matter of business size because these dozens, possibly hundreds, of concerns doing the processing, dyeing, weaving, finishing, cutting and sewing are largely *small* businesses.

In view of the foregoing, I feel that the comparison of cotton and nylon articles is not entirely fair. Moreover, I know of fine cotton shirts, imported and domestic, that cost as much or more than a nylon shirt. It should also be borne in mind that the cotton shirt industry is one of long standing and given to mass production methods to a degree which has not yet been attained in the case of nylon.

You have asked further why every nylon shirt is priced at $7.95. The same inquiry could be directed to the average cotton shirt, the price of which is, I believe, fairly uniform within various grades, or to a quart of milk, or a loaf of bread. I do not find anything peculiar in this for I am convinced that the American public will only pay for value received and will demand the best possible bargain. If the product of one manufacturer can be retailed for $1.00 all competitive articles must meet that price in order to sell. For your information, however, I have seen advertisements for nylon shirts at varying prices and only last Sunday in the New York Times they were offered by a department store at less than $6. I can't say that this necessarily implies anything because there may be a difference in quality, but it is mentioned to rebut your inference that all prices are the same.

Much more could be said on the subject, but quite frankly I did not intend to dwell at this length. I do hope that this information may in some measure clarify the situation for you.

Cordially yours,

C. H. Greenewalt
President

4. *U.S. News and World Report* Explains What the Baby Boom Means to the Economy, 1957

Each year, this country produces a crop of 4 million babies. Those babies—the customers of the future—will be in the market for goods and services over an average span of 70 years. Of the 4 million babies born, nearly 3 million represent net additions to the buying public.

It is this fact that today lies back of much of the planning for business expansion. Markets over the years ahead inevitably will grow as more people, with more wants and more money to spend, make their demands felt.

A lifetime of wants. What a crop of babies means in terms of goods during a lifetime can be seen [in the next section].

Here are but a few of the products that the individual consumes. At current rates of consumption, the individual demand for these basic products over an average lifetime is known. When that demand is multiplied by 4 million to take account of the crop of babies each year the result is shown in the startling figures [in the next section].

Industry in this country must be prepared to supply the wants of this growing population over a full lifetime. Each year, the potential of those wants rises. As the years go by, the population will tend to grow even more rapidly when the baby crops of earlier years reach maturity, marry and have babies of their own. A sharp rise in the number of families and the number of births already is seen for the 1960s. At that time the big crops of babies of the late 1940s will be reaching marriageable age and will be settling into homes of their own.

Lower standards? It is this rise in numbers of people that causes some students of population to suggest that the future may hold the threat of somewhat lower living standards. These assessors of the outlook see a population so large, with such astronomical demands, that there will be a shortage of resources out of which wants can be satisfied. America, in their view, might enter a period when population pressure will prevent further improvement in comfort and enjoyment.

However, such a period, if and when it comes, now appears to be distant. In the remaining years of this century, at least, population growth promises an expanding market for nearly everything that can be produced and consumed.

The huge figures presented [in the next section] are attracting serious attention and study from the men who have the job of planning industry's future. These figures form the basis for gauging the market that will develop in the years ahead and the share of that market that various industries can expect to get.

An end to surpluses. The annual addition of 4 million mouths to feed, for example, promises in time to solve the country's problem of farm surpluses. Analysts in the Department of Agriculture point out that over the long run American farmers may be hard put to satisfy the needs of the people. It is the same story when it comes to measuring the future demand for clothing, furniture, appliances, automobiles and everything else that goes to make up the high standard of American living. Home builders, for instance, who now are having difficulty after several years of

---

boom, can expect a renewed boom when the baby crop of the early postwar years begins to want new homes. That will come in the 1960s.

The managers of industry are constantly measuring their present capacity against the population they will have to support in the future. From these studies, they come to the conclusion that they will have to keep on building new plants, as well as improving the plants they have now.

A yearly crop of 4 million babies, in fact, is viewed as basic assurance that this country will be able to avoid any severe and extended depression in the foreseeable future. Temporary ups and downs in business conditions are expected, but the basic trend in activity promises to parallel the growth in population and, perhaps, even to exceed that growth as living standards improve.

The Babies of '57 as the Customers of Tomorrow

In their lifetimes, babies born in 1957 will need these things:

1,059,000,000 PAIRS OF SHOES—equal to nearly 2 years' production of all U.S. shoe factories. Wholesale value, in '56 prices: about 4 billion dollars.

91 BILLION GALLONS OF GASOLINE—that is about twice as much gasoline as the country's autos use in a year's time, now.

25 BILLION POUNDS OF BEEF—which means that 49 million steers will have to be born, fattened, [and] marketed, to feed this year's baby crop its steaks and roasts.

200 MILLION TONS OF STEEL—U.S. steel mills would have to work 1 year and 8 months to provide this much steel. Wholesale value, in '56 prices: about 15.4 billion dollars.

22 BILLION POUNDS OF PORK—this represents 165 million hogs, three times the number of hogs on farms today.

65.2 MILLION TONS OF PAPER—and that's assuming an average of 15 tons of paper for each baby of 1957, which is based on the '56 rate of usage. Actually, paper use is rising fast; lifetime need may average 25 tons or more per baby of 1957.

6.3 MILLION ELECTRIC REFRIGERATORS—a 1.7 billion-dollar market of the future, at 1956 prices, for refrigerator manufacturers. This is nearly 2 years' normal sales.

50 BILLION QUARTS OF MILK—an 11.8 billion-dollar order for the dairymen of the country, in terms of 1956 retail prices.

62.8 MILLION SUITS OF CLOTHES—for the men and women that 1957's babies will grow to be. These suits represent about 2 billion dollars' worth of clothes at '56 wholesale prices. Many more billions' worth of children's clothes, dresses, shirts, [and] other things will be needed.

10.8 MILLION NEW CARS—nearly 2 years' auto output, at the '56 rate of production. In addition to these new cars, the babies of 1957 will buy an even greater number of used cars, eventually.

THESE EXAMPLES give some idea of the effect of the birth rate on future markets. Estimates are conservative, based on 1956 rates of consumption. If the American standard of living continues to rise as expected, businesses and farms will be selling much more of these products, and other things, to the babies of 1957.

Note: Assumes 4.35 million births in 1957, with life expectancy of 70 years.

5. *Fortune* Credits Federal Policies for the Explosion of Motels, 1959

This year, when some 90 million Americans (10 per cent more than last year) take to the highways, the once frowzy motel industry will be doing almost as much business as all of the nation's hotels put together, and it may soon exceed them. A huge chunk of this business will be done by a spectacular type of stopping place that a new breed of motel investors have developed. These are not motels but Grand Motels. Typically, the grand motel is a vast assemblage of shrimp-pink barracks abutting a swimming pool, proclaiming in vivid neon lights: "Newest, Largest, Most Luxurious, Air-Conditioned, Free TV, Gourmet Restaurant, Cocktail Lounge . . ." Pastel palaces like these have mushroomed across the country—not only along the obvious highways and around airports but even in new residential and industrial suburbs. Edifices unbelievably "pretentious" (as one grand-motel man proudly describes his buildings) have crowded into resort areas like Atlantic City, Phoenix, Las Vegas, and Miami Beach. In a single two-and-a-half-mile stretch along Miami Beach—where tens of thousands of motorists will flock this summer to take advantage of the off-season rates—more than fifty grand motels, each basically a concrete blockhouse surrounding a communal bath, stand shoulder to shoulder behind façades suggesting Shinto temples, Moorish seraglios, and Mies van der Rohe mountain eyries.

The real rush of investors to the wayside-bedroom business began only five years ago. In 1954, according to the *Tourist Court Journal,* there were some 51,000 motels of varying sizes in the U.S., with about 816,000 rooms. For the most part fifteen-to-twenty-room operations, they represented a total investment of $3.9 billion and did a total business of $1.1 billion. By last year their numbers had increased to about 58,000, but the number of rooms had risen, in large part because of the growth of the grand motel, by over 50 per cent to 1,229,000. Total investment and business volume had more than doubled. Meanwhile, some 24,800 hotels (with 1,500,000 rooms), which had earned more than twice what motels earned in 1954, by 1958 were earning just 4 per cent more than the motels were. Investment in motels in 1958, according to FORTUNE's estimates, stood at $10 billion, and volume was up to some $2.2 billion.

Seymour Freedgood, "The Motel Free-for-All," *Fortune* 59 (June 1959): 119, 122–123, 171. Copyright © 1959 *Time* Inc. Reprinted by permission.

Big Money from Everywhere

The rise of the new caravansary has taken place in a riotous atmosphere reminiscent of a gold rush, which to some extent it is. Until recently, according to Stephen Brener, a leading New York motel broker, "the motel was like the stationery-store business. You had these thousands and thousands of little courts run by middle-aged, semiretired couples. They had the world by the tail—a market yelling for improvements—and they couldn't handle it. Then, almost overnight, the big money began to flood in from everywhere—and I mean from everywhere."

A decade of high prosperity, longer vacations, and vastly increased automobile travel had created a demand for better highway accommodations—a demand that neither the old motel nor the traditional in-town hotel was able to satisfy. Then two acts of Congress helped unloose the flood of new investment.

One was the $40-billion federal interstate highway program of 1956. By the time this 41,000-mile system of high-speed, limited-access throughways is completed in 1975, it is expected to put over half again as many cars on the road as there are today. This makes roadside business one of the most obvious "growth situations" in the U.S. economy, and has led to a real scramble for motel sites that, according to somebody's guess, are close to a future interchange or access road.

The second act was the provision in the 1954 tax code permitting a "fast write-off" on new construction and modernization. This was a stimulus to all kinds of commercial building, of course, but in the case of motels, it reinforced some powerful basic attractions: the relatively low costs of land, construction, and operation, and the high rates of occupancy. The return on investment from a grand motel is considerably higher than that from most other forms of real estate—and certainly higher than the returns from in-city hotels. Even the most optimistic hotel owner doesn't hope for much more than a 10 per cent return on his investment. In contrast, the return on a well-managed grand motel in an "unsaturated" area may sometimes run as high as 30 per cent.

So stimulated, big money began to flood in from everywhere, and as one grand-motel man puts it, "the game of creating obsolescence began." The eager players include a host of real-estate men, usually heading investor syndicates and often fortified by mortgage money from banks and conservative life-insurance companies like Prudential, Equitable, and John Hancock; a variety of general contractors, restaurant operators; institutional investors such as the trustees of the company welfare fund of U.S. Steel. Among the new motel men:

• Robert K. Lifton, a New York real-estate investor previously specializing in office buildings, who put together an eleven-man syndicate, including a shipowner, a commercial printer, a hosiery manufacturer, a department-store executive, a lawyer, an accountant, and a housewife. Since early this year the Lifton group has acquired $4 million worth of motel property, of which one example is a 100-room motel in Daytona Beach, Florida, costing $1 million. The group put up $250,000 in cash, got a Florida bank and the seller to finance the rest, expects a 14 per cent cash return annually. "You just don't get that kind of return on other kinds of real estate these days," Lifton observes. "There's plenty of money around, but not enough deals." He recently set up a company to lease a string of grand motels and operate them with professional management.

•   The Teamsters Union, which invested $1,600,000 in Miami Beach's 304-room Castaways Motel, and has taken $1,800,000 of the financing for Atlanta's five-story, $3-million Atlanta Cabana.

•   J. Willard Marriott, of Washington, D.C., owner of the Hot Shoppes restaurant chain, who opened the 375-room Marriott Motor Hotel across the Potomac from Washington in 1957 at a cost of $5 million. It has done so well that he has just completed a second grand motel in the same area, and is planning a third in Dallas for a total investment of $13 million.

The Trapped Hotel

And now in the forefront of the rush are, of all people, the hotelmen, who saw the handwriting on the wall. Ever since World War II, hotels have found themselves in increasingly awkward straits. Primarily built to serve the railroad stations, they have discovered themselves, in an era of frantic road building, galloping suburbanization, and declining rail travel, trapped without adequate parking facilities at the center of town. Between 1948 and 1958, while passenger-car registrations were increasing by over two-thirds, the national average of hotel occupancy fell from 85 per cent to 67 per cent—the worst showing since the last years of the depression.

The smaller hotels (under 500 rooms) in all but the very biggest cities and resorts have been hit the hardest. For one thing, branch plants, which supplied most of the business at the smaller city hotel, aren't downtown any more: they have moved out to the new industrial parks in the suburbs, thus managers and their visiting firemen rarely come to town at all. Motels on the outskirts of town have been the gainers; in addition to places to sleep and eat, they provide conference rooms, stenographic services, etc. They have become the new community center where, as likely as not, the Kiwanians now hold meetings, and suburban couples come for dinner, sometimes for the weekend. When the Louisiana legislature is in session at Baton Rouge, many state senators and representatives stay at motels, notably the Bellemont, which is now the convention center. Deals are worked out in smoke-filled motel rooms.

By last year the average occupancy of small in-town hotels had sunk to around 60 per cent, and many were going out of business. The larger hotels in big cities are in better shape. But even some of these are suffering: in 1958 occupancy rates for major downtown hotels in New York, Chicago, Los Angeles, Philadelphia, Boston, and San Francisco ranged from 83 per cent (San Francisco) to 63 per cent (Philadelphia).

Hotelmen have by no means conceded the end of their big metropolitan enterprises. As Spearl Ellison, Hilton Hotel Corp. vice president, observed recently, "There will always be a large enough concentration of people in the big cities and enough convention business to keep the big hotel going." Hotelmen are backing up this conviction by enlarging, modernizing, and air-conditioning many of their big-city properties (wherever possible, installing such motel-like features as free parking, special registration desks in the garage, and direct access to the upstairs rooms without going through the lobby), and a considerable number of new big-city hotels are being built.

Nevertheless, as Ellison observes, "We can hope for a 25 per cent return on a motor inn—about two and a half times that of a hotel," and this arithmetic is pulling more and more hotelmen into the motel field. Today all six of the big-city hotel chains—Hilton, Sheraton, Hotel Corp. of America, Western, Pick, and Knott—operate sub-chains of grand motels. Since 1955 Pick Hotels group has invested about $11 million in twelve luxury motels; H.C.A., which acquired its first Charterhouse (as it calls its motels) in 1957, has increased its chain to eight, with twenty-five now projected, among them an edifice in Cambridge, Massachusetts, six or seven stories high, on stilts, with parking underneath. Western Hotels of Seattle, which operates the plush Caravan Inn Motel in San Francisco, now has fourteen other Caravan Inns under construction in California and Arizona. Scores of smaller chains and individual hotel operators have also entered the field: Tisch Hotels, for example, owner of the $22-million Americana in Miami Beach, is opening two grand motels in Atlantic City this summer—one of them a 300-room job costing $4,500,000. . . .

Full Circle

The trouble is that within months after an astute operator builds the first grand motel at one of these locations he can expect it to be surrounded by a cluster of others. Knott's experience at Idlewild is typical. "We decided that 320 rooms was about right for the area," explains William B. Rasor, the company's executive vice president. "Before we knew it, there was a 100-room motel, a 112-room one, a 64-room one, all right next door to us, really. That is overbuilding. If this keeps up, people will start cutting prices and then everyone will suffer."

In New Orleans, according to Seymour Weiss, managing director of the Roosevelt Hotel, there has been so much motel building on the two main approaches to the city—100 motels as of this spring—that at least fifteen of the better ones are in financial trouble and up for sale. Meanwhile there is a flurry of motel building downtown, where land costs are high enough to keep most operators out of the field, zoning restrictions are tight, and there is a good potential convention business. Following the lead of such lavish New Orleans establishments as the Motel de Ville, the Ta Ma Na Ca, and the recently completed 200-room Fontainebleau in the move downtown, a group headed by Weiss is negotiating a forty-year lease for a $3,400,000, 265-room motel with a five-story parking garage to be built adjacent to the New Orleans civic center. A similar shift to the core of the city is taking place in Chicago, San Francisco, Atlanta, and other metropolitan centers. The trend, as one downtown New Orleans motelman observes hopefully, "will kill off a lot of the outlying motels."

Thus, a fifty-year cycle has come to a close. To protect itself against cutthroat competition and the risks of being bypassed by the new throughways, the outlying motel has penetrated the center of town. Here the motel has grown vertically and must now compete with the big city hotel on its own ground.

Spinning the Wheel

The question remains: How soon can the shoddier grand motels in the suburbs be expected to kill each other off and either go under the bulldozer or end up as highway shanty towns? In many cases the demise will be lengthy. Through the "fast write-off" provision in the 1954 tax code, it is quite possible for a motel that has ceased to give its original owner a healthy profit still to be of considerable value to a succession of sharp buyers.

Under the code, the owner is permitted to write off a declining amount of his investment as depreciation each year before payment of taxes: in the case of a building erected since 1954 in which he has invested $100,000, for example, he might deduct 10 per cent—$10,000—the first year. The second year he can deduct 10 per cent of the $90,000 balance and so on until nothing remains to be written off. So then he looks for a buyer. He will usually have no trouble finding one. In the first place, the tax law permits the new owner to give the depreciation wheel another spin—i.e., he too can start out by writing off 10 per cent of his full investment. For some entrepreneurs this tax advantage is compensation enough for reduced earnings, particularly when, as is the case with the big chain operators, they can afford to run a motel with a smaller return on investment than is possible for an owner whose entire livelihood depends on one property. And there will be an added incentive to a new buyer in the fact that land values in the area will probably have risen since the motel was built.

The net effect has been to encourage a brisk trade in second, third, and even fourth-hand grand motels, many of which would already have been junked under ordinary circumstances, and equally important, to encourage builders to put up junky motels. Undoubtedly, once the new highway system is stabilized, thus taking much of the risk out of motel building, the industry will take a longer lease on life, and will probably build more substantial and attractive hostelries. The big problem then will be how to get rid of the pastel slums.

6. Senator Hubert H. Humphrey Compares R&D Expenditures at Home and Abroad, 1962

I mentioned here a while ago, and I believe this is a roughly accurate figure, 65 percent of all R. & D. spending is Government today in the United States, Federal Government. . . .

With most of it going into military, the capital that is required to make this R. & D. apply in fact to new products and new goods, that capital follows the research and the scientific personnel, so that you have less capital going into what you call the civilian sector of your economy.

In Germany, 85 percent—85 cents out of every research dollar is private, and less than 15 percent goes into military and space. Eighty-five cents of that goes into the civilian economy, so that today the German plant competition for world markets of civilian goods is being automated, modernized, equipped in the latest and best fashion, and new products are developing, while we are developing new wrappings. We are the greatest packagers in the world. We package them beautifully. We have an artistic capacity second to none in cellophane wrappings, foils, and so forth, but the German is developing the thing inside of the package.

In Japan, it is about 85 to 15 again. That is a rough estimate. Eighty-five cents out of every research dollar is private and going into the civilian economy, with huge capital investments going into the Japanese civilian economy.

U.S. Senate Select Committee on Small Business, *Impact of Defense Spending on Labor Surplus Areas, 1962,* August 29, 1962, 87th Cong., 2nd sess. (Washington, D.C.: GPO, 1962), pp. 27–29.

In England, which also has a low rate of economic growth, as does our country, 60 cents out of every research dollar is governmental and goes into military and space, atomic energy, and 40 cents out of that research dollar goes into the private sector; about 35 percent.

This poses some problems here. I may be getting far afield. What happens in general terms, and these are at best "guesstimates," you know, just generalities. What you see happening is not so much just the profit squeeze that business talks about as holding back on investment, not even quite so much the necessity for investment tax credit like we voted yesterday, but the real truth of the fact is that scientific manpower, technological and scientific research, moneys and the facilities, attract capital, because that is where the money is to be made; that is where the new product is to come from; there is where you need the new plant, the new facility.

If your military budget provides most of this R. & D. fund and then the R. & D. funds are located in limited areas such as California, Texas, and Florida, which is partially true, at least in part, you have the tendency to follow the capital, the capital flowing into the area. . . . I would like to see the Council of Economic Advisers, your economic services in the Labor Department, . . . and the Defense Department economic consultants take a look at this picture. What is the relationship of the flow of private capital to . . . R. & D. . . . [versus military] research and development funds?

What is happening to our civilian economy as we plow more and more of our scientific personnel, our brains, into the military and into space and into atomic energy for military purposes? Where are we going to end up in this trade competition with these Belgians and these Dutch, who are clever, and the Germans who are very clever, who are spending more money for civilian aspects and will develop products cheaper, better, and more serviceable? Our rate of economic growth is nothing to be proud of. Look at the Italians, who put very, very little money into military—very, very little. We are paying the cost of military. They put 90 cents of their research dollar into the civilian economy. They talk about a miracle of Italian economy. It proves that if you put enough brains to work on something with money, you get it done.

7. Vietnam War Raises Business Hackles, 1971

Answer true or false:

1. Defense spending, rising almost continuously for twenty years, has been an important stimulant and crutch for American business. (*True.*)
2. American business has used its economic and political influence to perpetuate a large defense budget. (*True.*)
3. American business has used its economic and political influence to prevent settlement of military conflicts, because of their "pump-priming" benefits.

Despite the surface logic of answering true to the third statement as well, the Vietnamese War has shown that business and financial leaders look at cold wars and

James Clotfelter, "Millions for Defense, But . . . ," *The Nation* 212 (January 25, 1971): 108–110. Reprinted with permission from *The Nation*. For subscription information, call 1-800-333-8536. Portions of each week's *Nation* magazine can be accessed at http://www.thenation.com.

hot wars quite differently. Those accepting the military-industrial complex notion that money is the binder between defense policy makers and supportive industrial and labor groups ask how American business can find fault with a war which has cost $15 billion to $25 billion a year. Where there is that much money, there must be profit and eagerness for the war to continue—right?

The clear implication of the anti-war rally chant of "rich man's war, poor man's fight" is that American business, and the wealthy, best-schools-and-clubs men who run firms and own stock in them, profit from the war in Indochina—while poor draftees from our urban jungles are sent to die in somebody else's jungles. The war is, to a considerable extent, a "poor man's fight"—economic class affects one's prospects for getting drafted and killed, of course—and equally, a "rich man's war"— some individuals and companies have profited substantially. But the economic class interpretation of the war should not be taken so seriously as to obscure the distinction between cold-war defense business (until recently, very profitable) and hot-war defense business (seen as more trouble than it is worth).

This distinction, although rarely made by businessmen in public statements, is a real one for them, judging from their recent behavior on the war issue. While most national labor leaders hold to the view that high defense budgets and wars are necessary for high employment, the financial leadership has become a potent anti-war lobby. Business' position on the war, however, has been obscured because it simultaneously lobbies for the perpetuation of strategic arms competition (e.g., the campaign for ABM).

By fall 1970 it should have become clear that Middle America is not forcing the government to "cut and run" from the Vietnamese War, despite domestic costs. Business and Wall Street, however, increasingly are saying what many dovish politicians have not yet said publicly: the war must be liquidated, by whatever means necessary, and the devil take the domino theory.

"The most important reason for . . . optimism," Stock Exchange firm partner Heinz H. Biel wrote in *Forbes,*

> is the apparent fact that President Nixon has become more fully aware of the close inter-relationship between Vietnam, social and political tensions, business conditions and the stock market. The key, obviously, is Vietnam, which *must be de-escalated and terminated at almost any price* if we are to avoid major calamities at home. . . . Is it possible that [Nixon] has forgotten this? Or has he, like his predecessors, been taken in by the persuasive power of the generals whose one-sided views and unwarranted confidence in our military prowess have led us deeper and deeper into a hopeless quagmire? [*Italics mine.*]

Anti-war rhetoric has not yet recognized that attitudes of financial interests toward the war differ sharply from their attitudes toward defense spending, although it has been apparent for two years that friendly statements from Hanoi could do more for the stock market than reassuring statements from the White House. The economic stimulation of anti-war sentiment has been given too little attention, perhaps because of the mutual uneasiness of the intellectual and business communities at finding themselves on the same side.

Simply stated, the Vietnamese War is not popular among businessmen because its costs exceed its benefits even for companies in the "complex," *even for companies directly benefiting from war spending.* Many other companies benefit very little from war spending, yet are surrounded by higher costs, taxes and debt, and by decreasing markets.

What makes hot wars less profitable is that they cannot be calibrated carefully to meet industry's capital investment and research and development timetables. Defense spending for strategic deterrence underwrites technological innovation for the aircraft, electronics and communications "growth" industries, and supports long-range industrial planning. Spending on Vietnam, on the other hand, is for items like bomb casings and uniforms. In the past, an important economic benefit of wars was that equipment was destroyed, and thus had to be replaced. Technological obsolescence performs this function in cold-war periods, of course, and with less unpleasant side effects. Until recent Vietnam-related cancellations and stretchouts, cold-war business has been profitable—more so than most commercial business.

What has the war meant to the economy? The 1965–66 troop buildup increased employment in the United States by about 1 million persons, according to the U.S. Chamber of Commerce. There was a sharp (but temporary) increase in business for supplemental airlines and helicopter and munitions manufacturers, for example, and a more limited increase for most major industries. But the Vietnam prosperity was shortlived: by late 1966 the adverse economic effects were beginning to be felt by most businessmen and stockholders. By early 1968 peace rumors had become the leading bullish stimuli for Wall Street, and by mid-1970 the litany of economic damage had become familiar: the end of the 1960s prosperity, the worst inflation and the highest interest rates since the Civil War and before, the stock market collapse, little available credit, rising unemployment (especially, of course, among minority group workers only recently hired), a gold outflow and declining international trade surplus, the loss of the investment tax credit, higher taxes, tighter government budgets (thus less money for everything from road construction to textbooks), declining profit margins for companies and declining real income for workers.

As *Moody's Stock Survey* warned:

> The war has been at the root of many of our present difficulties, including inflation, balance-of-payments problems, rising taxes, and the recurrent spector of wage, price or credit controls. . . . The economy would be hard put to digest the burden of increased military spending [for Cambodia] without suffering some serious dislocations.

Thomas Watson of International Business Machines testified against the war before a Congressional committee and press reports indicated that many bankers and business leaders were conveying anti-war opinions to the Administration in language less delicate than *Moody's*. The would-be "complex" cabalists looked at Japanese capitalism, for example, unburdened by heavy war spending, and told themselves that peace means prosperity.

War casualties included "faith in paper currencies" around the world (Terrence McCarthy); the government's authority in maintaining wage and price stability (J. K. Galbraith); and American business's freedom of investment abroad (Charles Percy). It led to the 1966 money panic and the 1970 liquidity crisis; the resulting distortion in the interest rate structure, with its impact on the essential construction industry, may be a long-term phenomenon.

By 1969 the total cost of the war (including debt interest and future veterans' benefits) was estimated by James L. Clayton in "Vietnam: the 200-Year Mortgage" [*The Nation,* May 26, 1969] at $330 billion to $350 billion to date. Other estimates, including indirect inflation and balance-of-payments costs, have exceeded a half trillion dollars. And this does not begin to deal with social costs of lower spending on urban and welfare problems, education and health.

It is a cliché that the stock market reflects people's hopes and fears, and the decline since Richard Nixon's election seems to be both a result and a cause of growing disenchantment among important economic groups with the Administration's Southeast Asia policies. Many people think most clearly with their money, and the stock market and declining consumer purchasing among higher income groups do not reflect "blank check" public confidence in the Administration. Stock brokers report, for example, that war-motivated college disruptions in May discouraged some people from buying, because the alienation of the young leads to loss of faith in the future of the American society and economy.

Disillusionment with a quagmire war cannot, of course, be equated with anti-defense-spending attitudes within the business community, although there have been some cautious beginnings in that direction. But this should not detract from the significance of business's position on Vietnam.

On the war, the public has more patience than Wall Street. For many Americans, the war's economic impact (prewar home mortgages carried interest rates of 5.25 per cent and the "widows' and orphans'" Telephone stock sold in the mid-70s), has not been translated into resentment against war policies. Wall Street's attitude, however, is reminiscent of turn-of-the-century business pacifism; international adventures were opposed not because they were "bad" but because they did not pay. Wars simply were uneconomic and outmoded forms of competition. Norman Angell's pacifist *The Great Illusion* reflects businessmen's attitudes more faithfully now than it has in sixty years. Thus the irony that if and when the war is terminated, it may be as much because of pressure from business and financial elites (its presumed beneficiaries), as from The People.

 E S S A Y S

In the first essay, Lizabeth Cohen, the Howard Mumford Jones Professor of American Studies at Harvard University and the author of *A Consumers' Republic: The Politics of Mass Consumption in Postwar America* (2003), examines the transformation of the marketplace after World War II. Cohen's case study focuses on small urban businesses and middle-class consumers in northern New Jersey, close to two upscale shopping centers built at Paramus during the 1950s. In different ways, both groups lamented the demise of town centers, decried the commercial shift to the suburbs, and tried to counter the economic decline caused by the new malls. Do Cohen's conclusions apply to the nation at large? What factors encouraged New Jersey retailers and other businesses to move from the cities to the suburbs? Would studies of blue-collar consumers, commercial strips, or other regions of the United States be likely to support or contradict Cohen's thesis?

Next, Bruce J. Schulman, professor of history at Boston University and author of *From Cotton Belt to Sunbelt: Federal Policy, Economic Development, and the Transformation of the South, 1938–1980,* rev. ed. (1994), considers the impact of defense spending on regional economic development in postwar America. He shows how Dixie politicians used their influence in Washington to draw federal dollars into the poverty-stricken South, materializing the upswing envisioned by New Dealers in the 1930s. The growing obsolescence of manufacturing plants in the Northeast and Midwest inadvertently aided these efforts, pushing defense dollars into the West and the South. Although Florida, Georgia, and Texas never rivaled California as Pentagon contractors, these states came to rely heavily on military dollars to support their textile, aircraft, and electronics factories, military bases, and National Aeronautics and Space Administration (NASA) facilities. What does Schulman's story about Fortress Dixie reveal about the political economy of postwar America? How does his essay relate to Joel Davidson's discussion of the military-industrial complex in Chapter 11? How does it dovetail with Hubert H. Humphrey's observations in Document 6?

From Town Center to Shopping Center: The Reconfiguration of Marketplaces in Postwar America

LIZABETH COHEN

When the editors of *Time* magazine set out to tell readers in an early January 1965 cover story why the American economy had flourished during the previous year, they explained it in terms that had become the conventional wisdom of postwar America. The most prosperous twelve months ever, capping the country's fourth straight year of economic expansion, were attributable to the American consumer, "who continued spending as if there were no tomorrow." According to *Time*'s economics lesson, consumers, business, and government "created a nonvicious circle: spending created more production, production created wealth, wealth created more spending." In this simplified Keynesian model of economic growth, "the consumer is the key to our economy." As R. H. Macy's board chair Jack Straus explained to *Time*'s readers, "When the country has a recession, it suffers not so much from problems of production as from problems of consumption." And in prosperous times like today, "Our economy keeps growing because our ability to consume is endless. The consumer goes on spending regardless of how many possessions he has. The luxuries of today are the necessities of tomorrow." A demand economy built on mass consumption had brought the United States out of the doldrums of the Great Depression and World War II, and its strength in the postwar period continued to impress those like retail magnate Straus whose own financial future depended on it.

Although Straus and his peers invested great energy and resources in developing new strategies for doing business in this mass-consumption economy, historians have paid far less attention to the restructuring of American commercial life in the postwar period than to the transformation of residential experience. An impressive literature documents the way the expansion of a mass consumer society encouraged a larger and broader spectrum of Americans to move into suburban communities after the war. Between 1947 and 1953 alone, the suburban population increased by 43 percent, in contrast to a general population increase of only 11 percent. At an

Lizabeth Cohen, "From Town Center to Shopping Center: The Reconfiguration of Community Marketplaces in Postwar America," *American Historical Review* 101, no. 4 (October 1996): 1050–1081 (excerpt, pp. 1050–1053, 1061–1068). Reprinted by permission of American Historical Association and the author.

astonishing pace, the futuristic highways and mass-built, appliance-equipped, single-family homes that had been previewed at the New York World's Fair in 1939–1940 seemed to become a reality. Thanks to a shortage in urban housing, government subsidies in highway building and home construction or purchase, and pent-up consumer demand and savings, a new residential landscape began to take shape in metropolitan areas, with large numbers of people commuting into cities for work and then back to homes in the suburbs. (Increasingly as the postwar era progressed, suburbanites worked, not just lived, outside cities.)

Less explored by historians and slower to develop historically was the restructuring of the consumer marketplace that accompanied the suburbanization of residential life. New suburbanites who had themselves grown up in urban neighborhoods walking to corner stores and taking public transportation to shop downtown were now contending with changed conditions. Only in the most ambitious suburban tracts built after the war did developers incorporate retail stores into their plans. In those cases, developers tended to place the shopping district at the core of the residential community, much as it had been in the pre-war planned community of Radburn, New Jersey, and in the earliest shopping centers, such as Kansas City's Country Club Plaza of the 1920s. These precedents, and their descendents in early postwar developments in Park Forest, Illinois, Levittown, New York, and Bergenfield, New Jersey, replicated the structure of the old-style urban community, where shopping was part of the public space at the settlement's core and residences spread outward from there. But most new suburban home developers made no effort to provide for residents' commercial needs. Rather, suburbanites were expected to fend for themselves by driving to the existing "market towns," which often offered the only commerce for miles, or by returning to the city to shop. Faced with slim retail offerings nearby, many new suburbanites of the 1940s and 1950s continued to depend on the city for major purchases, making do with the small, locally owned commercial outlets in neighboring towns only for minor needs.

It would not be until the mid-1950s that a new market structure appropriate to this suburbanized, mass-consumption society prevailed. Important precedents existed in the branch department stores and prototypical shopping centers constructed between the 1920s and 1940s in outlying city neighborhoods and in older suburban communities, which began the process of decentralizing retail dollars away from downtown. But now the scale was much larger. Even more significant, the absence or inadequacy of town centers at a time of enormous suburban population growth offered commercial developers a unique opportunity to reimagine community life with their private projects at its heart.

By the early 1950s, large merchandisers were aggressively reaching out to the new suburbanites, whose buying power was even greater than their numbers. The 30 million people that *Fortune* magazine counted as suburban residents in 1953 represented 19 percent of the U.S. population but 29 percent of its income. They had higher median incomes and homeownership rates, as well as more children fourteen and under than the rest of the metropolitan population, all indicators of high consumption.

Merchandisers also realized that postwar suburbanites were finally living the motorized existence that had been predicted for American society since the 1920s. As consumers became dependent on, virtually inseparable from, their cars, traffic congestion and parking problems discouraged commercial expansion in central business districts of cities and smaller market towns, already hindered by a short supply of developable space. Reaching out to suburbanites where they lived, merchandisers at first built stores along the new highways, in commercial "strips" that consumers could easily reach by car. By the mid-1950s, however, commercial developers—many of whom owned department stores—were constructing a new kind of marketplace, the regional shopping center aimed at satisfying suburbanites' consumption *and* community needs. Strategically located at highway intersections or along the busiest thoroughfares, the regional shopping center attracted patrons living within half an hour's drive, who could come by car, park in the abundant lots provided, and then proceed on foot (although there was usually some bus service as well). Here was the "new city" of the postwar era, a vision of how community space should be constructed in an economy and society built on mass consumption. Well-designed regional shopping centers would provide the ideal core for a settlement that grew by adding residential nodes off of major roadways rather than concentric rings from downtown, as in cities and earlier suburban communities. After spending several months in the late 1950s visiting these "modern-day downtowns," *Women's Wear Daily* columnist Samuel Feinberg was moved to invoke Lincoln Steffens's proclamation on his return from the Soviet Union in the 1920s: "I have seen the future and it works."

This essay will analyze the larger social and political implications of the shift in community marketplace from town center to shopping center. Although I draw on national evidence, I pay special attention to the case of Paramus, New Jersey, a postwar suburb seven miles from the George Washington Bridge that sprouted virtually overnight in the vegetable fields of Bergen County and became the home of the largest shopping complex in the country by the end of 1957. Within six months, R. H. Macy's Garden State Plaza and Allied Stores Corporation's Bergen Mall opened three quarters of a mile from each other at the intersection of Routes 4, 17, and the soon-to-be-completed Garden State Parkway. Both department store managements had independently recognized the enormous commercial potential of Bergen and Passaic counties; although the George Washington Bridge connected the area to Manhattan in 1931, the Depression and the war postponed major housing construction until the late 1940s. By 1960, each shopping center had two to three department stores as anchors (distinguishing it from many pre-war projects built around a single anchor), surrounded by fifty to seventy smaller stores. Attracting half a million patrons a week, these shopping centers dominated retail trade in the region. . . .

If developers and retailers envisioned the regional shopping center as the new American city of postwar suburbia, what actually happened? How successful were shopping centers in attracting patrons and displacing existing urban centers? By investigating the behavior of consumers, on the one hand, and retail businessmen on the other, we can assess the impact of Bergen Mall and Garden State Plaza on the commercial and community life of Bergen County.

Consumer surveys of the late 1950s and early 1960s, carried out by sociologists and market researchers interested in evaluating the changes wrought by the new regional shopping centers, provide a remarkably good picture of consumer behavior in the era. Before the Bergen Mall and Garden State Plaza opened in 1957, Bergen

County shoppers satisfied their immediate needs on the main streets of Hacken-sack and of smaller surrounding towns such as Ridgewood, Fair Lawn, Bergenfield, and Englewood. For more extensive shopping, people went to branches of Sears and Arnold Constable in Hackensack, Meyer Brothers and Quackenbush's department stores in Paterson, Bamberger's, Hahne's, and Kresge's in Newark, and quite often to the big stores in Manhattan. Even before the regional shopping centers opened, the huge influx of new suburban dwellers had raised retail sales in Bergen County from $400 million in 1948 to $700 million in 1954, an increase of 79 percent; by 1958, sales had increased another 23 percent to $866 million. Nonetheless, Bergen County residents in 1954 were still spending $650 million outside the county, almost as much as inside.

Samuel and Lois Pratt, professors at Fairleigh Dickinson University, surveyed Bergen County consumers living within a ten-minute drive of the two new shopping centers in 1957, 1958, and 1959 to follow changes in their shopping habits over time. Prior to the opening of the shopping centers, seven in ten suburban families surveyed shopped in New York City to some extent. One year after the centers opened, the numbers shopping in New York dropped to six in ten, and two years after, fewer than five in ten families shopped there at all. In other words, one-fourth of the entire sample formerly had shopped in New York City but had now entirely stopped. . . . Nation-wide, the trend was the same; retail sales in central business districts declined dra-matically between 1958 and 1963, while overall metropolitan sales mushroomed from 10 to 20 percent.

The reasons consumers routinely gave for shifting from downtown stores to shopping centers varied, but the overwhelming motivation they articulated was convenience—the ability to drive and park easily, more night hours, improved store layouts, increased self-selection, and simplified credit like the charge plate. The Pratts concluded that shoppers were not so much dissatisfied with New York and Hackensack stores as attracted to the ease and "progressiveness" of shopping-center shopping. People seemed to share the developers' sense that shopping centers were the modern way to consume. . . .

While it is hard to evaluate the extent to which people viewed the shopping centers as more than places to shop—as community centers—anecdotal evidence suggests that they did. Many reporters writing stories in the late 1950s and 1960s on the way malls were becoming central to the nation's culture made this point, and they routinely introduced their readers to people like Ernest J. Weinhold, a retired designer, who said that he and his wife came to the Cherry Hill Mall in southern New Jersey four days a week. "I love it here—there are things going on that you don't find anywhere else. I don't shop every day but what I do buy I get here." The general man-ager of Willowbrook Mall, a shopping center not far from Paramus, explained that the Ernest Weinholds of the suburban world made it easy to program activities about forty-five weeks a year. "Whether it's charity fairs, 4-H exhibits, meetings of the Weight-Watchers or the concert by the local barbershop quartet, we find that people respond—and that's what counts." In the new public place of the shopping center, consuming and leisure were becoming inseparably intertwined, constructing com-munity experiences around the cultural tastes of white middle-class suburbanites.

The response of businessmen in the existent town centers of northern New Jersey provides further evidence of the crisis confronting local retailers with the arrival of the shopping centers in the late 1950s. As the openings of the Bergen Mall and Garden State Plaza neared, and particularly once they were a reality, Main Street retailers in Hackensack, Paterson, and other shopping towns told interviewers that they knew they had to improve their own stores and work cooperatively with other merchants to promote downtown. In 1957, Hackensack's Chamber of Commerce launched the first of many campaigns to make shopping in Hackensack more attractive, featuring the covering of downtown meters at Christmas time so customers could park free. Paterson, four miles away, formed the Commercial Development Fund for Paterson's Future, which raised $65,000 to promote downtown through marketing and advertising; at the same time, the Municipal Parking Authority issued $1.8 million in bonds to double the capacity of Paterson's downtown parking lots, raising the total to 800. (By contrast, each shopping center offered parking for more than 8,000 cars!) . . .

Recognizing the limits of what they could do alone, or through their volunteer merchants' organizations, local Bergen County retailers endorsed two strategies for improving their situation, both of which mobilized the authority and resources of government on their behalf. First, they joined a coalition of other interests—including churches and citizens concerned with traffic congestion—to pass blue laws prohibiting Sunday sales. If the shopping centers were allowed to open on Sunday, small, family-run stores for whom a seven-day week was a great hardship would suffer a handicap. If all stores were required to close, the score would be somewhat even. "It's easy for the big stores to open, but it's different for the independents," explained the owner of a men's clothing store in Hackensack, adding that he and most of his staff of ten worked six days a week. "We are truly a service store, which consists of all full-time people. If you open seven days, you might have to hire part-timers. Our customers want to find a familiar face. They don't want to hear that the person they expect to see is off today." The best defense that downtown retailers had against the shopping centers—service—would thus be jeopardized.

Losing no time, Paramus prohibited Sunday sales of virtually all goods except "necessities" (food, drugs, gasoline, newspapers) in 1957, the year the shopping centers opened; violators were subject to a $200 fine per offense or ninety days in jail, or both, which finally put teeth into a longstanding statute on the state books. Although the merchants in highway shopping centers protested and sued to have the ordinance revoked, arguing all the way to the New Jersey Supreme Court that their ability to compete with stores in neighboring towns was undermined, they lost. Meanwhile, agitation continued for an effective state-wide restriction of Sunday shopping so as not to penalize particular locales with blue laws, and the New Jersey legislature finally agreed to allow counties to hold referenda on the question. In November 1959, voting took place in fifteen of the state's twenty-one counties; twelve counties, including Bergen, voted a Sunday ban into law. Although highway discount stores appealed, the State Supreme Court eventually upheld the law, as did the U.S. Supreme Court indirectly when it ruled in 1961 on four companion cases concerning the constitutionality of Sunday closing laws in Maryland, Massachusetts, and Pennsylvania. The Supreme Court held that such laws did not violate freedom of religion as protected under the First Amendment or the equal protection guarantees of the Fourteenth Amendment and thereby left it to individual states and localities to regulate Sunday selling as they wished. Due, no doubt, to strong advocacy by influential local businessmen, Bergen County was reputed to have made the greatest effort at enforcing blue laws of any county in New Jersey; a local magistrate even ordered that cigarette vending machines in a Howard Johnson restaurant be unplugged on Sunday. Nationwide during the late 1950s and early 1960s, retailers skirmished over Sunday closing laws, not so much defending traditional mores as using the separation of church and state to veil intense struggles over the extent to which discount stores, shopping centers, and chain stores could capture millions of dollars in retail business through restructuring consumer markets.

The second way that downtown business people sought to harness the power of the state in fighting the shopping centers involved the use of federal funds for urban renewal. The 1954 National Housing Act and the 1956 Federal Highway Act made it possible for cities to use urban renewal grants for rehabilitation of commercial areas; the federal government pledged from two-thirds to three-quarters of the cost of acquiring land and demolishing structures. Paterson proved the most aggressive of the cities in Bergen and Passaic counties in pursuing this strategy, joining with at least sixteen other communities in the metropolitan New York area. . . . [C]ivic leaders founded PLAN (Paterson Looks Ahead Now) in the early 1960s to develop 121 acres at the core of downtown. PLAN implemented a design by Victor Gruen, who had become an early advocate of the revival of downtowns through careful commercial planning, much as he had pioneered the development of regional shopping centers, themselves the source of many cities' economic ills.

Bringing many of the characteristics of Bergen County shopping centers to the Paterson city center, Gruen designed wide, landscaped pedestrian areas, accessible through loop roadways tied in with six parking garages accommodating 4,500 cars. With Uncle Sam committed to footing three-quarters of the $24 million bill, local civic leaders headed by PLAN president Raymond J. Behrman, owner of a downtown luggage and women's accessories store, worked to reverse a drastic decline: by 1962, the number of Paterson shoppers had fallen to half what it had been in 1940, despite all the population growth in the region. Soon, Hackensack was talking about applying for urban renewal funds as well. But this injection of federal dollars failed as a remedy. In 1971, shopping centers in the Paterson/Passaic metropolitan area captured 79 percent of all retail trade, well beyond the average of 50 percent for the nation's twenty-one largest metropolitan areas. In 1950, Paterson was a major shopping district, while retail in Paramus hardly existed: twenty years later, Paterson found itself suffering from long-term economic decline, ignored by recently constructed parkways, turnpikes, and interstates and facing intense competition from shopping centers, while Paramus was well on its way to becoming one of the largest retail centers in the world. As the segmentation of consumer markets became the guiding principle in postwar commerce, no amount of revitalization could make a city whose population was becoming increasingly minority and poor attractive to the white middle-class shoppers with money to spend.

While local merchants in Bergen and Passaic counties struggled, the big New York and Newark stores developed their own strategy for dealing with the competition from the new suburban shopping centers: they opened branch stores. Rather than be eclipsed by the postwar shift in population, they followed it. By the late 1950s, branch stores—once a rarity—had become a national trend among large department stores. When department stores with annual net sales of $10 million or more were considered, the percentage of branch sales skyrocketed from 4 percent of total sales in 1951 to 32 percent by 1959; specialty stores with sales over $1 million made a comparable shift from 6 percent of sales through branches to 33 percent over the same period. By 1959, the very success of a regional shopping center like Bergen Mall or Garden State Plaza depended on the quality of the department-store branches that served as its anchors. In time, branch stores evolved from small outlets of Fifth Avenue flagship stores into full-fledged department stores carrying a wide range of merchandise. In the early 1970s, in fact, Bergen Mall's Stern Brothers took the dramatic step of closing its New York City stores, investing everything in its more profitable shopping-center branches. Sterns was not alone; by 1976, branch sales amounted to nearly 78 percent of total department-store business nationwide. The huge postwar investment in suburban stores had significant consequences for consumers, for local retailers, and . . . for department store employees as well.

By the 1960s, the mass-consumption economy had brought about a major restructuring of consumer markets. As retail dollars moved out of major cities and away from established downtowns within suburban areas, regional shopping centers became the distinctive public space of the postwar landscape. Suburban populations increasingly looked to the mall for a new kind of community life—consumption-oriented, tightly controlled, and aimed at citizen-consumers who preferably were white and middle class. This commercialization of public space during the postwar era had profound effects, perhaps the most important of which was the struggle to define what kind of political behavior was permissible in the new, privately owned public place.

Fortress Dixie: Defense Spending and the Rise of the Sunbelt

BRUCE J. SCHULMAN

"Time was," the first number of *Southern Exposure* recalled, "when the only way for a poor southerner—black or white—to escape the region's poverty was to join the Army. Now, if he's lucky, he can get a job in a defense plant in one of the small, rural towns that punctuate the southern landscape." Or, an impoverished southerner could migrate to "a New South metropolis and look for a factory or warehouse job; but even here, he would likely find himself working in an industry that got (or gets) its stimulus from the demand of nearby military bases or far-off wars." In 1973 more southerners worked in defense-related industries than in textiles, synthetics, and apparel combined. Defense dollars permeated nearly every town in the region.

Defense dependency perpetuated itself over the postwar years. For practical reasons, such as the existence of already constructed facilities, defense dollars tended to stick where they first hit. The dormant Michoud Aircraft plant, a holdover from Andrew Jackson Higgins's wartime exploits, drew several military ventures to New

Bruce J. Schulman, *From Cotton Belt to Sunbelt: Federal Policy, Economic Development, and the Transformation of the South, 1938–1980,* rev. ed. (Durham, N.C.: Duke University Press, 1994), pp. 140–151 (excerpt, pp. 140–143, 145–151).

Orleans, including the Apollo rocket assembly factory. The government-owned Bell Bomber plant in Marietta, Georgia, then the largest factory in the South, was reopened by Lockheed in 1951.

Political considerations reinforced the geographic concentration of defense industries. Local constituencies and favored contractors fought to keep defense facilities operating. Moreover, regional specialization in defense resembled other forms of economic specialization, gearing the local political economies of many southern communities to the war plant in the same way they had previously centered around the textile mill or the cotton plantation. Marietta, Georgia, for instance, the home of Lockheed-Georgia, the largest single industrial organization in the Southeast in the 1960s and 1970s, employed workers in fifty-five of Georgia's 159 counties. With more than 90 percent of its business in defense contracts, Lockheed-Georgia not only paid several hundred million dollars a year in wages and salaries, but also served as the state's largest customer and supporter of technical universities. The aircraft giant purchased everything from soft drinks to metal parts from local suppliers.

In addition to subcontracts and expanded demand for industrial, consumer, and public goods, federally subsidized industries occasionally introduced innovations which altered what economists term the "production functions" of extant regional industry. That is, they changed the relative proportions of capital and labor used by a firm. The aircraft industry, for example, pursued and perfected numerically controlled computer automation of production in the 1950s and 1960s. The new processes offered advantages in performance and in management control of the workplace, but were not cost effective. Without cost-plus military contracts, the industry might not have pursued numerical control. Whether or not the new technology represented the most efficient course is debatable; considerable evidence suggests that it did not. But developments in aircraft manufacture pointed up the peculiar nature of the defense market, with its barriers to exit and entry, guaranteed profits, and subsidies for innovations that could not proceed in the open market.

Defense production was also vulnerable to cyclic fluctuations. Partially shielded from the business cycle, defense orders ebbed and flowed as political factors influenced the military budget. For instance, in 1964, Defense Secretary Robert McNamara closed 95 military bases and embarked on an aggressive cost cutting plan. A wartime build-up followed in the late 1960s, succeeded by another round of cuts in connection with procurement scandals in 1970.

Southern politicians fought to insulate the region from these fluctuations and maintain a steady flow of contracts. This strategy, however unwittingly, preserved the region's ancient role as commissary to the nation and its armed forces. The South provided the Pentagon with textiles, tobacco, coal, and food. The region did so happily because the military's demand for such items remained stable; it was far more secure and predictable than the lucrative "weapons roller coaster," even if less stimulating economically. In no other region did weapons account for so small a share of total defense contracts.

Ultimately, these peculiarities of the defense economy might derail southern and national economic progress. Certainly, the heady proclamations that space and defense research would spin off new consumer goods and industrial technologies proved false. With the exception of the aircraft industry, efforts to translate military technology to commercial use failed. Defense contractors lacked marketing skills and the ability to produce high volume at low unit costs. By the late 1960s, commentators acknowledged the "locked-in nature of defense resources." They argued that space and defense industry drained talent from the private sector and railroaded the American economy down a dead-end track. Defense spending did not set off the chain reaction of interactive innovation and economic growth that propelled the American economy in the nineteenth century. Nonetheless, the South had no choice but to hitch its economy to the defense train. No other source offered the technological community and the skilled employment opportunities the region desired.

The effects of that intervention were so pronounced as to lend credence to the warning of John Crowe Ransom, the unregenerate Nashville Agrarian of the 1930s. With Cassandra-like prescience, Ransom had beseeched the South to avoid participation in the nascent military-industrial complex. "Our vast industrial machine," Ransom had warned in 1930, "with its laboratories of experimentation, and its far-flung organs of mass production, is like a Prussianized State which is organized strictly for war and can never consent to peace."

Whatever its economic dependence on the national security state, Ransom's region, the agrarian South, became fortress Dixie. During the 1970s, the *New York Times* reported that defense was the single largest employer in four southern states, outpacing agriculture, textiles, lumber, and all the others. And of America's top ten defense contractors, seven, including Lockheed, McDonnell-Douglas, General Dynamics, and Rockwell, operated large installations in the South.

The changing geography of defense production reflected the changing character of defense demand during the postwar decades. In fiscal year 1953, tanks, vehicles, weapons, and ammunition constituted more than half of military hard goods delivered; they made up only 12 percent of prime contract awards in FY 1961. Meanwhile, expenditures on missiles soared from less than one percent to more than one-third of the military budget. The shift from conventional ordnance to missiles, electronics, and aircraft coincided with the regional migration of defense work and the enlistment of new firms as major contractors. In the decade after the conclusion of the Korean War, contracts did not leave the North for the South and West. Rather, the Pentagon terminated standing contracts for unnecessary tanks and vehicles, while offering new contracts for missiles and electronics. The conspiracy of international tensions, weapons developments, and increasing military budgets launched a competition for entirely new defense-related industries.

This competition accelerated broader developments in the national economy. Changing military demand reinforced the shift from heavy manufacturing to electronics and services. The economic stream was flowing away from industries such as steel, which required proximity to raw materials and to rail or water transport. Combined with the expansion of the highway system, this shift allowed the migration of economic activity. "Footloose" businesses could take advantage of the South's cheap land, surplus labor, and warm climate. These "dynamics of deconcentration," as a federal government report termed the phenomenon, were intensified by the long period of postwar economic growth. This sustained prosperity, driven in part and regulated by federal macroeconomic policy, kept up continual pressure for expansion of existing plants and the construction of new facilities. Over time, the obsolescence of old plants in the Frost Belt and the high costs of doing business there pushed new capacity toward the Sunbelt. Defense procurement was one part of this process. For instance, when the Kennedy administration heated up the economy by stepping up spending for military equipment without raising taxes, electronics and aerospace firms built new capacity in central Florida to exploit the area's cheap land and amenities.

The South and West won the decade-long battle for new contracts. New England held its own and conducted a major comeback after 1970. The mid-Atlantic and Midwest regions suffered the greatest losses. Texas's success in securing the new military aircraft industry was so great that visitors, like Secretary of Commerce Luther H. Hodges in 1962, could hardly distinguish between what was "new in Texas and what's new in air power." Since the aircraft and missile businesses were rapid-growth, research-based, automated industries with a history of low unionization, the South's victory in the battle for new military capacity proved a harbinger of its future. . . .

. . . [T]he South had developed . . . a political alliance with the Pentagon that brought economic bounty to the region in return for Congressional support of the Defense Department. In part, that alliance merely continued the heritage of World War II. Federal officials had made a concerted effort to deploy war industries in the service of regional development. During the war, they built an infrastructure of industrial plant[s], testing facilities, and military bases that remained after 1945. The Defense Department could not be faulted for developing that foundation.

The arrangement also betrayed the region's lingering suspicion of federal intervention. It reflected the South's traditional desire to control federal activity, to steer the benefits of federal aid toward the region's leadership and away from its dispossessed people. The South's Congressional delegation resisted the tide of whiggery longer than its statehouses. And even the new Whigs preferred federal aid without cumbersome regulations and Washington administrators. Only the Pentagon offered relatively unrestricted federal dollars. The South's "dependence on the federal military dole," proclaimed the liberal journal *Southern Exposure* in 1973, "is deepening the push from this region, not for humane domestic programs, but for a continued policy of growth that is both stimulated and secured through massive military spending." . . .

. . . [T]he Congressional seniority system granted the South the political power to deliver large defense budgets. In so doing, southern hawks saw to it that their roosts were well-furnished. The postwar growth of the Pentagon and its demand for new goods and services like missiles offered potential bonanzas to southern legislators. They had little to trade but their influence in the Congress and they dealt that influence shrewdly. Such efforts made South Carolina congressman L. Mendel Rivers legendary. As one journalist put it, Rivers, as the second-ranking member and eventually as chairman of the House Armed Services Committee, "transmogrified Charleston into a microcosm of military-industrial civilization." Into his district, Rivers poured an Air Force base, a naval base, a Polaris Missile maintenance center, a naval shipyard and ballistic submarine training station, a naval hospital, a Coast Guard station, a mine warfare center, and the Sixth Naval District Headquarters. McDonnell-Douglas, Avco, GE, and Lockheed all established factories in the district during Rivers's chairmanship. By some estimates, as much as one-third of the income in the area and half the employment was defense-related. Representative Carl Vinson (D-Ga), Rivers's mentor and predecessor as Armed Forces chairman once joked that "you put anything else down there in your district, Mendel, it's gonna sink."

Rivers gave as well as he received; he was an influential and steadfast supporter of the military. He repeatedly squelched debate on the defense budget and occasionally even appropriated more funds than the military brass had requested. Before military audiences, Rivers routinely mocked liberal civilians: "The only powder those people have ever smelled is talcum powder. The only war they have been in is bood-war."

Rivers's only rivals for Pentagon spoils hailed from neighboring Georgia—the home of both Senate Armed Forces Committee chairman Richard Russell and his opposite number in the House, Representative Carl Vinson. They made defense the largest employer in Georgia. By 1960 the two men had secured fifteen military installations for their home state. After Vinson's retirement, Russell ensured a steady supply of prime contracts for the Lockheed plant in Marietta, the largest private employer in the state.

While some southern politicians, like Rivers, viewed this alliance as just another game of pork barrel, many others saw it as a main chance for their region. Military spending not only promised jobs, but permanent high paying jobs, which demanded and fashioned a skilled workforce. Defense plants also pioneered new production techniques and brought industrial prestige and additional investment to the region.

The space program was a case in point. Before *Sputnik,* southern politicians displayed little enthusiasm for rocketry. In fact, Albert Thomas (D-Tex), the Houston area congressman and the chairman of the subcommittee that handled space appropriations, waged a one-man war against the program. Thomas was the nemesis of the National Advisory Committee for Aeronautics (NACA), the principal space agency before NASA. Thomas believed in a balanced budget and found rocketry unimportant. NACA's failure to place a facility in his district reinforced that animosity. But "No sooner had *Sputnik*'s first beep-beep been heard," one Defense Department official recalled, "than the nation's legislators leaped forward like heavy drinkers hearing a cork pop." Texas naturally hosted the biggest celebration for the biggest "drinkers." Charles Brewton, a former assistant to Alabama senator Lister Hill, journeyed to Austin and passed a memorandum to Lyndon Johnson's closest aide. That memo suggested that *Sputnik* could cripple the Republicans, save the Democrats from a divisive battle over race relations, and land LBJ in the White House. Seeking such political advantages, Texans led the fight for an expanded space program. Johnson, the Senate Majority leader, held public hearings and roasted witnesses like NACA chief Jimmy Doolittle. In his inimitable style, LBJ taunted the old flying hero that "he'd rather be dead than broke" and remain "a solvent if moribund bloke." Across Capitol Hill, Johnson found allies in Speaker Sam Rayburn, Representative Thomas, a sudden convert to the importance of space, and another Texan, House Space Committee chairman Olin Teague. They steered a space bill through the Congress in 1958. In addition to its southern constituency, the principal feature that distinguished the new space agency—the National Aeronautics and Space Administration—from its predecessor was its enormous budget. As one pundit put it, NA¢A became NA$A.

But the space program represented more than a political coup for southern Democrats, and more than a chance at palm-greasing. Even though NASA would invest only a fraction of the resources that the Pentagon invested in the South, southern leaders saw the space program as a conduit to a new "New South" of science and technology-based enterprise. The glamor of the program in the early 1960s, especially of the desperate race to reach the moon before the Soviets, convinced many Americans that space research held the key to the nation's economic and political future. Southern politicians as diverse as Mississippi senator John Stennis, Lyndon Johnson, and Florida congressman Donald Fuqua envisioned NASA as the Moses who would lead the South to a high-tech promised land. If NASA administrator James Webb, an Oklahoman who owed his appointment to LBJ, did not share that view, he did nothing to disabuse southern legislators of it. NASA even pledged to include blacks in the regional reconstruction. The space agency promised to employ blacks in technical capacities at all its southern installations.

The hopes for space-based economic development were largely borne out in several southern communities. First, NASA almost single-handedly supported scientific research in universities across the South. In 1962, despite the shortage of universities and doctorates in the South, NASA placed fifty-seven of its 130 grants and research contracts in the southern states. In terms of dollar awards, NASA placed the largest chunk of its research dollars with the nation's "Big 20" colleges and universities, but the public universities of Alabama, Georgia, and Florida stood among the top recipients.

No southern university benefited more than the University of Alabama-Huntsville. The space program practically established the university in the first place and did indeed sustain the booming metropolis that housed it. A sagging textile town of 16,000 when Wernher Von Braun and the German rocket team arrived in 1950, Huntsville claimed 72,000 residents, but little else, when the Marshall Space Flight Center opened in 1960. The Huntsville Research Institute followed in 1961. The Cummings Research Park opened a year later. Two industrial parks, housing IBM and Rockwell, opened in 1964 and 1965. The University of Alabama-Huntsville, which NASA officials began lobbying for in 1964, held its first classes in 1969. In 1966, six years after NASA arrived, per capita personal income in Huntsville outdistanced the rest of Alabama by 20 percent. The city's population nearly doubled between 1960 and 1970. The influx converted an overwhelmingly agricultural workforce into a diversified one, with many government and service workers. Almost a third of the city's 1966 labor force had come there since 1960. Huntsville, according to the Information director at the Redstone arsenal, "was high tech when high tech wasn't cool." The city represented the economic treasure chest that southern leaders sought with space.

Houston was a more luminous jewel. In September 1961, NASA announced its decision to construct the Manned Spacecraft Center (now the Johnson Space Center), a $60 million installation on land donated by Rice University for the purpose. Politics certainly played into the location decision; the space agency did not underestimate the influence of Johnson, Rayburn, and Thomas. But whatever the political calculation, NASA policy dictated a dispersal of facilities away from the East and West coast, and the necessity of water transport probably ensured a Gulf site. Twelve of the 18 locations NASA considered were in the South. A year after the decision, before construction of the Center had been completed, 29 space-related companies had opened up shop in the Houston area. By 1965, Houston ranked first in the Southwest in population, manufacturing payroll, value added, and as an industrial and consumer market. Moreover, it began a dozen-year spurt of growth in science and market-oriented industries that promised to end its dependence on natural resources. Unlike Huntsville, Houston did not depend exclusively on the space center for its growth, but business leaders agreed that the center both accelerated and reshaped that development. The city's boosters never failed to remind visitors that the first phrase spoken from the surface of the moon was not "the Eagle has landed," but "Houston?"

The Apollo program, the moon expedition, was the grand prize in the aerospace bonanza. Largest of the space programs, Project Apollo spread its operations in a crescent from Florida to Texas. And after completing its lunar expeditions, NASA maintained its southern base. In 1985, five of the space agency's nine facilities were in the South, including the Marshall and Johnson Centers, the Kennedy Space Center at Cape Canaveral, the Michoud Assembly facility in New Orleans, and the Mississippi Test facility at Bay St. Louis. According to NASA administrator James Webb, space programs, whether on the steppes of the Soviet Union or the South's Gulf Coast, dragged "the whole economy up behind this penetrating wedge of advanced technology."

If any symbol of the national defense state's involvement in the South shone brighter than those space facilities, it was the region's surfeit of military bases. As it did during World War II, the region remained the nation's boot camp throughout the postwar era. In fiscal 1975, for example, the South drew one and a half times the national average in defense salaries. Forts, naval stations, and airfields translated into numerous service jobs in the base towns; the Defense Department estimated that every soldier stimulated three service sector jobs. Accordingly, base towns reported high ratios of service to nonservice employment. Military bases also carried increased federal aid to the affected communities. Beginning in 1950, the federal government picked up the costs of educating the children of servicemen. Washington also provided subsidies to compensate for loss of tax revenues that federally owned lands represented.

But military bases have exerted an uncertain influence on regional economic growth. When a military facility closed, the guidelines for federal aid ensured that the community lost its financial support just as its largest employer closed shop. In Mobile, Alabama, the closing of the Mobile Matériel Area at Brookley Air Force Base shocked the local economy. The number of employed dropped almost overnight by more than 5 percent, the unemployment rate soared, and many residents departed the area. The catastrophe highlighted the fact that no major employer had moved to Mobile in the decade before the base closure. The shutdown of Fort Donaldson in Greenville, South Carolina, on the other hand, sparked an aggressive and successful redevelopment campaign so that Greenville escaped Mobile's fate. The experience led the Greenville *News* to editorialize, "From where we look at it now, we wish we had another military installation like Donaldson for the Pentagon to close, and for the city to redevelop for the good of the local and regional economy." As different as they were, in both cases, the presence of military bases had arrested industrial growth. Without pulling dynamic industries in their wake, military installations contributed little to regional development. Georgia politicians came to that conclusion in the late 1970s. State leaders realized that Georgia's five major bases provided few economic dividends for Georgia. They successfully lobbied the Pentagon to shift base operations toward army electronics and to work more closely with the research institute at Georgia Tech in Atlanta.

Despite their limited economic influence, military bases constituted a large share of defense spending in the South from 1955 to 1980. That fact underlines the limits of defense spending in fostering regional economic growth. The South, while faring quite well in the distribution of prime contracts, never rivaled California. The resurgence of New England in recent years only reinforced the South's leadership in bases and salaries rather than contracts. Moreover, the South continued to receive a large portion of its contracts for food, textiles, cigarettes, and coal. These contracts neither developed new skills in the area nor challenged the dominance of the traditional low wage southern industries. So, until the 1970s, defense nourished high-technology industry less in the South than the region's leaders had supposed. Los Angeles, not Atlanta or Houston, represented the nation's biggest defense city. Not surprisingly, then, journalists, mesmerized by the highly visible bases, tended to exaggerate the direct economic effects of defense spending in the South, while economists, in search of quantifiable measures of economic stimuli, downplayed the role of military spending in Dixie.

Neither the journalists nor the economists, however, emphasized the marginal impact of defense activities in the region. The net level of spending obscured the pivotal role of Pentagon involvement. Unlike the industrial North, the South received far more in federal spending than it paid in federal taxes. Defense accounted for almost all the regional disparities in that "balance of payments." Moreover, while the South did not win the most defense dollars between 1955 and 1980, the funds it received mattered more than in other regions. They energized the South's take off, transformed its political institutions, and shaped the direction of its development.

The crucial point is not that defense dollars developed the South at the expense of other regions, as Frostbelt leaders charged during the 1970s. Nor is it that the South received the lion's share of defense largesse because of its political influence. It is not even the marginal impact that matters most—the fact that dollar for dollar, a defense base meant more for Alabama than a lucrative prime contract meant for California, even if the base (unlike the contract) did not contribute to an economic take off. It was not defense spending per se that so reshaped the postwar South, but the peculiar operation of a series of programs, many only tangentially related to defense but all under the aegis of the defense establishment.

This constellation of defense-related programs provided maneuvering room for Whig politicians. It provided access to funds and jobs in a region of slender resources, a region deeply suspicious of non-defense programs. It allowed for close cooperation between defense agencies and influential southern Congressional committee chairmen. And it disbursed federal dollars with a minimum of interference—either in race relations or in economic arrangements. Southern business progressives could develop their states without providing economic opportunities for blacks or the poor.

Federal action, then, forged a new sort of southern political economy. It permitted the South to pursue development through federal investments, as southern New Dealers had envisioned, but without liberal politics or redistributionist economic policy—without support for welfare, labor, blacks. The alliance between the South and the defense state brought with it highways and airports—old favorites of southern business progressives—but also funds for research facilities and higher education. It provided little in the way of welfare, job training, or primary education.

Furthermore, the activities of the national military establishment directly affected the various components of growth. Southern politicians recognized that relation, even if other analysts neglected it. In 1977, Florida governor Reubin Askew noted that tax levels, wage rates, degrees of unionization, transportation facilities—all of the seemingly independent determinants of economic development—were linked in some way to government policy. And no part of the government exerted a stronger influence on these components of growth than the national security establishment.

FURTHER READING

Baughman, James L. *Henry R. Luce and the Rise of the American News Media* (1987).

Bird, William L., Jr. *Better Living: Advertising, Media, and the New Vocabulary of Business Leadership, 1935–1955* (1999).

Blaszczyk, Regina Lee, and Mimi Minnick. "Setting the Precedent: Four Women Who Excelled in Business." Website, Smithsonian National Museum of American History, Archives Center, launched 2002. http://americanhistory.si.edu/archives/WIB-tour.

Buderi, Robert. *The Invention That Changed the World: How a Small Group of Radar Pioneers Won the Second World War and Launched a Technological Revolution* (1996).

Clarke, Alison J. *Tupperware: The Promise of Plastic in 1950s America* (1999).

Cohen, Lizabeth. *A Consumers' Republic: The Politics of Mass Consumption in Postwar America* (2003).

Fones-Wolf, Elizabeth A. *Selling Free Enterprise: The Business Assault on Labor and Liberalism, 1945–1960* (1994).

Galambos, Louis, with Jane Eliot Sewell. *Networks of Innovation: Vaccine Development at Merck, Sharp & Dohme, and Mulford, 1895–1995* (1995).

Graham, Margaret B. W., and Alec T. Schuldiner. *Corning and the Craft of Innovation* (2001).

Hanchett, Thomas W. "U.S. Tax Policy and the Shopping-Center Boom of the 1950s and 1960s." *American Historical Review* 101, no. 4 (October 1996): 1082–1110.

Handley, Susannah. *Nylon: The Story of a Fashion Revolution* (1999).

Hardwick, M. Jeffrey. *Mall Maker: Victor Gruen, Architect of an American Dream* (2004).

Heinrich, Thomas. "Cold War Armory: Military Contracting in Silicon Valley." *Enterprise and Society* 3 (June 2002): 247–284.

Hounshell, David A., and John Kenly Smith, Jr. *Science and Corporate Strategy: Du Pont R&D, 1902–1980* (1988).

Lécuyer, Christophe. *Making Silicon Valley: Innovation and the Growth of High-Tech, 1930–1970* (2006).

Leslie, Stuart W. *The Cold War and American Science: The Military-Industrial-Academic Complex at MIT and Stanford* (1993).

Lotchin, Roger W. *Fortress California, 1910–1961: From Warfare to Welfare* (1992).

McQuaid, Kim. *Uneasy Partners: Big Business in American Politics, 1945–1990* (1994).

Melman, Seymour. *Pentagon Capitalism: The Political Economy of War* (1970).

Nelson, Richard R., and Gavin Wright. "The Rise and Fall of American Technological Leadership: The Postwar Era in Historical Perspective." *Journal of Economic Literature* 30 (December 1992): 1931–1964.

Roland, Alex. *The Military-Industrial Complex* (2001).

Rose, Mark H. *Interstate: Express Highway Politics, 1939–1989,* rev. ed. (1990).

Rosenbloom, Richard S., and William J. Spencer, eds. *Engines of Innovation: U.S. Industrial Research at the End of an Era* (1996).

Vatter, Harold G., and John F. Walker, eds. *History of the U.S. Economy Since World War II* (1996).

Zunz, Olivier. *Why the American Century?* (1998).

C H A P T E R
13

Business and the Public Interest: Corporate Responsibility for Environment, Health, and Safety, 1945–2005

In August 1978, the New York Times *alerted readers to the tragedy of Love Canal. This neighborhood in Niagara Falls, New York, was built on an abandoned industrial dump that was now exuding dangerous chemicals. The story, previously reported by Buffalo-area newspapers, became a national sensation. Over the course of the 1970s, the hundred families living in this 1950s development had experienced unusually high rates of cancer, miscarriage, birth defects, and mortality. Dogs playing in the streets were coming home with bleeding paws, while backyard trees were withering. In 1976, after six years of high rain, a peculiar, foul-smelling liquid began oozing up from the ground into Love Canal's playgrounds, lawns, gardens, swimming pools, and basements.*

Alarmed resident Karen Schroeder, who had a child born with a cleft palate, a third row of teeth, and mental retardation, protested to the Niagara Falls Gazette *and her congressman. Over two days in 1978, local authorities pumped 17,500 gallons of toxic waste out of Schroeder's yard, transferring it to a disposal site in Ohio. The Environmental Protection Agency (EPA) analyzed the air in Schroeder's house, finding high amounts of nine chemical compounds, including two carcinogens. Buried beneath the ground at Love Canal, barrels filled with 150,000 tons of toxic waste had started to leak and discharge their contents.*

The New York Times *article attracted the attention of the national media. Television, radio, and print jumped on the bandwagon to launch a two-decade crusade against the American chemical industry, which in some eyes symbolized all that was notorious about "Corporate America." Environmental, health, and government organizations supported the charge in the press and the courts. Some critics blamed the Hooker Chemical Company, which had used Love Canal as a*

408

toxic dump in the 1940s and 1950s. Others pointed to Niagara Falls authorities, who built a school on the site and parceled the land out to developers, while ignoring Hooker's warnings about the site's toxicity. Multiple lawsuits dragged on until 1999. Ultimately, Occidental Chemical (OxyChem), the firm that had absorbed Hooker and two other chemical companies, assumed the primary responsibility for the cleanup. The U.S. chemical industry responded in 1988 through the American Chemistry Council (ACC), implementing a Responsible Care initiative to improve its environmental, health, and safety performance.

In some respects, the Love Canal episode echoed aspects of earlier attacks on "the corporation" issued by William M. Gouge, Henry Demarest Lloyd, Louis D. Brandeis, the Senate Munitions Investigating Committee, and others. The critics argued: Yet again, business is putting profits above the people's welfare. But Love Canal captured the public imagination in the 1970s because it came on the heels of several important postwar failures in American business ethics. In 1952, Reader's Digest *published "Cancer by the Carton," an essay describing medical research that linked cigarettes to lung disease, sending a loud message to the tobacco companies. In 1962, Rachel Carson's* Silent Spring *warned Americans about industrial pollutants and poisons, giving birth to the contemporary environmental movement and eventually to a ban on DDT, a carcinogenic insecticide. A few years later, Washington lawyer Ralph Nader lashed out against negligent Detroit automakers in* Unsafe at Any Speed. *With a bestseller under his belt, Nader began testifying at congressional hearings, and he established a law firm dedicated to consumer advocacy. The march against "Corporate America" swelled, infused in part by the social movements that reshaped the American consciousness in the 1960s and 1970s: civil rights, black power, counterculture, antiwar, and feminism.*

These sagas suggest that simple questions do not lead to simple answers. Exactly who is to blame for Love Canal? Which chemicals adversely affect plants, animals, and people? How much research is needed before a new material, product, or drug is released? Who should bear the costs of research or cleanup? How clean is clean air? Should tobacco companies encourage smoking among minority groups? Are fast-food companies responsible for the obesity epidemic of our own time? Does "Corporate America" really exist? Or is the concept a convenient scapegoat? What is the proper role of regulatory agencies and the courts? Is a manager's first responsibility to stockholders, or is there something greater? Heroes and villains are hard to find, and the ethical concerns are not easy.

 # D O C U M E N T S

During the late twentieth century, Americans built on liberal tradition in their efforts to mesh private enterprise with the public interest. For some businesses, trade and industry associations continued to function as mechanisms for self-regulation, as demonstrated by the ACC's Responsible Care program. In other cases, government agencies continued to perform the watch-dog duties deemed appropriate by liberal policymakers in the Progressive Era. In matters of the environment and consumer safety, the regulatory state expanded its reach during the 1970s and 1980s, giving rise to agencies such as the EPA and legislation such as the Clean Air Acts. By the 1980s, Americans frustrated by government bureaucracy increasingly turned to the courts to adjudicate corporate social responsibility. The documents in this chapter explore elements of these transitions.

Documents 1 and 2 contain two speeches made at the 1949 national meeting of the U.S. Chamber of Commerce. Created in 1912 to represent business in Washington, the Chamber was the nation's largest trade association by the postwar era. It provided members with a forum for debate and encouraged self-regulation. During the 1949 meeting, members discussed postwar economic growth, including diminishing supplies of natural resources. In Document 1, guest speaker Fairfield Osborn, president of the New York Zoological Society and author of the 1948 book, *Our Plundered Planet,* surveys industry's conservation practices. This outspoken conservationist is wary, but hopeful. In Document 2, businessman J. Philip Weyerhaeuser, president of the Weyerhaeuser Timber Company in Tacoma, Washington, describes the lumber trade's conservation efforts and examines the U.S. Forest Service's interventionist practices. What do these documents reveal about the ecological consciousness of American business in the postwar years?

Next, consumer activist Ralph Nader indicts the American automobile industry in the preface to his 1965 book, *Unsafe at Any Speed.* Appalled at the safety record of the Chevrolet Corvair, Nader investigated dozens of lawsuits filed against General Motors by plaintiffs like Rose Pierini of Santa Barbara, California. In 1961, Pierini's Corvair flipped over while she drove it at thirty-five miles per hour along a highway, severing her right arm from her body. Several years later, General Motors settled Pierini's case out of court, fearful of the publicity. Other such cases revealed engineering flaws in the Corvair, designed by GM to compete on the market as a sporty roadster. Nader's book explored the auto industry's decision to focus on styling rather than safety, and probed the ethical implications of that choice.

In Document 4, John D. Harper, chief executive at the Aluminum Company of America (Alcoa), responds to the 1960s critique of American business by such activists as Rachel Carson and Ralph Nader. Harper speaks about the imperative for balancing the demands of stockholders with the needs of society at large. Harper started working at Alcoa in 1925, becoming president in 1963 and CEO in 1965. During the late 1960s and early 1970s, he led a movement among American executives committed to advancing a code of social responsibility. How do Harper's ideas dovetail with those of Weyerhaeuser in Document 2?

Next, Milton Friedman, a champion of free-market economics who won the 1976 Nobel Prize, lashes out against the doctrine of social responsibility as articulated by executives like John Harper. In Document 5, Friedman argues that the only responsibility of a corporation is to make money for its stockholders. In his view, the job of tending to social needs should fall to government officials and private philanthropists. Friedman's ideas enjoyed great currency with Republican administrations that came to power beginning in the 1980s and have remained a mantra in some business circles in our own time.

During the seventies, Americans reeled under the impact of *stagflation,* as economic *stag*nation and soaring *in*flation eroded jobs, buying power, and savings. From October 1973 to March 1974, the Arab-dominated oil cartel, OPEC (Organization of Petroleum-Exporting Countries), embargoed oil shipments to the United States in retaliation for its pro-Israeli policies on the Mideast. Oil shortages and skyrocketing gas prices focused public attention on the nation's energy needs. Yet well before the oil shock, a "crisis in energy" preoccupied businessmen. In Document 6, Sun Oil Company executive T. A. Burtis addresses the situation in a speech to his sales staff in March 1973. As president of Sun's Product Group, Burtis was responsible for marketing gasoline, heating oil, lubricants, jet fuel, and chemicals to the oil company's customers. What strategies does Burtis propose for the nation, the petroleum industry, and Sun Oil? How does government fit into the picture?

Love Canal and similar disasters focused media attention on toxic waste and impelled President Jimmy Carter in June 1979 to propose the creation of a "superfund" to clean up the mess. In Document 7, the Republican senator from Vermont, Robert T. Stafford, who helped to write the 1980 Comprehensive Environmental Response,

Compensation, and Liability Act (CERCLA), commonly known as Superfund, explains the need for the law. Despite good intentions, enormous costs soon overwhelmed Superfund. In 1992, *Business Week* reported that $11 billion had been spent by the federal government and culpable companies to detoxify a mere 84 of the 1,200 worst sites.

Next, Dr. Therman Evans, vice president and corporate medical director at CIGNA Corporation, a major insurance company, addresses a gathering of the American Lung Association on the relationship between cigarette advertising and African American health (Document 8). Evans, a black physician, directly blames tobacco companies such as R. J. Reynolds and Philip Morris for the high percentage of smokers among minorities. How does Evans build his case against the cigarette companies? What do Evans's ideas reveal about the "business community" and tobacco?

Finally, two Hawaiian interest groups, the Maui Pueo Coalition and Maui Tomorrow, take opposing sides in a public debate over a proposal to expand the runway at Kahului Airport in Document 9. Both associations share concerns about introducing alien species harmful to agriculture, while disagreeing about tourism, the mainstay of Maui's economy. The Maui Pueo Coalition—comprised of business groups, unions, and farm organizations—argues that airport enlargement is essential to sustaining the tourist trade, while Maui Tomorrow—a group of citizen environmentalists—holds that runway expansion will lead to unsustainable growth.

1. A Prominent Zoologist Speaks About the Threat of the Modern Economy, 1949

Ever since President Zachary Taylor was in the White House, just a hundred years ago, we as a nation have prodigally used and spent these life-supporting resources with little if any thought for the future. Our national economy has been anything but good economy because we are breaking the primary rule of all business, namely, living to a great degree upon our capital account in that we have been steadily drawing upon our reserves. To this degree, our famed high standard of living is neither a true one nor a permanent one. Obviously, our nation cannot continue to do this much longer. Already we can sense oncoming scarcities—for example, in water resources and in lumber. These make it obvious, even to the casual observer, that the day of "reorganization" is at hand. . . .

About one-half of American industry today—whether stated in terms of plants or jobs or output—relies directly on . . . renewable resources for its principal raw materials; over one-third of the nation's power is hydroelectric; about one-fifth of the industrial kilowatt hours are devoted to processing organic resource material; nearly one-fifth of the revenue freight of the nation's railroads derives from the carriage of these raw materials alone. The future of our country's wellbeing depends upon our getting on a sustained-yield basis. This is now evident to all of us. Every element in the life of our nation has got to get into this game of Conservation.

Now, let's take a quick summary review of some of our errors and abuses. As to forests, we have in the last 40 years reduced our reserves of saw timber by more than

Fairfield Osborn, "Modern Economy's Threat to Our Resources," Chamber of Commerce, Minutes of the 37th Annual Meeting, Washington, D.C., May 2–5, 1949, pp. 326–328, in box 10, series 1, acc. 1960: Chamber of Commerce of the United States of America Papers, Hagley Museum and Library, Wilmington, Del.

40%. Today our annual consumption of this, the biggest drain upon our forests, exceeds annual growth by more than one-half. At the present rate of drain, assuming there are no other changing factors, we will not have a stick of saw timber left in this country in another 87 years.

A great deal of this loss is preventable. For example, it is estimated that of the total wood-drain in our country 35% is being lost by wastage.

This points up the unpalatable fact that waste has been a national characteristic since the days when 40 million buffalo were slaughtered for their hides and innumerable carcasses were left to rot on the plains. Oh, the romantic glories of prodigality!

Granted that saw timber is only one element in our forest needs, this is obviously a drain that must be corrected. Within the last 16 years the general commodities index has risen about 100%. In the same period the price of lumber has risen more than 250%, a direct reflection in prices of what has been taking place.

Of our billion acres of rangelands, farm pasturelands and croplands we have ruined or severely impoverished approximately one-quarter by misuse. Such losses are totally preventable. Paradoxically, by extra-ordinary advancements in agricultural techniques we have substantially stepped up crop production both in the aggregate as well as in the average per acre. This fact appears to discredit those individuals such as myself who take the position that our conservation practices do not as yet begin to be adequate. Quantity production, unless soil productivity is preserved, is good for today, but fatal for tomorrow. . . .

What's on the bright side of the picture? A great deal. First and foremost, we are waking up as a nation to the situation we are discussing today. There is nothing in this country that we cannot accomplish if public opinion really becomes sufficiently aroused. Further, wonderful advances have been made in methods of agriculture. Science triumphant in the physical areas is exploring methods of supplementing the biological processes of nature. It must do so. The situation calls for scientific exploration even into uncharted channels from which new sources of organic material can be drawn—sources of either land or marine origin. The net of the situation today is that we have the "know how." In turn, there is ample evidence that the renewable resource problem can be solved in this country. We have only to follow the pattern of what is already being accomplished in certain agricultural regions or take a leaf, on a nationwide basis, from the book of some of the great lumber companies, who are successfully getting their forest reserves on a sustained-yield basis. In this regard, however, 75% of all privately owned forest lands is in the hands of 4,200,000 owners, with an average size of holdings of only 62 acres. The introduction of proper forestry methods on these holdings is essential.

I am to be followed by speakers of the highest competence in these matters. In hearing them you will realize that we have the technical "know-how" as well as an enlightened point of view of the responsibilities of ownership. In listening to them, however, please let me point this out. It is *not* that we do not have the skills; it is *not* that we do not have many examples of responsible ownership. The question is the extent to which sound Conservation practices can be adopted throughout our entire country and how soon we can reach this great objective. Isolated leaders, whether in skills or in trusteeship, are impotent unless they are supported and followed by public opinion and by the army of our citizenship in government, in organized labor, business and industry, and in education, who too are prepared to serve.

2. Weyerhaeuser Explains the Forest Industry's Practices, 1949

Those who insist America is heading down a one-way street to forest oblivion obviously haven't bothered to check all the facts. Certainly they have not examined the prevailing trends in modern industrial forestry. The basic concept of the timber operators has long since changed from one of migratory trade and temporary holdings to one of permanence based on long range planning and scientific land operation. Our modern economy, rather than posing a growing threat to forest resources, is, for the first time, providing the economic incentive to grow trees as a crop.

The realization that timber is renewable was slow in developing. True it is that tree farming and treating timber as a crop became the practice only after it became economically in the interest of timberland owners to do so. . . . Until sometime after the Great Depression of 1932, one could purchase more trees whenever needed at less than the cost of growing them.

Our 345 million acres of private forestlands capable of producing a commercial crop represent over four million different ownerships. Our 116 million acres of similar publicly-owned forestland contain a large percentage (45%) of the present inventory of mature timber, but are by and large less capable of growing a large annual crop of timber than the more accessible and fertile private lands. The forest industry, which owns 84 million acres out of this total of 461 million acres of commercial timberland in the country, depends for its existence upon the renewal and wise use of *all* these lands. Industry's own lands are being treated with increasing care for regrowth, as evidenced by the employment in industry of more than 2,000 forest school graduates at this writing. Wood-using industries' statements of policy increasingly stress the importance of timber cropping. . . .

Constructive work in this direction has been done by an industry agency called American Forest Products Industries. Its "Tree Farm Program" has spread the tree-farm movement from a single beginning in the State of Washington in 1941 by our Company to 23 states of the Union, where there are 1,738 organized tree farms covering 17,593,129 acres. Its current "Trees for America Program" is aimed at persuading the four million small owners of 261 million acres of commercial forestland that they have a paramount and financially profitable interest in managing their forestland on a crop basis, much as other cropped lands are managed. At the present rate of organization, American Forest Products Industries, Inc., which sponsors these programs in behalf of lumber, pulp, and paper industries, expects to have 30,000,000 acres in organized, carefully supervised tree farms by 1951. . . .

Reference to hundreds of millions of acres and millions of owners calls attention to the fact that appraisal of our forest inventory and its use is such a Gargantuan task that no one feels equal to it except government. All parties to an argument about America's forests perforce go to the United States Forest Service for factual data.

J. Philip Weyerhaeuser, "Answering the Threat of Forest Depletion," Chamber of Commerce, Minutes of the 37th Annual Meeting, Washington, D.C., May 2–5, 1949, pp. 339–342, in box 10, series 1, acc. 1960: Chamber of Commerce of the United States of America Papers, Hagley Museum and Library, Wilmington, Del.

We must recognize that since its organization under [Gifford] Pinchot the Forest Service itself has almost continuously "viewed the situation with alarm." It was predicted in 1907 for instance, that the Southern pineries would be cut out by 1920, though the 1946 resurvey found in the 11 southern states 323 billion board feet of sawtimber and an annual growth amounting to 19 billion board feet. In 1919 the Chief of the Forest Service predicted that should another war emergency arise by 1934 we would have very great embarrassment in obtaining even the lumber needed for general construction. Yet the record of war supply was remarkable and not limited by the timber supply.

Interpretation of Forest Service data often seems to us in industry to lean toward the thesis that the public must be frightened into acceptance of the big, all-powerful "Let's pass a law" federal approach, offering subsidies and incentives in one hand and threats of federal regulation in the other. This means more and more taxes and more thousands of federal employees who would render ostensibly free services not only on forestry, but also on how to conduct our businesses. . . .

We are all agreed on growing more trees for America. Recent years have seen great strides in that direction. Not the least of the actuating forces has been that same rise in values of prime forest material which many of us have viewed askance. The use of lower valued, though more expensively handled, material has been accelerated by the rise in stumpage values. Industry's technological improvements have made possible the transmutation of small and previously unmarketable pieces or species of wood into pulp for paper, board, or chemical uses. A wide market for the trees we are all growing will continue to be of utmost importance to forestry.

Out in the West, we're just beginning to find markets for those so-called "wastes" for which the industry has been criticized. No one is going to legislate those markets for us. Hard work in product development and sales as the result of self-interest will produce them. The necessary investment risks also will be taken if the business climate permits, but not via the "crack-the-whip" method. Neither can the millions of forestland owners be so actuated.

Our modern economy is providing a background leading to voluntary renewal of our timber resources, and, instead of being a threat, it furnishes the greatest assurance that those resources will both be renewed and used for the greatest benefit of all the people.

3. Ralph Nader Blames Detroit Carmakers for Automotive Accidents, 1965

For over half a century the automobile has brought death, injury, and the most inestimable sorrow and deprivation to millions of people. With Medea-like intensity, this mass trauma began rising sharply four years ago reflecting new and unexpected ravages by the motor vehicle. A 1959 Department of Commerce report projected that 51,000 persons would be killed by automobiles in 1975. That figure will probably be reached in 1965, a decade ahead of schedule.

Ralph Nader, *Unsafe at Any Speed: The Designed-in Dangers of the American Automobile* (New York: Grossman, 1965), pp. vii–xi.

A transportation specialist, Wilfred Owen, wrote in 1946, "There is little question that the public will not tolerate for long an annual traffic toll of forty to fifty thousand fatalities." Time has shown Owen to be wrong. Unlike aviation, marine, or rail transportation, the highway transport system can inflict tremendous casualties and property damage without in the least affecting the viability of the system. Plane crashes, for example, jeopardize the attraction of flying for potential passengers and therefore strike at the heart of the air transport economy. They motivate preventative efforts. The situation is different on the roads.

Highway accidents were estimated to have cost this country in 1964, $8.3 billion in property damage, medical expenses, lost wages, and insurance overhead expenses. Add an equivalent sum to comprise roughly the indirect costs and the total amounts to over two per cent of the gross national product. But these are not the kind of costs which fall on the builders of motor vehicles (excepting a few successful law suits for negligent construction of the vehicle) and thus do not pinch the proper foot. Instead, the costs fall to users of vehicles, who are in no position to dictate safer automobile designs.

In fact, the gigantic costs of the highway carnage in this country support a service industry. A vast array of services—medical, police, administrative, legal, insurance, automotive repair, and funeral—stand equipped to handle the direct and indirect consequences of accident injuries. Traffic accidents create economic demands for these services running into billions of dollars. It is in the post-accident response that lawyers and physicians and other specialists labor. This is where the remuneration lies and this is where the talent and energies go. Working in the area of prevention of these casualties earns few fees. Consequently our society has an intricate organization to handle direct and indirect aftermaths of collisions. But the true mark of a humane society must be what it does about *prevention* of accident injuries, not the cleaning up of them afterward.

Unfortunately, there is little in the dynamics of the automobile accident industry that works for its reduction. Doctors, lawyers, engineers and other specialists have failed in their primary professional ethic: to dedicate themselves to the prevention of accident-injuries. The roots of the unsafe vehicle problem are so entrenched that the situation can be improved only by the forging of new instruments of citizen action. When thirty practicing physicians picketed for safe auto design at the New York International Automobile Show on April 7, 1965, their unprecedented action was the measure of their desperation over the inaction of the men and institutions in government and industry who have failed to provide the public with the vehicle safety to which it is entitled. The picketing surgeons, orthopedists, pediatricians and general practitioners marched in protest because the existing medical, legal and engineering organizations have defaulted.

A great problem of contemporary life is how to control the power of economic interests which ignore the harmful effects of their applied science and technology. The automobile tragedy is one of the most serious of these manmade assaults on the human body. The history of that tragedy reveals many obstacles which must be overcome in the taming of any mechanical or biological hazard which is a by-product of industry or commerce. Our society's obligation to protect the "body rights" of its citizens with vigorous resolve and ample resources requires the precise, authoritative articulation and front-rank support which is being devoted to civil rights.

This country has not been entirely laggard in defining values relevant to new contexts of a technology laden with risks. The postwar years have witnessed a historic broadening, at least in the courts, of the procedural and substantive rights of the injured and the duties of manufacturers to produce a safe product. Judicial decisions throughout the fifty states have given living meaning to Walt Whitman's dictum, "If anything is sacred, the human body is sacred." Mr. Justice Jackson in 1953 defined the duty of the manufacturers by saying, "Where experiment or research is necessary to determine the presence or the degree of danger, the product must not be tried out on the public, nor must the public be expected to possess the facilities or the technical knowledge to learn for itself of inherent but latent dangers. The claim that a hazard was not foreseen is not available to one who did not use foresight appropriate to his enterprise."

It is a lag of almost paralytic proportions that these values of safety concerning consumers and economic enterprises, reiterated many times by the judicial branch of government, have not found their way into legislative policy-making for safer automobiles. Decades ago legislation was passed, changing the pattern of private business investments to accommodate more fully the safety value on railroads, in factories, and more recently on ships and aircraft. In transport, apart from the motor vehicle, considerable progress has been made in recognizing the physical integrity of the individual. There was the period when railroad workers were killed by the thousands and the editor of *Harper's* could say late in the last century: "So long as brakes cost more than trainmen, we may expect the present sacrificial method of car-coupling to be continued." But injured trainmen did cause the railroads some operating dislocations; highway victims cost the automobile companies next to nothing and the companies are not obliged to make use of developments in science-technology that have demonstrably opened up opportunities for far greater safety than any existing safety features lying unused on the automobile companies' shelves.

A principal reason why the automobile has remained the only transportation vehicle to escape being called to meaningful public account is that the public has never been supplied the information nor offered the quality of competition to enable it to make effective demands through the marketplace and through government for a safe, nonpolluting and efficient automobile that can be produced economically. The consumer's expectations regarding automotive innovations have been deliberately held low and mostly oriented to very gradual annual style changes. The specialists and researchers outside the industry who could have provided the leadership to stimulate this flow of information by and large chose to remain silent, as did government officials.

The persistence of the automobile's immunity over the years has nourished the continuance of that immunity, recalling Francis Bacon's insight: "He that will not apply new remedies must expect new evils, for time is the greatest innovator."

The accumulated power of decades of effort by the automobile industry to strengthen its control over car design is reflected today in the difficulty of even beginning to bring it to justice. The time has not come to discipline the automobile for safety; that time came over four decades ago. But that is not cause to delay any longer what should have been accomplished in the nineteen-twenties.

4. Alcoa CEO Explains the Public Responsibility of Private Enterprise, 1967

Many of the problems that trouble our society today were created, at least in part, or aggravated by the very same business enterprise system that has made our society the most comfortable and prosperous on earth.

Of course, the several agencies of our society—among them business—didn't deliberately set out to plague the public with dirty water or air that's hardly fit to breathe, nor did they somehow conspire to cause urban congestion, traffic jams, and technological unemployment. All these problems, and more, arose from the very nature of our cultural and economic development, from changing values and standards, from the concentration of industrial plants in advantageous centers, from technological progress, from the sheer size and success of our free enterprise system. And, especially, they have arisen with the growth of our population.

Nobody, for instance, really wanted to poison the fish in the rivers or to contaminate the air that all of us have to breathe, but it happened. It happened in part because we only have such problems with a growing population, in part because we have lacked satisfactory techniques for control of contamination, and in part because responsibility is like a hot poker that nobody really wants to grasp.

In any event, we today have very little choice in the matter. Business is involved right up to the neckline in hundreds of public problems, and the public—that is to say our customers, our neighbors, our employees and our stockholders—expect us to accept the responsibility of helping to solve those problems. And in so doing, we protect the very system that permits us all to prosper.

Whatever justification there may have been for ignoring such problems in the past, we cannot justify apathy or inaction today. . . .

Charity Is Private Concern

Please note the phrase "intelligent exercise of public responsibility." Business should not go galloping off in all directions performing all kinds of good works at the expense of its primary function—which is, to produce and sell at a profit goods of the quality and quantity required by the consumer. We are not in business to compete with the Salvation Army. Charity for its own sake is, I hope, a private concern of each of us; it is not the task we are paid to perform.

The intelligent exercise of public responsibility is something quite different. It involves, first of all, a recognition that a business is a citizen in a very real sense and must behave like a citizen in return for being allowed to operate within the community.

Just as an individual citizen can't throw rocks through his neighbor's picture window without landing in jail, so the corporate citizen cannot wantonly abuse the public interest without public retaliation. A business, for instance, cannot disregard

---

John D. Harper, "Private Enterprise's Public Responsibility," *Public Relations Journal* (August 1967): 8–10.

the fire and health laws, or deliberately make false claims in advertising. At least in that minimum sense, therefore, public responsibility is not an optional chore for business.

Extremes of Approach

Quite frankly, and unfortunately for all of us, there are some businessmen who still believe that public responsibility means living up to the letter of the law and not one inch beyond. These are the same fellows whose smokestacks will go right on belching soot into your office windows and on your wife's laundry until the city council passes a law against it. Their disregard for the public interest inevitably leads to public clamor for repressive or restrictive legislation, which may cause problems for all of us.

Businessmen are perhaps the most vocal members of society in complaining about regulation. We must remember that we can prevent further regulation best by anticipating needs and meeting them voluntarily.

At the other end of the spectrum is the man who would like to make his company an extension of his own personal social conscience. Sixty or seventy years ago, in the era of family ownership, it was perfectly proper to donate millions of dollars to any charity that appealed to the leader. He owned the business and could do as he pleased with his profits. Today's corporate leader has no such privilege; he cannot dispense corporate funds for social purposes, however worthy, without proper regard for the interests of his stockholders. If he lacks that regard, they will find a new manager.

Somewhere in between those two extremes is the enlightened business leader of today, of the 1960's, the professional executive who balances his company's public and private responsibilities, who undertakes an appropriate range of projects in the public sphere with full awareness of the fact that his company has other public responsibilities beyond its profit responsibility.

Profit Is Prime Factor

Let me repeat. The number one public responsibility of private enterprise is to operate at a profit. That's a cliche, of course, but it became a cliche because it is true. And every last one of us—social worker, scientist, politician, educator, clergymen, union member or corporate manager—should be ready to fight to the last ditch for that profit incentive, because that is what provides our jobs, our taxes, all the wealth that makes social progress possible. Never let us forget that profit is the basis of our free enterprise economy. . . .

Despite what we may hear from time to time from some critics of our system, there is no contradiction between making a profit and meeting other public responsibilities. The business community has long recognized the relationship between social and economic progress. I, for one, am troubled when I hear a prominent news commentator—as I did recently—express surprise that business today is actively concerned with such public responsibilities as health and education, delinquency, poverty, air and water pollution, or the physical deterioration of our cities. I am chiefly surprised that he is surprised. I find myself wondering where he has been all this time. Have we business leaders failed so completely to get our message across to the public? Perhaps we should reexamine our communications. It may be that some of us have forgotten to turn on the microphone. We might discover that we have been talking only to ourselves.

It would seem evident that business—free private enterprise—will flourish and prosper best in a healthy environment, where its employees are educated and productive, where the consumers of its goods and services are sufficiently cultivated and sufficiently well-off to seek a continually higher standard of living.

If you drive through a brawling ghetto on your way to the office in the morning, and back home again at night, it doesn't take much imagination to recognize that something is wrong. You don't have to be a social scientist to realize that slums don't generate much business for you. The bright young men you want for future executive jobs aren't going to beat a path through crime-ridden slums to get to your door. Nor will they want to live in a deteriorating city in order to work for you.

Community Projects Pay

It makes sense to participate—with corporate money, talent and energy—in a community project to improve conditions in the slums. In the long run, such participation will prove to be beneficial to your own business. Because if you reduce delinquency, crime and illiteracy, you reduce your own corporate tax load, and you convert welfare cases into productive workers. You may even pick up some new customers in the bargain!

Supporting a symphony orchestra, or a theater group, or an art collection might sound impractical as an avenue of corporate philanthropy. But it can be good business for the company that is trying to recruit university graduates who seek to live in a community where they and their families can enjoy the arts. Such activities also return benefits in the form of increased stature in the community, an intangible reward of no small value. This can be a contribution to the upgrading of the cultural well-being of the community. It can result in enhancing our reputation in a way that advertising can never accomplish.

In each of those instances, self-interest coincides with public interest. And that's the way it should be. The business dollar that goes to meet public responsibility must be a productive dollar if it is to be of real benefit to the society we purport to help. And, I submit that any dollar spent that successfully meets our dual responsibility to shareholders and to the community is a productive dollar.

More and more, American business is recognizing that it has a unique public responsibility, because of the fact that it is the source of all our productive wealth—and because it is the beneficiary of our society. The real dilemma for today's businessman is not whether he should or should not accept that responsibility. His dilemma, rather, is how to identify the public areas in which he can properly and helpfully operate. And I suggest that his problem could be greatly simplified by applying the test of productivity.

I am not saying that we should put public responsibility on a strictly C.O.D., "What's in it for me?" basis. I *am* saying that we have got to be selective in what we undertake, that we have got to avoid overcommitting our resources. A bankrupt business offers mighty few job opportunities and it makes a mighty poor taxpayer, even if it's headed by the busiest do-gooder in all America. . . .

Act on Public Policy

I do not believe it can be said too often or too emphatically that a primary public responsibility of the principal management officers of American business is to speak up on legislation and other government actions that affect their business.

We can all agree that company presidents and board chairmen are a fairly busy breed of men. But that simply explains—and does not excuse—the top business executive who delegates responsibility in matters of public policy to his subordinates or his trade associations.

This delegation of responsibility just won't work. Not in this time of our lives, at any rate. We are moving into an era of business-government relationships in which there is no room for the indifferent executive, when more of our top people have simply *got* to find time to express themselves to the members of Congress and to the executive branch on all matters that involve their own interests. There is no substitute for that kind of responsibility. It just can't be delegated.

It would be a wonderful world if somebody else could establish peace on earth, eliminate poverty, ignorance, crime and disease, settle all labor disputes before they start, lower taxes, and guarantee all of us everlasting prosperity—without disturbing our golf game. But it just doesn't come out that way.

Responsibility is something each of us must accept. We must use the resources, talents and energies of business wisely and effectively to advance the public interest and the system of private enterprise upon which it depends. We must accept personal responsibility for our own stewardship as managers of business.

Great tides of change are on the move today, and the business system of this nation must move with them, must help to direct them through exercising its public responsibility.

5. Economist Milton Friedman Urges Business to Focus on Profits, 1970

When I hear businessmen speak eloquently about the "social responsibilities of business in a free-enterprise system," I am reminded of the wonderful line about the Frenchman who discovered at the age of 70 that he had been speaking prose all his life. The businessmen believe that they are defending free enterprise when they declaim that business is not concerned "merely" with profit but also with promoting desirable "social" ends; that business has a "social conscience" and takes seriously its responsibilities for providing employment, eliminating discrimination, avoiding pollution and whatever else may be the catchwords of the contemporary crop of reformers. In fact they are—or would be if they or anyone else took them seriously—preaching pure and unadulterated socialism. Businessmen who talk this way are unwitting puppets of the intellectual forces that have been undermining the basis of a free society these past decades.

The discussions of the "social responsibilities of business" are notable for their analytical looseness and lack of rigor. What does it mean to say that "business" has responsibilities? Only people can have responsibilities. A corporation is an artificial

---

person and in this sense may have artificial responsibilities, but "business" as a whole cannot be said to have responsibilities, even in this vague sense. The first step toward clarity in examining the doctrine of the social responsibility of business is to ask precisely what it implies for whom.

Presumably, the individuals who are to be responsible are businessmen, which means individual proprietors or corporate executives. Most of the discussion of social responsibility is directed at corporations, so in what follows I shall mostly neglect the individual proprietor and speak of corporate executives.

In a free-enterprise, private-property system, a corporate executive is an employe of the owners of the business. He has direct responsibility to his employers. That responsibility is to conduct the business in accordance with their desires, which generally will be to make as much money as possible while conforming to the basic rules of the society, both those embodied in law and those embodied in ethical custom. Of course, in some cases his employers may have a different objective. A group of persons might establish a corporation for an eleemosynary purpose—for example, a hospital or a school. The manager of such a corporation will not have money profit as his objective but the rendering of certain services.

In either case, the key point is that, in his capacity as a corporate executive, the manager is the agent of the individuals who own the corporation or establish the eleemosynary institution, and his primary responsibility is to them.

Needless to say, this does not mean that it is easy to judge how well he is performing his task. But at least the criterion of performance is straightforward, and the persons among whom a voluntary contractual arrangement exists are clearly defined.

Of course, the corporate executive is also a person in his own right. As a person, he may have many other responsibilities that he recognizes or assumes voluntarily—to his family, his conscience, his feelings of charity, his church, his clubs, his city, his country. He may feel impelled by these responsibilities to devote part of his income to causes he regards as worthy, to refuse to work for particular corporations, even to leave his job, for example, to join his country's armed forces. If we wish, we may refer to some of these responsibilities as "social responsibilities." But in these respects he is acting as a principal, not an agent; he is spending his own money or time or energy, not the money of his employers or the time or energy he has contracted to devote to their purposes. If these are "social responsibilities," they are the social responsibilities of individuals, not of business.

What does it mean to say that the corporate executive has a "social responsibility" in his capacity as businessman? If this statement is not pure rhetoric, it must mean that he is to act in some way that is not in the interest of his employers. For example, that he is to refrain from increasing the price of the product in order to contribute to the social objective of preventing inflation, even though a price increase would be in the best interests of the corporation. Or that he is to make expenditures on reducing pollution beyond the amount that is in the best interests of the corporation or that is required by law in order to contribute to the social objective of improving the environment. Or that, at the expense of corporate profits, he is to hire "hardcore" unemployed instead of better-qualified available workmen to contribute to the social objective of reducing poverty.

In each of these cases, the corporate executive would be spending someone else's money for a general social interest. Insofar as his actions in accord with his "social responsibility" reduce returns to stockholders, he is spending their money. Insofar as his actions raise the price to customers, he is spending the customers' money. Insofar as his actions lower the wages of some employes, he is spending their money.

The stockholders or the customers or the employes could separately spend their own money on the particular action if they wished to do so. The executive is exercising a distinct "social responsibility," rather than serving as an agent of the stockholders or the customers or the employes, only if he spends the money in a different way than they would have spent it.

But if he does this, he is in effect imposing taxes, on the one hand, and deciding how the tax proceeds shall be spent, on the other.

This process raises political questions on two levels: principle and consequences. On the level of political principle, the imposition of taxes and the expenditure of tax proceeds are governmental functions. We have established elaborate constitutional, parliamentary and judicial provisions to control these functions, to assure that taxes are imposed so far as possible in accordance with the preferences and desires of the public—after all, "taxation without representation" was one of the battle cries of the American Revolution. We have a system of checks and balances to separate the legislative function of imposing taxes and enacting expenditures from the executive function of collecting taxes and administering expenditure programs and from the judicial function of mediating disputes and interpreting the law.

Here the businessman—self-selected or appointed directly or indirectly by stockholders—is to be simultaneously legislator, executive and jurist. He is to decide whom to tax by how much and for what purpose, and he is to spend the proceeds—all this guided only by general exhortations from on high to restrain inflation, improve the environment, fight poverty and so on and on.

The whole justification for permitting the corporate executive to be selected by the stockholders is that the executive is an agent serving the interests of his principal. This justification disappears when the corporate executive imposes taxes and spends the proceeds for "social" purposes. He becomes in effect a public employe, a civil servant, even though he remains in name an employe of a private enterprise. On grounds of political principle, it is intolerable that such civil servants—insofar as their actions in the name of social responsibility are real and not just window-dressing—should be selected as they are now. If they are to be civil servants, then they must be selected through a political process. If they are to impose taxes and make expenditures to foster "social" objectives, then political machinery must be set up to guide the assessment of taxes and to determine through a political process the objectives to be served.

This is the basic reason why the doctrine of "social responsibility" involves the acceptance of the socialist view that political mechanisms, not market mechanisms, are the appropriate way to determine the allocation of scarce resources to alternative uses. . . .

Whether blameworthy or not, the use of the cloak of social responsibility, and the nonsense spoken in its name by influential and prestigious businessmen, does clearly harm the foundations of a free society. I have been impressed time and again by the schizophrenic character of many businessmen. They are capable of being extremely far-sighted and clear-headed in matters that are internal to their businesses. They are incredibly short-sighted and muddle-headed in matters that are outside their businesses but affect the possible survival of business in general. This short-sightedness is strikingly exemplified in the calls from many businessmen for wage and price guidelines or controls or incomes policies. There is nothing that could do more in a brief period to destroy a market system and replace it by a centrally controlled system than effective governmental control of prices and wages.

The short-sightedness is also exemplified in speeches by businessmen on social responsibility. This may gain them kudos in the short run. But it helps to strengthen the already too prevalent view that the pursuit of profits is wicked and immoral and must be curbed and controlled by external forces. Once this view is adopted, the external forces that curb the market will not be the social consciences, however highly developed, of the pontificating executives; it will be the iron fist of Government bureaucrats. Here, as with price and wage controls, businessmen seem to me to reveal a suicidal impulse.

The political principle that underlies the market mechanism is unanimity. In an ideal free market resting on private property, no individual can coerce any other, all cooperation is voluntary, all parties to such cooperation benefit or they need not participate. There are no "social" values, no "social" responsibilities in any sense other than the shared values and responsibilities of individuals. Society is a collection of individuals and of the various groups they voluntarily form.

The political principle that underlies the political mechanism is conformity. The individual must serve a more general social interest—whether that be determined by a church or a dictator or a majority. The individual may have a vote and a say in what is to be done, but if he is overruled, he must conform. It is appropriate for some to require others to contribute to a general social purpose whether they wish to or not.

Unfortunately, unanimity is not always feasible. There are some respects in which conformity appears unavoidable, so I do not see how one can avoid the use of the political mechanism altogether.

But the doctrine of "social responsibility" taken seriously would extend the scope of the political mechanism to every human activity. It does not differ in philosophy from the most explicitly collectivist doctrine. It differs only by professing to believe that collectivist ends can be attained without collectivist means. That is why, in my book "Capitalism and Freedom," I have called it a "fundamentally subversive doctrine" in a free society, and have said that in such a society, "there is one and only one social responsibility of business—to use its resources and engage in activities designed to increase its profits so long as it stays within the rules of the game, which is to say, engages in open and free competition without deception or fraud."

6. Sun Oil Executive Outlines the Nation's Energy Dilemmas, 1973

Natural gas, which has been a preferred fuel for home and industry in this country for a good many years, is now so tight that the suppliers are cutting off some customers completely, rationing others, and in many areas of the country refusing to take any new accounts even for home heating. These measures help to spread the existing

Sun Oil Company, "Speech for Regional Sales Meetings," by T. A. Burtis, May 1973, in accession 1317: Sun Oil Company Papers, series 2: Senior Management, subseries F: T. A. Burtis Series, box 167, Hagley Museum and Library, Wilmington, Del. Courtesy of Hagley Museum and Library.

supply, but they do nothing to produce another single cubic foot of gas. So the major gas pipeline companies are spending huge amounts of money to liquefy gas in Africa and import it into the United States at a cost roughly six to seven times that of the wellhead price of gas produced here. Further, they are scrambling to secure supplies of naphtha and crude oil to convert to pipeline quality gas—the so-called SNG—which also carries the same kind of price tag. This puts more pressure on crude supply, since an SNG plant with a capacity of 250MMCF a day requires on the order of 55,000 barrels a day of naphtha charge stock, or its equivalent in crude.

Our crude oil situation doesn't present any more attractive picture. Domestic crude production peaked out last year and is now beginning to decline. Efforts to find more crude in the most promising areas, particularly off-shore on the Continental shelf, have been severely hindered by failure of the government to hold lease sales as scheduled, and by the opposition of the environmentalists. There is a great deal of crude abroad, most of it in the Middle East, specifically Iran, Kuwait, and Saudi Arabia. This is not of much immediate use to us for two reasons. First, much of it is in undeveloped reserves and not available for immediate production. Secondly, most Middle East crude is sour, that is, it has a high sulfur content. Unfortunately few U.S. refineries are able to process sour crude, because of the lack of alloy protection in the equipment, the inability to meet product specifications, or the lack of equipment to keep the sulfur out of the atmosphere. On top of that the producing countries have recently banded together to raise prices, so that the day of the so-called "cheap foreign crude" is behind us. Some sweet African crudes landing in the U.S. today are priced above domestic crude.

Finally, refined products, as you are all particularly aware, are in short supply. We decided that we had to allocate gasoline to our customers beginning May 1 and it is very likely that distillates will have to be allocated during the next heating season. On May 10, a "voluntary" system was formulated by the Federal Government. Demand is increasing at a much higher than expected rate—about 6% for gasoline—while today there is not a single refinery now actually under construction in the United States, although some expansions have been announced. Some distillate may be brought in from abroad, but the likelihood of significantly supplementing our supplies of gasoline from off-shore are remote. What little is available has been quoted at prices in the order of 18–22¢/gal. in Europe.

This is where we are, and the question is, "How did we get here"? . . .

First, our natural gas situation came about because in the fifties the Federal Power Commission [FPC] asserted the power to regulate the price of gas at the wellhead, whereas before this time its authority was limited to the regulation of rates charged by the interstate transmission companies. When this authority was upheld by the Courts, the FPC clamped a tight lid on prices, basing their pricing policy on cost of production rather than the value of the fuel. Two things happened as a result of this action. Consumers were encouraged to use this clean, cheap fuel in all kinds of applications. Not only did homeowners flock to gas heat, with the assistance and support of the gas companies, but many factories and power plants were designed to run on gas. The demand increased fantastically. At the same time, however, the tight lid clamped on prices eliminated any incentive for the industry to go out and search for gas. Inevitably, demand for gas grew at a rate even faster than the growth of the economy, while practically no effort was being made to find additional supplies.

For many years the United States was able to produce more crude than it needed to satisfy its own requirements and dominated worldwide production. During the fifties, however, huge discoveries of crude were made in the Middle East and later in North Africa. Unlike our own producing fields, where the average well pumped a few hundred barrels a day, the Middle East fields were tremendously prolific and production from a single well characteristically was more than 5,000 barrels a day. This made the cost of discovery and production of foreign crude very low and it came onto the market at prices often on the order of half that of domestic crude. Had this low-cost material been allowed to flow in unlimited quantities into the United States, it is clear that our our production industry would have disappeared, and the U.S. would then have become completely dependent on foreign sources. Because of the national security problems and the desire to maintain the viability of the industry, a mandatory oil import program was enacted in the late 1950's. In its time and for its purposes this was probably a reasonable policy, but the situation began to change and the changes were not well recognized, particularly in the government. When the 6-Day War broke out in 1967 and the Suez Canal was closed, Europe was for a time shut off from crude. Supplies had to come from the United States and, therefore, the fields were allowed to produce at capacity. When this happened we found that we really did not have the excess producing capacity that we thought we had, and it became evident to the industry—although not to the government—that some steps were going to have to be taken to find more domestic reserves. The cost of exploration and production by that time, however, had gone up substantially, so that to justify the major effort which would be required, crude prices had to rise. The Federal Government still maintained a policy of providing energy at very low cost, however, and effectively prevented the finding of new reserves by threatening to open up the import gates whenever a crude price rise was attempted.

Consequently, in recent years exploration for new crude in the U.S. has declined and production from existing fields has peaked out and is declining. . . . [F]oreign producers have raised the price of foreign crude approximately to parity with the U.S.

The situation with refineries is what one might expect from all this. The cost of building refineries has been rising at a rate of 8–10% a year, while product prices have remained low. It has simply been impossible to justify the investment of the $200MM required to build a modern 150,000 barrel per day refinery in the face of rising costs and low product prices. Where companies have found the economic justification, it has been nearly impossible in recent years to find an acceptable refinery site because of the environmental restrictions put upon us. . . . The Mobil refinery in Joliet, Illinois, completed last year has a capacity of 160,000 barrels a day. Estimates of demand say that we should be building at least 5 of those every year.

Well, what are we going to do about getting ourselves out of this tight situation we're in? As a nation, as an industry, and particularly Sun Oil Company.

The first national priority has to be the establishment of a cohesive national energy policy. It should be aimed at assuring an adequate supply of energy, particularly hydrocarbons, at a price to the public which will reflect the cost of production, the value of the product, and the risk undertaken by the producers. We are going to have to find a way to establish a realistic cost/benefit relationship when imposing and enforcing pollution controls and other environmental restrictions.

Some useful actions have been recommended in . . . [President Nixon's] Energy Message. Imports are being opened up, and properly so. No one can in good conscience demand that imports be restricted when we are unable to supply from domestic sources. At the same time we need to protect against the further export of refining capacity, and this is handled in the President's message and last week's "voluntary" allocation program by the application of special fees—higher for products than for crude—in the hope that it will encourage domestic companies to build refineries. Whether or not the difference is enough to accomplish this end is questionable at the moment, but at least it's a step in the right direction. As a nation we do need to encourage further U.S. exploration and production. One of the key steps would be to speed up the leasing of off-shore federal lands, particularly in the Gulf and probably on the Atlantic Coast. This, too, is recommended in the President's message. We need to provide suitable ports for importing crude in very large cargo carriers. It is perfectly ridiculous for a country our size to be forced to bear the cost of shipping in small vessels because there is no port in the United States capable of handling the supertankers. There are no doubt great environmental battles to be fought over this, but it is an inevitable step that must be taken. The same is true of refineries. We simply must provide for the increasing demand, whatever the crude source, and the preferable way is to do it in U.S. refineries rather than exporting the jobs abroad. This will require a policy to permit the siting of refineries as well as a realistic view at prices to justify their economics. The decontrol of newly-found gas is a step in the right direction and hopefully in time will add to our supplies. There is general consensus that we have the resources, but they need to be found and converted first into proved reserves and then into production. And finally, the research and development into alternate sources, as for example, coal gasification, coal liquefaction, shale oil, is going to need some Federal support simply because the magnitude of the problem is so great.

These are all national steps—but what is Sun Oil Company going to do[?] *The one thing we are not going to do is sit back and cry about our problems.* Because the most obvious and pressing need is for added crude supplies, the corporation has decided to take a big gamble. Bob Sharbaugh calls this an "elephant hunt," in that we are going to spend our money in areas where the risks are high but the prospects of major discoveries are the best. You will see that we have been extremely aggressive in bidding for the off-shore leases and are making a major effort right now in off-shore exploration both in the U.S. and the North Sea. We have just concluded an agreement with the Algerian Government under which we have a long-term concession in that country in an area which we believe will be highly productive (the first well is being drilled). Our Canadian exploration has been stopped in the lower part of the country and we are moving into the highest risk area of all the Canadian Arctic Islands. Here the costs and difficulties are almost beyond belief, and yet the geological formations promise that major crude supplies should be there. For the near term we must be able to buy sweet crude somewhere on the World Market. This is a tough one, but . . . if it flows and burns, we'll buy it. . . .

Given success in finding crude supplies, we obviously must someday have more refining capacity if we are to meet our responsibilities to the public and to our shareholders. Our present plans are of necessity based on a constant product supply. This is a tough one because of the uncertainties of crude cost, continuity of supply and the product pricing restrictions we are under. Nevertheless, we are working hard at finding ways to justify an increase in our product supply. If we find crude and can make a processing agreement with some refiner with spare capacity, we *will do so.* We have on the drawing boards now plans for expanding capacity at several of our refineries, and I am sure that when we can see the economics are favorable, we will be knocking at the corporation's door asking for the capital to build. . . .

We have a stake in the development of alternate fuels and certainly will support Federal efforts to get this moving. We already own coal reserves in the West suitable for gasification or liquefaction, and we are actively pursuing the possibility of a shale oil development. And Sun, of course, was the pioneer in developing alternate sources through our enormously expensive experiment at Great Canadian Oil Sands. Sun Limited is actively pushing to have our allowable production at that plant raised from 45,000 bbls. a day to the neighborhood of 60,000 bbls. a day.

We are making strenuous efforts both to increase our crude and product supply. I would be less than candid with you, however, if I did not acknowledge that we are in a tight spot for a while and that it's unlikely that we will see a substantial loosening of product supply for at least a year—probably longer. There is a bright side, to the extent that the price structure seems to be firm and likely to remain so, and thus we have the opportunity to generate some of the capital that this corporation is going to need to accomplish its objectives. The Marketing Division is the ultimate revenue generator, so we have a responsibility to make the maximum contribution we can. The one thing we have to avoid is any feeling of complacency because of the ability to sell all product at attractive prices. Someday the shortage will end, and when that day comes Sun Oil Company is going to have to be in the position of once more vigorously competing for the market. My crystal ball is no more clear than anyone else's—but one thing I am convinced of is that this is, and will remain a very competitive business. Sun Oil Company, particularly its Marketing Division, is going to succeed only if we can be as efficient, low-cost, innovative and imaginative a competitor as there is in the market. Getting ourselves into that position is the crucial job we have to accomplish over the next couple of years.

7. A Lawmaker Explains the Necessity for Superfund, 1981

The country has waited a long time for the Superfund law dealing with chemical poisons in the environment. What we have now is, in my judgment, the major preventative health law passed by the Congress in the past four years.

Together with the other members of the Senate Committee on Environment and Public Works, I worked on this legislation for nearly three years. I will not say that it was a labor of love, because the process was trying. We were beset with problems at nearly every turn.

But it has been a three-year trial well worth it. Eighty percent of the American people wanted some legislation. That sentiment was reflected in the Senate, where 24 Senators joined as sponsors of the legislation. And, judging from what we know,

Robert T. Stafford, "Why Superfund Was Needed," *EPA Journal* (June 1981), accessed at http://www .epa.gov/history/topics (December 2004).

those concerns are well founded. The Surgeon General of the United States considers toxic chemicals to pose the major threat to health in the United States for the decade of the 1980s. . . .

The legacy of past haphazard disposal of chemical wastes and the continuing danger of spills and other releases of dangerous chemicals pose what many call the most serious health and environmental challenges of the decade. Chemical spills capable of inflicting environmental harm occur about 3,500 times each year, and an estimated $65 million to $260 million is needed to clean them up. More than 2,000 dump sites containing hazardous chemicals are believed by the Environmental Protection Agency to pose threats to the public health. The cost of containing their contents is estimated to be an average of $3.6 million per site. . . .

The acceptance of man-made chemicals—to the extent that they are hardly recognized as such anymore—has become a fact of daily life in the United States. We are dependent on synthetic chemicals for health, livelihood, housing, transportation, food, and for our funerals.

But within recent years, there has been a realization that what is our meat may also be our poison. Here are some examples:

•   In a report dated March 1980, the Library of Congress concluded that damages to natural resources of the United States because of toxic chemicals were "substantial and enduring." The report identified damaged resources ranging from all five of the Great Lakes to the aquifer underlying the San Joaquin Valley, possibly the richest agricultural area in the United States.

•   In a report to the President of the United States, the Toxic Substances Strategy Committee concluded that the cancer death rate in the United States had increased sharply and that "occupational exposure to carcinogens is believed to be a factor in more than 20 percent of all cases of cancer."

•   In a report released in the spring of 1980 by the Congressional Office of Technology Assessment, agricultural losses because of chemical contamination were placed at $283 million. The report said the value was based on economic data from only six of the 50 States and was therefore "likely to be a gross underestimation of the actual costs."

•   In 1979, the total production of chemicals in the United States was 565 billion pounds. Of this amount, 347 billion pounds was of chemicals officially classified by the United States Government as hazardous. Production growth was increasing at a rate of 7.6 percent in 1979. At that rate, production will double in 10 years.

This is not to say that chemicals are necessarily bad. On the contrary, they have contributed mightily to American prosperity. . . . In fact, most chemicals are benign. Only a small number of them cause cancer, birth defects, or other illnesses. But the fact remains that, small though the relative number of these dangerous chemicals may be, they can cause terrible damage when set loose on the public. Moreover, because we do use these substances in such a large volume, the number of incidents involving them has increased dramatically in the recent past. . . .

Using existing documentation, the Environmental Protection Agency identified some 250 hazardous waste sites involving damages or significant threats of damages. Among the reported incidents were 27 sites associated with actual damages to health (kidneys, cancer, mutations, aborted pregnancies, etc.), 32 sites which have resulted in the closure of public and private drinking water wells, 130 sites with contaminated ground waters and 74 sites where natural habitats have been damaged and are adversely affecting indigenous species.

The preliminary findings of a joint States/EPA survey of pits, ponds, and lagoons used to treat, store, and dispose of liquid wastes identify 11,000 industrial sites with 25,000 such surface impoundments. At least one-half of the sites are believed to contain hazardous wastes. The survey found that virtually no monitoring of ground water was being conducted and that 30 percent of the impoundments, or 2,455 of the 8,221 sites assessed, are unlined, overlie usable groundwater aquifers, and have intervening soils which would freely allow liquid wastes to escape into groundwater. . . .

Some examples of the type of accidents that have resulted from spills and other non-waste disposal incidents include:

• PCBs, a cancer-causing insulating fluid whose manufacture is now banned, leaked from an out-of-service transformer, entered the food chain and spread through 19 States and two foreign countries. Hundreds of thousands of hogs, chickens, turkeys, and a large quantity of other food stuffs had to be destroyed.

• One-third to one-half of the drinking water and irrigation wells in the San Joaquin Valley have been contaminated by a pesticide, DBCP. In sufficient amounts, this pesticide is known to cause sterility in males. It is suspected also of causing cancer. . . .

• Portions of Lakes Ontario and Erie have been closed to commercial fishing because of chemical contamination. The taking of coho salmon, stocked through the lakes to encourage a viable commercial and sport fishery, is banned because of chemical contamination. . . .

What I have just described is the scope of the toxics problem in the United States. The scope is not just of inactive hazardous waste disposal sites, as tragic as Love Canal may be. Nor is the scope confined to accidental spills into rivers, as disastrous as they may be. The problem is just as broad as the benefit.

I am not suggesting, nor have the members of my Committee suggested, that chemicals be banned. What we have proposed through legislation is that we reduce the number of people who may become victims of chemical poisoning incidents.

8. CIGNA Doctor Critiques Tobacco Advertising, 1987

Year in and year out, for decades, going on centuries, ad nauseum, the health picture of African Americans relative to the rest of America, has been a disproportionate burden characterized by receipt of "more to most of the bad" and, "less to least of the good" this society has to offer. Smoking related disease, disability and death is another scene being painted in this same sickening picture.

The high black disease, disability and death rate from all causes is due largely to the set of circumstances in existence since the status of slavery, since the emancipation proclamation, since the era of the Jim Crow laws and the black codes, since the yet unfulfilled promise of "forty acres and a mule." This set of circumstances

Tobacco Industry Federal Relations Report, October 6, 1987, "Black Health Choices and Advertising: The Critical Connection," reprinted from *Congressional Record* (October 5, 1987), pp. E 3828–3830. Accessed from the Legacy Tobacco Documents Library, University of California at San Francisco, San Francisco, Calif., http://legacy.library.ucsf.edu (December 2004).

can be nut-shelled by the present relatively lower educational, political and socio economic conditions of black people. These inferior conditions, a direct result of decades of active, overt, oppressively discriminatory behavior by whites, have contributed to a poor health status. The victims, seeking relief, in many instances have adopted lifestyle behaviors that provide immediate gratification, but, in the long run, and sometimes in the short run, contribute to worsening the situation from which relief is being sought. So, through negative, non-productive lifestyle habits, like substance abuse (including cigarette smoking) black people, are co-partners in their self-destruction. This is especially true with respect to smoking cigarettes, as the tobacco industry is the other co-partner. I say this because it is clear that the tobacco industry is targeting the African-American and Hispanic communities for cigarette sales. This targeting effort is clearly identified in advertising strategy manifested in recent years by cigarette makers. This point is supported by Dr. Alan Blum, in an article written for the *Washington Post* on June 8, 1986 called, "Tobacco Ads Aim At Blacks." In this article Dr. Blum makes several points:

Cigarette ads now account for about 25% of billboard advertising. In some communities, especially the low income areas, more than 50% of the billboards carry cigarette ads.

Advertising Age lists Phillip Morris as the leading marketer to the 17 million Americans for whom Spanish is their first language.

In the Black community 3 brands: Newport by Loews; Kool by Brown & Williamson; and Salem by R J Reynolds have been promoted for maximum consumption. These account for more than 60% of cigarettes purchased by Blacks.

Cigarette advertising, along with those of alcohol, are the mainstay of such African-American oriented publications as *Jet* and *Ebony*. A minimum of 12% of the color advertisements in each issue of *Essence* are for cigarettes, second only to advertisements for alcohol—20%.

Black and Hispanic publications, publishers, neighborhoods, social, cultural, and political events, educational and community based institutions have been supported as a part of this strategy.

Cigarette makers have been targeting events and outlets that have a significant focus on youth. . . .

Though cigarette maker representatives say that their sponsorship of African American organizational events (which includes in many instances, giving away free samples of cigarettes) is simply, "the right thing to do," the apparent results of this advertising strategy (more blacks than whites smoke cigarettes) suggests that it is the wrong thing to do.

Can it be said that the cigarette advertising targeted towards blacks, brings a return in the form of either increased purchases of cigarettes, or, more black people hooked on the idea of smoking? . . .

. . . Our society is making some progress towards decreasing the number of people who smoke. However, African Americans are still suffering a disproportionate burden from the behavior of cigarette smoking. In the face of smoking related excess morbidity and mortality among African Americans, what can, or should be done?

1. African Americans must be encouraged to discontinue smoking. This must be done in as intense a fashion as possible. Just as tobacco companies are advocates for

the health and well being of their product, it is incumbent upon leaders who are black to be advocates for the health and well being of black people.

The encouragement to stop smoking should be a part of an information/education campaign designed to simply and clearly identify the health hazards of smoking and the excess burden black people are bearing. To best achieve this, all segments of the African American community should be vigorously involved. The religious, academic, business, entertainment, political and communications areas all can play a role, and should. None of us can afford the foot dragging hesitancy to speak out, born of the conflict between receipt of tobacco company support and, the right thing to do, advocacy of discontinuance of smoking.

2. Government should address the issue of allowing the advertising of a product/behavior that, when used as advertised, causes serious harm to health. I find it disturbing and distressing that government, with its many sets of laws, rules and regulations cannot manage to help protect the health and well being of its citizens through restricting the advertising of a product/behavior that, when used as advertised, causes serious health hazards. According to a March 19, 1987 *New England Journal of Medicine* article, "A Ban on The Promotion of Tobacco Products" by Kenneth Warner, smoking is the leading cause of premature death causing more deaths than the combined total caused by all illicit drugs and alcohol, all accidents, and all homicides and suicides. Regarding the issue of free speech, on July 1, 1986 the U.S. Supreme Court decided in *Posadas v. Tourism Co. of Puerto Rico,* that Puerto Rico could prohibit advertising of casino gambling to its residents, even though gambling was legal. Chief Justice Rehnquist wrote the decision, and a remark was included indicating that states could ban or restrict advertising "of products or activities deemed harmful, such as cigarettes, alcoholic beverages and prostitution."

3. African American communities should organize to limit, curtail, indeed, eliminate the targeted exposure of black people by cigarette companies, to cigarette smoking. This will certainly involve some measure of sacrifice, as substantial amounts of advertising dollars are being spent by tobacco companies to sponsor African American cultural, social, and sporting events and, to reach African Americans through specific print media.

From a health perspective, the tobacco industry sponsorship of African American cultural, social, fundraising and sports events is metaphorically analogous to foxes warming up to the chickens by stating and expressing concern and support for chicken welfare but, with a main focus on fox welfare. Chicken dependence on fox statements and expressions of concern and support always result in the demise of the chicken. Those who consider themselves Leader Roosters and Head Hens should know better and should be crowing and clucking about the dangers associated with the gifts and services being offered by the foxes. Millions of people in America are addicted to cigarette smoking. In a real sense, an addiction is an imprisonment. The individual is physically and psychologically locked into a cycle of dependency on a substance, more and more of which, is required to achieve the same levels of satisfaction. It is not easy to free oneself from this imprisonment. In the case of cigarette smoking, testimony to this point is the many persons who have made many attempts, without success, to free themselves of the imprisoning addiction that accompanies the habit. The recent introduction of a "smokeless cigarette," is, in my view, analogous to simply improving the conditions of imprisonment. Persons who are in jail may be made to feel better about jail life by wall-to-wall carpet, chandeliers, and improved food, the bottom line is, they are still in jail. They are still imprisoned by an addiction that costs time, money and maybe even the same health hazards as before.

Each of us can help with this problem. How? We can write letters. Whenever we see advertisements fostering the habit of smoking we can communicate with the outlet for the message, with another message: Why are you fostering the self-destructive habit of smoking on our people?

Certainly more of us would be up in arms if the advertising of other drugs was being targeted at African Americans. Consider what the impact of the following would be: "Crack into the big time with crack." "It's an inexpensive way to get an expensive high." "And it's more healthy than cigarettes." Or, how about, "mellow out with marijuana." "For a low monthly cost you can maintain mellowness with Marijuana Melody." "It's more healthy than cigarettes."

Subsequent to such messages, the cries of genocide would be loud and clear and frequent. Yet the above substances have not been shown to be responsible for as much morbidity and mortality as cigarette smoking.

9. Hawaiians Debate Airport Expansion on Maui, 1996

Maui Pueo Coalition, *"Statement of Positions on Kahului Runway Extension"*

The position of Maui Pueo Coalition and a majority of citizens on Maui is that a longer runway is essential to the long-term economic health of Maui, the safety of all passengers using the airport, the maintenance of a high quality of life and a clean environment.

The Economy

Foreign Competition—In a changing world, old travel patterns no longer apply. Maui must compete in an increasingly international tourism market. According to Hawaii Visitors Bureau projections, by the year 2000 more than 50 percent of all visitors to Hawaii will be from foreign countries.

Domestic and Local Competition—Less dependence on Maui's traditional West Coast markets will be gained through an extended runway. The ability to encourage direct flights to Maui from the Mid West and East Coast will ensure greater stability for our number one industry—tourism. Locally, the impact of extending the runway at Keahole on the Big Island has already been felt. United is now flying 747s direct to the Big Island, flights which are reported to be full. United has stated

U.S. Department of Transportation, Federal Aviation Administration, and Hawaii Department of Transportation, Airports Division, *Draft Environmental Impact Statement,* vol. 2: *Kahului Airport Improvements, Kahului, Maui, Hawaii, March 1996,* Maui Pueo Coalition, "Statement of Positions on Kahului Runway Extension," pp. 1–3; Maui Tomorrow, "Testimony to the Federal Aviation Administration Regarding the Preparation of an Environmental Impact Statement for the Proposed Expansion and Runway Extension at Kahului Airport," pp. 2–3.

that these jets would have been routed to Maui instead if Kahului's runway had been of adequate length.

Airline Viability—Airlines have clearly stated that Kahului's 7,000 ft. runway is too short for economically feasible operations. Maui has a long history of aircraft fuel capacity problems. . . . A 9,600 ft. runway is the minimum length necessary for sustainable aircraft operations. In the competitive international visitor marketplace airlines will not service a destination with an inadequate airport. Maui's entire economy is dependent on efficient air access. . . .

Jobs—More than 43,000 jobs on Maui are directly or indirectly dependent on tourism. As the local population grows, the job base must expand or the next generation will leave for other states. Keeping tourism and new emerging industries healthy will assure job opportunities.

Agriculture—Farmers support the extension of the runway to 9,600 ft. because it is essential for reliable air service to export their crops without cargo being bumped and produce spoiling. Efficient air lift capacity is vital to the survival of the pineapple industry and Maui's produce farmers. Farm viability is in itself a protection against development—if a farm fails someone will need to make the land pay and that usually means development.

Economic Diversification—Maui's growing hi-tech industries must have consistent air service to the U.S. Mainland and Asia. Kahului Airport is the linchpin for Maui's growing software, graphic design and small manufacturing industries. Regular International air service is vital to their success. (See study *"The Role of Air Transportation in Maui's Economic Future,"* researched and produced by The Maui Economic Development Board.)

Quality of Life

Uncontrolled Growth a Myth—The runway extension in and of itself will not cause growth. The airport is a facility which services the normal demands of our society. . . . Opposition claims that an extended runway will cause a massive influx of visitors or new development pressures are false and a distraction from the reality. The majority believe a modern airport will *enhance* the quality of life.

Citizens Support Runway—Most Maui residents, as evidenced in a SMS Research survey commissioned by *The Maui News* (October 11, 1992) support a longer runway for convenience and safety. The airport is an essential part of Maui's infrastructure; it is zoning and General Plan controls which determine growth.

Hotel Rooms—The runway extension is needed to service existing hotels which are experiencing low occupancies. The runway has nothing to do with spurring new hotel growth.

Safety

Present Runway Dangerous—While the runway officially meets *minimum* FAA standards most pilots in the 40,000 member Airline Pilots Association consider it only marginally safe. . . .

Longer Runway Safer—Maui Pueo Coalition believes that the likelihood of a crash is decreased with a longer runway regardless of size of jets coming in.

Wide-bodies jets are currently landing at Kahului. A crash of a DC10 would exceed Maui Memorial Hospital's capacity and this is all the more reason to take a preventative posture by lengthening the runway to make it safer.

The Environment

Alien Species a Concern—Maui Pueo Coalition is deeply concerned about the introduction of alien pests and urges more controls at harbors and airports. Maui Pueo Coalition supports all creative ideas for intercepting alien species and we recommend some portion of landing fees be devoted to conservation efforts. Maui Pueo Coalition would also support introducing an appropriation request (possibly $1 million) to thoroughly study alien species introduction, particularly in regard to airports and harbors. It is the Coalition's belief that substantially more alien species are introduced through harbors than airports and the goal of the study would be to determine real facts as to how pests enter the state. The study would be a cooperative effort between University of Hawaii entomologists, a group such as The Nature Conservancy of Hawaii and the State Dept. of Agriculture. An expert would be appointed to coordinate the study. A report to the Legislature would recommend levels of future funding for alien species interdiction and control.

    Runway Would Not Worsen Problem—Maui Pueo Coalition takes the position that a longer runway would not significantly increase alien pest introduction any more than we experience now. Pests are already entering at Honolulu Airport, a substantial amount through the military facilities which do not have controls. In fact if fewer inter-island flights land as a result of direct flights the risk of pests coming in from Oahu is lessened.

    Kanaha Pond—There is no evidence that existing flights have impacted bird life at Kanaha Pond. . . .

    Noise Abatement—Maui Pueo Coalition supports adopting into law current recommendations for noise abatement at Kahului. Maui Pueo Coalition encourages cooperation from Aloha Airlines on specific flight paths and timing for night cargo operations until such time as new quieter equipment is brought on line.

Environmental Advantages of a Longer Runway—

•   In the case of international flights, establishment of customs facility at Kahului would *strengthen* interception of smuggled fruits, the main source of alien pests.
•   A longer runway would allow for stage 3 aircraft which are quieter and more fuel efficient. This would lessen noise impact and pollution.
•   A longer runway will strengthen the local economy allowing government, businesses and citizens to contribute more resources to conservation efforts.
•   A longer runway would allow an earlier take off point further away from Spreklesville homes, reducing noise impact. . . .

*   *   *

Maui Tomorrow, *"Testimony to the Federal Aviation Administration"*

It has not yet been shown that the net effect of the runway extension would be diversification of Maui's economic base. Indeed, if the runway extension is more of a stimulus to tourism than it is to agriculture, the result will be a less diversified economy. . . .

An examination should be made of the possibility that runway extension would disrupt agricultural and social pursuits, and of whether the County's natural resources will be further depleted. The EIS [Environmental Impact Survey] should study the potential that further growth in tourism would accelerate the decline of the agricultural and manufacturing sectors of our economy.

Agricultural pests would severely hamper efforts to diversify our economic base by making it harder (more costly) for diversified agriculture to succeed.

Recent pest introductions, otherwise known as "species pollution," on Maui include yellow jackets and a new species of crab spiders; and mullein, a weed species that is capable of destroying the habitat of silverswords and other endangered plant species in Haleakala National Park. . . .

Economics and the environment are inseparable when it comes to Maui's visitor industry. Lengthening of the runway at Kahului will hurt, rather than help, our main industry. Maui must be careful not to let the success of tourism degrade the natural environment and quality of life upon which that tourism depends. Otherwise, we will have "tourism killing tourism."

Visitors love our beautiful scenery, the climate, the ocean and beaches, all in the context of the Hawaiian culture. Preserving these things can actually be profitable. What turns visitors off is the commercialization and overdevelopment of these irreplaceable resources. Facilitating an unconstrained projection will facilitate broad and numerous impacts, all of which must be analyzed.

Tourism on Maui has already passed the point of diminishing returns. According to State figures provided by the airport consultants, we have 42 visitors for every hundred residents on an average day, triple the tourist density of any other island in the State. Let's not lose the vision that we on Maui previously had of keeping quality up, while keeping the quantity of tourism, and its adverse impacts on residents, relatively low. Other destinations, such as Bermuda, have done so and prospered. Let us not go down the path of Coney Island in New York, or of Mallorca in the Mediterranean. The EIS should evaluate potential mitigation measures such as those implemented by Bermuda, and negative impacts such as those experienced by Mallorca.

 # E S S A Y S

In the first essay, David B. Sicilia, an associate professor of history at the University of Maryland–College Park and coeditor of *Constructing Corporate America: History, Politics, Culture* (2004), surveys the challenges faced by American chemical and tobacco companies during the late twentieth century. Sicilia examines the chemical industry's proactive approach to environmental issues, including its effort to "go green," and the tobacco industry's accommodationist response to a series of health scares. How did these two industries deal with alarm and criticism?

Next, Mansel G. Blackford, professor of history at the Ohio State University and author of *Fragile Paradise: The Impact of Tourism on Maui, 1959–2000* (2001), provides a case study about corporate social responsibility from Hawaii in the 1980s and 1990s. His analysis draws on the primary sources in Document 9 and similar materials. How does Blackford use this evidence? How might he have used it differently?

The Corporation Under Siege

DAVID B. SICILIA

The tobacco, chemical, and nuclear industries responded to the attacks they sustained in the postwar decades in a variety of ways, depending on the perceived nature and seriousness of the threat. But there was an overarching pattern to the corporate responses. In the short term, a few companies and industry associations stepped forward in an attempt to defend themselves and discredit their challengers. Some assumed a bunker mentality, hunkering down and reducing communication with potentially harmful outside interest groups. Overall, a sense of frustration and confusion reigned among business leaders in these three industries.

But, after a decade or so, the industries under attack devised ways of regaining a greater sense of control over their external political and social environments. They did this by making some concessions to their critics and by employing new, specialized forms of public relations. For both reasons, the industries under siege began to claim many of their former opponents' issues for themselves. By the 1990s, all three industries had moved decisively from a reactive to a much more proactive posture toward the social movement activists, regulators, and government agencies who had challenged them in earlier decades.

The immediate response of some chemical industry representatives to *Silent Spring* was shrill hyperbole. To accept [Rachel] Carson's ideas, proclaimed one of its outspoken critics, would lead to "the end of all human progress, reversion to a passive social state devoid of technology, scientific medicine, agriculture, sanitation. It means disease, epidemics, starvation, misery, and suffering." A few ordinarily low-profile companies could not resist joining the fray. Monsanto, according to its corporate historian, "responded [to *Silent Spring*] in non-Monsanto style—with a rebuttal which burst upon the scene like a skyfull [*sic*] of skyrockets." The October following *Silent Spring*'s publication, Monsanto published "The Desolate Year" in *Monsanto Magazine,* a story that speculated about a world without pesticides. Ironically, Monsanto then manufactured some selective weed-killers, but was not a leading producer of insecticides (except parathion) and had discontinued making DDT years earlier.

Most chemical companies, however, quietly went about the business of adapting to the new regulations. Du Pont, the nation's largest chemical producer, had conducted toxicological research at its Haskell Laboratory since 1935, which now was expanded dramatically; its budget grew from $2.1 million in 1970 to $13.3 million in 1979. Hercules—whose agricultural pesticide toxaphene was indicted in *Silent Spring* as particularly destructive to fish—began monitoring legal developments in the area, set up an Environmental Health Committee with "pollution abatement coordinators" to liaison with plant operations, testified before House and Senate committees about toxaphene, and invested large sums in new toxicological testing and waste air and water treatment. Most other companies relied on technical solutions aimed at treating plant waste—the so-called "end-of-the-pipe" solutions.

David B. Sicilia, "The Corporation Under Siege: Social Movements, Regulation, Public Relations, and Tort Law Since the Second World War," in Kenneth Lipartito and David B. Sicilia, eds., *Constructing Corporate America: History, Politics, Culture* (New York: Oxford University Press, 2004), pp. 204–209. Copyright © 2004. Reprinted by permission of Oxford University Press.

Over the course of a decade or so, however, this "compliance mentality" gave way to a more sophisticated, public relations-oriented approach. A few firms and industry associations moved early in this direction. Midwest Agricultural Chemical Association was founded in 1958 to address public concern about agricultural pesticides. Foreshadowing the kind of industry approaches that would become commonplace, the MACA promoted a growth ideology by working to "control the language of public debate," by cooperating closely with presumably neutral institutions, such as land grant colleges, and by exerting influence over the local political process.

In both practical and rhetorical ways, the U.S. chemical industry in the 1970s and 1980s started "going green." Some firms simply pursued business opportunities in environmentally related businesses such as the manufacture of water treatment chemicals and industrial catalytic converters. This was a rapidly growing global business, one with strong advantages for first-movers. Because the United States was lagging behind Europe in the environmental area, for example, American industry had to import 70 percent of its air pollution control equipment after the passage of the more stringent 1990 Clean Air Act. A growing roster of U.S. chemical companies now saw opportunities to exploit niches in this field. On the other hand, a number of companies moved in the opposite direction by outsourcing their environmental functions. As one consultant observed, compliance is a "data-intensive" process that requires "a large bureaucracy" and can "lead to staff burnout, yield little or no competitive advantage, and have a high cost."

On the rhetorical front, consultants became a growing force behind the chemical industry's new proactive approach. Some were recruited from the ranks of environmental activists. Others, such as Burson–Marstellar, were retained to manage the aftermath of crises, in this case the Exxon Valdez oil leak and the devastating Union Carbide gas leak in Bhopal, India. They had learned their lessons from the adversarial 1960s and 1970s. In those days, according to an executive for Bechtel Environmental, Inc., public relations had been "defensive and reactive—and not very successful." But in the 1990s, he argued, to be effective public relations needed to be continuous and "truly two-way"; chemical companies should "furnish reliable information, apologize when necessary, open your doors." Arguably, the leading environmental consultant to the chemical industry was E. Bruce Harrison, who literally wrote the book on this subject, with the revealing title *Going Green: How to Communicate Your Company's Environmental Commitment* (1993). Harrison's approach was thoroughly accommodationist, as summarized in his "Three Steps to the Green":

1. Commit to pollution prevention beyond what the current laws require of you;
2. Team up with people outside your organization to solve general environmental problems, including those you do not cause; and
3. Take the initiative in dialogue that ensures continuous environmental improvement.

Sounding much like a 1970s environmentalist's agenda, these principles worked to [defuse] an immeasurable amount of anti-industry criticism. But many skeptical critics were only inflamed by the industry's "going green" campaign. They pointed to industry efforts designed to confuse and obfuscate, such as the 1990 fight over Proposition 128 in California, an environmental protection act also known as "Big Green." Working in cooperation with timber and utility interests, the chemical industry spent some

$16 million to defeat the measure by a two-to-one margin. As part of its campaign, the industry introduced the Consumer Pesticide Enforcement Act, otherwise known as "Big Brown," which, according to environmental writer and consultant Jacqueline Switzer, "had the dual purpose of confusing voters because of [its name] and making it seem as if the state were being overcome with environmental legislation."

Switzer was one of a growing cadre of journalists and academics who wrote about what they call "green backlash." The term applies mainly to political and corporate efforts to discredit environmentalists, and so should be distinguished from the accommodationist approach described here. For chemical industry opponents, the industry's green positions posed a more subtle challenge: how to separate the rhetoric from the reality.

The tobacco industry's responses to its adversaries changed with the nature of the attacks it sustained. But cigarette producers came very late to the kind of accommodationist position exemplified by the chemical industry. The "health scare" of the 1950s evoked several responses. One was a market response: cigarette makers came out with scores of new brands, most with higher filtration, lower tar and nicotine yields, or both. The most illustrative case is Lorillard's Kent brand. In March 1952, Lorillard introduced its first filtered cigarette, named for its soon-to-retire president, Herbert A. Kent. Lorillard then supplied only about 5.5 percent of the U.S. cigarette market. But with the first "cancer scare" in 1953, Kents flew off the shelves. *Reader's Digest* gave the brand another big boost in 1957, when it identified Kent as the lowest tar and nicotine cigarette of the major brands. That year Lorillard announced with great fanfare a reformulated Kent with a space-age "micronite" filter. The filter was made of asbestos (although asbestos was not yet associated with respiratory disease). Between 1956 and 1958, Lorillard's profits grew sixfold. But in 1960, *Financial World* declared that "The boom in Kent sales [is] over." The larger cigarette producers had launched competing brands that squeezed out Kent, not only because of their marketing power, but because the competing brands were more "flavorful." Kent's filter worked too well; most smokers preferred a "full bodied" cigarette, and the industry had responded. At the same time, the FTC stepped in to restrict health-related claims, thereby preventing smaller competitors such as Lorillard from competing on the basis of lower tar and nicotine yields.

The second tobacco industry response to the "health scare" came on the public relations front. In 1953, the industry retained Hill & Knowlton to formulate a strategy for coping with its increasingly hostile environment. The following year, on the advice of Hill & Knowlton, the industry established the Tobacco Industry Research Committee (renamed the Council for Tobacco Research–U.S.A. a decade later) to conduct research into the health effects of cigarette smoke, although industry critics have characterized TIRC as purely a lobbying and public relations front. The TIRC took the position that scientific evidence indicating that smoking caused cancer and other illnesses was "inconclusive," which remained the industry's central stance on smoking and health for decades.

In response to the growing fervor about cigarette advertising, the tobacco industry also attempted voluntary self-regulation. On January 1, 1965, the major producers put into effect a self-imposed "Cigaret Advertising Code," which—because it included fines for non-compliance—was dubbed the first move of its kind in advertising history. The code was approved by the Justice Department, which agreed to exempt compliant companies from criminal (but not civil) prosecution. But like the FTC's new advertising rules, the "Cigaret Advertising Code" became moot with the passage of the Cigarette Labeling and Advertising Act of 1965.

The industry's response to the threat of growing federal and state regulation was, generally, to make jurisdictional and broad constitutional arguments about federal agency powers and free speech. . . . [T]he tobacco makers fared well at the federal level, especially against the FTC, but lost considerable ground against the wave of tightening state laws and municipal codes to restrict or prohibit smoking. As for First Amendment issues, the tobacco industry continued to argue for the protection of advertising as free speech, and for the protection of smokers' civil rights. Following the early FTC and Congressional controls over advertising to minors, the industry never took an official position regarding the marketing of cigarettes to children, although critics continued to allege that the companies were not doing enough to discourage smoking by youths.

The cigarette industry's fifth and sixth strategic responses to the challenges of the 1950s and 1960s—by far the most important economically—were diversification and globalization. In 1955, each of the Big Six was solely in the tobacco business. Five years later, Philip Morris had moved into packaging products, industrial products, shaving products, and paper products, while Reynolds had begun making wrapping materials. By 1970, all six firms were solidly diversified, mostly in consumer household products and alcohol. (Lorillard had been acquired by Loew's, itself a diversified company.) Accordingly, the tobacco portion of the Big Six's total sales declined significantly. At the same time, five of the Big Six (again Lorillard, which sold its international operations to BAT, was the exception) moved aggressively to expand their cigarette exports. In 1950 they collectively exported roughly 15 billion cigarettes; by 1980, nearly 80 billion; and by 1995, the number topped 225 billion. To be sure, the 1960s and early 1970s were an age of conglomerates (unrelated diversified firms) and international expansion for American big business. But as corporate strategy analyst Robert Miles has shown, these two strategies for the tobacco companies were "domain creation" moves largely in reaction to the increasingly hostile political and social environment in which the companies found themselves.

The other four strategies were "domain defense" moves, and the industry sustained them with relatively little change for decades. When the CEOs of the nation's leading cigarette companies testified at the Congressional hearings on the regulation of tobacco in March 1994, their equivocation about whether smoking causes cancer and their uniform statements, "I believe nicotine is not addictive," harkened back to the companies' stance on smoking and health in the early 1950s.

All of this changed within a few short years. In the late 1990s and after, the tobacco companies—like the chemical and nuclear industries before them—agreed with most of the arguments of their critics. Philip Morris now not only acknowledges, but aggressively promotes positions on smoking and health that are almost indistinguishable from those of its staunchest critics of twenty or even ten years ago. Its corporate web site is not so much a resource for and about the company as it is a statement of the company's position on smoking, health, and advertising. There and elsewhere one finds the Philip Morris positions on long-disputed issues stated clearly and unequivocally: "cigarette smoking causes lung cancer, heart disease, emphysema and other serious diseases"; "smoking is addictive"; to reduce these health effects, the best thing to do is quit, not smoke fewer or lower-tar and nicotine cigarettes; lower-tar and nicotine brands are neither "safe" nor "safer" than other brands; the FDA should regulate cigarettes and "assess their toxicological effect"; the public should take the advice of public health officials regarding smoking; adults should not smoke around children. Big Tobacco, too, arrived at the accommodationist position.

The Controversy Over the Kahului Airport

MANSEL G. BLACKFORD

Growing Conflict in the 1980s and Early 1990s

Owned and operated by the State of Hawai'i as part of a statewide airport system, the Kahului Airport covered about 1,450 acres by the early 1980s and was by far the most important airport on Maui. In 1982 the state put forward a master plan for the development of the Kahului Airport based on the assumption that it would handle only interisland flights, as specified in the county's development plan. The airport plan retained a 7,000-foot limit on the length of runway 2-20, the airport's longest runway, content to propose a slight extension to a shorter runway and several other minor airport improvements. The deregulation of the U.S. airline industry quickly made this plan obsolete, however, as several airlines scheduled direct flights, mainly for the benefit of tourists, from the West Coast to Maui in 1983.

As Maui developed into a premier tourist destination in the mid-1980s, the state revisited airport issues and in 1988 drafted a new master plan. This airport scheme consisted of a short-term plan for changes to be made through 1990 and a long-term plan for alterations through 2005. Based on the assumption that the Kahului Airport would handle both interisland and overseas flights—a real change from earlier airport plans—the 1988 plan called for extensions to the airport's two major runways. The plan to enlarge Maui's airport was part of a larger scheme to expand much of the state's airport system. In a plan approved in 1990, some $2.5 billion were allocated for the purpose, with most of the funding going to upgrade Honolulu's airport. At the time, political leaders projected a 33 percent increase in the number of tourists coming to the Hawaiian Islands by the year 2000, with most of them passing through Honolulu.

The preparation of an environmental impact statement accompanied the 1988 airport plan. Objecting to what they thought would be environmental damage resulting from the implementation of the 1988 plan, individuals and environmental groups filed suit to block any airport changes, charging that the environmental impact statement was inadequate and calling for the preparation of a more complete one. This litigation resulted in a court-ordered stipulation in 1991 that such a study be made.

Over the next several years conflict shifted to the county level. Maui's residents adopted a new ten-year general development plan, which, like its predecessor,

Mansel G. Blackford, "The Controversy over the Kahului Airport," in *Fragile Paradise: The Impact of Tourism on Maui, 1959–2000* (Lawrence: University Press of Kansas, 2001), pp. 170–190 (excerpt, pp. 174–177, 181–186, 189–190). Reprinted by permission of University Press of Kansas.

stipulated that the longest runway be restricted to 7,000 feet and that other alterations be limited. These limitations placed the county plan at odds with the 1988 state airport plan. However, in early 1992 Mayor Linda Lingle asked for an immediate reconsideration of the county plan. With Maui's economy slumping as a result of a falloff in tourism, Lingle called for airport additions, including an extension to the main runway. As the *Maui News* observed at the time, "A deepening recession, higher unemployment and concern about tourism and the economy set the stage for reconsideration." At this point, supporters and opponents of airport alterations began mobilizing as organized groups, making their positions clear in public statements and hearings.

Leading support for the runway extension was the Maui Pueo Coalition headed by Jimmy Rust. A Native Hawaiian who lent the coalition the name of his family's *'aumakua* (personal totem), the *pueo* or Hawaiian owl, Rust was a heavy-equipment driver and representative of the Hawaii Operating Engineers on Maui. The Pueo Coalition was an umbrella organization composed of twenty major bodies including business groups (the Maui Chamber of Commerce, the Maui Visitors Bureau [MVB], the Maui Economic Development Board [MEDB], and the Maui Hotel Association [MHA]), labor unions (the International Longshore and Warehouse Union [ILWU] Local 142, the Laborers' International Local 368, and the Hawaii Carpenters Union Local 745), and several farm organizations (the Maui County Farm Bureau, for example). . . .

Led by Dana Naone and Isaac Hall, many of the opponents of airport expansion formed the Maui No Ka Oi Coalition. . . . Dana Naone Hall was (and remains) a Hawaiian rights activist. In fact, she had to return early from a protest meeting on Kaho'olawe to testify against the airport extensions. Criticizing Mayor Lingle for not upholding Maui County's general plan, members of the Maui No Ka Oi Coalition claimed that the expansion would bring too many new visitors to Maui, straining the island's already overstressed infrastructure of roads, sewers, water sources, and supplies of electricity. Then, too, unwanted pests—snakes, insects, and plants—might, they feared, hitch rides on planes from South Pacific islands and Southeast Asia, flourish on Maui, and threaten the island's native flora and fauna. . . .

Conflict Over the Airport Intensifies

The 1996 environmental impact statement embraced considerable input from Maui's many concerned business, labor, and environmental groups. In written correspondence and in public hearings the groups that had been emerging in the early 1990s elaborated their positions, with different views of what economic growth, environmental responsibility, and the "good life" meant coming to the fore during the intensifying debate.

Chaired by Rust, the Pueo Coalition led the charge for runway extensions, expanding on arguments made four years before. Its economic message was blunt. "Without one-stop flights to Maui from major world airports," Rust claimed, "we will see decreased tourism which will lead to fewer jobs and a reduced tax revenue base." Thousands of jobs were, Rust averred, at risk. Unless airport extensions took place soon, "the next generation will leave for other states." Toni Rust, Jimmy Rust's twenty-three-year-old daughter, lamented what many people her age were saying: that after completing her college education at the University of Hawai'i, she would have to go to the mainland, because there were "no adequate job opportunities" in the islands.

Jimmy Rust argued that the proposed airport changes would diversify Maui's economy. The tourist business would become less dependent on a seasonal influx from the West Coast. "The ability to encourage direct flights to Maui from the Mid West and East Coast," he said, "will ensure [greater] stability for our number one industry—tourism." Nor was that all. Farmers and high-technology businesses— Rust singled out "Maui's growing software, graphic design, and small manufacturing industries"—would also benefit from better air connections. Picking up on the point raised by the Rusts, Carolann Guy, who had just stepped down as president of the Maui Chamber of Commerce, wondered if there would be enough jobs available on her island in the future. Maui, she worried, "lacked the economic opportunities and diversity . . . to attract her children back to Maui's shores." Further, Guy queried, "Have we considered what a community built without young adults will become? The common term—brain drain?"

Representatives of numerous business entities, including many belonging to the Pueo Coalition, rallied to Rust's support. The head of the MVB, who was also vice-chair of the Pueo Coalition, observed that Maui was in increasing competition with other destinations worldwide for tourists and business and that airport alterations "will help us counter the onslaught, enabling us to reach out to new markets domestically and internationally." The executive director of the MHA echoed such sentiments, saying that "we have to do what we can to keep [tourism] healthy" and noted that "even to diversify our economy, and we are certainly not opposed to that, we will need to be able to compete with other areas of the world with regard to ease of getting in and out for both people and products." The general manager of the Stouffer Wailea Hotel was outspoken: "Make no mistake about it: we are all part of tourism and tourism is part of us." The president of the Maui County Farm Bureau wrote that a longer runway was needed, "because exports represent such a significant part of the total market for our agricultural production."

Members of the Pueo Coalition downplayed environmental dangers. Rust stated that his group was "deeply concerned about the introduction of alien pests" and supported "all creative ideas for intercepting alien species," without, however, putting forward much in the way of specific plans to do so. Rust argued that the arrival of more nonstop flights on Maui would benefit the island, for the number of interisland flights would fall, thus lowering the risk of the importation of insect pests from O'ahu. The president of the Maui County Farm Bureau added that he thought that "individual farmers should be responsible for pest management on their own farms." Claiming that "there is no evidence that existing flights have impacted bird life at Kanaha Pond"—by this time the former fish pond had become a nature preserve near the airport that was the home of three endangered species of birds—Rust doubted that the runway extension would have any negative impact, either. . . .

Environmental issues were at the forefront of the minds of many opponents, and of these the topic of alien pests generated the most discussion. Maui's residents recoiled in horror from the possibility of a brown tree snake invasion and from the possibility of unwanted insects getting loose on their island. "It is imperative," stated Isaac Hall, "that a program be developed in the [economic impact statement], that can be implemented *prior* to extending any runways and *prior* to internationalizing the airport to prevent the introduction of further alien species. . . . Any increased introductions," he observed, harm "Maui's farmers, endangered species and parks." Members of the Sierra Club raised similar objections. The superintendent of the Haleakalā National Park observed that his domain was "the home of more endangered and threatened species than any other national park" and concluded that "new introductions of alien species arriving aboard foreign aircraft" would greatly harm his park's integrity. . . .

Opponents also raised economic issues, many of which were intertwined with the environmental ones. Jeffrey Parker—owner of the Tropical Orchid Farm, the largest exporter of live orchids from Maui, and an outspoken opponent of the Waena power plant—greatly feared "the very real threats to Maui's eco-system and agriculture which could arise from direct overseas flights." Alien slugs and thrips were already damaging his flowers, he said. Similarly, the owner of a papaya farm feared "the insects and pests that come into the islands." Thus, far from all of Maui's farmers agreed with the Maui County Farm Bureau that runway extensions would help agriculturists. For growers of specialized fruits, vegetables, and flowers the prospect of unwanted insects was even more terrifying than their fears of brown tree snakes. . . .

For others the economic stakes were broader. Maui Tomorrow led much of the fight against airport alterations by stressing the need to diversify Maui's economy and pointing out that the airport improvements would not do so. Mark Sheehan, the group's president, argued that it had "not yet been shown that the net effect of the runway extension would be diversification of Maui's economic base." To the contrary, "if the runway extension is more of a stimulus to tourism than it is to agriculture," he observed, "the result will be a less diversified economy." Moreover, Sheehan pointed out that economic and environmental issues were closely linked, for the importation of agricultural pests could "hamper efforts to diversify our economic base by making it harder (more costly) for diversified agriculture to succeed." Then, too, he argued that even tourism, far from being helped, might be hurt by airport extensions. The influx of too many tourists would, Sheehan feared, overwhelm the island. "Maui must be careful," he warned, "not to let the success of tourism degrade the natural environment and quality of life upon which that tourism depends." Dick Mayer added that "a particular issue is the question of home rule." Airport extensions, he feared, would "give much greater control to people off this island and even outside this state, even outside this country"—much the same argument he mounted against building the Waena power plant.

For many opponents there was more at stake than economic or environmental issues. Cherished ways of life seemed to hang in the balance. For no people was this truer than for Native Hawaiians. As Dorothy Pyle, a faculty member teaching Hawaiian history at Maui Community College and head of the Maui County Cultural Commission, observed, the Hawaiian sovereignty issue was "important," with Native Hawaiians disliking "being dictated to by outside interests." One Native Hawaiian wrote, "The expansion of the Kahului airport will devastate the unique natural beauty of my island home, Maui" and concluded that "Maui's beauty and lifestyle is unparalleled and must be preserved." He stressed his fear the brown tree snake might enter Maui and then destroy Maui's native bird life. Another Native Hawaiian, a fisherman, objected to having public hearings at the airport. "Why couldn't we have the hearing down in the Maui Community Center, where it's common ground?" he asked. "Am I to be someone talking about spirituality, cultural resources, the environment where you choose it to be?" he wondered. Charles Maxwell, the Native Hawaiian leader, called the plans for the expansion of the airport "one of the worst things that's happened to Maui."

Native Hawaiians and their supporters were not alone in their concerns. "Magic Maui," many were afraid, might be overwhelmed by construction projects and become another Waikīkī. With too many people, the island's infrastructure would crumble, and the quality of life for residents would decline. Airport alterations acted as a lightning rod for such fears. With more planes and people arriving on more and longer runways at the Kahului Airport, prophesied the head of Maui Tomorrow, "quality of life will deteriorate, property values will decline, and as the island becomes a less attractive place [in which] to reside and to vacation, the decrease in revenues will transform this thriving community into a morass of social and environmental ills." . . .

Resolution

Many of Maui's residents saw the question of whether to expand the Kahului Airport as the most disruptive local political issue of the 1990s. Sally Raisbeck, the retired scientist turned environmentalist, spoke for many when she called the airport controversy "very divisive." The fallout from the debate on Maui reached to the other Hawaiian Islands. In the summer of 1999 consideration was given to lengthening the runway of the airport at Lī'hue on Kaua'i. Fearing that his island's residents would be divided the way those on Maui had been, one of the county council members for Kaua'i called upon the Center for Alternative Dispute Resolution to help those on Kaua'i reach consensus.

Still, as the 1990s came to a close, compromise on Kahului Airport matters seemed closer than before, despite the continuing debates before meetings of the State Land Use Commission. The long recession on Maui may have led some of the island's residents to look upon airport expansion more favorably. Alice Lee, a member of the Maui County Council, thought so. Noting that while there were "very strong feelings on both sides," she believed that "the seven-year recession has changed people's minds about the extension of the runway . . . because now jobs are at stake, abilities to pay mortgages are at stake." Reaching a satisfactory compromise was also more likely than earlier because grassroots environmental and Native Hawaiian rights groups had had a real impact on the airport plans. Efforts to mitigate the invasion of Maui by alien pests, resulting from pressures emanating from environmental groups, had become more stringent. Maui's experience with airport expansion shows just how important public involvement in the planning process can be. By participating in hearings on the various environmental impact statements and by the astute use of court challenges, opponents of airport extensions had a measurable impact on the outcome.

Like most of the other matters examined in this study, the debate about the Kahului Airport serves as a reminder about just how interlinked economic, environmental, and cultural issues are. The airport controversy reveals the complexity of the situation, showing that much more joined and separated people than simply economic issues. Economic matters merged with cultural and ideological concerns. Differing views about Native Hawaiian rights and the physical environment of the island divided groups of Maui's residents. At the root of controversy lay competing visions about the quality of life on Maui and the roles different types of economic changes might play.

In the end, however, it was economics that decided matters. With concession fees from shops in airports drastically declining and with airlines reluctant to pick up the shortfall in the form of higher landing fees, funds to expand the Kahului Airport were not available, and in March 2000 the state abandoned efforts to win approval for runway extensions. Had opponents won a major victory? Perhaps. "I am pleased that the runway extension plan has been cancelled," enthused Dick Mayer. "I believe this is a wonderful way for Maui to keep its reputation as the No. 1 tourist area in the world and it also means that housing prices and other difficulties that the people of Maui would have had if their airport had been extended will be kept under control." Still, there was more to the situation. A new generation of efficient, lighter airplanes such as the Boeing 777 could fly long distances. They could offer direct flights to and from places far from Maui, using the existing runway at the Kahului Airport, ensuring that debates over how best to mitigate the impacts of those flights would continue.

 F U R T H E R   R E A D I N G

Anderson, Terry H. "The New American Revolution: The Movement and Business." In *The Sixties: From Memory to History*, ed. David Farber (1994).

Bradshaw, Thornton, and David Vogel, eds. *Corporations and Their Critics: Issues and Answers to the Problems of Corporate Social Responsibility* (1981).

Clark, John G. *Energy and the Federal Government: Fossil Fuel Policies, 1900–1946* (1987).

Colten, Craig E., and Peter N. Skinner. *The Road to Love Canal: Managing Industrial Waste Before EPA* (1996).

Gorman, Hugh S. *Redefining Efficiency: Pollution Concerns, Regulatory Mechanisms, and Technological Change in the U.S. Petroleum Industry* (2001).

Hays, Samuel P. *Beauty, Health, and Permanence: Environmental Politics in the United States, 1955–1985* (1987).

Hoffman, Andrew J. *From Heresy to Dogma: An Institutional History of Corporate Environmentalism* (1997).

Hurley, Andrew. *Environmental Inequalities: Class, Race, and Industrial Pollution in Gary, Indiana, 1945–1980* (1995).

Kluger, Richard. *Ashes to Ashes: America's Hundred-Year Cigarette War, the Public Health, and the Unabashed Triumph of Philip Morris* (1997).

McEvoy, Arthur F. *The Fisherman's Problem: Ecology and Law in the California Fisheries, 1850–1890* (1986).

McNeil, Donald G., Jr. "Upstate Waste Site May Endanger Lives: Abandoned Dump in Niagara Falls Leaks Possible Carcinogens." *New York Times*, August 2, 1978, pp. A1, B9.

Perrow, Charles, ed. *The Radical Attack on Business* (1972).

Pratt, Joseph A., et al. *Voice of the Marketplace: A History of the National Petroleum Council* (2002).

Rabin, Robert J., and Stephen D. Sugarman, eds. *Regulating Tobacco* (2001).

Sabin, Paul. *Crude Politics: The California Oil Market, 1900–1940* (2005).

Schrepfer, Susan R., and Philip B. Scranton, eds. *Industrializing Organisms: Introducing Evolutionary History* (2004).

Schulman, Bruce J. *The Seventies: The Great Shift in American Culture, Society, and Politics* (2001).

Sellers, Christopher C. *Hazards of the Job: From Industrial Disease to Environmental Health Science* (1997).

Silk, Leonard, and David Vogel. *Ethics and Profits: The Crisis of Confidence in American Business* (1976).

Sobel, Robert. *They Satisfy: The Cigarette in American Life* (1978).

Stine, Jeffrey K., and Joel A. Tarr. "At the Intersection of Histories: Technology and the Environment." *Technology and Culture* 39 (1998): 601–640.

Stradling, David. *Smokestacks and Progressives: Environmentalists, Engineers and Air Quality in America, 1881–1951* (1999).

Vietor, Richard H. K. *Energy Policy in America Since 1945: A Study of Business-Government Relations* (1984).

———. *Environmental Politics and the Coal Coalition* (1980).

Walker, J. Samuel. *Three Mile Island: A Nuclear Crisis in Historical Perspective* (2004).

Weems, Robert E., Jr. *Desegregating the Dollar: African American Consumerism in the Twentieth Century* (1998).

Wright, Gavin. "The Civil Rights Revolution as Economic History." *Journal of Economic History* 59, no. 2 (June 1999): 267–289.

Yergin, Daniel. *The Prize: The Epic Quest for Oil, Money, & Power* (1991).

Zeusse, Eric. "Love Canal: The Truth Seeps Out." *Reason*, February 1981, accessed at http://www.reason.com (December 2004).

CHAPTER
14

The Great Transition from Manufacturing to Services, 1945–2005

Between 1981 and 2001, John Francis "Jack" Welch, Jr., served as chief executive officer of General Electric. Jack Welch inherited a blue chip business created during the great merger movement of the 1890s when Edison General Electric and Thomson-Houston were consolidated to form the General Electric Company (GE). During the early twentieth century, GE and its chief rival, Westinghouse, formed an electrical duopoly that controlled the market for light bulbs and electrical equipment. GE invested heavily in industrial science, engineering, and product development to create electrical appliances, x-ray machines, fluorescent lighting, diesel-electric locomotives, jet engines, nuclear power plants, synthetic diamonds, new plastics, and novelties like Silly Putty. By 1981, GE had $27 billion in revenues, more than 400,000 employees, and dozens of separate businesses. As an industrial concern that grew by emphasizing the 3Ms—manufacturing, marketing, and management—GE epitomized American big business as described in Chapter 1 by Alfred D. Chandler, Jr.

Jack Welch changed much at GE. Sizing up the firm, he saw shrinking margins in manufacturing, rising union wages, increasing international competition, and an entrenched bureaucracy. In a whirl of housecleaning, Welch shut down plants, dismantled businesses, and eliminated jobs. In the mid-1980s, he bought the conglomerate RCA, sold its electronics and recording businesses, and kept its NBC television network to gain a major share of American broadcasting. The move portended a big shift in GE's core business. As Welch traded companies, he reshaped GE into a major player in the growing service sector. At the start of Welch's tenure, GE earned most of its revenues from manufacturing. When he left, the tables were turned, with GE owing 58 percent of its revenues to services.

In 2002, GE's annual report showed that 41 percent of the company's $131.7 billion in revenues came from GE Capital Services, a subsidiary dedicated to insurance, equipment financing, real estate, and aircraft leasing. Another 17 percent came from divisions like NBC-TV and services provided by GE's remaining manufacturing businesses. Divisions that produced jet engines, power systems, appliances, and medical imaging devices contributed to the service income on GE's financial statements by *delivering, installing, and maintaining high-technology equipment for its customers. Remarkably, Welch had remade a classic big business dedicated to fabricating things into a services company that continued to generate the high profits characteristic of the manufacturing sector.*

The makeover at GE coincided with a transformation in American business at large. From the late 1960s through the early 1990s, shock waves rippled through the U.S. economy. A series of crises—Vietnam, Watergate, two OPEC embargoes, energy shortages, the Japanese miracle, Detroit's woes, the federal bailouts of Chrysler and New York City, deindustrialization, the savings-and-loan debacle, and more— wreaked havoc with the status quo. The United States exited World War II as the world's capitalist superpower, with unrivaled industrial might. By the seventies, all of that seemed to be crumbling.

Historians now understand that the three decades from the 1970s to the 1990s were a period of realignment for American business. Change meant that older industries adjusted or failed, while newer organizational forms—conglomerates, franchises, and dot-coms—gained a toehold. Change meant that the U.S. economy depended less on manufacturing and more on services: information processing, insurance, food distribution, retailing, leisure, health, and entertainment. Change also deepened the divide between "the haves" and "the have-nots." The shift to services went hand-in-hand with the decline of large industrial unions. There are few such mediators in the service economy.

In 1955, Fortune *published its first "500," a list of the nation's top manufacturing and mining concerns. At the pinnacle were General Motors, Standard Oil of New Jersey, U.S. Steel, General Electric, and Swift. Forty years later,* Fortune *acknowledged the major transition, expanding the "500" to include service companies. In the 2004 list, two-thirds of the top fifty were service companies, including household names such as Wal-Mart, GE, Citigroup, Verizon Communications, Home Depot, Berkshire Hathaway, State Farm Insurance, Kroger, and Fannie Mae. This massive transition would certainly have amazed Thomas Edison.*

 D O C U M E N T S

As a scholar at the National Bureau of Economic Research, a nonprofit, nonpartisan think tank, Victor R. Fuchs was an early authority on the rise of the service sector. In a 1965 article published in the *Journal of Business,* Fuchs presented data showing the shift from manufacturing and mining to services in the post–World War II era. He wrote that the United States "is pioneering a new stage of economic development. We are now a 'service economy,'—that is, we are the first nation in the history of the world in which more than half of the employed population is not involved in the production of food, clothing, houses, automobiles, and other tangible goods." By 2005, the breakdown in the United States was even more dramatic, as reported by *The Economist:* 1.4 percent agriculture, 20.3 percent industry, and 78.3 percent services. Document 1 is an excerpt from Fuchs's seminal article, discussing the implications of the shift from industry to services. He predicts ten important changes. How accurate was Fuchs's forecast?

The computer industry was a new type of business in the postwar years. From the first electronic computer installation in 1951, the industry grew significantly over the next decade so that there were some 12,000 computers being used by the early 1960s. This growth rate was twice that of the electronics industry as a whole. Pioneers such as International Business Machines (IBM) developed, manufactured, and leased proprietary electronic computers, with compatible software and peripherals, which only IBM technicians had the know-how to service. In this regard, early computer companies such as IBM and Control Data inhabited a middle ground between manufacturing and services.

During the 1960s, the computer was primarily a tool for business, government, and military applications. Early computers were costly, difficult to program, and limited in capability. These devices were good at doing repetitive tasks like tracking payrolls, census data, tax returns, and vital statistics. In Document 2, the Investment Bankers Association of America explores the computer's potential, with reference to government, insurance, banking, and retailing.

In Document 3, Bill Veeck, former owner-operator of three major league baseball clubs, speaks about his sport as an "entertainment business" in response to declining attendance. During the early 1960s, Veeck's farsighted ideas were criticized by contemporaries in the baseball business. Decades later, they embraced many of his proposals to remake the sport as a vital segment of the entertainment industry. How does Veeck account for baseball's demise? How might club owners reverse the trend?

Next, McDonald's founder Ray Kroc discusses his early childhood, his discovery of the McDonald Brothers, and his experience with franchising (Document 4). This interview with *Nation's Business,* a magazine published by the U.S. Chamber of Commerce, lays down the basic story that became the basis of the "McLore" that remains part of McDonald's corporate culture.

Document 5 examines the dark side of the economic shifts during the 1970s and 1980s. Journalists for *The Philadelphia Inquirer,* Donald L. Bartlett and James Steele won a 1991 Pulitzer Prize for their nine-part series, "America: What Went Wrong?" This excerpt from their follow-up book with the same title describes the experiences of transportation workers in the wake of airline deregulation. It stands in contrast to Richard H. K. Vietor's essay in this chapter, written from the perspective of top executives at American Airlines.

Finally, the primary sources in Documents 6 and 7 present opposing views on Wal-Mart stores. In Document 6, founding entrepreneur Sam Walton outlines "Sam's Rules for Building a Business," in his 1992 autobiography, *Made in America.* A self-made man, Walton worked his way up in the retail world, establishing a series of deep-discount stores in postwar rural Arkansas. Eventually, he expanded Wal-Mart into a national chain, still remaining committed to family values and small-town America. How do Walton's prescriptions for success compare with those of Andrew Carnegie, outlined in Chapter 6? How might a business executive put Walton's generalizations into practice? In Document 7, Congressman George Miller, a member of the U.S. House Committee on Education and the Workforce, explores the labor practices at Wal-Mart stores in the new millennium. Miller's report challenges some fundamental assumptions about the service economy. What are those assumptions? How do they dovetail with Fuchs's earlier predictions? With Sam Walton's vision of partnership?

1. Economist Victor R. Fuchs Highlights the Growth of Services, 1965

Between 1929 and 1963 employment in the service sector grew 1.7 per cent per annum faster than in the goods sector. At some point during the past decade the United States became the first "service economy" in the history of the world, that is, the first economy in which more than half of the employed population is not involved in the production of tangible goods. The more rapid growth of services was observed for individual industries as well as the sector aggregates and for occupations as well

Victor R. Fuchs, "The Growing Importance of the Service Industries," *Journal of Business* 38 (October 1965): 344–373 (excerpt, p. 372). Reprinted by permission of The University of Chicago Press.

as industries. This shift represents an acceleration of a trend that has persisted for at least the past century.

Numerous conceptual and statistical problems in the measurement of real output make it difficult to explain precisely why service industry employment has grown so rapidly. The data examined in this paper appear to reject the hypothesis that the growth of real income per capita was a major explanation. The demand for services, compared with goods, may have been slightly more elastic with respect to income (principally because of the low elasticity for agriculture), but this was not an important reason for the shift of employment. Sector differences in the rate of growth of real output were probably very small; differences in the rate of growth of real output per man were probably very large.

The differential in the rate of growth of real output per man reflects a moderate differential change in productivity, in the sense of efficiency in the use of resources, but this is not the only or major explanation. It also reflects a more rapid decline in hours per man in services, a more rapid rise in the quality of labor in goods industries, and a more rapid rise in capital per worker in the goods sector.

The shift of employment to services has many important implications. The trends discussed here may be offset by other changes that are also taking place in the economy, but they serve to indicate the likely effects of the relative growth of services, other things remaining the same. These trends include:

1. Growing employment opportunities for women and older workers.
2. Growing opportunities for part-time employment and urban self-employment.
3. Growing need for workers with more formal education.
4. Possible decreasing importance of unions and growing importance of professional organizations.
5. Possible trend toward greater personalization of work.
6. Growing importance of small firms.
7. Growing importance of nonprofit organizations (public and private).
8. Declining relative importance of physical capital.
9. Growing stability in employment and, to a lesser extent, in output.
10. Possible increase in cyclical variability in output per man-hour.

2. Investment Bankers Association Predicts a Computer Boom, 1963

From practically no installations or sales in 1951, the industry has grown to a point where there are now 10–12,000 computers in use, with yearly shipments on the order of $1.5 billion. Within the short period of ten years, this industry now finds ranking among the billion dollar industries. There are no official industry statistics available, but it has been estimated that the computer market has been growing twice as fast as the market for office business machines, and on the basis of a 25% annual growth rate since 1957, is growing twice as fast as the electronic industry as a whole. . . .

Industrial Securities Committee, Investment Bankers Association of America, "A Survey and Study of the Computer Field: Part 1," *Computers and Automation* 13, no. 1 (January 1963): 15–16, 21–23.

Economic justification for the utilization of computers is based on the savings effected in such areas as clerical personnel and inventory. Computer usage has led to savings of 10–25% in clerical costs in many cases, and savings of 10–20% in inventory costs. The greatest payoff, however, will be in sophisticated total management information systems, employing such advanced management science techniques as operations research and linear programming. Costly decisions of the past, such as Ford's Edsel model, and General Dynamics' Convair 990, might be avoided with these techniques. There are over 500 areas in which computers are finding an application today, and these are growing every day. Future applications will include income tax processing, weather forecasting, medical analysis and diagnosis, traffic control and automatic classroom instruction, amongst many others.

Competitive Conditions

The computer industry has developed some very definite patterns and characteristics during its ten year life period. Of the nine major companies manufacturing computers, only two are showing any profits. One of these companies is IBM, which accounts for approximately 80% of the computer market. Large capital investments and research and development expenditures are required to remain competitive, and the breakeven point for most companies still appears to be 2 to 3 years away. This profit picture becomes critical in view of the capital requirements necessary for effective competition. Another industry characteristic is that 80% of the computer installations are leased. The huge investment required to carry rented equipment is straining the budgets of even the largest companies in the industry. . . .

Public Acceptance

As the communications problem between man and machine improves with the utilization of packaged language programs offered by computer manufacturers, the computer could one day become as easy to use as a desk calculator. This will open vast, untapped markets. Computers appear to be today where the automobile was when it generally gained public acceptance. Electronic data processing will lead to a dramatic increase in technological progress as it extends man's capabilities and intellect. Computers will help to channel man's efforts into areas and directions promising the greatest profits and rate of return on investment. These machines will not only aid in the restoration of former profit levels for business as a whole, but will be an invaluable tool in meeting the serious challenge our country faces in international trade competition. . . .

Government. The Government is the largest single user of computers, with a total of 1,006 installations as of June 1962, excluding special military computers. Operating costs in 1961 (rental, amortization, personnel, etc.) were approximately $597 million, and probably in excess of $1.5 billion with the inclusion of military operational applications. Today there are over 45,000 employees in positions related to management or operation of computers in the Federal Government. The Bureau of the Budget has estimated that by 1966, 1,500 computers will be installed by the government.

Computers are being used for a number of new applications by the government in the non-military field. The Internal Revenue Service has turned to computers to process its 95 million tax returns. These tax returns have grown from 20 million two decades ago, and could reach 135 million in 1980. The only logical means to handle all this paper work is high-speed electronic equipment. The system will be in full effect in 1965, and should prove a very effective means of catching up with tax evaders. The Social Security Administration is using computers to speed the processing of claims for social security benefits. District offices transmit data via AT&T's Data-Phone system to a computer center in Baltimore. Information is produced on magnetic tape, which can be fed directly to the computing center for further processing. . . .

The military has been the largest developer and user of computer technology to date. The military value of improved computer characteristics has led to the support of government-sponsored research projects which the computer industry would not have undertaken on its own. Due to the requirements of space, speed, and reliability, military control and command systems are far more sophisticated than commercial systems. However, many of the techniques developed by the military are adaptable to business systems. . . .

Insurance.   The first computer was installed in this industry eight years ago, and since then it has been one of the nation's biggest users of electronic data processing equipment. No large life insurance company could operate competitively today without an electronic data processing installation. More than three-fourths of the nation's 120-million policyholders are now on tape. It is estimated that more than 75 large-scale computers, approximately 200 medium-size machines and many hundreds of small units are now operating in life company offices. These numbers are growing every day. In addition to its normal functions, [the] computer will be used increasingly as an analytical tool in providing life companies with marketing analysis and financial forecasts. Operations research techniques will be used to provide life companies with scientific reports. . . .

Investment Banking.   In the financial community, computers are used in such applications as payroll, margin and cash accounting, customer statements, trade confirmations, commissions, dividends, and a host of allied management reports. Computers are also used to speed up such routine work as figuring portfolio market values and yields, and making records of company earnings, dividends and profit margins. A number of firms are experimenting with these machines for security analysis work. . . .

Computers are also widely used in the various stock exchanges. The Midwest Stock Exchange is developing an electronic centralized bookkeeping service which will reduce back office expenses by more than 70% per order, and will save member firms an estimated $3 million a year in labor and machines. The NYSE's Stock Clearing Corporation uses computers to verify and clear thousands of transactions each day. A computer system which will automate the Exchange's ticker and quotation service is expected to go into operation early in 1965. . . .

Retailing.   The potential for computing equipment in the retailing industry is considered very large, but will not attain fruition until three elements are more fully developed—optical scanners; methods of inexpensive data transmission; and larger, less expensive random-access memory devices. A number of retailing firms have installed computers to handle accounts payable, payroll, sales audit and accounts receivable. Notable savings are being achieved in these areas alone. For example, Stix, Baer and Fuller of St. Louis is projecting a five-year savings of $400,000 primarily in clerical savings, by employing two computers. The extension of computers into merchandise control, inventory control, and market analysis could prove to be even more significant in terms of savings. In this respect, retailing firms could very well follow the pattern set by such apparel companies as Bobbie Brooks, which is speeding up its inventory turnover by 30–40%, and expects to save over $1 million in the process over the next five years. . . .

These are just a few areas in which computers are finding applications today. In addition, there are a number of areas with large, but relatively untapped potential, which appear to be ready markets for computers. These include service organizations (hospitals, hotels), the transportation field (airlines, trucking, traffic control), local government, information retrieval, medicine, advertising, and law. The uses for computers appear limited only by man's imagination. Eventually, computers could become as commonplace as the office telephone.

3. Bill Veeck Assesses Baseball's Marketing, 1963

Q: Mr. Veeck, is the baseball business in trouble?

A: Well, let's say it isn't booming. I think it has been losing ground.

Q: What's wrong? Are people losing interest in the game?

A: No, I don't think that's true. Here you have a strange paradox. More people —certainly more youngsters—are playing baseball today than ever before. You have all these Little Leagues and Babe Ruth Leagues and Junior Leagues for youngsters. More high schools have baseball teams now—and far more colleges. But all this interest in baseball is not being translated into dollars at the big-league box offices— and certainly not in the minor leagues. This is the paradox.

Q: How do you explain it?

A: Oh, there are several things that contribute.

One reason is that big-league baseball games are not as entertaining as they used to be.

Another reason is that there is more sports participation by people today than there used to be. More people play golf and tennis and handball, go swimming, fishing or boating or bowling. When you increase the number of active participants, you reduce the number of spectators.

Q: What's the solution for baseball?

A: I believe baseball should concentrate on providing entertainment.

Q: Hasn't it always been entertainment?

A: In the past, baseball has tried to sell its game on the won-and-lost column— on the standings. How many games your team has won has determined, almost, how many people you were going to draw. Well, it's fine to win. But, obviously, under this standard, there are going to be only three or four clubs in each league that draw big crowds, because the rest of the clubs are losers.

Baseball should sell its game as entertainment. Really, there is no nicer way to spend an afternoon or an evening than by going to a baseball game. This is a delightful form of entertainment. And it can be made even more delightful.

Q: Mr. Veeck, in your career as an owner of big-league clubs in Cleveland, St. Louis and Chicago, you acquired a reputation as an innovator—a man with ideas. What would you do to make baseball more attractive?

A: I would aim at putting on a better show, recognizing that I am in the entertainment business. I'd try to draw not just the dyed-in-the-wool baseball fans, but a lot of people who simply would like to be entertained. Baseball should become a family sport.

I would modernize the ball parks. I would improve services and accommodations at the ball parks. Next to a winning ball club, the most important thing in a ball park is the ladies' rooms. Why, in Chicago at Comiskey Park we had the finest ladies' rooms in the city—full-length mirrors, the whole treatment.

I would use the public-address system to explain any complicated play. It's ridiculous to have people in your ball park not knowing as much about what's going on as the people sitting at home listening to the television announcer explain things.

Q: Would you change the game itself?

A: I would try to improve the game from the spectator's standpoint by squeezing some of the dead air out of it.

Q: What do you mean—"dead air"?

A: You hear a lot of people complain that ball games are too long. I don't believe that to be true. It isn't that the games are too long, but that there are too-long periods of inactivity in a game. You check by a stopwatch and you'll find that maybe 20 minutes out of every hour are taken up by a pitcher simply standing on the mound and holding the ball. Now, this is hardly exciting. If you're watching the game at home on TV you can go out to the kitchen and get a can of beer and be back before the pitcher throws the ball. This may be good for sponsors—but not for baseball. . . .

Q: Is baseball being passed by other sports? Is it losing its claim to be America's "national pastime"?

A: I don't know who gave baseball this claim in the first place. I think you'll find that actually more people pay to see basketball than any other sport, because there are more basketball teams. And football crowds are larger, on a per game average, than baseball crowds. But you can get trapped in an endless go-around in these comparisons. There's room for all sports.

There is one change, though, that's affecting baseball.

Q: What's that?

A: Baseball, by and large, has been the game of the working people. Football, because of its college origin, was more a game of the employer class—the wealthier, better-educated people. And the people who used to make up the suburban population were more of that class, and football was their game. It was the fellow who lived in town who supported the baseball clubs.

Now, you take the charts you published recently in your own magazine, and you'll see that the populations of the suburbs are growing immensely as against the populations inside cities. This means that many of the people who had been baseball fans are moving out to the suburbs. And when they arrive in the suburbs they become more "suburban" than the ones who originally lived there. So, for them, the thing to do is to be a football fan. And they build an outdoor grill, and they just don't make the trip into town to see the game they used to support.

So the result is that when these people move out to suburbia you have lost a hard core of your baseball attendance. And the people who replace them in the city are often in the lowest income bracket and the least likely to buy baseball tickets. . . .

Q: How much does it cost to set up a ball club?

A: Take the four new clubs that have been added to the big leagues. I think their original expenditure was something like 3 million dollars each. But I venture that each of them has spent at least an additional 2 million dollars since coming into existence. So I would figure that about 5 million dollars would be a reasonable total.

Q: Does that include the cost of the stadium?

A: No.

Q: Why are nearly all the recently built stadiums built with public funds rather than private capital?

A: Most of the new stadiums are designed not only for baseball, but for other sports—a variety of purposes. They are municipal projects, and baseball is only a tenant. Many cities have come to the conclusion—and I think with considerable reason—that it is a good thing to have a place for sporting events. There is nothing I know that gives a city as much "face" as a big-league ball club. . . .

Q: Do you see further expansion ahead for the big leagues?

A: I think ultimately, yes—but not for some time.

Q: How about a third major league? Do you expect that?

A: No. What I do think will happen ultimately is that you will have two 12-club leagues divided into two sections of six teams each—like pro football.

But before that happens, I think that big leagues will finally—at long last—come to interleague play.

Q: How do you mean?

A: Teams from the American League will play teams from the National League, not only at World Series time but in the course of the regular season.

Q: What would be the reason for that?

A: Right now you have only three cities with teams in both major leagues—New York, Chicago and Los Angeles. That means there are 14 cities where people only get to see teams from one major league. I think people would turn out to see teams from the other league, for a change.

4. Ray Kroc Explains How He Built the McDonald's Empire, 1968

How come the chain isn't called Kroc's, instead of McDonald's?

Because the formula didn't originate with me. I borrowed it from two McDonald brothers, Mac and Dick. They had opened a barbecue parlor in San Bernardino, Calif. They had pork, beef, ham and chicken on the menu. But they said Mrs. Jones, who was a real good customer, would say:

"Mac, that pork is awfully greasy today."

Or, "The barbecue beef is stringy," or "It's tough."

Mac and Dick said to each other: "Some day we are going to find a food item that is the same every day of the year—never tough, never too tender, never dry, never greasy, never stringy—always just the same. An item we can sell for 15 cents, and make a profit."

Finally, they hit on it—the hamburger.

How did you run into the McDonalds?

At the time, I was selling a multiple malted-milk mixer. I had exclusive distribution of it. . . .

It mixed five malts at a time—and it never broke down.

The McDonalds had eight of my multimixers in one store. I didn't have another customer with that many.

I said, "This I have to see."

So I went to San Bernardino. It was terrific. They had people standing in line clamoring for more. . . .

What did you do then?

I thought, "Well, jeepers, maybe the way for me to sell multimixers is to open up these sure-fire hamburger units all over the country myself. So I signed a 99-year contract with the McDonald brothers to represent them exclusively.

I agreed to pay them one half of one per cent of all gross receipts from the units. . . .

Where was your first unit?

In Des Plaines, Ill., a suburb of Chicago. It was opened April 15, 1955.

I opened the second place in Fresno, Calif., in August or September, 1955, the third place, in Reseda, Calif., in November or December. . . .

What was your first franchised restaurant?

In Fresno, Calif.

Does the man who franchised it still run it?

Yes, his name is Art Bender.

And the man who was my first manager in Des Plaines, Ill., is Ed MacLuckie. They are both millionaires today. . . .

How do you pick your franchisees?

We prefer someone with a business background—and ambition. We are also interested in his character, his attitude toward family life, his level-headedness and whether he can stand prosperity.

Some people reach their level of expectations pretty quickly.

We want someone who will get totally involved in the business. If his ambition is to reach the point where he can play golf four days a week, or play gin rummy for a cent a point, instead of a tenth, we don't want him in a McDonald's restaurant.

Is previous business experience a must?

No, we put our franchisees through a training school. Then we open the store for them, help them get it going and do everything under the sun to help them boost their sales. We have fun in this business. Our operators eat and sleep it.

We insist on all of our people, whether they be franchisees or company personnel, being dedicated to what we call "QSC"—that is, quality, service and cleanliness. The best advertising and public relations are meaningless without these three fundamentals. We at McDonald's believe in these fundamentals and really live by them.

Sure, there is competition, but if we stick to these basics and do everything else right, the way we have been doing for the past 13 years, we know we will stay on top.

Do you have any trouble getting applicants?

No, we have a permanent waiting list of about 100 applicants. We keep it at that level. They come from all walks of life—former dentists, retired Navy officers, and a former Assistant Secretary of Labor, John Gibson. . . .

Is there a danger that you will run out of places to build restaurants or people to eat McDonald's hamburgers?

I don't think so.

We have more than 1,000 units now, and are growing fast. In 1967, these units grossed over $266 million. In 1960, we grossed $6 million.

We have sold more than four billion hamburgers. My publicity men tell me it would take one man 40,000 years to eat them all—if he ate one every five minutes.

It took 400,000 head of cattle to produce the top quality beef for those hamburgers.

Most of them were served with catsup, mustard, pickles and onion. The catsup and mustard alone would fill the Mississippi River.

As we build up consumer acceptance, we have a broader and broader market.

What's your goal now?

We're shooting for 2,000 units. About 15 per cent of them are owned by the McDonald's Corp., the rest by franchisees. The average unit grosses about $297,000 a year.

What's the secret of McDonald's success?

Several things. For one, it's largely a franchise operation. That permits you to grow fast, because much of the capital for expansion is put up by the franchisee.

Then we have worked the business out to a science.

It takes an average of 50 seconds to serve a hamburger, a milk shake and an order of French fries in a McDonald's restaurant.

We've worked out the precise formula for making a hamburger to the public's liking, down to the exact size of the bun, three and three-quarter inches, and how much onions go on it—one fourth of an ounce.

And then we supervise all units carefully to insure quality.

For example, French fries are thrown away if they are seven minutes old. That's long enough for them to get stale.

Hamburgers are discarded for the same reason.

Whom do you cater to?

We aim at the local family trade.

When we look for a site, we count church steeples, rather than autos, signs of substantial family neighborhoods. That's where we get 90 per cent of our business.

We try to build up that image, too. That's why we never allow a jukebox, a ciga-ret [*sic*] machine, a vending device, a pinball game or a telephone in a McDonald's restaurant. . . .

What made you so sure this venture would succeed?

Well, I suppose we are all gamblers, to a certain extent.

If I am convinced of something beyond a question of doubt, and I have complete convictions in my own mind, then I am going to go ahead. And I had that feeling about the McDonald's hamburger restaurant formula. . . .

Didn't you have any doubts at all?

Yes, I wasn't too sure whether we could stay open in winter.

I remember a telephone call from a fellow in Minneapolis. He owned a drive-in theater and he was interested in a McDonald's franchise.

He said, "Of course, you would open about April 1 and close about the end of November."

I said, "No, no. This is based on a year-round operation."

"You must be nuts," he replied.

I wasn't too sure I wasn't. So this was the only question I had—what about the bad weather? But I went ahead.

When did you discover your misgivings were groundless?

After the first winter in Des Plaines.

What I didn't realize was that there are nice winter days, when the wind isn't howling and the streets are dry. And there are always people out at noon, like sales-men, who are in a hurry, and they want a hamburger and a cup of coffee and some French fries.They can take the food into their car and the car is warm.

And people in the neighborhood send over for hamburgers and French fries and shakes. One person might bring back $4 or $5 worth.

After the first winter I had no doubts.

5. Journalists Probe Transportation Workers' Lives in the Wake of Deregulation, 1992

Since deregulation of the trucking industry in 1980, more than 100 once-thriving trucking companies have gone out of business. More than 150,000 workers at those companies lost their jobs.

Since deregulation of the airlines in 1978, a dozen airline companies have merged or gone out of business. More than 50,000 of their employees lost their jobs.

Since deregulation of the savings and loan industry in 1982, about 650 thrifts have folded, with at least 400 more in serious trouble. The bailout will leave tax-payers stuck with a half-trillion-dollar tab.

Now, the people who rewrote the government rule book to deregulate airlines, trucking and savings and loans are about to rewrite the rules on banks. They call it

Donald L. Bartlett and James B. Steele, *America: What Went Wrong?* (Kansas City, Mo.: Andrews and McMeel, 1992), pp. 106–108.

banking reform. President Bush spelled out the plans in February 1991: "Regulatory reform is long overdue. Our banking reform proposals . . . address the reality of the modern financial marketplace by creating a U.S. financial system that protects taxpayers, serves consumers and strengthens our economy."

Sound familiar? It should. The arguments for deregulating banks are much the same as those that were made in the 1970s and 1980s for the other industries: Removing government restrictions on the private sector would let free and open competition rule the marketplace. Getting rid of regulations would spur the growth of new companies. Existing companies would become more efficient or perish. Competition would create jobs, drive down prices and benefit consumers and businesses alike.

That's the theory. The gritty reality, as imposed on the daily lives of the men and women most directly affected, is a little different.

For Christopher E. Neimann of Fort Smith, Arkansas, deregulation meant the loss of health insurance as he was battling cancer. Neimann, who worked for a trucking company, was diagnosed with a rare bone cancer in November 1987. He went on medical leave two months later. In August 1988 his company, Smith's Transfer Corporation, entered bankruptcy, a victim of deregulation's rate wars. Its checks began bouncing, including ones paying for Neimann's treatment at the M.D. Anderson Cancer Center in Houston.

On Apr. 11, 1989, the hospital sent Neimann a stern letter asking him to pay his bill, which totaled $30,128. When the bedridden, gravely ill Neimann couldn't make payments, the hospital began pressuring his wife, Billie.

"The hospital called me one night and told me they were going to dip into the estate," she said. "And he wasn't dead. He was still alive. I knew he was going to die. And they knew he was going to die. I just cried and I said, 'I beg your pardon. Could I ask you what estate are you talking about?' And they said, 'Well, his estate.' And I said, 'Ma'am, at thirty-one years old, you don't have an estate. You don't have anything to go into an estate. At this age, we're just starting out.' I said, 'You can dip all you want. Dip right in and get some of the bills, too. Because there won't be anything left.' "

After a battle of a year and a half, Neimann died on June 6, 1989, aged thirty-one, leaving behind a young wife and an infant daughter. The calls from M.D. Anderson's collection department continued.

"They kept calling and told me that I was still liable," said his wife, who has since remarried. "I was so upset that eventually I talked to my lawyer and he told me to give them his name. I don't know what's happened, but lately they haven't called."

For Leslie Wagner of Flower Mound, Texas, deregulation meant seven years of relentlessly shrinking paychecks—and, ultimately, no paycheck. At twenty-three, she went to work as a flight attendant for Braniff International Airlines. That was in 1969, when the Dallas-based carrier was the nation's eighth largest airline. By 1982 her base salary was $19,300 a year. That year, the fourth year of airline deregulation, Braniff asked workers to accept wage cuts and other concessions.

Even after employees agreed to reductions, Braniff still could not pay its bills and the airline was forced to seek protection in United States Bankruptcy Court in May 1982. The action grounded Braniff and put 9,000 employees, including Leslie Wagner, out of work. Two years later a scaled-down Braniff, Inc., under new owners, emerged from bankruptcy court and resumed service. Former employees were offered jobs, but at reduced pay. When Wagner returned to work in 1985, her new base pay was $15,600 a year—19 percent less than she earned in 1982.

By 1989, with Braniff still in financial trouble, employees were asked to take another pay cut. Wagner's base pay went down again—to $14,400. On Sept. 28, 1989, Braniff was forced into bankruptcy court for the second time in seven years. Its assets were auctioned off to pay creditors, and the airline's remaining 4,800 employees were let go. After absorbing pay cuts of 25 percent during the years when the cost of living rose 28 percent, Leslie Wagner was out of work. The company resumed limited service in July 1991, but Wagner was not recalled. It didn't matter. Braniff was back in bankruptcy court a month later, for the third time in a decade. . . .

And finally, for you, the American taxpayer and consumer, deregulation has meant fewer airlines and higher air fares, more unsafe trucks on the highways, and more of your tax money diverted to pay for the savings and loan debacle. That last one is going to cost you for years to come.

6. Sam Walton, Ten Rules That Worked for Me, 1992

For what they're worth, here they are. Sam's Rules for Building a Business:

RULE 1: COMMIT to your business. Believe in it more than anybody else. I think I overcame every single one of my personal shortcomings by the sheer passion I brought to my work. I don't know if you're born with this kind of passion, or if you can learn it. But I do know you need it. If you love your work, you'll be out there every day trying to do it the best you possibly can, and pretty soon everybody around will catch the passion from you—like a fever.

RULE 2: SHARE your profits with all your associates, and treat them as partners. In turn, they will treat you as a partner, and together you will all perform beyond your wildest expectations. Remain a corporation and retain control if you like, but behave as a servant leader in a partnership. Encourage your associates to hold a stake in the company. Offer discounted stock, and grant them stock for their retirement. It's the single best thing we ever did.

RULE 3: MOTIVATE your partners. Money and ownership alone aren't enough. Constantly, day by day, think of new and more interesting ways to motivate and challenge your partners. Set high goals, encourage competition, and then keep score. Make bets with outrageous payoffs. If things get stale, cross-pollinate; have managers switch jobs with one another to stay challenged. Keep everybody guessing as to what your next trick is going to be. Don't become too predictable.

RULE 4: COMMUNICATE everything you possibly can to your partners. The more they know, the more they'll understand. The more they understand, the more they'll care. Once they care, there's no stopping them. If you don't trust your associates to know what's going on, they'll know you don't really consider them partners.

Sam Walton with John Huey, "Ten Rules That Worked for Me," in *Sam Walton: Made in America: My Story* (New York: Doubleday, 1992), pp. 246–249. Copyright © 1992 by Estate of Samuel Moore Walton. Used by permission of Doubleday, a division of Random House, Inc.

Information is power, and the gain you get from empowering your associates more than offsets the risk of informing your competitors.

RULE 5: APPRECIATE everything your associates do for the business. A paycheck and a stock option will buy one kind of loyalty. But all of us like to be told how much somebody appreciates what we do for them. We like to hear it often, and especially when we have done something we're really proud of. Nothing else can quite substitute for a few well-chosen, well-timed, sincere words of praise. They're absolutely free—and worth a fortune.

RULE 6: CELEBRATE your successes. Find some humor in your failures. Don't take yourself so seriously. Loosen up, and everybody around you will loosen up. Have fun. Show enthusiasm—always. When all else fails, put on a costume and sing a silly song. Then make everybody else sing with you. Don't do a hula on Wall Street. It's been done. Think up your own stunt. All of this is more important, and more fun, than you think, and it really fools the competition. "Why should we take those cornballs at Wal-Mart seriously?"

RULE 7: LISTEN to everyone in your company. And figure out ways to get them talking. The folks on the front lines—the ones who actually talk to the customer—are the only ones who really know what's going on out there. You'd better find out what they know. This really is what total quality is all about. To push responsibility down in your organization, and to force good ideas to bubble up within it, you *must* listen to what your associates are trying to tell you.

RULE 8: EXCEED your customers' expectations. If you do, they'll come back over and over. Give them what they want—and a little more. Let them know you appreciate them. Make good on all your mistakes, and don't make excuses—apologize. Stand behind everything you do. The two most important words I ever wrote were on that first Wal-Mart sign: "Satisfaction Guaranteed." They're still up there, and they have made all the difference.

RULE 9: CONTROL your expenses better than your competition. This is where you can always find the competitive advantage. For twenty-five years running—long before Wal-Mart was known as the nation's largest retailer—we ranked number one in our industry for the lowest ratio of expenses to sales. You can make a lot of different mistakes and still recover if you run an efficient operation. Or you can be brilliant and still go out of business if you're too inefficient.

RULE 10: SWIM upstream. Go the other way. Ignore the conventional wisdom. If everybody else is doing it one way, there's a good chance you can find your niche by going in exactly the opposite direction. But be prepared for a lot of folks to wave you down and tell you you're headed the wrong way. I guess in all my years, what I heard more often than anything was: a town of less than 50,000 population cannot support a discount store for very long.

Those are some pretty ordinary rules, some would say even simplistic. The hard part, the real challenge, is to constantly figure out ways to execute them. You can't just keep doing what works one time, because everything around you is always changing. To succeed, you have to stay out in front of that change.

7. A Congressman Explores Wal-Mart's Labor Practices in the United States and Asia, 2004

Since the recession began in March 2001, the United States has lost 2.4 million jobs. In every recession, since the Great Depression, jobs were recovered within the first 31 months after the recession began—until now. The latest recession began 34 months ago and officially ended in November 2001, but the jobs have not been recovered. For American working families, by all accounts, the "jobless recovery" has been of little benefit to them. While GDP growth was strong or solid in the third and fourth quarters of 2003, real wages for workers remained stagnant and even declined.

Indeed, of the jobs that remain, the pay is low. The country has seen a dramatic shift from high-paying jobs to low-paying jobs. For instance, in New Hampshire, which still has not recovered the number of jobs it lost in the recession, new jobs pay 35 percent lower wages than lost jobs. In Delaware, those wages are 43 percent lower; in Colorado, 35 percent lower; in West Virginia, 33 percent lower. In fact, the low-pay shift has hit all but two of the fifty states.

Moreover, these changes in the labor market reveal themselves in a marked decline in living standards for low- and middle-income workers. The real weekly earnings for full-time workers age 25 and older fell for the bottom half of the workforce between the fourth quarters of 2002 and 2003. In particular, workers in the 10th percentile saw their weekly earnings fall 1.2 percent; in the 20th percentile, by 0.5 percent, in the 50th percentile, by 0.1 percent. Conversely, earners in the top percentiles of income experienced growth. The 90th percentile, for instance, saw a 1.1 percent increase in weekly earnings. As the Economic Policy Institute points out: "This pattern of earnings growth suggests that while the economy is expanding, the benefits of growth are flowing to those at the top of the wage scale."

These lower-paying jobs are largely service sector jobs, like retail, replacing traditionally higher-paying and unionized manufacturing jobs. Between January 1998 and August 2003, the nation experienced a net loss of 3 million manufacturing jobs. During the "recovery," 1.3 million manufacturing jobs disappeared. American manufacturers find it increasingly difficult to keep jobs in the U.S., given the availability of cheap labor abroad. In 2003, the U.S. trade deficit hit a record high of $551 billion, increasing 15 percent from 2002 and exceeding 5 percent of GDP.

Wal-Mart plays a curiously illustrative role in this jobs phenomenon—not just in the creation of low-paying jobs and the downward pressure on wages and benefits, but also in the export of existing manufacturing jobs to foreign countries offering cheap labor. Wal-Mart markets itself with a patriotic, small-town, red-white-and-blue

U.S. House Committee on Education and the Workforce, *Everyday Low Wages: The Hidden Price We All Pay for Wal-Mart,* pp. 11–13. Report prepared by George Miller. 108th Cong., 1st sess., 2004.

advertising motif. But Wal-Mart's trade practices are anything but small-town. Indeed, Wal-Mart conducts international trade in manufactured goods on a scale that can bring down entire nations' economies.

While the red-white-and-blue banners remain, long-gone are the days when Wal-Mart abided by the mottos of "Buy American" and "Bring It Home to the USA." In 1995, Wal-Mart claimed only 6 percent of its merchandise was imported. Today an estimated 50–60 percent of its products come from overseas. In the past five years, Wal-Mart has doubled its imports from China. In 2002, the company bought 14 percent of the $1.9 billion of clothes exported by Bangladesh to the United States. Also in 2002, the company purchased $12 billion in merchandise from China, or 10 percent of China's total U.S.-bound exports, a 20 percent increase from the previous year. In 2003, these Chinese purchases jumped to $15 billion, or almost one-eighth of all Chinese exports to the United States. Today, more than 3,000 supplier factories in China produce for Wal-Mart.

Wal-Mart maintains an extensive global network of 10,000 suppliers. Whether American, Bangladeshi, Chinese, or Honduran, Wal-Mart plays these producers against one another in search of lower and lower prices. American suppliers have been forced to relocate their businesses overseas to maintain Wal-Mart contracts. Overseas manufacturers are forced to engage in cutthroat competition that further erodes wages and working conditions of what often already are sweatshops. To keep up with the pressure to produce ever cheaper goods, factories force employees to work overtime or work for weeks without a day off. A Bangladeshi factory worker told the *Los Angeles Times* that employees at her factory worked from 8 A.M. to 3 A.M. for 10 and 15 day stretches just to meet Wal-Mart price demands. And still, Wal-Mart's general manager for Bangladesh complained of his country's factories, telling the *Los Angeles Times,* "I think they need to improve. When I entered a factory in China, it seemed they [were] very fast."

While low-wage jobs displace higher-paid manufacturing jobs in the United States, undercutting living standards at home, living standards abroad are not reaping the benefits one might expect. Reports indicate that Wal-Mart's bargaining power is able to maintain low wages and poor working conditions among its foreign suppliers. The *Washington Post* has explained: "As capital scours the globe for cheaper and more malleable workers, and as poor countries seek multinational companies to provide jobs, lift production, and open export markets, Wal-Mart and China have forged themselves into the ultimate joint venture, their symbiosis influencing the terms of labor and consumption the world over." Thanks to a ban on independent trade unions and a lack of other basic human rights, China offers Wal-Mart a highly-disciplined and cheap workforce. A Chinese labor official who asked to remain anonymous for fear of punishment told the *Washington Post* that "Wal-Mart pressures the factory to cut its price, and the factory responds with longer hours or lower pay. And the workers have no options."

One employee of a Chinese supplier described the difficulties of surviving on $75 per month. She could rarely afford to buy meat, and her family largely subsisted on vegetables. Over four years, she had not received a single salary increase.

Wal-Mart has countered that it insists that its suppliers enforce labor standards and comply with Chinese law. One-hundred Wal-Mart auditors inspect Chinese plants, and the company has suspended contracts with about 400 suppliers, mainly for violating overtime limits. An additional 72 factories were permanently blacklisted in 2003 for violating child labor standards. Still, critics point out that Wal-Mart does not regularly inspect smaller factories that use middlemen to sell to the company. Nor does it inspect the factories of subcontractors. A Chinese labor organizer explained that the inspections are "ineffective," since Wal-Mart usually notifies the factories in advance. The factories "often prepare by cleaning up, creating fake time sheets and briefing workers on what to say."

The factories themselves complain that, because Wal-Mart demands such low prices, they have slim profit margins—if any. A manager of one Chinese supplier told the *Washington Post,* "In the beginning, we made money. . . . But when Wal-Mart started to launch nationwide distribution, they pressured us for a special price below our cost. Now, we're losing money on every box, while Wal-Mart is making more money." Obviously, one way to regain a profit for such suppliers would be to begin cutting back on labor costs.

 # E S S A Y S

Thomas S. Dicke, a history professor at Southwest Missouri State University, and author of *Franchising in America: The Development of a Business Method, 1840–1980* (1992), presents a case study of Domino's Pizza to consider how the franchising system was adapted by a fast-food vendor serving a market comprised of college students. Perfected by the Ford Motor and Sun Oil companies in the early twentieth century, franchising was a ubiquitous feature of the business landscape by the late 1960s. Franchising gives large corporations a mechanism for selling directly to consumers, while providing local entrepreneurs with a standardized, proven system for merchandising a range of products, including sewing machines, agricultural equipment, cars and trucks, gasoline, and fast food. In many respects, the franchising system meshes big business and small business, maximizing their complementarities.

In the next essay, Richard H. K. Vietor, the Senator John Heinz Professor of Environmental Management at the Harvard Business School and author of *Contrived Competition: Regulation and Deregulation in America* (1994), examines how two American Airlines executives—CEO Albert V. Casey and president Robert Crandall—made their carrier competitive following deregulation. In the unregulated market filled with low-cost competitors, American Airlines's profits declined. Between 1980 and 1985, Casey and Crandall revamped various operations, from fleet management to labor productivity, to put the airline back on track. In part, the carrier's automated reservation system, SABRE—the world's largest real-time computer system created jointly by American and IBM—enabled the firm to develop innovations like Ultimate Super Saver fares and the AAdvantage frequent flyer program.

Finally, Simon Head, director of the Project on Technology and the Workplace at the Century Foundation, examines Wal-Mart, the world's largest retailer. In 2002, Wal-Mart bumped General Motors from the top slot on the *Fortune* 500, becoming the first retailing firm to achieve this status or size. Head scrutinizes the cost-cutting strategies that enabled Wal-Mart's growth, including automated inventory control and discriminatory labor practices. How does Head's analysis intersect with Sam Walton's biography and Congressman George Miller's report, found in Documents 6 and 7?

We Deliver: Domino's Pizza and the Franchising Method

THOMAS S. DICKE

In most ways, Domino's Pizza is a typical franchise industry firm. The company came into being at the start of franchising's transition from a method of distribution to a separate industry and over the next twenty-five years followed a pattern common to successful franchisers. In the beginning Domino's was a traditional small business; it became a franchiser only after its product and the system for its production were well developed. Tom Monaghan, one of Domino's founders, turned to franchising in 1967 because of the success of McDonald's. But as often happens with new franchisers, Monaghan did not fully realize that he had entered a new business and so failed to develop adequate training programs for franchisees and other services that now made up his main product. As a result, the company underwent a crisis that lasted until Domino's had built the infrastructure and developed the techniques required for its new market. Once the company possessed a system to produce franchises with the same efficiency it had earlier used to manufacture pizzas, it was able to begin the rapid expansion characteristic of a successful franchise industry firm. By the late 1970s Domino's was opening more than three new outlets a week. . . .

Tom and Jim Monaghan founded Domino's in December 1960, when they purchased a small pizza shop in Ypsilanti, Michigan, for $500 cash and agreed to assume the store's $8,000 debt. . . . The brothers bought the shop from Dominick DeVarti, a friend of Jim's and a restaurateur from the nearby city of Ann Arbor. . . . Faced with the prospect of a lean period, Jim, who had never given up his job at the post office, finally tired of the long hours and sold Tom his half of the business in 1961 for full ownership of the firm's delivery car, a 1959 Volkswagen Beetle. . . .

The profits and appearance of the original store were unimpressive, but in a rough way it already contained the key elements of Domino's future format. Its location next to the Eastern Michigan University campus proved to be well suited to Domino's products, and to this day the company continues to concentrate on reaching the student market. Like modern Domino's outlets, the original store was small, had a limited menu, and relied on takeout and free delivery for the bulk of its business. . . .

The process of refining Domino's system for making pizza proceeded in a piecemeal fashion and by the mid-1960s had come to include almost every aspect of the business. As part of the original purchase arrangement, DeVarti had given the Monaghans recipes and lessons in pizza making, but these brief sessions left the brothers unprepared for the complexities of operating and managing even their single outlet. Painfully aware of his lack of experience, Tom spent much of his time visiting pizzerias in other cities to get advice on recipes and operations. Among the first fruits of these visits, which by 1969 had taken him to over three hundred stores, was a new sauce recipe from an operator in nearby Lansing. Other changes included

Thomas S. Dicke, *Franchising in America: The Development of a Business Method, 1840–1980* (Chapel Hill: University of North Carolina Press, 1992), pp. 131–141, 143–144, 146–149. Copyright © 1992 by the University of North Carolina Press. Used by permission of the publisher.

the installation of a "ferris wheel" type of revolving oven, which could accommodate more pies in less space than conventional ovens, and the practice of placing pizzas on rigid screens rather than directly on the oven shelves, which allowed for faster, easier handling and reduced the losses from misshaped pies.

Monaghan's own experiences in the shop led to further refinements. Before the end of the first year, he restructured the interior of the store and rearranged counters, coolers, and work areas to improve the flow of work in all phases of the operation from order taking to delivery. When completed, Monaghan's system was reminiscent of those developed by the managers of White Castle Hamburgers in the 1920s, the McDonald brothers in the 1940s, and other fast-food pioneers. In each case, success depended on adapting the techniques of mass production to the restaurant business. In taking this approach, Monaghan, like the others, viewed the production process as a unified whole, requiring the standardization of materials, thoughtful placement of equipment, and detailed division of labor—all geared to achieve continuous production of a limited product line. And as in the case of other fast-food pioneers, Monaghan's marketing strategy of speedy service and uniform quality led him to a mass-production system. He found that during peak times, the only way to ensure fast delivery was to create a comprehensive and coordinated system of production that covered every step in the pizza-making process. Domino's entered the franchise industry in 1967 with a significant advantage[;] its production system was standardized and therefore more easily reproducible. . . .

. . . [That year,] Monaghan sold his first three franchises. By then Domino's was well placed to begin franchising. Its emphasis on uniform quality and rapid delivery had given it a unique and complete system for operating a pizza shop. The company had a clear, well-established local identity, and its management was experienced, if not yet professional, in the tasks supporting store openings, such as site selection and lease negotiation. It also had the beginnings of a supply and administrative system. To save space and enhance quality control at its company stores, Domino's prepared all raw materials off-site and delivered them to the outlets daily. The accounts of all four stores were likewise centralized, with the home office processing the outlets' financial records. This gave Monaghan's staff at least some experience with collecting and organizing financial data from a number of stores.

During the first two years as a franchiser, Monaghan moved slowly and avoided problems. In his first sale, for example, he sidestepped difficulties with site selection, remodeling, and equipment supply by selling the licensee an existing outlet. This method was clearly unsuitable for any major expansion, however, and in the next sale, he took responsibility for locating, leasing, remodeling, and equipping the outlet and training the franchisee. Once the outlet opened, Domino's was committed to furnish the owner with all supplies needed to produce and package the pizza, to provide advertising, and to keep all financial records. In exchange, Domino's received a franchise fee of $4,475, a royalty of 2½ percent on gross to be paid monthly, a 2 percent advertising fee to be used for the general benefit of all members of the Domino's system, a 1 percent bookkeeping fee, and the profits from equipment and supply sales.

Tom Monaghan quickly threw himself into the franchise business with gusto and fell into the overexpansion trap that often destroys new business-format franchisers.

His first mistake was to commit his company to providing too many services to his franchisees. His second was his failure to create an infrastructure capable of producing the services he promised. Like many new franchisers, Monaghan did not realize that he was in a new business. After 1969 his main product was pizza shops, not pizza. That demanded new production techniques, which he was slow to develop.

As late as 1969, Monaghan still viewed franchises as products that could be made using what amounted to craft production techniques. The terms of his franchise agreements varied, stores were located without any formal analysis of traffic patterns or neighborhood demographics, and owners were expected to run their stores after only a few weeks of informal instruction. To be successful, a franchise industry firm needs to produce the bundle of services that make up its product in high volume at a relatively low cost. This, in turn, requires an organization capable of providing a uniform product using techniques that approximate economies of scale and scope. Domino's did not develop such a system until a near-failure prompted the company to reorganize its franchise production system. . . .

In 1969 Monaghan launched a campaign to make Domino's "the MacDonald's [*sic*] of the pizza industry," and for a brief time his goal seemed realistic. Between the opening of corporate stores, the sale of single-store franchises, and the efforts of a few area franchisees who had the exclusive right to develop Domino's stores in a given territory, the company was opening one store a week. In June 1969, with twenty-two stores already open, Monaghan confidently predicted that "by the time the Christmas party season arrives we'll have 100 [stores] in operation." Instead, by Christmas Domino's had opened only forty-four stores and faced a nearly crushing $1.5 million debt.

Domino's crash of 1969 came suddenly. Ever the optimist, Tom Monaghan had relied heavily on credit to finance expansion and operating costs and to cover the lavish spending by the home office, which after too many lean years did not always use its newfound wealth wisely. When royalty payments and supply profits from spottily trained and poorly supported franchisees were lower than anticipated and franchise sales lagged, Domino's found itself unable to pay its approximately $1.5 million debt. . . .

At the center of the problems leading to the crash was the lack of an organized franchise production system. The company came out with its then-famous "Domino's people are pizza people, period" advertising slogan in 1969, but by that time this statement was no longer true. The home office's primary job was the manufacture and sale of the host of services that made up the Domino's franchise, and the company was only beginning to professionalize its operations in these areas. Without a strong production and control system, quality suffered, and this in turn drew down royalty payments and supply profits. Company sales, for example, rose from $2 million in 1968 to $4 million in 1969, a 100 percent increase. At the same time, however, sales per store dropped about 45 percent. The growing confusion at the home office probably also accounted for some of the slump in franchise sales, as the company recruited most of its franchisees from within and those employees already had first-hand knowledge of Domino's problems. . . .

In an effort to correct the problems that had led to the crash of 1969 . . . , management began to build a system that would make the company into a true franchise industry firm. Over the next eight years, it redesigned and refined its corporate infrastructure until it could provide the services its franchisees had contracted for in high volume at a relatively low cost. . . .

One of the first major changes undertaken by Monaghan was to shift some of the burdens of franchisee recruiting and development to his existing franchisees. Prior to 1969, most of Domino's expansion came through the sale of single-unit franchises, which granted the holder the right to operate a single store. This allowed the company greater control and produced higher per-unit profits, but it also put too great a burden on the firm in training, supply, and service. In the early 1970s Domino's did not have the personnel or the organization to carry out these functions on a large scale. Therefore, as many franchisers do in their early years, Domino's began to push the sale of larger territories. As a general rule, it sold the rights to build and operate stores in an entire city, but in some cases it granted the rights to develop entire states.

From Monaghan's standpoint, the main attraction of the area franchise was not the slightly larger fee that Domino's charged, but rather its potential for rapid expansion. The company could keep its initial fee fairly low ($10,000 in 1973) because area franchisees had to "license, appoint, establish, train, supervise and control all DOMINO Pizza stores" in their particular area. In effect, it formed a series of partnerships with its area franchisees giving them greater profits in exchange for assuming much of the responsibility for managing a given territory according to company standards. . . .

In looking back at the reasons for the crash of 1969, Monaghan believed that one of the chief causes for the uneven performance of Domino's outlets was the decision to market franchises to people from outside the company. These new franchisees, he thought, had lacked adequate experience and training. Given the sketchy training franchisees actually received, he may have been right. But one of the main reasons people buy a franchise is so training can substitute for experience, at least in the critical first few years when most small businesses fail. Thus, if Domino's wished to become a true franchise industry firm, it had to provide better training.

To correct problems in training, Domino's reverted back to its original policy of selling most franchises internally. It also formalized its training program to make sure that future franchise holders, whether internal or not, received adequate instruction to master Domino's methods. . . .

One of Monaghan's most important changes occurred in 1973, when he established the "College of Pizzarology." Modeled after McDonald's famous "Hamburger University," Domino's school combined classroom instruction with in-store training. The curriculum changed somewhat between 1973 and 1978, but generally it consisted of a number of short but intensive courses in management and operations and several weeks of paid apprenticeship, when franchisees observed and performed every task associated with operating a store. By formalizing the initial training and taking it out of the shop, Monaghan not only captured economies of scale and enhanced uniformity but also guaranteed that the focus would be on training because instructors no longer had to divide their attention between training franchisees and serving customers. Once trainees had mastered the basics, the formal apprenticeship in a company-owned outlet was a vital part of the instructional program, giving new franchisees familiarity with the rhythms of the business and an understanding of how Domino's techniques worked in practice. . . .

From the earliest days of the business, Monaghan had encouraged corporate store managers to purchase a part interest in the stores they operated, so the move from manager to franchisee was often a short and logical step. During the late 1970s, however, the company made two specific changes to codify this system and increase franchise sales. The first action, taken in 1979, was the establishment of a sponsorship program, whereby the company agreed to pay existing franchisees either $15,000 in one lump sum or a percentage of the royalties produced by any qualified managers during the first five years following their purchase of a Domino's franchise. The rationale for this move was that existing franchisees had already provided Domino's with a service by training the new store owner; if the firm compensated them for the loss of experienced personnel, owners might be more willing to encourage employees to establish outlets of their own. . . .

Overall, the internal recruiting programs were very effective. In the early 1980s Monaghan estimated that 92 percent of Domino's franchise holders were former company employees. Moreover, as the company expanded, so did its pool of potential internal candidates. Despite the preponderance of internal franchisees, Domino's did sell franchises to outsiders and, like so many of the company's operations, this system became more organized in the late 1970s. In 1978 the firm appointed its first full-time director of franchise marketing and began to market franchises to the general public. . . .

One of the most valuable services that Domino's offered its new franchisees was a greatly improved operations manual. Franchisees have been known to refer to their operations manual as "the bible"—and with good reason. Running almost any business is a complicated affair and no matter how thorough their training, most franchisees are likely to need occasional assistance in determining procedures and policies. At these times, the operations manual serves as the final authority. Domino's drew up its first manual in 1972. Designed as a reference work rather than a unified explanation of outlet operations, the manual defies easy summary. By the late 1970s it was roughly two inches thick and described the correct procedure for every aspect of store operations down to the smallest detail, from checking the quality of supplies through the actual delivery of a pizza. . . .

An additional motive for standardizing the equipment and appearance of outlets seems to have been the desire to recapture some of the lucrative supply business for the company or, at the very least, to increase its level of service and hence the franchisees' reliance on the home office. Like most other franchisers, Domino's offered a full line of equipment and supplies to its dealers; however, . . . it had allowed them to purchase from whatever sources they wished as long as they met the company's standards for quality. Domino's managers believed that with the advantages of bulk purchasing, coupled with the firm's ability to provide its outlets with a full line of equipment and supplies at a competitive price, they would be able to capture most of this lucrative market. After 1978, when Monaghan expanded his commissary system, this did, in fact, happen. By speeding up deliveries, reducing prices, and simplifying ordering, the company increased franchisee use from 63 percent in 1978 to over 90 percent by the early 1980s. And even though some franchisees chose not to use the commissary service, Domino's still gained because simply having it made the franchises more salable. People buy franchises because they offer advantages over independent ownership. Instead of having to shop for equipment and then deal with a multitude of supplies once the outlet was established, franchisees could buy everything they needed from the company and have it delivered on the same truck.

By the late 1970s, then, Monaghan had made great strides in reorienting his business and building a solid system to provide a complete package of services designed to virtually guarantee franchise success. Improvements in training, store design, and outlet supply operations all strengthened the power of the home office by increasing its ability to make a uniform product, the Domino's Pizza shop, in high volume and at a relatively low cost. As typically occurs with mature business-format franchisers, the completion of a corporate infrastructure to provide these services led to a policy restricting the authority of large area franchises. This change reflected the enhanced capabilities of the home office, the desire of its managers to gain economies of scale and scope, and perhaps Monaghan's increased awareness that ultimately Domino's success rested on its ability to provide the public with a uniform product and its franchisees with the means to satisfy this demand. In 1979, when its training program was perfected, its operations and identity manuals were complete, and its supply system was reorganized, Domino's decided to curtail the sale of large area franchises.

In place of the old area franchisees, where the terms of the agreement varied as to the number of outlets franchise holders could open and the specific services they must provide were vaguely defined, Domino's new multiunit franchise limited the holder to a maximum of five stores per contract, set a rigid timetable for store openings, and increased home office control over training, store operations, and supervision. Under the new contracts, Domino's agreed to pay the cost of site selection for the first shop and to allow the $29,500 franchise fee to cover all five stores. In return, the franchise holder agreed to open the five units at set intervals, with the last store to be opened just under two years of the first. In addition, the multiunit franchisee had to absorb the costs of site selection for all units after the first, for remodeling, and for advertising his or her grand opening. . . .

Domino's shift to small multiunit franchises reflected abilities and concerns that were typical of a mature business-format franchiser. In the late 1960s, while trying to establish himself in the market, Monaghan willingly sacrificed a measure of control and profits for rapid expansion. By the late 1970s he no longer needed to rely as much on area franchisees and could supply franchisee services more efficiently in any case. More importantly, consolidation of control, training, advertising, operations, and supply not only guaranteed greater uniformity, but it also diminished the threat that any single franchisee or group of franchisees might become powerful enough to defy the parent company. . . .

By 1979, when the company had nearly 300 stores in operation, Tom Monaghan attempted a second major expansion. Unlike in 1969, this time he achieved considerable success. Between 1979 and 1985, Domino's and its area franchisees opened over 2,500 outlets, or slightly more than one store per day. Monaghan could do this because in the years between 1969 and 1979 he had reoriented the company and developed an infrastructure that was capable of providing training, support, and supplies in high volume and at a relatively low cost. . . .

In more general terms, Domino's and other franchise industry firms succeeded because of changes in the basic structure of the economy. With the creation of the modern economy came dozens of managerial innovations and specialized services designed to assist the large-scale enterprises that have dominated the American economic landscape during the twentieth century. These were the basic services that the business-format franchise provided small business owners. Because they typically did not use elaborate managerial tools such as cost accounting or inventory control systems and because they lacked the capital for specialized services such as professional advertising or specially designed outlets, small businesses were often thought to have little or no need for these services. As perceptive entrepreneurs came to realize in the 1950s, however, most of these services were neither irrelevant nor impractical for the small business owner if they could be provided at an affordable price.

The franchise contract provided the perfect tool for this purpose. By the 1950s product franchisees had already demonstrated that the franchise contract offered an invaluable organizational tool that was capable of combining large and small business into a single administrative unit. Through this unique form of organization, big business produced small businesses and in doing so did, in fact, create a system that combined the economic efficiency and security of big business with the independence of small business. Although substantial debate continues on exactly how independent this new breed of small business owner really is, the economic benefits of the franchise system are indisputable. Recently, more than one-half of all independent businesses have failed within five years. In contrast, fewer than 5 percent of franchised businesses have suffered the same fate.

American Airlines Competes After Deregulation

RICHARD H. K. VIETOR

The first year of airline deregulation "was one of the most difficult and tumultuous years of our history," commented Bob Crandall. "As an industry, we seemed bent on giving away the store." But 1979 paled in comparison to the first half of 1980, when all but two of the major carriers ran operating losses. American's half-year loss of $121 million was the worst in the industry. Passenger traffic had slumped throughout the industry. The price of jet fuel had doubled. And intense competition for key routes, with wild discounting of fares, had squeezed yields and forced load factors below the break-even point, turning the industry's bottom line red.

Not all of these problems could be attributed to deregulation. Like the previous period of airline crisis, macroeconomic conditions had a significant effect. In fact, without the managerial freedoms afforded by deregulation, airline industry performance might well have been worse at this time.

On the supply side, the second oil shock had a devastating impact on costs. The Iranian Revolution broke out just as deregulation was initiated. Between October 1978 and July 1980, crude oil prices increased from $12.45 to $30.00 per barrel; the price of jet fuel increased from 40 to 90 cents a gallon. In 1979 the domestic trunk airlines together spent $5.9 billion for fuel—about 25 percent of total operating costs. With the general inflation rate at 10.1 percent in 1980, airline labor costs reached astronomical levels: $26,691 per employee. . . . And with the prime rate at 19 percent, acquisition of new aircraft became prohibitively expensive. On the demand

Richard H. K. Vietor, *Contrived Competition: Regulation and Deregulation in America* (Cambridge, Mass.: The Belknap Press of Harvard University Press, 1994), pp. 57–61, 64–66, 68–69, 72–77. Copyright © 1994 by the President and Fellows of Harvard College. Reprinted by permission of the publisher.

side, a recession induced by the tight money policy of the Federal Reserve Board cut GNP growth to an annual rate of –0.7 percent. Airline passenger traffic dropped 4 percent. . . .

To make matters worse, the major carriers were grossly unprepared for deregulation. At the very least, they had expected a gradual, semiorderly process. So had Congress. But neither the Civil Aeronautics Board nor the host of new entrants followed the plan. Neither, for that matter, did the established carriers themselves.

Before the end of 1978, the board had begun reallocating dormant route authorities and had adopted a zone for fares, ranging from 70 percent below existing standard fares to 10 percent above. In 1979 the board implemented simplified procedures for route abandonment, approved some mergers . . . and virtually eliminated entry restrictions. "By the spring of 1980," claimed the board, "carriers were essentially free to determine the routes they served and the prices they charged."

New entry by low-cost, no-frills, point-to-point carriers caused immediate shock. Former intrastates, charters, commuter airlines, and new ventures all sensed tremendous opportunities to make money, entering ill-served intercity markets or high-density markets where trunk carriers had maintained high prices. With low overhead, nonunion labor, used aircraft, leased ground facilities, and few extraneous services, these companies put intense competitive pressure, at least in the short run, on the established carriers. . . .

In May 1979 the "Transcon Wars" broke out. Previously, discount-price promotions such as American's Super Saver had been carefully limited by restrictive conditions. But now, World Airways touched off an unrestricted price war with a one-way fare of $108 between New York and California. "The top two transcontinental markets (New York–Los Angeles and New York–San Francisco)," explained Tom Plaskett, American's vice-president for marketing, "represented about $750 million in revenues for the industry." With American's share of this at $250 million, these were "the highest stakes in the deregulation saga."

Next Capitol entered, and TWA expanded the war to the "semitranscon" market, announcing a fare of $119 for Chicago–San Francisco. When American matched this in March 1980, TWA cut its price to $99. Pricing "madness" went from bad to worse when Eastern tried breaking into the "transcon" market with a one-way unrestricted fare of $99. At this point, entry skirmishes were transformed into internecine warfare. All of the major carriers—American, United, and TWA—matched Eastern's offer, but World reduced its fare to $88. Similar fares spread to the "peripheral transcon" markets of Boston, Washington, and Philadelphia.

Now the majors themselves began dropping unprofitable routes and entering the potentially profitable routes of their competitors. This put pressure on the more profitable, business-traveler segment of the market, forcing a dilution of yield (effective revenue per revenue-passenger mile), in turn raising break-even load factors. . . . As yields fell, break-even load factors rose; American's reached 66.8 percent by mid-1980.

Acceleration of "hubbing" (concentrating connecting flights at a particular airport) was a related and immediate competitive response to deregulation. This practice had been used to a limited extent since the 1960s, and increasingly since the first oil shock had intensified pressure on operating costs. Both Delta and Eastern had developed significant "hub" operations at Atlanta; United at Chicago; American at Dallas;

and Allegheny Airlines (now US Air) at Pittsburgh. Regulation, however, had severely constrained the use of hub-and-spoke route structure as an operating strategy. . . .

The hub-and-spoke route arrangement offered airlines several advantages. Most obvious were the economies of scale achieved by focusing labor resources and surface assets at a single point and increasing their utilization. . . .

Not until deregulation were these economic efficiencies fully recognized, much less compelling. But after receiving route flexibility, the major carriers began shifting toward more concentrated hub operations. As they did so, they also began to realize the operational, competitive, and strategic aspects as well. And those that moved fastest, like American, benefited most by gaining invaluable first-mover advantages.

But "in a deregulated world," as Robert Crandall put it, "an airline's route system is essentially determined by its fleet composition," at least in the short run. This shift away from long, nonstop, city-pair routes only highlighted the inappropriateness and inefficiency of existing aircraft fleets. Most of the larger trunk carriers were now stuck with aged, fuel-inefficient fleets of diverse aircraft types, including too few smaller aircraft and too many widebodies. As Crandall explained this situation in 1980, "The established carriers bought their airplanes years ago expecting to operate them over a stable and franchised route system developed within the structure of Civil Aeronautics Board regulations. Critical decisions about which airplanes to buy, and in what numbers, were based on marketing assumptions that seemed reasonable at the time. They could not—and did not—anticipate the free-for-all we have today." . . .

. . . [I]n June 1980, American . . . reported a six-month operating loss of $121 million. American was in even worse shape than most of its principal rivals. Its route structure was the most fragmented. It served 120 cities in five very different types of markets: transcontinental, northeast business, Dallas and Chicago connecting hubs, Caribbean vacation islands, and miscellaneous city pairs. Its average trip length was among the highest in the industry (a problem only when load factor was low).

American's fleet, Crandall also knew, "was less fuel efficient than the fleet of almost any other carrier." American's seating configuration was the least dense of all the major carriers, and it was operating under a disadvantageous, long-term fuel contract. Older engine technology, too many engines per aircraft, and inappropriate route assignments all contributed to American's problem. . . .

American, of course, had planned to modernize this fleet. Casey had already placed a firm order for thirty Boeing 767s (with options on twenty more). These twin-engine aircraft would deliver 33 percent greater fuel efficiency (than the 707s), had 199 seats, and used state-of-the-art technology, allowing two rather than three pilots. Casey had placed another order for fifteen 757s, pending financial arrangements.

These commitments, together with investments in surface equipment, gates, and terminals, added up to $5.7 billion over the next five years. This much capital was more than American could earn in the new competitive environment or raise from conventional sources. The company would need a 5 percent operating margin and annual growth of 24 percent to support borrowing of this magnitude. Since this was unlikely, some sort of cutbacks on modernization, together with dramatically new sources of capital, would be necessary.

American's labor costs and productivity posed an even greater comparative disadvantage. Its wage cost per employee was higher than average, while its productivity (revenue-ton miles per employee) was lower than average. About 59 percent of its employees were represented by labor unions. The Transport Workers Union, representing 11,000 people in maintenance, stores, flight instruction, and dispatch, was the largest. Nearly 4,000 pilots were organized in a company union (the Allied Pilots Association), but flight engineers were organized separately (the Flight Engineers International, an AFL-CIO affiliate). American's 5,600 flight attendants, renowned for their high-quality service, were represented by the Association of Professional Flight Attendants.

American's contracts provided comparatively high wages and extensive work rules. Under earlier management regimes, neither had been priorities. For flight crews, work rules (backed by "safety") and seniority limited "stick time"—the time pilots actually worked at flying airplanes—to about forty-four hours a month, and made flexible scheduling difficult. Similarly, work hours for flight attendants had declined to about fifty-three per month. Especially problematic was the contract negotiated with the Transport Workers Union that prohibited part-time work or any significant job crossover. Thus, underutilized tractor drivers could not assist with baggage handling, which in turn was separate from cabin preparation, refueling, and so on.

Despite its severe problems, American had a few competitive advantages, or potential advantages: size (it was the second largest company, after United), dominance in some of the most important routes, elaborate training facilities and a well-trained work force, a tradition of and reputation for service, and a strong computerized reservation system. In the early months of competition, American had managed to hold customers, relative to most of its competitors. . . . American's problem was not that it couldn't sell its services; it just couldn't make any money doing so. Its problem, clearly, was cost.

Between June and October 1980, American's management decided what to do. The "Profit Improvement Plan" was a short-term strategy for restructuring, consonant with a longer-term goal of remaining a viable, full-service, national airline. Its five parts addressed fleet, route structure, fuel and other operating costs, service, and marketing. As it unfolded over the next eighteen months, this prosaic plan turned out to be a necessary but insufficient purgative.

Crandall grounded the 707s. These fifty-three aircraft had been scheduled for phasing out over the subsequent four years, but they were losing money each time they took off. This action (taken over the next few months) effectively reduced American's fleet by 22 percent. Acquisition of some used 727-200s from Braniff left American with a net capacity reduction of about 11 percent. This decision—to shrink the airline—was a drastic step . . . although its effect would be less severe now that price competition was permitted. At the same time, Casey had to cancel the 757 order, since financing was clearly unavailable. . . .

. . . Now, with the reduction in its fleet and the regulatory flexibility to abandon routes, American had the opportunity to reconfigure its route system into a more efficient, hub-and-spoke network.

The issue, from a route-planning perspective, was whether to expand the Dallas–Fort Worth hub, with the expense and operating difficulties that would entail, or focus on Chicago, or develop a hub in some other city. American's operating skills had already been challenged by its nineteen-aircraft complex. Wesley Kaldahl, American's chief planner, took a careful look at the economies of scale and scope, the available cities, airport gates and weather conditions, traffic patterns and demographic trends, and, above all, at competitors' systems. Delta provided the yardstick. The Civil Aeronautics Board had given Delta many routes in the southeast that the company had organized around a hub at Atlanta. With a forty-two-plane complex, Delta could spread gate- and surface-operating costs over 1,764 city pairs—nearly four times as many as American's largest complex. Revenue generation from additional connectivity worked the same way.

Once the economies of hubbing were completely clear, the other issues fell into place. The Dallas–Fort Worth Airport was the largest in the United States. . . . Kaldahl recommended a major expansion, focusing 50 percent of American's traffic at the Dallas–Fort Worth "Superplex." The number of transcontinental and semi-transcontinental nonstop flights was reduced; two dozen miscellaneous routes, nine Mexican routes, and six more northeast business routes were discontinued. But through Dallas–Fort Worth, twenty-two new destinations would be served, increasing city-pair combinations from 655 to 1,519 and hub departures to 213 daily. . . .

Reducing the size of the fleet, combined with restructuring the routes, made possible significant cost savings, through more efficient use of flight crews, ground personnel, and equipment. Layoffs, combined with an early retirement program, reduced airline personnel from 41,000 to 35,500 by the end of 1981. Labor productivity, in every job classification, was reviewed and improved, to the extent allowed by labor contracts and the need to maintain good customer service. . . .

To address the fuel problem, long-term contracts were renegotiated as soon as possible. While seating density was increased, weight was reduced by using new slimline seating designs. The company initiated other weight-reduction efforts, as well as more fuel-efficient flying and fuel-loading procedures. It modified and repainted its aircraft to reduce drag, and in some instances retrofitted them with new fuel-efficient engines.

Even with its cost-control efforts, American could not compete on cost. Since competition tended to drive air travel toward a commodity basis, American had to differentiate itself and segment the market. It needed to retain nondiscretionary business travelers through its hub, at premium fares, minimizing or redefining the service degradation implicit in hub (rather than nonstop) operations. Brand loyalty somehow had to be promoted. At the same time, however, American needed to fill empty seats with discretionary travelers—students and vacationers—using discount fares. Any revenue dilution across fare classes had to be avoided.

The competitive aspects of hubbing, together with American's service and information advantages, led American's marketing managers logically, but not easily, to adopt a brilliant three-pronged marketing plan that was clear by 1981. The plan's strategic components were traffic control, product distribution, and service.

Competition made traffic control essential; hubbing made it possible. Only by gathering traffic and retaining control from end to end could American afford to serve smaller, lower-density markets. . . .

Pricing was the other aspect of traffic control. A more differentiated and flexible price structure, managed by SABRE, could help maximize revenue and fill seats. Peak-load prices needed to be higher than off-peak—daily, weekly, and seasonally. Promotional pricing needed to be targeted to each type of discretionary traveler, but with sufficient restrictions to prevent business travelers from crossing over. To compete with new entrants such as People Express, American developed the Ultimate

Super Saver—a fare that matched People's lowest, but with a precision that prevented dilution of other markets. SABRE's programmers worked closely with American's marketing and route-planning people to enhance SABRE's capabilities. Before long, the system was indeed able to manage this more complex fare structure, allocating seats to five different categories and shifting allocations on a daily basis.

SABRE not only facilitated the pricing aspects of traffic control; it soon became the industry's largest, most sophisticated distribution system. Even before deregulation, the importance of independent travel agencies had been growing. But the extraordinary instability of prices and schedules after 1978 made this channel a necessity for the perplexed traveler. By 1981, the airlines were deriving 63 percent of their traffic from travel agencies. . . .

Service was the least innovative piece of American's marketing plan, but still played an important role. Since American continued to target business travelers, its service had to be as good as or better than that of the other carriers, especially its archrival, United. Reservations, ticketing, advance boarding passes, check-in, baggage handling, in-flight services, and on-time flights would continue to be operating priorities. Cost cutting would not be allowed to interfere with these. . . .

To cap the marketing plan, American had been studying various schemes to create brand loyalty among frequent flyers, to wed them to the hub. Throughout the spring of 1980, discussions among people in marketing, operations, and information systems gradually focused on a "loyalty fare," aimed at frequent flying. It could not be a simple discount, however, since that could dilute revenue and was too easily matched by competitors. It had to shift customers from competitors to American, and then lock them in. Making use of SABRE's ability to "track" customers with an assigned number and mileage record, the "AAdvantage" program was conceived.

AAdvantage, tested in the second half of 1980 and rolled out in 1981, gave mileage credits for flying American that could accumulate to "award" levels, where a customer became eligible for free round-trip tickets. . . .

. . . AAdvantage proved to be a huge success. With a two-year lead over competitors, the program enabled American to capture a significant, one-time share change and eventually enrolled more than 6.3 million subscribers. For the airline industry as a whole, competitive frequent-flyer programs would become one of the many unanticipated consequences of deregulation—a nightmare of elaborate bookkeeping, "award wars," demand for first-class seats, and a free-travel liability equivalent to at least $1 billion by 1988.

This first phase of American's strategic and structural adjustment was designed to eliminate losses. But even before it was fully implemented, Crandall had begun to implement a second, longer-term program to make American Airlines a successful competitor in the unregulated market. As it unfolded between 1981 and 1985, this phase of adjustment had three key elements: labor productivity enhancement and cost reduction, fleet modernization, and expansion and reentry into eastern markets.

Even before deregulation, Crandall knew that American's labor costs and restrictive work rules posed a serious competitive problem. He also understood that labor's attitudes and practices were deeply entrenched; there was little he could do right away. American's contracts would not expire for at least two years, and management had no particular leverage. In fact, American's service-oriented strategy made it especially important that Crandall achieve change "without a sledgehammer."

In 1981, starting with his "President's Conferences" (a tour of cities in which he met with local employees), Crandall began an intense campaign to educate employees about the implications of competition. . . . This strategy of approaching employees directly, rather than through union channels, was designed to bypass bureaucratic resistance to contract renegotiations. Crandall took aim at work rules, rather than at wage or benefit give-backs, to minimize the impact on employee relations. He believed that when employees really understood what competition was about, they would see the need to concede some work rules.

In the spring of 1982, Crandall's message began to take a sharper edge, comparing the potential benefits of work-rule changes with the unattractive alternatives—namely, a significant capacity reduction, grounding a portion of the fleet (the 727-100s), closing a significant number of stations, or shutting down the airline. For each alternative, employees were presented with detailed quantitative estimates of cash flow, cost savings, and layoffs. The deep recession that struck in 1982, with record-high levels of unemployment, helped make these alternatives painfully real. Management's alternatives were a growing airline and three concrete benefits for employees: guaranteed job security, profit sharing, and early retirement.

At this point American Airlines made its first tentative approach to the unions, starting with the Transport Workers Union, American's largest. The union was asked to allow cross-utilization of employees and part-time work. Pilots were asked for fifty-five hours of productive flying time each month, and flight attendants were asked to reopen contract negotiations on productivity gains. For most of 1982, American made little progress with union officials, who clearly viewed Crandall and his work-rule initiative as a major threat. . . .

By the end of 1983, the company had negotiated new contracts with the flight attendants and pilots, including significant work-rule gains and a two-tier wage structure. In Crandall's words, this virtually created an "airline within an airline." As American expanded, new employees would start at a much lower, "market wage," reflecting the realities of competition rather than the era of regulation. New entrants, with nonunion labor, would no longer be able (as one of American's executives put it), "to blow American out of the market based on cost."

Once American had succeeded in restructuring its labor costs and work rules, it was able to refocus on healthy expansion. And the timing was perfect. The economy had begun to recover late in 1983, and under the stimulus of lower prices the airline business was booming.

Now Crandall implemented the second part of his long-term strategy. In the spring of 1984, he startled the industry by ordering sixty-seven MD Super 80s, with a price-protected option on one hundred more—making this one of the largest orders in aviation history. The MD-80 . . . could deliver 32 percent lower operating costs (per seat-mile) than the 727-100. . . .

The previous year, American had acquired twenty of the MD-80s, to replace its oldest 727-100s. In order to keep its assembly line operating, McDonnell Douglas had agreed to an extremely favorable short-term lease rate, as well as an option for American to return the aircraft after five years without penalty, or to extend the lease for eighteen years. This not only made the deal affordable for American, but insured against the risk of technological obsolescence. Moreover, American found that the new aircraft performed extremely well. . . .

With the aircraft it needed, with its Dallas–Fort Worth and Chicago hubs expanded, with a dominant reservation system, and especially with a declining cost structure, American was ready for its third strategic thrust: a new hub. Throughout 1984 and the first half of 1985, Wes Kaldahl's planning group carefully studied the options for route expansion. As they saw it, there were at least six: (1) transcontinental nonstops, (2) West Coast business markets, (3) a hub for northeast business markets, (4) a third east-west hub, (5) a north-south hub in the East, and (6) Europe. . . .

Denver would give American complete market coverage in the West, with no strong hubs nearby. This could, however, precipitate a confrontation with United, and possibly a price war with Frontier and Continental. . . . The combination of Nashville and Raleigh-Durham, on the other hand, offered a capacity of about thirty-five gates, a central location in the north-south markets of the East, and virtually no overlap with American's existing traffic. Competitively, Nashville and Raleigh-Durham straddled the two dominant hubs in the region: Charlotte (Piedmont) and Atlanta (Delta). . . .

In July 1985, American's board of directors approved the decision to open two new hubs, at Nashville and Raleigh-Durham. With this move, American had set a course to become the largest and most profitable domestic airline.

Inside Wal-Mart

SIMON HEAD

Throughout the recent history of American capitalism there has always been one giant corporation whose size dwarfs that of all others, and whose power conveys to the world the strength and confidence of American capitalism itself. At mid-century General Motors was the undisputed occupant of this corporate throne. But from the late 1970s onward GM shrank in the face of superior Japanese competition and from having outsourced the manufacture of many car components to independent suppliers. By the millennium GM was struggling to maintain its lead over Ford, its long-standing rival.

With the technology boom of the 1990s, the business press began writing about Microsoft as if it were GM's rightful heir as the dominant American corporation. But despite its worldwide monopoly as the provider of software for personal computers, Microsoft has lacked the essential qualification of size. In *Fortune*'s 2004 listings of the largest U.S. corporations, Microsoft ranks a mere forty-sixth, behind such falling stars as AT&T and J. C. Penney. However, *Fortune*'s 2004 rankings also reveal the clear successor to GM, Wal-Mart. In 2003 Wal-Mart was also *Fortune*'s "most admired company."

Wal-Mart is an improbable candidate for corporate gorilla because it belongs to a sector, retail, that has never before produced America's most powerful companies. But Wal-Mart has grown into a business whose dominance of the corporate world rivals GM's in its heyday. With 1.4 million employees worldwide, Wal-Mart's workforce is now larger than that of GM, Ford, GE, and IBM combined. At $258 billion in 2003, Wal-Mart's annual revenues are 2 percent of U.S. GDP, and eight

Simon Head, "Inside the Leviathan," *New York Review of Books* (December 16, 2004): 80–81, 85–86, 88–89. Copyright © 2004 NYREV, Inc. Reprinted with permission.

times the size of Microsoft's. In fact, when ranked by its revenues, Wal-Mart is the world's largest corporation. . . .

Within the corporate world Wal-Mart's preeminence is not simply a matter of size. In its analysis of the growth of U.S. productivity, or output per worker, between 1995 and 2000—the years of the "new economy" and the high-tech bubble on Wall Street—the McKinsey Global Institute has found that just over half that growth took place in two sectors, retail and wholesale, where, directly or indirectly, Wal-Mart "caused the bulk of the productivity acceleration through ongoing managerial innovation that increased competition intensity and drove the diffusion of best practice." This is management-speak for Wal-Mart's aggressive use of information technology and its skill in meeting the needs of its customers.

In its own category of "general merchandise," Wal-Mart has taken a huge lead in productivity over its competitors, a lead of 44 percent in 1987, 48 percent in 1995, and still 41 percent in 1999, even as competitors began to copy Wal-Mart's strategy. Thanks to the company's superior productivity, Wal-Mart's share of total sales among all the sellers of "general merchandise" rose from 9 percent in 1987 to 27 percent in 1995, and 30 percent in 1999, an astonishing rate of growth which recalls the rise of the Ford Motor Company nearly a century ago. McKinsey lists some of the leading causes of Wal-Mart's success. For example, its huge, ugly box-shaped buildings enable Wal-Mart "to carry a wider range of goods than competitors" and to "enjoy labor economies of scale."

McKinsey mentions Wal-Mart's "efficiency in logistics," which make it possible for the company to buy in bulk directly from producers of everything from toilet paper to refrigerators, allowing it to dispense with wholesalers. McKinsey also makes much of the company's innovative use of information technology, for example its early use of computers and scanners to track inventory, and its use of satellite communications to link corporate headquarters in Arkansas with the nationwide network of Wal-Mart stores. Setting up and fine-tuning these tracking and distribution systems has been the special achievement of founder Sam Walton's (the "Wal" of Wal-Mart) two successors as CEO, David Glass and the incumbent Lee Scott.

Throughout its forty-year existence Wal-Mart has also shown considerable skill in defining its core customers and catering to their needs. One of Sam Walton's wisest decisions was to locate many of his earliest stores in towns with populations of fewer than five thousand people, communities largely ignored by his competitors. This strategy gave Wal-Mart a near monopoly in its local markets and enabled the company to ride out the recessions of the 1970s and 1980s more successfully than its then larger competitors such as K-Mart and Sears. Wal-Mart has also been skillful in providing products that appeal to women with low incomes.

Although her book *Selling Women Short* is a powerful indictment of how Wal-Mart has treated its female employees, Liza Featherstone nonetheless acknowledges the lure of the Wal-Mart store for female shoppers, who delight "in spending as little as possible, all in one place." At a Wal-Mart "supercenter"

> you can change a tire, buy groceries for dinner, and get a new pair of shoes and some yard furniture—a set of errands that once would have required a long afternoon of visits to far-flung merchants.

All these innovations contribute to Wal-Mart's remarkable productivity record, and this in turn has opened up another major source of competitive advantage for the company, its policy of "Every Day Low Prices" ("EDLP"), which makes it possible for it to undersell its competitors by an average of as much as 14 percent. Here the picture darkens because Wal-Mart's ability to keep prices low depends not just on its productivity but also on its ability to contain, or even reduce, costs, above all labor costs. As Sam Walton wrote in his memoirs:

> You see: no matter how you slice it in the retail business, payroll is one of the most important parts of overhead, and overhead is one of the most crucial things you have to fight to maintain your profit margin.

One of the ways to win this particular fight is to make sure that the growth of labor's productivity well exceeds the growth of its wages and benefits, which has in fact been the dominant pattern for U.S. corporations during the past decade.

From a corporate perspective, this is a rosy outcome. When the productivity of labor rises and its compensation stagnates, then, other things being equal, the cost of labor per unit of output will fall and profit margins will rise. Wal-Mart has carried this strategy to extremes. While its workforce has one of the best productivity records of any U.S. corporation, it has kept the compensation of its rank-and-file workers at or barely above the poverty line. As of last spring, the average pay of a sales clerk at Wal-Mart was $8.50 an hour, or about $14,000 a year, $1,000 below the government's definition of the poverty level for a family of three. Despite the implied claims of Wal-Mart's current TV advertising campaign, fewer than half—between 41 and 46 percent—of Wal-Mart employees can afford even the least-expensive health care benefits offered by the company. To keep the growth of productivity and real wages far apart, Wal-Mart has reached back beyond the New Deal to the harsh, abrasive capitalism of the 1920s.

At a retail business such as Wal-Mart the methods used to increase employee productivity differ from those used "on the line" at a manufacturing plant producing automobiles or computers, where work can be rigorously defined, and higher productivity can be achieved by simplifying tasks so that they are performed more quickly. At Wal-Mart most employees are not engaged in single, repetitive tasks. The location and timing of work at a Wal-Mart store is determined by the flow of goods entering the store through the back entrance, and the flow of customers entering the store through the front.

Neither of these flows is constant or entirely predictable, and workers may have to be moved from one task to another as the flows change. An employee may begin the day by unloading and unpacking goods at the receiving dock; she may then transfer to shifting goods from the dock into the store; then to stacking goods on shelves or in special displays; and then finally to registering the sale of goods at one of the many checkout counters and making change. . . .

Since there is no assembly line at Wal-Mart its senior management uses blunter methods to achieve higher levels of productivity from the workforce. These methods are governed by a simple principle: when deciding how many workers to employ, Wal-Mart management relies on a formula guaranteeing that the growth of the labor budget will lag behind the growth in store sales, so that every year there will be more work for each employee to do. . . .

The harshness of the working conditions at Wal-Mart helps to account for the exceptionally high employee turnover at the company. Some 50 percent of Wal-Mart workers employed at the beginning of 2003 had left the company by the end of the year. At the retailer Costco, where employees are better treated, turnover in 2003 was just 24 percent. But Wal-Mart's harshness is not simply a consequence of management's efforts to extract maximum productivity from its workforce at minimum cost. There are also employees and groups of employees that management particularly mistrusts, and these have often been subjected to relentless harassment. Hundreds of employees have testified against Wal-Mart in the many class-action lawsuits brought against the corporation, and their sworn depositions provide a detailed account of what it is like to work at Wal-Mart day by day, even hour by hour.

Perhaps the best evidence we have of this selective harassment is to be found in the depositions of 115 women who have testified against Wal-Mart in the *Dukes* case, a class-action lawsuit brought in 2001 by six female employees and named for one of the six, Betty Dukes, a Wal-Mart employee in Pittsburg, California. Most of the witnesses in the case have since either left Wal-Mart or been fired, but Betty Dukes herself continues to work as a greeter at the Pittsburg Wal-Mart. The suit, which alleges systematic discrimination by Wal-Mart both in the pay and promotion of women, is brought on behalf of 1.6 million female employees of Wal-Mart past and present, the largest civil rights case of its kind in U.S. history. On June 22, 2004, U.S. District Judge Martin Jenkins of San Francisco held that the *Dukes* lawsuit could proceed to trial, although a date has not been set. . . .

The *Dukes* case depositions show how ruthless and inventive Wal-Mart managers can be in keeping troublesome women in their place. To discipline the workforce, Wal-Mart managers can use a variety of formidable penalties and punishments. There are written reprimands in the form of "pink slips"; spoken reprimands in the form of "coachings"; "decision making days" when an employee must explain why he or she should not be fired; and, finally, summary dismissal. Women who inquire about promotion are often told they must conform to rules or qualifications that are invented on the spur of the moment and have never been required of male employees. Claudia Renati, a marketing specialist at a Roseville, California, Wal-Mart, was told by her boss that she could not join a management training course unless she could first prove to him that she could lift fifty-pound bags of dog food. "When I told him I could not repeatedly lift 50 pounds, he told me that there was nothing he could do for me." Renati was also told that she was not eligible for management training unless she was prepared to sell her house in Roseville and move immediately to Alaska. . . .

Wal-Mart has also set off a particularly destructive form of competition among corporations, which seek competitive advantage by pushing down the wages and benefits of employees. A clear example of this has been the conflict provoked by Wal-Mart's decision in 2002 to enter the southern California grocery market with forty of its "supercenters"—where the shopper can buy everything from tomatoes to deck furniture and spare tires. Although Wal-Mart has not yet opened any of these new stores, the response of California supermarkets, led by Safeway, has been to demand cuts in their employees' wages and benefits, with the cuts falling heavily on newly hired workers. This posed a serious threat to the supermarket employees, 70,000 of whom are members of the Union of Food and Commercial Workers (UFCW) and have benefited from its bargaining with employers. While a sales clerk at Wal-Mart earns only $8.50 an hour, a worker holding a similar job at Safeway or Albertson could earn $13 an hour along with full health care benefits. For employees that could make the difference between minimal financial security and a life spent scraping by on the poverty line.

After the UFCW called a large-scale strike against the Safeway stores last winter, two other retailers, Kroger and Albertsons, locked out their workforce—and replaced it with temporary employees—as a demonstration of support for Safeway even though their workers were not on strike themselves. Taking full advantage of their right to hire replacements for striking and nonstriking workers, the supermarket owners beat the Safeway strike and forced the UFCW to accept cuts in wages and benefits.

The failure of the California grocery strike, not to mention the history of labor relations at Wal-Mart, points to the urgent need for reform of labor law in the United States. Wal-Mart is a ferociously anti-union company, and the UFCW has yet to organize a Wal-Mart store. Every store manager at Wal-Mart is issued a "Manager's Toolbox to Remaining Union Free," which warns managers to be on the lookout for signs of union activity, such as "frequent meetings at associates' homes" or "associates who are never seen together . . . talking or associating with each other."

The "Toolbox" provides managers with a special hotline so that they can get in touch with Wal-Mart's Bentonville headquarters the moment they think employees may be planning to organize a union. A high-powered union-busting team will then be dispatched by corporate jet to the offending store, to be followed by days of compulsory anti-union meetings for all employees. In the only known case of union success at Wal-Mart, in 2000 workers at the meat-cutting department of a Texas Wal-Mart somehow managed to circumvent this corporate FBI, and voted to join the UFCW in an election certified by the National Labor Relations Board. A week later Wal-Mart closed down the meat-cutting department and fired the offending employees, both illegal acts under the National Labor Relations Act. The NLRB ordered Wal-Mart to reopen the department, reemploy the fired workers, and bargain with the union, but Wal-Mart has appealed the NLRB decision and the litigation continues.

Unions are needed at Wal-Mart for much the same reasons that they were needed at Ford and GM in the 1930s—to prevent the mistreatment of employees, and to obtain for them fair, living wages. Unions are also needed to curb the unedifying "race to the bottom" among corporations. If Wal-Mart had been a union company and its employees had the same wages and benefits as other California store employees, Safeway and Albertsons could not have used Wal-Mart's planned entry into the California market as an excuse to beat down employee wages and benefits.

As things stand now, the National Labor Relations Act, the toothless federal law governing the right to organize, allows union-busting corporations like Wal-Mart to break the law with virtual impunity. Since 1995 the U.S. government has issued sixty complaints against Wal-Mart at the National Labor Relations Board, citing the illegal firing of pro-union employees, as well as the unlawful surveillance and intimidation of employees. But under the present law persistent violators of government rules such as Wal-Mart are responsible only for restoring the lost pay of fired workers—in most cases, not more than a few thousand dollars—and these penalties do not increase with successive violations. So long as U.S. law makes it possible for Wal-Mart to crush efforts to organize unions it will continue to treat its more than a million workers shabbily, while the company no doubt continues to be celebrated in the business press as a model of efficient modern management.

FURTHER READING

Aleutta, Ken. *Media Man: Ted Turner's Improbable Empire* (2004).

Baughman, James L. *The Republic of Mass Culture: Journalism, Filmmaking, and Broadcasting in America Since 1941,* 2d ed. (1997).

Bell, Daniel. *The Coming of Post-Industrial Society: A Venture in Social Forecasting* (1973).

Birch, David L. *Job Creation in America: How Our Smallest Companies Put the Most People to Work* (1987).

Bluestone, Barry, and Bennett Harrison. *The Deindustrialization of America: Plant Closings, Community Abandonment, and the Dismantling of Basic Industry* (1982).

Caves, Richard E. *Creative Industries: Contracts Between Art and Commerce* (2000).

Ceruzzi, Paul E. *A History of Modern Computing,* 2d ed. (2003).

Chandler, Alfred D., Jr., and James W. Cortada, eds. *A Nation Transformed by Information: How Information Has Shaped the United States from Colonial Times to the Present* (2000).

Cherny, Lynn, et al., eds. *Wired Women: Gender and New Realities in Cyberspace* (1996).

Cortada, James W. *The Digital Hand: How Computers Changed the Work of American Manufacturing, Transportation, and Retail Industries* (2004).

Davis, Clark. *Company Men: White-Collar Life and Corporate Cultures in Los Angeles, 1892–1941* (2000).

Dyer, Davis. *TRW: Pioneering Technology and Innovation Since 1900* (1998).

Ensmenger, Nathan L. "From 'Black Art' to Industrial Discipline: The Software Crisis and the Management of Programmers." Ph.D. dissertation, University of Pennsylvania, 2001.

Fuchs, Victor R. *The Service Economy* (1968).

Gates, Bill, with Collins Hemingway. *Business @ the Speed of Thought: Using a Digital Nervous System* (1999).

Head, Simon. *The New Ruthless Economy: Work & Power in the Digital Age* (2003).

Kenny, Charles C. *Riding the Runaway Horse: The Rise and Decline of Wang Laboratories* (1992).

Kroc, Ray, and Robert Anderson. *Grinding It Out: The Making of McDonald's* (1977).

Light, Ivan, and Edna Bonacich. *Immigrant Entrepreneurs: Koreans in Los Angeles, 1965–1982* (1988).

Lubar, Steven D. *InfoCulture: The Smithsonian Book of Information Age Inventions* (1993).

Mason, David L. *From Buildings and Loans to Bail-Outs: A History of the American Savings and Loan Industry, 1831–1995* (2004).

McKenna, Christopher D. "The World's Newest Profession: Management Consultancy in the Twentieth Century." Ph.D. dissertation, The Johns Hopkins University, 2000.

O'Boyle, Thomas F. *At Any Cost: Jack Welch, General Electric, and the Pursuit of Profit* (1998).

Sobel, Robert. *RCA* (1986).

Vance, Sandra Stringer, and Roy V. Scott. *Wal-Mart: A History of Sam Walton's Retail Phenomenon* (1994).

Vietor, Richard H. K., and Davis Dyer, eds. *Telecommunications in Transition* (1986).

Wallace, James, and Jim Erickson. *Hard Drive: Bill Gates and the Making of the Microsoft Empire* (1992).

CHAPTER
15

American Business in the World,

1945–2005

At first glance, the worldwide economic shifts of the past sixty years seem dramatically new—and frightening. In the United States, the visible elements of the sea change known as "globalization" seem to portend the demise of the American way of life. How are we to interpret the rise of gargantuan ports like Miami and Long Beach, permanent and growing trade deficits, and the spread of sweatshops, part-time jobs, and outsourcing? Overseas, the questions are similar. What are we to make of multinational corporations like Disney and Wal-Mart, which inject American culture into distant markets? In 1999, historian William Leach observed in Country of Exiles *that globalization is dangerously eroding the sense of place that once anchored Americans to local communities and united them through a common national culture. Around the same time, political scientist Benjamin R. Barber, author of* Jihad vs. McWorld, *denounced global capitalism as a threat to democracy. To Leach, Barber, and like-minded analysts, globalization is breaking down national borders, making corporations more powerful than nation-states, and causing widespread cultural dislocation. In their eyes, globalization is a harmful force that needs to be curtailed.*

Other scholars see the recent wave of globalization as far less sinister, acknowledging that the global economy is the latest manifestation of a process that has been underway for centuries. People have always looked beyond their home territories, traveling to distant and exotic lands for the sake of expanding empires, religion, and commerce. For nearly fifteen centuries beginning around the birth of Christ, the Silk Route connected Europe, the Middle East, and China. In the 1500s, the first circumnavigation of the globe opened the entire world to explorers, colonizers, missionaries, and commercial adventurers. By the 1700s, trade networks linking five continents—the Americas, Europe, Asia, and Africa—had created a global market *for some products, setting the stage for the emergence of a* global economy. *In the eighteenth century, however, economic convergence was stymied by the lack of technologies, institutions, and financial instruments that could generate huge quantities of goods, truncate great distances, and operate across national boundaries.*

In Multinationals and Global Capitalism: From the Nineteenth to the Twenty-first Century *(2005), business historian Geoffrey Jones explains how a global market yielded to a global economy after 1800. Jones divides globalization into two periods, showing that the "first global economy" prospered until the outbreak of World War I, was partially restored in the 1920s, and collapsed after 1929. It was superseded by the "second global economy," which took shape after 1945 and flourished after 1980. Thousands of multinational enterprises—some giant firms and many smaller companies that own and control business in more than one country—played a key role in both waves of globalization. In Jones's account, multinationals are agents of economic change that may have positive or negative outcomes on economies. Successful firms learn to accommodate host cultures, to a greater or lesser extent. By diffusing brands and technologies, they also reshape societies.*

Jones's story about the rise and fall of the first global economy follows a clear outline. By the early 1800s, the industrializing western nations—England, the United States, Germany, and France—sought new markets for their products, raw materials for their factories, and food for their growing populations. Numerous factors, from reduced transportation costs to the implementation of the gold standard, further encouraged international trade and investment. Throughout the industrial world, many companies began to develop and sustain foreign investments. Between the 1880s and 1910s, multinationals grew in number, scale, and reach. Both foreign direct investment (FDI)—investment by a corporation that gives it management control over a business in another country—and foreign portfolio investment (FPI)—the purchase of overseas securities and bonds by individuals and firms—increased to a scale that was, in relative terms, not matched until the 1990s. This converged with huge trade flows and the substantial movement of immigrants to create the first global economy.

The two world wars and the Great Depression put the brakes on the first wave of globalization. According to Jones, World War I disrupted the international monetary system, shifting control of world finance from Great Britain to the United States and throwing Germany out of the mix. While this transition enabled the United States to play a greater role in the world economy, other factors contributed to a backlash. In the interwar years, nations licking wartime wounds adopted policies that dampened internationalism. The mobility of trade and capital was destroyed by exchange controls and protectionism, and the former integration of markets was reversed. As the first global economy dissolved, some American multinationals— Ford Motor Company, General Motors Corporation, Standard Oil of New Jersey, United Fruit Company, and others—continued to prosper overseas. However, the Great Depression sounded the death knell for the first global economy.

In this chapter, an excerpt from Jones's book, Multinationals and Global Capitalism, *explains the rise of the second global economy that dominates our lives today. As you read, take some time to evaluate the second global economy. What roles do the U.S. government and multinationals play? Have global firms "Americanized" the world, as suggested by Barber? How does Leach's theory about dislocation and homogeneity hold up?*

 ## D O C U M E N T S

In the first document, Henry R. Luce's business magazine, *Fortune*, puts forth its founder's vision about the proper goal for American business in the postwar years: advance industrial growth in the United States and abroad to win prosperity at home and freedom for the world. While denouncing communism, this 1947 article praises the General Agreement on Tariffs and Trade (GATT) as the harbinger of a new era. How does *Fortune*'s approach compare with the *Magazine of Wall Street*'s 1938 analysis in

Chapter 11? Who are *Fortune*'s heroes and villains? In *Fortune*'s view, how will the postwar exportation of American capital and management expertise differ from earlier efforts along these lines?

As one of America's older industries, steel was on shaky ground by the 1960s. Like textiles and glass, steel suffered a blow during the Great Depression followed by a boom during World War II. By 1968, however, mounting troubles prompted the trade journal *Steel* to probe the crisis (Document 2). What is *Steel*'s position on America's "basic industries"? How did steel manufacturers make technological choices in the 1950s? What was the impact? How does the magazine depict labor unions, government, and international trade?

During the 1960s, John F. Kennedy's administration pressed for trade liberalization by lobbying GATT for more tariff reductions. From 1964 to 1967, the "Kennedy Round" of trade negotiations involved more than fifty nations. After the deliberations, the National Industrial Conference Board (NICB) surveyed the international business community on the new agreement (Document 3). Founded in 1916, the NICB served as research institute and information clearing-house for major American corporations. How do the executives interviewed by the NICB react to the reduction of trade barriers? How do the organization's views on international trade compare with the steel industry's perspective, found in Document 2?

As more U.S. companies sought international markets in the postwar years, American managers discovered the challenges of doing business in a cross-cultural context. Maxwell Gordon was one such executive. A scientist-manager at pharmaceutical giant Bristol-Myers during the 1970s, Gordon had broad responsibility for acquiring potential products through cooperative research and licensing agreements. In Document 4, Gordon recalls his experience negotiating licenses with companies and research institutions in Japan and the Soviet Union. How did cultural conventions in the host country affect the negotiations? How did American expectations shape the deliberations?

Another major problem of the mid-1980s was record agricultural surpluses. In 1986, *Time* magazine studied the situation and the inadequate solutions offered during the period (Document 5). What agricultural products are specifically affected, and what others are omitted from the discussion? Where are small farmers in this picture? How is it possible that the United States is importing more agricultural products than it is exporting?

During the 1990s, globalization became a hot topic among politicians, academics, environmentalists, labor groups, and journalists. In many respects, globalization provided a new battleground for debates that had preoccupied Americans since the founding years of the republic: How far should capitalism reach, and how does international trade affect the notion of business's social responsibility?

The debate over globalization pitted the advocates of free-market ideology, emphasizing business as the driving economic force, against the proponents of the progressive tradition, stressing the continued need for government mediation. Questions revolved around classic issues of jobs, prices, and living standards and new concerns like environment and culture. By the mid-1990s, the mass media—newspapers, magazines, books, and cable news shows—discovered that globalization hit the right buttons with the public. Globalization had become the new economic system—and the new business buzzword.

Building his career in this context, journalist Thomas L. Friedman offered an interpretation of globalization that tried to balance both sides of the debate. In Document 6, Friedman outlines his now-famous "Golden Arches Theory" in the *New York Times* in 1996, laying the groundwork for his 1999 bestseller, *The Lexus and the Olive Tree*. What is the "Golden Arches Theory," and how does it explain globalization? How does Friedman's discussion of "Americanization" intersect with the ideas advanced by *Fortune* in Document 1?

Finally, Documents 7 and 8 present opposing points of view on the impact of the North American Free Trade Agreement (NAFTA), which liberalized trade between the United States, Canada, and Mexico during the mid-1990s. Putting globalization at the center of U.S. foreign policy, George Bush advocated NAFTA, and Bill Clinton made it law in 1993, creating the world's largest free trade zone on January 1, 1994. Clinton furthered the U.S. commitment to free trade in 1994 when he joined other international leaders to sign an agreement that abolished quotas, lowered tariffs, and created the World Trade Organization (WTO) to succeed GATT.

As instruments of globalization, NAFTA and the WTO sparked controversy. Once leaders defined the terms of these agreements, some Americans protested in the press and on the streets. NAFTA had an immediate effect on U.S. employment. By 1994, the nation had lost some 12,000 jobs in older manufacturing industries while gaining 130,000 new jobs in sectors that produced exports for the Mexican market. Thus as unemployment and the budget deficit declined, Clinton could point to NAFTA's success during negotiations over the WTO.

After a decade, Americans are beginning to reassess NAFTA's impact. Documents 7 and 8 present evidence compiled by the Economic Policy Institute (EPI), a Washington think tank, and the U.S. Department of Agriculture (USDA), respectively. The EPI offers statistics on jobs, while the USDA analyzes export trends. What challenges do these sources present to historians?

1. *Fortune* Urges Business to Export Capitalism and Democracy, 1947

If, as the editors of FORTUNE believe, the fate of world freedom hangs upon American response to the challenge of world need and world Communism, how and where shall we begin?

Our primary job, obviously and beyond argument, is to carry the Industrial Revolution forward at home. We shall win few converts to capitalism and democracy, and perhaps not even keep them for ourselves, unless an overwhelming majority of us are content with the kind of lives that they make possible. And even if Marx and Lenin and Stalin had never been born, the path of the U.S. toward greater and more stable prosperity would still clearly lie in the direction of increasing world trade.

The prosperity of the world, as we discovered in the 1930's, rests on our economic vigor: our ability to buy, to sell, to lend, to invest. The Russians are counting on a U.S. depression to weaken our will and our ability to intervene for freedom in Europe and elsewhere. And the world's crying need today is not for our dollars but for our production; our dollars are useless unless there are goods to be bought with them. . . .

At Geneva, Under Secretary of State Will Clayton and his staff are laboring with representatives of seventeen other nations to scale down world trade barriers and create an International Trade Organization to keep those barriers within reasonable bounds. Success in diminishing these controls and resuming a freer flow of world trade will open the way for the greatest contribution that the U.S. can make toward stemming the Communist revolution. For world prosperity cannot be restored by

"The U.S. Opportunity," *Fortune* 35, no. 6 (June 1947): 83–85, 187, 192. Copyright 1947 *Time* Inc. Reprinted by permission.

governments alone, unless the world is to yield to the Communist philosophy of state control. The real U.S. job of re-establishing private enterprise firmly in the world's regard must, by definition, be done by U.S. private enterprisers.

The U.S. must lend some of its capital and its capital goods, to be sure. But it must also, if it is really to lead the way to world freedom, lend the world some of its industrial know-how. Americans with the needed knowledge and resourcefulness must go over the earth, as investors and managers and engineers, as makers of mutual prosperity, as missionaries of capitalism and democracy.

From Mexico to Arabia

This is no utopian dream; American businessmen are doing it now. The classic current example is the development of the Middle East's vast oil deposits by U.S. oil companies. . . . Communists are busily suggesting that the Truman Doctrine is nothing but another example of "dollar imperialism": a bold plot to let U.S. capitalists, at the point of U.S. guns, plunder the riches of a few small, primitive, helpless nations. The fact that Soviet Russia recently tried to grab some Middle Eastern oil through an attempted coup in Azerbaijan is, like all such facts, conveniently ignored. And this time the Communist propaganda job is relatively easy; except perhaps for "munitions," no word more vividly suggests sinister international plotting by greedy titans than "oil." Americans are particularly vulnerable; the sorry history of U.S. oil adventuring in Mexico still sits uneasily on the national conscience.

These are the suspicions. Let us examine the facts.

The story of Mexican oil epitomizes almost all of the worst that can be said about American business enterprise abroad. Early in this century a number of U.S. oil companies took advantage of Mexican ignorance and need to acquire Mexican oil lands for a fraction of their worth. They saw to it, with every device at their command, that Mexico kept little of the riches they took from the Mexican earth. When mere bribing and buying of Mexican politicians was not enough, they helped finance a revolution. The exploiters (including great Standard of New Jersey) flouted Mexican laws and did little to improve their workers' health or education or enjoyment of living. As a result, they poisoned U.S.-Mexican relations for three decades, created a bitter distrust of the U.S. that still exists throughout Latin America, and in the end lost their holdings through expropriation. Standard of New Jersey's loss was $22 million, plus hoped-for profits. Its only gain was a valuable lesson in world citizenship.

This is what the Communists are talking about. It makes potent propaganda. . . . Just as Mexico epitomizes the worst of the past, so the operations of U.S. oilmen in the Middle East illustrate at its best the new spirit of American enterprise abroad, the spirit of *mutual* benefit.

Today a group of U.S. oil companies, organized as Aramco (Arabian American Oil Co.) and prospectively including Standard of New Jersey, is preparing to double its $150-million investment in Saudi Arabian oil production. The equation is spectacularly simple. The Arabs have the oil, but were helpless to get at it, or even find it. The Americans found the oil and have the money, the equipment, and the technical knowledge and experience to build and operate the necessary wells, pipelines, refineries, tankers, and a deepwater port. Result, if all goes well: the oil companies can supply the increasing demands of their European and Asiatic markets (Russia can buy as freely and cheaply as anyone else), conserve war-depleted Western Hemisphere oil deposits for Western Hemisphere use, and make money. The golden flood of royalties into King Ibn Saud's depleted treasury, at 22 cents a barrel, may swell to some $100,000 a day.

Some Americans suspect that the blessings of their country's gadget-ridden civilization are of doubtful benefit to simpler societies. But the realities of Arabian life are considerably different from the Hollywood version of it. Arab tribesmen and their children, ridden by ancient poverty, filth, malnutrition, disease, and illiteracy, are encountering their first modern schools and hospitals, new housing, new foods, modern sanitary methods—all supplied by Aramco. American royalties and wages are being used to buy American power generators, automobiles, radios, refrigerators, and candy.

All this is only a beginning. The Arabs, said the London *Economist* recently, "should be offered the resources of Western technique in making their deserts once more blossom like the rose. Western democracy claims that it stands for a synthesis of enterprise, forethought, and trusteeship. It will never have a better chance to prove its case." Aramco executives earnestly agree. The first of King Ibn Saud's irrigation projects, supervised in the beginning by Aramco engineers, has already restored 3,000 desert acres to fertility.

Why this dramatic change of policy from early Mexican days? Pure altruism? No. Self-interest? Certainly. But enlightened self-interest; a change of heart has accompanied, if it did not precede, the change of policy. The first article of the capitalist faith is that men do learn by experience that they best serve their own self-interest, including their personal happiness, by sharing the benefits of their enterprise. Aramco's managers expect to make a profit—but not at somebody else's expense.

American oilmen learned in Mexico that, in the long run, ruthless exploitation simply does not pay. They will not repeat that mistake. Standard of Jersey has learned in its worldwide operations in 115 countries that to give local people a stake in its prosperity, a direct stake in the management and directorship as well as in the labor of its subsidiaries, is the best means of ensuring its prosperity and stability. Standard has learned abroad, as it long ago learned at home, that well-fed, well-housed, well-clothed, healthy, educated workers are better workers, more productive, less likely to botch or sabotage the job. Standard has learned, too, that well-paid workers contribute directly to its prosperity and stability by buying more of its own products, more of its customers' goods. . . .

The Role of Policy

. . . [Only] a handful of U.S. corporations operate on the scale of the American oil companies in Saudi Arabia. Gigantic as it is, Aramco's problem is obviously simpler than most. It is dealing with a single natural resource in a country without onerous trade restrictions. It is so powerful that it can deal with that country almost as one government to another. Its joint resources, organization, and experience in foreign operations are tremendous; its component companies are accustomed to large risks and a long pull.

But the pattern . . . is one within which thousands of American businessmen must work if the U.S. is to win the world to capitalism and democracy. How can they do it? What, specifically, is the government's role in making their great adventure a success?

What every foreign trader needs most from the U.S. Government is a firm, consistent foreign policy, particularly as it affects the rights and interests of Americans abroad. This calls, in turn, for a revolutionary change, by the government and by the whole American people, in the traditional U.S. attitude toward foreign trade.

The British Government and people have long recognized that foreign trade is their lifeblood. They know that they must have it to prosper, or even to survive, on their little island. This is why young Britons have been eager to seek their fortunes abroad, and why the British Government has maintained a consistent policy in support of British business enterprises abroad, no matter what party was in power at home. This is why the whole spirit of the British Board of Trade and Foreign Office in regard to foreign trade is so different from that of the U.S. Commerce and State departments.

In colonial times, and in their early nationhood, Americans were foreign traders as eager and necessitous as the British. But as the great U.S. industrial plant was built, we turned away from the sea and came gradually to regard our foreign trade as nonessential, no more important to our national economy than "imported" knickknacks were to the well-to-do American who bought them. Economists knew that this was false, that the 10 per cent of our national income which resulted from foreign trade was essential to our prosperity. But most of us were engrossed in what was becoming the world's greatest free-trade area.

We know now that U.S. peace and prosperity are inseparable from the rest of the world's. Unlike the British, we do not and will not have to trade abroad just to keep on eating, so we are in little danger of imitating the less attractive aspects of old-time British imperialism. But in the direction in which our vital interest lies, the direction of mutual prosperity and freedom, American commercial policy must be as steadfast as ever Britain's was. The recent action of the Republican Congress in authorizing Will Clayton to carry on the Roosevelt-Hull reciprocal-tariff policy at Geneva was a heartening token to new U.S. consistency transcending partisanship. . . .

A New National Purpose.   A man could ask for many other things: a chance to mind his own business, to dig in his garden or lie in the sun without having to worry about the Koreans and the Azerbaijanis. No one could blame him for desiring such pleasures[;] all of us do. But the man who expects to enjoy them any time soon was born in the wrong century.

There have been, as a matter of fact, only a few years when Americans could, or wanted to, live for themselves alone. For nearly three centuries American life had a meaning and purpose beyond individual gain and individual pleasure. Our fathers believed that Providence had sent them into the wilderness to build not merely a new nation but a new kind of nation, one that would show the whole world how to be free *and* prosperous. Every American, whether he was clearing a patch in the forest or laying a railroad across the continent, could feel in his heart that while he sought his own fortune he was also serving that national purpose.

After the first world war, in which we grew to national maturity, we were offered a chance to lead the world, as well as point the way, toward freedom and prosperity. We refused it, and no American need look further than into his own heart to know the effect of that shirking on our national happiness. Now we have a second chance. If we accept the challenge of world need and world Communism not as misfortune but as an opportunity greater than any a nation has ever been offered, we may in time regain our fathers' sense of purpose and the peace of mind it gave them. We have the power; if we also have the will, we can turn our plight into the promise of a new life for mankind.

2. High Labor Costs and Foreign Competition Confound Steelmakers, 1968

The steel industry was once king. It was the leader of all industry.

Today it is not. Other industries are growing faster. Most others are more profitable.

But the industry is a leader in one respect. It is one of the first to feel the lash from the modern, growing industries of nations that are coming of age. Its problems suggest that the U.S. will not always be No. 1 on product and price.

This year, the world outside the U.S. can turn out 60 million tons more steel than it can use. And this excess will grow about 10 million tons a year for the next several years.

Imports could climb to such a height in the next five years that they might jeopardize more than half a million of the best paying jobs in the country. It could also mean the loss of a market for hundreds of supplier companies and the cutting out of more jobs. It could make other industries dependent on foreign sources for steel and materials know-how.

Other metalworkers are growing concerned as they see more and more of their home markets being lost to foreign manufacturers. The loss of a basic industry such as steel is certainly a national problem—not simply that industry's problem. The potential loss of other industries suggests that perhaps our entire economic system needs a reappraisal.

As the largest steel consuming nation, the U.S. is the prime target for the world's excess capacity.

And the market is receptive. One reason: "The price differential for domestic buyers between domestic and imported steel appears to be in a range of $20 to $25 (per ton)," concludes the steel imports study conducted for the Senate Committee on Finance and coordinated by Dr. Robert M. Weidenhammer. . . .

In ability to produce efficiently, U.S. steelmakers have maintained their edge. It takes fewer manhours to produce a ton of steel here than abroad. But we lag far behind in labor costs—or rather we are far in the lead. Our prosperous economy has raised wages, and our standard of living is high. The rub comes when we try to match other nations product for product. Too often we are priced out of the market. The trick is to be in a position to supply those items which are not made in the countries with lower cost structures.

But what do we do about a basic product that can neither be sold abroad nor in our own country because it is "overpriced"? Do we drop it from our production lines? Basic rules of international economics tell us this is the most efficient thing to do. But laws of self-preservation warn us that certain basic industries cannot be

---

"Steel's Fight for Survival," *Steel: The Metalworking Management Weekly* (June 17, 1968): 60, 62–65, 72–74.

allowed to fall by the wayside or the entire economy will become dependent on outside sources of supply.

The steel industry's illness raises still other questions that will be basic in the shaping of our economics and politics for years to come. Should our government, like others, aid ailing industries? Should our government place fewer restrictions on business and permit a no-holds-barred fight between free enterprise and other economic systems? Will the laws and customs designed for domestic business work in a world market?

How did the steel industry get into such a predicament? The trouble began at the close of World War II. The industry began scrapping some of the old equipment used through the war. But the postwar business boom caused a shortage of steel. The government threatened to build its own steel plants. The industry was forced to a decision on large scale expansion. "This was a difficult decision for the industry to make because during the years 1940–50 replacement costs of its facilities had more than doubled, and cash flow from legally permitted depreciation based on original costs was insufficient to replace outworn facilities," says the Weidenhammer report. "Profits had, therefore, been in part fictitious and taxed instead of being available for dividends or expansion."

Years of Critical Decisions

Because the stock market saw the truth about overstated profits, it couldn't be tapped for new funds. Depreciation reform was many years into the future. The industry was afraid of going farther into debt after the experience of the thirties. The only resource for obtaining the capital funds needed was to raise prices.

More pressure was put on the race for cash when the industry faced exhaustion of its chief iron ore source, the Mesabi Range. In the early fifties, the industry spent $5 billion for plants to beneficiate and pelletize lower grade ores and to develop new ore deposits as well as the elaborate transportation systems needed.

Because steel was so much in demand, producers found it paid to remain as production-minded as they had been during the war. They became "order takers" with the attitude "we'll ship it when we're ready."

In the early fifties, the industry was asked by government to expand capacity in the event the Korean War mushroomed. This prompted a critical decision. The industry was aware of the potential efficiencies needed here. It chose not to gamble on the new technology for this critical buildup.

Again in the midfifties steelmakers came to a critical point. They were forecasting a surge in demand in the sixties, says Alan Greenspan, president, Townsend Greenspan & Co., New York. They asked themselves, "Can we trust the new technologies?" Again they played it safe—a decision for which they are severely criticized today. "The risk mix pointed to staying with old technology," believes Mr. Greenspan.

Right Choice, Wrong Time

Although the industry may have made the right choice, the unfortunate thing is that it felt compelled to make any decision at that time. Forecasts of expanding demand failed to materialize. After the 1958 recession, steel consumption did not bounce back. Steel was caught in a materials battle the likes of which had never been seen. Aluminum for example, was coming of age. The steel industry cannot go blameless for its lack of vision, however. In sizing up the aluminum threat, one steel executive scoffed, "We measure production in tons, aluminum producers measure theirs in pounds."

Inevitable Import Problem

Another error occurred in sizing up the threat from abroad. However, there may have been little within the industry's grasp to use as a defense anyway. "The import problem was in the cards no matter what we would have spent," says the Rev. Fr. William Hogan, S.J., economist at Fordham University, New York.

The import problem came not only as the result of significantly lower prices on foreign steel but because of the inadequate supply of domestic steel during the labor negotiation periods. Users stocked heavily to protect themselves against a possible strike in 1959. Imports soared from 1.2 million tons in 1957 to 1.7 million in 1958 and 4.4 million in 1959.

That was the foot in the door. Since then imports have climbed to account for 1 out of every 8 tons consumed in this country. Each round of labor negotiations brings on a new spurt. This year, imports will reach 14 million to 15 million tons—and possibly more. . . .

Labor Troubles

"The growth of steel imports has to be largely laid to labor-management difficulties in the steel industry," says George S. Arneson, president, Vendo Co., Kansas City, Mo. "Many companies tried foreign steel for the first time when shortages, or possible shortages, appeared."

Labor costs have climbed faster than in other manufacturing industries. Since World War II, the steel industry's unit labor costs have increased 3.9% a year vs. 2% for all manufacturing.

The industry has also grown more and more capital intensive. The plant and equipment needed to generate a dollar of value added by manufacture has doubled in the postwar years vs. a decline in other manufacturing industries. In addition, an increasing proportion of its workforce is of the whitecollar variety. This tends to raise the percentage of costs which are "fixed."

With high fixed costs and wild swings in production every three years due to labor negotiations, the industry's profits are erratic. . . .

Backs to the Wall

. . . Partly through its own fault and partly through the fault of labor with government assistance, the industry has its back to the wall on imports. Some of the blame must go unplaced, too, for the industry is simply the victim of a changing world. The U.S. is encountering economic competition from other nations unlike anything it has ever experienced. Manufacturing goods with a high labor content and a high degree of sophistication is no longer the exclusive domain of U.S. manufacturers.

"Ours is the only steel industry in the world that operates as an entirely private industry," says Edmund F. Martin, chairman, Bethlehem Steel Corp. In other countries, steel industries are government owned or otherwise get assistance to make them competitive in a world market.

Japan: The Contender

In Japan, for example, the industry benefits from a unique combination of industry, banking, and government. Steel output was hiked by 15 million tons to 68 million tons last year and will reach 90 million tons by 1972. The industry's profits appear low (about 2% on assets vs. triple that here) but "owners" realize their return through the heavy debt that is carried at high interest rates. The nation encourages formation of large companies.

"We don't have a free trade world," assert steel executives. "You can't pit a private industry against a government-run economy."

Problem for All Industry

The steel import situation is only an "indication of what will happen in other industries," says Robert Tyson, chairman of the finance committee, U.S. Steel Corp. "This is a national problem that has to be solved for all industry." . . .

After scrapping a tariff proposal, steelmakers are pushing hard to get an import quota system enacted. Quotas would limit the supply of steel in the U.S. but would neither expand the market nor lower production costs. They might also isolate us from world markets; retaliation by foreigners might close important markets to other metalworkers. . . .

The top echelon, too, knows that a quota would be only a stopgap measure. Hopefully, it would provide time to let other developments solve the basic problems. And it might force steel producing nations to get together to learn how to cope with excess capacity and establish a truly free trade world. "There seems little virtue in our being asked to be crucified on the cross of free trade when so little of the rest of the world seems to be dedicated to the faith," says U.S. Steel's [executive vice president,] Mr. [R. Heath] Larry. . . .

"Leave Us Alone"

Steel company leaders basically agree with Mr. [John] Lobb [president, Crucible Steel Corp.] when he says, "We don't want government help; we want government to leave us alone."

"If the steel industry could settle its problems with unions without federal interference, it would be able to compete with foreign steel producers," says John Saunders of General Fireproofing.

Face the Changing World

Government should not abandon its free trade policies. But it should permit our industries to take the shape they need to fight back. We must examine the laws and customs that worked internally but are failing in new world competition. We must ask ourselves where we draw the line on imports when a basic industry is threatened with failure. We must ask what would happen to prices in an industry if imports became dominant; would imports continue to be a "bargain"?

We—our government, our unions, all of us—must face up to changes in the world's economy.

The steel industry is finally changing its notion that "steel is different." Whether is survives, however, will depend as much on how we shape it as on its own efforts to change. One thing is sure—the steel industry will never be the same again.

3. National Industrial Conference Board Evaluates the General Agreement on Tariffs and Trade (GATT), 1969

The General Agreement on Tariffs and Trade (GATT) was signed in 1947 as a "provisional and temporary device" for international trade cooperation. The original contracting parties numbered 23. Through the years, GATT has grown to include 86 contracting parties and has sponsored six rounds of tariff negotiations. GATT serves both as a forum for multilateral trade and tariff negotiations and to promote fair international trading practices.

The Kennedy Round, sixth round of GATT tariff negotiations, with over 50 countries participating, began in 1964 and ended in 1967. Nine countries (Austria, Denmark, Finland, Norway, Sweden, Switzerland, Japan, the United Kingdom, and the United States) and the EEC (negotiating as a unit) participated on a "linear" basis, that is, they agreed in advance to reduce tariff levels in broad product categories on an across-the-board basis rather than on an item-by-item basis. The goal for across-the-board tariff reductions was set at 50%. Other countries—primarily developing and less-developed nations—agreed to grant concessions on a reciprocal and item-by-item basis but not on a linear basis. A few less-developed nations participated in Kennedy Round talks but did not offer to make any reciprocal tariff reductions.

Nations participating on a *linear* basis were requested to submit exception lists of industrial items for which they would not consider 50% across-the-board tariff cuts, and to submit offer lists for agricultural products. Multilateral and bilateral negotiations proceeded on the basis of the excepted items and the offers of all the negotiating countries.

At the conclusion of the Kennedy Round, worldwide tariff reductions approximated 35% on over 6,000 products, primarily manufactured goods. In some cases tariffs were completely eliminated—e.g., on some tropical food products from less-developed nations—and the 50% goal was reached on many industrial products. However, a number of products—among them steel, textiles, and foodstuffs—were not touched by tariff cuts or received only modest cuts.

Karen Kraus Bivens, *After the Kennedy Round: Outlook for World-wide Trade Liberalization* (n.p.: National Industrial Conference Board, [ca. 1969]), pp. 5, 2–3.

The Agreement provides that the tariff reductions will be made in instalments from 1968 to 1972. The "most-favored-nation" clause of the Agreement provides that all tariff reductions made during the negotiations between individual nations will be automatically extended to all GATT members. . . .

The tariff reductions of the Kennedy Round are expected to have an over-all favorable impact on total world trade and economic development. Many survey respondents believe that free flow of goods and economic integration brought about by such a major international trade liberalization must necessarily benefit all nations, despite any short-range unfavorable effects on individual nations. They feel that all nations will be better off in a world of expanding trade and growing interdependence.

Business leaders who view the impact of the Kennedy Round from a global standpoint believe that the sizable tariff reductions will increase the flow of goods among nations, and that an increase in the total volume of world trade will stimulate higher economic activity and standards of living throughout the world. In the words of a Canadian executive, "The link between multilateral trade liberalization and international affluence hardly requires elaboration." Similarly, a United States businessman writes:

> "A freer flow of goods within and among nations can be expected to have significant effects. It is not for nothing, for example, that the countries of the European Economic Community, which have benefited so greatly by the reduction of trade barriers among its members, are commonly referred to as the Common Market. Similarly, it is well known that a major U.S. economic advantage is derived from the free flow of goods that exists within its large domestic market. The Kennedy Round was a substantial step in this direction for the whole world."

Another benefit expected to apply to all nations is freer competition among the world's producers. The chairman of an Italian firm maintains that many nations participating in the Kennedy Round could have predicted serious competition against their products. Therefore the tariff reductions that were made were, in his words, "a demonstration of faith in the capacity of free international trade to make a decisive contribution to increase prosperity amongst the nations."

As a consequence of freer access to all markets and of freer competition within markets, some business leaders forecast more meaningful and more efficient integration of the world economy. The point is made that a free and natural flow of goods will motivate individual nations to increase trade in those goods which they can produce most efficiently. The inevitable result, say executives, is progress toward true international division of labor and regional specialization. A United States business leader expresses this view:

> "Efforts to bring about a reduction in tariffs through the Kennedy Round negotiations were prompted by a firm conviction that lower tariffs would be beneficial to all countries, including the U.S. As tariffs are gradually lowered over the next five years, there will be greater opportunity and incentive for each country to transfer resources from less productive to more productive uses. The reason why this is so is that lower tariffs, unless offset by the erection of other trade barriers, will serve to broaden each country's foreign markets for the goods it can produce most efficiently. The end result: greater world specialization in production, greater efficiency, and a faster rise in world standards of living."

4. Pharmaceutical Giant Bristol-Myers Encounters Cultural Differences in Japan and the USSR in the 1970s

At Bristol-Myers I had a broad mandate to combine science and commerce and to acquire products on the basis of their scientific and commercial potential. Our licensing efforts, which included intensive discussions worldwide, led to the successful development of new pharmaceuticals, as described below.

Of all our negotiations, those we did in Japan and the USSR were the longest and most grueling. They demonstrate how our steadfast approach to licensing allowed us to surpass our rivals and become the leader in the field of cancer drugs.

Negotiations in Japan

Bristol's relationship with the Japanese began when Amel Menotti, my predecessor at Bristol, started supporting the research of Hamao Umezawa of the Microbial Chemistry Research Foundation (MCRF) in Tokyo; when Menotti retired in the early 1970s, I took over the contract. In exchange for financial support, Bristol obtained marketing rights worldwide (except for Japan) to drugs developed at the MCRF. The first such compound was kanamycin, an antibiotic; the second was an antibiotic used in cancer chemotherapy, bleomycin. Umezawa's business partner for bleomycin in Japan was the firm Nippon Kayaku, and thus the negotiations involved three parties: Bristol-Myers, the MCRF, and Nippon Kayaku.

Negotiations lasted for about 14 years. They typically ran through the day and into the night, when all the negotiating parties would adjourn to a local restaurant. We came to know it as the "bleomycin restaurant," and today I can no longer remember its true name. During the "bleomycin discussions," the negotiations constantly seemed to be going in circles: we would reach an apparent agreement in one session, adjourn, and then resume the next day, or week, or month to find that the demands had changed. This behavior was not unique to Nippon Kayaku. Much of the delay may have been due to the Japanese tradition of trying to achieve internal consensus on every point.

Development of bleomycin—running clinical trials, getting FDA approval, and so forth—continued in the United States while negotiations continued in Japan, and Bristol in fact lost no time in putting the drug on the U.S. market in 1973. Umezawa was of great help in pushing Nippon Kayaku to reach a final agreement: he pointed out that our real purpose was to make drugs available on the market, not to have endless debates.

Bristol-Myers also negotiated for the rights to another antibiotic, mitomycin C, which was discovered by Toju Hata, a professor at the Kitasato Institute in Tokyo. He made the discovery under a grant from the Japanese Antibiotics Research Association (JARA), which was actually funded by Bristol-Myers. During the 1960s and 1970s Bristol developed widespread contacts with Japanese university professors and

Maxwell Gordon, "Licensing, Negotiations—and Stale Cookies: Another Side of the Pharmaceutical Industry," *Chemical Heritage* 22, no. 4 (Winter 2004/5): 12–13, 37–39 (excerpt, pp. 13, 37–38). Copyright © 2005 Chemical Heritage Foundation. Reprinted with permission from the Chemical Heritage Foundation.

drug companies (contacts that have not, unfortunately, been fully maintained in recent years). JARA was a nonprofit volunteer association of companies, individuals, and universities that shared an interest in antibiotic research. Professors at national universities were not allowed to accept money from industry, but companies could feed money to professors through nonprofit organizations like JARA—an important route to commercializing Japanese university discoveries.

Because the Kyowa Hakko Company had acquired the mitomycin C patent for development in Japan, licensing discussions for the U.S. market involved both Hata and Kyowa Hakko. Negotiations with the professor presented no problem, but the discussions with Kyowa Hakko—like the bleomycin discussions with Nippon Kayaku—also went on for 14 years.

In May 1972 Bristol filed a new drug application on mitomycin C; the firm received approval in May 1974 and put the drug on the U.S. market in 1974, before reaching an agreement. Kyowa Hakko would not agree that Bristol had rights and therefore refused to accept royalty payments for U.S. sales, which were accordingly deposited in an escrow account. Finally, our Bristol team went to Tokyo and argued that neither company could operate in the United States without the other, since Kyowa Hakko owned the patent on the compound and Bristol had an approved new-drug application. After intensive negotiations, we hammered out an equitable agreement, and Bristol's U.S. sales of bleomycin and mitomycin C ultimately exceeded sales of the drugs in Japan. . . .

USSR Adventures in Licensing

As our success and reputation grew, we were able to license more compounds abroad. Our licensing experiences in the Soviet Union in the 1970s are worth recording, though unrewarding in terms of marketed products. We were initially interested in the anti-cancer drug Ftorafur (tegafur), a 5-fluorouracil analog that breaks down to 5-fluorouracil when metabolized. This compound had been synthesized at the Institute of Organic Synthesis in Riga, Latvia, then one of the Soviet republics. Through an obscure chain of circumstances, Ftorafur was licensed to the Japanese company Taiho, in whose hands it became very successful under the name of Futraful in Japan, where it was still a major product 20 years later.

Although tegafur was a success in Japan, its clinical efficacy was in question. We wanted an agreement that would allow us to evaluate the compound clinically before marketing it. A number of U.S. companies had also expressed an interest in the compound, but no doubt our record—with half a dozen cancer drugs on the market—persuaded the Soviets that we were the most suitable company to develop tegafur in the United States and in most of Europe.

We found the Soviet negotiators even more difficult to deal with than their Japanese counterparts. At one point we were convinced we would spend 14 years in the Soviet Union, as we did in Japan. Fortunately we did not, but we did spend several months negotiating during successive visits over four years. A major problem was that Soviet licensing involved multiple organizations. We negotiated with Medexport for supplies of tegafur and with Licensintorg for a license for the tegafur patent application. We had to have an agreement that was satisfactory to both organizations, but the two would not sit down together with us, because they reported to different ministries in the government. We constantly had to tell one group what the other had told us. To make matters worse, often one group would say something at one meeting and retract it at the next, leaving us in a bad position with the other group. We felt like a ping-pong ball being batted back and forth between the two agencies.

Bureaucratic obstacles existed at an even deeper level. For our first visit to the USSR, we had made arrangements to meet with a group of scientists. When we arrived in Moscow, we were told that the group was not ready to see us, and we were forced to go back to New York. When we met with the scientists on our next visit, they asked why we did not show up for the first meeting. They had all assembled and waited for us but were not informed that we had been sent on our way. After that fiasco the Soviet government advised us to sign a protocol with the Central Committee of the Soviet Union, which has jurisdiction over all scientific academies. In effect we negotiated a treaty with the Soviets.

Our counterparts in the Soviet Union could be suspicious and reluctant to speak freely to foreigners, especially about technical matters. After we received the specific protocol signed by the Central Committee of the USSR, laboratory scientists felt freer to talk to us because we had been "certified" at the highest level as official friends of the Soviet Union. Individual scientists were quite professional and helpful in their discussions and welcomed the opportunity to break out of their scientific isolation. But our own isolation was often severe, compounded by the lack of news available in English—except for the *Daily Worker*. Visitors really had to rely on each other for company.

Negotiations were bleak. We typically held discussions in one of the offices of Medexport or Licensintorg, arriving early in the morning and negotiating until noon, when the first Soviet team would leave and a second team would arrive to continue talks until 5 or 6 P.M. The Soviets never provided us with any lunch; on a good day they served us tea and cookies. The meeting rooms were unheated, so we were uncomfortable as well as hungry. We believe the discomfort was a deliberate tactic to wear us down—whereas the Japanese seemed to rely on sumptuous meals to melt our resistance.

Food became a concern generally. Once when we were put up at the Metropole Hotel for a return visit, we said, "Let's eat here. It can't be as bad as we remember it." It was even worse. First the staff refused to seat us because the kitchen was closed. When we pointed out that it was only 8:30 P.M., they relented and brought out soup that tasted like dishwater. We ended up with tea and stale cookies for dinner. On subsequent trips to the USSR we carried two suitcases—a large one for food and a small one for clothes.

5. *Time* Documents the Agricultural Surplus, 1986

Across the farm belt last week, it was clear that another bumper crop is on the way. In Illinois, the corn is already seven feet high in spots and not close to topping out. Some corn is tasseling weeks ahead of schedule, and an early harvest is in prospect. Soybeans have also benefited from perfect weather; many plants are waist high and flowering ahead of time. Good, dry planting weather came early this year across

Iowa and Nebraska, and even scattered flooding has not hurt the promise of a bountiful harvest. Elsewhere in the Midwest, it is much the same, a year so good that Dennis Vercler, news director of the Illinois Farm Bureau, calls it "absolutely phenomenal."

Yet the great bounty of U.S. agriculture continues to be a curse as well as a blessing. As the corn rises speedily, so does a forest of new silos that signals a crop-storage problem of epic proportions. All across the corn belt, from Indiana to Nebraska and Missouri to Minnesota, a binge of bin and silo building is in full swing. Reason: by the end of summer, U.S. farmers and the Department of Agriculture will be buried under more excess wheat, corn, rice and other products than ever before in history. Last week the immensity of the surplus became clear in the marketplace, as commodities traders sent the price of corn futures plunging to $1.71 per bu., the lowest level in twelve years.

While farmers fret about how to store the huge harvest, much tougher questions will loom as unavoidably as tarpaulin-covered mountains of wheat. The unsentimental truth is that America's farm industry, once a source of pride and power, has become an economic burden. Because so many other countries have improved their agricultural output, maintaining America's vast farming capacity is now a costly exercise in excess. During fiscal 1986 the expense to taxpayers for supporting farm programs will reach, according to the Government's estimates, $24 billion—a 36% increase over last year. As exports shrivel and imports increase, the U.S. agricultural industry no longer even produces the hefty foreign exchange earnings that farmers once provided.

To put the situation in order, the Government is allowing thousands of farmers to fail but is spending billions to boost foreign sales and prop up incomes for those who survive. Yet the adjustment process is a bitter one that promises hardship not only for farm families but for the thousands of already troubled farm-oriented businesses, including machinery builders, petrochemical companies, seed producers and the mom-and-pop shops that keep small rural towns alive.

This year's corn crop will be the most dramatic example of U.S. agriculture's relentless surpluses. Because of the almost perversely ideal weather, with exactly the right amount of rain at the proper intervals, says Illinois' Vercler, "crop development is just about the best ever." Last year's corn crop was the largest in history, 8.9 billion bu., of which a record 5 billion bu. is left over in storage. The expected bumper harvest of 8 billion bu. this year, smaller in volume than 1985's because an increasing number of farmers have taken some acreage out of production to qualify for Government support programs, will send prices plummeting even further into the cellar.

Other vast surpluses abound. At the beginning of last month, the U.S. held 1.9 billion bu. of wheat, a record overstock, and 847 million bu. of soybeans, almost 40% more than at the same time last year. Kansas alone held 178.8 million bu. of grain sorghum, a livestock feed, almost 80% more than in June 1985. The U.S. is producing a huge excess of milk as well, a problem reduced only partly by the USDA's program this year to pay thousands of dairy farmers some $1.8 billion to send their herds to slaughter or export markets.

The Midwest's surplus is so stubbornly large that even this year's severe drought in the South will fail to boost depressed farm prices. The sad result: farmers in those states will face a double bind of low prices and small harvests, which could push many of them over the financial brink. Last week's heat wave, which reached 105° F in parts of the Carolinas, further scorched crops and killed more than 500,000 chickens. "This could put us completely out of business," laments Dairy Farmer Charlie Bouldin, of Chatham County, N.C., who expects less than 30% of his hay and corn crops to survive.

But for most farmers, the problem is a lack of customers. Foreign sales of U.S. farm products have faltered because dozens of countries from Brazil to China have become more self-sufficient, while heavily indebted Third World nations lack the money to buy significant imports. This year total U.S. farm exports are expected to dip to $27.5 billion, down 12% from fiscal 1985 and 37% from 1981. At the same time, U.S. imports of such products as fish, fruit and vegetables have increased. Earlier this month the USDA announced that during May the U.S. became a net importer of farm products for the first time since 1959, except for occasions when dockworkers were on strike. May's farm deficit was $348.7 million. Although the USDA predicts a $7.5 billion agricultural-trade surplus for the year as a whole, the historic one-month deficit outraged farm-state legislators. Said Senate Majority Leader Robert Dole of Kansas: "Something is radically wrong when the greatest food producer in the world is buying more agricultural commodities than it is selling. This trend simply cannot continue."

6. Journalist Thomas L. Friedman Describes McDonald's Global Expansion, 1996

So I've had this thesis for a long time and came here to Hamburger University at McDonald's headquarters to finally test it out. The thesis is this: No two countries that both have a McDonald's have ever fought a war against each other.

The McDonald's folks confirmed it for me. I feared the exception would be the Falklands war, but Argentina didn't get its first McDonald's until 1986, four years after that war with Britain. Civil wars don't count: McDonald's in Moscow delivered burgers to both sides in the fight between pro- and anti-Yeltsin forces in 1993.

Since Israel now has a kosher McDonald's, since Saudi Arabia's McDonald's closes five times a day for Muslim prayer, since Egypt has 18 McDonald's and Jordan is getting its first, the chances of a war between them are minimal. But watch out for that Syrian front. There are no Big Macs served in Damascus. India-Pakistan? I'm still worried. India, where 40 percent of the population is vegetarian, just opened the first beefless McDonald's (vegetable nuggets!), but Pakistan is still a Mac-free zone.

Obviously, I say all this tongue in cheek. But there was enough of a correlation for me to ask James Cantalupo, president of McDonald's International and its de facto Secretary of State, what might be behind this Golden Arches Theory of Conflict Prevention—which stipulates that when a country reaches a certain level of economic development, when it has a middle class big enough to support a McDonald's, it becomes a McDonald's country, and people in McDonald's countries don't like to fight wars; they like to wait in line for burgers. Or as Mr. Cantalupo puts it: "We

Thomas L. Friedman, "Big Mac I," *The New York Times,* December 8, 1996; *idem,* "Big Mac II," *idem,* December 11, 1996. Copyright © 1996 by The New York Times Co. Reprinted with permission.

focus our development on the more well-developed economies—those that are growing and those that are large—and the risks involved in being adventuresome [for those growing economies] are probably getting too great."

In the 1950's and 60's developing countries thought that having an aluminum factory and a U.N. seat was what made them real countries, but today many countries think they will have arrived only if they have their own McDonald's and Windows 95 in their own language. This year McDonald's went into its 100th country and for the first time it earned more revenue from McDonald's overseas than from McDonald's America.

Said Mr. Cantalupo: "I feel these countries want McDonald's as a symbol of something—an economic maturity and that they are open to foreign investments. I don't think there is a country out there we haven't gotten inquiries from. I have a parade of ambassadors and trade representatives in here regularly to tell us about their country and why McDonald's would be good for the country."

The question raised by the McDonald's example is whether there is a tip-over point at which a country, by integrating with the global economy, opening itself up to foreign investment and empowering its consumers, permanently restricts its capacity for troublemaking and promotes gradual democratization and widening peace. Francis Fukuyama, author of the classic work "The End of History," argued to me that a country's getting its own McDonald's was probably not a good indicator of that tip-over point, because the level of per capita income needed in a country to host a McDonald's is too low. "I would not be surprised if in the next 10 years several of these McDonald's countries go to war with each other," he said.

Yes, there will be conflicts, but more inside countries than between them. No question, the spread of McDonald's (a new one opens every three hours) is part of this worldwide phenomenon of countries integrating with the global economy and submitting to its rules, but this is not a smooth linear process. It produces a backlash inside countries from those who do not benefit from this globalization, who feel that their traditional culture will be steamrolled by it and who fear that they won't eat the Big Mac, the Big Mac will eat them.

How well governments and global companies manage these frustrations will be the real determinant of whether economic development will lead to wider democratization and wider peace. Here again McDonald's is an intriguing pioneer. When the riots broke out in Los Angeles one of the few commercial buildings not trashed was McDonald's. Wednesday's column will explore why.

Sunday's column explored why no two countries that both have a McDonald's have ever fought a war against each other. This examines why McDonald's became a "glocal" company—both global and local.

The folks at McDonald's like to tell the story about the young Japanese girl who arrived in Los Angeles, looked around and said to her mother: "Look, mom, they have McDonald's here too."

You could excuse her for being surprised that McDonald's was an American company. With 2,000 restaurants in Japan, McDonald's Japan, a.k.a. "Makadonaldo," is the biggest McDonald's franchise outside the U.S. The McDonald's folks even renamed Ronald McDonald in Japan "Donald McDonald" because there's no "R" sound in Japanese.

"You don't have 2,000 stores in Japan by being seen as an American company," said James Cantalupo, head of McDonald's International. "Look, McDonald's serves meat, bread and potatoes. They eat meat, bread and potatoes in most of the world. It's how you package it and the experience you offer that counts."

The way McDonald's has packaged itself is to be a "multi-local" company. That is, by insisting on a high degree of local ownership, and by tailoring its products just enough for local cultures, McDonald's has avoided the worst cultural backlashes that some other U.S. companies have encountered. Not only do localities now feel a stake in McDonald's success, but more important, countries do. Poland for instance has emerged as one of the largest regional suppliers of meat, potatoes and bread for McDonald's in Central Europe. That is real power. Because McDonald's is gradually moving from local sourcing of its raw materials to regional sourcing to global sourcing. One day soon, all McDonald's meat in Asia might come from Australia, all its potatoes from China. Already, every sesame seed on every McDonald's bun in the world comes from Mexico. That's as good as a country discovering oil.

This balance between local and global that McDonald's has found is worth reflecting upon. Because this phenomenon we call "globalization"—the integration of markets, trade, finance, information and corporate ownership around the globe—is actually a very American phenomenon: it wears Mickey Mouse ears, eats Big Mac's, drinks Coke, speaks on a Motorola phone and tracks its investments with Merrill Lynch using Windows 95. In other words, countries that plug into globalization are really plugging into a high degree of Americanization.

People will only take so much of that. Therefore, to the extent that U.S.-origin companies are able to become multi-local, able to integrate around the globe economically without people feeling that they are being culturally assaulted, they will be successful. To the extent they don't, they will trigger a real backlash that will slam not only them but all symbols of U.S. power. Iran now calls the U.S. "the capital of global arrogance."

People in other cultures cannot always distinguish between American power, American exports, American cultural assaults and globalization. That's why you already see terrorists lashing out at U.S. targets not for any instrumental reason, but simply to reject this steamroller of globalization/Americanization, which has become so inescapable. (The McDonald's people have a saying: Sooner or later McDonald's is in every story. Where did O.J. eat just before the murder of Nicole? McDonald's. What did Commerce Secretary Ron Brown serve U.S. troops just before he died? McDonald's . . .)

"You try to shut the door and it comes in through the window," says the historian Ronald Steel about globalization. "You try to shut the window and it comes in on the cable. You cut the cable, it comes in on the Internet. And it's not only in the room with you. You eat it. It gets inside you."

The only answer is multi-localism—democratizing globalization so that people everywhere feel some stake in how it impacts their lives. "McDonald's stands for a lot more than just hamburgers and American fast food," argued Mr. Cantalupo. "Cultural sensitivity is part of it too. There is no 'Euroburger.' . . . We have a different chicken sandwich in England than we do in Germany. We are trying not to think as a cookie cutter."

7. Washington Think Tank Calculates NAFTA's Impact on Jobs, 2001 (table and map)

U.S. Trade with Canada and Mexico, 1993–2000, Totals for All Commodities (Millions of Constant 1992 Dollars)

	1993	2000	Change Since 1993 Dollars	Change Since 1993 Percent	Jobs Lost or Gained
Canada					
Domestic exports	$90,018	$149,214	$59,196	66%	563,539
Imports for consumption	108,087	193,725	85,638	79	962,376
Net exports	(18,068)	(44,511)	(26,443)	146	(398,837)
Mexico					
Domestic exports	$39,530	$97,509	$57,979	147%	574,326
Imports for consumption	38,074	132,439	94,364	248	941,520
Net exports	1,456	(34,930)	(36,386)	n.a.	(367,193)
Mexico and Canada					
Domestic exports	$129,549	$246,723	$117,174	90%	1,137,865
Imports for consumption	146,161	326,164	180,003	123	1,903,896
Net exports	(16,612)	(79,441)	(62,828)	378	(766,030)

Robert E. Scott, "NAFTA's Hidden Costs: Trade Agreement Results in Job Losses, Growing Inequality, and Wage Suppression for the United States" (Washington, D.C.: Economic Policy Institute, 2001), p. 4, accessed at http://epinet.org (December 2004). Reprinted by permission of EPInet.org.

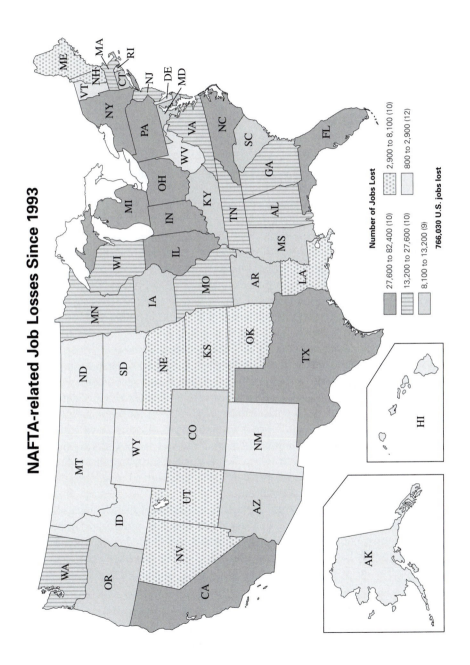

NAFTA-related Job Losses Since 1993

Number of Jobs Lost

- 27,600 to 82,400 (10)
- 13,200 to 27,600 (10)
- 8,100 to 13,200 (9)
- 2,900 to 8,100 (10)
- 800 to 2,900 (12)

766,030 U.S. jobs lost

8. USDA Reports NAFTA's Benefits
to Agricultural Exports, 2001

The continued strength of North American Free Trade Agreement (NAFTA) markets has been one of the brightest spots for U.S. farmers, agricultural exporters, and the industries that support them. Together, our NAFTA partners, Canada and Mexico, purchase 27 percent of U.S. agricultural exports.

Farmers in the United States, Canada, and Mexico *all* benefit from NAFTA. Two-way agricultural trade between the United States and Mexico increased more than 55 percent since 1994, reaching more than $11.6 billion last year.

Two-way agricultural trade between the United States and Canada increased more than 50 percent in the same time frame reaching $16.3 billion in 2000.

Although U.S. imports have grown under NAFTA, so have U.S. exports. Without NAFTA, the United States would have lost these expanded export opportunities.

Since implementation of the U.S.-Canada Free Trade Agreement, U.S. agricultural exports to Canada have doubled. Canada is the No. 2 market for U.S. agricultural exports, purchasing $7.6 billion worth last year.

Since NAFTA was approved in 1993, U.S. agricultural exports to Mexico have nearly doubled. Mexico imported $6.5 billion of U.S. agricultural products in 2000, making it our third largest agricultural market.

Canada took record levels of many key U.S. commodities in 2000: fresh vegetables, fresh fruits, snack foods, poultry meat, live animals, pet foods, dairy foods, vegetable oils, planting seeds, breakfast cereals, tree nuts, nursery products, and red meats.

Record U.S. exports to Mexico in 2000 included red meats, processed fruits and vegetables, poultry meat, snack foods, fresh fruits and vegetables, juices, tree nuts, pet foods, feeds and fodder, and rice. This broad cross section of commodities suggests the benefits of NAFTA are widely distributed across U.S. agriculture.

Import competition has increased under NAFTA for some commodities, a not-unexpected development when barriers to trade begin to come down and trade is subject to open marketing conditions. As the largest of the NAFTA countries and with a booming economy and strong currency, it is not surprising that U.S. imports have grown strongly, providing American consumers with a broader array of competitively priced, high-quality products.

In 1993, U.S. goods faced an average tariff barrier at the Mexican border of about 10 percent, five times the 2.07 percent rate that the United States imposed on Mexican goods. With NAFTA, Mexico's average tariff has already fallen to about 2 percent. Import licensing and other nontariff barriers have been eliminated and more than two-thirds of U.S. exports now enter duty-free.

Some Positive Stories From NAFTA

U.S. pork producers credit NAFTA with their gains in market share in Mexico for pork products which increased 130 percent between 1994 and 2000.

U.S. Department of Agriculture, "Benefits of NAFTA," FASonline, accessed at http://www.fas.usda.gov (December 2004).

The volume of U.S. beef and veal exports to Canada increased 26 percent between 1990 and 2000 and increased over fivefold to Mexico during 1993 to 2000.

Sales of U.S. corn to Canada increased more than 127 percent in volume between 1990 and 2000 and increased nearly eighteenfold to Mexico during 1993 to 2000. Mexico chose to expedite its market openings for corn under NAFTA in order to provide lower cost food to its increasingly urban population and to ensure it had sufficient animal feed. The volume of U.S. soybean exports to Canada increased 15 percent between 1990 and 2000 and doubled for Mexico during 1993 to 2000.

Exports of U.S. horticultural products to Canada have increased almost 30 percent since 1994, reaching $3.3 billion in 2000.

 E S S A Y S

First, Geoffrey Jones, the Joseph C. Wilson Professor of Business Administration at the Harvard Business School, probes the relationship between international business and the global economy since 1945. Jones highlights the reasons behind the reemergence of the international movement of capital, trade, and people in the postwar era and examines the intensification of globalization beginning in the 1980s. He also considers the distribution of economic power between North America, Western Europe, and Japan, and explores the role of multinational corporations in driving the integration of the global economy.

In the second essay, Martin Baily, a Senior Fellow at the Institute for International Economics and a Senior Advisor to the McKinsey Global Institute (MGI), and Diana Farrell, Director of MGI, consider one of the business trends redefining the global economy in the twenty-first century: offshoring. While businesses see offshoring as a way to boost profits, politicians, unionists, and workers decry the loss of American industrial jobs. Baily and Farrell focus on the big picture, drawing on MGI research that demonstrates gains to the U.S. economy through corporate savings, repatriated profits by American multinationals, increased international trade, greater productivity, and net gains to employment. What criticisms could be made of this view?

Multinationals and Globalization

GEOFFREY JONES

Restoring a Global Economy, 1950–80

The 1950s onwards saw the beginning of the reconstruction of a new global economy. Between 1950 and 1973 the annual real GDP [Gross Domestic Product] growth of developed market economies averaged around 5 percent. This growth was smooth, with none of the major recessions seen in the interwar years. World War II left the United States in a uniquely powerful position. While Europe and Asia had experienced extensive destruction and loss of life, no battles had been fought on the soil of the United States. The U.S. dollar became the world's major reserve currency. U.S. corporations assumed leading positions in many industries. Europe and Japan had to spend the immediate postwar decade undergoing extensive reconstruction, heavily dependent on official aid from the United States, yet over time Europe and Japan closed the technological and productivity gap with the United States. The emergence of a U.S. deficit on its balance of trade in the 1960s, and the devaluation of the U.S. dollar, and the end of its convertibility into gold in 1971, provided symbolic signs of the ending of an era.

There remained many restrictions on the flow of capital, trade, and people across borders. Foreign companies were entirely excluded from the Communist world. In the twenty years after 1945 the European colonial empires were dismantled. In some cases, decolonization was followed by an aggressive reaction against the businesses of the former colonial power, and sometimes all foreign investment. The relatively small number of expropriations without compensation until the late 1960s—when a period of large-scale expropriation began—reflected the power and determination of the United States to protect foreign investments, but Western countries were unable to re-establish an international legal regime which guaranteed the property rights of international investors. Even in the developed countries, receptivity towards multinationals fell. In Europe and the United States, whole sectors were closed to foreign companies. The Japanese economy grew so fast that it had become the world's second largest capitalist economy by the 1970s, but its governments systematically discouraged wholly owned FDI [Foreign Direct Investment] and restricted it to a low level.

During the 1940s and early 1950s only the U.S. dollar was available as a major convertible currency. Elsewhere exchange controls regulated capital movements. They were often the instruments used by governments to screen or monitor FDI flows. The worldwide controls over capital movements were related to balance of payments concerns and the system of fixed exchange rates established at Bretton Woods. It was not until 1958 that most European countries adopted nonresident convertibility, which permitted foreigners to move funds for current account purposes freely from one country to another. This was the key development in the establishment of a liberal and open international economy. It had an immediate impact on FDI flows, with an increase of U.S. FDI into Europe. However, most developing countries continued to exercise tight controls over capital movements. Even most developed countries retained some exchange controls.

It was only after the collapse of the Bretton Woods system of fixed exchange rates in the early 1970s that controls over capital movements began to be slowly dismantled. The advent of floating exchange rates permitted a huge explosion in international financial markets from the 1970s, but these capital flows were different than before 1914, for they largely occurred between rich countries. In 1900 Asia, Latin America, and Africa had accounted for 33 percent of global liabilities. In the 1990s, they accounted for 11 percent.

World trade barriers were reduced under the auspices of the General Agreement on Tariffs and Trade (GATT) signed in 1947. This process peaked in the 1960s, when the Kennedy Administration in the United States made major efforts to secure radical reductions in tariff rates. During the middle of this decade there was a comprehensive reduction of barriers to trade in manufactured goods. By the end of the 1960s, however, the U.S.-inspired drive for trade liberalization showed a loss of momentum, as U.S. balance of payments deficits began to cause concern about the scale of foreign imports. Nontariff barriers spread in the following decade. Most developing countries in Latin America, Asia, and Africa became progressively closed to international trade from the 1950s to the 1980s. Even the richest and most developed countries maintained very high levels of protection for agricultural products, far higher than before 1913.

The formation of regional trading blocs was both a part of the process of reducing trade barriers and a limitation on it. The European Economic Community (later known as the EC, and, from 1993, the European Union) was formed in 1957, and initially consisted of six Western European countries. It developed common tariffs against external imports. An extreme case was the Common Agricultural Policy, adopted in 1966, which severely restricted U.S. agricultural exports to Europe. However, within Europe, free trade was established between the member countries, even though nontariff barriers persisted. The creation of such a large "Common Market" attracted many U.S. companies to Western Europe.

Technology made it easier than ever before for companies to move people, knowledge, and goods around the world. There were new waves of innovations in transport and communications. In 1958 the first commercial jet made an Atlantic crossing. This was followed by a phenomenal increase in air traffic. The development of telex was a considerable advance over telephones in facilitating international communications and coordinating of multinational business. In 1965 the first satellite for commercial telecommunications was launched. During the 1970s the use of the facsimile machine took off. The movement of goods across the world was facilitated by the development of larger ocean-going ships or super-freighters, and the growth of containerization.

The flow of migrants across borders remained constrained by immigration policies. Although the number of migrants were considerable—there were 3.2 million immigrants to the United States in the 1960s—they were much smaller relative to the host population than in the early twentieth century. The proportion of foreign-born in the U.S. population was less than 5 percent in 1970. There was also a major shift in the geographical source of emigrants. Europeans were much less important, although they moved within their home region. The proportion of Europeans and Canadians to total immigrants in the United States fell from 78 percent in the 1940s to 13 percent in the 1980s. Over the same decades the proportion of Latin Americans rose from 18 percent to 47 percent, and the proportion of Asians from 4 percent to 37 percent.

By 1980, the integration of worldwide capital, commodity and labor markets remained limited compared to the late nineteenth century.

The Resumption of Multinational Growth

The expansion of the world economy prompted a recovery in the growth rate of world FDI. The system of international cartels was dismantled. By 1960 the world stock of FDI had reached $60 billion. By 1980 it was over $500 billion. These were the decades when the term "multinational" was invented, and when economic theorists turned their attention to explaining their existence.

Between 1945 and the mid-1960s the United States may have accounted for 85 percent of all new FDI flows. By 1980 it held 40 percent of total stock. In the twenty years after the end of World War II both German and Japanese FDI remained low, but growth during the 1970s gave the two countries an overall share of world FDI of 8 percent and 7 percent respectively. The German share finally surpassed that of the Netherlands by that date. By 1980 almost two-thirds of world FDI was located in Western Europe and North America. Latin America and Asia had declined very sharply in their relative importance as host economies. By 1980 there was no multinational investment in China, and almost none in India. Even Japan in that year accounted for less than 1 percent of world inward FDI stock.

The relative shift of world FDI to Western Europe and North America reflected the many barriers to foreign multinationals elsewhere. In agriculture and mining, and later in petroleum, foreign firms lost the ownership of production facilities in many countries, even if they remained very powerful in the transportation, processing, and marketing of commodities. By 1980 manufacturing FDI was larger than the natural resource and service sectors combined. In services, while transport and utility investments were no longer important, from the 1960s multinational banks, trading companies, and international commodity dealers began rapid international expansion.

. . . [T]here were two different trends evident in this era. On the one hand, much of the multinational investment dating from the first global economy in resources and utilities was swept away. The high levels of integration seen in many commodities was broken by nationalizations and other forms of government intervention. Formerly large host economies including Russia, China, and even India—which retained a quasi-capitalist economy—were isolated from the world economy. On the other hand, new types of firms expanded abroad. These included management consultants which transferred knowledge across borders, and fast food restaurants and hotels, which transferred lifestyles. They were particularly important in diffusing U.S. management and marketing techniques to other economies, although they were typically adapted in their new hosts. In Europe, firms also began to respond to European integration by building European-wide organizations, and integrating previously autonomous national subsidiaries.

By 1979 the overall size of multinational investment was still smaller in relation to the world economy as a whole than in 1914. This reflected the barriers to foreign ownership erected in many countries, and in many sectors, such as utilities, and the disappearance of hugely capital-intensive investments in mining and petroleum. During the first global economy, much of the growth had been driven by the exchange of manufactured goods made in the developed world for the resources found elsewhere. The emergent new global economy was driven by trade, investment, and knowledge flows between Europe, North America, and Japan.

The New Global Economy: Borderless, Regional, or Semiglobal?

During the 1980s the pace of globalization intensified. By then the overwhelming influence of the United States on the world economy had given away to a situation whereby wealth was distributed more equally between the Triad of North America, Western Europe, and Japan, which accounted for around three-fourths of world manufacturing production. Paradoxically, the United States became the single "superpower" following the end of the Cold War. Although the importance of the Triad in the global economy persisted or even grew after 1980, there were significant shifts. Japan's share of world manufacturing increased from 5 percent in the early 1960s to 20 percent thirty years later, but thereafter the Japanese economy stagnated for a decade in the wake of the collapse of its speculative "bubble economy." In contrast, during the 1990s the United States experienced a surge of growth, apparently driven by the productivity gains of a "New Economy" associated with a boom in Internet and other high technology companies. This growth also ground to a halt at the end of the decade. The twenty-first century began with a major recession, scandals over auditing irregularities in large firms, major acts of international terrorism, and war.

National restrictions over cross-border capital flows were largely swept away as financial deregulation spread. The most striking changes were in emerging markets. Countries abandoned state planning and import substitution and sought export-led growth. Multinationals were increasingly seen as a means to develop new technologies, products and skills. China's adoption of market-oriented policies in 1979 is the appropriate chronological starting point for the new, or second global economy. The collapse of Communism in Russia and eastern Europe a decade later reopened further huge parts of the globe to foreign firms. Deregulation and privatization opened further opportunities, including in services such as air transport, tourism, and telecommunications which had long been closed to foreign companies. Multinationals now faced few risks of expropriation, but the international property rules of the nineteenth century were not restored. In China, eastern Europe, and elsewhere, multinationals faced enormous uncertainties regarding their legal rights and the enforcement of contracts.

However, governments did not withdraw from the market for capital flows in the way they had before 1914. Practically every government on the planet offered incentives for multinationals to invest. There also continued to be barriers to multinational investment in many resource and service industries. Although only some developing countries had exchange controls, world exchange markets continued to see continual and sometimes massive intervention in efforts to influence exchange rates.

A worldwide trend towards tariff reduction made possible further growth in trade, and deeper levels of economic integration. By the end of the century, tariffs on manufactured goods were lower than in 1913, although this was not true for a number of populous developing countries, including India and China. Nontariff barriers also fell from the late 1980s. However, there was no return to nineteenth-century free-trade. International trade in many commodities was distorted by tariffs and subsidies. Both the United States and the EU gave their farmers huge subsidies to grow cotton, oils, and many other commodities rather than import the much cheaper products of developing countries. The rich countries were also quite prepared to erect tariffs if domestic vested interests seemed threatened. The United States heavily protected its domestic textile industry, and in 2003 imposed "emergency" tariffs to protect its steel industry.

In part, falling tariffs reflected the further growth of regional trading blocs. The EU was enlarged in 1973, 1981, 1986, 1995, and 2004. Barriers to the movement of goods and services within Europe declined sharply, and over time, barriers to the movement of capital and people were also removed. EU law took precedence over that of member states. In 2002, twelve members of the EU even abolished their national currencies and adopted the new Euro currency. The United States, Canada, and Mexico formed the North American Free Trade Agreement (NAFTA) in 1994, although this remained primarily a free trade area. In the following year the Mercosur customs union was launched by Brazil, Paraguay, Uruguay, and Argentina.

The real costs and risks of managing at a distance were sharply reduced by changes in communications and transport technologies. Developments in information technology revolutionized communications. The use of "geo-stationary" satellites, which orbited the earth at heights of between 12,000 and 25,000 miles, permitted simultaneous cheap voice, data, and video links worldwide. Optical fiber cables provided an alternative means of transmitting very large volumes of information at very high speeds. The 1980s saw the appearance of the personal computer (PC).

The Internet began to be created after 1969 through the interlinking of computer networks in the United States, but it remained exotic for several decades. In 1990 the World Wide Web was born when a researcher at CERN, the high-energy physics laboratory in Geneva, Switzerland, developed hypertext markup language (HTML). Four years later the Internet was formally separated from the U.S. government's auspices and became open to commercial activity. The number of Internet users in the United States increased from 6 million to 159 million between 1993 and 2002. There was a rapid worldwide diffusion. The number of Internet users in China increased . . . to 59 million over the same period, although in sub-Saharan Africa there were only 6.2 million by 2002.

Although information could cross borders almost instantaneously, people could not. There remained tight restrictions on migrant flows. The majority of immigrants to developed countries during the 1980s and 1990s were admitted through family reunification schemes or as refugees. Although both Europe and Japan had ageing populations combined with birth rates falling below replacement rates, there were few pressures on governments to relax controls, and xenophobic reactions to ethnic minorities became more rather than less frequent. However, diaspora formed a dynamic component of the global economy. There was also considerable illegal migration, especially from eastern Europe and Latin America. Emigrant remittances grew as important components of global capital flows. In 2003 estimated emigrant remittances to Latin America and the Caribbean reached $38 billion. This was more than the total of inward FDI and official aid.

The pressure on rich countries to permit higher immigration was relaxed because technological change permitted companies to export jobs to locations with lower labor costs rather than import workers from such countries. From the 1990s there was a growth in offshoring, involving the relocation of labor-intensive service industry functions from rich countries to remote locations with skilled workforces but much lower wages. Among the functions to be offshored first were back-end processing, call centers, accounting, and software maintenance and development. The geographical flows of offshoring were heavily influenced by language. U.S. businesses dominated the global share of offshoring, and British companies accounted for much of the remainder. It was located mainly in countries where English was the main business language, especially India, but also the Philippines and Israel.

The benefits of global capitalism were not spread evenly between nations and within nations. For many citizens in North America, Europe, and Japan, human indicators such as life expectancy continued to improve. Rapid income gains were also experienced by some East and Southeast Asian economies. The lead was taken by the "four tigers"—Hong Kong, Singapore, South Korea, and Taiwan—which from the 1960s achieved high rates of economic growth and structural transformation. Between 1966 and 1990 Singapore grew by an average 8.5 percent per annum, or three times as fast as the United States. The "four tigers" were followed by a second wave of Asian economies, including Malaysia and Thailand, although a major currency crisis in 1997, which began in Thailand, provided a major shock. Subsequent currency crises in Russia in 1998 and Argentina in 2001 demonstrated the vulnerability of the global system to such shocks.

The sustained growth of the Chinese economy marked the most important shift of economic power in the new global economy. China's real GDP between 1979 and 2003 grew at 9 percent per annum. China's re-entry into the global economy had profound implications for the rest of the world. By 2004 China's steel production was larger than the United States and Japan combined, and the country had become the world's second largest importer of oil after the United States. Foreign trade growth averaged almost 15 percent between 1979 and 2003. In 2001, by which time China's GDP was larger than that of Italy and approaching the size of France and Britain, the country joined the WTO. China was by then the largest manufacturer in the world of many products, including DVD players, cellular phones, desktop PCs, cameras, and refrigerators. However, China's GDP per head, at purchasing power parity, was only one-sixth that of the United States in 2004. After 1991, policy liberalization in India was also followed by a more gradual but significant improvement in that country's economic performance.

There were also visible losers. While globalization was good for Asia, most of Africa experienced declining incomes. In the 1990s half of Africa's population lived in absolute poverty. While some Latin American countries including Chile appeared to benefit, others such as Argentina were rewarded for their participation in the global economy by economic crisis and the threat of social meltdown. At the end of the twentieth century most of the world's population beyond Western Europe and East Asia lived in countries where income levels were a lower percentage of the U.S. level . . . in 1950. Some scholars ascribed this situation to poorly functioning institutions which were hard to change because of embedded customs and traditions. Others pointed to the downsides of globalization. Economic restructuring, liberalization and competition led to increased insecurity and impoverishment for some. Even in developed countries workers with few skills, and even skilled industrial and white-collar workers, faced uncertain futures.

Unlike the first global economy, a substantial part of the world was left out of the globalization process. Most economic activity was concentrated in North America, Europe, and East Asia. . . .

Multinationals and the New Global Economy

Multinationals became the leading driver of the integration of the global economy. During the 1980s the average annual growth rate for FDI outflows reached 14 percent. Between 1996 and 2000 it reached 40 percent per annum. This was far faster than both the annual growth of world exports (4.2 percent) and of world output (1.2 percent). The huge sums of multinational investment were the result of cross-border mergers and acquisitions which had become the principal vehicle for FDI. These were driven by the new opportunities for globalization, Internet-related technological change, and the very high levels of stock valuation seen in global equity markets. The total stock of world FDI reached $6.8 trillion by 2001, before stagnating over the following two years as world share prices fell.

In 2004 the United States remained, by a considerable margin, the largest home economy. Yet the once-dominant trio of the United States, Britain, and the Netherlands only accounted for two-fifths of world FDI stock. German, French, and other European firms also held large shares of FDI. The surge in Japanese FDI, which had begun in the 1970s, increased rapidly following a sharp appreciation of the yen in 1985. Japan held almost 13 percent of world FDI in the early 1990s, but a decade later this share had fallen to 5 percent. There was also a relatively small amount of FDI from emerging markets, including South Korea.

The stock of multinational investment remained largely located in North America and Western Europe, but there was a striking rise of flows into China. For much of the 1990s China was the second largest recipient of FDI worldwide after the United States. This sum did not include Hong Kong, which reverted from being a British colony to part of the People's Republic of China in 1997, albeit administratively distinct for fifty years. From 1979 until 2000 China absorbed, on a cumulative basis, over $346 billion of FDI. Although inward FDI only represented around 5 percent of Chinese GDP during the second half of the 1990s, and amounted to less than one-seventh of total investment, foreign multinationals accounted for one half of gross exports. In India, the amount of FDI was so small even after 1991 that it had little impact on overall growth. However, Indian diaspora may have been significantly directing outsourcing opportunities to their country of origin. The fast development of the IT industry in Bangalore has been attributed to business linkages with Indians working in Silicon Valley.

While services represented around a quarter of the total world stock at the beginning of the 1970s, they accounted for at least one half by 2000. Although there are a large and diverse group of service sector activities, 85 percent of service FDI was in trade-related activities and financial services. The same percentage of the stock was located in developed countries, where they took advantage of the growing demand for consumer services from rising real incomes, the growing technological, information and knowledge component of many activities, and the new opportunities offered by deregulation and liberalization.

By 2004 if the level of world FDI was related to the world output, the globalization of international business was approaching that obtained before World War I. Corporations had a much greater flexibility to locate different parts of their value-added activities in different parts of the world. Production of goods and services became internationalized at a deeper level than in the past. A striking manifestation of these trends was a rapid growth of intrafirm trade in manufacturing, especially in high technology industries such as automobiles and machinery which had experienced the greatest rationalization on a world scale. In 1970 intrafirm trade was estimated to account for around 20 percent of world trade. By 2000 the share was over 40 percent. Multinationals were the drivers of world trade growth.

As the integration of international production by multinationals proceeded, organizational forms evolved. Although in many industries giant corporations were created by mergers, boundaries of firms also became more porous, as they had been in the first global economy. During the 1970s and 1980s many large U.S. and European-owned M-form corporations suffered from growing managerial diseconomies caused by size and diversification. Large corporations, although spending large sums on R&D, experienced growing problems achieving successful innovation. The result was a general trend towards divestment of "non-core" businesses, outsourcing of many value-added activities once performed within corporate borders, and the formation of many alliances with other firms, which acted as suppliers and customers, or as partners in innovation. The new global economy was complex. Large corporations were power-houses of innovation spending and market power. Yet the economy could also be seen as a "worldwide web of inter-firm connections."

It remained less evident that the global economy had spawned a multitude of "global firms." Trade flows remained more regional than global. Only a handful of large multinationals really operated on a "global scale." In most instances, firms continued to generate a high proportion of their revenues from their home regions. A study of the 500 largest companies in the world in 2000 identified 380 for whom the geographical distribution of sales existed. Defining "global" as a firm having 20 percent of its sales in each three parts of the Triad, but less than 50 percent in any one region, Rugman and D'Cruz (2000) could only find nine "global firms." These were mostly in the computer, telecom, and high-tech sectors, such as IBM, Sony, and Intel, but included Coca-Cola. In the new global economy, one study concluded, the multinational was a "national corporation with international operations." As global competition intensified, geography and location remained central to corporate strategy.

Exploding the Myths About Offshoring

MARTIN N. BAILY AND DIANA FARRELL

Total U.S. employment has fallen by over 2 million since 2000. While employment is rising again as the economy recovers, the pace of job growth has been agonizingly slow. Many people blame "offshoring," or the nation's growing trade in services with emerging markets. Because of the digital revolution and the dramatic fall in international telecommunication costs, white-collar jobs that once were insulated from global competition can now be performed in low-wage nations like India for as little as one-tenth of the cost of U.S. labor. Employees with jobs as diverse as call-center agents, data processors, medical technicians, and software programmers are thought to be at risk.

Even self-proclaimed free-trade advocates have wavered in their beliefs, and critics warn that as hiring favors the enormous supply of highly educated Indian and Chinese workers, millions of Americans will become jobless. In response to these concerns, Congress included in the fiscal 2004 omnibus spending bill a provision that prohibits federal agencies from outsourcing some kinds of work to private

Martin N. Baily and Diana Farrell, *Exploding the Myths About Offshoring* (n.p.: McKinsey Global Institute, 2004), pp. 1–8. Reprinted by permission of McKinsey Global Inst. McKinsey & Co.

companies that use workers abroad. Over thirty states are considering similar restrictions; at least four have already passed them. . . .

However, the current debate is misplaced, because the problem is neither trade itself nor globalization more broadly, but the question of how the nation should allocate the benefits of global trade. The global labor market, like other international trade, benefits the nation as a whole by making the economic pie bigger and raising the standard of living. For some businesses, outsourcing jobs abroad will allow them to remain profitable, thereby preserving other U.S. jobs. Many companies use the savings from outsourcing to lower prices and offer consumers new and better types of services. By increasing productivity, offshoring enables companies to invest more in the next-generation technologies and business ideas that will create new jobs. With the most flexible and innovative economy in the world, the United States is uniquely positioned to benefit from the trend. After all, despite a large overall trade deficit, the United States has consistently run a surplus in its international trade in services.

Many people believe that the money U.S. companies spend on services abroad is lost to the U.S. economy, but a 2003 study by the McKinsey Global Institute shows that offshoring creates wealth for the United States as well as for the country receiving the jobs. For every dollar of corporate spending that is outsourced to a low-wage nation, the spending economy captures more than three-quarters of the benefit and gains as much as $1.14 in return. Far from being a zero-sum game, offshoring is instead a story of mutual economic gain.

Of course, what is good for the economy as a whole may not be good for particular individuals. Based on economic history, we can expect that some U.S. workers will indeed lose their jobs. But this painful reality does not weaken the case for free trade. The United States can enjoy the significant benefits of free trade while protecting individuals with programs that help workers make the transition to new jobs. These programs might include job retraining opportunities and generous severance packages, portable health and pension benefits, and wage insurance. Given the benefits of offshoring, the logical response is to make the U.S. labor force and economy more flexible and able to cope with change.

How the U.S. Benefits

The offshoring trend prompted us to look into what happens to a dollar of U.S. corporate spending when a company moves a service job to India. We found that the receiving economy (India) captures 33 cents, in the form of wages paid to local workers, profits earned by local outsourcing providers and their suppliers, and taxes collected from second- and third-tier suppliers to the outsourcing companies. (Today, both foreign and local outsourcing providers in India enjoy a tax holiday from the government.)

Corporate Savings.   The gains to the U.S. economy are much larger. The most obvious source of value is the cost savings enjoyed by U.S. companies. For every dollar of corporate spending that moves offshore, U.S. companies save 58 cents. Companies can reinvest the savings in new business opportunities, pay additional earnings out to shareholders, or both. Often, U.S. companies and customers obtain better-quality services from abroad. Because wages are lower, companies can hire more and more highly qualified people to do the same job, and spend more on supervision and training. Some companies have found that offshore workers are more highly motivated and perform better, particularly for low-skilled jobs that lack prestige and suffer from high turnover in the U.S. One British bank's call-center agents in India process 20 percent more transactions than their counterparts in the United Kingdom and have a 3 percent higher accuracy level.

Ultimately, in a competitive economy such as the United States, consumers benefit as companies pass on savings in the form of lower prices. Consumers also benefit directly from trade, since they can acquire goods and services at lower prices. New research by Catherine Mann of the Institute for International Economics found that global sourcing of components in the computer hardware industry has reduced the cost of IT hardware by as much as 30 percent, thereby boosting demand and adding up to $230 billion to U.S. GDP since 1995. Trade in services will do the same. A technician in India, for instance, can read an MRI or CT scan at a fraction of the cost to do the job in the United States. Transferring that position to India may cause an American medical technician to be laid off, but lower prices for these life-saving technologies will enable many more sick people to receive them.

Additional Exports.   Offshoring benefits the U.S. economy in other ways as well. First, Indian companies that provide offshore services will also buy goods and services, ranging from computers and telecommunications equipment to legal, financial, and marketing expertise. Often, they buy these from U.S. companies. A call center in Bangalore is likely to be filled with HP computers, Microsoft software, and telephones from Lucent and to be audited by PricewaterhouseCoopers. We estimate that for every dollar of corporate spending that moves offshore, suppliers of offshore services buy five cents' worth of goods and services from the United States. Furthermore, young Indian workers employed by outsourcing firms also buy goods imported from abroad. Thanks to these corporate and individual buyers, exports from the United States to India stood at $4.1 billion in 2002, compared with less than $2.5 billion in 1990. In the last quarter of 2003, exports to India grew by 26 percent.

Repatriated Profits.   In addition, the U.S. economy benefits because many Indian outsourcing firms are owned in whole or in part by U.S. companies such as GE and EDS, which repatriate their earnings back to the United States. Such companies generate 30 percent of the revenues of the Indian offshore industry. In this way, another four cents of every dollar spent on offshoring returns to the U.S. economy.

Productivity and New Jobs.   The direct benefits to the United States from corporate savings, new exports, and repatriated profits total $0.67—twice the benefit to India. But the gains don't end here. Corporate savings can be invested in new business opportunities, and this investment will boost productivity as well as create new jobs. Based on historical experience, these new jobs will have on average higher value-added than the ones they replaced. Carriage makers were replaced by auto assemblers, and farmers by factory workers. Indeed, this is exactly the pattern over the past two decades as manufacturing jobs moved offshore. The Bureau of Labor Statistics reports that U.S. manufacturing employment shrank by two million jobs in the past 20 years—but net employment increased by 43 million jobs in other areas, such as educational and health services, professional and business services, trade and transport, government, leisure and hospitality, and financial services. Over the same period, manufacturing output has increased, meaning that factories are more productive than before. Higher productivity means more national income and a higher standard of living for Americans.

The same thing is likely to happen again as jobs in call centers, back-office operations, and some IT functions go offshore. Opportunities to redeploy labor and invest capital to generate opportunities in higher-value-added occupations will appear, although we can't predict exactly where. The Bureau of Labor Statistics estimates that from 2000 to 2010, there will be a net creation of 22 million new U.S. jobs, mostly in business services, health care, social services, transportation, and communications. The BLS also predicts that computer-related occupations—often thought to be at high risk of offshoring—will be among the fastest-growing jobs in the country. While code writing can be done abroad, many other IT functions, like systems integration, cannot. In addition, there will undoubtedly be jobs we can't even fathom today. Twenty years ago, for example, no one could have imagined the ubiquity of the cellular phone, an industry employing nearly 200,000 workers in the United States.

The view that new jobs will be created as old jobs disappear is not an article of faith; it is based on repeated experience. Most recently, in the 1990s, trade expanded rapidly, with increases in offshoring of both manufacturing and service-sector jobs. At the same time, overall employment soared, unemployment fell to 4 percent, and real wages increased.

We estimate that offshoring will create an additional 45 to 47 cents of value to the U.S. economy as labor is redeployed. This is a conservative estimate, based on historical figures of job loss due to trade. White-collar employees at risk of offshoring today are generally more highly educated and tend to find jobs faster than do workers in the service sector as a whole. Far from being bad for the United States, offshoring thus creates net value for the economy—to the tune of $1.12 to $1.14 for every dollar that goes abroad.

Offshoring in Perspective

To assess offshoring's impact on employment rationally, we must put it in perspective. Forrester Research predicts that by 2015, roughly 3.3 million U.S. business-processing jobs will be performed abroad. Even though this number may seem startlingly large, it is only a piece of a much larger picture.

The United States today has more than 150 million employed workers. Technological change, economic recessions, shifts in consumer demand, and other changes result in continuous job turnover. Each month, roughly 2 million Americans change jobs—a figure that dwarfs even the most aggressive predictions of job loss due to offshoring. The number of service jobs that may be lost to free trade is small even compared with the mass layoffs prompted by corporate mergers and restructuring when the economy is growing. In 1999 alone—at the peak of the bubble economy—1.15 million workers lost their jobs through mass layoffs as companies restructured their operations. Job churn is part of life, even in a growing economy.

Liberalized, competitive economies with flexible labor markets can cope with the natural process of job creation and destruction. The U.S. economy, the world's most dynamic, is arguably in the best position to do so. According to the Organisation for Economic Co-operation and Development, the United States has the highest rate of reemployment of any OECD country by a factor of almost two.

Most workers who lose their positions find another within six months. Over the past ten years, 3.5 million private-sector jobs have been created each year, on average, for a total of 35 million new jobs—and job growth was fastest, according to the OECD, among high-wage jobs.

A flexible job market and the mobility of U.S. workers will enable the United States to create new jobs faster than offshoring eliminates them. Consider how the U.S. semiconductor industry reinvented itself after losing out to Japanese competitors that entered the market during the late 1980s. The Japanese quickly dominated many segments, including memory, and spurred a public outcry over "unfair" Japanese competition and the loss of high-paying, white-collar U.S. jobs. The big U.S. players—Intel, Texas Instruments, and Motorola—all exited the memory business. But this prompted them to invest more aggressively in the production of microprocessors and logic products—the next growth wave in semiconductors. Intel became the dominant global player in microprocessors, Texas Instruments in DSPs (Digital Signal Processors, the "brain" in mobile phones), and Motorola gained a strong position in communications devices. Throughout this shift toward higher-value-added activities, the total number of U.S. jobs in semiconductors and closely related electronics held constant at around half a million.

Separating Fact from Fiction

Muddling the public debate over white-collar offshoring are a number of myths and half-truths. Most troubling are statements by self-proclaimed free-trade advocates who argue that the current offshoring phenomenon is different. The overwhelming evidence among economists is that trade contributes to faster economic growth. Skeptics argue that trade in services is somehow different from trade in goods and will be less beneficial to the U.S. economy, but given the strength of the U.S. services industries, increased trade in services is even more likely to be a substantial plus for Americans.

The United States has always and continues to run a trade surplus in services, even with India. It has the most productive and developed service sector of any country in the world, and unlike manufacturing, it continues to hold a comparative advantage in these knowledge-based industries. American banks, law firms, accounting firms, IT integrators, and consultants, to name a few, have established themselves as global competitors. As a result, U.S. trade policy has consistently demanded more openness on the part of other countries in these areas. The declining U.S. dollar will undoubtedly help boost service exports even higher.

Others argue that the massive number of potential workers in China and India is so massive that integrating them into the global economy will cause persistent unemployment in the United States and Europe. Certainly, both countries have a large supply of productive workers. But they also have fast-growing appetites for goods and services. The great majority of the enormous workforces in these economies will be producing goods and services for their own economies. They are bringing new demand to the world economy about as fast as they are adding to supply. As is true in other countries, only a small portion of their workforce produces goods for export. Provided they allow their exchange rates to adjust, China and India will not be a net drain on economic activity or jobs in the rest of the world.

Equally untenable is the notion that low-wage nations are taking American jobs. The fact is that many of the jobs in India today are viable only in a low-wage environment and would not exist in the United States. That half a million people are now employed in India's outsourcing industry does not mean that there could be 500,000 more jobs in the United States. Without offshoring, companies would scale back or stop offering services like 24/7 customer help. Companies are also using technology to replace many of the jobs at risk in the United States. Automated voice response units are replacing call-center workers, online hotel and airline booking systems are replacing live operators and travel agents, and imaging software is replacing data-entry workers.

A related myth is that service-sector offshoring is responsible for the anemic job creation during this economic recovery. Critics frequently point out that more than two million American jobs have been lost since 2000. But nearly all jobs lost were actually in manufacturing, not service sectors. Moreover, employment in IT, which is supposedly one of the hardest hit by offshoring, has actually grown since 1999. While it is true that 70,000 computer programmers have lost their jobs, most of these losses were due to the bursting of the IT bubble. In addition, more than 115,000 higher-paid software engineering jobs were created during that period. Jobs for computer support specialists and systems analysts and administrators grew by roughly 83,000.

The Challenge for Policymakers

Arguments about the greater good and the long-term health of the economy do not, of course, ease the plight of people who lose their jobs or find themselves in lower-wage employment. While free trade creates wealth and improves a nation's standard of living, not all groups benefit, particularly in the short term. Today, globalization is creating a higher level of turnover in the workforce than ever before. Rather than a single career with just one or two companies, as those in previous generations could expect, most people today will have many employers, and a growing number will switch their careers as well. Job change is a much larger part of life than it used to be, and the challenge for policymakers is to make it easier and less painful.

 F U R T H E R   R E A D I N G

Barber, Benjamin R. *Jihad vs. McWorld* (1996).

Bonin, Hubert, et al., eds. *Ford, 1903–2003: The European History* (2003).

Cowie, Jefferson R. *Capital Moves: RCA's 70-Year Search for Cheap Labor* (1999).

Friedman, Thomas L. *The Lexus and the Olive Tree: Understanding Globalization* (1999).

Gabel, Medard, and Henry Bruner. *Global Inc.: An Atlas of the Multinational Corporation* (2003).

Harrison, Bennett. *Lean and Mean: The Changing Landscape of Corporate Power in the Age of Flexibility* (1997).

Hoerr, John P. *And the Wolf Finally Came: The Decline of the American Steel Industry* (1988).

Leach, William. *Country of Exiles: The Destruction of Place in American Life* (1999).

McArthur, John R. *The Selling of Free Trade: NAFTA, Washington, and the Subversion of American Democracy* (2000).

O'Rourke, Kevin H., and Jeffrey G. Williamson. *Globalization and History: The Evolution of a Nineteenth-Century Atlantic Economy* (1999).

Pitti, Stephen J. *The Devil in Silicon Valley: Northern California, Race, and Mexican Americans* (2003).

Streeten, Paul. *Globalisation: Threat or Opportunity?* (2001).

Tiffany, Paul. *The Decline of American Steel* (1988).

Wilkins, Mira. *The Emergence of Multinational Enterprise: American Business Abroad From the Colonial Era to 1914* (1970).

———. *The History of Foreign Investment in the United States, 1914–1945* (2004).

———. *The History of Foreign Investment in the United States to 1914* (1989).

———. *The Maturing of Multinational Enterprise: American Business Abroad From 1914 to 1970* (1974).

———, and Frank Ernest Hill. *American Business Abroad: Ford on Six Continents* (1964).